A FIRST COURSE IN MACHINE LEARNING

Second Edition

Chapman & Hall/CRC
Machine Learning & Pattern Recognition Series

SERIES EDITORS

Ralf Herbrich
Amazon Development Center
Berlin, Germany

Thore Graepel
Microsoft Research Ltd.
Cambridge, UK

AIMS AND SCOPE

This series reflects the latest advances and applications in machine learning and pattern recognition through the publication of a broad range of reference works, textbooks, and handbooks. The inclusion of concrete examples, applications, and methods is highly encouraged. The scope of the series includes, but is not limited to, titles in the areas of machine learning, pattern recognition, computational intelligence, robotics, computational/statistical learning theory, natural language processing, computer vision, game AI, game theory, neural networks, computational neuroscience, and other relevant topics, such as machine learning applied to bioinformatics or cognitive science, which might be proposed by potential contributors.

PUBLISHED TITLES

BAYESIAN PROGRAMMING
Pierre Bessière, Emmanuel Mazer, Juan-Manuel Ahuactzin, and Kamel Mekhnacha

UTILITY-BASED LEARNING FROM DATA
Craig Friedman and Sven Sandow

HANDBOOK OF NATURAL LANGUAGE PROCESSING, SECOND EDITION
Nitin Indurkhya and Fred J. Damerau

COST-SENSITIVE MACHINE LEARNING
Balaji Krishnapuram, Shipeng Yu, and Bharat Rao

COMPUTATIONAL TRUST MODELS AND MACHINE LEARNING
Xin Liu, Anwitaman Datta, and Ee-Peng Lim

MULTILINEAR SUBSPACE LEARNING: DIMENSIONALITY REDUCTION OF MULTIDIMENSIONAL DATA
Haiping Lu, Konstantinos N. Plataniotis, and Anastasios N. Venetsanopoulos

MACHINE LEARNING: An Algorithmic Perspective, Second Edition
Stephen Marsland

SPARSE MODELING: THEORY, ALGORITHMS, AND APPLICATIONS
Irina Rish and Genady Ya. Grabarnik

A FIRST COURSE IN MACHINE LEARNING, SECOND EDITION
Simon Rogers and Mark Girolami

STATISTICAL REINFORCEMENT LEARNING: MODERN MACHINE LEARNING APPROACHES
Masashi Sugiyama

MULTI-LABEL DIMENSIONALITY REDUCTION
Liang Sun, Shuiwang Ji, and Jieping Ye

REGULARIZATION, OPTIMIZATION, KERNELS, AND SUPPORT VECTOR MACHINES
Johan A. K. Suykens, Marco Signoretto, and Andreas Argyriou

ENSEMBLE METHODS: FOUNDATIONS AND ALGORITHMS
Zhi-Hua Zhou

Chapman & Hall/CRC
Machine Learning & Pattern Recognition Series

A FIRST COURSE IN MACHINE LEARNING
Second Edition

Simon Rogers

University of Glasgow
United Kingdom

Mark Girolami

University of Warwick
United Kingdom

CRC Press
Taylor & Francis Group
Boca Raton London New York

CRC Press is an imprint of the
Taylor & Francis Group, an **informa** business

A CHAPMAN & HALL BOOK

MATLAB® is a trademark of The MathWorks, Inc. and is used with permission. The MathWorks does not warrant the accuracy of the text or exercises in this book. This book's use or discussion of MAT-LAB® software or related products does not constitute endorsement or sponsorship by The MathWorks of a particular pedagogical approach or particular use of the MATLAB® software.

CRC Press
Taylor & Francis Group
6000 Broken Sound Parkway NW, Suite 300
Boca Raton, FL 33487-2742

First issued in paperback 2020

© 2017 by Taylor & Francis Group, LLC
CRC Press is an imprint of the Taylor & Francis Group, an informa business

ISBN 13: 978-0-367-57464-2 (pbk)
ISBN 13: 978-1-4987-3848-4 (hbk)

Visit the Taylor & Francis Web site at
http://www.taylorandfrancis.com

and the CRC Press Web site at
http://www.crcpress.com

Contents

List of Tables

List of Figures

Preface to the First Edition

Machine learning is rapidly becoming one of the most important areas of general practice, research and development activity within computing science. This is reflected in the scale of the academic research area devoted to the subject and the active recruitment of machine learning specialists by major international banks and financial institutions as well as companies such as *Microsoft, Google, Yahoo and Amazon.*

This growth can be partly explained by the increase in the quantity and diversity of measurements we are able to make of the world. A particularly fascinating example arises from the wave of new biological measurement technologies that have followed the sequencing of the first genomes. It is now possible to measure the detailed molecular state of an organism in manners that would have been hard to imagine only a short time ago. Such measurements go far beyond our understanding of these organisms and machine learning techniques have been heavily involved in the distillation of useful structure from them.

This book is based on material taught in a machine learning course in the School of Computing Science at the University of Glasgow, UK. The course, presented to final year undergraduates and postgraduates, is made up of 20 hour-long lectures and 10 hour-long laboratory sessions. In such a short teaching period, it is impossible to cover more than a small fraction of the material that now comes under the banner of machine learning. Our intention when teaching this course therefore, is to present the core mathematical and statistical techniques required to understand some of the most popular machine learning algorithms and then present a few of these algorithms that span the main problem areas within machine learning: classification, clustering and projection. At the end of the course, the students should have the knowledge and confidence to be able to explore the machine learning literature to find methods that are more appropriate to them. The same is hopefully true of readers of this book.

Due to the varying mathematical literacy of students in the course, we assume only very minor mathematical prerequisites. An undergraduate student from computer science, engineering, physics or any other numerical subject should have no problem. This does not exclude those without such experience – additional mathematical explanations appear throughout the text in comment boxes. In addition, important equations have been highlighted – it is worth spending time understanding these equations before proceeding.

Students attending this course often find the practical sessions very useful. Experimenting with the various algorithms and concepts helps transfer them from an abstract set of equations into something that could be used to solve real problems. We have attempted to transfer this to the book through an extensive collection of MATLAB®/Octave[1]/R/Python scripts, available from the associated web page and referenced throughout the text. These scripts enable the user to recreate plots that appear in the book and investigate changing model specifications and parameter values.

Finally, the machine learning methods that are covered in this book are our choice of those that we feel students should understand. In limited space and time, we think that it is more worthwhile to give detailed descriptions and derivations for a small number of algorithms than attempting to cover many algorithms at a coarser level of detail – many people will not find their favourite algorithms within this book!

Simon Rogers and Mark Girolami.

---

[1]A free mathematical software environment, available from `www.gnu.org/software/octave/`

Preface to the Second Edition

Since the first edition was published in late 2011, interest in machine learning has grown substantially. It is increasingly difficult to find a problem area in research or industry in which machine learning methods have not been applied. Interest in university courses in this area has, at least in our experience, grown enormously (the course on which this book is based has increased in size tenfold since 2010). We hope that this book will continue to be useful to anyone without a machine learning background who wants to give themselves a solid foundation in this area.

In this edition, we have added three chapters of new material. The book now consists of two sections. Section I, which is the original content, and Section II, the new, more advanced material. The advanced material is all probabilistic – Gaussian processes, Markov chain Monte Carlo sampling and extensions to mixture modeling (including Dirichlet processes). These are all topics that have seen considerable development in the last 5 years and, arguably, are joining the collection of techniques that practitioners could be expected to have some knowledge or experience of (it is no coincidence that these are also areas in which we have a research interest!).

As well as new material, we have also updated the accompanying code, including examples in Python and R as well as the original MATLAB. Python and R code is provided via Jupyter notebooks and all code is available on the accompanying web page.

Finally, we would like to take this opportunity to thank all those who have contributed to this book so far. Rónán Daly, Lisa Hopcroft, Keith Harris and Gary MacIndoe did a great job of proofreading and critiquing the first edition. Tamara Polajner did a great job of designing the cover for the second edition. Thanks to Francois-Xavier Briol and Jon Cockayne for translating the code into R. Thanks also to all those who have provided valuable feedback (too many to mention by name) or (unfortunately) spotted the errors that creep in (that have now hopefully all been fixed).

Simon Rogers and Mark Girolami.

I

Basic Topics

CHAPTER 1

Linear Modelling: A Least Squares Approach

An important and general problem in machine learning, which has wide application, is *learning* or *inferring* a functional relationship between a set of *attribute* variables and associated *response* or *target* variables so that we can predict the response for any set of attributes. For example, we may wish to build a model that can perform disease diagnosis. To do this we would use a dataset comprised of measurements (attributes; e.g. blood pressure, heart rate, weight, etc.) taken from patients with known disease state (responses; healthy or diseased). In a completely different example, we may wish to make recommendations to customers. In this case, we could build a model from descriptors of items a particular customer had previously bought (attributes) and whether or not the customer ultimately liked the product (response). This would enable us to predict which objects a customer would like and hence make recommendations. There are many more important application areas that we will come across throughout this text.

1.1 LINEAR MODELLING

To begin with we will consider, using a practical example, the most straightforward of *learning* problems, linear modelling[1] – learning a linear relationship between attributes and responses. Figure 1.1 shows the gold medal winning time for the men's 100 m at each of the Olympic Games held since 1896. Our aim is to use this data to *learn* a model of the functional dependence (if one exists) between Olympic year and 100 m winning time and use this model to make predictions about the winning times in future games. Clearly the year

---

[1]The type of modelling we will consider here is often known as *regression* and was originally used in the context of genetics by Francis Galton (1877) when studying how intelligence is passed on (or not as the case may be) from generation to generation. The term was then adopted by statisticians who developed Galton's work within a statistical context.

is not the only factor that affects the winning time and if we are interested in using our predictions seriously we may want to take other things into account (the recent form of the main competitors is an obvious example). However, examining Figure 1.1 we can see that there is at least a statistical dependence between year and winning time (it may not be a *causal* dependence – elapsing years are not directly *causing* the drop in winning times) and this is enough to help us introduce and develop the main ideas of linear modelling.

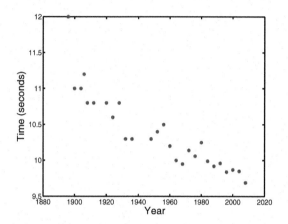

FIGURE 1.1   Winning men's 100 m times at the Summer Olympics since 1896. Note that the two world wars interrupted the games in 1914, 1940 and 1944.

1.1.1   Defining the model

We can begin by defining our model as a function which maps our *input* attributes, in this case Olympic year, to our *output* or target values – winning time. For our attributes, we will use the numerical value of the year – e.g. 1980 – although there are alternative formulations (e.g. years since the first modern games, $1980 - 1896 = 84$) that would make no real difference to the underlying assumptions.

There are many **functions** that could be used to define this mapping. In general, this function will take as an input x (the Olympic year) and will return t (the winning time in seconds). In other words, t is a function of x. Mathematically, we will write this as $t = f(x)$. In some cases, all we will need to know to evaluate our function is x. For example, if $f(x) = \sin(x)$ or, say, $f(x) = x$, we can compute t for any x. In general, we will need to be more flexible and it is likely that our model will have a set of associated **parameters**. For example, $t = ax$ has a parameter called a that needs to be defined somehow. Learning model parameters from a suitable dataset is a common theme in machine learning. We will use $t = f(x; a)$ to denote a function $f(\cdot)$ that acts on x and has a parameter a.

Comment 1.1 – Linear relationships: The equation

$$y = mx + c,$$

where m and c are constant, defines a linear relationship between x and y. It is called linear because the relationship between x and y could be visualised as a straight line. The following equations are non-linear due to the more complex forms in which we find the variables x and y:

$$y = mx^2 + c, \quad y = \sin(x), \quad \sqrt{y} = mx + c.$$

The values of m and c do not affect the linearity of the relationship. For example, the following still represent linear relationships between x and y:

$$y = mx + c^2, \quad y = x\sin(m) + c.$$

1.1.2 Modelling assumptions

To help us choose which particular model to use, we need to make some assumptions. Our principal assumption at this stage is the following:

The relationship between x and t is linear (see Comment 1.1).

This could be stated alternatively as

The data in Figure 1.1 could be adequately modelled with a straight line.

Or

The winning time drops by the same amount every M years.

Examining Figure 1.1 we can see that this assumption is not perfectly satisfied. However, it is our hope that it is adequate and will produce a model that is useful in the sense that it can make predictions regarding winning times in the future.

The simplest model that satisfies our assumptions is

$$t = f(x) = x,$$

the winning time is equal to the Olympic year. The fact that x takes values greater than or equal to 1880 and t values less than or equal to 12, and that the winning time is decreasing as the year increases tells us that this model is inadequate. Adding a single parameter results in

$$t = f(x; w) = wx,$$

where w can be either positive or negative. This enhanced model lets us produce a straight line with any gradient through the choice of w. This is an increase in flexibility but it is still limited by the fact that, at year 0, the model predicts a winning time of $w \times 0 = 0$. Looking at the data we can see that this is not realistic –

following the general trend of the data, the winning time at year 0 is actually going to be quite a large number. Adding one more parameter to the model overcomes this limitation:

$$t = f(x; w_0, w_1) = w_0 + w_1 x. \tag{1.1}$$

This is the standard equation for a straight line that many readers will have encountered before. The *learning* task now involves using the data in Figure 1.1 to choose suitable values for the two parameters w_0 and w_1. These two parameters are often known as the intercept (w_0; where the line intercepts the t-axis) and the gradient (w_1; the gradient of the line) and the effect of varying them can be seen in Figure 1.2 (MATLAB script: `plotlinear.m`) (see Exercise 1.1).

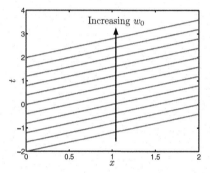

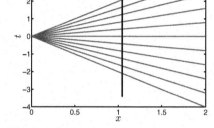

(a) Increasing w_0 changes the point at which the line crosses the t axis.

(b) Increasing w_1 changes the gradient of the line.

FIGURE 1.2 Effect of varying w_0 and w_1 in the linear model defined by Equation 1.1.

1.1.3 Defining a *good* model

In order to choose values of w_0 and w_1 that are somehow *best*, we need to define what *best* means. Common sense would suggest that the *best* solution consists of the values of w_0 and w_1 that produce a line that passes as close as possible to *all* of the data points. A common way of measuring how close a particular model gets to one of the data points is the squared difference between the true winning time and the winning time predicted by the model. Using x_n, t_n to denote the nth Olympic year and winning time, respectively, the squared difference is defined as

$$(t_n - f(x_n; w_0, w_1))^2.$$

The smaller this number is, the closer the model, at x_n, is to t_n. Squaring the difference is important. Without it, we could indefinitely reduce this quantity by continually increasing $f(x_n; w_0, w_1)$.

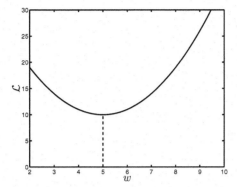

FIGURE 1.3 Example loss function of one parameter (w). The dashed line shows the value of w that minimised the loss $(w = 5)$.

This expression is known as the *squared loss function*, as it describes how much accuracy we are losing through the use of $f(x_n; w_0, w_1)$ to model t_n. Throughout this text, we will use $\mathcal{L}_n()$ to denote loss functions. In this case,

$$\mathcal{L}_n(t_n, f(x_n; w_0, w_1)) = (t_n - f(x_n; w_0, w_1))^2 \qquad (1.2)$$

is the loss for year n. Loss is always positive and the lower the *loss*, the better our function describes the data. As we want a low *loss* for all of the N years, we consider the *average loss* across the whole dataset, given as

$$\mathcal{L} = \frac{1}{N} \sum_{n=1}^{N} \mathcal{L}_n(t_n, f(x_n; w_0, w_1)). \qquad (1.3)$$

This is the average of the loss values at each of the N years. The lower it is, the better. We will therefore tune w_0 and w_1 to produce the model that results in the lowest value of the average loss, $\mathcal{L}$. Finding these *best* values for w_0 and w_1 can be expressed mathematically as

$$\underset{w_0, w_1}{\operatorname{argmin}} \frac{1}{N} \sum_{n=1}^{N} \mathcal{L}_n(t_n, f(x_n; w_0, w_1)).$$

The term argmin is the mathematical shorthand for 'find the argument that minimises...'. In this instance, the argument(s) are the values of w_0 and w_1 and the expression to be minimised is the average loss. Figure 1.3 shows a hypothetical loss that is a function of a single parameter, w. The value of w that minimises $\mathcal{L}$ is $w = 5$. Historically, minimisation of the squared loss is the basis of the *least-squares* errors method of function approximation, which dates back to methods developed by Gauss and Legendre (1809) when predicting planetary motion.

Other loss functions exist that are suitable for regression. For example, a common alternative is the absolute loss:

$$\mathcal{L}_n = |t_n - f(x_n; w_0, w_1)|.$$

The squared loss is a very common choice, in part due to the fact that it makes finding the best values of w_0 and w_1 relatively straightforward – we can derive an **analytical** solution. However, modern computational power has reduced the importance of mathematical convenience – there is no longer any excuse for choosing a convenient loss function over one more suited to the data. This notwithstanding, our aim is to introduce general modelling concepts for which the squared loss will be adequate. It is worth bearing in mind that others are available and, in many cases, will be more appropriate.

1.1.4 The least squares solution – a worked example

To recap, our dataset consists of $n = 1, \ldots, N$ observations, each of which consists of a year x_n and a time in seconds t_n.

We are going to attempt to find a functional relationship using a linear model defined as

$$f(x; w_0, w_1) = w_0 + w_1 x \tag{1.4}$$

and we have decided that we will use the least squares loss function to choose suitable values of w_0 and w_1. Substituting the linear model into the expression for average loss and multiplying out the brackets results in

$$
\begin{aligned}
\mathcal{L} &= \frac{1}{N} \sum_{n=1}^{N} \mathcal{L}_n(t_n, f(x_n; w_0, w_1)) \\
&= \frac{1}{N} \sum_{n=1}^{N} (t_n - f(x_n; w_0, w_1))^2 \\
&= \frac{1}{N} \sum_{n=1}^{N} (t_n - (w_0 + w_1 x_n))^2 \\
&= \frac{1}{N} \sum_{n=1}^{N} (w_1^2 x_n^2 + 2 w_1 x_n w_0 - 2 w_1 x_n t_n + w_0^2 - 2 w_0 t_n + t_n^2) \\
&= \frac{1}{N} \sum_{n=1}^{N} (w_1^2 x_n^2 + 2 w_1 x_n (w_0 - t_n) + w_0^2 - 2 w_0 t_n + t_n^2). \tag{1.5}
\end{aligned}
$$

> **Comment 1.2 – Turning points:** We can find turning points (that might correspond to minima) of a function, $f(w)$, by searching for points where the gradient of the function, $\frac{\delta f(w)}{\delta w}$, is zero. To determine whether or not a turning point corresponds to a maximum, minimum or saddle point, we can examine the second derivative, $\frac{\delta^2 f(w)}{\delta w^2}$. If, at a turning point $\hat{w}$, the second derivative is positive, we know that this turning point is a minimum. The following three plots show three example functions along with their first and second derivatives.
>
>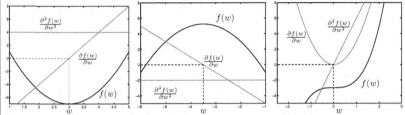
>
> In general, a function may have several turning points. An interesting special case is functions whose second derivative is a positive constant – these correspond to functions that have only one minimum.

Differentiating the loss function   At a minimum of $\mathcal{L}$, the **partial derivatives** with respect to w_1 and w_0 must be zero (see Comment 1.2). Therefore, computing the partial derivatives, equating them to zero and solving for w_0 and w_1 will give us a potential minimum. Starting with w_1, we know that terms in Equation 1.5 that do not include w_1 can be ignored (as their partial derivative with respect to w_1 will be zero). Removing these terms leaves

$$\frac{1}{N} \sum_{n=1}^{N} [w_1^2 x_n^2 + 2w_1 x_n w_0 - 2w_1 x_n t_n].$$

Before we take the partial derivatives, we will rearrange the expression to make it a little simpler. In particular, taking terms that are not indexed by n outside of the sum and rearranging results in

$$w_1^2 \frac{1}{N} \left(\sum_{n=1}^{N} x_n^2 \right) + 2w_1 \frac{1}{N} \left(\sum_{n=1}^{N} x_n (w_0 - t_n) \right).$$

Taking the partial derivative with respect to w_1 gives us the expression

$$\frac{\partial \mathcal{L}}{\partial w_1} = 2w_1 \frac{1}{N} \left(\sum_{n=1}^{N} x_n^2 \right) + \frac{2}{N} \left(\sum_{n=1}^{N} x_n (w_0 - t_n) \right). \tag{1.6}$$

Now we do the same for w_0. Removing non w_0 terms leaves

$$\frac{1}{N} \sum_{n=1}^{N} [w_0^2 + 2w_1 x_n w_0 - 2w_0 t_n].$$

Again, we will rearrange it a bit before we differentiate. Moving terms not indexed by n outside of the summation (noting that $\sum_{n=1}^{N} w_0^2 = N w_0^2$) results in

$$w_0^2 + 2w_0 w_1 \frac{1}{N} \left(\sum_{n=1}^{N} x_n \right) - 2w_0 \frac{1}{N} \left(\sum_{n=1}^{N} t_n \right).$$

Taking the partial derivative with respect to w_0 results in

$$\frac{\partial \mathcal{L}}{\partial w_0} = 2w_0 + 2w_1 \frac{1}{N} \left(\sum_{n=1}^{N} x_n \right) - \frac{2}{N} \left(\sum_{n=1}^{N} t_n \right). \tag{1.7}$$

Equating the derivatives to zero We now have expressions for the partial derivatives of the loss with respect to both w_0 and w_1. To find the values of w_0 and w_1 that correspond to a turning point (hopefully a minimum), we must set these expressions to zero and solve for w_0 and w_1. It's easiest to start with the expression for w_0. Setting Equation 1.7 to zero and solving for w_0:

$$2w_0 \quad + \quad 2w_1 \frac{1}{N} \left(\sum_{n=1}^{N} x_n \right) - \frac{2}{N} \left(\sum_{n=1}^{N} t_n \right) = 0$$

$$2w_0 \quad = \quad \frac{2}{N} \left(\sum_{n=1}^{N} t_n \right) - w_1 \frac{2}{N} \left(\sum_{n=1}^{N} x_n \right)$$

$$w_0 \quad = \quad \frac{1}{N} \left(\sum_{n=1}^{N} t_n \right) - w_1 \frac{1}{N} \left(\sum_{n=1}^{N} x_n \right).$$

Denoting the average winning time as $\bar{t} = \frac{1}{N} \sum_{n=1}^{N} t_n$ and the average Olympic year as $\bar{x} = \frac{1}{N} \sum_{n=1}^{N} x_n$, we can rewrite our expression for the value of w_0 at the turning point $(\widehat{w_0})$ as

$$\widehat{w_0} = \bar{t} - w_1 \bar{x}. \tag{1.8}$$

What insight can we gain from this expression? This new expression is a rearrangement of our original model $(t_n = w_0 + w_1 x_n)$ where t_n and x_n have been replaced by their average values $\bar{t}$ and $\bar{x}$. Consider the value of our function averaged over the N data points. This is given by

$$\frac{1}{N} \sum_{n=1}^{N} f(x_n; w_0, w_1) = \frac{1}{N} \sum_{n=1}^{N} (w_0 + w_1 x_n) = w_0 + w_1 \bar{x}.$$

The average winning time is given by $\bar{t}$ so, in using Equation 1.8, we are choosing $\widehat{w_0}$ to ensure that the average value of the function is equal to the average winning time. Intuitively, matching the averages in this way seems very sensible.

Before we use Equation 1.6 to get an expression for $\widehat{w_1}$ (the value of w_1 at the turning point – see Comment 1.2), it is worth briefly examining the second derivatives to ensure that this is a minimum. Differentiating Equation 1.6 again with respect to w_1 and Equation 1.7 again with respect to w_0 results in

$$\frac{\delta^2 \mathcal{L}}{\delta w_1^2} = \frac{2}{N} \sum_{n=1}^{N} x_n^2$$

$$\frac{\delta^2 \mathcal{L}}{\delta w_0^2} = 2. \tag{1.9}$$

Both of these quantities must be positive. This tells us that there will be only one turning point and it will correspond to a minimum of the loss.

This process has supplied us with an expression for the value of $\widehat{w_0}$ – the value of w_0 that minimises the loss. This expression depends on w_1 implying that, for any particular w_1, we know the best w_0. Substituting our expression for the best w_0 value (Equation 1.8) into Equation 1.6 and rearranging, we obtain an expression that only includes w_1 terms:

$$\begin{aligned}
\frac{\partial \mathcal{L}}{\partial w_1} &= w_1 \frac{2}{N} \left(\sum_{n=1}^{N} x_n^2 \right) + \frac{2}{N} \left(\sum_{n=1}^{N} x_n (\widehat{w_0} - t_n) \right) \\
&= w_1 \frac{2}{N} \left(\sum_{n=1}^{N} x_n^2 \right) + \frac{2}{N} \left(\sum_{n=1}^{N} x_n (\bar{t} - w_1 \bar{x} - t_n) \right) \\
&= w_1 \frac{2}{N} \left(\sum_{n=1}^{N} x_n^2 \right) + \bar{t} \frac{2}{N} \left(\sum_{n=1}^{N} x_n \right) - w_1 \bar{x} \frac{2}{N} \left(\sum_{n=1}^{N} x_n \right) - \frac{2}{N} \left(\sum_{n=1}^{N} x_n t_n \right).
\end{aligned}$$

We can simplify this expression by using $\bar{x} = (1/N) \sum_{n=1}^{N} x_n$ as before and gathering together w_1 terms:

$$\frac{\partial \mathcal{L}}{\partial w_1} = 2 w_1 \left[\left(\frac{1}{N} \sum_{n=1}^{N} x_n^2 \right) - \bar{x}\bar{x} \right] + 2\bar{t}\bar{x} - 2 \frac{1}{N} \left(\sum_{n=1}^{N} x_n t_n \right).$$

Finally, we can get an expression for $\widehat{x_1}$ by setting this partial derivative to zero and solving for w_1:

$$2 w_1 \left[\left(\frac{1}{N} \sum_{n=1}^{N} x_n^2 \right) - \bar{x}\bar{x} \right] + 2\bar{t}\bar{x} - 2 \frac{1}{N} \left(\sum_{n=1}^{N} x_n t_n \right) = 0$$

$$2 w_1 \left[\left(\frac{1}{N} \sum_{n=1}^{N} x_n^2 \right) - \bar{x}\bar{x} \right] = 2 \frac{1}{N} \left(\sum_{n=1}^{N} x_n t_n \right) - 2\bar{t}\bar{x}$$

$$\widehat{w_1} = \frac{\frac{1}{N} \left(\sum_{n=1}^{N} x_n t_n \right) - \bar{t}\bar{x}}{\left(\frac{1}{N} \sum_{n=1}^{N} x_n^2 \right) - \bar{x}\bar{x}}.$$

It is helpful to now define some new average quantities. The first, $(1/N) \sum_{n=1}^{N} x_n^2$ is the average squared value of the data and we will denote this $\overline{x^2}$. Note that this quantity is not the same as $(\bar{x})^2$. The second is $(1/N) \sum_{n=1}^{N} x_n t_n$ (which, similarly, is not the same as $\bar{x}\bar{t}$). We will denote this as $\overline{xt}$. Substituting these into our expression for w_1 gives

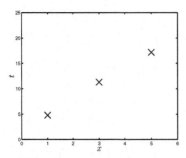

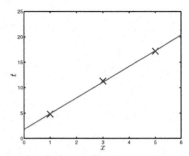

(a) The three synthetic data points described in Table 1.1.

(b) The least squares fit defined by $f(x; w_0, w_1) = 1.8 + 3.1x$.

FIGURE 1.4 Data and function for the worked example of Section 1.1.5.

$$\widehat{w_1} = \frac{\overline{xt} - \bar{x}\bar{t}}{\overline{x^2} - (\bar{x})^2} \tag{1.10}$$

Equations 1.10 and 1.8 provide everything required to compute the best parameter values. Firstly $\widehat{w_1}$ from Equation 1.10, which is then substituted into Equation 1.8 to calculate $\widehat{w_0}$ (MATLAB script: `fitlinear.m`).

1.1.5 Worked example

Before we fit the linear model to the Olympic data, it is useful to provide a worked example on a smaller dataset. Assume we observe $N = 3$ data points, provided in Table 1.1. The final row also gives the various averages required to compute $\widehat{w_0}$ and $\widehat{w_1}$: $\bar{x}$, $\bar{t}$, $\overline{xt}$ and $\overline{x^2}$. The three data points are plotted in Figure 1.4.

TABLE 1.1 Synthetic dataset for linear regression example.

n	x_n	t_n	$x_n t_n$	x_n^2
1	1	4.8	4.8	1
2	3	11.3	33.9	9
3	5	17.2	86	25
$(1/N) \sum_{n=1}^{N}$	3	11.1	41.57	11.67

Substituting these values into Equation 1.10 gives

$$\begin{aligned} w_1 &= \frac{41.57 - 3 \times 11.1}{11.67 - 3 \times 3} \\ &= \frac{8.27}{2.67} \\ &= 3.1 \end{aligned}$$

and

$$w_0 = 11.1 - 3.1 \times 3 = 1.8.$$

Our best linear function is therefore

$$f(x; w_0, w_1) = 1.8 + 3.1x,$$

and it is shown in Figure 1.4(b).

1.1.6 Least squares fit to the Olympic data

The data for the Olympic 100 m dataset (shown in Figure 1.1) is summarised in Table 1.2. Applying exactly the same methodology to this data, we obtain the following

TABLE 1.2 Olympic men's 100 m data.

n	x_n	t_n	$x_n t_n$	x_n^2
1	1896	12.00	22752.0	3.5948×10^6
2	1900	11.00	20900.0	3.6100×10^6
3	1904	11.00	20944.0	3.6252×10^6
4	1906	11.20	21347.2	3.6328×10^6
5	1908	10.80	20606.4	3.6405×10^6
6	1912	10.80	20649.6	3.6557×10^6
7	1920	10.80	20736.0	3.6864×10^6
8	1924	10.60	20394.4	3.7018×10^6
9	1928	10.80	20822.4	3.7172×10^6
10	1932	10.30	19899.6	3.7326×10^6
11	1936	10.30	19940.8	3.7481×10^6
12	1948	10.30	20064.4	3.7947×10^6
13	1952	10.40	20300.8	3.8103×10^6
14	1956	10.50	20538.0	3.8259×10^6
15	1960	10.20	19992.0	3.8416×10^6
16	1964	10.00	19640.0	3.8573×10^6
17	1968	9.95	19581.6	3.8730×10^6
18	1972	10.14	19996.1	3.8888×10^6
19	1976	10.06	19878.6	3.9046×10^6
20	1980	10.25	20295.0	3.9204×10^6
21	1984	9.99	19820.2	3.9363×10^6
22	1988	9.92	19721.0	3.9521×10^6
23	1992	9.96	19840.3	3.9681×10^6
24	1996	9.84	19640.6	3.9840×10^6
25	2000	9.87	19740.0	4.0000×10^6
26	2004	9.85	19739.4	4.0160×10^6
27	2008	9.69	19457.5	4.0321×10^6
$(1/N) \sum_{n=1}^{N}$	1952.37	10.39	20268.1	3.8130×10^6

values for w_1 and w_0 (note that our final values were worked out in MATLAB – if you work through, you might get slightly different results due to rounding errors):

$$
\begin{aligned}
w_1 &= \frac{20268.1 - 1952.37 \times 10.39}{3.8130 \times 10^6 - 1952.37 \times 1952.37} \\
&= \frac{-16.3}{1225.5} \\
&= -0.0133 \\
w_0 &= 10.39 - (-0.0133) \times 1952.37 \\
&= 36.416.
\end{aligned}
$$

Therefore, our best linear function is

$$
f(x; w_0, w_1) = 36.416 - 0.013x. \tag{1.11}
$$

The function is plotted in Figure 1.5 (see Exercise 1.2). Do these values agree with the approximations you made in Exercise 1.1? (MATLAB script: `fitolympic.m`)

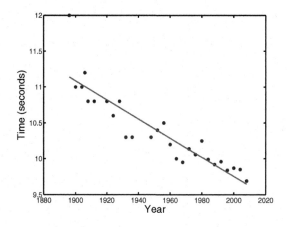

FIGURE 1.5 The least squares fit $(f(x; w_0, w_1) = 36.416 - 0.013x)$ to the men's 100 m Olympic dataset.

1.1.7 Summary

It is worth recapping the topics covered so far. We have introduced the idea of creating a model (in particular, a linear one) that encapsulates the relationship between a set of attributes and a set of responses. To enable us to fit (or learn) this model from data, we defined a *loss* function as a way of objectively identifying how good a particular model was. Using the squared loss, we derived exact expressions for the values of the model parameters that minimised the loss and therefore corresponded to the best function. Finally, we applied this technique to two different datasets. We shall now see how we can use the model to make predictions.

1.2   MAKING PREDICTIONS

Now that we have a model relating the Olympic year to the winning 100 m sprint time, we can use it to predict the winning time for a year that we have not yet observed. For example, to predict the winning times at the 2012 and 2016 Olympics, t^{2012} and t^{2016}, we plug $x = 2012$ and $x = 2016$ into our formula.

$$
\begin{aligned}
f(x; w_0 = 36.416, w_1 = -0.0133) &= 36.416 - 0.0133x \\
t^{2012} = f(2012; w_0, w_1) &= 36.416 - 0.0133 \times 2012 = 9.595\,\text{s} \\
t^{2016} = f(2016; w_0, w_1) &= 36.416 - 0.0133 \times 2016 = 9.541\,\text{s}
\end{aligned}
$$

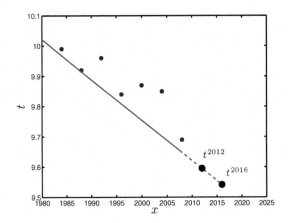

FIGURE 1.6   Zoomed in plot of the winning time in the Olympic men's 100 m sprint from 1980 showing predictions for both the 2012 and 2016 Olympics.

These predictions can be seen in Figure 1.6 (MATLAB script: olymppred.m). They tell us that, based on our linear regression model, we might expect a winning time of 9.595 s in London in 2012. This value is very precise. It seems unlikely that *any* model would be able to predict the outcome of such a complex event to such a high degree of accuracy, least of all one based on nothing more than a straight line. Our model is not even able to predict data that it has seen very precisely, as can be seen by the distance of some points to the line in Figure 1.5. Assuming that it will become more precise into the future seems particularly foolish.

Precise predictions are only of limited use in situations where our model is not perfect (almost all situations). In general, it is more useful to be able to express a range of values rather than any particular one. We shall see how to do this in Chapter 2 and beyond.

1.2.1   A second Olympic dataset

A second dataset, related to the first, is shown in Table 1.3 and is plotted, along with the linear model that minimises the squared loss, in Figure 1.7 (see Exercise 1.6

TABLE 1.3 Olympic women's 100 m data.

n	x_n	t_n	$x_n t_n$	x_n^2
1	1928	12.20	23521.6	3.7172×10^6
2	1932	11.90	22990.8	3.7326×10^6
3	1936	11.50	22264.0	3.7481×10^6
4	1948	11.90	23181.2	3.7947×10^6
5	1952	11.50	22448.0	3.8103×10^6
6	1956	11.50	22494.0	3.8259×10^6
7	1960	11.00	21560.0	3.8416×10^6
8	1964	11.40	22389.6	3.8573×10^6
9	1968	11.00	21648.0	3.8730×10^6
10	1972	11.07	21830.0	3.8888×10^6
11	1976	11.08	21894.1	3.9046×10^6
12	1980	11.06	21898.8	3.9204×10^6
13	1984	10.97	21764.5	3.9363×10^6
14	1988	10.54	20953.5	3.9521×10^6
15	1992	10.82	21553.4	3.9681×10^6
16	1996	10.94	21836.2	3.9840×10^6
17	2000	11.12	22240.0	4.0000×10^6
18	2004	10.93	21903.7	4.0160×10^6
19	2008	10.78	21646.2	4.0321×10^6
$(1/N) \sum_{n=1}^{N}$	1970.74	11.22	22106.2	3.8844×10^6

and Exercise 1.7). The model for the women's data is (remember that you might find slight differences to these values due to rounding errors)

$$f(x; w_0, w_1) = 40.92 - 0.015x.$$

It is interesting to compare this with the model obtained for the men's data:

$$f(x; w_0, w_1) = 36.416 - 0.013x.$$

The women's model has a higher intercept (w_0) and a steeper negative gradient (w_1). If we plot the two models together, as seen in Figure 1.8, we see that the higher intercept and larger negative gradient mean that, at some point, the two lines will intercept. Using our models we can predict the first Olympic games when the women's winning time will be faster than the men's. According to our models this will be in the 2592 Olympics (the actual answer has been rounded up to the nearest Olympic year and has been computed in MATLAB using the exact data, so you might find slight differences due to rounding) (see Exercise 1.8).

As with the point predictions for individual models, we should not place too much confidence in this prediction coming about. Not only is the prediction incredibly precise, it is also a very long time from our last observed data point. Can we assume that the relationship between winning time and Olympic year will continue this far into the future? To assume that it can is also to assume that there will, eventually, be a winning time of 0 seconds and we know that this is impossible.

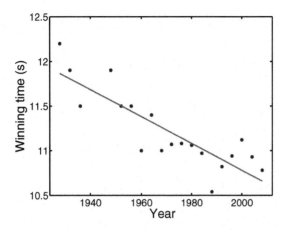

FIGURE 1.7 Women's Olympic 100 m data with a linear model that minimises the squared loss.

1.2.2 Summary

In the previous sections we have seen how we can fit a simple linear model to a small dataset and use the resulting model to make predictions. We have also described some of the limitations of making predictions in this way and we will introduce alternative techniques that overcome these limitations in later chapters. Up to this point, our attributes (x_n) have been individual numbers. We will now see how the linear model can be extended to larger sets of attributes, enabling us to model more complex relationships.

1.3 VECTOR/MATRIX NOTATION

In many applications, we will be interested in problems where each data point is described by a set of several attributes. For example, we might decide that using only the Olympic year is unsuitable for a model of Olympic sprint data. A model that used the Olympic year and each athlete's personal best might be more accurate. Using $s_1, s_2, \ldots, s_8$ to denote the personal best times for the athletes running in lanes 1 to 8, a possible linear model might consist of

$$
\begin{aligned}
t = f(x, s_1, \ldots, s_8; w_0, \ldots, w_9) \quad &= \quad w_0 + w_1 x + w_2 s_1 + w_3 s_2 + w_4 s_3 \\
&\quad + w_5 s_4 + w_6 s_5 + w_7 s_6 + w_8 s_7 + w_9 s_8.
\end{aligned}
$$

We could go through the analysis of the previous sections to find $\widehat{w_0}, \ldots, \widehat{w_9}$. After taking partial derivatives of the loss function, we would be left with 10 equations that would need to be rearranged and substituted into one another. This would be a time consuming exercise and would rapidly become infeasible as the number of variables we wanted to include increased further – machine learning applications with thousands of variables are not uncommon. Fortunately there is an alternative – using vectors and matrices.

As this is an area that some readers will find unfamiliar, we shall now devote some

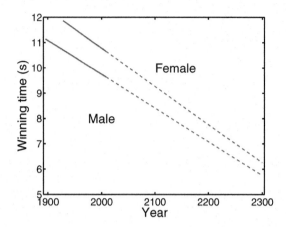

FIGURE 1.8 Male and female functions extrapolated into the future.

time to describing vector and matrix notation and how to perform mathematical operations with quantities in vector and matrix form. Readers familiar with these concepts could jump straight to Section 1.4.

> **Comment 1.3 – Scalars, vectors and matrices:** We will follow the standard convention of representing scalar values by letters (e.g. x), vectors by bold lowercase letters (e.g. $\mathbf{x}$) and matrices by bold uppercase letters (e.g. $\mathbf{X}$). Whilst we shall consistently stick to this notation, different communities have different ways of defining vectors. For example, $\overline{x}$ is common for a vector x.

The nine attributes for each data point (eight personal bests and Olympic year) can be combined into a single variable by stacking them together to form a vector. We will denote vectors with bold lower case letters, e.g. $\mathbf{x}_n$ (see Comment 1.3). Often we will need to refer to individual elements within a particular vector or matrix and will use *indices* to make it clear which element we're referring to. For example, the first element of the vector $\mathbf{x}_n$ would be denoted x_{n1}, the ith by x_{ni}.

If we want to show all of the elements in a vector, we write it out in a tabular fashion, surrounded by square brackets. Here are examples of vectors of length 2 and 4:

$$\mathbf{x}_n = \left[\begin{array}{c} x_{n1} \\ x_{n2} \end{array} \right], \ \mathbf{y} = \left[\begin{array}{c} y_1 \\ y_2 \\ y_3 \\ y_4 \end{array} \right].$$

Comment 1.4 – Vector transpose: The transpose of a vector $\mathbf{x}$, denoted $\mathbf{x}^\mathsf{T}$, is obtained by rotating the vector such that, rather than having one column and several rows, it has one row and several columns. For example

$$\mathbf{x} = \begin{bmatrix} 4 \\ 7 \\ 11 \\ -2 \end{bmatrix}, \quad \mathbf{x}^\mathsf{T} = [4, 7, 11, -2].$$

It is often a bit clumsy to keep drawing vectors as columns so we will often draw them as rows, and use the transpose operator (see Comment 1.4) to show that they should be rotated. If we assume that we have D attributes, we would define $\mathbf{x}_n$ as $\mathbf{x}_n = [x_{n1}, \ldots, x_{nD}]^\mathsf{T}$. In the case of our Olympic data, $\mathbf{x} = [\text{Year}, s_1, s_2, \ldots, s_8]^\mathsf{T}$.

Comment 1.5 – Matrix/vector dimensions and indexing: If we are quoting the size (or the dimension) of a matrix or vector, we give two numbers, starting with the number of rows. For example,

$$\mathbf{A} = \begin{bmatrix} a_{11} & a_{12} \\ a_{21} & a_{22} \\ a_{31} & a_{32} \end{bmatrix}$$

has dimension 3×2. A vector is a special case of a matrix where the second dimension is 1. For example,

$$\mathbf{y} = \begin{bmatrix} y_1 \\ y_2 \\ y_3 \\ y_4 \end{bmatrix}$$

could be thought of as a matrix with dimension 4×1.

When indexing elements within a vector, a single number is sufficient (e.g. y_3 for the third element in $\mathbf{y}$ above. When indexing a matrix, we will use two subscripts, starting with the row. For example, a_{21} represents the item in the second row and first column of $\mathbf{A}$ (above). Note that sometimes we will also have a subscript denoting the object index. For example, $\mathbf{x}_n$ is the vector holding the nth set of attributes. This index, if present, will always come first. It should be obvious from the context whether or not this index is present.

Before we embark on adding additional variables, it is worthwhile to repeat the analysis of the original model ($t = w_0 + w_1x$) in vector form. This will allow us to compare the expressions we obtain for $\widehat{w_0}$ and $\widehat{w_1}$ in both cases. The first step is to combine w_0 and w_1 into a single parameter vector $\mathbf{w}$ and create data vectors $\mathbf{x}_n$ by augmenting each x_n with a 1, i.e.

$$\mathbf{w} = \begin{bmatrix} w_0 \\ w_1 \end{bmatrix}, \quad \mathbf{x}_n = \begin{bmatrix} 1 \\ x_n \end{bmatrix}.$$

The model can be expressed in terms of $\mathbf{x}_n$ and $\mathbf{w}$ as (matrix/vector multiplication is defined in Comment 1.7)

$$f(x_n; w_0, w_1) = \mathbf{w}^\mathsf{T} \mathbf{x}_n = w_0 + w_1 x_n.$$

We can replace any instance of $w_0 + w_1 x$ by $\mathbf{w}^\mathsf{T}\mathbf{x}$. For example, our squared loss $\mathcal{L}$ can be expressed as

$$\mathcal{L} = \frac{1}{N} \sum_{n=1}^{N} (t_n - \mathbf{w}^\mathsf{T}\mathbf{x}_n)^2. \tag{1.12}$$

In actual fact, we can express this average loss as the following function of various vectors and matrices, which will be easier to manipulate:

$$\mathcal{L} = \frac{1}{N}(\mathbf{t} - \mathbf{X}\mathbf{w})^\mathsf{T}(\mathbf{t} - \mathbf{X}\mathbf{w}).$$

To see how this is equivalent to Equation 1.12, we start by combining all $\mathbf{x}_n$ into one matrix $\mathbf{X}$, and all t_n into one vector $\mathbf{t}$:

$$\mathbf{X} = \begin{bmatrix} \mathbf{x}_1^\mathsf{T} \\ \mathbf{x}_2^\mathsf{T} \\ \vdots \\ \mathbf{x}_N^\mathsf{T} \end{bmatrix} = \begin{bmatrix} 1 & x_1 \\ 1 & x_2 \\ \vdots & \vdots \\ 1 & x_N \end{bmatrix}, \quad \mathbf{t} = \begin{bmatrix} t_1 \\ t_2 \\ \vdots \\ t_N \end{bmatrix}.$$

Comment 1.6 – Matrix transpose: For a matrix, $\mathbf{X}$, the transpose, $\mathbf{X}^\mathsf{T}$, is formed by turning each row into a column and each column into a row. For example, if $\mathbf{Y} = \mathbf{X}^\mathsf{T}$, then $Y_{ij} = X_{ji}$.

$$\mathbf{X} = \begin{bmatrix} 1 & 4 \\ 3 & 6 \\ -2 & 11 \end{bmatrix}, \quad \mathbf{X}^\mathsf{T} = \begin{bmatrix} 1 & 3 & -2 \\ 4 & 6 & 11 \end{bmatrix}.$$

Comment 1.7 – Matrix multiplication: To proceed, we must introduce the concept of matrix multiplication. Taking the product, $\mathbf{AB}$, of an $N \times M$ matrix $\mathbf{A}$ and a $P \times Q$ matrix $\mathbf{B}$ is only possible if $M = P$, i.e. the number of columns in $\mathbf{A}$ is equal to the number of rows in $\mathbf{B}$. Assuming that this is the case, the product, $\mathbf{C} = \mathbf{AB}$ is the $N \times Q$ matrix defined such that

$$C_{ij} = \sum_k A_{ik} B_{kj}.$$

It is often helpful to draw the matrices. For example,

$$\begin{bmatrix} a_{11} & a_{12} \\ a_{21} & a_{22} \end{bmatrix} \begin{bmatrix} b_{11} & b_{12} & b_{13} \\ b_{21} & b_{22} & b_{23} \\ a_{11}b_{11} + a_{12}b_{21} & a_{11}b_{12} + a_{12}b_{22} & a_{11}b_{13} + a_{12}b_{23} \\ a_{21}b_{11} + a_{22}b_{21} & a_{21}b_{12} + a_{22}b_{22} & a_{21}b_{13} + a_{22}b_{23} \end{bmatrix}$$

where we can think of computing elements of $\mathbf{C}$ by working simultaneously across the relevant row of $\mathbf{A}$ and column of $\mathbf{B}$.

A special case that we will meet regularly is the *inner product* between two column vectors, defined as $z = \mathbf{x}^\mathsf{T}\mathbf{y}$, the result of which is a scalar. Both vectors must be of the same length and the transpose ensures that the number of columns in $\mathbf{x}$ is the same as the number of rows in $\mathbf{y}$. Applying the same technique as that for matrices, we see that

$$z = \sum_k x_k y_k.$$

Therefore, if we perform the matrix multiplication $\mathbf{Xw}$ we will end up with a vector which looks like this:

$$\mathbf{Xw} = \begin{bmatrix} 1 & x_1 \\ 1 & x_2 \\ \vdots & \vdots \\ 1 & x_N \end{bmatrix} \times \begin{bmatrix} w_0 \\ w_1 \end{bmatrix} = \begin{bmatrix} w_0 + w_1 x_1 \\ w_0 + w_1 x_2 \\ \vdots \\ w_0 + w_1 x_N \end{bmatrix}.$$

Subtracting this from $\mathbf{t}$ will give us

$$\mathbf{t} - \mathbf{Xw} = \begin{bmatrix} t_1 - w_0 - w_1 x_1 \\ t_2 - w_0 - w_1 x_2 \\ \vdots \\ t_N - w_0 - w_1 x_N \end{bmatrix}$$

and we can use a single multiplication and transpose to neatly perform the squaring and summation and obtain our original loss function:

$$\begin{aligned} (\mathbf{Xw} - \mathbf{t})^\mathsf{T}(\mathbf{Xw} - \mathbf{t}) &= (w_0 + w_1 x_1 - t_1)^2 + (w_0 + w_1 x_2 - t_2)^2 \\ &\quad + \cdots + (w_0 + w_1 x_N - t_N)^2 \\ &= \sum_{n=1}^{N} (w_0 + w_1 x_n - t_n)^2 \\ &= \sum_{n=1}^{N} (t_n - f(x_n; w_0, w_1))^2. \end{aligned}$$

Therefore, our loss can be written compactly as

$$\mathcal{L} = \frac{1}{N} (\mathbf{t} - \mathbf{Xw})^\mathsf{T} (\mathbf{t} - \mathbf{Xw}), \tag{1.13}$$

and the following loss expressions are all equivalent:

$$\mathcal{L} = \frac{1}{N} (\mathbf{t} - \mathbf{Xw})^\mathsf{T} (\mathbf{t} - \mathbf{Xw}) = \frac{1}{N} \sum_{n=1}^{N} (t_n - \mathbf{w}^\mathsf{T} \mathbf{x}_n)^2 = \frac{1}{N} \sum_{n=1}^{N} (t_n - (w_0 + w_1 x_n))^2.$$

Comment 1.8 – Transpose of a product: The transpose of a matrix product, $(\mathbf{Xw})^\mathsf{T}$, can be expanded by reversing the order of multiplication and transposing the two individual matrices

$$(\mathbf{Xw})^\mathsf{T} = \mathbf{w}^\mathsf{T} \mathbf{X}^\mathsf{T}.$$

To deal with more complex forms, we can apply the same result several times. For example,

$$\begin{aligned} (\mathbf{ABCD})^\mathsf{T} &= ((\mathbf{AB})(\mathbf{CD}))^\mathsf{T} \\ &= (\mathbf{CD})^\mathsf{T} (\mathbf{AB})^\mathsf{T} \\ &= \mathbf{D}^\mathsf{T} \mathbf{C}^\mathsf{T} \mathbf{B}^\mathsf{T} \mathbf{A}^\mathsf{T} \end{aligned}$$

It will be easier to work with this matrix loss once we have multiplied out the brackets. Noting that order is important in matrix multiplication (this is implied by the restriction on sizes discussed in Comment 1.7) and the definition for the transpose of a product given in Comment 1.8

$$
\begin{aligned}
\mathcal{L} &= \frac{1}{N}(\mathbf{Xw} - \mathbf{t})^{\mathsf{T}}(\mathbf{Xw} - \mathbf{t}) \\
&= ((\mathbf{Xw})^{\mathsf{T}} - \mathbf{t}^{\mathsf{T}})(\mathbf{Xw} - \mathbf{t}) \\
&= \frac{1}{N}(\mathbf{Xw})^{\mathsf{T}}\mathbf{Xw} - \frac{1}{N}\mathbf{t}^{\mathsf{T}}\mathbf{Xw} - \frac{1}{N}(\mathbf{Xw})^{\mathsf{T}}\mathbf{t} + \frac{1}{N}\mathbf{t}^{\mathsf{T}}\mathbf{t} \\
&= \frac{1}{N}\mathbf{w}^{\mathsf{T}}\mathbf{X}^{\mathsf{T}}\mathbf{Xw} - \frac{2}{N}\mathbf{w}^{\mathsf{T}}\mathbf{X}^{\mathsf{T}}\mathbf{t} + \frac{1}{N}\mathbf{t}^{\mathsf{T}}\mathbf{t}.
\end{aligned}
\tag{1.14}
$$

The two terms $\mathbf{t}^{\mathsf{T}}\mathbf{Xw}$ and $\mathbf{w}^{\mathsf{T}}\mathbf{X}^{\mathsf{T}}\mathbf{t}$ are the transpose of one another (using the identity for the transpose of a product) and also scalars (satisfy yourself that the result is a 1×1 matrix and hence a scalar). This implies that they must be the same and can therefore be combined.

Differentiating loss in vector/matrix form   We now require the value of the vector $\mathbf{w}$ corresponding to a turning point (minimum) of $\mathcal{L}$. To do this, we must take the partial derivate of $\mathcal{L}$ with respect to the *vector* $\mathbf{w}$. This involves taking partial derivatives of $\mathcal{L}$ with respect to each element of $\mathbf{w}$ in turn and then stacking the results into a vector. It is worth explicitly doing this in this instance, although we will see later that we can actually obtain $\frac{\partial \mathcal{L}}{\partial \mathbf{w}}$ directly in vector form. In our two-variable case, this vector is

$$
\frac{\partial \mathcal{L}}{\partial \mathbf{w}} = \left[\begin{array}{c} \frac{\partial \mathcal{L}}{\partial w_0} \\ \frac{\partial \mathcal{L}}{\partial w_1} \end{array} \right],
$$

the vector containing the partial derivatives of $\mathcal{L}$ with respect to w_0 and w_1. The two elements of this vector should be the same as Equations 1.7 and 1.6, respectively. We can check that our loss is indeed correct by manually differentiating Equation 1.13 with respect to the two parameters. Firstly, we need the multiplied out expression

$$
\mathcal{L} = \frac{1}{N}(\mathbf{w}^{\mathsf{T}}\mathbf{X}^{\mathsf{T}}\mathbf{Xw} - 2\mathbf{w}^{\mathsf{T}}\mathbf{X}^{\mathsf{T}}\mathbf{t} + \mathbf{t}^{\mathsf{T}}\mathbf{t}).
$$

The last term doesn't include either w_0 or w_1 so we can ignore it. When multiplied out, the first term is (see Exercise 1.3)

$$
w_0^2 \frac{1}{N}\left(\sum_{n=1}^{N} X_{n0}^2 \right) + 2w_0 w_1 \frac{1}{N}\left(\sum_{n=1}^{N} X_{n0}X_{n1} \right) + w_1^2 \frac{1}{N}\left(\sum_{n=1}^{N} X_{n1}^2 \right),
$$

where X_{n0} is the first element of the nth row of $\mathbf{X}$, i.e. the first element of the nth data object, and X_{n1} is the second (we've started numbering from zero to maintain the relationship with w_0). Similarly, the second term is equivalent to

$$
2w_0 \frac{1}{N}\left(\sum_{n=1}^{N} X_{n0}t_n \right) + 2w_1 \frac{1}{N}\left(\sum_{n=1}^{N} X_{n1}t_n \right).
$$

Combining these and noting that, in our previous notation, $X_{n0} = 1$ and $X_{n1} = x_n$ results in

$$w_0^2 + 2w_0w_1 \frac{1}{N} \left(\sum_{n=1}^{N} x_n \right) + w_1^2 \frac{1}{N} \left(\sum_{n=1}^{N} x_{n1}^2 \right) - 2w_0 \frac{1}{N} \left(\sum_{n=1}^{N} t_n \right) - 2w_1 \frac{1}{N} \left(\sum_{n=1}^{N} x_n t_n \right).$$

Recalling our shorthand for the various averages and differentiating with respect to w_0 and w_1 results in

$$\frac{\partial \mathcal{L}}{\partial w_0} = 2w_0 + 2w_1 \bar{x} - 2\bar{t}$$

$$\frac{\partial \mathcal{L}}{\partial w_1} = 2w_0 \bar{x} + 2w_1 \overline{x^2} - 2\overline{xt}.$$

It is left as an informal exercise to show that these are indeed equivalent to the derivates obtained from the non-vectorised loss function (Equations 1.7 and 1.6).

Fortunately, there are many standard identities that we can use that enable us to differentiate the vectorised expression directly. Those that we will need are shown in Table 1.4.

TABLE 1.4 Some useful identities when differentiating with respect to a vector.

$f(\mathbf{w})$	$\frac{\partial f}{\partial \mathbf{w}}$
$\mathbf{w}^\mathsf{T}\mathbf{x}$	$\mathbf{x}$
$\mathbf{x}^\mathsf{T}\mathbf{w}$	$\mathbf{x}$
$\mathbf{w}^\mathsf{T}\mathbf{w}$	$2\mathbf{w}$
$\mathbf{w}^\mathsf{T}\mathbf{C}\mathbf{w}$	$2\mathbf{C}\mathbf{w}$

From these identities, and equating the derivative to zero, we can directly obtain the following:

$$\frac{\partial \mathcal{L}}{\partial \mathbf{w}} = \frac{2}{N}\mathbf{X}^\mathsf{T}\mathbf{X}\mathbf{w} - \frac{2}{N}\mathbf{X}^\mathsf{T}\mathbf{t} = 0$$

$$\mathbf{X}^\mathsf{T}\mathbf{X}\mathbf{w} = \mathbf{X}^\mathsf{T}\mathbf{t}. \tag{1.15}$$

Comment 1.9 – Identity matrix: we will regularly come across the identity matrix $\mathbf{I}_N$. It is the $N \times N$ matrix with ones on the diagonal and zeros elsewhere.

$$\mathbf{I}_1 = 1, \quad \mathbf{I}_2 = \begin{bmatrix} 1 & 0 \\ 0 & 1 \end{bmatrix}, \quad \mathbf{I}_3 = \begin{bmatrix} 1 & 0 & 0 \\ 0 & 1 & 0 \\ 0 & 0 & 1 \end{bmatrix}.$$

Often, the size of the identity matrix will be obvious from the expression it's found in. In these cases, we will omit the size subscript.

A key property of the identity matrix is that any vector or matrix multiplied by a suitably sized identity matrix is equal to the original matrix or vector. For example, if $\mathbf{y} = [y_1, \ldots, y_D]^\mathsf{T}$ and $\mathbf{I}_D$ is the $D \times D$ identity matrix,

$$\mathbf{y}^\mathsf{T} \mathbf{I}_D = \mathbf{y}, \quad \mathbf{I}\mathbf{y} = \mathbf{y}.$$

Similarly, for an $N \times M$ matrix,

$$\mathbf{A} = \begin{bmatrix} a_{11} & a_{12} & \ldots & a_{1M} \\ a_{21} & a_{22} & \ldots & a_{2M} \\ \vdots & \vdots & \ddots & \vdots \\ a_{N1} & a_{N2} & \ldots & a_{NM} \end{bmatrix}$$

$$\mathbf{A}\mathbf{I}_M = \mathbf{A}, \quad \mathbf{I}_N \mathbf{A} = \mathbf{A}.$$

Multiplying a scalar by an identity results in a matrix with the scalar value on each diagonal element. An example that crops up a lot is

$$\sigma^2 \mathbf{I}_M = \begin{bmatrix} \sigma^2 & 0 & \ldots & 0 \\ 0 & \sigma^2 & \ldots & 0 \\ \vdots & \vdots & \ddots & \vdots \\ 0 & 0 & \ldots & \sigma^2 \end{bmatrix}.$$

Comment 1.10 – Matrix inverse: The inverse of a matrix $\mathbf{A}$ is defined as the matrix $\mathbf{A}^{-1}$ that satisfies $\mathbf{A}^{-1}\mathbf{A} = \mathbf{I}$. We don't provide the general form for inverting a matrix here, but from school mathematics, a 2×2 matrix can be inverted with the following formula:

$$\mathbf{A} = \begin{bmatrix} a & b \\ c & d \end{bmatrix}, \quad \mathbf{A}^{-1} = \frac{1}{ad - bc} \begin{bmatrix} d & -b \\ -c & a \end{bmatrix}.$$

A special case that we will come across regularly is the inverse of a matrix that only has values on the diagonal (i.e. all off-diagonal elements are zero). The inverse of such a matrix is another diagonal matrix where each diagonal element is simply the inverse of the corresponding element in the original. For example,

$$\mathbf{A} = \begin{bmatrix} a_{11} & 0 & \cdots & 0 \\ 0 & a_{22} & \cdots & 0 \\ \vdots & \vdots & \ddots & \vdots \\ 0 & 0 & \cdots & a_{DD} \end{bmatrix}, \quad \mathbf{A}^{-1} = \begin{bmatrix} a_{11}^{-1} & 0 & \cdots & 0 \\ 0 & a_{22}^{-1} & \cdots & 0 \\ \vdots & \vdots & \ddots & \vdots \\ 0 & 0 & \cdots & a_{DD}^{-1} \end{bmatrix}.$$

It is worth noting that this definition implies that the inverse of an identity matrix (see Comment 1.9) is simply another identity matrix:

$$\mathbf{I}^{-1} = \mathbf{I}.$$

The final step in deriving an expression $\widehat{\mathbf{w}}$, the optimum value of $\mathbf{w}$, is rearranging Equation 1.15. We cannot divide both sides by $\mathbf{X}^\mathsf{T}\mathbf{X}$ (division isn't defined for matrices) but we can premultiply both sides by a matrix that will cancel the $\mathbf{X}^\mathsf{T}\mathbf{X}$ from the left (leaving only an identity matrix, see Comment 1.9). This matrix is called the matrix inverse of $\mathbf{X}^\mathsf{T}\mathbf{X}$ (see Comment 1.10) and is denoted by $(\mathbf{X}^\mathsf{T}\mathbf{X})^{-1}$. Premultiplying both sides of (1.15) with $(\mathbf{X}^\mathsf{T}\mathbf{X})^{-1}$, we obtain

$$\mathbf{I}\mathbf{w} = (\mathbf{X}^\mathsf{T}\mathbf{X})^{-1}\mathbf{X}^\mathsf{T}\mathbf{t}.$$

As $\mathbf{I}\mathbf{w} = \mathbf{w}$ (from the definition of the identity matrix), we are left with a matrix equation for $\widehat{\mathbf{w}}$, the value of $\mathbf{w}$ that minimises the loss:

$$\widehat{\mathbf{w}} = (\mathbf{X}^\mathsf{T}\mathbf{X})^{-1}\mathbf{X}^\mathsf{T}\mathbf{t}. \tag{1.16}$$

1.3.1 Example

We can check that our matrix equation is doing exactly the same as the scalar equations we got previously by multiplying it out. In two dimensions,

$$\mathbf{X}^\mathsf{T}\mathbf{X} = \begin{bmatrix} \sum_{n=1}^N x_{n0}^2 & \sum_{n=1}^N x_{n0}x_{n1} \\ \sum_{n=1}^N x_{n1}x_{n0} & \sum_{n=1}^N x_{n1}^2 \end{bmatrix}.$$

Using $\bar{x}$ to denote averages, this can be rewritten as

$$\mathbf{X}^\mathsf{T}\mathbf{X} = N \begin{bmatrix} \overline{x_0^2} & \overline{x_0 x_1} \\ \overline{x_1 x_0} & \overline{x_1^2} \end{bmatrix}.$$

The identity for the inverse of a 2×2 matrix (see Comment 1.10) enables us to invert this

$$(\mathbf{X}^\mathsf{T}\mathbf{X})^{-1} = \frac{1}{N} \frac{1}{\overline{x_0^2}\,\overline{x_1^2} - \overline{x_1 x_0}\,\overline{x_0 x_1}} \begin{bmatrix} \overline{x_1^2} & -\overline{x_0 x_1} \\ -\overline{x_1 x_0} & \overline{x_0^2} \end{bmatrix}.$$

We need to multiply this by $\mathbf{X}^\mathsf{T}\mathbf{t}$, which is (jumping straight to the average notation),

$$N \begin{bmatrix} \overline{x_0 t} \\ \overline{x_1 t} \end{bmatrix}.$$

Now, we know that x_{n0} is 1 always and redefining x_{n1} as x_n (to be consistent with the scalar notation), we need to evaluate

$$\widehat{\mathbf{w}} = \frac{1}{N} \frac{1}{\overline{x^2} - \overline{x}\,\overline{x}} \begin{bmatrix} \overline{x^2} & -\overline{x} \\ -\overline{x} & 1 \end{bmatrix} \times N \begin{bmatrix} \overline{t} \\ \overline{xt} \end{bmatrix},$$

which is

$$\widehat{\mathbf{w}} = \begin{bmatrix} \widehat{w_0} \\ \widehat{w_1} \end{bmatrix} = \left(\frac{1}{\overline{x^2} - \overline{x}\,\overline{x}} \right) \begin{bmatrix} \overline{x^2}\,\overline{t} - \overline{x}\,\overline{xt} \\ -\overline{x}\,\overline{t} + \overline{xt} \end{bmatrix}. \tag{1.17}$$

Starting with $\widehat{w_1}$ (the second line),

$$\widehat{w_1} = \frac{\overline{xt} - \overline{x}\,\overline{t}}{\overline{x^2} - \overline{x}\,\overline{x}},$$

exactly as before. $\widehat{w_0}$ requires a little more rearrangement and it is easier to work backwards. Starting from our original expression and substituting this new expression for $\widehat{w_1}$,

$$\begin{aligned}
\widehat{w_0} &= \overline{t} - \widehat{w_1}\overline{x} \\
&= \overline{t} - \overline{x}\frac{\overline{xt} - \overline{x}\,\overline{t}}{\overline{x^2} - \overline{x}\,\overline{x}} \\
&= \overline{t}\left(\frac{\overline{x^2} - \overline{x}\,\overline{x}}{\overline{x^2} - \overline{x}\,\overline{x}} \right) - \overline{x}\frac{\overline{xt} - \overline{x}\,\overline{t}}{\overline{x^2} - \overline{x}\,\overline{x}} \\
&= \frac{\overline{t}\,\overline{x^2} - \overline{t}\,\overline{x}\,\overline{x} - \overline{x}\,\overline{xt} + \overline{x}\,\overline{x}\,\overline{t}}{\overline{x^2} - \overline{x}\,\overline{x}} \\
&= \frac{\overline{t}\overline{x^2} - \overline{x}\,\overline{xt}}{\overline{x^2} - \overline{x}\,\overline{x}},
\end{aligned}$$

which is exactly the first line in Equation 1.17, as required.

1.3.2 Numerical example

To help those readers who are not familiar with working with vectors and matrices, we will now repeat the synthetic linear regression example we saw in the previous section. The data, in matrix notation is

$$\mathbf{X} = \begin{bmatrix} 1 & 1 \\ 1 & 3 \\ 1 & 5 \end{bmatrix}, \quad \mathbf{t} = \begin{bmatrix} 4.8 \\ 11.3 \\ 17.2 \end{bmatrix}.$$

Examining Equation 1.16 we see that the first quantity we need to calculate is $\mathbf{X}^\mathsf{T}\mathbf{X}$:

$$\mathbf{X}^\mathsf{T}\mathbf{X} = \begin{bmatrix} 1 & 1 & 1 \\ 1 & 3 & 5 \end{bmatrix} \times \begin{bmatrix} 1 & 1 \\ 1 & 3 \\ 1 & 5 \end{bmatrix} = \begin{bmatrix} 3 & 9 \\ 9 & 35 \end{bmatrix}.$$

Using the formula provided above, we compute the inverse as

$$(\mathbf{X}^\mathsf{T}\mathbf{X})^{-1} = \frac{1}{24} \begin{bmatrix} 35 & -9 \\ -9 & 3 \end{bmatrix}.$$

Multiplying by $\mathbf{X}^\mathsf{T}$,

$$(\mathbf{X}^\mathsf{T}\mathbf{X})^{-1}\mathbf{X}^\mathsf{T} = \frac{1}{24} \begin{bmatrix} 35 & -9 \\ -9 & 3 \end{bmatrix} \times \begin{bmatrix} 1 & 1 & 1 \\ 1 & 3 & 5 \end{bmatrix} = \frac{1}{24} \begin{bmatrix} 26 & 8 & -10 \\ -6 & 0 & 6 \end{bmatrix}.$$

Finally, we multiply this matrix by $\mathbf{t}$:

$$\left((\mathbf{X}^\mathsf{T}\mathbf{X})^{-1}\mathbf{X}^\mathsf{T}\right)\mathbf{t} = \frac{1}{24} \begin{bmatrix} 26 & 8 & -10 \\ -6 & 0 & 6 \end{bmatrix} \times \begin{bmatrix} 4.8 \\ 11.3 \\ 17.2 \end{bmatrix} = \begin{bmatrix} 1.8 \\ 3.1 \end{bmatrix}.$$

Therefore, our formula is $f(x; w_0, w_1) = 1.8 + 3.1x$, exactly as before.

1.3.3 Making predictions

Given a new vector of attributes, x_{new}, the prediction from the model, t_{new}, is computed as

$$t_{\mathsf{new}} = \widehat{\mathbf{w}}^\mathsf{T}\mathbf{x}_{\mathsf{new}}.$$

1.3.4 Summary

In the previous sections, we have described our linear model in terms of vectors and matrices. The result is a very useful model – our expression for $\widehat{\mathbf{w}}$ makes no assumptions as to the number of parameters included in $\widehat{\mathbf{w}}$ (its length). We can therefore compute $\widehat{\mathbf{w}}$ and make predictions for any linear model of the form

$$t_n = w_1 x_{n1} + w_2 x_{n2} + w_3 x_{n3} + \ldots$$

This is a powerful tool – many real datasets are described by more than one attribute and for many, a linear model of this type will be appropriate. We have also learnt that predictions from this model are very precise and that this is not always sensible. We shall see how to overcome this in later chapters.

The attributes that make up $\mathbf{x}_n$ could be measurements of different properties (e.g. winning times and personal bests). Alternatively, they could be the result of applying a set of functions to an individual attribute like the Olympic year: x_n. This allows us to extend our armoury beyond models corresponding to straight lines and is the subject of the next section.

1.4 NON-LINEAR RESPONSE FROM A LINEAR MODEL

At the start of this chapter, we made the assumption that we could model the relationship between time and Olympic 100 m sprint times using a linear function. In many real applications, this is too restrictive. Even for the 100 m data it could be argued that it is far too simplistic – the linear model predicts that in the year 3000, the time will be -3.5 seconds! Fortunately, we can use exactly the same framework we have already described to fit a family of more complex models through a transformation of the attributes.

The linear model we have seen thus far,

$$f(x; \mathbf{w}) = w_0 + w_1 x,$$

is linear in both the parameters (w) and the data (x) (see Comment 1.1). The linearity in the parameters is desirable from a computational point of view, as the solution that minimises the squared loss can be found exactly via Equations 1.8 and 1.10. Consider augmenting our data matrix $\mathbf{X}$ with an additional column, x_n^2:

$$\mathbf{x}_n = \begin{bmatrix} 1 \\ x_n \\ x_n^2 \end{bmatrix}, \quad \mathbf{X} = \begin{bmatrix} 1 & x_1 & x_1^2 \\ 1 & x_2 & x_2^2 \\ \vdots & \vdots & \vdots \\ 1 & x_N & x_N^2 \end{bmatrix}$$

and adding an extra parameter to $\mathbf{w}$:

$$\mathbf{w} = \begin{bmatrix} w_0 \\ w_1 \\ w_2 \end{bmatrix},$$

resulting in

$$f(x; \mathbf{w}) = \mathbf{w}^\mathsf{T} \mathbf{x} = w_0 + w_1 x + w_2 x^2.$$

As the model is still linear in the parameters, we can use Equation 1.16 to find $\mathbf{w}$ but the function we are fitting is **quadratic** in the data. Figure 1.9 shows an example of using exactly this method to fit a function quadratic in the data to a suitable dataset (solid line) (MATLAB script: `synthquad.m`). Also shown is the function we get if we try and fit our original linear (in the data) model (dashed line, $t = w_0 + w_1 x$). It is clear from the quality of the fit to the data that the quadratic model is a more appropriate model for this data.

More generally, we can add as many powers of x as we like to get a **polynomial** function of any order. For a Kth order polynomial, our augmented data matrix will be

$$\mathbf{X} = \begin{bmatrix} x_1^0 & x_1^1 & x_1^2 & \cdots & x_1^K \\ x_2^0 & x_2^1 & x_2^2 & \cdots & x_2^K \\ \vdots & \vdots & \vdots & \cdots & \vdots \\ x_N^0 & x_N^1 & x_N^2 & \cdots & x_N^K \end{bmatrix} \tag{1.18}$$

(where $x^0 = 1$) and our function can be written in the more general form

$$f(x; \mathbf{w}) = \sum_{k=0}^{K} w_k x^k.$$

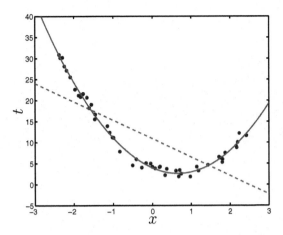

FIGURE 1.9 Example of linear (dashed) and quadratic (solid) models fitted to a dataset generated from a quadratic function.

Figure 1.10 shows the effect of fitting an eighth-order polynomial function to the 100 m sprint data that we have seen previously (MATLAB script: olymppoly.m). Comparing with Figures 1.5 and 1.6, does the eighth-order model look better than the first-order model? To answer this question, we need to be more precise about what we mean by better. For models built to make predictions, the best model is arguably the one that produces the best predictions. We shall return to the issue of model selection in more detail in Section 1.5. However, two things are immediately apparent and warrant description. Firstly, the eighth-order polynomial gets closer to the observed data than the first-order polynomial (original model). This is reflected in a lower value of the loss function: $\mathcal{L}^8 = 0.459$, $\mathcal{L}^1 = 1.358$ (where $\mathcal{L}^k$ is the loss achieved with a kth order polynomial). In fact, increasing the polynomial order will always result in a model that gets closer to the training data. Secondly, the predictions (shown by the dashed line) do not look sensible, particularly outside the range of the observed data.

We are not restricted to polynomial functions. We are free to define any set of K functions of x, $h_k(x)$:

$$\mathbf{X} = \begin{bmatrix} h_1(x_1) & h_2(x_1) & \cdots & h_K(x_1) \\ h_1(x_2) & h_2(x_2) & \cdots & h_K(x_2) \\ \vdots & \vdots & \cdots & \vdots \\ h_1(x_N) & h_2(x_N) & \cdots & h_K(x_N) \end{bmatrix}$$

which can be anything that we feel may be appropriate for the data available. For example, there appears to be a slight periodic trend in the 100 m data. A suitable

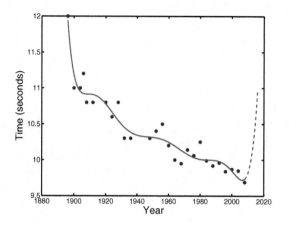

FIGURE 1.10 Eighth-order polynomial fitted to the Olympic $100\,\text{m}$ men's sprint data.

set of functions might be:

$$
\begin{aligned}
h_1(x) &= 1 \\
h_2(x) &= x \\
h_3(x) &= \sin\left(\frac{x-a}{b}\right) \\
f(x;\mathbf{w}) &= w_0 + w_1 x + w_2 \sin\left(\frac{x-a}{b}\right).
\end{aligned}
$$

This model has five parameters – w_0, w_1, w_2, a, b. Unfortunately, only the first three can be inferred using the procedures that we have developed. The last two, a and b, appear inside a non-linear (sine) function. As such, taking partial derivatives with respect to these parameters and equating to zero will not result in a set of equations that can be solved analytically. There are many ways of overcoming this problem, the simplest being a search over all values of a and b in some sensible range. However, we will ignore this problem for now and assume that we know of suitable values. If a and b are fixed, we can set the remaining parameters (w_0, w_1, w_2) using the expressions we derived previously. Assuming a and b are fixed ($a = 2660, b = 4.3$), Figure 1.11 shows a least squares fit using this model. In this case $\mathcal{L} = 1.1037$ so it is fitting the observed data better than the first order polynomial but not as well as the eighth order polynomial. The various model components are clearly visible in Figure 1.11: the constant term ($w_0 = 36.610$), the downward linear trend ($w_1 = -0.013$) and the non-linear sinusoidal term ($w_3 = -0.133$) causing oscillations. Notice also how the values for w_0 and w_1 are very similar to those for the first order polynomial model (c.f. Figure 1.5) – we have added an oscillating component around our original linear model.

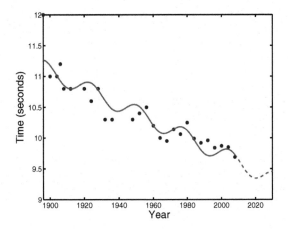

FIGURE 1.11 Least squares fit of $f(x; \mathbf{w}) = w_0 + w_1 x + w_2 \sin\left(\frac{x-a}{b}\right)$ to the $100\,\mathrm{m}$ sprint data $(a = 2660, b = 4.3)$.

1.5 GENERALISATION AND OVER-FITTING

In Section 1.4, we posed the question of which was better, the first- or eighth-order polynomial. Given that our original aim in building these models was to make predictions, it makes sense that the best model is the one which is able to make the most accurate predictions. Such a model will be one that can *generalise* beyond the examples we have for *training* (our Olympic data up to 2008, for example). Ideally, we would like to choose the model that performs best (i.e. minimises the loss) on this unseen data but, by the very nature of the problem, this data is unavailable.

Figure 1.10 gave an early indication that we should be very suspicious of using the loss on the training data to choose a model that will be used to make predictions. The plot shows an eighth-order polynomial fit to the men's $100\,\mathrm{m}$ data which has a much lower loss on the training data than a first order polynomial. At the same time, the predictions for future Olympics are very poor. For this data, a model based on an eighth-order polynomial pays too much attention to the training data (it *overfits*) and as a result does not generalise well to new data. As we make models more and more complex, they will be able to get closer and closer to the data that we have already seen. Unfortunately, beyond a certain point, the quality of the predictions can deteriorate rapidly. Determining the optimal model complexity such that it is able to generalise well without **over-fitting** is very challenging. This tradeoff is often referred to as the bias-variance tradeoff and we will briefly mention this in Section 2.9.

1.5.1 Validation data

One common way to overcome this problem is to use a second dataset, often referred to as a **validation** set. It is so called as it is used to validate the predictive performance of our model. The validation data could be provided separately or we could create it by removing some data from the original *training* set. For example, in our 100 m data, we could remove all Olympics since 1980 from the training set and make these the validation set. To choose between a set of models, we train each one on the reduced training set and then compute their loss on the validation set. Plots of the training and (log) validation losses can be seen in Figure 1.12(a) and Figure 1.12(b), respectively. The training loss decreases **monotonically** as the polynomial order (and hence **model complexity**) increases. However, the validation loss increases rapidly as the polynomial order increases, suggesting that a first-order polynomial has the best **generalisation** ability and will produce the most reliable predictions. This hypothesis is easily tested. In Figure 1.13 we can see the data (labelled as training and validation) and first-, fourth- and eighth-order polynomial functions (MATLAB script: `olympval.m`). It is clear to see that, for this data, had we been performing this task in 1979, a first-order model would indeed have given the best predictions.

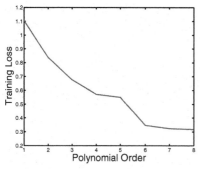

(a) Training loss for the Olympic men's 100 m data.

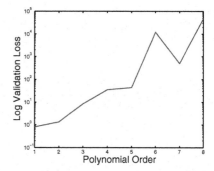

(b) Log validation loss for the Olympic men's 100 m data. When using the squared loss, this is also known as the squared predictive error and measures how close the predicted values are to the true values. Note that the log loss is plotted as the value increases so rapidly.

FIGURE 1.12 Training and validation loss for Olympic men's 100 m data.

1.5.2   Cross-validation

The loss that we calculate from validation data will be sensitive to the choice of data in our validation set. This is particularly problematic if our dataset (and hence our validation set) is small. **Cross-validation** is a technique that allows us to make more efficient use of the data we have.

K-fold cross-validation splits the data into K equally (or as close to equal as possible) sized blocks, illustrated in Figure 1.14. Each block takes its turn as a validation set for a training set comprised of the other $K - 1$ blocks. Averaging over the resulting K loss values gives us our final loss value. An extreme case of K-fold cross-validation is where $K = N$, the number of observations in our dataset: each data observation is held out in turn and used to test a model trained on the other

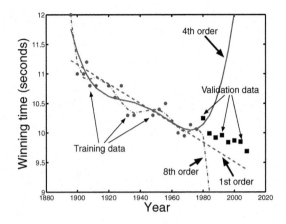

FIGURE 1.13 Generalisation ability of first-, fourth- and eighth-order polynomials on Olympic men's 100 m data.

$N - 1$ objects. This particular form of cross-validation is given the name Leave-One-Out Cross-Validation (LOOCV). The average squared validation loss for LOOCV is

$$\mathcal{L}^{CV} = \frac{1}{N} \sum_{n=1}^{N} (t_n - \widehat{\mathbf{w}}_{-n}^{\mathsf{T}} \mathbf{x}_n)^2, \tag{1.19}$$

where $\widehat{\mathbf{w}}_{-n}$ is the estimate of the parameters without the nth training example.

The mean LOOCV error for the Olympic men's 100 m data can be seen in Figure 1.15. This plot suggests that a third-order polynomial would be best. This is in disagreement with the value obtained from using the last few data points as a validation set. Disagreement like this is not uncommon – **model selection** is a very difficult problem. However, the two methods do agree on one thing – the model certainly shouldn't be sixth-order or above.

One drawback of illustrating model selection on a real dataset is that we don't know what the 'true' model is and therefore don't know if our selection techniques are working. We can overcome this by generating a synthetic dataset. Fifty input-target pairs were generated from a noisy third-order polynomial function and used to learn polynomial functions of increasing order (from first to seventh). Ideally, we hope to see minimum validation loss for the true polynomial order of three. A further 1000 input-target pairs were generated from the true function and are used as an independent test set with which to compute an additional, independent loss. This very large dataset will give us a good approximation to the true expected loss against which we can compare the LOOCV loss.

The results can be seen in Figure 1.16 (MATLAB script: cv_demo.m). As we have already discovered, the training loss keeps decreasing as the order increases. The LOOCV loss and the test loss decrease as the order is increased to 3 and then increase as the order is increased further. Either of these validation methods would have predicted the correct model order. Unfortunately, we will rarely be able to call

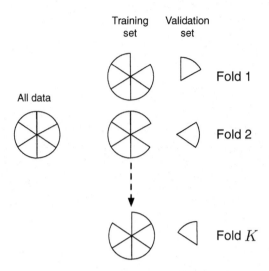

FIGURE 1.14 Cross-validation. The dataset is depicted on the left as a pie chart. In each of the K folds, one set of data points is removed from the training set and used to validate or test the model.

upon 1000 independent points from outside our training set and will heavily rely on a cross-validation scheme, often LOOCV.

1.5.3 Computational scaling of K-fold cross-validation

LOO cross-validation appears to be a good means of estimating our expected loss from the training data, allowing us to explore and assess various alternative models. However, consider implementing LOOCV. We need to train our model N times, which will take roughly N times longer than training it once on all of the data (it is not exactly the same, as we will be training it on one less data point). For some models, particularly if we have a lot of data, this might be infeasible.

The simplest way to alleviate this problem is to use $K \ll N$. For example, in 10-fold cross-validation, we would leave out 10% of the data for validation and use the remaining 90% for training. This reduces the number of training loops from N to 10 – a considerable saving if $N \gg 10$. A popular choice is to use N-fold cross-validation and repeat it several times with the data partitioned differently into the N groups, allowing averages to be taken across both folds and repetitions.

1.6 REGULARISED LEAST SQUARES

In the previous section, we discussed how predictions on data that was not part of the training set could be used to ensure good predictive performance (good generalisation) and prevent the model from over-fitting. In essence, this stops our model

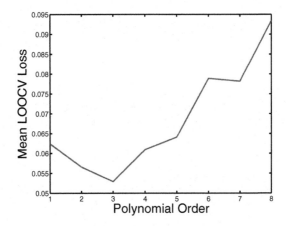

FIGURE 1.15 Mean LOOCV loss as polynomials of increasing order are fitted to the Olympic men's 100 m data.

becoming too complex. However, there is another way that this can be done, known as **regularisation**.

Consider a trivial model, defined by $f(\mathbf{x}; \mathbf{w}) = \mathbf{w}^\mathsf{T}\mathbf{x}$ where $\mathbf{w} = [0, 0, \ldots, 0]^\mathsf{T}$ – the model always predicts a value of 0. This is the simplest model possible. Any change we make to the elements of $\mathbf{w}$ increases their absolute value and makes the model more complex. Specifically, consider the fifth order polynomial model

$$f(x; \mathbf{w}) = w_0 + w_1 x + w_2 x^2 + w_3 x^3 + w_4 x^4 + w_5 x^5.$$

If we start with all of the elements of $\mathbf{w}$ being zero, the function always predicts a value of zero. Now imagine we set w_0 to some non-zero value. The model now predicts a constant (w_0). Leaving w_0 at its new value, we can set w_1 to some value. The model has become more complex, and, as each additional parameter is given a non-zero value, the model becomes more complex still. In general, we could consider that the higher the sum of the absolute values in $\mathbf{w}$, the more complex the model (note that it is the absolute value – we don't want the positive values to cancel with the negative ones). Alternatively, because absolute values tend to make the maths a bit harder, we could define the complexity of our model as

$$\sum_i w_i^2$$

or, in vector form,

$$\mathbf{w}^\mathsf{T}\mathbf{w}.$$

As we don't want our model to become too complex, it makes sense to try and keep this value low. So, rather than just minimising the average squared loss $\mathcal{L}$, we could minimise a regularised loss $\mathcal{L}'$ made by adding together our previous loss and a term penalising overcomplexity:

$$\mathcal{L}' = \mathcal{L} + \lambda \mathbf{w}^\mathsf{T}\mathbf{w}. \tag{1.20}$$

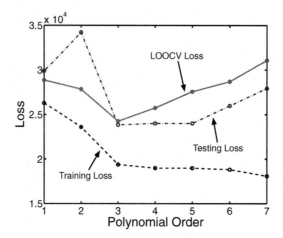

FIGURE 1.16 The training, testing and leave-one-out loss curves obtained for a noisy cubic function where a sample size of 50 is available for training and LOOCV estimation. The test error is computed using 1000 independent samples.

The parameter λ controls the trade-off between penalising not fitting the data well ($\mathcal{L}$) and penalising overly complex models ($\mathbf{w}^\mathsf{T}\mathbf{w}$). We can find the optimal value of $\mathbf{w}$ in exactly the same way as before. Adding the regularisation term to our original squared loss (Equation 1.14) gives

$$\mathcal{L}' = \frac{1}{N}\mathbf{w}^\mathsf{T}\mathbf{X}^\mathsf{T}\mathbf{X}\mathbf{w} - \frac{2}{N}\mathbf{w}^\mathsf{T}\mathbf{X}^\mathsf{T}\mathbf{t} + \frac{1}{N}\mathbf{t}^\mathsf{T}\mathbf{t} + \lambda\mathbf{w}^\mathsf{T}\mathbf{w}.$$

Taking partial derivatives with respect to $\mathbf{w}$,

$$\frac{\partial \mathcal{L}'}{\partial \mathbf{w}} = \frac{2}{N}\mathbf{X}^\mathsf{T}\mathbf{X}\mathbf{w} - \frac{2}{N}\mathbf{X}^\mathsf{T}\mathbf{t} + 2\lambda\mathbf{w}.$$

Setting this expression to zero and solving for $\mathbf{w}$ gives

$$\frac{2}{N}\mathbf{X}^\mathsf{T}\mathbf{X}\mathbf{w} - \frac{2}{N}\mathbf{X}^\mathsf{T}\mathbf{t} + 2\lambda\mathbf{w} = 0$$
$$(\mathbf{X}^\mathsf{T}\mathbf{X} + N\lambda\mathbf{I})\mathbf{w} = \mathbf{X}^\mathsf{T}\mathbf{t}.$$

Hence, the regularised least squares solution is given by

$$\widehat{\mathbf{w}} = (\mathbf{X}^\mathsf{T}\mathbf{X} + N\lambda\mathbf{I})^{-1}\mathbf{X}^\mathsf{T}\mathbf{t}. \tag{1.21}$$

Clearly, if $\lambda = 0$, we retrieve the original solution. We can see the effect of increasing λ with a synthetic example. Figure 1.17 shows six synthetic data points. A fifth-order polynomial function can fit the six data points exactly and we can see this if we set $\lambda = 0$ (in general N data points can be perfectly fitted by an $(N-1)$th order polynomial). If we increase λ, we begin to see the regularisation taking effect.

$\lambda = 1e - 06$ follows the general shape of the exact fifth-order polynomial but without as much variability and subsequently is further from the data points. $\lambda = 0.01$ and $\lambda = 0.1$ continue this trend – the function becomes less complex (MATLAB script: `regls.m`).

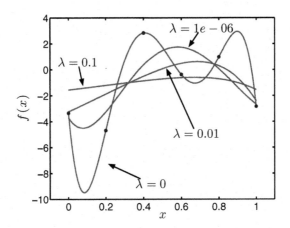

FIGURE 1.17 Effect of varying the regularisation parameter λ for a fifth-order polynomial function.

Choosing the value of λ presents us with the same over-fitting/generalisation trade-off we had when choosing the polynomial order. If it is too small, our function is likely to be too complex. Too large, and we will not capture any useful trends in the data. Fortunately, we can use exactly the validation techniques introduced in the previous section to determine the best value of λ. In particular, it is common to use cross-validation to choose the value of λ that gives the best predictive performance (see Exercise 1.12).

1.7   EXERCISES

1.1   By examining Figure 1.1 estimate the kind of values we should expect for w_0 and w_1 (e.g. High? Low? Positive? Negative?).

1.2   Write a MATLAB script that can find w_0 and w_1 for an arbitrary dataset of x_n, t_n pairs.

1.3   Show that

$$\mathbf{w}^\mathsf{T}\mathbf{X}^\mathsf{T}\mathbf{X}\mathbf{w} = w_0^2 \left(\sum_{n=1}^{N} x_{n1}^2 \right) + 2w_0w_1 \left(\sum_{n=1}^{N} x_{n1}x_{n2} \right) + w_1^2 \left(\sum_{n=1}^{N} x_{n2}^2 \right),$$

where

$$\mathbf{w} = \begin{bmatrix} w_0 \\ w_1 \end{bmatrix}, \quad \mathbf{X} = \begin{bmatrix} x_{11} & x_{12} \\ x_{21} & x_{22} \\ x_{31} & x_{32} \\ \vdots & \vdots \\ x_{N1} & x_{N2} \end{bmatrix}.$$

(Hint – it's probably easiest to do the $\mathbf{X}^\mathsf{T}\mathbf{X}$ first!)

1.4 Using $\mathbf{w}$ and $\mathbf{X}$ as defined in the previous exercise, show that $(\mathbf{Xw})^\mathsf{T} = \mathbf{w}^\mathsf{T}\mathbf{X}^\mathsf{T}$ by multiplying out both sides.

1.5 When multiplying a scalar by a vector (or matrix), we multiply each element of the vector (or matrix) by that scalar. For $\mathbf{x}_n = [x_{n1},\ x_{n2}]^\mathsf{T}$, $\mathbf{t} = [t_1, \ldots, t_N]^\mathsf{T}$, $\mathbf{w} = [w_0,\ w_1]^\mathsf{T}$ and

$$\mathbf{X} = \begin{bmatrix} \mathbf{x}_1^\mathsf{T} \\ \mathbf{x}_2^\mathsf{T} \\ \vdots \\ \mathbf{x}_N^\mathsf{T} \end{bmatrix},$$

show that

$$\sum_n \mathbf{x}_n t_n = \mathbf{X}^\mathsf{T}\mathbf{t}$$

and

$$\sum_n \mathbf{x}_n \mathbf{x}_n^\mathsf{T} \mathbf{w} = \mathbf{X}^\mathsf{T}\mathbf{X}\mathbf{w}.$$

1.6 Using the data provided in Table 1.3, find the linear model that minimises the squared loss.

1.7 Using the model obtained in the previous exercise, predict the women's winning time at the 2012 and 2016 Olympic games.

1.8 Using the models for the men's and wmen's 100 m, find the Olympic games when it is predicted for women to run a faster winning time than men. What are the predicted winning times? Do they seem realistic?

1.9 Load the data stored in the file synthdata.mat. Fit a fourth-order polynomial function – $f(x; \mathbf{w}) = w_0 + w_1 x + w_2 x^2 + w_3 x^3 + w_4 x^4$ – to this data. What do you notice about w_2 and w_4? Use 10-fold cross-validation to choose the polynomial order (between 1 and 4).

1.10 Derive the optimal least squares parameter value, $\hat{\mathbf{w}}$, for the total training loss

$$\mathcal{L} = \sum_{n=1}^{N}(t_n - \mathbf{w}^\mathsf{T}\mathbf{x}_n)^2.$$

How does the expression compare with that derived from the average loss?

1.11 The following expression is known as the *weighted* average loss:

$$\mathcal{L} = \frac{1}{N}\sum_{n=1}^{N} \alpha_n(t_n - \mathbf{w}^\mathsf{T}\mathbf{x}_n)^2$$

where the influence of each data point is controlled by its associated α parameter. Assuming that each α_n is fixed, derive the optimal least squares parameter value $\hat{\mathbf{w}}$.

1.12 Using K-fold cross-validation, find the value of λ that gives the best predictive performance on the Olympic men's 100 m data for (a) a firstorder polynomial (i.e. the standard linear model) and (b) a fourth-order polynomial.

1.8 FURTHER READING

[1] F. Galton. Regression towards mediocrity in hereditary stature. *Anthopological Miscellanea*, 15:246–263, 1886.

> The term "regression" was first used in the context of genetics by Francis Galton. This is one of Galton's original genetics papers on regression from 1886.

[2] T. Hastie, R. Tibshirani, and J. Friedman. *The Elements of Statistical Learning: Data Mining, Inference, and Prediction.* Springer-Verlag, second edition edition, 2009.

> This book includes a detailed chapter on least squares techniques which would be a good starting point to explore this area further.

[3] K. B. Petersen and M. S. Pedersen. The matrix cookbook. http://www2.imm.dtu.dk/pubdb/p.php?3274, October 2008.

> An excellent free resource that provides many matrix identities. Particularly useful for manipulating, and taking expectations with respect to, multivariate Gaussian densities.

CHAPTER 2

Linear Modelling: A Maximum Likelihood Approach

In the previous chapter, we introduced the idea of learning the parameters of a model by defining and minimising a loss function. By the end of this chapter, we will have derived exactly the same equation for the optimal parameter values from a different starting point. In particular, we will explicitly model the **noise** (the errors between the model and the observations) in the data by incorporating a **random variable**. We will demonstrate the considerable advantages of incorporating a noise term into our model. A large section of this chapter (Sections 2.2 to 2.5) is an introduction to random variables and **probability** which can be skipped by readers already familiar with these concepts.

2.1 ERRORS AS NOISE

In Figure 1.5 we saw the result of minimising the squared loss function to model the Olympic 100 m data with a linear model. The linear model appears to capture an interesting downward trend but is unable to explain each data point perfectly – there are errors between the model and the true values. These errors are highlighted in Figure 2.1.

When building our model, we assumed that there was a linear relationship between years and winning times. This model appeared to capture the general trend in the data whilst ignoring the, sometimes large, deviation between the model and the observed data. From a modelling perspective, ignoring these errors is hard to defend. If we know they are going to be present, we should make an effort to build them into our model.

In this chapter we will see the benefits of explicitly modelling these errors. In particular, it allows us to express the level of uncertainty in our estimate of the model parameters, **w** – if we change **w** a bit, do we still have a *good* model? This in turn allows us to express a degree of uncertainty in our predictions – 'we believe the winning time will be between a and b' rather than 'we believe the winning time will be exactly c'.

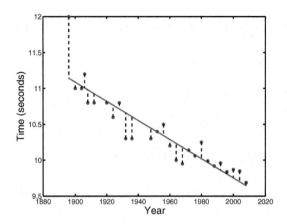

FIGURE 2.1 Linear fit to the Olympic men's 100 m data with errors highlighted.

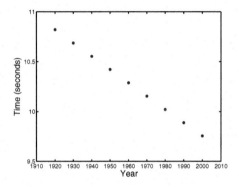

FIGURE 2.2 Dataset generated from the linear model.

2.1.1 Thinking generatively

The process that generated this particular dataset is very complex – we couldn't even begin to make a near-perfect model of one sprinter and the events surrounding his preparation and performance, let alone several of them *and* all of the other factors. However, it is still useful to think of our modelling problem as a **generative** one: can we build a model that could be used to create (or generate) a dataset that *looks* like ours? Although we are happy to accept that this isn't in fact how the data were generated, we shall see that this is a useful strategy.

How might we go about generating data from our current model? We have an equation, $f(\mathbf{x}; \mathbf{w}) = \mathbf{w}^\mathsf{T}\mathbf{x}$, that, if we plug in the values for $\mathbf{w}$ that we found in the previous chapter could be used to *generate* a winning time for any particular year. Figure 2.2 shows winning times generated in this way for a number of years between

1920 and 2000. It doesn't look much like the data in Figure 2.1. To make it more realistic, we need to add some errors. Examining Figure 2.1, we notice a couple of important features of the errors:

1. They are different at each year. Some are positive, some negative and they all have different magnitudes.

2. There does not seem to be any obvious relationship between the size (or direction) of the error and the year. The error does not appear to be a function of x, the Olympic year.

If we had a method for generating a random amount of time (in seconds) that could be either positive or negative and was, on average, roughly the same size as the errors in Figure 2.1, we could generate one such value for each data point we wished to generate, and add it to $\mathbf{w}^\mathsf{T}\mathbf{x}$. The tools that we will need to incorporate this variability into our model come from statistics. In the next section we will introduce random variables and some of the ways in which they can be manipulated. Readers already familiar with this can jump straight to Section 2.7.

2.2 RANDOM VARIABLES AND PROBABILITY

Any model we build will be a simplification of the real system that generated the data we observe. This will lead to a discrepancy between the model and reality which the tools presented in this section will help us to model and understand. As we must start with the basics, it may at first seem slightly disconnected from the particular problem of adding errors to our generated $100\,\mathrm{m}$ data and being able to express uncertainties in our predictions, but the connection will become clearer as we progress.

2.2.1 Random variables

The equation

$$y = 5x - 2$$

has two variables, x and y. If we were given a value for one (say $y = 8$) we could solve for the other ($x = 2$). *Random* variables are very different. They allow us to assign numerical values to random events. For example, I would like to model the outcome of a coin toss. As a starting point, I create a variable called X to which I will assign the value 1 if the coin lands heads and 0 if it lands tails. X is a random variable – the 'variable' part describes the fact that it can take a number of different values (in this case, 0 and 1) and the 'random' part is so called because we don't know what value X will take before the coin toss takes place – we couldn't express the outcome as a function of standard variables (e.g. $y = 5x - 2$). It is a common convention to use upper-case letters to describe random variables and lower-case ones for possible values that the random variable can take.

There are two types of random variable and they must be treated slightly differently. Discrete random variables are the easiest to conceptualise, as they are used for random events for which we can systematically list (or count) all possible outcomes. A discrete random variable could be used to, for example, describe a coin toss (possible outcomes are 0 and 1) or the rolling of a die (1, 2, 3, 4, 5 or 6). The collection of possible outcomes is known as the sample space.

It might seem that being able to systematically write all of the possible events in order should be true of almost anything. In fact, there are many possible events for which this is not the case. Taking our Olympic 100 m example and assuming that the winning time is going to be between 9 and 10 seconds, we could attempt to systematically write down all possibilities:

$$9,9.1,9.2,\ldots$$

at which point, we realise that we've missed some out (all the ones between 9 and 9.1 for example) so we start again:

$$9,9.01,9.02,\ldots,9,1,\ldots$$

But what about all the ones between 9 and 9.01? Starting a third time,

$$9,9.001,9.002,9.003,\ldots,9.01,\ldots\text{etc.}$$

The possible outcomes of this event cannot be systematically listed (after writing down any two values, someone could point out the missing ones in between). For events like this, we must use **continuous** random variables.

Table 2.1 gives examples of events or quantities that we might wish to model with random variables and whether or not they are discrete or continuous. We will now introduce some important concepts through discrete random variables before extending the ideas to the continuous case.

TABLE 2.1 Events we might want to model with random variables.

Process	Discrete or continuous
Toss of a coin	Discrete
Roll of a die	Discrete
Outcome of a 100 m race	Continuous
Failure of a node in a computer network	Discrete
Outcome of a court case	Discrete
Height of a human	Continuous
Mass of a pebble	Continuous
Score in a football match	Discrete
Errors in our 100 m linear regression model	See Exercise 2.1

2.2.2 Probability and distributions

Let Y be a random variable that represents the toss of a coin. If the coin lands heads, $Y = 1$ and if tails, $Y = 0$. To model this event (the coin toss), we need to be able to quantify how likely either outcome is. For discrete random variables, we do this by defining the probabilities of the different outcomes. One intuitive way of thinking about the probability of a particular outcome is to imagine that it represents the proportion of times this outcome would happen if the event were to be repeated many times. If a fair (i.e. not biased to land either way) coin were tossed 1000 times, we might expect to see heads roughly half of the time (and tails the rest of time). It would seem sensible to define the probability of seeing a head, which we will denote

$P(Y = 1)$, as a half, or 0.5. If the coin doesn't land as a head, it lands as a tail (there are only two options in our sample space) and so the proportion of tails must be one minus the proportion of heads. Therefore, $P(Y = 0) = 1 - P(Y = 1) = 0.5$.

Conceptualising probabilities as the proportion of times a particular outcome would occur if an event were repeated many times is not the only way they can be thought of. It is not always the most natural analogy, particularly for events that can only occur once. It will be sufficient for our needs, but the reader is encouraged to investigate this interesting area further.

From our short discussion on proportions, we can write down two important rules governing probabilities:

- Probabilities must be greater than or equal to 0 (a proportion cannot be negative) and less than or equal to 1.

- The sum of the probabilities of each possible individual outcome must be equal to 1.

$$\text{e.g. for a coin:} \qquad P(Y = 1) + P(Y = 0) = 1$$
$$\text{For a die:} \qquad P(Y = 1) + P(Y = 2) + \cdots + P(Y = 6) = 1$$

The mathematical equivalents of these statements are:

$$0 \le P(Y = y) \le 1, \tag{2.1}$$

$$\sum_y P(Y = y) = 1 \tag{2.2}$$

where the lower case y is used, by convention, to represent values that the random variable Y can take. Note that we will often need to write summations over the values that a random variable can take – to keep notation concise, $\sum_y$ will be used to denote a sum over all of the possible values that can be taken by a random variable Y.

$P(Y = y)$ is a scalar value – the probability that the random variable Y has outcome y. This notation can sometimes become unwieldy and so we will sometimes use the following shorthand:

$$P(Y = y) = P(y).$$

The set of all of the possible outcomes (all of the ys) and their probabilities, $P(y)$, is known as a probability **distribution**. It tells us how the total probability (1) is distributed (or shared out) over all possible outcomes.

Often, we can use Equations 2.1 and 2.2 to define probabilities based on some fundamental assumptions. For example, in the coin example, we might assume that the two outcomes are equally likely: $P(Y = 1) = P(Y = 0) = r$. Plugging this into Equation 2.2 and remembering that r must lie between 0 and 1 (Equation 2.1), we can use some algebra to work out the value of r (See Exercise 2.2):

$$\begin{aligned} P(Y = 0) + P(Y = 1) &= 1 \\ 2r &= 1 \\ r &= \frac{1}{2}. \end{aligned}$$

2.2.3 Adding probabilities

Let Y be a random variable for modelling the outcome of rolling a fair die. If we encode our assumption that the die is fair by assuming that all outcomes are equally likely, we know enough from the previous section to compute the probabilities of each possible outcome – 1, 2, 3, 4, 5 or 6. The die is rolled and the result is a 4. If it is rolled again, what is the probability of the result being lower than 4? Maybe we are playing a betting game and want to know whether the odds on offer are acceptable. The outcomes that are lower than 4 are 1, 2 and 3, suggesting that we need to be able to calculate the probability that the die lands 1 *or* 2 *or* 3. If the die were to be rolled many times, we could compute the proportion of times that this was the case. The proportion of times the die lands 1 or 2 or 3 is equal to the proportion of times the die lands 1 *plus* the proportion of times the die lands 2 *plus* the proportion of times the die lands 3. This leads us to the following additive law of probability:

$$P(Y < 4) = P(Y = 1) + P(Y = 2) + P(Y = 3).$$

Exactly the same result applies if the outcomes in which I'm interested are not in order. For example, the probability that I roll a 1 or a 6 would be $P(Y = 1) + P(Y = 6)$. It is also not just restricted to individual outcomes. For example, the probability that I don't roll a 4 could be computed as

$$
\begin{aligned}
P(Y \neq 4) &= P(Y < 4) + P(Y > 4) \\
&= P(Y = 1) + P(Y = 2) + P(Y = 3) + P(Y = 5) + P(Y = 6).
\end{aligned}
$$

As an aside, it is worth remembering that there is generally more than one way to compute any probability. In this example, it would in fact be easier to make use of Equation 2.2 and compute

$$
\begin{aligned}
P(Y \neq 4) + P(Y = 4) &= 1 \\
P(Y \neq 4) &= 1 - P(Y = 4).
\end{aligned}
$$

2.2.4 Conditional probabilities

Often one event will affect the outcome of another. For example, I toss a coin and then tell you what the result was (you cannot see the coin). There are two events – the first is tossing the coin, the second is me communicating the outcome of the coin toss to you. Let's assume that these two events are represented by two random variables. X is 1 if the coin lands heads and 0 if tails. Y is 1 if I tell you heads, and zero if I tell you tails. Unless I'm behaving very strangely, the outcome of Y will depend on the outcome of X. We can use **conditional probabilities** to express the probability that Y takes a particular value given that X has taken a particular value. We express this as

$$P(Y = y | X = x), \tag{2.3}$$

which reads as the probability that Y has the outcome y given that X has the outcome x. As for unconditional probabilities, we will also make use of the following shorthand:

$$P(Y = y | X = x) = P(y|x).$$

In our example, if we assume that I always tell the truth, the probability that I say heads if the coin lands heads is 1 (it will always happen):

$$P(Y = 1|X = 1) = 1.$$

Similarly for tails:

$$P(Y = 0|X = 0) = 1.$$

Using Equation 2.2 and these probabilities, we can deduce $P(Y = 0|X = 1)$ and $P(Y = 1|X = 0)$:

$$
\begin{aligned}
P(Y = 0|X = 1) + P(Y = 1|X = 1) &= 1 \\
P(Y = 0|X = 1) = 1 - P(Y = 1|X = 1) &= 0. \\
P(Y = 1|X = 0) + P(Y = 0|X = 0) &= 1 \\
P(Y = 1|X = 0) = 1 - P(Y = 1|X = 1) &= 0.
\end{aligned}
$$

Things get a bit more interesting if I'm not so truthful. Let's assume that, if the coin lands tails, I always tell the truth but the proportion of times I tell the truth if it lands heads is 0.8. This implies that, if the coin lands heads, I'll say heads with probability 0.8 and tails with probability 0.2. The full list of conditional probabilities under this assumption is

$$
\begin{aligned}
P(Y = 1|X = 1) &= 0.8 \\
P(Y = 0|X = 1) &= 0.2 \\
P(Y = 1|X = 0) &= 0 \\
P(Y = 0|X = 0) &= 1.
\end{aligned}
$$

Just as in non-conditional probabilities, Equation 2.2 must be satisfied, i.e. $\sum_y P(Y = y|X = x) = 1$. We can check this for the values just computed:

$$
\begin{aligned}
\sum_y P(Y = y|X = 1) &= P(Y = 1|X = 1) + P(Y = 0|X = 1) = 0.8 + 0.2 = 1 \\
\sum_y P(Y = y|X = 0) &= P(Y = 1|X = 0) + P(Y = 0|X = 0) = 0 + 1 = 1
\end{aligned}
$$

Armed with the conditional probabilities and assuming that $P(X = 1) = P(X = 0) = 0.5$ (i.e., our coin is fair), we might ask 'what is the probability that the coin lands heads *and* I say heads?' This is different from $P(Y = 1|X = 1)$; the conditional distribution assumes that $X = 1$ has already happened and the only uncertainty that remains is what will happen with Y whereas my question concerns both events. If neither has happened, what is the probability that they will both have a particular outcome? Other interesting quantities that we may want to evaluate are $P(Y = 1)$ and $P(Y = 0)$, the probability that I say heads or tails. To compute any of these, we need to understand probabilities and distributions of more than one variable.

2.2.5 Joint probabilities

Given two (or more) random variables, we may wish to know the probability that they each take a particular value. Continuing our previous coin tossing example, we might want to know the probability that the coin shows heads *and* I say heads or the probability that the coin shows heads *and* I say tails. These are joint probabilities and are denoted as

$$P(Y = y, X = x) \tag{2.4}$$

(or, in functional form, $p(y, x)$). How we deal with these joint distributions depends on whether or not the random variables are *dependent*. In our example, Y (what I say) depends on X (how the coin lands). This is the case even when I'm not always being truthful – how the coin lands determines how I *decide* what to say. If there is no dependence between the variables (e.g. if two random variables represent different coin tosses, the outcome of one is unlikely to affect the outcome of the other), the **joint probability** can be computed by multiplying the individual probabilities together:

$$P(Y = y, X = x) = P(Y = y) \times P(X = x).$$

The probability that Y takes value y *and* X takes value x is equal to the probability that Y takes value y multiplied by the probability that X takes value x. More generally (and here we switch to the functional form – $p(y_1, \ldots, y_J)$ rather than $P(Y_1 = y_1, \ldots Y_J = y_j)$ for convenience), for a family of J random variables $Y_1, \ldots, Y_J$,

$$P(y_1, y_2, \ldots, y_J) = P(y_1) \times p(y_2) \times \cdots \times P(y_J) = \prod_{j=1}^{J} P(y_j). \tag{2.5}$$

If the events are dependent, we cannot decompose the joint probability in this manner. However, if we can create conditional distributions, we can decompose the joint probability using the following definitions:

$$P(Y = y, X = x) = P(Y = y|X = x) \times P(X = x) \tag{2.6}$$

or as

$$P(Y = y, X = x) = P(X = x|Y = y) \times P(Y = y). \tag{2.7}$$

So, the probability that the coin lands heads *and* I say heads is

$$P(Y = 1, X = 1) = P(Y = 1|X = 1) \times P(X = 1) = 0.8 \times 0.5 = 0.4$$

or, in other words, if we repeated this many times, the proportion of times that the coin landed heads and I said heads is 0.4. The fact that I occasionally lie when the coin shows heads has reduced the probability that you will hear heads from 0.5 (if I were always honest) to 0.4.

There are four possible combinations of X and Y and hence four possible outcomes of the event. Equation 2.2 tells us that, if we sum the probabilities of all four of these events, we should get 1:

$$\sum_{x,y} P(X = x, Y = y) = 1. \tag{2.8}$$

(Note that $\sum_{x,y}$ corresponds to a summation over all possible combinations of x and y). We can test this by working them all out from Equation 2.6. We already know $P(X = 1, Y = 1) = 0.4$. The others are

$$
\begin{aligned}
P(Y = 0, X = 1) &= P(Y = 0|X = 1)P(X = 1) = 0.2 \times 0.5 = 0.1 \\
P(Y = 1, X = 0) &= P(Y = 1|X = 0)P(X = 0) = 0 \times 0.5 = 0 \\
P(Y = 0, X = 0) &= P(Y = 0|X = 0)P(X = 0) = 1 \times 0.5 = 0.5.
\end{aligned}
$$

Adding these together gives $0.4 + 0.1 + 0 + 0.5 = 1$, as required.

Before we move on, we will quickly consider these three values. The first (0.1) gives the probability that I say tails and the coin lands heads. This has increased from the truthful case (it would be zero if I always told the truth) because I sometimes lie if the coin is heads. The second (0) is the probability that I say heads when the coin is actually tails. This is zero because I never lie if the coin is tails. The final value is the probability that I say tails and the coin lands tails. This is 0.5 – the coin lands tails half the time and if it does, I always tell the truth.

2.2.6 Marginalisation

If you recorded the proportion of times I said heads or tails, you would in effect be computing $P(Y = 1)$ and $P(Y = 0)$. These expressions do not involve X – they just refer to what I say. $P(Y = y)$ can be obtained by **marginalising** out X from the joint distribution $P(Y = y, X = x)$. This is done by summing the joint probabilities over all possible values of X:

$$
P(Y = y) = \sum_x P(Y = y, X = x). \tag{2.9}
$$

In our coin example, X can take one of two values, so this summation would become

$$
P(Y = y) = P(Y = y, X = 0) + P(Y = y, X = 1).
$$

In general, for joint probabilities of J random variables, to get $P(Y_j = y_j)$, the marginal distribution of one of them is given by

$$
P(Y_j = y_j) = P(y_j) = \sum_{y_1, \dots, y_{j-1}, y_{j+1}, \dots, y_J} P(y_1, \dots, y_J). \tag{2.10}
$$

The summation in this expression looks a bit strange. It is summing over all combinations of the remaining $J - 1$ variables (y_j is missing). For example, if $J = 3$ and each variable can take only the values 0 or 1, to compute $P(Y_1 = y_1) = p(y_1)$ would require summation over four different combinations of y_2 and y_3:

y_2	y_3
0	0
0	1
1	0
1	1

If $J = 4$, this increases to 8:

y_2	y_3	y_4
0	0	0
0	0	1
0	1	0
0	1	1
1	0	0
1	0	1
1	1	0
1	1	1

In general, for binary variables, the number of combinations will be 2^{J-1}, which rapidly increases with J. If our random variables have more than two outcomes, it gets even worse (e.g. 6^{J-1} for a die). Marginalisation is important in some probabilistic areas of Machine Learning and can be very challenging, inspiring approximation methods such as those that we shall see in Chapter 4.

Returning to our coin example, $P(Y = 1)$ is

$$
\begin{aligned}
P(Y = 1) &= \sum_x P(Y = 1, X = x) \\
&= P(Y = 1, X = 0) + P(Y = 1, X = 1) \\
&= 0 + 0.4 = 0.4
\end{aligned}
$$

and $P(Y = 0)$ is

$$
\begin{aligned}
P(Y = 0) &= \sum_x P(Y = 0, X = x) \\
&= P(Y = 0, X = 0) + P(Y = 0, X = 1) \\
&= 0.5 + 0.1 = 0.6.
\end{aligned}
$$

We could also have computed $P(Y = 0)$ by using the value for $P(Y = 1)$ and Equation 2.2. These probabilities tell us the proportion of times I say heads and tails. They are different from the proportion of times that the coin lands heads or tails $(P(X = 1) = P(X = 0) = 0.5)$. This discrepancy is due to the uncertainty in my communication of the results – in the context of this chapter, I am effectively a source of noise or errors. A further example of conditional probabilities and marginalisation is provided in Comment 2.1.

Comment 2.1 – Conditional probabilities and marginalisation – an example: Let's assume that we have a fair coin and two dice (one of which is a little unusual). We will generate a coin toss (X) and a dice roll (Y) using the following procedure. Firstly, toss the coin. If it gives heads, roll die 1. If it gives tails, roll die 2. Die 1 and die 2 are different, with probabilities defined in the following table:

	1	2	3	4	5	6	
Die 1	$\frac{1}{6}$	$\frac{1}{6}$	$\frac{1}{6}$	$\frac{1}{6}$	$\frac{1}{6}$	$\frac{1}{6}$	$= P(y\|X = H)$
Die 2	$\frac{1}{12}$	$\frac{1}{6}$	$\frac{1}{4}$	$\frac{1}{4}$	$\frac{1}{6}$	$\frac{1}{12}$	$= P(y\|X = T)$

So, the probability of rolling say a 3 is 1/6 with die 1 and 1/4 with die 2. As we roll die 1 if our coin showed heads and dice 2 if tails, we have the following conditional distributions:

$$P(y|X = H), \ P(y|X = T),$$

i.e. the distribution over Y depends on the outcome of X. The joint distribution is given as (Equation 2.6)

$$p(y, x) = p(y|x)p(x).$$

We can use this to compute the probability of rolling a 3 *and* a head:

$$P(Y = 3, x = H) = P(Y = 3|X = H)P(X = H) = \frac{1}{6} \times \frac{1}{2} = \frac{1}{12}.$$

Alternatively, a 3 *and* a tail:

$$P(Y = 3, X = T) = P(Y = 3|X = H)P(X = T) = \frac{1}{4} \times \frac{1}{2} = \frac{1}{8}.$$

Perhaps more interestingly, we can compute the marginal distribution for Y. From our definition (Equation 2.9)

$$P(y) = \sum_x P(y, x) = \sum_x P(y|x)P(x).$$

Therefore, the probability of rolling a 3 is

$$
\begin{aligned}
P(Y = 3) &= \sum_x P(Y = 3|x)P(x) \\
&= P(Y = 3|X = H)P(X = H) + P(Y = 3|X = T)P(X = T) \\
&= \frac{1}{6} \times \frac{1}{2} + \frac{1}{4} \times \frac{1}{2} = \frac{5}{24}.
\end{aligned}
$$

2.2.7 Aside – Bayes' rule

Although we won't need it in this chapter, it is worth introducing Bayes'[1] rule, as it will feature heavily from Chapter 3 onwards. The left hand sides of Equations 2.6

---

[1] Named after the Reverend Thomas Bayes, a British mathematician and Presbyterian minister, who first proposed this reversing of conditional probabilities.

and 2.7 are identical so we can also equate the right hand sides:

$$P(Y = y|X = x)P(X = x) = P(X = x|Y = y)P(Y = y).$$

Rearranging, we can get an expression for the probability of X conditioned on a particular value of Y ($P(X = x|Y = y)$) that depends on the probability of Y conditioned on a particular value of X ($P(Y = y|X = x)$), which is known as Bayes' rule:

$$P(X = x|Y = y) = \frac{P(Y = y|X = x)P(X = x)}{P(Y = y)}. \tag{2.11}$$

In our example, this is the probability that the coin landed in a particular way given (or conditioned on) what I said. This is likely to be of interest to you if you want to make predictions about how the coin actually landed. Substituting our numerical values, we can work out $P(X = 1|Y = 1)$,

$$P(X = 1|Y = 1) = \frac{P(Y = 1|X = 1)P(X = 1)}{P(Y = 1)} = \frac{0.8 \times 0.5}{0.4} = 1$$

from which we can also deduce that $P(X = 0|Y = 1) = 0$ (Equation 2.2 again). Similarly, we can compute $P(X = 0|Y = 0)$,

$$P(X = 0|Y = 0) = \frac{P(Y = 0|X = 0)P(X = 0)}{P(Y = 0)} = \frac{1 \times 0.5}{0.6} = 0.83,$$

from which we can deduce that $P(X = 1|Y = 0) = 0.17$.

The first two values give the probabilities of the true coin toss if I say heads (i.e. $Y = 1$) and the second two the true probabilities if I say tails ($Y = 0$). $P(X = 1|Y = 1) = 1$ tells us that my saying heads must mean that heads was the true outcome of the coin toss. $P(X = 0|Y = 0) = 0.83$ tells us that, if tails is heard, it is more likely that the coin was tails (probability 0.83) than heads (probability 0.17). Reversing the conditioning in this way is very useful when building models and is something that we shall return to in Chapter 3 and beyond.

2.2.8 Expectations

When dealing with random variables, it is useful to summarise a distribution with a value or values that encapsulate its characteristics. An obvious example is the mean value – the average value that we expect the random variable to take. The mean is an example of an **expectation**. An expectation tells us what value we would expect some function $f(X)$ of a random variable X to take and is defined (for discrete random variables) as

$$\mathbf{E}_{P(x)}\{f(X)\} = \sum_x f(x)P(x). \tag{2.12}$$

For example, if we're interested in the expected value of X (the mean), $f(X) = X$, and the expression becomes

$$\mathbf{E}_{P(x)}\{X\} = \sum_x xP(x).$$

For a fair die ($P(x) = 1/6$), the expected value of X would be

$$\mathbf{E}_{P(x)}\left\{X\right\} = \sum_x x\frac{1}{6} = \frac{1}{6} + \frac{2}{6} + \ldots + \frac{6}{6} = \frac{21}{6} = 3.5.$$

Notice from this example that the expected value doesn't have to be one of the values that the random variable can take (we can never roll 3.5).

Expected values of other functions are computed in exactly the same manner. For example, the expected value of $f(X) = X^2$ is

$$\mathbf{E}_{P(x)}\left\{X^2\right\} = \sum_x x^2\frac{1}{6} = \frac{1}{6} + \frac{4}{6} + \ldots + \frac{36}{6} = \frac{91}{6}.$$

It is important to realise that the expected value of a function of X is not in general the function evaluated at the expected value of X. Mathematically, $\mathbf{E}_{P(x)}\left\{f(X)\right\}$ does not necessarily equal $f\left(\mathbf{E}_{P(x)}\left\{X\right\}\right)$. As an example, we've just computed $\mathbf{E}_{P(x)}\left\{X^2\right\} = 91/6$, which is not equal to $\left(\mathbf{E}_{P(x)}\left\{X\right\}\right)^2 = (21/6)^2$. One situation where the two are equal is when the function is just a constant multiplied by X. In this case, doing a little algebra allows us to show that the two are equivalent:

$$
\begin{aligned}
f(X) &= aX \\
\mathbf{E}_{P(x)}\left\{f(X)\right\} &= \sum_x axP(x) \\
&= a\sum_x xP(x) \\
&= a\mathbf{E}_{P(x)}\left\{X\right\} \\
&= f\left(\mathbf{E}_{P(x)}\left\{X\right\}\right).
\end{aligned}
$$

Another important case is when the function is simply a constant. In this case, the expectation disappears due to the fact that the distribution has to sum to 1 over all possible outcomes:

$$
\begin{aligned}
f(X) &= a \\
\mathbf{E}_{P(x)}\left\{f(X)\right\} &= \sum_x aP(x) \\
&= a\sum_x P(x) \\
&= a.
\end{aligned}
$$

A final special case that will prove useful is that the expectation of a sum of different functions is equal to a sum of the individual expectations:

$$
\begin{aligned}
\mathbf{E}_{P(x)}\left\{f(X) + g(X)\right\} &= \sum_x (f(x) + g(x))P(x) \\
&= \sum_x f(x)P(x) + \sum_x g(x)P(x) \\
&= \mathbf{E}_{P(x)}\left\{f(X)\right\} + \mathbf{E}_{P(x)}\left\{g(X)\right\}.
\end{aligned}
$$

The two most common expectations that we will come across are the mean ($\mathbf{E}_{P(x)}\left\{X\right\}$ as defined above) and the **variance**. Variance is a measure of how variable the random variable is and is defined as the expected squared deviation from the mean:

$$\text{var}\{X\} = \mathbf{E}_{P(x)}\left\{\left(X - \mathbf{E}_{P(x)}\{X\}\right)^2\right\}. \tag{2.13}$$

Multiplying out the bracket gives us the following convenient expression for the variance of a random variable:

$$
\begin{aligned}
\text{var}\{X\} &= \mathbf{E}_{P(x)}\left\{\left(X - \mathbf{E}_{P(x)}\{X\}\right)^2\right\} \\
&= \mathbf{E}_{P(x)}\left\{X^2 - 2X\mathbf{E}_{P(x)}\{X\} + \mathbf{E}_{P(x)}\{X\}^2\right\} \\
&= \mathbf{E}_{P(x)}\left\{X^2\right\} - 2\mathbf{E}_{P(x)}\{X\}\mathbf{E}_{P(x)}\{X\} + \mathbf{E}_{P(x)}\{X\}^2.
\end{aligned}
$$

To get from the second to third lines, we have used the fact that

$$\mathbf{E}_{P(x)}\left\{\mathbf{E}_{P(x)}\{f(X)\}\right\} = \mathbf{E}_{P(x)}\{f(X)\}.$$

The result of $\mathbf{E}_{P(x)}\{f(X)\}$ is a constant (all X terms are removed by the expectation). The outer expectation is the expected value of a constant, which we have already shown is equal to the constant. Collecting together the $\mathbf{E}_{P(x)}\{X\}^2$ terms gives

$$\text{var}\{X\} = \mathbf{E}_{P(x)}\left\{X^2\right\} - \mathbf{E}_{P(x)}\{X\}^2. \tag{2.14}$$

Random variables with high variance would, on average, take values further away from their mean than random variables with low variance.

Comment 2.2 – Vector random variables: It will often be necessary to define probability distributions over vectors. This is nothing more than a shorthand way of defining large joint distributions. For example, the values that could be taken on by random variables $X_1, X_2, \ldots, X_N$ can be expressed as the vector $\mathbf{x} = [x_1, x_2, \ldots, x_N]^\mathsf{T}$. Using this shorthand:

$$p(\mathbf{x}) = p(x_1, x_2, \ldots, x_N) = P(X_1 = x_1, X_2 = x_2, \ldots, X_N = x_N).$$

Even though $\mathbf{x}$ is a vector, $p(\mathbf{x})$ is a scalar quantity, just as $P(X_1 = x_1, X_2 = x_2, \ldots, X_N = x_N)$ is.

Expectations are computed for vector random variables (see Comment 2.2) in exactly the same way. For a random variable X that can take vector values $\mathbf{x}$, expectations are defined as

$$\mathbf{E}_{P(\mathbf{x})}\{f(\mathbf{x})\} = \sum_{\mathbf{x}} f(\mathbf{x})P(\mathbf{x})$$

where the sum is over all possible values of the vector $\mathbf{x}$. Therefore, the mean vector is defined as

$$\mathbf{E}_{P(\mathbf{x})}\{\mathbf{x}\} = \sum_{\mathbf{x}} \mathbf{x}P(\mathbf{x}).$$

When dealing with vectors, the concept of variance is generalised to a **covariance** matrix. This is defined as

$$\text{cov}\{\mathbf{x}\} = \mathbf{E}_{P(\mathbf{x})}\left\{\left(\mathbf{x} - \mathbf{E}_{P(\mathbf{x})}\{\mathbf{x}\}\right)\left(\mathbf{x} - \mathbf{E}_{P(\mathbf{x})}\{\mathbf{x}\}\right)^\mathsf{T}\right\} \tag{2.15}$$

If $\mathbf{x}$ is a vector of length D, then $\text{cov}\{\mathbf{x}\}$ is a $D \times D$ matrix. The diagonal elements correspond to the variance of the individual elements of $\mathbf{x}$ whilst the off-diagonal elements tell us to what extent different elements of $\mathbf{x}$ co-vary, that is, how dependent they are on one another. A high positive value between, say, elements x_d and x_e, suggests that if x_d increases, so does x_e. A high negative value suggests that they are related but move in opposite directions (x_d increases whilst x_e decreases) and a value of (or close to) zero suggests that there is no relationship between them (they are independent). We give some examples of covariance matrices and the associated densities in Section 2.5.4. Just as for variance, the covariance expression can be manipulated into a more convenient form as follows:

$$\begin{aligned}
\text{cov}\{\mathbf{x}\} &= \mathbf{E}_{P(\mathbf{x})}\left\{\left(\mathbf{x} - \mathbf{E}_{P(\mathbf{x})}\{\mathbf{x}\}\right)\left(\mathbf{x} - \mathbf{E}_{P(\mathbf{x})}\{\mathbf{x}\}\right)^{\mathsf{T}}\right\} \\
&= \mathbf{E}_{P(\mathbf{x})}\left\{\mathbf{x}\mathbf{x}^{\mathsf{T}} - 2\mathbf{x}\mathbf{E}_{P(\mathbf{x})}\{\mathbf{x}\}^{\mathsf{T}} + \mathbf{E}_{P(\mathbf{x})}\{\mathbf{x}\}\mathbf{E}_{P(\mathbf{x})}\{\mathbf{x}\}^{\mathsf{T}}\right\}.
\end{aligned}$$

Rearranging this expression results in

$$\text{cov}\{\mathbf{x}\} = \mathbf{E}_{P(\mathbf{x})}\left\{\mathbf{x}\mathbf{x}^{\mathsf{T}}\right\} - \mathbf{E}_{P(\mathbf{x})}\{\mathbf{x}\}\mathbf{E}_{P(\mathbf{x})}\{\mathbf{x}\}^{\mathsf{T}}. \tag{2.16}$$

2.3 POPULAR DISCRETE DISTRIBUTIONS

In all of our examples thus far, we have worked with random variables for which we can list the probabilities of each possible outcome. This is useful for explanative purposes but rapidly becomes infeasible as the number of possible outcomes increases. In reality, we will often work with well-known families of distributions. Each family is suitable for particular types of events and in general these distributions have parameters that can be tuned to change their characteristics. In this section we will describe some common discrete distributions that you are likely to come across in Machine Learning.

2.3.1 Bernoulli distribution

We have already come across the Bernoulli distribution several times without realising it. It is used for events like a coin toss that have two possible outcomes. For a random variable X that can take two values, 0 or 1 (a binary random variable), where the probability that it takes the value 1 is defined as q, the Bernoulli distribution is

$$P(X = x) = q^x(1 - q)^{1-x}. \tag{2.17}$$

The Bernoulli distribution is also a special case of the **binomial** distribution (see below) when $N = 1$.

2.3.2 Binomial distribution

The binomial distribution extends the Bernoulli distribution to define the probability of observing a certain number of heads in a total of N tosses. More generally, we might think of events that have two outcomes (success or failure). If we have N such events, the binomial random variable Y can take values from 0 (no successes) to N (N successes). The probability of observing a particular number of successes is given by

$$P(Y = y) = P(y) = \begin{pmatrix} N \\ y \end{pmatrix} q^y (1-q)^{N-y}. \tag{2.18}$$

The second part of this expression looks very similar to the Bernoulli expression we have already seen. In fact, if we define the N binary outcomes as $x_1, \ldots, x_N$, the second part of the binomial expression is the product of the N binomial probabilities:

$$\prod_{n=1}^{N} q^{x_n} (1-q)^{1-x_n} = q^{\sum_n x_n} (1-q)^{N-\sum_n x_n}$$
$$= q^y (1-q)^{N-y},$$

where $y = \sum_n x_n$: the number of successes (a success corresponds to $x_n = 1$). The first part of the binomial expression is required because there is potentially more than one set of $x_1, x_2, \ldots, x_N$ that corresponds to, say, $y = 3$. $q^y (1-q)^{N-y}$ gives us the probability of just one of these sets. Summing over all possible sets is equivalent to multiplying by the number of such sets, given by the combinations function, $\begin{pmatrix} N \\ y \end{pmatrix}$ (read as N choose y – see Comment 2.3 for details). Figure 2.3 shows an example of the distribution function when $N = 50$ and $q = 0.7$.

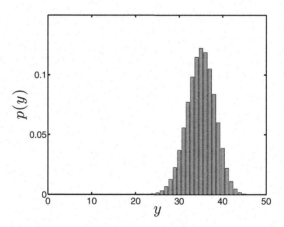

FIGURE 2.3 An example of the probability distribution function for a binomial random variable when $N = 50$ and $q = 0.7$ (see Equation 2.18).

2.3.3 Multinomial distribution

Our previous two examples have been distributions over scalar random variables – we will now look at a distribution that assigns probabilities to vectors of discrete values. The fundamental ideas are exactly the same – the distribution assigns a probability to every possible vector and the sum of these probabilities must equal 1. As a motivation for vector random variables, imagine you were building a machine that would produce random documents of N words and you wanted to define a distribution over these documents. This isn't as foolish as it might sound – Machine Learning techniques are often used to analyse text data by defining distributions over documents in just this manner. One way of representing a document would be with a vector of word counts. Assuming J possible words in our vocabulary, the vector would be of length J and the jth element would hold the number of times the jth word appears in the document. The **multinomial** distribution allows us to define a distribution over such vectors. Let Y be a random variable that represents a document. An instance of this random variable is a vector of word counts $\mathbf{y} = [y_1, \ldots, y_J]^\mathsf{T}$; the multinomial distribution defines the probability of $\mathbf{y}$ as

$$P(Y = \mathbf{y}) = P(\mathbf{y}) = \frac{N!}{\prod_j y_j!} \prod_j q_j^{y_j} \tag{2.19}$$

where q_j are the parameters of the multinomial distribution and represent the probabilities of the individual words ($\sum_j q_j = 1$).

Comment 2.3 – Combinations: N choose y, written as

$$\binom{N}{y}$$

is mathematical shorthand for the number of ways in which y distinct objects can be chosen from a set of N objects. For example, $\binom{4}{1}$ would be 4 – there are 4 ways I can choose one object from four objects – object 1 on its own, object 2 on its own, object 3 on its own or object 4 on its own. $\binom{4}{2}$ is 6 – the possible choices are 1 and 2, 1 and 3, 1 and 4, 2 and 3, 2 and 4 or 3 and 4. In general,

$$\binom{N}{y} = \frac{N!}{y!(N-y)!}$$

where $N!$ (read N factorial) is

$$\prod_{i=1}^{N} i = N \times (N-1) \times (N-2) \times \ldots \times 1.$$

2.4 CONTINUOUS RANDOM VARIABLES – DENSITY FUNCTIONS

We saw at the start of this section that we are unable to systematically write down all possible outcomes of a continuous random variable. Unfortunately, this precludes us from assigning probabilities to particular values. To overcome this, we work with the probabilities of the outcome falling within some range or interval. For example, given a continuous random variable X that can take on any value between minus infinity and infinity, it makes sense to try and work out

$$P(x_1 \leq X \leq x_2)$$

but not
$$P(X = x).$$

When working with continuous random variables, we need a continuous analogue to the probability distribution (recall that this, for a discrete random variable, was the set of outcomes (x) and the probabilities of each outcome, expressed as a function of x, $p(x)$). This is provided by a **probability density function** (pdf), also denoted $p(x)$. To compute the probability that X lies in a particular range, we compute the definite integral (see Comment 2.4) of $p(x)$ with respect to x over this range:

$$P(x_1 \leq X \leq x_2) = \int_{x_1}^{x_2} p(x)dx.$$

If our random variable may only take values in the range $x_1 \leq X \leq x_2$, it stands to reason that the probability that it lies in this range must be 1. This leads us to the continuous equivalent of Equation 2.2:

$$\int_{x_1}^{x_2} p(x)dx = 1 \quad \text{where } x_1 \leq X \leq x_2. \tag{2.20}$$

Equation 2.1 also has a continuous equivalent,

$$p(x) \geq 0, \tag{2.21}$$

that tells us that a pdf can never be negative. Note that there is no upper bound on the value of the pdf – it is not a probability and so can (and often will) be higher than 1 for a particular value of x.

Comment 2.4 – Definite Integrals: When differentiating a function including a constant term, the term disappears, e.g.

$$\frac{d}{dx}(x^2 + 3) = 2x.$$

Hence, when we are integrating a function, we have to admit the possibility that there might be a constant term

$$\int 2x \, dx = x^2 + C.$$

This is called an indefinite integral, as we don't know the value of C.

Often we will be interested in using integration to compute the area under a curve. For example, here we are interested in computing the area under the curve $y = 2x$ between $x = 2$ and $x = 3$, as shown in the plot on the right. This is calculated as

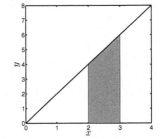

$$\int_2^3 2x \, dx = [x^2 + C]_2^3$$

where the $[\cdot]_a^b$ means take the value of the object inside the brackets when $x = a$ away from the value when $x = b$. In this case, this suggests

$$(3^2 + C) - (2^2 + C) = 9 - 4 + C - C = 5.$$

This is a definite integral – the constants cancel out and the answer is exact.

Joint and conditional continuous densities   Just as with the discrete case, we can define joint probability density functions over several continuous random variables. For example, $p(x, y)$ is the joint density of two random variables X and Y, and $p(\mathbf{w})$, is the density of a vector, $\mathbf{w}$ which could be thought of as the joint density of $p(w_0, w_1, \dots)$ – random variables representing each element in the vector. Although we cannot compute $P(X = x, Y = y)$, we can compute

$$P(x_1 \leq X \leq x_2, y_1 \leq Y \leq y_2) = \int_{x=x_1}^{x_2} \int_{y=y_1}^{y_2} p(x, y) \, dx \, dy.$$

The same applies for conditional distributions, although the conditioning is done on an exact value (as this event is assumed to have happened). For example, we would compute

$$P(x_1 \leq X \leq x_2 | Y = y) = \int_{x=x_1}^{x_2} p(x|Y = y) \, dx.$$

Often we will use the shorthand $p(x|y)$ to describe the density function of X given that $Y = y$.

Marginalisation   You may have already guessed that to marginalise over a continuous random variable, we replace the summation from the discrete case with an integral. For example, the pdf $p(y)$ can be computed from $p(y, x)$ as follows:

$$p(y) = \int_{x=x_1}^{x_2} p(y, x) \, dx$$

where $x_1 \leq X \leq x_2$ describes the sample space of X.

Expectations   Expectations with respect to continuous random variables are performed by integrating over the range of values that the random variable can take:

$$\mathbf{E}_{p(x)}\{f(x)\} = \int f(x)p(x)dx. \tag{2.22}$$

All of the expressions derived in Section 2.2.8 are identical in the continuous case.

   In many practical scenarios, we will not be able to perform this integral – we may not know the exact form of $p(x)$ or it might simply be impossible to integrate. However, if we can generate samples from $p(x)$, it can be approximated by

$$\mathbf{E}_{p(x)}\{f(x)\} \approx \frac{1}{S} \sum_{s=1}^{S} f(x_s) \tag{2.23}$$

where x_s is one of the S samples from $p(x)$. This is an example of a **Monte Carlo** approximation to an integral which we will see a lot more of in subsequent chapters.

2.5   POPULAR CONTINUOUS DENSITY FUNCTIONS

Just as for the discrete case, there are several common families of continuous density functions that we will often come across. In this section, we will describe three of them.

2.5.1   The uniform density function

The simplest continuous density function is the uniform density function. The uniform density function, $p(y) = \mathcal{U}(a, b)$, is constant between a and b and zero elsewhere:

$$p(y) = \begin{cases} r & \text{for } a \leq y \leq b \\ 0 & \text{otherwise.} \end{cases} \tag{2.24}$$

An example where $a = 3$ and $b = 8$ can be seen in Figure 2.4. We can compute the value of r for any values of a and b by remembering that the integral of the pdf over the sample space must be equal to 1 by definition. In this case,

$$\begin{aligned} P(a \leq Y \leq b) = 1 &= \int_{y=a}^{b} p(y) \, dy = \int_{y=a}^{b} r \, dy \\ &= [yr]_a^b = rb - ra = r(b - a) \\ r &= \frac{1}{b - a}. \end{aligned}$$

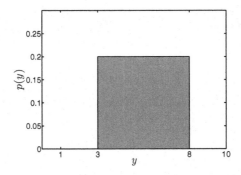

FIGURE 2.4   An example of the uniform pdf.

This is quite intuitive – it is the total probability available – 1 – divided by the length of the interval in which the variables must lie $(b - a)$. We can also easily define multidimensional uniform random variables. For example, if $\mathbf{y} = [y_1, y_2]^\mathsf{T}$,

$$p(\mathbf{y}) = \begin{cases} r & \text{for } a \le y_1 \le b \text{ and } c \le y_2 \le d \\ 0 & \text{otherwise} \end{cases}$$

and we can compute r in just the same way:

$$\begin{aligned} P(a \le y_1 \le b, c \le y_2 \le d) = 1 &= \int_{y_1=a}^{b} \int_{y_2=c}^{d} r \, dy_1 \, dy_2 \\ &= \int_{y_1=a}^{b} [ry_2]_c^d \, dy_1 = \int_{y_1=a}^{b} r(d-c) dy_1 \\ &= [r(d-c)y_1]_a^b = r(d-c)(b-a) \\ r &= \frac{1}{(d-c)(b-a)}. \end{aligned}$$

Again, this is intuitive – it is the total probability – 1 – divided by the area of the interval in which the variables must lie $(d - c)(b - a)$.

As an aside, Equation 2.23 shows how we can approximate expectations by taking samples (realisations of the random variable) from the appropriate distribution. We will demonstrate this approach by computing the expected value of y^2 analytically and via sampling. The analytical result is given by

$$\begin{aligned} \mathbf{E}_{p(y)} \{y^2\} &= \int_{y=a}^{b} y^2 p(y) \, dy = \int_{y=a}^{b} \frac{y^2}{b-a} \, dy \\ &= \left[\frac{y^3}{3(b-a)} \right]_a^b = \frac{b^3 - a^3}{3(b-a)}. \end{aligned}$$

Substituting $a = 0, b = 1$ gives

$$\mathbf{E}_{p(y)} \{y^2\} = \frac{1}{3}.$$

To compute the sample based approximation, we need to be able to draw samples from $\mathcal{U}(0,1)$. In MATLAB, the command **rand** generates samples from this distribution. If we generate S samples, y_s, we can approximate the expectation as

$$\mathbf{E}_{p(y)}\left\{y^2\right\} \approx \frac{1}{S}\sum_{s=1}^{S} y_s^2. \tag{2.25}$$

Figure 2.5 shows how this approximation improves as we increase the number of samples from 1 to 10^4. The true value, $\frac{1}{3}$, is shown as the dashed line (MATLAB script: **approx_expected_value.m**). After only 100 samples, the approximation is reasonably good. Approximating expectations with samples will be used extensively in later chapters (see Exercise 2.4).

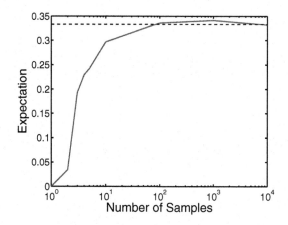

FIGURE 2.5 Effect of increasing the number of samples on the approximation to the expectation given in Equation 2.25 where $p(y) = \mathcal{U}(0,1)$. The dashed line is the true value of $1/3$. Note the log scale on the x-axis.

2.5.2 The beta density function

The beta density function can be used for continuous random variables that are restricted to between 0 and 1. The beta density function is defined as

$$p(r) = \frac{\Gamma(\alpha + \beta)}{\Gamma(\alpha)\Gamma(\beta)} r^{\alpha-1}(1-r)^{\beta-1}, \tag{2.26}$$

where α and β are parameters that control the shape of the density function, both of which must be positive. $\Gamma(z)$ is known as the gamma function and we will omit a discussion here except to say that it can be computed in MATLAB using the inbuilt function **gamma**. Figure 2.6 shows the beta pdfs corresponding to three different sets of parameters. We will use the beta density function considerably in Chapter 3 and so will leave more discussion until then.

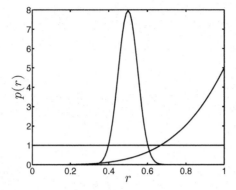

FIGURE 2.6 Examples of beta pdfs with three different pairs of parameters.

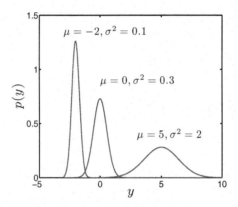

FIGURE 2.7 Three Gaussian pdfs with different means and variances.

2.5.3 The Gaussian density function

Gaussian random variables are used in many continuous applications. One reason is the ease with which the Gaussian pdf can be manipulated in certain, useful situations. The Gaussian distribution is defined over a sample space that includes all real numbers (i.e. all numbers between $-\infty$ and ∞) and has a pdf for a random variable Y defined as

$$p(y|\mu,\sigma^2) = \frac{1}{\sigma\sqrt{2\pi}} \exp\left\{-\frac{1}{2\sigma^2}(y-\mu)^2\right\} \tag{2.27}$$

and is characterised by two variables – the mean (μ) and variance (σ^2). Figure 2.7 shows three Gaussian pdfs with different μ, σ^2 values. The highest value of the pdf is obtained when $y = \mu$ and the density is symmetric about this point. The width of the density is controlled by σ^2 – the higher the value, the wider the density. If we used the leftmost Gaussian in Figure 2.7 to generate instances of a random variable, we would only expect values from a small range around -2. For the rightmost Gaussian, we would anticipate values from quite a large range around 5. A common shorthand for the Gaussian pdf is $\mathcal{N}(\mu, \sigma^2)$. Therefore, if Y has a Gaussian pdf, we could write

$$p(y|\mu, \sigma^2) = \mathcal{N}(\mu, \sigma^2),$$

which reads as 'the density function for the random variable Y is normal (Gaussian and normal are used interchangeably) with mean μ and variance σ^2'.

2.5.4 Multivariate Gaussian

The Gaussian distribution can also be generalised to define a density function over continuous vectors. This multivariate Gaussian density for a vector $\mathbf{x} = [x_1, \ldots, x_D]^\mathsf{T}$ is something we will use a great deal in subsequent chapters. The density function is defined as

$$p(\mathbf{x}) = \frac{1}{(2\pi)^{D/2}|\boldsymbol{\Sigma}|^{1/2}} \exp\left\{ -\frac{1}{2}(\mathbf{x} - \boldsymbol{\mu})^\mathsf{T} \boldsymbol{\Sigma}^{-1} (\mathbf{x} - \boldsymbol{\mu}) \right\} \qquad (2.28)$$

where the mean $\boldsymbol{\mu}$ is now a vector (of the same size as $\mathbf{x}$), the dth element of which tells us the mean value of x_d, and the variance has become a $D \times D$ covariance matrix. A graphical example is perhaps the best way of getting a feel for this density and the effects of the parameters $\boldsymbol{\mu}$ and $\boldsymbol{\Sigma}$. The first example is shown in the top line of Figure 2.8. In this example, the parameters are

$$\boldsymbol{\mu} = [2, \; 1]^\mathsf{T}, \; \boldsymbol{\Sigma} = \begin{bmatrix} 1 & 0 \\ 0 & 1 \end{bmatrix}$$

This is a special case of the multivariate Gaussian where the two variables (say x_1 and x_2) are independent. To show this, we note that $\boldsymbol{\Sigma} = \mathbf{I}$. So,

$$p(\mathbf{x}) = \frac{1}{(2\pi)^{D/2}|\mathbf{I}|^{1/2}} \exp\left\{ -\frac{1}{2}(\mathbf{x} - \boldsymbol{\mu})^\mathsf{T} \mathbf{I}^{-1} (\mathbf{x} - \boldsymbol{\mu}) \right\}.$$

Now, $\mathbf{I}^{-1} = \mathbf{I}$ (see Comment 1.10), allowing us to manipulate this expression to obtain a product over univariate Gaussian pdfs. Starting with the expression above (having swapped the $\mathbf{I}^{-1}$ for $\mathbf{I}$), we can convert the matrix product inside the exponential into a sum over the D different elements (see Exercise 2.5):

$$
\begin{aligned}
p(\mathbf{x}) &= \frac{1}{(2\pi)^{D/2}|\mathbf{I}|^{1/2}} \exp\left\{ -\frac{1}{2}(\mathbf{x} - \boldsymbol{\mu})^\mathsf{T} \mathbf{I} (\mathbf{x} - \boldsymbol{\mu}) \right\} \\
&= \frac{1}{(2\pi)^{D/2}|\mathbf{I}|^{1/2}} \exp\left\{ -\frac{1}{2} \sum_{d=1}^{D} (x_d - \mu_d)^2 \right\}.
\end{aligned}
$$

Comment 2.5 – Matrix determinant: The determinant of a square matrix, denoted $|\mathbf{A}|$ for matrix $\mathbf{A}$, is a useful quantity, especially when dealing with multivariate Gaussians. For large matrices, it is too cumbersome to calculate by hand but it can be done for small matrices. For example, for a 2×2 matrix

$$\mathbf{A} = \begin{bmatrix} a & b \\ c & d \end{bmatrix}, \quad |\mathbf{A}| = ad - bc,$$

but for anything bigger than this it is safest to resort to a computer unless the matrix has a special structure. One special matrix that we will see a lot of is a square matrix that only has diagonal elements (all off-diagonal elements are zero). In this case, the determinant is simply the product of these elements. For example,

$$\mathbf{A} = \begin{bmatrix} a_{11} & 0 & \cdots & 0 \\ 0 & a_{22} & \cdots & 0 \\ \vdots & \vdots & \ddots & \vdots \\ 0 & 0 & \cdots & a_{DD} \end{bmatrix}, \quad |\mathbf{A}| = \prod_{d=1}^{D} a_{dd}.$$

It is not easy to gain an intuition into what the determinant represents. Its role in the normalisation constant of the multivariate Gaussian leads us to think of it as related to the volume of the Gaussian unnormalised Gaussian (remember that the normalised volume must be equal to 1) and it may be useful to think of it in this way.

The exponential of a sum is a product of exponentials, allowing us to rewrite the expression as follows:

$$p(\mathbf{x}) \quad = \quad \frac{1}{(2\pi)^{D/2}|\mathbf{I}|^{1/2}} \prod_{d=1}^{D} \exp\left\{ -\frac{1}{2}(x_d - \mu_d)^2 \right\}.$$

$|\mathbf{I}|$ is the determinant of $\mathbf{I}$, which, from the discussion of diagonal matrices in Comment 2.5, is equal to 1. The other constant term, $(2\pi)^{D/2}$, could be written as $\prod_{d=1}^{D}(2\pi)^{1/2}$ and so our expression can be rewritten as

$$p(\mathbf{x}) = \prod_{d=1}^{D} \frac{1}{(2\pi)^{1/2}} \exp\left\{ -\frac{1}{2}(x_d - \mu_d)^2 \right\}.$$

Each term in the product is a univariate Gaussian (with mean μ_d and variance 1) and therefore, by the definition of independence, the elements of $\mathbf{x}$ are independent. This result doesn't just hold for $\Sigma = \mathbf{I}$, it holds for any covariance matrix that has non-zero elements only in the diagonal positions. These diagonal elements will be the variances of the individual, univariate Gaussians (see Exercises 2.5 and 2.6 for further exercises and practice at this kind of Gaussian manipulation).

The second row in Figure 2.8 gives another example, with parameters:

$$\boldsymbol{\mu} = [2, \ 1]^{\mathsf{T}}, \ \Sigma = \begin{bmatrix} 1 & 0.8 \\ 0.8 & 1 \end{bmatrix}.$$

In this example, we could not write the pdf as a product of univariate Gaussians,

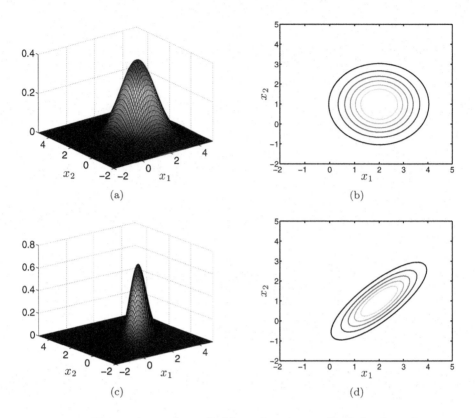

FIGURE 2.8 Example surface (left) and contour (right) plots for two different two-dimensional Gaussian pdfs.

suggesting that the elements of **x** are not independent. We can also see the dependence between them in the contour plot (bottom right of Figure 2.8). If x_1 and x_2 are independent, $p(x_2|x_1)$ should not vary with different values of x_1. Imagine that $x_1 = 3$. It looks, from Figure 2.8, that when $x_1 = 3$, values for x_2 are grouped around 2. If $x_1 = 1$, the values are grouped around 0. Clearly we expect different values of x_2 in both cases and, intuitively, x_1 and x_2 are dependent (MATLAB script: **gauss_surf.m**). Experiment with the values in the covariance matrix to see the effect this has on the surface and contour plots.

A nice feature of the multivariate Gaussian is that the conditional density function $p(x_2|x_1)$ is another Gaussian for which we can easily obtain the mean and variance.

2.6 SUMMARY

This completes our brief introduction to random variables and probability. Although we have only skimmed the surface of an enormous subject, the material presented in the previous few sections is sufficient for us to extend our model to explicitly measure the discrepancy between predictions and measurements. In the remainder of this chapter, we will add a random variable to our model that will model the error between the linear model and our data. Assuming that the random variable follows a Gaussian density, we will end up with exactly the equation for $\hat{\mathbf{w}}$ (the optimum parameter value) as in Chapter 1. However, the inclusion of the noise term allows us to obtain degrees of confidence in both our parameter values and predictions.

2.7 THINKING GENERATIVELY...CONTINUED

We now have a sufficient grounding in random variables to be able to handle the errors in our linear model (as shown in Figure 2.1). In Section 2.1.1 we began thinking about how we could generate data that looks like the data that we have observed. In particular, we considered generating the nth winning time from a function of the form $\mathbf{w}^\mathsf{T}\mathbf{x}_n$ and then adding a random quantity that we shall call ϵ_n – a random variable.

Our model now takes the following form:

$$t_n = \mathbf{w}^\mathsf{T}\mathbf{x}_n + \epsilon_n. \tag{2.29}$$

To complete the definition of this model, we need to decide on a distribution for ϵ_n. Firstly, it should be clear that the difference between the model and the actual winning times is a continuous quantity. Therefore, ϵ_n is a continuous random variable. We also do not just have one random variable, but one for each observed Olympic year. It seems reasonable to assume that these values are independent:

$$p(\epsilon_1, \ldots, \epsilon_N) = \prod_{n=1}^{N} p(\epsilon_n).$$

The final assumption is the form of $p(\epsilon_n)$. We will assume that this is a Gaussian (or normal) distribution with zero mean and variance σ^2. We will not make much effort to justify this assumption here except to say that this allows ϵ_n to be both positive and negative (allows data to lie both above and below the line $\mathbf{w}^\mathsf{T}\mathbf{x}$) and has interesting modelling properties that link it to the squared loss that we used in Chapter 1. As for the choice of loss functions discussed in Section 1.1.3, in a real modelling situation one should be much more careful to properly justify this choice.

Using a normal density for ϵ, i.e. $p(\epsilon) = \mathcal{N}(\mu, \sigma^2)$ (see Section 2.5.3), with a mean (μ) of zero and a variance of $\sigma^2 = 0.05$ (don't worry about the particular value here for now), we obtain a much more realistic looking dataset, shown in Figure 2.9 (MATLAB script: `genolymp.m`).

Our model now consists of two components:

1. A **deterministic** component ($\mathbf{w}^\mathsf{T}\mathbf{x}_n$), sometimes referred to as a *trend* or *drift*.

2. A random component (ϵ_n), sometimes referred to as *noise*.

We have already pointed out that we are not restricted to noise from a Gaussian distribution. We are also not restricted to *additive* noise. For some applications, a multiplicative term might be more appropriate (in which case, $t = f(\mathbf{x}; \mathbf{w})\epsilon$). For example, degradation of image pixels is often modelled with multiplicative noise.

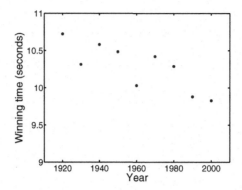

FIGURE 2.9 Dataset generated from a linear model with Gaussian errors.

However, as we shall see in the following sections, choosing additive Gaussian noise allows us to obtain exact expressions for the optimal parameter value $\widehat{\mathbf{w}}$.

2.8 LIKELIHOOD

Our model is of the following form:

$$t_n = f(\mathbf{x}_n; \mathbf{w}) + \epsilon_n, \ \epsilon_n \sim \mathcal{N}(0, \sigma^2).$$

As in Chapter 1, we need to find the optimal value of $\mathbf{w}$, $\widehat{\mathbf{w}}$. We also have an additional parameter σ^2 that needs to be set. In Chapter 1 we found the value of $\mathbf{w}$ that minimised the loss. The loss measured the difference between the observed values of t and those predicted by the model. The effect of adding a random variable to the model is that the output of the model, t, is now itself a random variable. In other words, there is no single value of t_n for a particular $\mathbf{x}_n$. As such, we cannot use the loss as a means of optimising $\mathbf{w}$ and σ^2.

Adding a constant $(\mathbf{w}^\mathsf{T}\mathbf{x}_n)$ to a Gaussian random variable is equivalent to another Gaussian random variable with the mean shifted by the same constant:

$$\begin{aligned} y &= a + z \\ p(z) &= \mathcal{N}(m, s) \\ p(y) &= \mathcal{N}(m + a, s) \end{aligned}$$

Therefore, the random variable t_n has the density function

$$p(t_n | \mathbf{x}_n, \mathbf{w}, \sigma^2) = \mathcal{N}(\mathbf{w}^\mathsf{T}\mathbf{x}_n, \sigma^2).$$

Note the conditioning on the left hand side – the density of t_n depends on particular values of $\mathbf{x}_n$ and $\mathbf{w}$ (they determine the mean) and σ^2 (the variance).

To see how we can use this to find optimal values of $\mathbf{w}$ and σ^2, consider one of the years from our dataset – 1980. Based on the model (w_0, w_1) found in the previous chapter and assuming again that $\sigma^2 = 0.05$, we can plot $p(t_n | x_n = 1980, \mathbf{w}, \sigma^2)$ as a function of t_n, shown Figure 2.10. The solid line shows

$$p(t_n | \mathbf{x}_n = [1, \ 1980]^\mathsf{T}, \mathbf{w} = [36.416, -0.0133]^\mathsf{T}, \sigma^2 = 0.05),$$

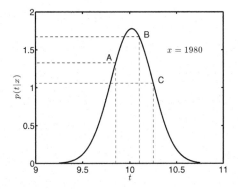

FIGURE 2.10 Likelihood function for the year 1980.

which is a Gaussian density with mean $\mu = 36.416 - 0.0133 \times 1980 = 10.02$ and variance $\sigma^2 = 0.05$. Recall that, for a continuous random variable, t, $p(t)$ cannot be interpreted as a probability. The height of the curve at a particular value of t can be interpreted as how *likely* it is that we would observe that particular t for $x = 1980$. The most *likely* winning time in 1980 would be 10.02 seconds (for a Gaussian, the most likely (highest) point corresponds to the mean). Also shown on the plot, are three example times – A, B and C. Of these, B is the most likely and C the least likely.

The actual winning time in the 1980 Olympics is C (10.25 seconds). The density $p(t_n | \mathbf{x}_n, \mathbf{w}, \sigma^2)$ evaluated at $t_n = 10.25$ is an important quantity, known as the **likelihood** of the nth data point. We cannot change $t_n = 10.25$ (this is our data) but we can change $\mathbf{w}$ and σ^2 to try and move the density so as to make it as high as possible at $t = 10.25$. The idea of finding parameters that maximise the likelihood in this way is a key concept in Machine Learning.

2.8.1 Dataset likelihood

In general, we are not interested in the likelihood of a single data point but that of all of the data. If we have N data points, we are interested in the joint conditional density:

$$p(t_1, \ldots, t_N | \mathbf{x}_1, \ldots, \mathbf{x}_N, \mathbf{w}, \sigma^2).$$

This is a joint density over all of the responses in our dataset (see Section 2.2.5). We will write this compactly (using vector notation and $\mathbf{X}$ as defined in Chapter 1) as $p(\mathbf{t} | \mathbf{X}, \mathbf{w}, \sigma^2)$. Evaluating this density at the observed data points gives a single likelihood value for the whole dataset, which we can optimise by varying $\mathbf{w}$ and σ^2.

The assumption that the noise at each data point is independent ($p(\epsilon_1, \ldots, \epsilon_N) = \prod_n p(\epsilon_n)$) enables us to factorise this density into something more manageable. In particular, this joint conditional density can be factorised into N separate terms, one for each data object:

$$L = p(\mathbf{t} | \mathbf{X}, \mathbf{w}, \sigma^2) = \prod_{n=1}^{N} p(t_n | \mathbf{x}_n, \mathbf{w}, \sigma^2) = \prod_{n=1}^{N} \mathcal{N}(\mathbf{w}^\mathsf{T} \mathbf{x}_n, \sigma^2). \qquad (2.30)$$

Note that we haven't gone as far as saying that the t_n values are themselves completely independent. This is not the case – the t_n values are, on average, decreasing over time, suggesting a clear statistical dependence between them. If they were completely independent, it would not be worthwhile actually trying to model the data at all. In fact, they are **conditionally independent** – given a value for $\mathbf{w}$ (the deterministic part of the model), the t_n are independent; without them they are not. If this sounds a bit strange, think of it in the following way: Imagine that we had values for all of the Olympic years and winning times except one of the ones in the middle – say 1960. For simplicity, we shall use $\mathbf{X}, \mathbf{t}$ to denote all Olympic years and winning times excluding 1960. If we want to use $\mathbf{X}$ and $\mathbf{t}$ to learn something about t_{1960}, we are interested in the conditional distribution

$$p(t_{1960}|\mathbf{x}_{1960}, \mathbf{X}, \mathbf{t}).$$

From the definition of conditional distributions, this is given by

$$p(t_{1960}|\mathbf{x}_{1960}, \mathbf{X}, \mathbf{t}) = \frac{p(t_{1960}, \mathbf{t}|\mathbf{x}_{1960}, \mathbf{X})}{p(\mathbf{t}|\mathbf{X})}.$$

Assuming that the elements of $\mathbf{t}$ are independent results in t_{1960} only depending on $\mathbf{x}_{1960}$:

$$p(t_{1960}|\mathbf{x}_{1960}, \mathbf{X}, \mathbf{t}) = \frac{p(t_{1960}|\mathbf{x}_{1960}) \prod_n p(t_n|\mathbf{x}_n)}{\prod_n p(t_n|\mathbf{x}_n)} = p(t_{1960}|\mathbf{x}_{1960}).$$

However, for our model to be any use, t_{1960} must, in some sense, be dependent on the other data. This dependence is encapsulated in the parameter $\mathbf{w}$. The deterministic part of our model captures this dependence. If we know $\mathbf{w}$, all that remains is the errors between the observed data and $\mathbf{w}^\mathsf{T}\mathbf{x}_n$. These errors are assumed to be independent. Hence, conditioned on $\mathbf{w}$, the observations are independent. Without a model (and therefore a $\mathbf{w}$), the observations are not independent.

We will now show how we can find the values of $\mathbf{w}$ and σ^2 that maximise the likelihood.

2.8.2   Maximum likelihood

Equation 2.30 gives us a single value that tells us how likely our dataset is, given the current model (by model, we mean choice of $\mathbf{w}$ and σ^2). As our dataset is fixed, varying the model will result in different likelihood values. A sensible choice of model would be that which maximised the likelihood. In other words, we will select the model parameters that will make our observations most likely.

For analytical reasons, we will maximise the **natural logarithm** of the likelihood (we will follow the Machine Learning convention of using $\log(y)$ to denote the natural logarithm of y, often denoted elsewhere as $\ln(y)$). We can do this because the estimated arguments $\widehat{\mathbf{w}}$ and $\widehat{\sigma^2}$ that maximise the log-likelihood will also maximise the likelihood.

Substituting the expression for the Gaussian density function (Equation 2.27) and separating the various terms gives us an expression that will be easier to deal with:

$$
\begin{aligned}
\log L &= \sum_{n=1}^{N} \log \left(\frac{1}{\sqrt{2\pi\sigma^2}} \exp\left\{ -\frac{1}{2\sigma^2}(t_n - f(\mathbf{x}_n; \mathbf{w}))^2 \right\} \right) \\
&= \sum_{n=1}^{N} \left(-\frac{1}{2}\log(2\pi) - \log\sigma - \frac{1}{2\sigma^2}(t_n - f(\mathbf{x}_n, \mathbf{w}))^2 \right) \\
&= -\frac{N}{2}\log 2\pi - N\log\sigma - \frac{1}{2\sigma^2}\sum_{n=1}^{N}(t_n - f(\mathbf{x}_n; \mathbf{w}))^2.
\end{aligned}
$$

Substituting our particular deterministic component $f(\mathbf{x}_n; \mathbf{w}) = \mathbf{w}^\mathsf{T}\mathbf{x}_n$ gives us the log-likelihood expression that we will work with:

$$
\log L = -\frac{N}{2}\log 2\pi - N\log\sigma - \frac{1}{2\sigma^2}\sum_{n=1}^{N}(t_n - \mathbf{w}^\mathsf{T}\mathbf{x}_n)^2. \tag{2.31}
$$

As for the least squares solution derived in Chapter 1, we can find the optimal parameters by taking derivatives, equating them to zero and solving for turning points, in a manner similar to that in Section 1.1.4. For $\mathbf{w}$ (noting that $\mathbf{w}^\mathsf{T}\mathbf{x}_n = \mathbf{x}_n^\mathsf{T}\mathbf{w}$),

$$
\begin{aligned}
\frac{\partial\log L}{\partial \mathbf{w}} &= \frac{1}{\sigma^2}\sum_{n=1}^{N}\mathbf{x}_n(t_n - \mathbf{x}_n^\mathsf{T}\mathbf{w}) \\
&= \frac{1}{\sigma^2}\sum_{n=1}^{N}\mathbf{x}_n t_n - \mathbf{x}_n\mathbf{x}_n^\mathsf{T}\mathbf{w} = \mathbf{0}.
\end{aligned}
$$

Note that $\frac{\partial\log L}{\partial \mathbf{w}}$ is a vector and so we equate it to $\mathbf{0}$, a vector of zeros of the same size. Recall the shorthand matrix/vector forms we used in Chapter 1:

$$
\mathbf{X} = \begin{bmatrix} \mathbf{x}_1^\mathsf{T} \\ \mathbf{x}_2^\mathsf{T} \\ \vdots \\ \mathbf{x}_N^\mathsf{T} \end{bmatrix} = \begin{bmatrix} 1 & x_1 \\ 1 & x_2 \\ \vdots & \vdots \\ 1 & x_N \end{bmatrix}, \quad \mathbf{t} = \begin{bmatrix} t_1 \\ t_2 \\ \vdots \\ t_N \end{bmatrix}.
$$

In this notation, $\sum_{n=1}^{N}\mathbf{x}_n t_n$ can be written as $\mathbf{X}^\mathsf{T}\mathbf{t}$ and similarly $\sum_{n=1}^{N}\mathbf{x}_n\mathbf{x}_n^\mathsf{T}\mathbf{w}$ as $\mathbf{X}^\mathsf{T}\mathbf{X}\mathbf{w}$ (see Exercise 1.5). This allows us to write the derivative in the more convenient vector/matrix form:

$$
\frac{\partial\log L}{\partial \mathbf{w}} = \frac{1}{\sigma^2}(\mathbf{X}^\mathsf{T}\mathbf{t} - \mathbf{X}^\mathsf{T}\mathbf{X}\mathbf{w}) = \mathbf{0}. \tag{2.32}
$$

Solving this expression for $\mathbf{w}$ will lead to an expression for the optimal value:

$$
\begin{aligned}
\frac{1}{\sigma^2}(\mathbf{X}^\mathsf{T}\mathbf{t} - \mathbf{X}^\mathsf{T}\mathbf{X}\mathbf{w}) &= 0 \\
\mathbf{X}^\mathsf{T}\mathbf{t} - \mathbf{X}^\mathsf{T}\mathbf{X}\mathbf{w} &= 0 \\
\mathbf{X}^\mathsf{T}\mathbf{X}\mathbf{w} &= \mathbf{X}^\mathsf{T}\mathbf{t} \\
\mathbf{w} &= (\mathbf{X}^\mathsf{T}\mathbf{X})^{-1}\mathbf{X}^\mathsf{T}\mathbf{t}.
\end{aligned}
$$

This is the **maximum likelihood** solution for $\mathbf{w}$:

$$\widehat{\mathbf{w}} = \left(\mathbf{X}^{\mathsf{T}}\mathbf{X}\right)^{-1}\mathbf{X}^{\mathsf{T}}\mathbf{t}. \tag{2.33}$$

Remarkably, this solution is *exactly* that which we have already derived for the least squares case in Chapter 1 (Equation 1.16). Minimising the squared loss is equivalent to the maximum likelihood solution if the noise is assumed to be Gaussian. Also, the noise variance, σ^2, does not appear in this expression at all – it scales the likelihood but doesn't affect the value of $\widehat{\mathbf{w}}$ corresponding to its maximum.

To obtain an expression for σ^2 (assuming $\mathbf{w} = \widehat{\mathbf{w}}$), we can follow the same procedure. Taking partial derivatives and equating to zero results in

$$\frac{\partial \log L}{\partial \sigma} = -\frac{N}{\sigma} + \frac{1}{\sigma^3}\sum_{n=1}^{N}(t_n - \mathbf{x}^{\mathsf{T}}\widehat{\mathbf{w}})^2 = 0. \tag{2.34}$$

Rearranging gives $\widehat{\sigma^2}$, the maximum likelihood estimate for σ^2:

$$\widehat{\sigma^2} = \frac{1}{N}\sum_{n=1}^{N}(t_n - \mathbf{x}^{\mathsf{T}}\widehat{\mathbf{w}})^2. \tag{2.35}$$

This expression makes perfect sense – the variance is simply the average squared error. We would prefer this in matrix notation so, using the fact that $\sum_{n=1}^{N}(t_n - \mathbf{x}^{\mathsf{T}}\widehat{\mathbf{w}})^2$ is equivalent to $(\mathbf{t} - \mathbf{X}\widehat{\mathbf{w}})^{\mathsf{T}}(\mathbf{t} - \mathbf{X}\widehat{\mathbf{w}})$,

$$\sigma^2 = \frac{1}{N}(\mathbf{t} - \mathbf{X}\widehat{\mathbf{w}})^{\mathsf{T}}(\mathbf{t} - \mathbf{X}\widehat{\mathbf{w}}) \tag{2.36}$$

$$= \frac{1}{N}(\mathbf{t}^{\mathsf{T}}\mathbf{t} - 2\mathbf{t}^{\mathsf{T}}\mathbf{X}\widehat{\mathbf{w}} + \widehat{\mathbf{w}}^{\mathsf{T}}\mathbf{X}^{\mathsf{T}}\mathbf{X}\widehat{\mathbf{w}}).$$

This can be further simplified by substituting $\widehat{\mathbf{w}} = \left(\mathbf{X}^{\mathsf{T}}\mathbf{X}\right)^{-1}\mathbf{X}^{\mathsf{T}}\mathbf{t}$ (note that $\widehat{\mathbf{w}}^{\mathsf{T}} = \mathbf{t}^{\mathsf{T}}\mathbf{X}(\mathbf{X}^{\mathsf{T}}\mathbf{X})^{-1}$ because $(\mathbf{X}^{\mathsf{T}}\mathbf{X})^{-1}$ is **symmetric** and is therefore equal to its own transpose):

$$\widehat{\sigma^2} = \frac{1}{N}(\mathbf{t}^{\mathsf{T}}\mathbf{t} - 2\mathbf{t}^{\mathsf{T}}\mathbf{X}(\mathbf{X}^{\mathsf{T}}\mathbf{X})^{-1}\mathbf{X}^{\mathsf{T}}\mathbf{t} + \mathbf{t}^{\mathsf{T}}\mathbf{X}(\mathbf{X}^{\mathsf{T}}\mathbf{X})^{-1}\mathbf{X}^{\mathsf{T}}\mathbf{X}(\mathbf{X}^{\mathsf{T}}\mathbf{X})^{-1}\mathbf{X}^{\mathsf{T}}\mathbf{t})$$

$$= \frac{1}{N}(\mathbf{t}^{\mathsf{T}}\mathbf{t} - 2\mathbf{t}^{\mathsf{T}}\mathbf{X}(\mathbf{X}^{\mathsf{T}}\mathbf{X})^{-1}\mathbf{X}^{\mathsf{T}}\mathbf{t} + \mathbf{t}^{\mathsf{T}}\mathbf{X}(\mathbf{X}^{\mathsf{T}}\mathbf{X})^{-1}\mathbf{X}^{\mathsf{T}}\mathbf{t})$$

$$= \frac{1}{N}(\mathbf{t}^{\mathsf{T}}\mathbf{t} - \mathbf{t}^{\mathsf{T}}\mathbf{X}(\mathbf{X}^{\mathsf{T}}\mathbf{X})^{-1}\mathbf{X}^{\mathsf{T}}\mathbf{t})$$

$$\widehat{\sigma^2} = \frac{1}{N}(\mathbf{t}^{\mathsf{T}}\mathbf{t} - \mathbf{t}^{\mathsf{T}}\mathbf{X}\widehat{\mathbf{w}}). \tag{2.37}$$

Using the Olympic 100 m data, our optimal parameter values (for a first-order (linear) polynomial) are

$$\widehat{\mathbf{w}} = [36.4165, \ -0.0133]^{\mathsf{T}}, \ \widehat{\sigma^2} = 0.0503.$$

$\widehat{\mathbf{w}}$ is the same as the least squares solution provided in the previous chapter (they are both computed using the same expression). $\widehat{\sigma^2}$ tells us the variance of the Gaussian noise that we have assumed is used to corrupt our data. Later in this chapter we will see that modelling the noise in this way provides several benefits over loss minimisation. Before we do, we shall first look at some of the characteristics of the solution.

2.8.3 Characteristics of the maximum likelihood solution

In Chapter 1, we used the second derivatives of the loss function to ensure that we had found a minimum. We will now do a similar thing with the second derivatives of the likelihood to ensure that we have found a maximum. Our derivatives are now with respect to a vector, and to examine the second derivatives, we construct the **Hessian matrix** (see Comment 2.6). Each entry in this matrix is the second derivative with respect to a pair of elements of $\mathbf{w}$. To be sure that we have found a maximum, we must show that the Hessian matrix is *negative definite* (see Comment 2.7).

Comment 2.6 – Hessian matrix: A Hessian matrix is square matrix containing all of the second-order partial derivatives of a function. For example, the Hessian matrix for a function $f(\mathbf{x}; \mathbf{w})$ with parameters $\mathbf{w} = [w_1, \ldots, w_K]^T$ would be

$$\mathbf{H} = \begin{bmatrix} \frac{\partial^2 f}{\partial w_1^2} & \frac{\partial^2 f}{\partial w_1 \partial w_2} & \cdots & \frac{\partial^2 f}{\partial w_1 \partial w_K} \\ \frac{\partial^2 f}{\partial w_2 \partial w_1} & \frac{\partial^2 f}{\partial w_2^2} & \cdots & \frac{\partial^2 f}{\partial w_2 \partial w_K} \\ \vdots & \vdots & \ddots & \vdots \\ \frac{\partial^2 f}{\partial w_K \partial w_1} & \frac{\partial^2 f}{\partial w_K \partial w_2} & \cdots & \frac{\partial^2 f}{\partial w_K^2} \end{bmatrix}.$$

We can use the Hessian to tell us something about turning points in $f(\mathbf{x}; \mathbf{w})$. For example, if the Hessian is *negative definite* (see Comment 2.7) at some turning point $\widehat{\mathbf{w}}$, then we know that that turning point corresponds to a maximum.

The Hessian matrix of second-order partial derivatives can be computed by differentiating Equation 2.32 with respect to $\mathbf{w}^T$:

$$\frac{\partial^2 \log L}{\partial \mathbf{w} \partial \mathbf{w}^T} = -\frac{1}{\sigma^2} \mathbf{X}^T \mathbf{X}. \qquad (2.38)$$

If we substitute $\mathbf{x}_n = [1, \ x_n]^T$, the diagonal elements of this matrix are equivalent (they differ by multiplication by a constant) to the second derivatives obtained in Equation 1.9 (see Exercise 2.7).

Comment 2.7 – Negative definite matrices: A real-valued matrix $\mathbf{H}$ is negative definite if

$$\mathbf{x}^T \mathbf{H} \mathbf{x} < 0$$

for all vectors of real values $\mathbf{x}$.

To be sure this is a maximum, we need to determine whether or not this matrix is negative definite. We can do this by showing that

$$-\frac{1}{\sigma^2} \mathbf{z}^T \mathbf{X}^T \mathbf{X} \mathbf{z} < 0$$

for any vector $\mathbf{z}$ or equivalently (because σ^2 must be positive) that

$$\mathbf{z}^T \mathbf{X}^T \mathbf{X} \mathbf{z} > 0$$

for any vector $\mathbf{z}$. At this stage, it is probably worth showing how this can be done. We will assume that each $\mathbf{x}_n$ is two dimensional so that we can explicitly multiply out the various terms. To be more general, we will define $\mathbf{X}$ slightly differently from before as

$$
\mathbf{X} = \begin{bmatrix} \mathbf{x}_1^\mathsf{T} \\ \mathbf{x}_2^\mathsf{T} \\ \vdots \\ \mathbf{x}_N^\mathsf{T} \end{bmatrix} = \begin{bmatrix} x_{11} & x_{12} \\ x_{21} & x_{22} \\ \vdots & \vdots \\ x_{N1} & x_{N2} \end{bmatrix}.
$$

Thus, $\mathbf{X}^\mathsf{T}\mathbf{X}$ is

$$
\mathbf{X}^\mathsf{T}\mathbf{X} = \begin{bmatrix} \sum_{i=1}^N x_{i1}^2 & \sum_{i=1}^N x_{i1}x_{i2} \\ \sum_{i=1}^N x_{i2}x_{i1} & \sum_{i=1}^N x_{i2}^2 \end{bmatrix}.
$$

Pre- and postmultiplying by an arbitrary real vector $\mathbf{z} = [z_1, z_2]^\mathsf{T}$,

$$
\begin{aligned}
\mathbf{z}^\mathsf{T}\mathbf{X}^\mathsf{T}\mathbf{X}\mathbf{z} &= \left[z_1 \sum_{i=1}^N x_{i1}^2 + z_2 \sum_{i=1}^N x_{i2}x_{i1}, \; z_1 \sum_{i=1}^N x_{i1}x_{i2} + z_2 \sum_{i=1}^N x_{i2}^2 \right] \mathbf{z} \\
&= z_1^2 \sum_{i=1}^N x_{i1}^2 + 2z_1z_2 \sum_{i=1}^N x_{i1}x_{i2} + z_2^2 \sum_{i=1}^N x_{i2}^2.
\end{aligned}
$$

Because the first and last terms must be positive, proving that this expression is greater than zero is equivalent to proving that their combined value is larger than the middle term:

$$
z_1^2 \sum_{i=1}^N x_{i1}^2 + z_2^2 \sum_{i=1}^N x_{i2}^2 > 2z_1z_2 \sum_{i=1}^N x_{i1}x_{i2}.
$$

Defining $y_{i1} = z_1 x_{i1}$ and $y_{i2} = z_2 x_{i2}$ and substituting into our expression gives

$$
\sum_{i=1}^N (y_{i1}^2 + y_{i2}^2) > 2 \sum_{i=1}^N y_{i1}y_{i2}.
$$

Now, considering some arbitrary i,

$$
\begin{aligned}
y_{i1}^2 + y_{i2}^2 &> 2y_{i1}y_{i2} \\
y_{i1}^2 - 2y_{i1}y_{i2} + y_{i2}^2 &> 0 \\
(y_{i1} - y_{i2})^2 &> 0
\end{aligned}
$$

which will only not be the case if $y_{i1} = y_{i2}$ and therefore $x_{i1} = x_{i2}$ – something unlikely to happen in practice. So, if $y_{i1}^2 + y_{i2}^2 > 2y_{i1}y_{i2}$ holds for any i, the summation of any number of these terms must also satisfy the inequality. Hence, $\mathbf{z}^\mathsf{T}\mathbf{X}^\mathsf{T}\mathbf{X}\mathbf{z}$ is always positive, our Hessian is negative definite and the solution corresponds to a maximum of the likelihood.

To ensure that our expression for $\widehat{\sigma^2}$ corresponds to a maximum of the likelihood, we differentiate Equation 2.34 again with respect to σ:

$$
\frac{\partial^2 \log L}{\partial \sigma^2} = \frac{N}{\sigma^2} - \frac{3}{\sigma^4}(\mathbf{t} - \mathbf{X}\widehat{\mathbf{w}})^\mathsf{T}(\mathbf{t} - \mathbf{X}\widehat{\mathbf{w}}).
$$

We can simplify this by substituting the value for $\widehat{\sigma^2}$ given in Equation 2.36, resulting in

$$
\begin{aligned}
\frac{\partial^2 \log L}{\partial \sigma^2} &= \frac{N}{\widehat{\sigma^2}} - \frac{3}{(\widehat{\sigma^2})^2} N \widehat{\sigma^2} \\
&= -\frac{2N}{\widehat{\sigma^2}},
\end{aligned}
$$

which is always negative and hence $\widehat{\sigma^2}$ corresponds to a maximum.

2.8.4 Maximum likelihood favours complex models

Plugging the expression for $\widehat{\sigma^2}$ (Equation 2.35) into the log-likelihood expression (Equation 2.31) gives us the value of the log-likelihood at the maximum:

$$
\begin{aligned}
\log L &= -\frac{N}{2}\log 2\pi - \frac{N}{2}\log\widehat{\sigma^2} - \frac{1}{2\widehat{\sigma^2}}N\widehat{\sigma^2} \\
&= -\frac{N}{2}(1 + \log 2\pi) - \frac{N}{2}\log\widehat{\sigma^2}.
\end{aligned}
$$

This tells us that the maximum value of L will keep increasing as we decrease $\widehat{\sigma^2}$. Recall that σ^2 is the variance of the noise incorporated into the model to capture effects that the deterministic part of our model (i.e. $f(\mathbf{x}; \mathbf{w})$) cannot. One way to decrease σ^2 is to modify $f(\mathbf{x}; \mathbf{w})$ so that it can capture more of the variability in the data – i.e., make it more flexible. For example, revisiting the Olympic men's 100 m data, we can investigate the increase in likelihood as model flexibility (or complexity) increases by fitting increasingly higher-order polynomial functions. Figure 2.11(a) shows that $\log L$ increases as polynomials of increasing order are fitted to the Olympic men's 100 m data (MATLAB script: olymplike.m). If we were to use $\log L$ to help choose which particular model to use, it would always point us to models of increasing complexity. This might seem like a sensible strategy – as $\widehat{\sigma^2}$ decreases, the deterministic part of our model must be capturing more of the variability in our data. However, consider the task of predicting the winning time for a year that we have not yet observed (e.g. 2016). Figure 2.11(b) shows first (dashed line) and eighth (solid line) order polynomial fits as well as their predictions for 2016 (shown as large dark circles). The more complex model makes a prediction of a winning time of close to 11 seconds (it would be one of the slowest ever) whereas the simpler model makes a much more realistic prediction. To the human eye, it looks like the simpler model has captured the important relationship in the data (the general downward trend) whilst the more complex model has not. This is a nice example of the trade-off between generalisation and over-fitting that we saw in Section 1.5. The simpler model is better able to generalise than the more complex one. The more complex model is over-fitting – we have given the model too much freedom and it is attempting to make sense out of what is essentially noise. In Section 1.6 we showed how regularisation could be used to penalise overcomplex parameter values. The same can be done with probabilistic models through the use of **prior distributions** on the parameter values. This will be introduced in the next chapter.

2.9 THE BIAS-VARIANCE TRADE-OFF

The trade-off between generalisation and over-fitting discussed in Section 1.5 is also sometimes described as the bias-variance trade-off. Imagine that we had access to the distribution from which the data were sampled, $p(\mathbf{x}, t)$. Using this distribution, we could, in theory, compute the expected value of the squared error between estimated parameter values and the true values. We would like this value, $\bar{\mathcal{M}}$, to be as low as

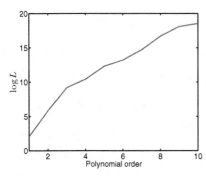

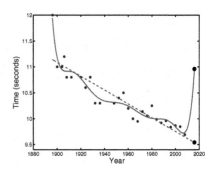

(a) Increase in log-likelihood as the polynomial order increases.

(b) First- and eighth- order polynomial functions fitted to the Olympic men's 100 m data. Large dark circles correspond to predictions for the 2016 Olympics.

FIGURE 2.11 Model complexity example with Olympic men's 100 m data.

possible. It can be decomposed into two terms called the bias $\mathcal{B}$ and the variance $\mathcal{V}$:

$$\bar{\mathcal{M}} = \mathcal{B}^2 + \mathcal{V}.$$

The bias describes the systematic mismatch between our model and the process that generated the data. A model that is too simple will have a high bias (underfitting). We can therefore decrease the bias and its contribution to the $\bar{\mathcal{M}}$ by making the model more complex. Unfortunately, more complex models have higher variance, thus increasing the $\mathcal{V}$ component of $\bar{\mathcal{M}}$. Finding the correct balance between generalisation and over/underfitting can thus also be thought of as finding the correct balance between bias and variance.

We omit further details here, but more details can be found in the suggested reading at the end of this chapter.

2.9.1 Summary

In the previous sections we have introduced a number of new concepts. Firstly, we made a case for explicitly modelling the noise (or errors) in our dataset. Making the assumption that these errors could be adequately modelled by a Gaussian random variable, we showed that we could compute a quantity called the *likelihood* that describes how likely our data is as a function of our model parameters. This is a reasonable quantity to maximise when choosing our parameters, and maximising the likelihood and minimising the squared loss give identical expressions for the optimal parameter values when we assume that the noise is Gaussian. In the remainder of the chapter we will look at two important benefits of explicitly modelling the noise: the ability to quantify the uncertainty in our parameters and the ability to express uncertainties in our predictions.

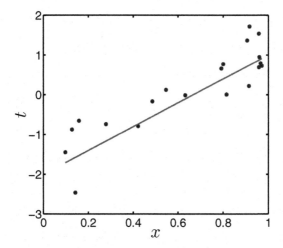

FIGURE 2.12 Data generated from the model given in Equation 2.39 and the true function.

2.10 EFFECT OF NOISE ON PARAMETER ESTIMATES

In this section we shall derive expressions for how much confidence we should place in our parameter estimates – how much could we change the straight line and still have a *good* model. If there is a lot of noise (σ^2 is high), it is likely that we could tolerate reasonably large changes in $\widehat{\mathbf{w}}$. If there is very little noise, the quality of the fit will deteriorate rapidly. Before we derive these expressions, it is useful to explore the variability in $\widehat{\mathbf{w}}$ by generating synthetic data. In particular, we shall generate lots of datasets with the same true $\mathbf{w}$ and σ^2 and see how our maximum likelihood estimate $\widehat{\mathbf{w}}$ varies. Consider the following model:

$$t_n = w_0 + w_1 x_n + \epsilon_n, \ \epsilon_n \sim \mathcal{N}(0, \sigma^2). \tag{2.39}$$

Assuming that the true parameter values are $w_0 = -2, w_1 = 3$ and the noise variance is $\sigma^2 = 0.5^2$, we can generate as many sets of responses $(t_1, \ldots, t_N)$ as we like for a particular set of attributes $(x_1, \ldots, x_N)$ and compute $\widehat{\mathbf{w}}$ for each set. An example of one such dataset and the *true* function can be seen in Figure 2.12, where the set of attributes consists of 20 values drawn from a uniform distribution between 0 and 1, i.e. $p(x) = \mathcal{U}(0, 1)$. Figure 2.13 shows the results of generating 10,000 datasets and fitting $\widehat{\mathbf{w}}$ in each case. The left panel shows a histogram where the height of each bar represents the number of datasets that resulted in parameter values within a particular range, and the right panel shows the same information as a contour plot. We can see a wide variability around the true values in both $\widehat{w_0}$ and $\widehat{w_1}$. It is hard, from these values, to get a feel for how much variability this implies in the model, so examples of $\widehat{\mathbf{w}}$ from ten datasets as well as the true function are plotted in Figure 2.14.

If we assume our real data to have been generated by such a process, it is useful to be able to quantify how variable our resulting estimates are. Unfortunately, we don't have access to many datasets from which we can compare values of $\widehat{\mathbf{w}}$. In the

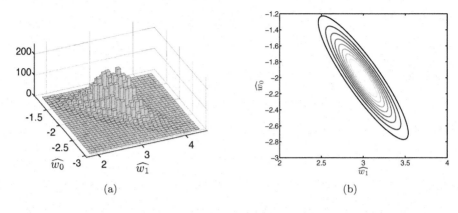

(a)   (b)

FIGURE 2.13 Variability in $\widehat{\mathbf{w}}$ for 10,000 datasets generated from the model described in Equation 2.39.

next section we will show how we can quantify this uncertainty using just the data that are available.

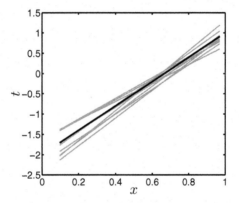

FIGURE 2.14 Functions inferred from ten datasets generated from the model given in Equation 2.39 as well as the true function (wider, darker line).

2.10.1 Uncertainty in estimates

We showed in the last section that the value we obtain for $\widehat{\mathbf{w}}$ is strongly influenced by the particular noise values in the data. In light of this, it would be useful to know how much uncertainty there was in $\widehat{\mathbf{w}}$. In other words, is this $\widehat{\mathbf{w}}$ unique in explaining the data well or are there many that could do almost as well?

To progress, we must be very clear about what $\mathbf{w}$ and $\widehat{\mathbf{w}}$ mean. We have hypothesised a model which was responsible for the data. This model is

$$t_n = \mathbf{w}^\mathsf{T}\mathbf{x}_n + \epsilon_n$$

where $\mathbf{w}$ represents the *true* value of the parameters and ϵ_n is a random variable that we have defined to be normally distributed. This assumption means that the *generating* distribution (or likelihood), $p(\mathbf{t}|\mathbf{X}, \mathbf{w}, \sigma^2)$, is a product of normal densities:

$$p(\mathbf{t}|\mathbf{X}, \mathbf{w}, \sigma^2) = \prod_{n=1}^{N} p(t_n|\mathbf{x}_n\mathbf{w}, \sigma^2) = \prod_{n=1}^{N} \mathcal{N}(\mathbf{w}^\mathsf{T}\mathbf{x}_n, \sigma^2).$$

In Section 2.5.4, we showed how a product of univariate Gaussian densities could be written as a multivariate Gaussian density with a diagonal covariance. It will be neater to work with a single multivariate Gaussian than a product over univariate ones. In this case, the multivariate Gaussian is

$$p(\mathbf{t}|\mathbf{X}, \mathbf{w}, \sigma^2) = \mathcal{N}(\mathbf{X}\mathbf{w}, \sigma^2\mathbf{I}).$$

Satisfy yourself that the mean and covariance terms are correct. Now, $\widehat{\mathbf{w}}$ is an estimate of the true parameter value $\mathbf{w}$. Computing the expectation (Section 2.2.8) of $\widehat{\mathbf{w}}$ with respect to the generating distribution will tell us what we expect $\widehat{\mathbf{w}}$ to be, on average:

$$\mathbf{E}_{p(\mathbf{t}|\mathbf{X}, \mathbf{w}, \sigma^2)}\{\widehat{\mathbf{w}}\} = \int \widehat{\mathbf{w}} p(\mathbf{t}|\mathbf{X}, \mathbf{w}, \sigma^2) d\mathbf{t}.$$

Substituting $\widehat{\mathbf{w}} = (\mathbf{X}^\mathsf{T}\mathbf{X})^{-1}\mathbf{X}^\mathsf{T}\mathbf{t}$ into this expression allows us to evaluate the integral:

$$= (\mathbf{X}^\mathsf{T}\mathbf{X})^{-1}\mathbf{X}^\mathsf{T} \int \mathbf{t} p(\mathbf{t}|\mathbf{X}, \mathbf{w}, \sigma^2) d\mathbf{t}$$

$$= (\mathbf{X}^\mathsf{T}\mathbf{X})^{-1}\mathbf{X}^\mathsf{T}\mathbf{E}_{p(\mathbf{t}|\mathbf{X}, \mathbf{w}, \sigma^2)}\{\mathbf{t}\}$$

$$= (\mathbf{X}^\mathsf{T}\mathbf{X})^{-1}\mathbf{X}^\mathsf{T}\mathbf{X}\mathbf{w}$$

$$= \mathbf{w}, \tag{2.40}$$

where we have used the fact that the expected value of a normally distributed random variable is equal to its mean ($\mathbf{E}_{p(\mathbf{t}|\mathbf{X}, \mathbf{w}, \sigma^2)}\{\mathbf{t}\} = \mathbf{X}\mathbf{w}$ because $p(\mathbf{t}|\mathbf{X}, \mathbf{w}, \sigma^2) = \mathcal{N}(\mathbf{X}\mathbf{w}, \sigma^2\mathbf{I})$).

This result tells us that the expected value of our approximation $\widehat{\mathbf{w}}$ is the true parameter value. We will consider this in more detail later in the chapter, but it means that our estimator is **unbiased** – it is not, on average, too big or too small.

This potential variability in the estimate of $\widehat{\mathbf{w}}$ is encapsulated in its *covariance matrix*. For our purposes, this covariance matrix provides us with two useful pieces of information. The diagonal elements (the variances of the individual elements in $\widehat{\mathbf{w}}$) tell us how much variability we might expect in the individual parameters – i.e. how well they are defined by the data. In our experiment above, the parameters appeared to vary quite a lot, suggesting that they were not defined very well by the data. The off-diagonal elements tell us how the parameters co-vary – if the values are high and positive, it tells us that increasing one will require an increase in the other to maintain a *good* model. Large negative values tell us the opposite – increasing one will cause a decrease in the other. Values close to zero tell us that the parameters are not dependent on one another. For the example described above, it looks (see Figure 2.13) like increasing w_1 causes a decrease in w_0 so we might expect the off-diagonal elements in the covariance matrix to be negative.

In Section 2.2.8, we derived a general expression for the covariance matrix (Equation 2.16). Substituting $\mathbf{t}$ and $p(\mathbf{t}|\mathbf{X}, \mathbf{w}, \sigma^2)$ into this expression, and using the previous result, $\mathbf{E}_{p(\mathbf{t}|\mathbf{X},\mathbf{w},\sigma^2)}\{\widehat{\mathbf{w}}\} = \mathbf{w}$, gives us

$$
\begin{aligned}
\text{cov}\{\widehat{\mathbf{w}}\} &= \mathbf{E}_{p(\mathbf{t}|\mathbf{X},\mathbf{w},\sigma^2)}\left\{\widehat{\mathbf{w}}\widehat{\mathbf{w}}^\mathsf{T}\right\} - \mathbf{E}_{p(\mathbf{t}|\mathbf{X},\mathbf{w},\sigma^2)}\{\widehat{\mathbf{w}}\}\, \mathbf{E}_{p(\mathbf{t}|\mathbf{X},\mathbf{w},\sigma^2)}\{\widehat{\mathbf{w}}\}^\mathsf{T} \\
&= \mathbf{E}_{p(\mathbf{t}|\mathbf{X},\mathbf{w},\sigma^2)}\left\{\widehat{\mathbf{w}}\widehat{\mathbf{w}}^\mathsf{T}\right\} - \mathbf{w}\mathbf{w}^\mathsf{T} \quad (2.41)
\end{aligned}
$$

where we have used the expectation of $\widehat{\mathbf{w}}$ that we derived above. To compute this quantity, we will start with the first term. It can expanded by substituting $\widehat{\mathbf{w}} = (\mathbf{X}^\mathsf{T}\mathbf{X})^{-1}\mathbf{X}^\mathsf{T}\mathbf{t}$ and all of the terms that do not involve $\mathbf{t}$ can be removed from the expectation:

$$
\begin{aligned}
\mathbf{E}_{p(\mathbf{t}|\mathbf{X},\mathbf{w},\sigma^2)}\left\{\widehat{\mathbf{w}}\widehat{\mathbf{w}}^\mathsf{T}\right\} &= \mathbf{E}_{p(\mathbf{t}|\mathbf{X},\mathbf{w},\sigma^2)}\left\{((\mathbf{X}^\mathsf{T}\mathbf{X})^{-1}\mathbf{X}^\mathsf{T}\mathbf{t})((\mathbf{X}^\mathsf{T}\mathbf{X})^{-1}\mathbf{X}^\mathsf{T}\mathbf{t})^\mathsf{T}\right\} \\
&= (\mathbf{X}^\mathsf{T}\mathbf{X})^{-1}\mathbf{X}^\mathsf{T}\, \mathbf{E}_{p(\mathbf{t}|\mathbf{X},\mathbf{w},\sigma^2)}\left\{\mathbf{t}\mathbf{t}^\mathsf{T}\right\}\mathbf{X}(\mathbf{X}^\mathsf{T}\mathbf{X})^{-1}. \quad (2.42)
\end{aligned}
$$

Now, $p(\mathbf{t}|\mathbf{X}, \mathbf{w}, \sigma^2) = \mathcal{N}(\mathbf{X}\mathbf{w}, \sigma^2\mathbf{I})$. Therefore, the covariance of $\mathbf{t}$ is, by definition, $\sigma^2\mathbf{I}$ and its mean is $\mathbf{X}\mathbf{w}$. By the same line of derivation that allowed us to reach Equation 2.41, we have

$$
\text{cov}\{\mathbf{t}\} = \sigma^2\mathbf{I} = \mathbf{E}_{p(\mathbf{t}|\mathbf{X},\mathbf{w},\sigma^2)}\left\{\mathbf{t}\mathbf{t}^\mathsf{T}\right\} - \mathbf{E}_{p(\mathbf{t}|\mathbf{X},\mathbf{w},\sigma^2)}\{\mathbf{t}\}\, \mathbf{E}_{p(\mathbf{t}|\mathbf{X},\mathbf{w},\sigma^2)}\{\mathbf{t}\}^\mathsf{T}.
$$

Therefore, we can rearrange this expression to obtain an expression for $\mathbf{E}_{p(\mathbf{t}|\mathbf{X},\mathbf{w},\sigma^2)}\left\{\mathbf{t}\mathbf{t}^\mathsf{T}\right\}$:

$$
\begin{aligned}
\mathbf{E}_{p(\mathbf{t}|\mathbf{X},\mathbf{w},\sigma^2)}\left\{\mathbf{t}\mathbf{t}^\mathsf{T}\right\} &= \mathbf{E}_{p(\mathbf{t}|\mathbf{X},\mathbf{w},\sigma^2)}\{\mathbf{t}\}\, \mathbf{E}_{p(\mathbf{t}|\mathbf{X},\mathbf{w},\sigma^2)}\{\mathbf{t}\}^\mathsf{T} + \sigma^2\mathbf{I} \\
&= \mathbf{X}\mathbf{w}(\mathbf{X}\mathbf{w})^\mathsf{T} + \sigma^2\mathbf{I} \\
&= \mathbf{X}\mathbf{w}\mathbf{w}^\mathsf{T}\mathbf{X}^\mathsf{T} + \sigma^2\mathbf{I}.
\end{aligned}
$$

Substituting this into Equation 2.42 gives

$$
\begin{aligned}
\mathbf{E}_{p(\mathbf{t}|\mathbf{X},\mathbf{w},\sigma^2)}\left\{\widehat{\mathbf{w}}\widehat{\mathbf{w}}^\mathsf{T}\right\} &= (\mathbf{X}^\mathsf{T}\mathbf{X})^{-1}\mathbf{X}^\mathsf{T}\mathbf{X}\mathbf{w}\mathbf{w}^\mathsf{T}\mathbf{X}^\mathsf{T}\mathbf{X}(\mathbf{X}^\mathsf{T}\mathbf{X})^{-1} \\
&\quad + \sigma^2(\mathbf{X}^\mathsf{T}\mathbf{X})^{-1}\mathbf{X}^\mathsf{T}\mathbf{X}(\mathbf{X}^\mathsf{T}\mathbf{X})^{-1} \\
&= \mathbf{w}\mathbf{w}^\mathsf{T} + \sigma^2(\mathbf{X}^\mathsf{T}\mathbf{X})^{-1}. \quad (2.43)
\end{aligned}
$$

Finally, substituting this into Equation 2.41 gives the expression for the covariance of $\widehat{\mathbf{w}}$:

$$
\begin{aligned}
\text{cov}\{\widehat{\mathbf{w}}\} &= \mathbf{w}\mathbf{w}^\mathsf{T} + \sigma^2(\mathbf{X}^\mathsf{T}\mathbf{X})^{-1} - \mathbf{w}\mathbf{w}^\mathsf{T} \\
&= \sigma^2(\mathbf{X}^\mathsf{T}\mathbf{X})^{-1} \quad (2.44)
\end{aligned}
$$

which is the negative of the inverse of the Hessian matrix of second derivatives derived previously (Equation 2.38), i.e.

$$\mathsf{cov}\{\widehat{\mathbf{w}}\} = \sigma^2 (\mathbf{X}^\mathsf{T}\mathbf{X})^{-1} = -\left(\frac{\partial^2 \log L}{\partial \mathbf{w}\partial \mathbf{w}^\mathsf{T}}\right)^{-1}. \tag{2.45}$$

This result tells us that the certainty/uncertainty in the parameters (as described by $\mathsf{cov}\{\widehat{\mathbf{w}}\}$) is directly linked to the second derivative of the log-likelihood. The second derivative of the log-likelihood tells us about the curvature of the likelihood function. Therefore, low curvature corresponds to a high level of uncertainty in parameters and high curvature to a low level. In other words, we have an expression that tells us how much **information** our data gives us regarding our parameter estimates. In fact, our matrix, $\sigma^2(\mathbf{X}^\mathsf{T}\mathbf{X})^{-1}$, is the inverse of something called the **Fisher Information Matrix** ($\mathcal{I}$). The Fisher Information Matrix is computed as the expected value of the martrix of second derivatives of the log-likelihood:

$$\mathcal{I} = \mathbf{E}_{p(\mathbf{t}|\mathbf{X},\mathbf{w},\sigma^2)}\left\{-\frac{\partial^2 \log p(\mathbf{t}|\mathbf{X},\mathbf{w},\sigma^2)}{\partial \mathbf{w}\partial \mathbf{w}^\mathsf{T}}\right\}.$$

We already know what the bit in the brackets is – it is the Hessian matrix we calculated earlier – so

$$\mathcal{I} = \mathbf{E}_{p(\mathbf{t}|\mathbf{X},\mathbf{w},\sigma^2)}\left\{\frac{1}{\sigma^2}\mathbf{X}^\mathsf{T}\mathbf{X}\right\}$$

which, because the argument of the expectation is a constant is just

$$\mathcal{I} = \frac{1}{\sigma^2}\mathbf{X}^\mathsf{T}\mathbf{X}. \tag{2.46}$$

The elements of $\mathcal{I}$ tell us how much information (the more negative the information value is, the more information is present) the data provides about a particular parameter (diagonal elements) or pairs of parameters (off-diagonal elements). Intuitively, if our data is very noisy, the information content is lower. In general, if the information content is high, the data can inform a very accurate parameter estimate and the covariance of $\widehat{\mathbf{w}}$ will be low ($\mathsf{cov}\{\widehat{\mathbf{w}}\} = \mathcal{I}^{-1}$). If the information content is low, the covariance will be high (see Exercises 2.13 and 2.14).

As an example, look at the top line in Figure 2.15. The left hand plot shows the data and the true function ($t = 3x - 2$) and the right hand plot shows the likelihood as a function of the two parameters. We can see that the likelihood function has a low curvature (contour lines are reasonably far apart) because of the large noise level, and, as such, many sets of parameters will result in a reasonable model. A low curvature should, from Equation 2.45, correspond to high covariance in $\widehat{\mathbf{w}}$. The Fisher information and covariance matrices are

$$\mathcal{I} = \begin{bmatrix} 50.0000 & 24.3311 \\ 24.3311 & 15.8953 \end{bmatrix}, \ \mathsf{cov}\{\widehat{\mathbf{w}}\} = \begin{bmatrix} 0.0784 & -0.1200 \\ -0.1200 & 0.2466 \end{bmatrix}.$$

It is difficult to know if these correspond to high or low information and covariance without context. This can be provided by comparing them with those obtained from the second dataset (second row in Figure 2.15). This dataset has much less noise and the corresponding likelihood curvature is much higher (the contour lines are closer together). In this case, the information and covariance matrices are

$$\mathcal{I} = \begin{bmatrix} 1.2500 \times 10^3 & 0.6083 \times 10^3 \\ 0.6083 \times 10^3 & 0.3974 \times 10^3 \end{bmatrix}, \ \mathsf{cov}\{\widehat{\mathbf{w}}\} = \begin{bmatrix} 0.0031 & -0.0048 \\ -0.0048 & 0.0099 \end{bmatrix}$$

which have significantly higher (in $\mathcal{I}$) and lower (in $\mathsf{cov}\{\widehat{\mathbf{w}}\}$) values.

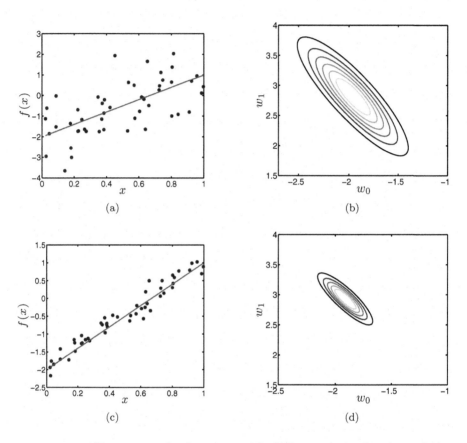

FIGURE 2.15 Two example datasets with different noise levels and the corresponding likelihood function.

2.10.2 Comparison with empirical values

At the start of Section 2.10 we generated many sets of responses for a set of attributes using the model (and associated noise distribution) given in Equation 2.39. If we use $\widehat{\mathbf{w}}_s$ to describe the parameters obtained from the sth dataset, the empirical covariance matrix can be computed as

$$\widehat{\text{cov}\{\widehat{\mathbf{w}}\}} = \frac{1}{S} \sum_{s=1}^{S} (\widehat{\mathbf{w}}_s - \widehat{\boldsymbol{\mu}})(\widehat{\mathbf{w}}_s - \widehat{\boldsymbol{\mu}})^{\mathsf{T}}$$

where

$$\widehat{\boldsymbol{\mu}} = \frac{1}{S} \sum_{s=1}^{S} \widehat{\mathbf{w}}_s.$$

Using the values shown in Figure 2.13, the empirical covariance matrix is

$$\widehat{\text{cov}\{\widehat{\mathbf{w}}\}} = \begin{bmatrix} 0.0627 & -0.0809 \\ -0.0809 & 0.1301 \end{bmatrix}.$$

Using Equation 2.44 and the true value of $\sigma^2 = 0.5^2$, the theoretical covariance matrix is

$$\text{cov}\{\widehat{\mathbf{w}}\} = \begin{bmatrix} 0.0638 & -0.0821 \\ -0.0821 & 0.1317 \end{bmatrix}$$

which is very close to our empirical value. Normally, we do not have access to a bottomless supply of data and so we can use the theoretical covariance matrix to help understand the variability present in our data. The off-diagonal elements are negative – increasing one of the parameters forces the other to decrease.

To compute the theoretical covariance matrix, we have used the true noise variance. If we take one arbitrary dataset, we can estimate the variance (using Equation 2.35) as $\sigma^2 = 0.2080$ (the true value is $\sigma^2 = 0.25$). The covariance matrix using the estimated variance is

$$\text{cov}\{\widehat{\mathbf{w}}\} = \begin{bmatrix} 0.0530 & -0.0683 \\ -0.0683 & 0.1095 \end{bmatrix}.$$

Because the estimated value of σ^2 is lower than the true value, the values in this matrix are lower than those when the true noise value is used. This suggests that the uncertainty is underestimated and our predictions will be overconfident. The systematic underestimation of noise variance in maximum likelihood is discussed more thoroughly in Section 2.11.2.

At the start of Section 2.10 we saw that changes in the exact values of the noise changed the parameter estimates. In reality we cannot generate many datasets with which to estimate this uncertainty in parameter values. However, we have derived an expression for the covariance of $\widehat{\mathbf{w}}$ that can be used to approximate the uncertainty in parameters. Before we move on to variability in predictions, we will look at the uncertainty present in the maximum likelihood estimations from the Olympic data.

2.10.3   Variability in model parameters – Olympic data

Using the now familiar men's Olympic 100 m data, and the standard linear function

$$f(\mathbf{x}; \mathbf{w}) = \mathbf{w}^\mathsf{T}\mathbf{x},$$

we know that the maximum likelihood value of $\mathbf{w}$, $\widehat{\mathbf{w}}$, will be $[36.4165, -0.0133]^\mathsf{T}$ (from Equation 2.33). The maximum likelihood variance value, $\widehat{\sigma^2}$, can be computed using Equation 2.37 and is $\widehat{\sigma^2} = 0.0503$. Using Equation 2.44, and using $\widehat{\sigma^2}$ as an estimate of σ^2, we can compute the covariance matrix of the estimate:

$$\mathsf{cov}\{\widehat{\mathbf{w}}\} = \begin{bmatrix} 5.7972 & -0.0030 \\ -0.0030 & 1.5204e - 06 \end{bmatrix}.$$

Taking the diagonal elements, we can see that the variance of $\widehat{w_0}$ (5.7972) is much higher than the variance in $\widehat{w_1}$ ($1.5204e - 06$), suggesting that we could tolerate bigger changes in $\widehat{w_0}$ than $\widehat{w_1}$ and still be left with a reasonably good model. Partly, this can be explained by the fact that $\widehat{w_0}$ has a much higher absolute value. The negativity of the off-diagonal elements tell us that, if we were to slightly increase either $\widehat{w_0}$ or $\widehat{w_1}$, we would have to slightly decrease the other. This is relatively intuitive – if we were to slightly increase $\widehat{w_0}$, the whole line would move up and the best value of $\widehat{w_1}$ would have to be decreased slightly (thereby producing a steeper negative gradient) to pass as close as possible to all of the data points.

Another way to get a feeling for the meaning of $\mathsf{cov}\{\widehat{\mathbf{w}}\}$ is to look at the variability in models that it suggests. To do this, we can assume that $\widehat{\mathbf{w}}$ is a random variable with a Gaussian distribution

$$\mathbf{w} \sim \mathcal{N}(\widehat{\mathbf{w}}, \mathsf{cov}\{\widehat{\mathbf{w}}\}). \tag{2.47}$$

From this density, we can sample several instances of $\mathbf{w}$ and plot the resulting models. An example of ten instances is shown in Figure 2.16. We can see that there is very little change in gradient (w_1) across the ten samples but that this small gradient change would, if we extrapolated back to year zero, result in quite a large change of w_0. This is reflected by the values in $\mathsf{cov}\{\widehat{\mathbf{w}}\}$, as already discussed. The idea of having a distribution over model parameters rather than a single *best* value is very important in Machine Learning and is introduced in the next chapter.

2.11   VARIABILITY IN PREDICTIONS

In Chapter 1 we made some predictions about 100 m winning times in future Olympics. We argued that these predictions were not very useful, as they took the form of exact values. It would seem more sensible to predict a range of values in which we think the winning time might fall. If we are quite certain about our prediction, this range might be small; if we are less certain, it might be large. So, as well as obtaining an indication of the variability of our parameter estimate, $\widehat{\mathbf{w}}$, it makes sense to provide indications of any variability or uncertainty in our predictions. Suppose we observe a new set of attributes, $\mathbf{x}_{\mathsf{new}}$. We would like to predict the output, t_{new}, and the variability associated with this output, σ^2_{new}.

To predict t_{new}, we multiply $\mathbf{x}_{\mathsf{new}}$ by the best set of model parameters, $\widehat{\mathbf{w}}$:

$$t_{\mathsf{new}} = \widehat{\mathbf{w}}^\mathsf{T}\mathbf{x}_{\mathsf{new}}. \tag{2.48}$$

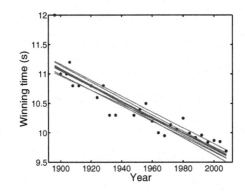

FIGURE 2.16 Ten samples of $\mathbf{w}$ using the distribution given in Equation 2.47.

To check that this is sensible, we can compute its expectation:

$$
\begin{aligned}
\mathbf{E}_{p(t|\mathbf{X},\mathbf{w},\sigma^2)}\{t_{\mathsf{new}}\} &= \mathbf{E}_{p(t|\mathbf{X},\mathbf{w},\sigma^2)}\{\widehat{\mathbf{w}}\}^{\mathsf{T}}\mathbf{x}_{\mathsf{new}} \\
&= \mathbf{w}^{\mathsf{T}}\mathbf{x}_{\mathsf{new}}
\end{aligned}
$$

where we have used Equation 2.40. The expected value of our prediction is the new data attribute multiplied by the *true* $\mathbf{w}$. In Section 2.2.8 we derived a general expression for variance. In our case, this is

$$
\sigma^2_{\mathsf{new}} = \mathsf{var}\{t_{\mathsf{new}}\} = \mathbf{E}_{p(t|\mathbf{X},\mathbf{w},\sigma^2)}\{t^2_{\mathsf{new}}\} - \left(\mathbf{E}_{p(t|\mathbf{X},\mathbf{w},\sigma^2)}\{t_{\mathsf{new}}\}\right)^2.
$$

To evaluate this expression, we need to first substitute $t_{\mathsf{new}} = \widehat{\mathbf{w}}^{\mathsf{T}}\mathbf{x}_{\mathsf{new}}$:

$$
\begin{aligned}
\mathsf{var}\{t_{\mathsf{new}}\} &= \mathbf{E}_{p(t|\mathbf{X},\mathbf{w},\sigma^2)}\left\{(\widehat{\mathbf{w}}^{\mathsf{T}}\mathbf{x}_{\mathsf{new}})^2\right\} - (\mathbf{w}^{\mathsf{T}}\mathbf{x}_{\mathsf{new}})^2 \\
&= \mathbf{E}_{p(t|\mathbf{X},\mathbf{w},\sigma^2)}\left\{\mathbf{x}^{\mathsf{T}}_{\mathsf{new}}\widehat{\mathbf{w}}\widehat{\mathbf{w}}^{\mathsf{T}}\mathbf{x}_{\mathsf{new}}\right\} - \mathbf{x}^{\mathsf{T}}_{\mathsf{new}}\mathbf{w}\mathbf{w}^{\mathsf{T}}\mathbf{x}_{\mathsf{new}}.
\end{aligned}
$$

Substituting our now familiar expression for $\widehat{\mathbf{w}}$,

$$
\mathsf{var}\{t_{\mathsf{new}}\} = \mathbf{x}^{\mathsf{T}}_{\mathsf{new}}(\mathbf{X}^{\mathsf{T}}\mathbf{X})^{-1}\mathbf{X}^{\mathsf{T}}\mathbf{E}_{p(t|\mathbf{X},\mathbf{w},\sigma^2)}\left\{\mathbf{t}\mathbf{t}^{\mathsf{T}}\right\}\mathbf{X}(\mathbf{X}^{\mathsf{T}}\mathbf{X})^{-1}\mathbf{x}_{\mathsf{new}} - \mathbf{x}^{\mathsf{T}}_{\mathsf{new}}\mathbf{w}\mathbf{w}^{\mathsf{T}}\mathbf{x}_{\mathsf{new}}.
$$

Using the expression for the $\mathsf{cov}\{\mathbf{t}\}$ (Equation 2.10.1) allows us to compute the expectation and simplify the expression:

$$
\begin{aligned}
\mathsf{var}\{t_{\mathsf{new}}\} &= \mathbf{x}^{\mathsf{T}}_{\mathsf{new}}(\mathbf{X}^{\mathsf{T}}\mathbf{X})^{-1}\mathbf{X}^{\mathsf{T}}(\sigma^2\mathbf{I} + \mathbf{X}\mathbf{w}\mathbf{w}^{\mathsf{T}}\mathbf{X}^{\mathsf{T}})\mathbf{X}(\mathbf{X}^{\mathsf{T}}\mathbf{X})^{-1}\mathbf{x}_{\mathsf{new}} - \mathbf{x}^{\mathsf{T}}_{\mathsf{new}}\mathbf{w}\mathbf{w}^{\mathsf{T}}\mathbf{x}_{\mathsf{new}} \\
&= \sigma^2\mathbf{x}^{\mathsf{T}}_{\mathsf{new}}(\mathbf{X}^{\mathsf{T}}\mathbf{X})^{-1}\mathbf{x}_{\mathsf{new}} + \mathbf{x}^{\mathsf{T}}_{\mathsf{new}}\mathbf{w}\mathbf{w}^{\mathsf{T}}\mathbf{x}_{\mathsf{new}} - \mathbf{x}^{\mathsf{T}}_{\mathsf{new}}\mathbf{w}\mathbf{w}^{\mathsf{T}}\mathbf{x}_{\mathsf{new}} \\
&= \sigma^2\mathbf{x}^{\mathsf{T}}_{\mathsf{new}}(\mathbf{X}^{\mathsf{T}}\mathbf{X})^{-1}\mathbf{x}_{\mathsf{new}}.
\end{aligned}
$$

Note that, by substituting our expression for $\mathsf{cov}\{\widehat{\mathbf{w}}\}$ (Equation 2.41), this expression can be rewritten as

$$
\sigma^2_{\mathsf{new}} = \mathbf{x}^{\mathsf{T}}_{\mathsf{new}}\mathsf{cov}\{\widehat{\mathbf{w}}\}\mathbf{x}_{\mathsf{new}}.
$$

To summarise, our prediction and associated variance are given as

$$t_{new} = \mathbf{x}_{new}^\mathsf{T}(\mathbf{X}^\mathsf{T}\mathbf{X})^{-1}\mathbf{X}^\mathsf{T}\mathbf{t} = \mathbf{x}_{new}^\mathsf{T}\widehat{\mathbf{w}}, \qquad (2.49)$$

$$\sigma_{new}^2 = \sigma^2 \mathbf{x}_{new}^\mathsf{T}(\mathbf{X}^\mathsf{T}\mathbf{X})^{-1}\mathbf{x}_{new}. \qquad (2.50)$$

σ^2 is the *true* variance of the dataset noise. In its place, we can use our estimate, $\widehat{\sigma^2}$.

2.11.1 Predictive variability – an example

Figure 2.17(a) shows the function $f(x) = 5x^3 - x^2 + x$ and data points sampled from this function and corrupted by Gaussian noise with mean zero and variance 1000. In Figures 2.17(b), 2.17(c) and 2.17(d) we can see $t_{new} \pm \sigma_{new}^2$ for linear, cubic and sixth-order models, respectively (MATLAB script: `predictive_variance_example.m`).

The linear model has very high predictive variance. It is unable to model the deterministic trend in the data very well, and much of the variability of the data is assumed to be noise. The cubic model is better able to model the trend (it is the correct order) and this is reflected in its much more confident predictions. The sixth-order model is over-complex – it has too much freedom and can therefore fit the data well for quite a large range of parameter values. This uncertainty in $\widehat{\mathbf{w}}$ feeds through to increased predictive variability – if we are less sure on the parameter values, we're going to be less sure of the predictions too. This point can be demonstrated by computing $\text{cov}\{\widehat{\mathbf{w}}\}$ for the third- and sixth-order models and then sampling functions just as we did in Section 2.10.3. Figure 2.18 shows 20 functions drawn from a Gaussian with mean $\widehat{\mathbf{w}}$ and covariance $\text{cov}\{\widehat{\mathbf{w}}\}$ for the third- and sixth-order models (the plot is zoomed into a small region of x and the darker line shows the true function) (MATLAB script: `predictive_variance_example.m`). The increased variability in possible functions caused by the increase in parameter uncertainty is clear for the sixth-order model.

A final interesting point is that, for all models, the predictive variance increases as we move towards the edge of the data. The model is less confident in areas where it has less data – an appealing property. In Chapter 1 we pointed out that making point indefinitely into the future (i.e. beyond the range of the training data) was not very sensible. We now have a model that will make predictions beyond the range of the training data, but will do so with increasing uncertainty, which is likely to be more useful. We also observe this effect towards the centre of the data (particularly Figure 2.17(d)) where there is a small gap (not many instances at around $x = 1$). Exercise 2.12 gives you the opportunity to investigate this effect further.

2.11.2 Expected values of the estimators

In Section 2.10.1 we computed the expected value of our estimate $\widehat{\mathbf{w}}$. This expectation is taken with respect to the generating density $p(\mathbf{t}|\mathbf{X}, \mathbf{w}, \sigma^2) = \mathcal{N}(\mathbf{X}\mathbf{w}, \sigma^2\mathbf{I})$

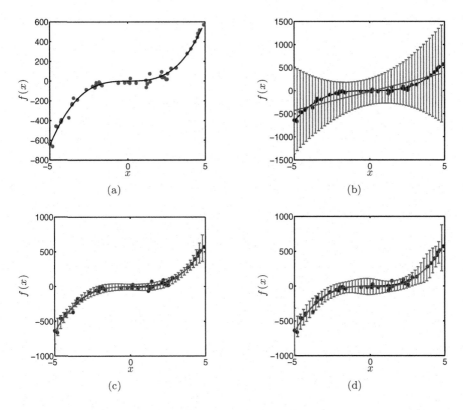

FIGURE 2.17 (a) Example data set. (b), (c) and (d) predictive error bars for a linear, cubic and sixth-order model, respectively.

and is repeated here:

$$
\begin{aligned}
\mathbf{E}_{p(\mathbf{t}|\mathbf{X},\mathbf{w},\sigma^2)}\{\widehat{\mathbf{w}}\} &= \mathbf{E}_{p(\mathbf{t}|\mathbf{X})}\left\{(\mathbf{X}^\mathsf{T}\mathbf{X})^{-1}\mathbf{X}^\mathsf{T}\mathbf{t}\right\} \\
&= (\mathbf{X}^\mathsf{T}\mathbf{X})^{-1}\mathbf{X}^\mathsf{T}\mathbf{E}_{p(\mathbf{t}|\mathbf{X})}\{\mathbf{t}\} \\
&= (\mathbf{X}^\mathsf{T}\mathbf{X})^{-1}\mathbf{X}^\mathsf{T}\mathbf{X}\mathbf{w} \\
&= \mathbf{I}\mathbf{w} = \mathbf{w}
\end{aligned}
$$

where we have used the expression for $\widehat{\mathbf{w}}$ ($\widehat{\mathbf{w}} = (\mathbf{X}^\mathsf{T}\mathbf{X})^{-1}\mathbf{X}^\mathsf{T}\mathbf{t}$) and the fact that the expected value of a Gaussian random variable ($\mathbf{t}$) is equal to the mean of the Gaussian ($\mathbf{Xw}$). So, the expected value of our estimate, $\widehat{\mathbf{w}}$, is the true value, $\mathbf{w}$. This is an important property of $\widehat{\mathbf{w}}$ – it tells us that $\widehat{\mathbf{w}}$ is an unbiased estimator – it is neither consistently too high nor too low. Another way of thinking about this is to think back to the experiment at the start of Section 2.10. There, for a set of attributes $x_1, \ldots, x_N$, we generated many sets of responses and looked at how much influence different particular noise values had on $\widehat{\mathbf{w}}$. Because $\widehat{\mathbf{w}}$ is unbiased, it should, on average, be correct. So, if we took the average of all of the different $\widehat{\mathbf{w}}$ values obtained in our experiment, it should be very close to the truth. In fact,

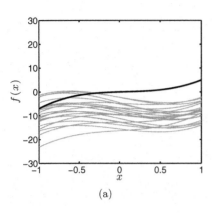
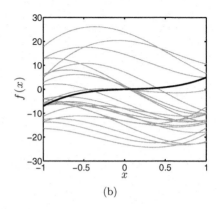

(a)   (b)

FIGURE 2.18 Examples of functions drawn with parameters from a Gaussian with mean $\widehat{\mathbf{w}}$ and covariance $\text{cov}\{\widehat{\mathbf{w}}\}$ for the example dataset shown in Figure 2.17(a).

taking this average, we get $\widehat{w_0} = -2.0007$ and $\widehat{w_1} = 3.0008$ which are both very close to the true values: $w_0 = -2, w_1 = 3$.

We can do the same for the estimate of the noise variance, $\widehat{\sigma^2}$. Recall the expression for $\widehat{\sigma^2}$ from Equation 2.37:

$$\widehat{\sigma^2} = \frac{1}{N}(\mathbf{t}^\mathsf{T}\mathbf{t} - \mathbf{t}^\mathsf{T}\mathbf{X}\widehat{\mathbf{w}}).$$

Taking the expectation with respect to $p(\mathbf{t}|\mathbf{X}, \mathbf{w}, \sigma^2)$ and doing some manipulation gives

$$
\begin{aligned}
\mathbf{E}_{p(\mathbf{t}|\mathbf{X},\mathbf{w},\sigma^2)}\left\{\widehat{\sigma^2}\right\} &= \frac{1}{N}\mathbf{E}_{p(\mathbf{t}|\mathbf{X},\mathbf{w},\sigma^2)}\left\{\mathbf{t}^\mathsf{T}\mathbf{t} - \mathbf{t}^\mathsf{T}\mathbf{X}\widehat{\mathbf{w}}\right\} \\
&= \frac{1}{N}\mathbf{E}_{p(\mathbf{t}|\mathbf{X},\mathbf{w},\sigma^2)}\left\{\mathbf{t}^\mathsf{T}\mathbf{t} - \mathbf{t}^\mathsf{T}\mathbf{X}(\mathbf{X}^\mathsf{T}\mathbf{X})^{-1}\mathbf{X}^\mathsf{T}\mathbf{t}\right\} \\
&= \frac{1}{N}\mathbf{E}_{p(\mathbf{t}|\mathbf{X},\mathbf{w},\sigma^2)}\left\{\mathbf{t}^\mathsf{T}\mathbf{t}\right\} \qquad (2.51) \\
&\quad -\frac{1}{N}\mathbf{E}_{p(\mathbf{t}|\mathbf{X},\mathbf{w},\sigma^2)}\left\{\mathbf{t}^\mathsf{T}\mathbf{X}(\mathbf{X}^\mathsf{T}\mathbf{X})^{-1}\mathbf{X}^\mathsf{T}\mathbf{t}\right\}.
\end{aligned}
$$

Comment 2.8 – Matrix trace: The trace of a square matrix $\mathbf{A}$, denoted $\mathsf{Tr}(\mathbf{A})$, is the sum of the diagonal elements of $\mathbf{A}$. For example, if

$$\mathbf{A} = \begin{bmatrix} A_{11} & A_{12} & \cdots & A_{1D} \\ A_{21} & A_{22} & \cdots & A_{2D} \\ \vdots & \vdots & \ddots & \vdots \\ A_{D1} & A_{D2} & \cdots & A_{DD} \end{bmatrix},$$

then

$$\mathsf{Tr}(\mathbf{A}) = \sum_{d=1}^{D} A_{dd}.$$

It follows that, if $\mathbf{A} = \mathbf{I}_D$, i.e. the $D \times D$ identity matrix,

$$\mathsf{Tr}(\mathbf{I}_D) = \sum_{d=1}^{D} 1 = D.$$

A useful identity that we will often use is that

$$\mathsf{Tr}(\mathbf{AB}) = \mathsf{Tr}(\mathbf{BA}).$$

Also, the trace of a scalar is just equal to the scalar value (a scalar could be thought of as a 1×1 matrix), i.e.

$$\mathsf{Tr}(a) = a,$$

or, if $\mathbf{w} = [w_1, \ldots, w_D]^\mathsf{T}$,

$$\mathsf{Tr}(\mathbf{w}^\mathsf{T}\mathbf{w}) = \mathbf{w}^\mathsf{T}\mathbf{w}$$

because the result of $\mathbf{w}^\mathsf{T}\mathbf{w}$ is a scalar.

We have seen the expectation of the form $\mathbf{t}\mathbf{t}^\mathsf{T}$ before but not $\mathbf{t}^\mathsf{T}\mathbf{t}$ $(= \mathbf{t}^\mathsf{T}\mathbf{I}\mathbf{t})$ or $\mathbf{t}^\mathsf{T}\mathbf{A}\mathbf{t}$. When $\mathbf{t}$ is a Gaussian random variable, expectations of the form $\mathbf{t}^\mathsf{T}\mathbf{A}\mathbf{t}$ are given by

$$\mathbf{t} \sim \mathcal{N}(\boldsymbol{\mu}, \boldsymbol{\Sigma})$$
$$\mathbf{E}_{p(\mathbf{t})}\left\{\mathbf{t}^\mathsf{T}\mathbf{A}\mathbf{t}\right\} = \mathsf{Tr}(\mathbf{A}\boldsymbol{\Sigma}) + \boldsymbol{\mu}^\mathsf{T}\mathbf{A}\boldsymbol{\mu},$$

where $\mathsf{Tr}()$ is the trace function (see Comment 2.8). For the first term on the right hand side of Equation 2.51, $\mathbf{A} = \mathbf{I}_N$ (note that $\mathbf{t}^\mathsf{T}\mathbf{t} = \mathbf{t}^\mathsf{T}\mathbf{I}_N\mathbf{t}$, where $\mathbf{I}_N$ is the $N \times N$ identity matrix) and in the second term, $\mathbf{A} = \mathbf{X}(\mathbf{X}^\mathsf{T}\mathbf{X})^{-1}\mathbf{X}^\mathsf{T}$. In both cases, $\boldsymbol{\mu} = \mathbf{X}\mathbf{w}$ and $\boldsymbol{\Sigma} = \sigma^2\mathbf{I}_N$. Substituting the necessary values into Equation 2.51 gives

$$\mathbf{E}_{p(\mathbf{t}|\mathbf{X},\mathbf{w},\sigma^2)}\left\{\widehat{\sigma^2}\right\} = \frac{1}{N}\left(\mathsf{Tr}(\sigma^2\mathbf{I_N}) + \mathbf{w}^\mathsf{T}\mathbf{X}^\mathsf{T}\mathbf{X}\mathbf{w}\right)$$
$$- \frac{1}{N}\left(\mathsf{Tr}(\sigma^2\mathbf{X}(\mathbf{X}^\mathsf{T}\mathbf{X})^{-1}\mathbf{X}^\mathsf{T}) + \mathbf{w}^\mathsf{T}\mathbf{X}^\mathsf{T}\mathbf{X}(\mathbf{X}^\mathsf{T}\mathbf{X})^{-1}\mathbf{X}^\mathsf{T}\mathbf{X}\mathbf{w}\right),$$

since $\mathbf{I}_N\mathbf{I}_N = \mathbf{I}_N$. Now, $\mathsf{Tr}(\sigma^2\mathbf{A}) = \sigma^2\mathsf{Tr}(\mathbf{A})$ and $\mathsf{Tr}(\mathbf{I_N}) = N$ by definition. Using these, we can simplify the expression to

$$\mathbf{E}_{p(\mathbf{t}|\mathbf{X},\mathbf{w},\sigma^2)}\left\{\widehat{\sigma^2}\right\} = \sigma^2 + \frac{1}{N}\mathbf{w}^\mathsf{T}\mathbf{X}^\mathsf{T}\mathbf{X}\mathbf{w} - \frac{\sigma^2}{N}\mathsf{Tr}(\mathbf{X}(\mathbf{X}^\mathsf{T}\mathbf{X})^{-1}\mathbf{X}^\mathsf{T}) - \frac{1}{N}\mathbf{w}^\mathsf{T}\mathbf{X}^\mathsf{T}\mathbf{X}\mathbf{w}$$

$$= \sigma^2 - \frac{\sigma^2}{N}\mathsf{Tr}(\mathbf{X}(\mathbf{X}^\mathsf{T}\mathbf{X})^{-1}\mathbf{X}^\mathsf{T})$$

$$= \sigma^2\left(1 - \frac{1}{N}\mathsf{Tr}(\mathbf{X}(\mathbf{X}^\mathsf{T}\mathbf{X})^{-1}\mathbf{X}^\mathsf{T})\right).$$

Finally, we need to use the fact that $\mathsf{Tr}(\mathbf{AB}) = \mathsf{Tr}(\mathbf{BA})$ and therefore the first $\mathbf{X}$ inside the trace function can be moved to be the last:

$$\mathbf{E}_{p(\mathbf{t}|\mathbf{X},\mathbf{w},\sigma^2)}\left\{\widehat{\sigma^2}\right\} = \sigma^2\left(1 - \frac{1}{N}\mathsf{Tr}((\mathbf{X}^\mathsf{T}\mathbf{X})^{-1}\mathbf{X}^\mathsf{T}\mathbf{X})\right)$$

$$= \sigma^2\left(1 - \frac{1}{N}\mathsf{Tr}(\mathbf{I}_D)\right)$$

$$= \sigma^2\left(1 - \frac{D}{N}\right), \tag{2.52}$$

where D is the number of attributes (the number of columns in $\mathbf{X}$).

Assuming that $D < N$ (i.e. the number of attributes we measure for each data point is smaller than the number of data points), then our estimate of the variance will, on average, be lower than the true variance:

$$\mathbf{E}_{p(\mathbf{t}|\mathbf{X},\mathbf{w},\sigma^2)}\left\{\widehat{\sigma^2}\right\} < \sigma^2.$$

Unlike $\widehat{\mathbf{w}}$, this estimator *is* **biased**.

We can see this bias by returning to our synthetic experiment. The average value of $\widehat{\sigma^2}$ over all of the datasets was 0.2264. The true value is $\sigma^2 = 0.5^2 = 0.25$. We can see that the average value is indeed too low. For this example, $D = 2$ and $N = 20$, so our theoretical expected value is

$$\mathbf{E}_{p(\mathbf{t}|\mathbf{X},\mathbf{w},\sigma^2)}\left\{\widehat{\sigma^2}\right\} = \sigma^2\left(1 - \frac{D}{N}\right) = 0.25\left(1 - \frac{2}{20}\right) = 0.2250$$

which is close to the observed average.

From Equation 2.52, we notice that one way to decrease the bias is to make D/N smaller. D is normally fixed, but we can increase N. In Figure 2.19 we can see the effect of increasing N from 20 to 10,000 (MATLAB script: w_variation_demo.m). The theoretical (dashed) curve and the empirical (solid) curve (created by rerunning our previous experiment with different numbers of observations, N) are in close agreement and converge towards the true value of $\sigma^2 = 0.25$ as the amount of data increases.

It is possible to provide an intuitive explanation for the bias in $\widehat{\sigma^2}$. The expression for the ML estimate of σ^2 is

$$\widehat{\sigma^2} = \frac{1}{N}\left(\mathbf{t}^\mathsf{T}\mathbf{t} - \mathbf{t}^\mathsf{T}\mathbf{X}\widehat{\mathbf{w}}\right). \tag{2.53}$$

It is possible to rearrange this to be equal to the sum of squared errors between the predictions and the true responses (see Exercise 2.11):

$$\widehat{\sigma^2} = \frac{1}{N}\sum_{n=1}^{N}(t_n - \mathbf{x}^\mathsf{T}\widehat{\mathbf{w}})^2.$$

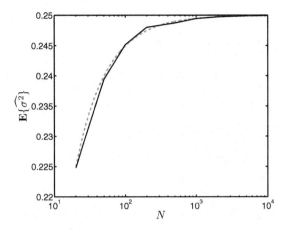

FIGURE 2.19 Evolution of the theoretical (dashed line) and empirical (solid line) estimates of $\mathbf{E}_{p(\mathbf{t}|\mathbf{X},\mathbf{w},\sigma^2)}\left\{\widehat{\sigma^2}\right\}$ as the number of data points increases.

This tells us that the closer the model gets to the data, the smaller $\widehat{\sigma^2}$. Now imagine the true value of $\mathbf{w}$ and our estimate $\widehat{\mathbf{w}}$. Which will get closer to the data? The maximum likelihood estimate, $\widehat{\mathbf{w}}$, is identical to the minimum loss estimate. It is, by definition, the set of parameters that gets closest to the data and therefore minimises $\widehat{\sigma^2}$. The value of $\widehat{\sigma^2}$ that we would get if we used the true value $\mathbf{w}$ instead of $\widehat{\mathbf{w}}$ in Equation 2.53 would have to be the same or higher than the value we get with $\widehat{\mathbf{w}}$. Because we are finding the value of $\mathbf{w}$ that minimises the noise, we will, on average, end up with a lower level of noise than the true value.

2.12 CHAPTER SUMMARY

In the preceding sections, we have covered a lot of material. An introduction to random variables provided the foundations required to be able to model the errors between the data and the proposed deterministic model. By explicitly modelling these errors, we have seen how the least squares solution from Chapter 1 is equivalent to the solution obtained by maximising a different quantity called the *likelihood* if the noise in the data is assumed to be normally distributed. The benefit of the likelihood approach is the ability to quantify the uncertainty in our parameter estimates and hence also, crucially, in our predictions. This allows us to move away from exact predictions (which will certainly be wrong) to ranges of values (e.g. $t_{\text{new}} \pm \sigma^2_{\text{new}}$). In most applications this will be much more useful. Finally, we looked at some theoretical properties of the maximum likelihood parameter values and saw that, although our estimate $\widehat{\mathbf{w}}$ is unbiased, $\widehat{\sigma^2}$ is, on average, biased to be too low.

2.13 EXERCISES

2.1 Would the errors in the 100 m linear regression (shown in Figure 2.1) be best modelled with a discrete or continuous random variable?

2.2 By using the fact that, when rolling a die, all outcomes are equally likely and by using the constraints given in Equations 2.1 and 2.2, compute the probabilities of the dice landing with each of the six faces facing up.

2.3 Y is a random variable that can take any positive integer value. The likelihood of these outcomes is given by the Poisson pdf

$$p(y) = \frac{\lambda^y}{y!} \exp\{-\lambda\}.$$

By using the fact that, for a discrete random variable, the pdf gives the probabilities of the individual events occurring and that probabilities are additive, (a) compute the probability that $Y \leq 4$ for $\lambda = 5$, i.e. $P(Y \leq 4)$.
(b) Using the result of (a) and the fact that one outcome has to happen, compute the probability that $Y > 4$. (Hint: one of the two events, $Y \leq 4$ and $Y > 4$, *has* to happen.)

2.4 Y is a random variable with a uniform density $p(y) = \mathcal{U}(a, b)$. Derive $\mathbf{E}_{p(y)} \{\sin(y)\}$. Note that $\int \sin(y) \, dy = -\cos(y)$. Compute $\mathbf{E}_{p(y)} \{\sin(y)\}$ for $a = 0, b = 1$. Modify `approx_expected_value.m` to compute a sample-based approximation to this value and observe how the approximation improves with the number of samples drawn.

2.5 Assume that $p(\mathbf{w})$ is the Gaussian pdf for a D-dimensional vector $\mathbf{w}$ given in Equation 2.28. By expanding the vector notation and rearranging, show that using $\boldsymbol{\Sigma} = \sigma^2 \mathbf{I}$ as the covariance matrix assumes independence of the D elements of $\mathbf{w}$. You will need to be aware that the determinant of a matrix that only has entries on the diagonal ($|\sigma^2 \mathbf{I}|$) is the product of the diagonal values and that the inverse of the same matrix is constructed by simply inverting each element on the diagonal. (Hint: a product of exponentials can be expressed as an exponential of a sum.)

2.6 Using the same setup as Exercise 2.5 above, see what happens if we use a diagonal covariance matrix with different elements on the diagonal, i.e.

$$\boldsymbol{\Sigma} = \begin{bmatrix} \sigma_1^2 & 0 & \cdots & 0 \\ 0 & \sigma_2^2 & \cdots & 0 \\ \vdots & \vdots & \ddots & \vdots \\ 0 & 0 & \cdots & \sigma_D^2 \end{bmatrix}.$$

2.7 Show that for a first-order polynomial, the diagonal elements of the Hessian matrix of second derivatives of the log-likelihood is equivalent to (they will differ by a multiplicative constant) the second derivatives in Equation 1.9.

2.8 Assume that a dataset of N values, $x_1, \ldots, x_N$, was sampled from a Gaussian distribution. Assuming that the data are IID, find the maximum likelihood estimate of the Gaussian mean and variance. (Hint: start by writing down the combined likelihood of all N data points and note that the product of an exponential function can be written as the exponential of a sum.)

2.9 Assume that a dataset of N binary values, $x_1, \ldots, x_N$, was sampled from a Bernoulli. Compute the maximum likelihood estimate for the Bernoulli parameter.

2.10 Obtain the maximum likelihood estimates of the mean vector and covariance matrix of a multivariate Gaussian density given N observations $\mathbf{x}_1, \ldots, \mathbf{x}_N$.

2.11 Show that the maximum likelihood estimate of the noise variance in our linear model,

$$\widehat{\sigma^2} = \frac{1}{N}\left(\mathbf{t}^\mathsf{T}\mathbf{t} - \mathbf{t}^\mathsf{T}\mathbf{X}\widehat{\mathbf{w}}\right),$$

can also be expressed as

$$\widehat{\sigma^2} = \frac{1}{N}\sum_{n=1}^{N}(t_n - \mathbf{x}_n^\mathsf{T}\mathbf{w})^2.$$

(Hint: work backwards from the second expression.)

2.12 Using `predictive_variance_example.m`, generate a dataset and remove all values for which $-1.5 \leq x \leq 1.5$. Observe the effect this has on the predictive variance in this range.

2.13 Compute the Fisher information for the parameter of a Bernoulli distribution.

2.14 Compute the Fisher information matrix for the components of the mean vector in a multivariate Gaussian density.

2.14 FURTHER READING

[1] Christopher Bishop. *Pattern Recognition and Machine Learning.* Springer, 2007.

This book is an excellent resource for many machine learning concepts. In particular, it includes a detailed discussion of the bias-variance trade-off.

[2] J. H. McColl. *Probability.* Elsevier, 1995.

A very accessible introduction to probability theory.

[3] Paul Meyer. *Introductory Probability and Statistical Applications.* Addison-Wesley, 1978.

An excellent resource for introductory probability theory.

[4] J. Rosenthal. *A First Look at Rigorous Probabillity Theory.* World Scientific Publishing Company, 2006.

This is a very accessible book to begin exploring measure theory – the branch of mathematics that underpins probability theory.

[5] Michael Tipping and Christopher Bishop. Probabilistic principal component analysis. *Journal of the Royal Statistical Society. Series B (Statistical Methodology)*, 61(3):611–622, 1999.

An interesting application of maximum likelihood. Here it is applied to one of the first probabilistic approaches to the the classical statistical problem of Principal Component Analysis.

CHAPTER 3

The Bayesian Approach to Machine Learning

In the previous chapter, we saw how explicitly adding noise to our model allowed us to obtain more than just point predictions. In particular, we were able to quantify the uncertainty present in our parameter estimates and our subsequent predictions. Once content with the idea that there will be uncertainty in our parameter estimates, it is a small step towards considering our parameters themselves as random variables. Bayesian methods are becoming increasingly important within Machine Learning and we will devote the next two chapters to providing an introduction to an area that many people find challenging. In this chapter, we will cover some of the fundamental ideas of Bayesian statistics through two examples. Unfortunately, the calculations required to perform Bayesian inference are often not analytically tractable. In Chapter 4 we will introduce three approximation methods that are popular in the Machine Learning community.

3.1 A COIN GAME

Imagine you are walking around a fairground and come across a stall where customers are taking part in a coin tossing game. The stall owner tosses a coin ten times for each customer. If the coin lands heads on six or fewer occasions, the customer wins back their £1 stake plus an additional £1. Seven or more and the stall owner keeps their money. The binomial distribution (described in Section 2.3.2) describes the probability of a certain number of successes (heads) in N binary events. The probability of y heads from N tosses where each toss lands heads with probability r is given by

$$P(Y = y) = \left(\begin{array}{c} N \\ y \end{array} \right) r^y (1 - r)^{N-y}. \tag{3.1}$$

You assume that the coin is fair and therefore set $r = 0.5$. For $N = 10$ tosses, the probability distribution function can be seen in Figure 3.1, where the bars corresponding to $y \leq 6$ have been shaded. Using Equation 3.1, it is possible to calculate the probability of winning the game, i.e. the probability that Y is less than or equal

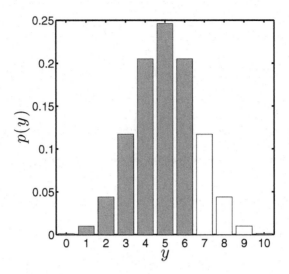

FIGURE 3.1 The binomial density function (Equation 3.1) when $N = 10$ and $r = 0.5$.

to 6, $P(Y \leq 6)$:

$$
\begin{aligned}
P(Y \leq 6) = 1 - P(Y > 6) &= 1 - [P(Y = 7) + P(Y = 8) \\
&\quad + P(Y = 9) + P(Y = 10)] \\
&= 1 - [0.1172 + 0.0439 + 0.0098 + 0.0010] \\
&= 0.8281.
\end{aligned}
$$

This seems like a pretty good game – you'll double your money with probability 0.8281. It is also possible to compute the expected return from playing the game. The expected value of a function $f(X)$ of a random variable X is computed as (introduced in Section 2.2.8)

$$
\mathbf{E}_{P(x)} \{f(X)\} = \sum_{x} f(x) P(x),
$$

where the summation is over all possible values that the random variable can take. Let X be the random variable that takes a value of 1 if we win and a value of 0 if we lose: $P(X = 1) = P(Y \leq 6)$. If we win, $(X = 1)$, we get a return of £2 (our original stake plus an extra £1) so $f(1) = 2$. If we lose, we get a return of nothing so $f(0) = 0$. Hence our expected return is

$$
f(1)P(X = 1) + f(0)P(X = 0) = 2 \times P(Y \leq 6) + 0 \times P(Y > 6) = 1.6562.
$$

Given that it costs £1 to play, you win, on average, $1.6562 - 1$ or approximately 66p per game. If you played 100 times, you'd expect to walk away with a profit of £65.62.

Given these odds of success, it seems sensible to play. However, whilst waiting you notice that the stall owner looks reasonably wealthy and very few customers seem to be winning. Perhaps the assumptions underlying the calculations are wrong. These assumptions are

1. The number of heads can be modelled as a random variable with a binomial distribution, and the probability of a head on any particular toss is r.

2. The coin is fair – the probability of heads is the same as the probability of tails, $r = 0.5$.

It seems hard to reject the binomial distribution – events are taking place with only two possible outcomes and the tosses do seem to be independent. This leaves r, the probability that the coin lands heads. Our assumption was that the coin was fair – the probability of heads was equal to the probability of tails. Maybe this is not the case? To investigate this, we can treat r as a parameter (like $\mathbf{w}$ and σ^2 in the previous chapter) and fit it to some data.

3.1.1 Counting heads

There are three people in the queue to play. The first one plays and gets the following sequence of heads and tails:

$$H,T,H,H,H,H,H,H,H,H,$$

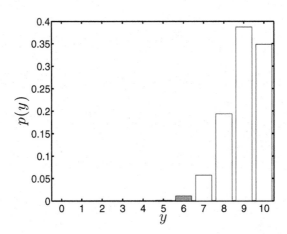

FIGURE 3.2 The binomial density function (Equation 3.1) when $N = 10$ and $r = 0.9$.

nine heads and one tail. It is possible to compute the maximum likelihood value of r as follows. The likelihood is given by the binomial distribution:

$$P(Y = y|r, N) = \binom{N}{9} r^y (1 - r)^{N-y}. \tag{3.2}$$

Taking the natural logarithm gives

$$L = \log P(Y = y|r, N) = \log \binom{N}{9} + y \log r + (N - y) \log(1 - r).$$

As in Chapter 2, we can differentiate this expression, equate to zero and solve for the maximum likelihood estimate of the parameter:

$$
\begin{aligned}
\frac{\partial L}{\partial r} &= \frac{y}{r} - \frac{N-y}{1-r} = 0 \\
y(1-r) &= r(N-y) \\
y &= rN \\
r &= \frac{y}{N}.
\end{aligned}
$$

Substituting $y = 9$ and $N = 10$ gives $r = 0.9$. The corresponding distribution function is shown in Figure 3.2 and the recalculated probability of winning is $P(Y \leq 6) = 0.0128$. This is much lower than that for $r = 0.5$. The expected return is now

$$
2 \times P(Y \leq 6) + 0 \times P(Y > 6) = 0.0256.
$$

Given that it costs £1 to play, we expect to make $0.0256 - 1 = -0.9744$ per game – a loss of approximately 97p. $P(Y \leq 6) = 0.0128$ suggests that only about 1 person in every 100 should win, but this does not seem to be reflected in the number of people who *are* winning. Although the evidence from this run of coin tosses suggests $r = 0.9$, it seems too biased given that several people *have* won.

3.1.2 The Bayesian way

The value of r computed in the previous section was based on just ten tosses. Given the random nature of the coin toss, if we observed several sequences of tosses it is likely that we would get a different r each time. Thought about this way, r feels a bit like a random variable, R. Maybe we can learn something about the distribution of R rather than try and find a particular value. We saw in the previous section that obtaining an exact value by counting is heavily influenced by the particular tosses in the short sequence. No matter how many such sequences we observe there will always be some uncertainty in r – considering it as a random variable with an associated distribution will help us measure and understand this uncertainty.

In particular, defining the random variable Y_N to be the number of heads obtained in N tosses, we would like the distribution of r conditioned on the value of Y_N:

$$
p(r|y_N).
$$

Given this distribution, it would be possible to compute the expected probability of winning by taking the expectation of $P(Y_{new} \leq 6|r)$ with respect to $p(r|y_N)$:

$$
P(Y_{new} \leq 6|y_N) = \int P(Y_{new} \leq 6|r)p(r|y_N)dr,
$$

where Y_{new} is a random variable describing the number of heads in a future set of ten tosses.

In Section 2.2.7 we gave a brief introduction to Bayes' rule. Bayes' rule allows us to reverse the conditioning of two (or more) random variables, e.g. compute $p(a|b)$ from $p(b|a)$. Here we're interested in $p(r|y_N)$, which, if we reverse the conditioning, is $p(y_N|r)$ – the probability distribution function over the number of heads in N

independent tosses where the probability of a head in a single toss is r. This is the binomial distribution function that we can easily compute for any y_N and r. In our context, Bayes' rule is (see also Equation 2.11)

$$p(r|y_N) = \frac{P(y_N|r)p(r)}{P(y_N)}.$$

(3.3)

This equation is going to be very important for us in the following chapters so it is worth spending some time looking at each term in detail.

The likelihood, $P(y_N|r)$ We came across likelihood in Chapter 2. Here it has exactly the same meaning: how likely is it that we would observe our data (in this case, the data is y_N) for a particular value of r (our model)? For our example, this is the binomial distribution. This value will be high if r could have feasibly produced the result y_N and low if the result is very unlikely. For example, Figure 3.3 shows the likelihood $P(y_N|r)$ as a function of r for two different scenarios. In the first, the data consists of ten tosses ($N = 10$) of which six were heads. In the second, there were $N = 100$ tosses, of which 70 were heads.

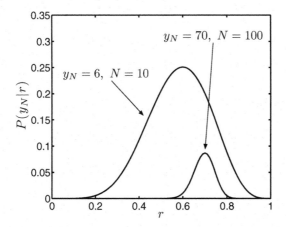

FIGURE 3.3 Examples of the likelihood $p(y_N|r)$ as a function of r for two scenarios.

This plot reveals two important properties of the likelihood. Firstly, it is not a probability density. If it were, the area under both curves would have to equal 1. We can see that this is not the case without working out the area because the two areas are completely different. Secondly, the two examples differ in how much they appear to tell us about r. In the first example, the likelihood has a non-zero value for a large range of possible r values (approximately $0.2 \leq r \leq 0.9$). In the second, this range is greatly reduced (approximately $0.6 \leq r \leq 0.8$). This is very intuitive: in the second example, we have much more data (the results of 100 tosses rather than 10) and so we *should* know more about r.

The prior distribution, $p(r)$ The prior distribution allows us to express any belief we have in the value of r *before* we see any data. To illustrate this, we shall consider the following three examples:

1. We do not know anything about tossing coins or the stall owner.
2. We think the coin (and hence the stall owner) is fair.
3. We think the coin (and hence the stall owner) is biased to give more heads than tails.

We can encode each of these beliefs as different prior distributions. r can take any value between 0 and 1 and therefore it must be modelled as a continuous random variable. Figure 3.4 shows three density functions that might be used to encode our three different prior beliefs.

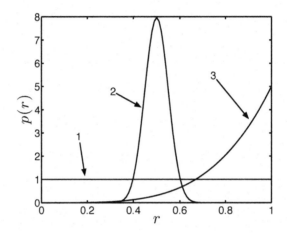

FIGURE 3.4   Examples of prior densities, $p(r)$, for r for three different scenarios.

Belief number 1 is represented as a uniform density between 0 and 1 and as such shows no preference for any particular r value. Number 2 is given a density function that is concentrated around $r = 0.5$, the value we would expect for a fair coin. The density suggests that we do not expect much variance in r: it's almost certainly going to lie between 0.4 and 0.6. Most coins that any of us have tossed agree with this. Finally, number 3 encapsulates our belief that the coin (and therefore the stall owner) is biased. This density suggests that $r > 0.5$ and that there is a high level of variance. This is fine because our belief is just that the coin is biased: we don't really have any idea how biased at this stage.

We will not choose between our three scenarios at this stage, as it is interesting to see the effect these different beliefs will have on $p(r|y_N)$.

The three functions shown in Figure 3.4 have not been plucked from thin air. They are all examples of beta probability density functions (see Section 2.5.2). The beta density function is used for continuous random variables constrained to lie between 0 and 1 – perfect for our example. For a random variable R with parameters α and β, it is defined as

$$p(r) = \frac{\Gamma(\alpha + \beta)}{\Gamma(\alpha)\Gamma(\beta)} r^{\alpha-1}(1-r)^{\beta-1}. \qquad (3.4)$$

$\Gamma(a)$ is known as the gamma function (see Section 2.5.2). In Equation 3.4 the gamma functions ensure that the density is normalised (that is, it integrates to 1 and is therefore a probability density function). In particular

$$\frac{\Gamma(\alpha)\Gamma(\beta)}{\Gamma(\alpha + \beta)} = \int_{r=0}^{r=1} r^{\alpha-1}(1-r)^{\beta-1} \, dr,$$

ensuring that

$$\int_{r=0}^{r=1} \frac{\Gamma(\alpha + \beta)}{\Gamma(\alpha)\Gamma(\beta)} r^{\alpha-1}(1-r)^{\beta-1} \, dr = 1.$$

The two parameters α and β control the shape of the resulting density function and must both be positive. Our three beliefs as plotted in Figure 3.4 correspond to the following pairs of parameter values:

1. Know nothing: $\alpha = 1$, $\beta = 1$.
2. Fair coin: $\alpha = 50$, $\beta = 50$.
3. Biased: $\alpha = 5$, $\beta = 1$.

The problem of choosing these values is a big one. For example, why should we choose $\alpha = 5$, $\beta = 1$ for a biased coin? There is no easy answer to this. We shall see later that, for the beta distribution, they can be interpreted as a number of previous, hypothetical coin tosses. For other distributions no such analogy is possible and we will also introduce the idea that maybe these too should be treated as random variables. In the mean time, we will assume that these values are sensible and move on.

The marginal distribution of y_N – $P(y_N)$

The third quantity in our equation, $P(y_N)$, acts as a normalising constant to ensure that $p(r|y_N)$ is a properly defined density. It is known as the marginal distribution of y_N because it is computed by integrating r out of the joint density $p(y_N, r)$:

$$P(y_N) = \int_{r=0}^{r=1} p(y_N, r) \, dr.$$

This joint density can be factorised to give

$$P(y_N) = \int_{r=0}^{r=1} P(y_N|r)p(r) \, dr,$$

which is the product of the prior and likelihood integrated over the range of values that r may take.

$p(y_N)$ is also known as the **marginal likelihood**, as it is the likelihood of the data, y_N, averaged over all parameter values. We shall see in Section 3.4.1 that it can be a useful quantity in model selection, but, unfortunately, in all but a small minority of cases, it is very difficult to calculate.

The posterior distribution – $p(r|y_N)$ This **posterior** is the distribution in which we are interested. It is the result of updating our prior belief $p(r)$ in light of new evidence y_N. The shape of the density is interesting – it tells us something about how much information we have about r after combining what we knew beforehand (the prior) and what we've seen (the likelihood). Three hypothetical examples are provided in Figure 3.5 (these are purely illustrative and do not correspond to the particular likelihood and prior examples shown in Figures 3.3 and 3.4). (a) is uniform – combining the likelihood and the prior together has left all values of r equally likely. (b) suggests that r is most likely to be low but could be high. This might be the result of starting with a uniform prior and then observing more tails than heads. Finally, (c) suggests the coin is biased to land heads more often. As it is a density, the posterior tells us not just which values are likely but also provides an indication of the level of uncertainty we still have in r having observed some data.

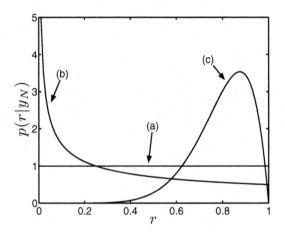

FIGURE 3.5   Examples of three possible posterior distributions $p(r|y_N)$.

As already mentioned, we can use the posterior density to compute expectations. For example, we could compute

$$\mathbf{E}_{p(r|y_N)}\left\{P(Y_{10} \le 6)\right\} = \int_{r=0}^{r=1} P(Y_{10} \le 6|r)p(r|y_N)\ dr,$$

the expected value of the probability that we will win. This takes into account the data we have observed, our prior beliefs and the uncertainty that remains. It will be useful in helping to decide whether or not to play the game. We will return to this later, but first we will look at the kind of posterior densities we obtain in our coin example.

Comment 3.1 – Conjugate priors: A likelihood-prior pair is said to be conjugate if they result in a posterior which is of the same form as the prior. This enables us to compute the posterior density analytically without having to worry about computing the denominator in Bayes' rule, the marginal likelihood. Some common conjugate pairs are listed in the table to the right.

Prior	Likelihood
Gaussian	Gaussian
Beta	Binomial
Gamma	Gaussian
Dirichlet	Multinomial

3.2 THE EXACT POSTERIOR

The beta distribution is a common choice of prior when the likelihood is a binomial distribution. This is because we can use some algebra to compute the posterior density exactly. In fact, the beta distribution is known as the **conjugate** prior to the binomial likelihood (see Comment 3.1). If the prior and likelihood are conjugate, the posterior will be of the same form as the prior. Specifically, $p(r|y_N)$ will give a beta distribution with parameters δ and γ, whose values will be computed from the prior and y_N. The beta and binomial are not the only conjugate pair of distributions and we will see an example of another conjugate prior and likelihood pair when we return to the Olympic data later in this chapter.

Using a conjugate prior makes things much easier from a mathematical point of view. However, as we mentioned in both our discussion on loss functions in Chapter 1 and noise distributions in Chapter 2, it is more important to base our choices on modelling assumptions than mathematical convenience. In the next chapter we will see some techniques we can use in the common scenario that the pair are non-conjugate.

Returning to our example, we can omit $p(y_N)$ from Equation 3.3, leaving

$$p(r|y_N) \propto P(y_N|r)p(r).$$

Replacing the terms on the right hand side with a binomial and beta distribution gives

$$p(r|y_N) \propto \left[\binom{N}{y_N} r^{y_N}(1-r)^{N-y_N} \right] \times \left[\frac{\Gamma(\alpha+\beta)}{\Gamma(\alpha)\Gamma(\beta)} r^{\alpha-1}(1-r)^{\beta-1} \right]. \quad (3.5)$$

Because the prior and likelihood are conjugate, we know that $p(r|y_N)$ has to be a beta density. The beta density, with parameters δ and γ, has the following general form:

$$p(r) = Kr^{\delta-1}(1-r)^{\gamma-1},$$

where K is a constant. If we can arrange all of the terms, including r, on the right hand side of Equation 3.5 into something that looks like $r^{\delta-1}(1-r)^{\gamma-1}$, we can be sure that the constant must also be correct (it has to be $\Gamma(\delta+\gamma)/(\Gamma(\delta)\Gamma(\gamma))$ because we know that the posterior density is a beta density). In other words, we know what the normalising constant for a beta density is so we do not need to compute $p(y_N)$.

Rearranging Equation 3.5 gives us

$$p(r|y_N) \propto \left[\binom{N}{y_N} \frac{\Gamma(\alpha+\beta)}{\Gamma(\alpha)\Gamma(\beta)} \right] \times \left[r^{y_N} r^{\alpha-1}(1-r)^{N-y_N}(1-r)^{\beta-1} \right]$$

$$\propto r^{y_N+\alpha-1}(1-r)^{N-y_N+\beta-1}$$

$$\propto r^{\delta-1}(1-r)^{\gamma-1}$$

where $\delta = y_N + \alpha$ and $\gamma = N - y_N + \beta$.

Therefore

$$p(r|y_N) = \frac{\Gamma(\alpha+\beta+N)}{\Gamma(\alpha+y_N)\Gamma(\beta+N-y_N)} r^{\alpha+y_N-1}(1-r)^{\beta+N-y_N-1} \qquad (3.6)$$

(note that when adding γ and δ, the y_N terms cancel). This is the posterior density of r based on the prior $p(r)$ and the data y_N. Notice how the posterior parameters are computed by adding the number of heads (y_n) to the first prior parameter (α) and the number of tails ($N - y_N$) to the second (β). This allows us to gain some intuition about the prior parameters α and β – they can be thought of as the number of heads and tails in $\alpha + \beta$ previous tosses. For example, consider the second two scenarios discussed in the previous section. For the fair coin scenario, $\alpha = \beta = 50$. This is equivalent to tossing a coin 100 times and obtaining 50 heads and 50 tails. For the biased scenario, $\alpha = 5, \beta = 1$, corresponding to six tosses and five heads. Looking at Figure 3.4, this helps us explain the differing levels of variability suggested by the two densities: the fair coin density has much lower variability than the biased one because it is the result of many more hypothetical tosses. The more tosses, the more we should know about r.

The analogy is not perfect. For example, α and β don't have to be integers and can be less than 1 (0.3 heads doesn't make much sense). The analogy also breaks down when $\alpha = \beta = 1$. Observing one head and one tail means that values of $r = 0$ and $r = 1$ are impossible. However, density 1 in Figure 3.4), suggests that all values of r are equally likely. Despite these flaws, the analogy will be a useful one to bear in mind as we progress through our analysis (see Exercises 3.1, 3.2, 3.3 and 3.4)

3.3   THE THREE SCENARIOS

We will now investigate the posterior distribution $p(r|y_N)$ for the three different prior scenarios shown in Figure 3.4 – no prior knowledge, a fair coin and a biased coin.

3.3.1   No prior knowledge

In this scenario (MATLAB script: `coin_scenario1.m`), we assume that we know nothing of coin tossing or the stall holder. Our prior parameters are $\alpha = 1$, $\beta = 1$, shown in Figure 3.6(a).

To compare different scenarios we will use the expected value and variance of r under the prior. The expected value of a random variable from a beta distribution with parameters α and β (the density function of which we will henceforth denote as $\mathcal{B}(\alpha, \beta))$ is given as (see Exercise 3.5)

$$\begin{aligned} p(r) &= \mathcal{B}(\alpha, \beta) \\ \mathbf{E}_{p(r)}\{R\} &= \frac{\alpha}{\alpha + \beta}. \end{aligned}$$

For scenario 1:

$$\mathbf{E}_{p(r)}\{R\} = \frac{\alpha}{\alpha + \beta} = \frac{1}{2}.$$

The variance of a beta distributed random variable is given by (see Exercise 3.6)

$$\mathrm{var}\{R\} = \frac{\alpha\beta}{(\alpha + \beta)^2(\alpha + \beta + 1)}, \tag{3.7}$$

which for $\alpha = \beta = 1$ is

$$\mathrm{var}\{R\} = \frac{1}{12}.$$

Note that in our formulation of the posterior (Equation 3.6) we are not restricted to updating our distribution in blocks of ten – we can incorporate the results of any number of coin tosses. To illustrate the evolution of the posterior, we will look at how it changes toss by toss.

A new customer hands over £1 and the stall owner starts tossing the coin. The first toss results in a head. The posterior distribution after one toss is a beta distribution with parameters $\delta = \alpha + y_N$ and $\gamma = \beta + N - y_N$:

$$p(r|y_N) = \mathcal{B}(\delta, \gamma).$$

In this scenario, $\alpha = \beta = 1$, and as we have had $N = 1$ tosses and seen $y_N = 1$ heads,

$$\begin{aligned} \delta &= 1 + 1 = 2 \\ \gamma &= 1 + 1 - 1 = 1. \end{aligned}$$

This posterior distribution is shown as the solid line in Figure 3.6(b) (the prior is also shown as a dashed line). This single observation has had quite a large effect – the posterior is very different from the prior. In the prior, all values of r were equally likely. This has now changed – higher values are more likely than lower values with zero density at $r = 0$. This is consistent with the evidence – observing one head makes high values of r slightly more likely and low values slightly less likely. The density is still very broad, as we have observed only one toss. The expected value of r under the posterior is

$$\mathbf{E}_{p(r|y_N)}\{R\} = \frac{2}{3}$$

and we can see that observing a solitary head has increased the expected value of r from $1/2$ to $2/3$. The variance of the posterior is (using Equation 3.7)

$$\mathrm{var}\{R\} = \frac{1}{18}$$

which is lower than the prior variance ($1/12$). So, the reduction in variance tells us that we have less uncertainty about the value of r than we did (we have learnt

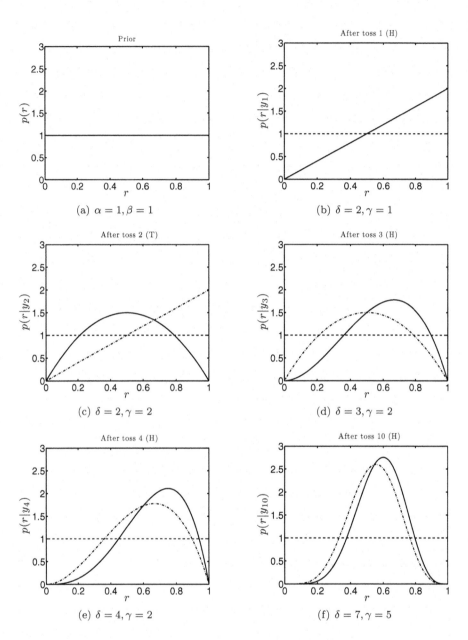

FIGURE 3.6 Evolution of $p(r|y_N)$ as the number of observed coin tosses increases.

something) and the increase in expected value tells us that what we've learnt is that heads are slightly more likely than tails.

The stall owner tosses the second coin and it lands tails. We have now seen one head and one tail and so $N = 2$, $y_N = 1$, resulting in

$$
\begin{aligned}
\delta &= 1 + 1 = 2 \\
\gamma &= 1 + 2 - 1 = 2.
\end{aligned}
$$

The posterior distribution is shown as the solid dark line in Figure 3.6(c). The lighter dash-dot line is the posterior we saw after one toss and the dashed line is the prior. The density has changed again to reflect the new evidence. As we have now observed a tail, the density at $r = 1$ should be zero and is ($r = 1$ would suggest that the coin always lands heads). The density is now curved rather than straight (as we have already mentioned, the beta density function is very flexible) and observing a tail has made lower values more likely. The expected value and variance are now

$$
\mathbf{E}_{p(r|y_N)}\{R\} = \frac{1}{2}, \ \mathrm{var}\{R\} = \frac{1}{20}.
$$

The expected value has decreased back to $1/2$. Given that the expected value under the prior was also $1/2$, you might conclude that we haven't learnt anything. However, the variance has decreased again (from $1/18$ to $1/20$) so we have less uncertainty in r and have learnt something. In fact, we've learnt that r is closer to $1/2$ than we assumed under the prior.

The third toss results in another head. We now have $N = 3$ tosses, $y_N = 2$ heads and $N - y_N = 1$ tail. Our updated posterior parameters are

$$
\begin{aligned}
\delta &= \alpha + y_N = 1 + 2 = 3 \\
\gamma &= \beta + N - y_N = 1 + 3 - 2 = 2.
\end{aligned}
$$

This posterior is plotted in Figure 3.6(d). Once again, the posterior is the solid dark line, the previous posterior is the solid light line and the dashed line is the prior. We notice that the effect of observing this second head is to skew the density to the right, suggesting that heads are more likely than tails. Again, this is entirely consistent with the evidence – we have seen more heads than tails. We have only seen three coins though, so there is still a high level of uncertainty – the density suggests that r could potentially still be pretty much any value between 0 and 1. The new expected value and variance are

$$
\mathbf{E}_{p(r|y_N)}\{R\} = \frac{3}{5}, \ \mathrm{var}\{R\} = \frac{1}{25}.
$$

The variance has decreased again reflecting the decrease in uncertainty that we would expect as we see more data.

Toss 4 also comes up heads ($y_N = 3, N = 4$), resulting in $\delta = 1 + 3 = 4$ and $\gamma = 1 + 4 - 3 = 2$. Figure 3.6(e) shows the current and previous posteriors and prior in the now familiar format. The density has once again been skewed to the right – we've now seen three heads and only one tail so it seems likely that r is greater than $1/2$. Also notice the difference between the $N = 3$ posterior and the $N = 4$ posterior for very low values of r – the extra head has left us pretty convinced that r is not 0.1 or lower. The expected value and variance are given by

$$
\mathbf{E}_{p(r|y_N)}\{R\} = \frac{2}{3}, \ \mathrm{var}\{R\} = \frac{2}{63} = 0.0317,
$$

where the expected value has increased and the variance has once again decreased. The remaining six tosses are made so that the complete sequence is

H,T,H,H,H,H,T,T,T,H,

a total of six heads and four tails. The posterior distribution after $N = 10$ tosses ($y_N = 6$) has parameters $\delta = 1 + 6 = 7$ and $\gamma = 1 + 10 - 6 = 5$. This (along with the posterior for $N = 9$) is shown in Figure 3.6(f). The expected value and variance are

$$\mathbf{E}_{p(r|y_N)}\{R\} = \frac{7}{12} = 0.5833, \ \mathrm{var}\{R\} = 0.0187. \tag{3.8}$$

Our ten observations have increased the expected value from 0.5 to 0.5833 and decreased our variance from $1/12 = 0.0833$ to 0.0187. However, this is not the full story. Examining Figure 3.6(f), we see that we can also be pretty sure that $r > 0.2$ and $r < 0.9$. The uncertainty in the value of r is still quite high because we have only observed ten tosses.

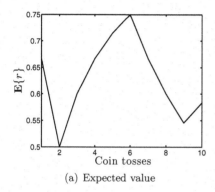

(a) Expected value

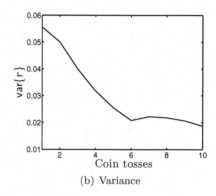

(b) Variance

FIGURE 3.7 Evolution of expected value (a) and variance (b) of r as coin toss data is added to the posterior.

Figure 3.7 summarises how the expected value and variance change as the 10 observations are included. The expected value jumps around a bit, whereas the variance steadily decreases as more information becomes available. At the seventh toss, the variance increases. The first seven tosses are

H,T,H,H,H,H,T.

The evidence up to and including toss 6 is that heads is much more likely than tails (5 out of 6). Tails on the seventh toss is therefore slightly unexpected. Figure 3.8 shows the posterior before and after the seventh toss. The arrival of the tail has forced the density to increase the likelihood of low values of r and, in doing so, increased the uncertainty.

The posterior density encapsulates all of the information we have about r. Shortly, we will use this to compute the expected probability of winning the game. Before we do so, we will revisit the idea of using point estimates by extracting a

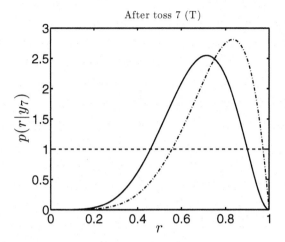

FIGURE 3.8 The posterior after six (light) and seven (dark) tosses.

single value $\widehat{r}$ of r from this density. We will then be able to compare the expected probability of winning with the probability of winning computed from a single value of r. A sensible choice would be to use $\mathbf{E}_{p(r|y_N)}\{R\}$. With this value, we can compute the probability of winning – $P(Y_{\text{new}} \leq 6|\widehat{r})$. This quantity could be used to decide whether or not to play. Note that, to make the distinction between observed tosses and future tosses, we will use Y_{new} as a random variable that describes ten future tosses.

After ten tosses, the posterior density is beta with parameters $\delta = 7, \gamma = 5$. $\widehat{r}$ is therefore

$$\widehat{r} = \frac{\delta}{\delta + \gamma} = \frac{7}{12}.$$

The probability of winning the game follows as

$$\begin{aligned}
P(Y_{\text{new}} \leq 6|\widehat{r}) &= 1 - \sum_{y_{\text{new}}=7}^{10} P(Y_{\text{new}} = y_{\text{new}}|\widehat{r}) \\
&= 1 - 0.3414 \\
&= 0.6586,
\end{aligned}$$

suggesting that we will win more often than lose.

Using all of the posterior information requires computing

$$\mathbf{E}_{p(r|y_N)}\{P(Y_{\text{new}} \leq 6|r)\}.$$

Rearranging and manipulating the expectation provides us with the following expression:

$$\begin{aligned}
\mathbf{E}_{p(r|y_N)}\left\{P(Y_{\text{new}} \leq 6|r)\right\} &= \mathbf{E}_{p(r|y_N)}\left\{1 - P(Y_{\text{new}} \geq 7|r)\right\} & (3.9) \\
&= 1 - \mathbf{E}_{p(r|y_N)}\left\{P(Y_{\text{new}} \geq 7|r)\right\} \\
&= 1 - \mathbf{E}_{p(r|y_N)}\left\{\sum_{y_{\text{new}}=7}^{y_{\text{new}}=10} P(Y_{\text{new}} = y_{\text{new}}|r)\right\} \\
&= 1 - \sum_{y_{\text{new}}=7}^{y_{\text{new}}=10} \mathbf{E}_{p(r|y_N)}\left\{P(Y_{\text{new}} = y_{\text{new}}|r)\right\}.
\end{aligned}$$

To evaluate this, we need to be able to compute $\mathbf{E}_{p(r|y_N)}\left\{P(Y_{\text{new}} = y_{\text{new}}|r)\right\}$. From the definition of expectations, this is given by

$$\begin{aligned}
\mathbf{E}_{p(r|y_N)}\left\{P(Y_{\text{new}} = y_{\text{new}}|r)\right\} &= \int_{r=0}^{r=1} P(Y_{\text{new}} = y_{\text{new}}|r)p(r|y_N)\, dr \\
&= \int_{r=0}^{r=1}\left[\binom{N_{\text{new}}}{y_{\text{new}}} r^{y_{\text{new}}}(1-r)^{N_{\text{new}}-y_{\text{new}}}\right]\left[\frac{\Gamma(\delta+\gamma)}{\Gamma(\delta)\Gamma(\gamma)}r^{\delta-1}(1-r)^{\gamma-1}\right]dr \\
&= \binom{N_{\text{new}}}{y_{\text{new}}}\frac{\Gamma(\delta+\gamma)}{\Gamma(\delta)\Gamma(\gamma)}\int_{r=0}^{r=1} r^{y_{\text{new}}+\delta-1}(1-r)^{N_{\text{new}}-y_{\text{new}}+\gamma-1}\, dr. & (3.10)
\end{aligned}$$

This integral looks a bit daunting. However, on closer inspection, the argument inside the integral is an unnormalised beta density with parameters $\delta + y_{\text{new}}$ and $\gamma + N_{\text{new}} - y_{\text{new}}$. In general, for a beta density with parameters α and β, the following *must* be true:

$$\int_{r=0}^{r=1} \frac{\Gamma(\alpha+\beta)}{\Gamma(\alpha)\Gamma(\beta)} r^{\alpha-1}(1-r)^{\beta-1} dr = 1,$$

and therefore

$$\int_{r=0}^{r=1} r^{\alpha-1}(1-r)^{\beta-1} dr = \frac{\Gamma(\alpha)\Gamma(\beta)}{\Gamma(\alpha+\beta)}.$$

Our desired expectation becomes

$$\mathbf{E}_{p(r|y_N)}\left\{P(Y_{\text{new}} = y_{\text{new}}|r)\right\} = \binom{N_{\text{new}}}{y_{\text{new}}}\frac{\Gamma(\delta+\gamma)}{\Gamma(\delta)\Gamma(\gamma)}\frac{\Gamma(\delta+y_{\text{new}})\Gamma(\gamma+N_{\text{new}}-y_{\text{new}})}{\Gamma(\delta+\gamma+N_{\text{new}})}$$

which we can easily compute for a particular posterior (i.e. values of γ and δ) and values of N_{new} and y_{new}.

After ten tosses, we have $\delta = 7, \gamma = 5$. Plugging these values in, we can compute the expected probability of success:

$$\begin{aligned}
\mathbf{E}_{p(r|y_N)}\left\{P(Y_{\text{new}} \leq 6|r)\right\} &= 1 - \sum_{y_{\text{new}}=7}^{y_{\text{new}}=10}\mathbf{E}_{p(r|y_N)}\left\{P(Y_{\text{new}} = y_{\text{new}}|r)\right\} \\
&= 1 - 0.3945 \\
&= 0.6055.
\end{aligned}$$

Comparing this with the value obtained using the point estimate, we can see that both predict we will win more often than not. This is in agreement with the evidence – the one person we have fully observed got six heads and four tails and hence won £2. The point estimate gives a higher probability – ignoring the posterior uncertainty makes it more likely that we will win.

Another customer plays the game. The sequence of tosses is

$$\text{H,H,T,T,H,H,H,H,H,H,}$$

eight heads and two tails – the stall owner has won. Combining all 20 tosses that we have observed, we have $N = 20$, $y_N = 6 + 8 = 14$ heads and $N - y_N = 20 - 14 = 6$ tails. This gives $\delta = 15$ and $\gamma = 7$. The posterior density is shown in Figure 3.9 where the light line shows the posterior we had after ten and the dashed line the prior. The expected value and variance are

$$\mathbf{E}_{p(r|y_N)}\{R\} = 0.6818, \text{var}\{R\} = 0.0094.$$

The expected value has increased and the variance has decreased (c.f. Equation 3.8). Both behaviours are what we would expect – eight heads and two tails should increase the expected value of r and the increased data should decrease the variance. We can now recompute $\mathbf{E}_{p(r|y_N)}\{P(Y_{\text{new}} \leq 6|r)\}$ in light of the new evidence. Plug-

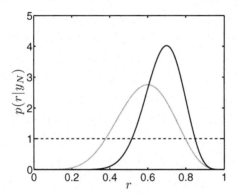

FIGURE 3.9 Posterior distribution after observing 10 tosses (light curve) and 20 tosses (dark curve). The dashed line corresponds to the prior density.

ging in the appropriate values, this is

$$\mathbf{E}_{p(r|y_N)}\{P(Y_{\text{new}} \leq 6|r)\} = 0.4045.$$

The new evidence has pushed the density to the right, made high values of r (and hence the coin landing heads) more likely and reduced the probability of winning. For completeness, we can also compute $P(Y_{\text{new}} \leq 6|\hat{r}) = 0.3994$.

This corresponds to an expected return of:

$$2 \times 0.4045 - 1 = -0.1910,$$

equivalent to a loss of about 20p per go.

In this example we have now touched upon all of the important components of Bayesian Machine Learning – choosing priors, choosing likelihoods, computing posteriors and using expectations to make predictions. We will now repeat this process for the other two prior scenarios.

3.3.2 The fair coin scenario

For the fair coin scenario (MATLAB script: coin_scenario2.m), we assumed that $\alpha = \beta = 50$, which is analogous to assuming that we have already witnessed 100 tosses, half of which resulted in heads. The first thing to notice here is that 100 tosses corresponds to much more data than we are going to observe here (20 tosses). Should we expect our data to have the same effect as it did in the previous scenario?

Figure 3.10(a) shows the prior density and Figures 3.10(b), 3.10(c), 3.10(d), 3.10(e) and 3.10(f) show the posterior after 1, 5, 10, 15 and 20 tosses, respectively. For this scenario, we have not shown the previous posterior at each stage – it is too close to the current one. However, in most cases, the change in posterior is so small that the lines almost lie right on top of one another. In fact, it is only after about ten tosses that the posterior has moved significantly from the prior. Recalling our analogy for the beta prior, this prior includes the evidential equivalent of 100 tosses and so it is not surprising that adding another ten makes much difference.

The evolution of $\mathbf{E}_{p(r|y_N)}\{R\}$ and $\mathsf{var}\{R\}$ as the 20 tosses are observed can be seen in Figure 3.11. We see very little change in either as the data appear compared to the changes we observed in Figure 3.6. Such small changes are indicative of a very *strong* prior density. The prior will dominate over the data until we've observed many more tosses – i.e., $p(r)$ dominates $p(y_N|r)$ in Equation 3.3. We have created a model that is stuck in its ways and will require a lot of persuasion to believe otherwise.

Just as in the previous section, we can work out $\mathbf{E}_{p(r|y_N)}\{P(Y_{\mathsf{new}} \leq 6|r)\}$. After all 20 tosses have been observed, we have $\delta = \alpha + y_N = 50 + 14 = 64$ and $\gamma = \beta + N - y_N = 50 + 20 - 14 = 56$. The expectation works out as

$$\mathbf{E}_{p(r|y_N)}\{P(Y_{\mathsf{new}} \leq 6|r)\} = 0.7579. \tag{3.11}$$

As before, we can also see how much difference there is between this value and the value obtained using the point estimate $\widehat{r}$, $P(Y_{\mathsf{new}} \leq 6|\widehat{r})$ (in this case, $\widehat{r} = 64/(64 + 56) = 0.5333$):

$$P(Y_{\mathsf{new}} \leq 6|\widehat{r}) = 0.7680.$$

Both quantities predict that we will win more often than not. In light of what we've seen about the posterior, this should come as no surprise. The data has done little to overcome the prior assumption that the coin is fair, and we already know that, if the coin is fair, we will tend to win (a fair coin will result in us winning, on average, 66p per game – see the start of Section 3.1).

As an aside, consider how accurate our approximation $P(Y_{\mathsf{new}} \leq 6|\widehat{r})$ is to the proper expectation in this scenario and the previous one. In the previous one, the difference between the two values was

$$|\mathbf{E}_{p(r|y_N)}\{P(Y_{\mathsf{new}} \leq 6|r)\} - P(Y_{\mathsf{new}} \leq 6|\widehat{r})| = 0.0531.$$

In this example, the values are closer:

$$|\mathbf{E}_{p(r|y_N)}\{P(Y_{\mathsf{new}} \leq 6|r)\} - P(Y_{\mathsf{new}} \leq 6|\widehat{r})| = 0.0101.$$

There is a good reason why this is the case – as the variance in the posterior decreases (the variance in scenario 2 is much lower than in scenario 1), the probability density becomes more and more condensed around one particular point. Imagine the variance

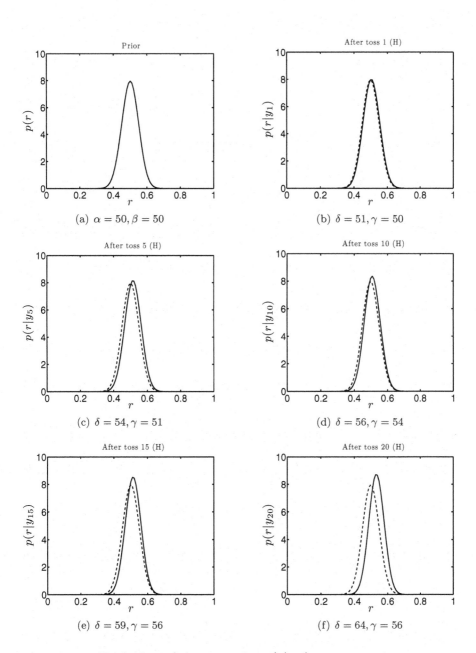

FIGURE 3.10 Evolution of the posterior $p(r|y_N)$ as more coin tosses are observed for the fair coin scenario. The dashed line shows the prior density.

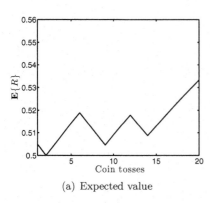

(a) Expected value

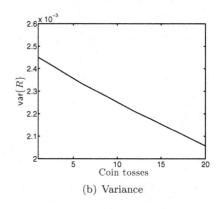

(b) Variance

FIGURE 3.11 Evolution of $\mathbf{E}_{p(r|y_N)}\{R\}$ (a) and $\mathsf{var}\{R\}$ (b) as the 20 coin tosses are observed for the fair coin scenario.

decreasing to such an extent that there was a single value of r that had probability 1 of occurring with $p(r|y_N)$ being zero everywhere else. The expectation we are calculating is

$$\mathbf{E}_{p(r|y_N)}\{P(Y_{\text{new}} \leq 6|r)\} = \int_{r=0}^{r=1} P(Y_{\text{new}} \leq 6|r)p(r|y_N)\ dr.$$

If $p(r|y_N)$ is zero everywhere except at one specific value (say $\hat{r}$), this becomes

$$\mathbf{E}_{p(r|y_N)}\{P(Y_{\text{new}} \leq 6|r)\} = P(Y_{\text{new}} \leq 6|\hat{r}).$$

In other words, as the variance decreases, $P(Y_{\text{new}} \leq 6|\hat{r})$ becomes a better and better approximation to the true expectation. This is not specific to this example – as the quantity of data increases (and uncertainty about parameters subsequently decreases), point approximations become more reliable.

3.3.3   A biased coin

In the final scenario we assume that the coin (and therefore the stall owner) is biased to generate more heads than tails (MATLAB script: `coin_scenario3.m`). This is encoded through a beta prior with parameters $\alpha = 5$, $\beta = 1$. The expected value is

$$\mathbf{E}_{p(r)}\{r\} = 5/6,$$

five coins out of every six will come up heads. Just as for scenario 2, Figure 3.12(a) shows the prior density and Figures 3.12(b), 3.12(c), 3.12(d), 3.12(e) and 3.12(f) show the posterior after 1, 5, 10, 15 and 20 tosses, respectively. Given what we've already seen, there is nothing unusual here. The posterior moves quite rapidly away from the prior (the prior effectively has only the influence of $\alpha + \beta = 6$ data points). Figure 3.13 shows the evolution of expected value and variance. The variance curve has several bumps corresponding to tosses resulting in tails. This is because of the strong prior bias towards a high r value. We don't expect to see many tails under

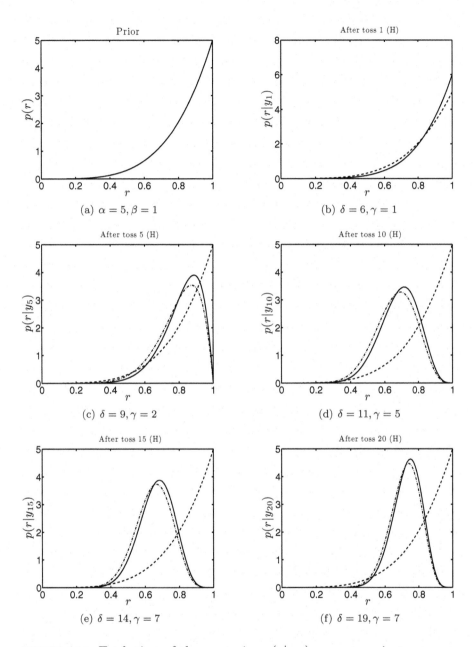

FIGURE 3.12 Evolution of the posterior $p(r|y_N)$ as more coin tosses are observed for the biased coin scenario. The dashed line shows the prior density and in the last four plots, the dash-dot line shows the previous posterior (i.e. the posterior after 4, 9, 14 and 19 tosses).

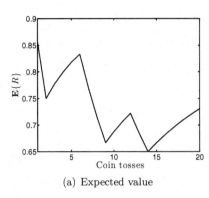

(a) Expected value

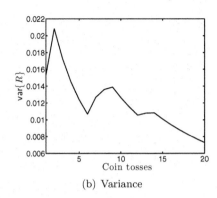

(b) Variance

FIGURE 3.13 Evolution of $\mathbf{E}_{p(r|y_N)}\{R\}$ (a) and $\mathsf{var}\{R\}$ (b) as the 20 coin tosses are observed for the biased coin scenario.

this assumption and so when we do, the model becomes less certain. Once again, we calculate the true quantity of interest, $\mathbf{E}_{p(r|y_N)}\{P(Y_{\mathsf{new}} \leq 6|r)\}$. The final posterior parameter values are $\delta = \alpha + y_N = 5 + 14 = 19$, $\gamma = 1 + N - y_N = 1 + 20 - 14 = 7$. Plugging these in,

$$\mathbf{E}_{p(r|y_N)}\{P(Y_{\mathsf{new}} \leq 6|r)\} = 0.2915.$$

The approximation, noting that $\hat{r} = 19/(19 + 7) = 0.7308$ is

$$P(Y_{\mathsf{new}} \leq 6|\hat{r}) = 0.2707.$$

Both values suggest we will lose money on average.

3.3.4 The three scenarios – a summary

Our three different scenarios have given us different values for the expected probability of winning:

1. No prior knowledge: $\mathbf{E}_{p(r|y_N)}\{P(Y_{\mathsf{new}} \leq 6|r)\} = 0.4045.$

2. Fair coin: $\mathbf{E}_{p(r|y_N)}\{P(Y_{\mathsf{new}} \leq 6|r)\} = 0.7579.$

3. Biased coin: $\mathbf{E}_{p(r|y_N)}\{P(Y_{\mathsf{new}} \leq 6|r)\} = 0.2915.$

Which one should we choose? We could choose based on which of the prior beliefs seems most plausible. Given that the stall holder doesn't look like he is about to go out of business, scenario 3 might be sensible. We might decide that we really do not know anything about the stall holder and coin and look to scenario 1. We might believe that an upstanding stall holder would never stoop to cheating and go for scenario 2. It is possible to justify any of them. What we have seen is that the Bayesian technique allows you to combine the data observed (20 coin tosses) with some prior knowledge (one of the scenarios) in a principled way. The posterior density explicitly models the uncertainty that remains in r at each stage and can be used to make predictions (see Exercises 3.7 and 3.8).

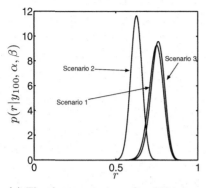

(a) The three posteriors after 100 tosses

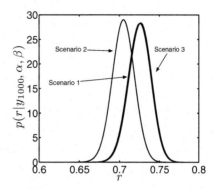

(b) The three posteriors after 1000 tosses

FIGURE 3.14 The posterior densities for the three scenarios after 100 coin tosses (left) and 1000 coin tosses (right).

3.3.5 Adding more data

Before we move on, it is worth examining the effect of adding more and more data. We have seen in each of our scenarios that the addition of more data results in the posterior diverging from the prior – usually through a decrease in variance. In fact, if we continue adding more data, we will find that the posteriors for all three scenarios start to look very similar. In Figure 3.14 we see the posteriors for the three scenarios after 100 and 1000 tosses. Compared with the posteriors for the three scenarios after small numbers of tosses have been observed (Figures 3.6(f), 3.10(d) and 3.12(d)), we notice that the posteriors are becoming more and more similar. This is particularly noticeable for scenarios 1 and 3 – by 1000 tosses they are indistinguishable. The difference between these two and the posteriors for scenario 2 is due to the high strength (low variance) of the prior for scenario 2 – the prior corresponds to a very strong belief and it will take a lot of contradictory data to remove that influence.

The diminishing effect of the prior as the quantity of data increases is easily explained if we look at the expression used to compute the posterior. Ignoring the normalising marginal likelihood term, the posterior is proportional to the likelihood multiplied by the prior. As we add more data, the prior is unchanged but the likelihood becomes a product (if the normal independence assumptions are made) of individual likelihood for more and more observations. This increase will gradually swamp the single contribution from the prior. It is also very intuitive – as we observe more and more data, beliefs we had before seeing any become less and less important.

3.4 MARGINAL LIKELIHOODS

Fortunately, subjective beliefs are not the only option for determining which of our three scenarios is best. Earlier in this chapter, when discussing the terms in Equation 3.3, we showed how the denominator $p(y_N)$ could be considered to be related to r as follows:

$$
\begin{aligned}
p(y_N) &= \int_{r=0}^{r=1} p(r, y_N) \, dr \\
&= \int_{r=0}^{r=1} p(y_N | r) p(r) \, dr.
\end{aligned} \tag{3.12}
$$

Now when considering different choices of $p(r)$, we need to be more strict about our conditioning. $p(r)$ should actually be written as $p(r | \alpha, \beta)$ as the density is conditioned on a particular pair of α and β values. Extending this conditioning through Equation 3.12 gives

$$
p(y_N | \alpha, \beta) = \int_{r=0}^{r=1} p(y_N | r) p(r | \alpha, \beta) \, dr. \tag{3.13}
$$

The marginal likelihood (so called because r has been marginalised), $p(y_N | \alpha, \beta)$, is a very useful and important quantity. It tells us how likely the data (y_N) is given our choice of prior parameters α and β. The higher $p(y_N | \alpha, \beta)$, the better our evidence agrees with the prior specification. Hence, for our dataset, we could use $p(y_N | \alpha, \beta)$ to help choose the best scenario: select the scenario for which $p(y_N | \alpha, \beta)$ is highest.

To compute this quantity, we need to evaluate the following integral:

$$
\begin{aligned}
p(y_N | \alpha, \beta) &= \int_{r=0}^{r=1} p(y_N | r) p(r | \alpha, \beta) \, dr \\
&= \int_{r=0}^{r=1} \binom{N}{y_N} r^{y_N} (1-r)^{N-y_N} \frac{\Gamma(\alpha+\beta)}{\Gamma(\alpha)\Gamma(\beta)} r^{\alpha-1} (1-r)^{\beta-1} \, dr \\
&= \binom{N}{y_N} \frac{\Gamma(\alpha+\beta)}{\Gamma(\alpha)\Gamma(\beta)} \int_{r=0}^{r=1} r^{\alpha+y_N-1} (1-r)^{\beta+N-y_N-1} \, dr.
\end{aligned}
$$

This is of exactly the same form as Equation 3.10. The argument inside the integral is an unnormalised beta density and so we know that by integrating it we will get the inverse of the normal beta normalising constant. Therefore,

$$
p(y_N | \alpha, \beta) = \binom{N}{y_N} \frac{\Gamma(\alpha+\beta)}{\Gamma(\alpha)\Gamma(\beta)} \frac{\Gamma(\alpha+y_N)\Gamma(\beta+N-y_N)}{\Gamma(\alpha+\beta+N)}. \tag{3.14}
$$

In our example, $N = 20$ and $y_N = 14$ (there were a total of 14 heads in the 2 sets of 10 tosses). We have three different possible pairs of α and β values. Plugging these values into Equation 3.14 gives

1. No prior knowledge, $\alpha = \beta = 1$, $p(y_N | \alpha, \beta) = 0.0476$.

2. Fair coin, $\alpha = \beta = 50$, $p(y_N | \alpha, \beta) = 0.0441$.

3. Biased coin, $\alpha = 5, \beta = 1$, $p(y_N | \alpha, \beta) = 0.0576$.

The prior corresponding to the biased coin has the highest marginal likelihood and the fair coin prior has the lowest. In the previous section we saw that the probability of winning under that scenario was $\mathbf{E}_{p(r|y_N, \alpha, \beta)} \{P(Y_{new} \leq 6 | r)\} = 0.2915$ (note that we're now conditioning the posterior on the prior parameters – $p(r | y_N, \alpha, \beta)$).

A word of caution is required here. Choosing priors in this way is essentially choosing the prior that best agrees with the data. The prior no longer corresponds to our beliefs *before* we observe any data. In some applications this may be unacceptable. What it does give us is a single value that tells us how much the data backs up the prior beliefs. In the above example, the data suggests that the biased coin prior is best supported by the evidence.

3.4.1 Model comparison with the marginal likelihood

It is possible to extend the prior comparison in the previous section to using the marginal likelihood to optimise α and β. Assuming that α and β can take any value in the ranges

$$0 \leq \quad \alpha \quad \leq 50$$
$$0 \leq \quad \beta \quad \leq 30,$$

we can search for the values of α and β that maximise $p(y_N|\alpha, \beta)$.

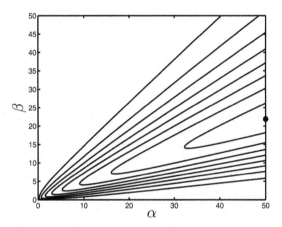

FIGURE 3.15 Marginal likelihood contours (as a function of the prior parameters, α and β) for the coin example. The circle towards the top right shows the optimum.

Figure 3.15 shows the marginal likelihood as α and β are varied in their respective ranges. The optimum value is $\alpha = 50, \beta = 22$, resulting in a marginal likelihood of 0.1694. Choosing parameters in this way is known as Type II Maximum Likelihood (to distinguish it from standard (i.e. Type I) Maximum Likelihood, introduced in Chapter 2).

3.5 HYPERPARAMETERS

The Bayesian analysis presented thus far has all been based on the idea that we can represent any quantities of interest as random variables (e.g. r, the probability of a coin landing heads). r is not the only parameter of interest in our example. α and β are also parameters – could we do the same thing with them? In some cases we can be directed towards particular values based on our knowledge of the problem (we might know that the coin is biased). Often we will not know the exact value that they should take and should therefore treat them as random variables. To do so, we need to define a prior density over all random variables – $p(r, \alpha, \beta)$. This factorises as (see Section 2.2.5)

$$p(r, \alpha, \beta) = p(r|\alpha, \beta)p(\alpha, \beta).$$

In addition, it will often be useful to assume that α and β are independent: $p(\alpha, \beta) = p(\alpha)p(\beta)$. The quantity in which we are interested is the posterior over all parameters in the model:

$$p(r, \alpha, \beta|y_N).$$

Applying Bayes' rule, we have

$$
\begin{aligned}
p(r, \alpha, \beta|y_N) &= \frac{p(y_N|r, \alpha, \beta)p(r, \alpha, \beta)}{p(y_N)} \\
&= \frac{p(y_N|r)p(r, \alpha, \beta)}{p(y_N)} \\
&= \frac{p(y_N|r)p(r|\alpha, \beta)p(\alpha, \beta)}{p(y_N)}.
\end{aligned}
$$

Note that, in the second step, we removed α and β from the likelihood $p(y_N|r)$. This is another example of conditional independence (see Section 2.8.1). The distribution over y_N depends on α and β but only through their influence on r. Conditioned on a particular value of r, this dependence is broken.

$p(\alpha, \beta)$ will normally require some additional parameters – i.e. $p(\alpha, \beta|\kappa)$ where κ controls the density in the same way that α and β control the density for r. κ is known as a **hyper-parameter** because it is a parameter controlling the prior on the parameters controlling the prior on r. When computing the marginal likelihood, we integrate over all random variables and are just left with the data conditioned on the hyperparameters:

$$p(y_N|\kappa) = \iiint p(y_N|r)p(r|\alpha, \beta)p(\alpha, \beta|\kappa) \ dr \ d\alpha \ d\beta.$$

Unfortunately, adding this extra complexity to the model often means that computation of the quantities of interest – the posterior $p(r, \alpha, \beta|y_N, \kappa)$ (and any predictive expectations) and the marginal likelihood $p(y_N|\kappa)$ – is analytically intractable and requires one of the approximation methods that we will introduce in Chapter 4.

At this point, one could imagine indefinitely adding layers to the model. For example, κ could be thought of as a random variable that comes from a density parameterised by other random variables. The number of levels in the hierarchy (how far we go before we fix one or more parameters) will be dictated by the data we are trying to model (perhaps we can specify exact values at some level) or how much computation we can tolerate. In general, the more layers we add the more complex it will be to compute posteriors and predictions.

3.6 GRAPHICAL MODELS

When adding extra layers to our model (hyperparameters, etc.), they can quickly become unwieldy. It is popular to describe them graphically. A **graphical model** is a network where nodes correspond to random variables and edges to dependencies

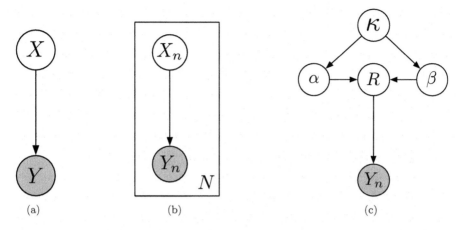

FIGURE 3.16 Graphical model examples. Nodes correspond to random variables, with the shaded nodes corresponding to things that we observe. Arrows describe the dependencies between variables and the plates describe multiple instances. For example, in (b), there are N random variables Y_n $(n = 1, \ldots, N)$ and each is dependent on a random variable X_n. (c) is a graphical representation of the model used in the coin example with the addition of a prior on α and β parameterised by κ.

between random variables. For example, in Section 2.2.4 we introduced various properties of random variables through a model that consisted of two random variables – one representing the toss of a coin (X) and one representing how I say the coin landed (Y). The model is defined through the conditional distribution $P(Y = y | X = x)$ and is represented graphically in Figure 3.16(a). The two nodes are joined by an aarrow to show that Y is defined as being conditioned on X. Note also that the node for Y is shaded. This is because, as far as the listener is concerned, this variable is *observed*. The listener does not see the coin actually landing and so doesn't observe X. Imagine that the procedure was repeated N times; we now have $2N$ random variables, $X_1, \ldots, X_N$ and $Y_1, \ldots, Y_N$. Drawing all of these would be messy. Instead we can embed the nodes within a **plate**. Plates are rectangles that tell us that whatever is embedded within them is repeated a number of times. The number of times is given in the bottom right corner, as shown in Figure 3.16(b).

Figure 3.16(c) shows a graphical representation of our coin toss model. It has a single (observed) random variable that represents the number of heads in N tosses, y_N. This is conditioned on a random variable R, which depends on random variables α and β. Finally, α and β are dependent on the hyper-parameter κ.

More information on graphical models can be found in the suggested reading at the end of the chapter.

3.7 SUMMARY

In the previous sections we have introduced many new concepts. Perhaps the most important is the idea of treating all quantities of interest as random variables. To do this we must define a prior distribution over the possible values of these quantities and then use Bayes' rule (Equation 3.3) to see how the density changes as we incorporate evidence from observed data. The resulting posterior density can be examined and used to compute interesting expectations. In addition, we have shown how the marginal likelihood (the normalisation constant in Bayes' rule) can be used to compare different models – for example, choosing the most likely prior in our coin tossing example – and discussed the possible pitfalls and objections to such an approach. Finally, we have shown how the Bayesian method can be extended by treating parameters that define the priors over other parameters as random variables. Additions to the hierarchy such as this often make analytical computations intractable and we have to resort to sampling and approximation based techniques, which are the subject of the next chapter.

3.8 A BAYESIAN TREATMENT OF THE OLYMPIC 100 m DATA

We now return to the Olympic 100 m data. In the previous chapters we fitted a linear (in the parameters) model by minimising the squared loss and then incorporated an explicit noise model and found optimal parameter values by maximising the likelihood. In this section, we will give the data a Bayesian treatment with the aim of making a prediction for the 2012 Olympics in London. This will involve several steps. Firstly, we will need to define the prior and likelihood (as we did in the coin example) and use these to compute the posterior density over the parameters of our model, just as we computed the posterior over r in the coin example. Once we've computed the posterior, we can use it to make predictions for new Olympic years.

3.8.1 The model

We will use the kth order polynomial model that was introduced in Chapter 1 with the Gaussian noise model introduced in Chapter 2:

$$t_n = w_0 + w_1 x_n + w_2 x_n^2 + \cdots + w_K x_n^K + \epsilon_n,$$

where $\epsilon_n \sim \mathcal{N}(0, \sigma^2)$. In vector form, this corresponds to

$$t_n = \mathbf{w}^\mathsf{T} \mathbf{x}_n + \epsilon_n$$

where $\mathbf{w} = [w_0, \ldots, w_K]^\mathsf{T}$ and $\mathbf{x}_n = [1, x_n, x_n^2, \ldots, x_n^K]^\mathsf{T}$. Stacking all of the responses into one vector $\mathbf{t} = [t_1, \ldots, t_N]^\mathsf{T}$ and all of the inputs into a single matrix, $\mathbf{X} = [\mathbf{x}_1, \mathbf{x}_2, \ldots, \mathbf{x}_N]^\mathsf{T}$ (just as in Equation 1.18), we get the following expression for the whole dataset:

$$\mathbf{t} = \mathbf{X}\mathbf{w} + \boldsymbol{\epsilon},$$

where $\boldsymbol{\epsilon} = [\epsilon_1, \ldots, \epsilon_N]^\mathsf{T}$.

In this example, we are going to slightly simplify matters by assuming that we know the true value of σ^2. We could use all of the methods introduced in this chapter to treat σ^2 as a random variable and we could get analytical results for the posterior

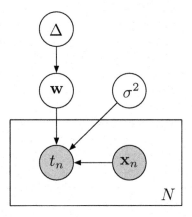

FIGURE 3.17 Graphical model for the Bayesian model of the Olympic men's 100 m data.

distribution but the maths is messier, which could detract from the main message. Substituting these various symbols into Bayes' rule gives

$$
\begin{aligned}
p(\mathbf{w}|\mathbf{t}, \mathbf{X}, \sigma^2, \Delta) &= \frac{p(\mathbf{t}|\mathbf{w}, \mathbf{X}, \sigma^2, \Delta)p(\mathbf{w}|\Delta)}{p(\mathbf{t}|\mathbf{X}, \sigma^2, \Delta)} \\
&= \frac{p(\mathbf{t}|\mathbf{w}, \mathbf{X}, \sigma^2)p(\mathbf{w}|\Delta)}{p(\mathbf{t}|\mathbf{X}, \sigma^2, \Delta)}
\end{aligned}
$$

where Δ corresponds to some set of parameters required to define the prior over $\mathbf{w}$ that will be defined more precisely below. The graphical model can be seen in Figure 3.17. Expanding the marginal likelihood we have

$$
p(\mathbf{w}|\mathbf{t}, \mathbf{X}, \sigma^2, \Delta) = \frac{p(\mathbf{t}|\mathbf{w}, \mathbf{X}, \sigma^2)p(\mathbf{w}|\Delta)}{\int p(\mathbf{t}|\mathbf{w}, \mathbf{X}, \sigma^2)p(\mathbf{w}|\Delta)\ d\mathbf{w}}. \tag{3.15}
$$

We are interested in making predictions which will involve taking an expectation with respect to this posterior density. In particular, for a set of attributes $\mathbf{x}_{\text{new}}$ corresponding to a new Olympic year, the density over the associated winning time t_{new} is given by

$$
p(t_{\text{new}}|\mathbf{x}_{\text{new}}, \mathbf{X}, \mathbf{t}, \sigma^2, \Delta) = \int p(t_{\text{new}}|\mathbf{x}_{\text{new}}, \mathbf{w}, \sigma^2)p(\mathbf{w}|\mathbf{t}, \mathbf{X}, \sigma^2, \Delta)\ d\mathbf{w}. \tag{3.16}
$$

Notice again the conditioning on the right hand side. The posterior density of $\mathbf{w}$ does not depend on $\mathbf{x}_{\text{new}}$ and so it does not appear in the conditioning. Similarly, when we make predictions, we will not be using Δ and so it doesn't appear in $p(t_{\text{new}}|\mathbf{x}_{\text{new}}, \mathbf{w}, \sigma^2)$. Predictions could also take the form of probabilities. For example, we could compute the probability that the winning time will be under 9.5 seconds:

$$
P(t_{\text{new}} < 9.5|\mathbf{x}_{\text{new}}, \mathbf{X}, \mathbf{t}, \sigma^2, \Delta) = \int P(t_{\text{new}} < 9.5|\mathbf{x}_{\text{new}}, \mathbf{w}, \sigma^2)p(\mathbf{w}|\mathbf{t}, \mathbf{X}, \sigma^2, \Delta)\ d\mathbf{w}. \tag{3.17}
$$

3.8.2 The likelihood

The likelihood $p(\mathbf{t}|\mathbf{w}, \mathbf{X}, \sigma^2)$ is exactly the quantity that we maximised in the previous chapter. Our model tells us that

$$\mathbf{t} = \mathbf{Xw} + \boldsymbol{\epsilon}$$

where $\boldsymbol{\epsilon} \sim \mathcal{N}(\mathbf{0}, \sigma^2\mathbf{I}_N)$. This is a Gaussian random variable ($\boldsymbol{\epsilon}$) plus a constant. We showed in Section 2.8 that this is equivalent to the Gaussian random variable with the constant added to the mean. This gives us our likelihood

$$p(\mathbf{t}|\mathbf{w}, \mathbf{X}, \sigma^2) = \mathcal{N}(\mathbf{Xw}, \sigma^2\mathbf{I}_N),$$

an N-dimensional Gaussian density with mean $\mathbf{Xw}$ and variance $\sigma^2\mathbf{I}_N$. The analogous expression in the coin example is the binomial likelihood given in Equation 3.2.

3.8.3 The prior

Because we are interested in being able to produce an exact expression for our posterior, we need to choose a prior, $p(\mathbf{w}|\Delta)$, that is conjugate to the Gaussian likelihood. Conveniently, a Gaussian prior is conjugate to a Gaussian likelihood. Therefore, we will use a Gaussian prior for $\mathbf{w}$. In particular,

$$p(\mathbf{w}|\boldsymbol{\mu}_0, \boldsymbol{\Sigma}_0) = \mathcal{N}(\boldsymbol{\mu}_0, \boldsymbol{\Sigma}_0),$$

where we will choose the parameters $\boldsymbol{\mu}_0$ and $\boldsymbol{\Sigma}_0$ later. This is analogous to Equation 3.4 in the coin example. From now on we will not always explicitly condition on $\boldsymbol{\mu}_0$ and $\boldsymbol{\Sigma}_0$ in our expressions. For example, for brevity, instead of writing $p(\mathbf{w}|\mathbf{t}, \mathbf{X}, \sigma^2, \boldsymbol{\mu}_0, \boldsymbol{\Sigma}_0)$ we will use $p(\mathbf{w}|\mathbf{t}, \mathbf{X}, \sigma^2)$ (see Exercise 3.10).

3.8.4 The posterior

We now turn our attention to computing the posterior. As in the coin example, we will use the fact that we *know* that the posterior will be Gaussian. This allows us to ignore the marginal likelihood in Equation 3.15 and just manipulate the likelihood and prior until we find something that is proportional to a Gaussian. As a first step, we can collect the terms in $\mathbf{w}$ together and ignore any term that does not include $\mathbf{w}$:

$$
\begin{aligned}
p(\mathbf{w}|\mathbf{t}, \mathbf{X}, \sigma^2) \;\propto\; & p(\mathbf{t}|\mathbf{w}, \mathbf{X}, \sigma^2)p(\mathbf{w}|\boldsymbol{\mu}_0, \boldsymbol{\Sigma}_0) \\
= \; & \frac{1}{(2\pi)^{N/2}|\sigma^2\mathbf{I}|^{1/2}} \exp\left(-\frac{1}{2}(\mathbf{t} - \mathbf{Xw})^\mathsf{T}(\sigma^2\mathbf{I})^{-1}(\mathbf{t} - \mathbf{Xw})\right) \\
& \times \frac{1}{(2\pi)^{N/2}|\boldsymbol{\Sigma}_0|^{1/2}} \exp\left(-\frac{1}{2}(\mathbf{w} - \boldsymbol{\mu}_0)^\mathsf{T}\boldsymbol{\Sigma}_0^{-1}(\mathbf{w} - \boldsymbol{\mu}_0)\right) \\
\propto \; & \exp\left(-\frac{1}{2\sigma^2}(\mathbf{t} - \mathbf{Xw})^\mathsf{T}(\mathbf{t} - \mathbf{Xw})\right) \\
& \times \exp\left(-\frac{1}{2}(\mathbf{w} - \boldsymbol{\mu}_0)^\mathsf{T}\boldsymbol{\Sigma}_0^{-1}(\mathbf{w} - \boldsymbol{\mu}_0)\right) \\
= \; & \exp\left\{-\frac{1}{2}\left(\frac{1}{\sigma^2}(\mathbf{t} - \mathbf{Xw})^\mathsf{T}(\mathbf{t} - \mathbf{Xw}) + (\mathbf{w} - \boldsymbol{\mu}_0)^\mathsf{T}\boldsymbol{\Sigma}_0^{-1}(\mathbf{w} - \boldsymbol{\mu}_0)\right)\right\}.
\end{aligned}
$$

Multiplying the terms in the bracket out and once again removing any that don't involve $\mathbf{w}$ gives

$$p(\mathbf{w}|\mathbf{t}, \mathbf{X}, \sigma^2) \propto \exp\left\{-\frac{1}{2}\left(-\frac{2}{\sigma^2}\mathbf{t}^\mathsf{T}\mathbf{X}\mathbf{w} + \frac{1}{\sigma^2}\mathbf{w}^\mathsf{T}\mathbf{X}^\mathsf{T}\mathbf{X}\mathbf{w} + \mathbf{w}^\mathsf{T}\boldsymbol{\Sigma}_0^{-1}\mathbf{w} - 2\boldsymbol{\mu}_0^\mathsf{T}\boldsymbol{\Sigma}_0^{-1}\mathbf{w}\right)\right\}.$$

We know that the posterior will be Gaussian. Therefore we can remove the constants (i.e. terms not involving $\mathbf{w}$) and rearrange an expression for a multivariate Gaussian to make it look something like the expression we have above:

$$\begin{aligned}
p(\mathbf{w}|\mathbf{t}, \mathbf{X}, \sigma^2) &= \mathcal{N}(\boldsymbol{\mu}_\mathbf{w}, \boldsymbol{\Sigma}_\mathbf{w}) \\
&\propto \exp\left(-\frac{1}{2}(\mathbf{w} - \boldsymbol{\mu}_\mathbf{w})^\mathsf{T}\boldsymbol{\Sigma}_\mathbf{w}^{-1}(\mathbf{w} - \boldsymbol{\mu}_\mathbf{w})\right) \\
&\propto \exp\left\{-\frac{1}{2}\left(\mathbf{w}^\mathsf{T}\boldsymbol{\Sigma}_\mathbf{w}^{-1}\mathbf{w} - 2\boldsymbol{\mu}_\mathbf{w}^\mathsf{T}\boldsymbol{\Sigma}_\mathbf{w}^{-1}\mathbf{w}\right)\right\}. \quad (3.18)
\end{aligned}$$

The terms linear and quadratic in $\mathbf{w}$ in Equation 3.8.4 must be equal to those in Equation 3.18. Taking the quadratic terms, we can solve for $\boldsymbol{\Sigma}_\mathbf{w}$:

$$\begin{aligned}
\mathbf{w}^\mathsf{T}\boldsymbol{\Sigma}_\mathbf{w}^{-1}\mathbf{w} &= \frac{1}{\sigma^2}\mathbf{w}^\mathsf{T}\mathbf{X}^\mathsf{T}\mathbf{X}\mathbf{w} + \mathbf{w}^\mathsf{T}\boldsymbol{\Sigma}_0^{-1}\mathbf{w} \\
&= \mathbf{w}^\mathsf{T}\left(\frac{1}{\sigma^2}\mathbf{X}^\mathsf{T}\mathbf{X} + \boldsymbol{\Sigma}_0^{-1}\right)\mathbf{w}
\end{aligned}$$

$$\boxed{\boldsymbol{\Sigma}_\mathbf{w} = \left(\frac{1}{\sigma^2}\mathbf{X}^\mathsf{T}\mathbf{X} + \boldsymbol{\Sigma}_0^{-1}\right)^{-1}.}$$

Similarly, equating the linear terms from Equations 3.8.4 and 3.18 (and using our new expression for $\boldsymbol{\Sigma}_\mathbf{w}$) we can get an expression for $\boldsymbol{\mu}_\mathbf{w}$:

$$\begin{aligned}
-2\boldsymbol{\mu}_\mathbf{w}^\mathsf{T}\boldsymbol{\Sigma}_\mathbf{w}^{-1}\mathbf{w} &= -\frac{2}{\sigma^2}\mathbf{t}^\mathsf{T}\mathbf{X}\mathbf{w} - 2\boldsymbol{\mu}_0^\mathsf{T}\boldsymbol{\Sigma}_0^{-1}\mathbf{w} \\
\boldsymbol{\mu}_\mathbf{w}^\mathsf{T}\boldsymbol{\Sigma}_\mathbf{w}^{-1}\mathbf{w} &= \frac{1}{\sigma^2}\mathbf{t}^\mathsf{T}\mathbf{X}\mathbf{w} + \boldsymbol{\mu}_0^\mathsf{T}\boldsymbol{\Sigma}_0^{-1}\mathbf{w} \\
\boldsymbol{\mu}_\mathbf{w}^\mathsf{T}\boldsymbol{\Sigma}_\mathbf{w}^{-1} &= \frac{1}{\sigma^2}\mathbf{t}^\mathsf{T}\mathbf{X} + \boldsymbol{\mu}_0^\mathsf{T}\boldsymbol{\Sigma}_0^{-1} \\
\boldsymbol{\mu}_\mathbf{w}^\mathsf{T}\boldsymbol{\Sigma}_\mathbf{w}^{-1}\boldsymbol{\Sigma}_\mathbf{w} &= \left(\frac{1}{\sigma^2}\mathbf{t}^\mathsf{T}\mathbf{X} + \boldsymbol{\mu}_0^\mathsf{T}\boldsymbol{\Sigma}_0^{-1}\right)\boldsymbol{\Sigma}_\mathbf{w} \\
\boldsymbol{\mu}_\mathbf{w}^\mathsf{T} &= \left(\frac{1}{\sigma^2}\mathbf{t}^\mathsf{T}\mathbf{X} + \boldsymbol{\mu}_0^\mathsf{T}\boldsymbol{\Sigma}_0^{-1}\right)\boldsymbol{\Sigma}_\mathbf{w}
\end{aligned}$$

$$\boxed{\boldsymbol{\mu}_\mathbf{w} = \boldsymbol{\Sigma}_\mathbf{w}\left(\frac{1}{\sigma^2}\mathbf{X}^\mathsf{T}\mathbf{t} + \boldsymbol{\Sigma}_0^{-1}\boldsymbol{\mu}_0\right),} \quad (3.19)$$

because $\boldsymbol{\Sigma}_\mathbf{w}^\mathsf{T} = \boldsymbol{\Sigma}_\mathbf{w}$ due to the fact that it must be symmetric. Therefore,

$$p(\mathbf{w}|\mathbf{t}, \mathbf{X}, \sigma^2) = \mathcal{N}(\boldsymbol{\mu}_\mathbf{w}, \boldsymbol{\Sigma}_\mathbf{w}) \quad (3.20)$$

where

$$\boldsymbol{\Sigma}_\mathbf{w} = \left(\frac{1}{\sigma^2}\mathbf{X}^\mathsf{T}\mathbf{X} + \boldsymbol{\Sigma}_0^{-1}\right)^{-1} \quad (3.21)$$

$$\boldsymbol{\mu}_\mathbf{w} = \boldsymbol{\Sigma}_\mathbf{w}\left(\frac{1}{\sigma^2}\mathbf{X}^\mathsf{T}\mathbf{t} + \boldsymbol{\Sigma}_0^{-1}\boldsymbol{\mu}_0\right) \quad (3.22)$$

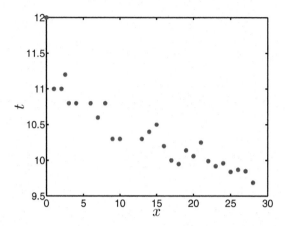

FIGURE 3.18 Olympic data with rescaled x values.

(see Exercise 3.12). These expressions do not look too far away from things we have seen before. In particular, compare Equation 3.22 with the regularised least squares solution given in Equation 1.21. In fact, if $\boldsymbol{\mu}_0 = [0, 0, \dots, 0]^{\mathsf{T}}$, the expressions are almost identical. Given that the posterior is a Gaussian, the single most likely value of $\mathbf{w}$ is the mean of the posterior, $\boldsymbol{\mu}_{\mathbf{w}}$. This is known as the **maximum a posteriori** (MAP) estimate of $\mathbf{w}$ and can also be thought of as the maximum value of the joint density $p(\mathbf{w}, \mathbf{t} | \mathbf{X}, \sigma^2, \Delta)$ (the likelihood multiplied by the prior). We have already seen that the squared loss considered in Chapter 1 is very similar to a Gaussian likelihood and it follows from this that computing the most likely posterior value (when the likelihood is Gaussian) is equivalent to using regularised least squares (see Exercise 3.9). This comparison can often help to provide intuition regarding the effect of the prior.

3.8.5 A first-order polynomial

We will illustrate the prior and posterior with a first-order polynomial, as it is possible to visualise densities in the two-dimensional parameter space. The input vectors also have two elements, $\mathbf{x}_n = [1, \ x_n]^{\mathsf{T}}$. To aid visualisation, we will rescale the Olympic year by subtracting the year of the first Olympics (1896) from each year and then dividing each number by 4. This means that x_1 is now 0, x_2 is 1, etc. The data with this new x scaling is plotted in Figure 3.18.

Returning to the fairground, the first step in our analysis is the choice of prior parameters $\boldsymbol{\mu}_0$ and $\boldsymbol{\Sigma}_0$. For $\boldsymbol{\mu}_0$, we will assume that we don't really know anything about what the parameters should be and choose $\boldsymbol{\mu}_0 = [0, 0]^{\mathsf{T}}$. For the covariance, we will use

$$\boldsymbol{\Sigma}_0 = \begin{bmatrix} 100 & 0 \\ 0 & 5 \end{bmatrix}.$$

The larger value for the variance of w_0 is due to the fact that we saw in the maximum likelihood estimate that the optimal value of w_0 was much higher than that for w_1. We have also assumed that the two variables are independent in the prior by setting

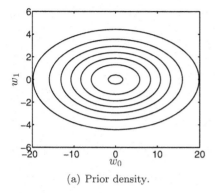

(a) Prior density.

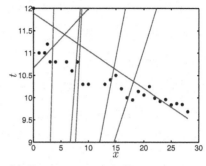

(b) Functions created from parameters drawn from prior.

FIGURE 3.19 Gaussian prior used for the Olympic 100 m data (a) and some functions created with samples drawn from the prior (b).

the off-diagonal elements in the covariance matrix to zero. This does not preclude them from being dependent in the posterior. The contours of this prior density can be seen in Figure 3.19(a). It's hard to visualise what this means in terms of the model. To help, in Figure 3.19(b) we have shown functions corresponding to several sets of parameters drawn from this prior. To create these, we sampled $\mathbf{w}$ from the Gaussian defined by $\boldsymbol{\mu}_0$ and $\boldsymbol{\Sigma}_0$ and then substituted these into our linear model – $t_n = w_0 + w_1 x_n$. The examples show that the prior admits the possibility of many very different models.

Using $\sigma^2 = 10$ for illustrative purposes (MATLAB script: olympbayes.m), we can now compute the posterior distribution when we observe one data point. Using the data point corresponding to the first Olympics, our data is summarised as $\mathbf{x} = [1, 0]^{\mathsf{T}}$, $\mathbf{X} = [1, 0]$, $\mathbf{t} = [12]$. Plugging these values along with our prior parameters and $\sigma^2 = 10$ into Equations 3.20–3.22, we obtain the posterior distribution shown in Figure 3.20(a). The posterior now has much more certainty regarding w_0 but still knows very little about w_1. This makes sense – we've provided a data point at $x = 0$ so this should be highly informative in determining the intercept but tells us very little about the gradient (one data point alone could never tell us much about the gradient). Some functions created with samples from this posterior are shown in Figure 3.20(b). They look quite different from those from the prior – in particular, they all pass quite close to our first data point.

Figures 3.20(c), 3.20(d) and 3.20(e) show the evolution of the posterior after 2, 5 and 10 data points, respectively. Just as in the coin example, we notice that the posterior becomes more condensed (we are becoming more certain about the value of $\mathbf{w}$). Also, as it evolves, the posterior begins to tilt. This is indicative of a dependence developing between the two parameters – if we increase the intercept w_0, we must decrease the gradient. Recall that, in the prior, we assumed that the two parameters were independent ($\boldsymbol{\Sigma}_0$ only had non-zero values on the diagonal) so this dependence is coming entirely from the evidence within the data. To help visualise what the posterior means at this stage, Figure 3.20(f) shows a set of functions made from parameters drawn from the posterior. When compared with Figure 3.20(b),

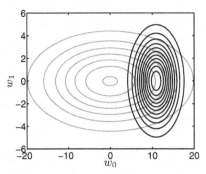

(a) Posterior density (dark contours) after the first data point has been observed. The lighter contours show the prior density.

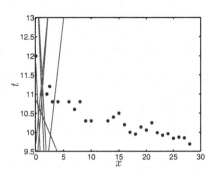

(b) Functions created from parameters drawn from the posterior after observing the first data point.

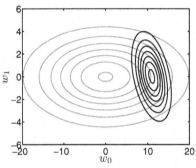

(c) Posterior density (dark contours) after the first two data points have been observed.

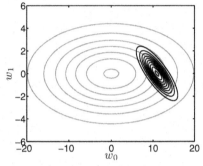

(d) Posterior density (dark contours) after the first five data points have been observed.

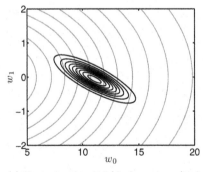

(e) Posterior density (dark contours) after the first ten data points have been observed. (Note that we have zoomed in.)

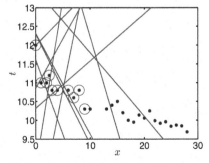

(f) Functions created from parameters drawn from the posterior after observing the first ten (highlighted) data points.

FIGURE 3.20 Evolution of the posterior density and example functions drawn from the posterior for the Olympic data as observations are added.

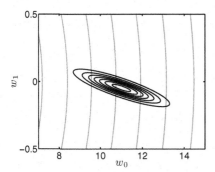

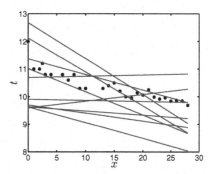

(a) Posterior density (dark contours) after all datapoints have been observed. The lighter contours show the prior density. (Note that we have zoomed in.)

(b) Functions created from parameters drawn from the posterior after observing all data points.

FIGURE 3.21 Posterior density (a) and sampled functions (b) for the Olympic data when all 27 data points have been added.

we see that the posterior density is beginning to favour parameters that correspond to models suited to our data. Finally, in Figure 3.21(a) we see the posterior after all 27 data points have been included and in Figure 3.21(b) we see functions drawn from this posterior. The functions are really now beginning to follow the trend in our data. There is still a lot of variability though. This is due to the relatively high value of $\sigma^2 = 10$ that we chose to help visualise the prior and posteriors. For making predictions, we might want to use a more realistic value. In Figure 3.22(a) we show the posterior after all data has been observed for $\sigma^2 = 0.05$ (this is roughly the maximum likelihood value we obtained in Section 2.8.2). The posterior is now far more condensed – very little variability remains in $\mathbf{w}$, as can be seen by the homogeneity of the set of functions drawn in Figure 3.22(b). We will now turn our attention to making predictions.

3.8.6 Making predictions

Given a new observation $\mathbf{x}_{\text{new}}$, we are interested in the density

$$p(t_{\text{new}}|\mathbf{x}_{\text{new}}, \mathbf{X}, \mathbf{t}, \sigma^2).$$

Notice that this is not conditioned on $\mathbf{w}$ – just as in the coin example, we are going to integrate out $\mathbf{w}$ by taking an expectation with respect to the posterior, $p(\mathbf{w}|\mathbf{t}, \mathbf{X}, \sigma^2)$. In particular, we need to compute

$$
\begin{aligned}
p(t_{\text{new}}|\mathbf{x}_{\text{new}}, \mathbf{X}, \mathbf{t}, \sigma^2) &= \mathbf{E}_{p(\mathbf{w}|\mathbf{t}, \mathbf{X}, \sigma^2)} \left\{ p(t_{\text{new}}|\mathbf{x}_{\text{new}}, \mathbf{w}, \sigma^2) \right\} \\
&= \int p(t_{\text{new}}|\mathbf{x}_{\text{new}}, \mathbf{w}, \sigma^2) p(\mathbf{w}|\mathbf{t}, \mathbf{X}, \sigma^2) \, d\mathbf{w}.
\end{aligned}
$$

This is analogous to Equation 3.9 in the coin example.

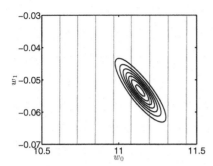

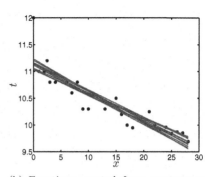

(a) Posterior density (dark contours) after all data points have been observed. The lighter contours show the prior density. (Note that we have zoomed in.)

(b) Functions created from parameters drawn from the posterior after observing all data points.

FIGURE 3.22 Posterior density (a) and sampled functions (b) for the Olympic data when all 27 data points have been added with more realistic noise variance, $\sigma^2 = 0.05$.

$p(t_{new}|\mathbf{x}_{new}, \mathbf{w}, \sigma^2)$ is defined by our model as the product of $\mathbf{x}_{new}$ and $\mathbf{w}$ with some additive Gaussian noise:

$$p(t_{new}|\mathbf{x}_{new}, \mathbf{w}, \sigma^2) = \mathcal{N}(\mathbf{x}_{new}^T\mathbf{w}, \sigma^2).$$

Because this expression and the posterior are both Gaussian, the result of the expectation is another Gaussian. In general, if $p(\mathbf{w}|\boldsymbol{\mu}, \boldsymbol{\Sigma}) = \mathcal{N}(\boldsymbol{\mu}, \boldsymbol{\Sigma})$, then the expectation of another Gaussian density $(\mathcal{N}(\mathbf{x}_{new}^T\mathbf{w}, \sigma^2))$ is given by

$$p(t_{new}|\mathbf{x}_{new}, \mathbf{X}, \mathbf{t}, \sigma^2) = \mathcal{N}(\mathbf{x}_{new}^T\boldsymbol{\mu}_\mathbf{w}, \sigma^2 + \mathbf{x}_{new}^T\boldsymbol{\Sigma}_\mathbf{w}\mathbf{x}_{new}).$$

For the posterior shown in Figure 3.22(a), this is

$$p(t_{new}|\mathbf{x}_{new}, \mathbf{X}, \mathbf{t}, \sigma^2) = \mathcal{N}(9.5951, 0.0572)$$

and is plotted in Figure 3.23.

This density looks rather like the predictive densities we obtained from the maximum likelihood solution in Chapter 2. However, there is one crucial difference. With the maximum likelihood we chose one particular model: the one corresponding to the highest likelihood. To generate the density shown in Figure 3.23, we have averaged over all models that are consistent with our data and prior (we averaged over our posterior). Hence this density takes into account all uncertainty that remains in $\mathbf{w}$ given a particular prior and the data.

3.9 MARGINAL LIKELIHOOD FOR POLYNOMIAL MODEL OR-DER SELECTION

In Section 1.5 we used a cross-validation procedure to select the order of polynomial to be used. The cross-validation procedure correctly identified that the dataset was

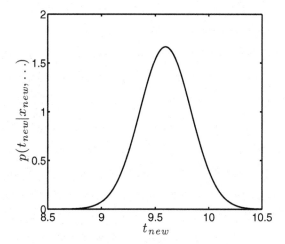

FIGURE 3.23 Predictive distribution for the winning time in the men's 100 m sprint at the 2012 London Olympics.

generated from a third-order polynomial. In Section 3.4 we saw how the marginal likelihood could be used to choose prior densities. We will now see that it can also be used to choose models. In particular, we will use it to determine which order polynomial function to use for some synthetic data.

The marginal likelihood for our Gaussian model is defined as

$$p(\mathbf{t}|\mathbf{X}, \boldsymbol{\mu}_0, \boldsymbol{\Sigma}_0) = \int p(\mathbf{t}|\mathbf{X}, \mathbf{w}, \sigma^2)p(\mathbf{w}|\boldsymbol{\mu}_0, \boldsymbol{\Sigma}_0) \, d\mathbf{w}.$$

This is analogous to Equation 3.14 in the coin example. It is of the same form as the predictive density discussed in the previous section and is another Gaussian,

$$p(\mathbf{t}|\mathbf{X}, \boldsymbol{\mu}_0, \boldsymbol{\Sigma}_0) = \mathcal{N}(\mathbf{X}\boldsymbol{\mu}_0, \sigma^2\mathbf{I}_N + \mathbf{X}\boldsymbol{\Sigma}_0\mathbf{X}^\mathsf{T}), \tag{3.23}$$

which we evaluate at $\mathbf{t}$ – the responses in the training set. Just as in Section 1.5, we will generate data from a noisy third-order polynomial and then compute the marginal likelihood for models from first to seventh-order. For each possible model, we will use a Gaussian prior on $\mathbf{w}$ with zero mean and an identity covariance matrix. For example, for the first-order model,

$$\boldsymbol{\mu}_0 = [0, 0]^\mathsf{T}, \ \boldsymbol{\Sigma}_0 = \begin{bmatrix} 1 & 0 \\ 0 & 1 \end{bmatrix}$$

and for the fourth-order model

$$\boldsymbol{\mu}_0 = [0, 0, 0, 0, 0]^\mathsf{T}, \ \boldsymbol{\Sigma}_0 = \begin{bmatrix} 1 & 0 & 0 & 0 & 0 \\ 0 & 1 & 0 & 0 & 0 \\ 0 & 0 & 1 & 0 & 0 \\ 0 & 0 & 0 & 1 & 0 \\ 0 & 0 & 0 & 0 & 1 \end{bmatrix}.$$

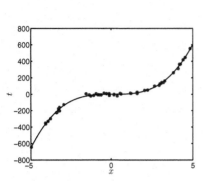

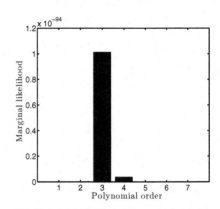

(a) Noisy data from a third-order polynomial.

(b) Marginal likelihood for models of different order.

FIGURE 3.24 Dataset sampled from the function $t = 5x^3 - x^2 + x$ (a) and marginal likelihoods for polynomials of increasing order (b).

The data and true polynomial are shown in Figure 3.24(a) (MATLAB script: `margpoly.m`). The true polynomial is $t = 5x^3 - x^2 + x$ and Gaussian noise has been added with mean zero and variance 150. The marginal likelihood for models from first to seventh order is calculated by plugging the relevant prior into Equation 3.23 and then evaluating this density at $\mathbf{t}$, the observed responses. The values are shown in Figure 3.24(b). We can see that the marginal likelihood value is very sharply peaked at the true third-order model. The advantage of this over the cross-validation method is that, for this model, it is computationally undemanding (we don't have to fit several different datasets). We can also use all the data. However, as we have already mentioned, calculating the marginal likelihood is, in general, very difficult and we will often find it easier to resort to cross-validation techniques.

The marginal likelihood is conditioned on the prior parameters and so changing them will have an effect on the marginal likelihood values and possibly the highest scoring model. To show the effect of this, we can define $\boldsymbol{\Sigma}_0 = \sigma_0^2 \mathbf{I}$ and vary σ_0^2. We have already seen the result for $\sigma_0^2 = 1$. If we decrease σ_0^2, we see higher-order models performing better. This can be seen in Figure 3.25. Decreasing σ_0^2 from 1 to 0.3 results in the seventh-order polynomial becoming the most likely model. By decreasing σ_0^2, we are saying that the parameters have to take smaller and smaller values. For a third order polynomial model to fit well, one of the parameters needs to be 5 (recall that $t = 5x^3 - x^2 + x$). As we decrease σ_0^2, this becomes less and less likely, and higher-order models with lower parameter values become more likely. This emphasises the importance of understanding what we mean by a model. In this example, the model consists of the order of polynomial *and* the prior specification and we must be careful to choose the prior sensibly (see Exercise 3.11).

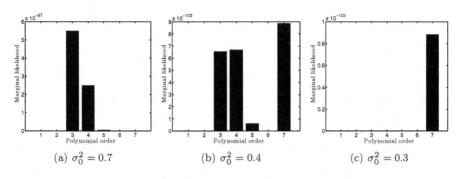

(a) $\sigma_0^2 = 0.7$ (b) $\sigma_0^2 = 0.4$ (c) $\sigma_0^2 = 0.3$

FIGURE 3.25 Marginal likelihoods for the third-order polynomial example with $\boldsymbol{\Sigma}_0 = \sigma_0^2 \mathbf{I}$ as σ_0^2 is decreased.

3.10 CHAPTER SUMMARY

This chapter has provided an introduction to the Bayesian way of performing Machine Learning tasks – treating all parameters as random variables. We have performed a Baysesian analysis for a coin tossing model and the linear regression model introduced in Chapters 1 and 2. In both cases, we defined prior densities over parameters, defined likelihoods and computed posterior densities. In both examples, the prior and likelihood were chosen such that the posterior could be computed analytically. In addition, we computed predictions by taking expectations with respect to the posterior and introduced marginal likelihood as a possible model selection criterion.

Unfortunately, these expressions are not often analytically tractable and we must resort to sampling and approximation techniques. These techniques are the foundations of modern Bayesian inference and form an important area of Machine Learning research and development. The next chapter will describe three popular techniques – point estimates, Laplace approximations and Markov chain Monte Carlo.

3.11 EXERCISES

3.1 For $\alpha, \beta = 1$, the beta distribution becomes uniform between 0 and 1. In particular, if the probability of a coin landing heads is given by r and a beta prior is placed over r, with parameters $\alpha = 1, \beta = 1$, this prior can be written as

$$p(r) = 1 \ (0 \le r \le 1).$$

Using this prior, compute the posterior density for r if y heads are observed in N tosses (i.e. multiply this prior by the binomial likelihood and manipulate the result to obtain something that looks like a beta density).

3.2 Repeat the previous exercise for the following prior, also a particular form of the beta density:

$$p(r) = \begin{cases} 2r & 0 \le r \le 1 \\ 0 & \text{otherwise} \end{cases}$$

What are the values of the prior parameters α and β that result in $p(r) = 2r$?

3.3 Repeat the previous exercise for the following prior (again, a form of beta density):

$$p(r) = \begin{cases} 3r^2 & 0 \leq r \leq 1 \\ 0 & \text{otherwise.} \end{cases}$$

What are the prior parameters here?

3.4 What are the effective prior sample sizes (α and β) for the previous three exercises (i.e. how many heads and tails are they equivalent to)?

3.5 If a random variable R has a beta density

$$p(r) = \frac{\Gamma(\alpha + \beta)}{\Gamma(\alpha)\Gamma(\beta)} r^{\alpha-1}(1-r)^{\beta-1},$$

derive an expression for the expected value of r, $\mathbf{E}_{p(r)}\{r\}$. You will need the following identity for the gamma function:

$$\Gamma(n+1) = n\Gamma(n).$$

Hint: Use the fact that

$$\int_{r=0}^{r=1} r^{a-1}(1-r)^{b-1} \, dr = \frac{\Gamma(a)\Gamma(b)}{\Gamma(a+b)}.$$

3.6 Using the setup in the previous exercise, and the identity

$$\text{var}\{r\} = \mathbf{E}_{p(r)}\{r^2\} - \left(\mathbf{E}_{p(r)}\{r\}\right)^2,$$

derive an expression for $\text{var}\{r\}$. You will need the gamma identity given in the previous exercise.

3.7 At a different stall, you observe 20 tosses of which 9 were heads. Compute the posteriors for the three scenarios, the probability of winning in each case and the marginal likelihoods.

3.8 Use MATLAB to generate coin tosses where the probability of heads is 0.7. Generate 100 tosses and compute the posteriors for the three scenarios, the probabilities of winning and the marginal likelihoods.

3.9 In Section 3.8.4 we derived an expression for the Gaussian posterior for a linear model within the context of the Olympic 100 m data. Substituting $\mu_0 = [0, 0, \ldots, 0]^{\mathsf{T}}$, we saw the similarity between the posterior mean

$$\mu_{\mathbf{w}} = \frac{1}{\sigma^2} \left(\frac{1}{\sigma^2}\mathbf{X}^{\mathsf{T}}\mathbf{X} + \Sigma_0^{-1}\right)^{-1} \mathbf{X}^{\mathsf{T}}\mathbf{t}$$

and the regularised least squares solution

$$\widehat{\mathbf{w}} = \left(\mathbf{X}^{\mathsf{T}}\mathbf{X} + N\lambda\mathbf{I}\right)^{-1} \mathbf{X}^{\mathsf{T}}\mathbf{t}.$$

For this particular example, find the prior covariance matrix Σ_0 that makes the two identical. In other words, find Σ_0 in terms of λ.

3.10 Redraw the graphical representation of the Olympic 100 m model to reflect the fact that the prior over $\mathbf{w}$ is actually conditioned on μ_0 and Σ_0.

3.11 In Figure 3.25 we studied the effect of reducing σ_0^2 on the marginal likelihood. Using MATLAB, investigate the effect of increasing σ_0^2.

3.12 When performing a Bayesian analysis on the Olympics data, we assumed that the prior was known. If a Gaussian prior is placed on $\mathbf{w}$ and an inverse gamma prior on the variance σ^2

$$p(\sigma^2|\alpha, \beta) = \frac{\beta^\alpha}{\Gamma(\alpha)}(\sigma^2)^{-\alpha-1}\exp\left\{-\frac{\beta}{\sigma^2}\right\},$$

the posterior will also be the product of a Gaussian and an inverse gamma. Compute the posterior parameters.

3.12 FURTHER READING

[1] Ben Calderhead and Mark Girolami. Estimating Bayes factors via thermodynamic integration and population MCMC. *Comput. Stat. Data Anal.*, 53:4028–4045, October 2009.

An article by the authors describing a novel approach for calculating the marginal likelihoods (Bayes factors) in models where it is not analytically tractable.

[2] Andrew Gelman, John B. Carlin, Hal S. Stern, and Donald B. Rubin. *Bayesian Data Analysis*. Chapman and Hall/CRC, second edition, 2004.

One of the most popular textbooks on Bayesian inference. Provides a detailed and practical description of Bayesian Inference.

[3] Michael Isard and Andrew Blake. Contour tracking by stochastic propagation of conditional density. In *European Conference on Computer Vision*, pages 343–356, 1996.

An interesting example of the use of Bayesian methods in the field of human computer interaction. The authors use a sampling technique to infer posterior probabilities over gestures being performed by users.

[4] Michael Jordan, editor. *Learning in Graphical Models*. MIT Press, 1999.

An introduction to the field of graphical models and how to use them for learning tasks.

[5] Christian Robert. *The Bayesian Choice: From Decision-Theoretic Foundations to Computational Implementation*. Springer, second edition edition, 2007.

[6] Tian-Rui Xu et al. Inferring signaling pathway topologies from multiple perturbation measurement of specific biochemical species. *Science Signalling*, 3(113), 2010.

A paper showing how Bayesian model selection via the marginal likelihood can be used to answer interesting scientific questions in the field of biology. It is also an interesting example of large-scale Bayesian sampling.

CHAPTER 4

Bayesian Inference

In the previous chapter we introduced the key concepts required to adopt a Bayesian approach to machine learning. Within the Bayesian framework, all unknown quantities are treated as random variables. Each parameter is described by a distribution rather than an individual value. Uncertainty in our parameter estimates is naturally channeled into any predictions we make. We saw two examples of *prior* and *likelihood* combinations that were *conjugate*, meaning that the *posterior* would be of the same form as the prior and could be computed analytically. Examples where we can justify the choice of a conjugate prior and likelihood combination are rare. In the remainder, we cannot compute the posterior and must resort to approximations. In this chapter, we will introduce three such approximation techniques.

4.1 NON-CONJUGATE MODELS

In the previous chapter we saw two models for which exact Bayesian inference was possible. In the first case, we were modelling the tossing of a coin and the combination of a beta prior and binomial likelihood meant that we could state that the posterior would also belong to the beta family. In the second example, a Gaussian prior coupled with a Gaussian likelihood resulted in a Gaussian posterior. The fact that we knew the form of the posterior meant that we didn't need to calculate the normalisation constant (the denominator in, for example, Equation 3.3). As long as we could find something proportional to the density of interest (i.e. proportional to a beta or a Gaussian), we could be certain that the normalisation would take care of itself. The beta-binomial and Gaussian-Gaussian combinations are not the only conjugate prior-likelihood pairs that we can use. Two other popular examples are the multinomial-Dirichlet and the gamma-Gaussian for discrete and continuous data, respectively.

For many models, it is not possible (or not justifiable from a modelling perspective) to pick a conjugate prior and likelihood, and we are forced to approximate. In this chapter, we will introduce three approximation techniques through a binary classification problem. Binary classification is a common problem within machine learning and one for which no conjugate prior and likelihood combination exists. The three techniques that we will look at are a point estimate, an approximate density, and sampling. All three are widely used within machine learning.

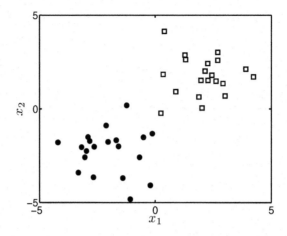

FIGURE 4.1 An example of a dataset with a binary response. Each object is defined by two attributes (x_1 and x_2) and a binary target, $t = \{0, 1\}$. Points with $t = 0$ are plotted as circles and those with $t = 1$ as squares.

4.2   BINARY RESPONSES

Figure 4.1 shows a dataset that looks a bit different from those we have seen so far. Each object is described by two attributes, x_1 and x_2, and has a binary response, $t = \{0, 1\}$. The objects are plotted with a symbol that depends on their response: if $t = 0$, the point is plotted as a circle, and, if $t = 1$, as a square. We will use this data to build a model that will enable us to predict the response (0 or 1; circle or square) for a new object. This task is known as classification – we want to be able to classify objects into one of a set of classes (in this case there are two classes). Classification is one of the major problems within machine learning, and we will introduce several other classification algorithms in Chapter 5.

4.2.1   A model for binary responses

We will work with the following vector and matrix representations of our data:

$$
\mathbf{x}_n = \left[\begin{array}{c} x_{n1} \\ x_{n2} \end{array} \right], \quad \mathbf{w} = \left[\begin{array}{c} w_1 \\ w_2 \end{array} \right], \quad \mathbf{X} = \left[\begin{array}{c} \mathbf{x}_1^\mathsf{T} \\ \mathbf{x}_2^\mathsf{T} \\ \vdots \\ \mathbf{x}_N^\mathsf{T} \end{array} \right].
$$

Our model (with parameters $\mathbf{w}$) will allow us to predict t_{new} for some new observation $\mathbf{x}_{\text{new}}$.

Just as in our Olympics example in Section 3.8, we will need to compute the posterior density over the parameters of the model. According to Bayes' rule, this is given by

$$p(\mathbf{w}|\mathbf{t}, \mathbf{X}) = \frac{p(\mathbf{t}|\mathbf{X}, \mathbf{w})p(\mathbf{w})}{p(\mathbf{t}|\mathbf{X})} \tag{4.1}$$

where the marginal likelihood $p(\mathbf{t}|\mathbf{X})$ is given by

$$p(\mathbf{t}|\mathbf{X}) = \int p(\mathbf{t}|\mathbf{X}, \mathbf{w})p(\mathbf{w}) \; d\mathbf{w}.$$

Prior: We shall use a Gaussian density for the prior, $p(\mathbf{w})$. In particular, $p(\mathbf{w}) = \mathcal{N}(\mathbf{0}, \sigma^2\mathbf{I})$. To be consistent, given that $p(\mathbf{w})$ depends on σ^2, we will denote the prior as $p(\mathbf{w}|\sigma^2)$. In previous chapters, the choice of a Gaussian density was often motivated by analytical convenience. Given that we are not going to be able to rely on conjugacy in this chapter, we are not restricted in our choice of prior density. However, our interest in this chapter is in the methods required to overcome non-conjugacy and for that, a Gaussian will suffice. Readers are recommended to try the methods introduced in this chapter with different forms of prior density, $p(\mathbf{w})$.

Likelihood: To make headway with the likelihood, $p(\mathbf{t}|\mathbf{X}, \mathbf{w})$, we start by assuming that the elements of $\mathbf{t}$ are conditionally independent (see Section 2.8.1), conditioned on $\mathbf{w}$:

$$p(\mathbf{t}|\mathbf{X}, \mathbf{w}) = \prod_{n=1}^{N} p(t_n|\mathbf{x}_n, \mathbf{w}).$$

t_n is a binary variable indicating the class (0 or 1) of the nth object, $\mathbf{x}_n$. In the Gaussian Olympics example in the previous chapter, we treated t_n as a Gaussian random variable with mean $\mathbf{w}^\mathsf{T}\mathbf{x}_n$ and variance σ^2, but this is only appropriate for real-valued t_n. Instead, we can model t_n as a binary random variable – a single coin toss for each n. Rather than a mean and variance, this random variable is characterised by the probability that the class is 1 (the probability of belonging to class 0 is 1 minus the probability of belonging to class 1). To avoid confusion, we will denote this random variable T_n (to distinguish it from the actual instance, t_n, that we observe). Therefore, we can write each of the n likelihood terms as a probability:

$$p(\mathbf{t}|\mathbf{X}, \mathbf{w}) = \prod_{n=1}^{N} P(T_n = t_n|\mathbf{x}_n, \mathbf{w}). \tag{4.2}$$

This likelihood function will be high if the model assigns high probabilities for class 1 when we observe class 1 and high probabilities for class 0 when we observe class 0. It has a maximum value of 1 where all of the training points are predicted perfectly.

Our task is now to choose a function of $\mathbf{x}_n$ and $\mathbf{w}$, $f(\mathbf{x}_n; \mathbf{w})$, that produces a probability. A popular technique is to take a simple linear function (e.g. $f(\mathbf{x}_n; \mathbf{w}) = \mathbf{w}^\mathsf{T}\mathbf{x}_n$) and then pass the result through a second function that *squashes* its output to ensure it produces a valid probability. One such squashing function is the sigmoid function shown in Figure 4.2. As $\mathbf{w}^\mathsf{T}\mathbf{x}$ increases, the value converges to 1 and as it decreases, it converges to 0. The sigmoid function is defined as

$$P(T_n = 1|\mathbf{x}_n, \mathbf{w}) = \frac{1}{1 + \exp(-\mathbf{w}^\mathsf{T}\mathbf{x}_n)}. \tag{4.3}$$

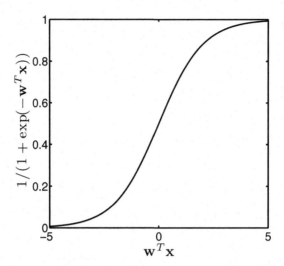

FIGURE 4.2 The sigmoid function that squashes a real value (e.g. $\mathbf{w}^\mathsf{T}\mathbf{x}$) to always be between 0 and 1.

This expression gives us the probability that $T_n = 1$. In our likelihood we require the probability of the actual observation, some of which will be zero. Because T_n can *only* take the value 0 or 1, we can easily compute $P(T_n = 0|\mathbf{x}, \mathbf{w})$ using Equation 2.2:

$$
\begin{aligned}
P(T_n = 0|\mathbf{x}_n, \mathbf{w}) &= 1 - P(T_n = 1|\mathbf{x}_n, \mathbf{w}) \\
&= 1 - \frac{1}{1 + \exp(-\mathbf{w}^\mathsf{T}\mathbf{x}_n)} \\
&= \frac{\exp(-\mathbf{w}^\mathsf{T}\mathbf{x}_n)}{1 + \exp(-\mathbf{w}^\mathsf{T}\mathbf{x}_n)}. \quad (4.4)
\end{aligned}
$$

We combine Equations 4.3 and 4.4 to produce a single expression for $P(T_n = t_n|\mathbf{x}_n, \mathbf{w})$ as follows:

$$
P(T_n = t_n|\mathbf{x}_n, \mathbf{w}) = P(T_n = 1|\mathbf{x}_n, \mathbf{w})^{t_n} P(T_n = 0|\mathbf{x}_n, \mathbf{w})^{1-t_n},
$$

where the observed data (t_n) switches the relevant term on and the other off.

Substituting this into Equation 4.2 gives us the likelihood for all n training points:

$$
\begin{aligned}
p(\mathbf{t}|\mathbf{X}, \mathbf{w}) &= \prod_{n=1}^{N} P(T_n = 1|\mathbf{x}_n\mathbf{w})^{t_n} P(T_n = 0|\mathbf{x}_n, \mathbf{w})^{1-t_n} \\
&= \prod_{n=1}^{N} \left(\frac{1}{1 + \exp(-\mathbf{w}^\mathsf{T}\mathbf{x}_n)}\right)^{t_n} \left(\frac{\exp(-\mathbf{w}^\mathsf{T}\mathbf{x}_n)}{1 + \exp(-\mathbf{w}^\mathsf{T}\mathbf{x}_n)}\right)^{1-t_n}. \quad (4.5)
\end{aligned}
$$

Posterior: This definition of the likelihood combined with the Gaussian prior we chose earlier are all we need, in theory, to work out the posterior density,

$p(\mathbf{w}|\mathbf{X}, \mathbf{t}, \sigma^2)$. Once we have the posterior density, we can predict the response (class) of new objects by taking an expectation with respect to this density:

$$P(t_{\text{new}} = 1|\mathbf{x}_{\text{new}}, \mathbf{X}, \mathbf{t}) = \mathbf{E}_{p(\mathbf{w}|\mathbf{X}, \mathbf{t}, \sigma^2)} \left\{ \frac{1}{1 + \exp(-\mathbf{w}^\mathsf{T}\mathbf{x}_{\text{new}})} \right\}.$$

In practice, this is not straightforward. The posterior is not of any standard form. To be able to evaluate it at a particular $\mathbf{w}$, we would need to evaluate both the numerator and denominator of Equation 4.1. The numerator is fine – we could evaluate the Gaussian prior density at $\mathbf{w}$ and the likelihood that we've just defined and multiply the two values together. The denominator is the problem, as we cannot analytically perform the integration required to compute the marginal likelihood:

$$Z^{-1} = p(\mathbf{t}|\mathbf{X}, \sigma^2) = \int p(\mathbf{t}|\mathbf{X}, \mathbf{w})p(\mathbf{w}|\sigma^2) \, d\mathbf{w}.$$

In other words, we have a function $g(\mathbf{w}; \mathbf{X}, \mathbf{t}, \sigma^2) = p(\mathbf{t}|\mathbf{X}, \mathbf{w})p(\mathbf{w}|\sigma^2)$ which we know is proportional to the posterior, $p(\mathbf{w}|\mathbf{X}, \mathbf{t}, \sigma^2) = Zg(\mathbf{w}; \mathbf{X}, \mathbf{t}, \sigma^2)$, but we do not know the constant of proportionality, Z^{-1} (note that this constant is traditionally defined as Z^{-1} rather than Z). We are left with three options:

1. Find the single value of $\mathbf{w}$ that corresponds to the highest value of the posterior. As $g(\mathbf{w}; \mathbf{X}, \mathbf{t}, \sigma^2)$ is proportional to the posterior, a maximum of $g(\mathbf{w}; \mathbf{X}, \mathbf{t}, \sigma^2)$ will also correspond to a maximum of the posterior. Z^{-1} is not a function of $\mathbf{w}$.

2. Approximate $p(\mathbf{w}|\mathbf{X}, \mathbf{t}, \sigma^2)$ with some other density that we can compute analytically.

3. Sample directly from the posterior $p(\mathbf{w}|\mathbf{X}, \mathbf{t}, \sigma^2)$, knowing only $g(\mathbf{w}; \mathbf{X}, \mathbf{t}, \sigma^2)$.

The first option is not very Bayesian – we will have to make predictions for new objects based on a single value of $\mathbf{w}$ and not a density. It is, however, easy to do and this makes it a popular technique. The second option leaves us with a density that is easy to work with (we can choose any density we like) but if the chosen density is very different from the posterior, our model will not be very reliable. The final option allows us to sample from the posterior (and hence get good approximations to any expectations that we might require) but can be difficult.

These are the three options that are open to us in any problem where we cannot directly compute the posterior density. All three options have good and bad points and the choice of one over another will depend on the specifications (and computational limitations) of the problem at hand. We will now describe each in turn.

4.3 A POINT ESTIMATE – THE MAP SOLUTION

In the previous section we showed that, whilst we could not compute the posterior density $p(\mathbf{w}|\mathbf{X}, \mathbf{t}, \sigma^2)$, we could compute something proportional to it, $g(\mathbf{w}; \mathbf{X}, \mathbf{t}, \sigma^2)$. This is equal to the prior multiplied by the likelihood. The value of $\mathbf{w}$ that maximises $g(\mathbf{w}; \mathbf{X}, \mathbf{t}, \sigma^2)$ will also correspond to the value at the maximum of the posterior. This will be the single most likely value of $\widehat{\mathbf{w}}$ (under the posterior) and is a sensible choice if we decide to use a point estimate. Chapter 2 was devoted to finding the value of $\widehat{\mathbf{w}}$ that maximised the likelihood. The idea here is very similar except now we are maximising the likelihood multiplied by the prior. This solution is the maximum a posteriori (MAP) estimate that we first saw in Section 3.8.4 and is common within machine learning.

Comment 4.1 – The Newton–Raphson method: The Newton–Raphson method (also known as the Newton method) is a general method for finding points where functions are equal to zero, i.e., finding points where the function $f(x) = 0$. Given a current estimate of the zero point, x_n, we update it by moving to the point where the tangent to the function at x_n passes through the x-axis. This point can be computed by approximating the gradient as a change in $f(x)$ divided by a change in x. Defining $\partial f(x)/\partial x$ as $f'(x)$,

$$f'(x_n) = \frac{f(x_n) - 0}{x_n - x_{n+1}}$$

$$(x_n - x_{n+1})f'(x_n) = f(x_n)$$

$$x_{n+1} = x_n - \frac{f(x_n)}{f'(x_n)}.$$

The method can also be used to find minima and maxima, as these are simply points where the gradient passes through zero. Therefore, we simply replace $f(x)$ with its derivative $f'(x)$ and $f'(x)$ with its derivative $f''(x)$:

$$x_{n+1} = x_n - \frac{f'(x_n)}{f''(x_n)}.$$

This is readily extendable to functions of a vector – say $\mathbf{x}$. In this instance, $f'(x_n)$ is replaced by the vector of partial derivatives evaluated at $\mathbf{x}_n$ and $1/f''(x_n)$ is replaced by the inverse of the Hessian matrix (see Comment 2.6) – $\partial^2 f(\mathbf{x})/\partial \mathbf{x}\partial \mathbf{x}^\mathsf{T}$ – evaluated at $\mathbf{x} = \mathbf{x}_n$.

As with finding the maximum likelihood solution, it is easiest to find the value of $\mathbf{w}$ that maximises $\log g(\mathbf{w}; \mathbf{X}, \mathbf{t})$ rather than $g(\mathbf{w}; \mathbf{X}, \mathbf{t})$:

$$\log g(\mathbf{w}; \mathbf{X}, \mathbf{t}) = \log p(\mathbf{t}|\mathbf{X}, \mathbf{w}) + \log p(\mathbf{w}|\sigma^2).$$

Unlike the maximum likelihood solution for the linear model, we cannot obtain an exact expression for $\mathbf{w}$ by differentiating this expression and equating it to zero. Instead, we can use any one of many optimisation algorithms that start with a guess for $\mathbf{w}$ and then keep updating it in such a way that $g(\mathbf{w}; \mathbf{X}, \mathbf{t})$ increases until a maximum is reached. The Newton–Raphson procedure (see Comment 4.1) is one such method that updates $\mathbf{w}$ using the following equation:

$$\mathbf{w}' = \mathbf{w} - \left(\frac{\partial^2 \log g(\mathbf{w}; \mathbf{X}, \mathbf{t})}{\partial \mathbf{w}\partial \mathbf{w}^\mathsf{T}}\right)^{-1} \frac{\partial \log g(\mathbf{w}; \mathbf{X}, \mathbf{t})}{\partial \mathbf{w}}. \tag{4.6}$$

The new version ($\mathbf{w}'$) of $\mathbf{w}$ is calculated by subtracting the inverse of the Hessian (see Comment 2.6) multiplied by the vector of partial derivatives. For any starting value of $\mathbf{w}$, this iterative procedure will update $\mathbf{w}$ until it reaches a point where the gradient is zero. To check that the point we have converged to corresponds to a maximum, we can check the Hessian to ensure that it is negative definite, just as we did for maximum likelihood in Section 2.8.3.

In order to compute the vector of first derivatives, we first expand our expression for $\log g(\mathbf{w}; \mathbf{X}, \mathbf{t})$ using Equations 4.2 and 4.5:

$$
\begin{aligned}
\log g(\mathbf{w}; \mathbf{X}, \mathbf{t}) \;&=\; \sum_{n=1}^{N} \log P(T_n = t_n | \mathbf{x}_n, \mathbf{w}) + \log p(\mathbf{w}|\sigma^2) \\
&=\; \sum_{n=1}^{N} \log \left[\left(\frac{1}{1 + \exp(-\mathbf{w}^\mathsf{T} \mathbf{x}_n)} \right)^{t_n} \left(\frac{\exp(-\mathbf{w}^\mathsf{T} \mathbf{x}_n)}{1 + \exp(-\mathbf{w}^\mathsf{T} \mathbf{x}_n)} \right)^{1-t_n} \right] \\
&\quad + \log p(\mathbf{w}|\sigma^2).
\end{aligned}
$$

To stop this expression becoming too complicated, we will use the following shorthand:

$$
P_n = P(T_n = 1 | \mathbf{w}, \mathbf{x}_n) = \frac{1}{1 + \exp(-\mathbf{w}^\mathsf{T} \mathbf{x}_n)}.
$$

Therefore, assuming that $\mathbf{w}$ is D-dimensional, we have the following expression:

$$
\begin{aligned}
\log g(\mathbf{w}; \mathbf{X}, \mathbf{t}) \;&=\; \log p(\mathbf{w}|\sigma^2) + \sum_{n=1}^{N} \log P_n^{t_n} + \log(1 - P_n)^{1-t_n} \\
&=\; -\frac{D}{2} \log 2\pi - D \log \sigma - \frac{1}{2\sigma^2} \mathbf{w}^\mathsf{T} \mathbf{w} \\
&\quad + \sum_{n=1}^{N} t_n \log P_n + (1 - t_n) \log(1 - P_n),
\end{aligned}
$$

where the first three terms are the log of the (Gaussian) prior. To find the vector of partial derivatives, we can use the chain rule (see Comment 4.2) to give an expression in terms of the partial derivatives of P_n:

$$
\begin{aligned}
\frac{\partial \log g(\mathbf{w}; \mathbf{X}, \mathbf{t})}{\partial \mathbf{w}} \;&=\; -\frac{1}{\sigma^2} \mathbf{w} + \sum_{n=1}^{N} \left(\frac{t_n}{P_n} \frac{\partial P_n}{\partial \mathbf{w}} + \frac{1 - t_n}{1 - P_n} \frac{\partial(1 - P_n)}{\partial \mathbf{w}} \right) \\
&=\; -\frac{1}{\sigma^2} \mathbf{w} + \sum_{n=1}^{N} \left(\frac{t_n}{P_n} \frac{\partial P_n}{\partial \mathbf{w}} - \frac{1 - t_n}{1 - P_n} \frac{\partial P_n}{\partial \mathbf{w}} \right), \qquad (4.7)
\end{aligned}
$$

where we have used the chain rule a second time to turn $\frac{\partial(1 - P_n)}{\partial \mathbf{w}}$ into $-\frac{\partial P_n}{\partial \mathbf{w}}$:

$$
\begin{aligned}
\frac{\partial(1 - P_n)}{\partial \mathbf{w}} \;&=\; \frac{\partial(1 - P_n)}{\partial P_n} \frac{\partial P_n}{\partial \mathbf{w}} \\
&=\; -\frac{\partial P_n}{\partial \mathbf{w}}.
\end{aligned}
$$

To calculate $\frac{\partial P_n}{\partial \mathbf{w}}$, we can use the chain rule once more:

$$
\begin{aligned}
\frac{\partial P_n}{\partial \mathbf{w}} &= \frac{\partial \left(1 + \exp(-\mathbf{w}^\mathsf{T}\mathbf{x}_n)\right)^{-1}}{\partial \left(1 + \exp(-\mathbf{w}^\mathsf{T}\mathbf{x}_n)\right)} \frac{\partial \left(1 + \exp(-\mathbf{w}^\mathsf{T}\mathbf{x}_n)\right)}{\partial \mathbf{w}} \\
&= -\frac{1}{\left(1 + \exp(-\mathbf{w}^\mathsf{T}\mathbf{x}_n)\right)^2} \exp(-\mathbf{w}^\mathsf{T}\mathbf{x}_n)(-\mathbf{x}_n) \\
&= \frac{\exp(-\mathbf{w}^\mathsf{T}\mathbf{x}_n)}{\left(1 + \exp(-\mathbf{w}^\mathsf{T}\mathbf{x}_n)\right)^2} \mathbf{x}_n \\
&= \frac{1}{1 + \exp(-\mathbf{w}^\mathsf{T}\mathbf{x}_n)} \frac{\exp(-\mathbf{w}^\mathsf{T}\mathbf{x}_n)}{1 + \exp(-\mathbf{w}^\mathsf{T}\mathbf{x})} \mathbf{x}_n \\
&= P_n(1 - P_n)\mathbf{x}_n.
\end{aligned}
\tag{4.8}
$$

Comment 4.2 – The chain rule: When taking partial derivatives, it is often convenient to use the chain rule. The chain rule states that

$$
\frac{\partial f(g(\mathbf{w}))}{\partial \mathbf{w}} = \frac{\partial f(g(\mathbf{w}))}{\partial g(\mathbf{w})} \frac{\partial g(\mathbf{w})}{\partial \mathbf{w}}.
$$

As an example, let

$$
f(\mathbf{w}) = t_n \log P_n
$$

where

$$
P_n = \frac{1}{1 + \exp(-\mathbf{w}^\mathsf{T}\mathbf{x}_n)}.
$$

To compute $\frac{\partial f(\mathbf{w})}{\partial \mathbf{w}}$, we can use the chain rule as follows:

$$
\frac{\partial f(\mathbf{w})}{\partial \mathbf{w}} = \frac{\partial f(\mathbf{w})}{\partial P_n} \frac{\partial P_n}{\partial \mathbf{w}} = \frac{t_n}{P_n} \frac{\partial P_n}{\partial \mathbf{w}}.
$$

Substituting Equation 4.8 into Equation 4.7 gives us the required vector of partial derivatives:

$$
\begin{aligned}
\frac{\partial \log g(\mathbf{w}; \mathbf{X}, \mathbf{t})}{\partial \mathbf{w}} &= -\frac{1}{\sigma^2}\mathbf{w} + \sum_{n=1}^{N} \left(\mathbf{x}_n t_n (1 - P_n) - \mathbf{x}_n(1 - t_n)P_n\right) \\
&= -\frac{1}{\sigma^2}\mathbf{w} + \sum_{n=1}^{N} \mathbf{x}_n (t_n - t_n P_n - P_n + t_n P_n) \\
&= -\frac{1}{\sigma^2}\mathbf{w} + \sum_{n=1}^{N} \mathbf{x}_n (t_n - P_n).
\end{aligned}
\tag{4.9}
$$

To compute the Hessian matrix of second derivatives, we differentiate this again with respect to $\mathbf{w}^\mathsf{T}$. Noting that $\frac{\partial P_n}{\partial \mathbf{w}^\mathsf{T}} = \left(\frac{\partial P_n}{\partial \mathbf{w}}\right)^\mathsf{T}$, we obtain the following expression:

$$
\begin{aligned}
\frac{\partial^2 \log g(\mathbf{w}; \mathbf{X}, \mathbf{t})}{\partial \mathbf{w} \partial \mathbf{w}^\mathsf{T}} &= -\frac{1}{\sigma^2}\mathbf{I} - \sum_{n=1}^{N} \mathbf{x}_n \frac{\partial P_n}{\partial \mathbf{w}^\mathsf{T}} \\
&= -\frac{1}{\sigma^2}\mathbf{I} - \sum_{n=1}^{N} \mathbf{x}_n \mathbf{x}_n^\mathsf{T} P_n(1 - P_n).
\end{aligned}
\tag{4.10}
$$

One thing to notice from the Hessian is that, because $0 \leq P_n \leq 1$, it will be negative definite for any set of $\mathbf{x}_n$ and for any $\mathbf{w}$ (see Section 2.8.3). Therefore,

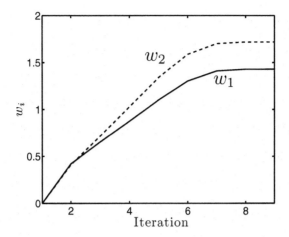

FIGURE 4.3 Evolution of the components of **w** throughout the Newton–Raphson procedure to find the **w** corresponding to the maximum of the posterior density.

there can only be one optimum and it must be a maximum. Whatever value of **w** the Newton–Raphson procedure converges to must correspond to the highest value of the posterior density. This is a consequence of the choice of prior and likelihood function, and changing either may result in a harder posterior density to optimise.

We now have everything we need to perform the Newton–Raphson procedure and find a potential optimal value of **w**. Starting with $\mathbf{w} = [0, 0]^{\mathsf{T}}$ and setting $\sigma^2 = 10$, the procedure converges (the change in **w** becomes insignificant) after only nine iterations (MATLAB script: `logmap.m`). The evolution of the two components of **w** over this period can be seen in Figure 4.3. Following the previous chapters, we will call the value of **w** that corresponds to the maximum $\widehat{\mathbf{w}}$.

Using $\widehat{\mathbf{w}}$, we can compute the probability that the response equals 1 for any **x**. In particular, if we observe $\mathbf{x}_{\mathsf{new}}$, a new set of attributes, the probability that it should be given a response of 1 (it belongs to the square class) is given by

$$P(T_{\mathsf{new}} = 1 | \mathbf{x}_{\mathsf{new}}, \widehat{\mathbf{w}}) = \frac{1}{1 + \exp(-\widehat{\mathbf{w}}^{\mathsf{T}} \mathbf{x}_{\mathsf{new}})}. \tag{4.11}$$

Given that there are two possible responses (or classes) for this new object, a sensible strategy might be to assign it to the square class ($T_{\mathsf{new}} = 1$) if the probability is greater than 0.5 and to the circle class ($T_{\mathsf{new}} = 0$) otherwise. In this case, the set of **x** values that correspond to $P(T = 1 | \mathbf{x}, \widehat{\mathbf{w}}) = 0.5$ will form a line that can be thought of as a **decision boundary** – points on one side of the line will belong to one class, and points on the other side to the other class. To plot the decision boundary, we make use of the fact that $P(T = 1 | \mathbf{x}, \widehat{\mathbf{w}}) = 0.5$ implies that $\widehat{\mathbf{w}}^{\mathsf{T}} \mathbf{x} = 0$ (see Exercise 4.5). If we expand this expression, we can obtain the decision boundary

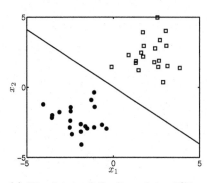

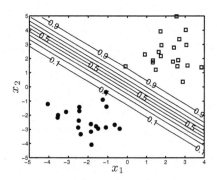

(a) The data and the line where $P(T = 1|\mathbf{x}, \widehat{\mathbf{w}}) = 0.5$. If we took 0.5 as a threshold, new points above the line would be classified as squares, below as circles.

(b) The contours show $P(T = 1|\mathbf{x}, \widehat{\mathbf{w}})$, the probability that a new object should be classified as a square, as a function of $\mathbf{x}$.

FIGURE 4.4 Inferred function in the binary response example.

as a function of x_1 and x_2:

$$
\begin{aligned}
0 &= \widehat{\mathbf{w}}^\mathsf{T}\mathbf{x} \\
&= \widehat{w_1}x_1 + \widehat{w_2}x_2 \\
\widehat{w_2}x_2 &= -\widehat{w_1}x_1 \\
x_2 &= -\frac{\widehat{w_1}x_1}{\widehat{w_2}},
\end{aligned}
$$

which is plotted in Figure 4.4(a). If we want to split the two classes with a straight line, this seems like quite a reasonable choice. In Figure 4.4(b) we plot contours of $P(T = 1|\mathbf{x}, \widehat{\mathbf{w}})$ as a function of $\mathbf{x}$ (MATLAB script: logmap.m). Close to the squares the probability is 1 (the squares are objects for which $t_n = 1$) and close to the circles it is 0. Between the two groups of data, the probability is around 0.5, reflecting the fact that objects here would be equidistant from both groups.

The outcome of this optimisation is that we have a model with which we can make predictions. The model is based on a point estimate, $\widehat{\mathbf{w}}$, of the parameters that we have obtained by finding the value of $\mathbf{w}$ that corresponds to a maximum of the posterior, $p(\mathbf{w}|\mathbf{X}, \mathbf{t}, \sigma^2)$. This MAP solution is common in machine learning because it is reasonably easy to find $\widehat{\mathbf{w}}$ in this way. One could follow the steps described above for any prior and likelihood combination and find an optimum value. The optimisations will not always be as well behaved as this – in some problems, the posterior might have several maxima (and maybe even some minima). It would be difficult to know if the maximum we had found using Newton–Raphson was the global optimum.

In Chapter 3 we have already seen the advantage of maintaining a density over $\mathbf{w}$ rather than collapsing onto a point estimate. With this in mind, we will now move on to our second option when faced with a posterior we cannot compute exactly – finding a density that approximates $p(\mathbf{w}|\mathbf{X}, \mathbf{t}, \sigma^2)$.

4.4   THE LAPLACE APPROXIMATION

There are various approximation methods used within machine learning to replace tricky posterior densities with approximations that are easier to handle. The most popular is the Laplace approximation.[1] The idea is to approximate the density of interest with a Gaussian. Given the ease with which we can manipulate Gaussians, this seems to be a sensible choice – the expectations required to make predictions are likely to be easy to calculate given a Gaussian posterior. However, we should always bear in mind that our predictions will then only be as good as our approximation. If our true posterior is not very Gaussian, our predictions will be easy to compute but not very useful.

The Gaussian density is defined by its mean and (co)variance. Using a Gaussian to approximate another density amounts to choosing suitable values for these parameters. To motivate the choices of parameters made by the Laplace approximation, imagine that, rather than having two parameters, our model has only one – w – and that we know $\widehat{w}$ – the value corresponding to the highest value of the posterior. Our first step is to approximate $\log g(w; \mathbf{X}, \mathbf{t}, \sigma^2)$ using a Taylor expansion (see Comment 4.3) around the maximum, $\widehat{w}$:

$$
\begin{aligned}
\log g(w; \mathbf{X}, \mathbf{t}, \sigma^2) \approx{}& \log g(\widehat{w}; \mathbf{X}, \mathbf{t}, \sigma^2) + \left.\frac{\partial \log g(w; \mathbf{X}, \mathbf{t}, \sigma^2)}{\partial w}\right|_{\widehat{w}} \frac{(w - \widehat{w})}{1!} \\
&+ \left.\frac{\partial^2 \log g(w; \mathbf{X}, \mathbf{t}, \sigma^2)}{\partial w^2}\right|_{\widehat{w}} \frac{(w - \widehat{w})^2}{2!} + \cdots
\end{aligned}
$$

The second term is the first derivative (i.e. the gradient) evaluated at the maximum point and must therefore be zero. Discarding this, and ignoring terms of third-order and above, we are left with the following expression:

$$
\log g(w; \mathbf{X}, \mathbf{t}, \sigma^2) \approx \log g(\widehat{w}; \mathbf{X}, \mathbf{t}, \sigma^2) - \frac{v}{2}(w - \widehat{w})^2, \tag{4.12}
$$

where v is the negative of the second derivative of $\log g(w; \mathbf{X}, \mathbf{t}, \sigma^2)$ evaluated at $w = \widehat{w}$:

$$
v = - \left.\frac{\partial^2 \log g(w; \mathbf{X}, \mathbf{t}, \sigma^2)}{\partial w^2}\right|_{\widehat{w}}.
$$

Now, the Gaussian density is defined as

$$
\frac{1}{\sqrt{2\pi}\sigma} \exp\left\{ -\frac{1}{2\sigma^2}(w - \mu)^2 \right\},
$$

the log of which is equal to

$$
\log(K) - \frac{1}{2\sigma^2}(w - \mu)^2,
$$

where K is the normalising constant. This looks very similar to Equation 4.12 with $\mu = \widehat{w}$ and $\sigma^2 = 1/v$. This is the Laplace approximation – we approximate the posterior with a Gaussian that has its mean at the posterior **mode** ($\widehat{w}$) and has variance inversely proportional to the curvature of the posterior (its second derivative) at its mode.

---

[1] Technically, it is actually a saddle-point approximation but has come to be known as the Laplace approximation within machine learning. In computational statistics, the Laplace approximation is a name given to something else entirely.

Comment 4.3 – Taylor expansions: The Taylor expansion is a way of approximating a function. The approximation is always made 'about' some value – the approximation will tend to diverge from the true function as we move away from that value. The definition of the Taylor series of $f(w)$ about $\widehat{w}$ is

$$f(w) = \sum_{n=0}^{\infty} \frac{(w - \widehat{w})^n}{n!} \left. \frac{\partial^n f(w)}{\partial w^n} \right|_{\widehat{w}}$$

where $\left. \frac{\partial^n f(w)}{\partial w^n} \right|_{\widehat{w}}$ is the nth derivative of $f(w)$ with respect to w, evaluated at $\widehat{w}$. When $n = 0$, this derivative is simply the function $f(w)$. If we only compute a finite number of terms, we will have an approximation to the function. A first-order approximation would just include terms $n = 0$ and $n = 1$ – an nth-order approximation includes all terms up to and including term n. For example, we can approximate $f(w) = \exp(w)$ at $\widehat{w} = 0$:

$$\exp(w) = \exp(\widehat{w}) + \frac{w}{1!} \exp(\widehat{w}) + \frac{w^2}{2!} \exp(\widehat{w}) + \dots$$

Now, $\exp(\widehat{w}) = 1$, so

$$\exp(w) = 1 + \frac{w}{1!} + \frac{w^2}{2!} + \frac{w^3}{3!} + \dots$$

The approximation will get better and better as we add more and more terms. This can be seen in the figure on the right.

This idea is easily extended to multivariate densities. In particular, the Laplace approximation to our true posterior $p(\mathbf{w}|\mathbf{X}, \mathbf{t}, \sigma^2)$ is

$$p(\mathbf{w}|\mathbf{X}, \mathbf{t}, \sigma^2) \approx \mathcal{N}(\boldsymbol{\mu}, \boldsymbol{\Sigma}),$$

where $\boldsymbol{\mu}$ is set to $\widehat{\mathbf{w}}$, and $\boldsymbol{\Sigma}$ is the negative of the inverse Hessian:

$$\boldsymbol{\mu} = \widehat{\mathbf{w}}, \quad \boldsymbol{\Sigma}^{-1} = -\left. \left(\frac{\partial^2 \log g(\mathbf{w}; \mathbf{X}, \mathbf{t})}{\partial \mathbf{w} \partial \mathbf{w}^{\mathsf{T}}} \right) \right|_{\widehat{\mathbf{w}}}. \tag{4.13}$$

4.4.1 Laplace approximation example: Approximating a gamma density

Before we look at what this approximation looks like in the binary response example, it is useful to look at an example where we know the true density (see also Exercises 4.1, 4.2 and 4.3) (MATLAB script: `lapexample.m`). This will allow us to see how good or bad the approximation is. The following is the gamma density for a random variable Y:

$$p(y|\alpha, \beta) = \frac{\beta^{\alpha}}{\Gamma(\alpha)} y^{\alpha-1} \exp\{-\beta y\}. \tag{4.14}$$

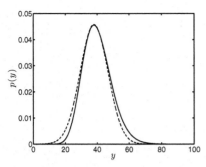
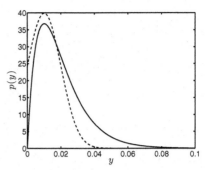

(a) $p(y|\alpha, \beta)$ (solid line) and approximating Gaussian (dashed line) for $\alpha = 20$, $\beta = 0.5$.

(b) $p(y|\alpha, \beta)$ (solid line) and approximating Gaussian (dashed line) for $\alpha = 2$, $\beta = 100$.

FIGURE 4.5 Examples of the Laplace approximation to the gamma density function given in Equation 4.14.

We will investigate how good the Laplace approximation is to this density. The gamma density has an analytic expression for its mode which means we do not need to go through an optimisation procedure similar to that in the last section. The mode, $\widehat{y}$, is defined as

$$\widehat{y} = \frac{\alpha - 1}{\beta}.$$

The Laplace approximation to $p(y|\alpha, \beta)$ takes the form of a Gaussian:

$$p(y|\alpha, \beta) \approx \mathcal{N}(\mu, \sigma^2).$$

The mean μ will be equal to the mode of $p(y|\alpha, \beta)$, which we've already defined. To find the variance, σ^2, of the approximating Gaussian, we need to find the second derivative of $\log p(y|\alpha, \beta)$ with respect to y. This is computed as follows:

$$\begin{aligned}
\log p(y|\alpha, \beta) &= \alpha \log \beta - \log(\Gamma(\alpha)) + (\alpha - 1) \log y - \beta y \\
\frac{\partial \log p(y|\alpha, \beta)}{\partial y} &= \frac{\alpha - 1}{y} - \beta \\
\frac{\partial^2 \log p(y|\alpha, \beta)}{\partial y^2} &= -\frac{\alpha - 1}{y^2}.
\end{aligned}$$

σ^2 will be equal to the negative inverse of this quantity evaluated at $y = \widehat{y}$. In particular

$$\sigma^2 = \frac{\widehat{y}^2}{\alpha - 1} = \frac{\alpha - 1}{\beta^2}.$$

In Figure 4.5 we can see two examples of $p(y|\alpha, \beta)$ and the corresponding Laplace approximation. In the first, $p(y|\alpha, \beta)$ looks rather like a Gaussian and the approximation is pretty good. In the second, $p(y|\alpha, \beta)$ does not look very much like a Gaussian and the approximation is not accurate. In both cases the approximation gets worse as we move away from the mode. This is because the approximation is based on the characteristics of the function *at* the mode. We will see this property again as we return to the binary response model.

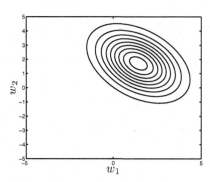

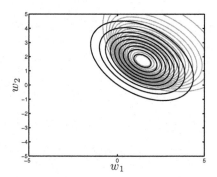

(a) Laplace approximation to the posterior.

(b) Laplace approximation to the posterior and the true unnormalised posterior (lighter lines).

FIGURE 4.6 The Laplace approximation for the binary problem.

4.4.2 Laplace approximation for the binary response model

Returning to our binary response model, we had to compute both the mode, $\widehat{\mathbf{w}}$ and the Hessian for the Newton–Raphson procedure. We therefore already have everything we need for the Laplace approximation to the posterior $p(\mathbf{w}|\mathbf{X}, \mathbf{t}, \sigma^2)$. In Figure 4.6(a) we can see the approximate posterior and in Figure 4.6(b) we can see the same approximation on top of $g(\mathbf{w}; \mathbf{X}, \mathbf{t})$, the unnormalised posterior. As for the gamma example in the previous section, the shape of the approximation is pretty good around the mode but diverges considerably from the true posterior as we move away from the mode. This is to be expected – the Laplace approximation only matches the shape (curvature) at the mode. We can also sample values of $\mathbf{w}$ from the approximate posterior and look at the decision boundaries that they correspond to. Twenty such boundaries are plotted in Figure 4.7(a). There appears to be a lot of variability in these boundaries, although all of them seem to split the classes reasonably well.

The final step is to use the approximate posterior to compute predictions. We now have a density over $\mathbf{w}$ rather than a single value and we know, from Chapter 3, that we compute a prediction by averaging over this density. In particular, we should be calculating the expected value of $P(T_{\text{new}} = 1|\mathbf{x}_{\text{new}}, \mathbf{w})$ with respect to the approximate posterior over $\mathbf{w}$ (which we've denoted as $\mathcal{N}(\boldsymbol{\mu}, \boldsymbol{\Sigma})$):

$$P(T_{\text{new}} = 1|\mathbf{x}_{\text{new}}, \mathbf{X}, \mathbf{t}, \sigma^2) = \mathbf{E}_{\mathcal{N}(\boldsymbol{\mu}, \boldsymbol{\Sigma})} \left\{ P(T_{\text{new}} = 1|\mathbf{x}_{\text{new}}, \mathbf{w}) \right\}.$$

Unfortunately, we cannot compute the integral over $\mathbf{w}$ required in this expectation. This might suggest that our choice of approximation was not sensible – we still cannot make predictions. However, we can easily sample from $\mathcal{N}(\boldsymbol{\mu}, \boldsymbol{\Sigma})$ and so (see Equation 2.23) we can approximate the expectation with

$$P(T_{\text{new}} = 1|\mathbf{x}_{\text{new}}, \mathbf{X}, \mathbf{t}, \sigma^2) = \frac{1}{N_s} \sum_{s=1}^{N_s} \frac{1}{1 + \exp(-\mathbf{w}_s^\mathsf{T} \mathbf{x}_{\text{new}})}, \qquad (4.15)$$

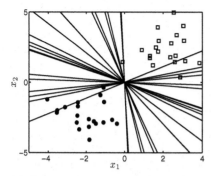

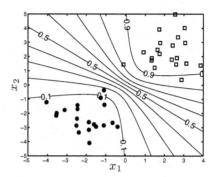

(a) Twenty decision boundaries corresponding to instances of **w** sampled from the Laplace approximation to the posterior.

(b) Contours of the probability of belonging to class 1 computed with a sample based approximation to $\mathbf{E}_{\mathcal{N}(\boldsymbol{\mu},\boldsymbol{\Sigma})}\{P(T_{\text{new}} = 1|\mathbf{x}_{\text{new}}, \mathbf{w})\}$.

FIGURE 4.7 Decision boundaries sampled from the Laplace approximation and the predictive probability contours.

where $\mathbf{w}_s$ is the sth of N_s samples drawn from the approximate posterior. Using $N_s = 1000$, the contours of $P(T_{\text{new}} = 1|\mathbf{x}_{\text{new}}, \mathbf{X}, \mathbf{t}, \sigma^2)$ can be seen in Figure 4.7(b) (MATLAB script: `loglap.m`). Compare this with Figure 4.4(b). There is a big difference – the contours are no longer straight lines. Averaging over the posterior density for **w** has had the effect of smudging the decision boundaries. The probabilities are now closer to 0.5 in all areas except those very close to the data objects. The model based on the point estimate, shown in Figure 4.4(b), could be said to be overconfident – take $x_1 = -3$, $x_2 = 5$ as an example. According to the predictions produced by the point estimate (Figure 4.4(b)), an object with these attributes would have a probability of approximately 1 of being a square despite the fact that it is quite distant from the other square objects. Compare this with the probability of approximately 0.6 given by the expectation with respect to the Laplace approximation to the posterior (Figure 4.7(b)). This value seems much more reasonable. Another way to understand the uncertainty that should be present in areas like this is to look at Figure 4.7(a) – there is very large variability in the possible decision boundaries at $x_1 = -3$, $x_2 = 5$. Some of these boundaries would classify this object as a square, some as a circle – the probability that it is a square, given the data that we have seen, is not 1.

In this section we have seen again that we should be wary of using point estimates. The Laplace approximation shown here can be used to approximate any density (over real-valued random variables) for which we can find the mode and compute the second derivative. The approach assumes that the posterior can be reasonably approximated by a Gaussian, something that is not always the case (see Figure 4.5). In our binary response model, the approximation did not allow us to compute the expectation necessary for making predictions exactly. However, the ease with which we can sample from a Gaussian meant that it was straightforward to obtain a sample-based approximation to the expectation. In the next section, we will extend this idea through the introduction of a technique that will enable us to sample directly from $p(\mathbf{w}|\mathbf{X}, \mathbf{t}, \sigma^2)$ despite the fact that we cannot compute the normalisation constant. The ability to generate these samples will allow us to use a sample-based approximation to the expectation without having to approximate the posterior.

4.5 SAMPLING TECHNIQUES

The Laplace approximation in the previous section provided us with a method for approximating the posterior density $p(\mathbf{w}|\mathbf{X}, \mathbf{t}, \sigma^2)$. Our interest in the posterior density is primarily to allow us to take all the uncertainty in $\mathbf{w}$ into account when making predictions. We do this by averaging over all potential values of $\mathbf{w}$ through the following expectation:

$$P(T_{\text{new}} = 1|\mathbf{x}_{\text{new}}, \mathbf{X}, \mathbf{t}, \sigma^2) = \mathbf{E}_{p(\mathbf{w}|\mathbf{X}, \mathbf{t}, \sigma^2)} \left\{ P(T_{\text{new}} = 1|\mathbf{x}_{\text{new}}, \mathbf{w}) \right\}.$$

Even substituting our approximation to the posterior into this expression, we could not analytically compute the integral required in this expectation. Fortunately, it was easy to sample from the Gaussian approximation, enabling us to use the sample based approximation given in Equation 4.15. In this instance, the benefit of making the approximation was that it enabled us to easily generate samples. In this section, we will look at a technique that enables us to cut out the approximation step and sample directly from the posterior. A set of samples from the true posterior generated in this way could be substituted directly into Equation 4.15 to compute the desired predictive probability, $P(T_{\text{new}} = 1|\mathbf{x}_{\text{new}}, \mathbf{X}, \mathbf{t}, \sigma^2)$. We're going to introduce a popular sampling technique known as the **Metropolis–Hastings** algorithm. However, before we go into this, it is perhaps useful to get more comfortable with the idea of sampling through a less abstract example.

4.5.1 Playing darts

In the game of darts, players take turns to throw three darts at a board like that shown in Figure 4.8. The darts are sharp and embed themselves into the board. The player receives a certain number of points for each dart, depending on where the dart lands. The scores from the three darts are added together and subtracted from the player's current total. Each player starts the game with the same total (normally 501) and the winner is the player who gets to zero first. The majority of the board is split into 20 segments and if the dart lands in the white parts of these segments, the score is equal to the number shown around the edge. If the dart lands in one of the shaded areas, the score is either double (lighter, outer shaded area) or triple (darker, inner area) the segment score. The circle in the centre of the board is known as the bull's-eye (50 points) and the circle around this as the bull (25 points). There is one slight complication to the rules – the player must get to zero with a double. So, for example, if a player currently has a total of 40, they could win by throwing a double 20 (the lightly shaded area just below the '20' label) or a single 20 (anywhere in the white bits of the '20' segment) followed by a double 10, etc. We will assume that the player does indeed need to score 40 to win, and has only one dart left with which to

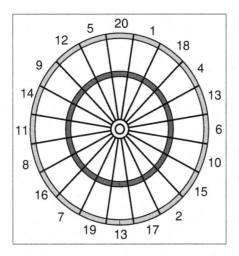

FIGURE 4.8 A dartboard.

do it. In other words, they need to hit the double 20 – what is the probability that they will succeed?

Assume that there exists some probability density function defined over the position that the dart will land. In other words, when a player is aiming for, say, double twenty, the position at which the dart will land could be considered as an instance of some random variable. We will use the vector $\mathbf{y}$ to describe this position and therefore the density will look something like $p(\mathbf{y}|\Delta)$. Δ ought to depend (at least to some extent) on where the player is aiming. The extent to which this dependence exists depends on the player's skill. For a professional trying to hit double twenty, we might expect the density to be tightly concentrated around the double twenty area. For a poor player, aiming might make very little difference to where the dart ends up. So, Δ depends on the skill of the player and the strength of their technique – making $p(\mathbf{y}|\Delta)$ very hard to define.

At this point it would be easy to give up. But, taking a step backwards, we are not directly interested in $p(\mathbf{y}|\Delta)$, just the probability that the player throws a double 20. Do we need to be able to write down an analytic expression for $p(\mathbf{y}|\Delta)$ to work this out? Before we answer this, let us satisfy ourselves that we could work it out if we could write down $p(\mathbf{y}|\Delta)$. Define the random variable $T = f(\mathbf{y})$ where $f(\mathbf{y})$ is 1 if $\mathbf{y}$ is inside the double twenty region and zero otherwise. T depends on $\mathbf{y}$ and hence depends on Δ. So, we're interested in the following probability: $P(T = 1|\Delta)$. This is nothing more than an expectation. In particular, it looks rather like the expectations we had to compute for the binary response model in the previous section:

$$P(T = 1|\Delta) = \mathbf{E}_{p(\mathbf{y}|\Delta)}\{f(\mathbf{y})\} = \int f(\mathbf{y})p(\mathbf{y}|\Delta)\ d\mathbf{y}. \tag{4.16}$$

In theory, if we could write down $p(\mathbf{y}|\Delta)$, we could work this out. However, we have also seen that we can compute quantities like this with a sample-based approximation. In particular, if $\mathbf{y}_s$ is the sth of N_s samples from $p(\mathbf{y}|\Delta)$, our approximation would look like:

$$P(T = 1|\Delta) \simeq \frac{1}{N_s} \sum_{s=1}^{N_s} f(\mathbf{y}_s).$$

So, we do not need to be able to write down $p(\mathbf{y}|\Delta)$ to be able to compute $P(T = 1|\Delta)$ as long as we can sample from it. Fortunately, sampling from $p(\mathbf{y}|\Delta)$ is pretty easy – we get our player, some darts and a board and we ask the player to aim for double twenty. The position of each dart thrown is a sample from $p(\mathbf{y}|\Delta)$. If we record $\mathbf{y}_s$ for each of N_s throws, we can compute the sample-based approximation given in Equation 4.16. In fact, in this case it works out as just the proportion of times the player throws a double twenty).

We can explicitly relate this procedure to our binary response model. Firstly, the quantity of interest in the darts case, $P(T = 1|\Delta)$ is analogous to the predictive probability in the binary response model: $P(T_{\text{new}} = 1|\mathbf{x}_{\text{new}}, \mathbf{X}, \mathbf{t}, \sigma^2)$. In both cases to compute this quantity, we must take an expectation with respect to some density: our darts distribution $p(\mathbf{y}|\Delta)$ is analogous to $p(\mathbf{w}|\mathbf{X}, \mathbf{t}, \sigma^2)$ – the posterior density over our parameters. In the darts case, we approximated this expectation by drawing samples directly from the posterior (despite the fact that we couldn't write it down). In the binary response case, we approximated the posterior with something we could sample from and then sampled. We will now see how we can sample directly from $p(\mathbf{w}|\mathbf{X}, \mathbf{t}, \sigma^2)$ (see Exercise 4.4).

4.5.2 The Metropolis–Hastings algorithm

In this section, we will introduce the Metropolis–Hastings[2] (MH) algorithm. Rather than go into too much detail we will introduce it as a recipe, describing the steps involved without proving why they work. References to further reading are provided at the end of the chapter.

Recall that we are attempting to sample from $p(\mathbf{w}|\mathbf{X}, \mathbf{t}, \sigma^2)$ so that we can approximate the following expectation:

$$\begin{aligned}
P(T_{\text{new}} = 1|\mathbf{x}_{\text{new}}, \mathbf{X}, \mathbf{t}, \sigma^2) &= \mathbf{E}_{p(\mathbf{w}|\mathbf{X}, \mathbf{t}, \sigma^2)} \{P(T_{\text{new}} = 1|\mathbf{x}_{\text{new}}, \mathbf{w})\} \\
&= \int P(T_{\text{new}} = 1|\mathbf{x}_{\text{new}}, \mathbf{w})p(\mathbf{w}|\mathbf{X}, \mathbf{t}, \sigma^2)\, d\mathbf{w},
\end{aligned}$$

with:

$$P(T = 1|\mathbf{x}_{\text{new}}, \mathbf{X}, \mathbf{t}, \sigma^2) \simeq \frac{1}{N_s} \sum_{s=1}^{N_s} P(T_{\text{new}} = 1|\mathbf{x}_{\text{new}}, \mathbf{w}_s).$$

Metropolis–Hastings generates a sequence of samples $\mathbf{w}_1, \mathbf{w}_2, \ldots, \mathbf{w}_{s-1}, \mathbf{w}_s, \ldots, \mathbf{w}_{N_s}$. Generating a sample (say $\mathbf{w}_s$) consists of two steps. In the first step, we need to *propose* a new sample – a candidate for $\mathbf{w}_s$. This is performed by proposing a movement from the previous sample ($\mathbf{w}_{s-1}$). Secondly, the proposed sample is tested to see whether or not it should be accepted. If accepted, it becomes our new sample

---

[2]Named after Nicholas Metropolis and W. Keith Hastings – a physicist and statistician, respectively, who developed the technique to tackle problems in an area of physics known as statistical mechanics.

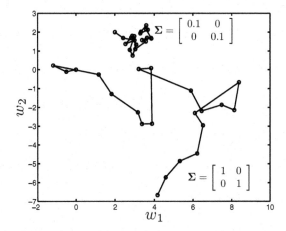

FIGURE 4.9 Two examples of random walks where the distribution over the next location is a Gaussian centred at the current location. The two walks have different covariance matrices, shown in the plot.

$\mathbf{w}_s$. If it is not accepted, our new sample is set to be equal to the previous one, $\mathbf{w}_s = \mathbf{w}_{s-1}$. This is continued until we have collected what we believe to be enough samples.

Now, if our proposal is based on a movement from the previous sample, what do we do for our first sample $\mathbf{w}_1$? It turns out that it doesn't matter where we start – $\mathbf{w}_1$ can be anything. As long as we sample for long enough, our sampler is guaranteed to converge to the distribution of interest. So, we can pluck a $\mathbf{w}_1$ from anywhere (sampling it from the prior would probably be a sensible choice), set the Metropolis–Hastings algorithm off, wait for it to converge to the correct distribution and then harvest as many samples as we need. A word of caution: the sampler is guaranteed to converge *in theory*. In practice, it is important to use one (or ideally more) of the methods available to test convergence before we start harvesting samples. We will now look at the proposal and acceptance steps in more detail.

Proposing a new sample Assume that we have already sampled $s - 1$ values using the MH scheme. We will propose a sample based on a movement from $\mathbf{w}_{s-1}$. Calling our proposed sample $\widetilde{\mathbf{w}}_s$ (we can only call it $\mathbf{w}_s$ once it has been accepted), we need to define a density:

$$p(\widetilde{\mathbf{w}}_s | \mathbf{w}_{s-1}).$$

This density does not have to have any connection with the posterior $p(\mathbf{w}|\mathbf{X}, \mathbf{t}, \sigma^2)$ from which we're trying to sample. We are free to define it as we please. In practice, the choice will have an impact on how long it will take the MH sampler to converge. A common choice is to use a Gaussian centred on the current sample, $\mathbf{w}_{s-1}$:

$$p(\widetilde{\mathbf{w}}_s | \mathbf{w}_{s-1}, \mathbf{\Sigma}) = \mathcal{N}(\mathbf{w}_{s-1}, \mathbf{\Sigma}).$$

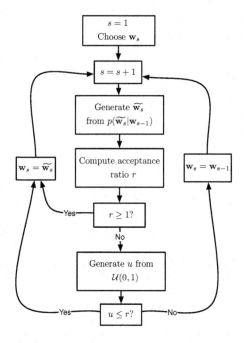

FIGURE 4.10 The Metropolis–Hastings algorithm.

Sampling a sequence of values like this creates what is known as a **random walk**. In Figure 4.9 we show two such walks (MATLAB script: `randwalks.m`). One starts from $\mathbf{w}_1 = [0,\ 0]^\mathsf{T}$ and has covariance $\mathbf{\Sigma} = \begin{bmatrix} 1 & 0 \\ 0 & 1 \end{bmatrix}$ whilst the other starts from $\mathbf{w}_1 = [2,\ 2]^\mathsf{T}$ and has covariance $\mathbf{\Sigma} = \begin{bmatrix} 0.1 & 0 \\ 0 & 0.1 \end{bmatrix}$. The latter walk moves less distance in each step due to the smaller diagonal (variance) elements in the covariance matrix. As we have already mentioned, the Gaussian is a popular choice for the proposal density. One reason is the ease with which we can sample from it – choosing a proposal distribution that was hard to sample from would make things unnecessarily complicated. Another reason is that it is symmetric: moving to $\widetilde{\mathbf{w}}_s$ from $\mathbf{w}_{s-1}$ is just as likely as moving from $\widetilde{\mathbf{w}}_s$ to $\mathbf{w}_{s-1}$:

$$p(\widetilde{\mathbf{w}}_s|\mathbf{w}_{s-1},\mathbf{\Sigma}) = p(\mathbf{w}_{s-1}|\widetilde{\mathbf{w}}_s,\mathbf{\Sigma}).$$

We will see the advantage of this as we move on to the acceptance step.

Accepting or rejecting   We now have $\widetilde{\mathbf{w}}_s$, a candidate for $\mathbf{w}_s$. We must now decide whether we should accept it or reject it. To do this, we compute the following ratio:

$$r = \frac{p(\widetilde{\mathbf{w}}_s|\mathbf{X},\mathbf{t},\sigma^2)}{p(\mathbf{w}_{s-1}|\mathbf{X},\mathbf{t},\sigma^2)}\frac{p(\mathbf{w}_{s-1}|\widetilde{\mathbf{w}}_s,\mathbf{\Sigma})}{p(\widetilde{\mathbf{w}}_s|\mathbf{w}_{s-1},\mathbf{\Sigma})}. \tag{4.17}$$

This is the ratio of the posterior density at the *proposed* sample to that at the old sample multiplied by the ratio of the proposal densities. The symmetry of the Gaussian proposal distribution discussed above allows us to ignore this last term, as it is always equal to 1. The first term is the ratio of posterior densities evaluated at the two different parameter values. We cannot compute the densities exactly because we cannot normalise them. However, because we are interested in a ratio, the normalisation constants cancel. So, we can substitute the ratio of posteriors with the ratio of the priors multiplied by the ratio of likelihoods. This leads us to the following expression:

$$r = \frac{g(\widetilde{\mathbf{w}}_s; \mathbf{X}, \mathbf{t}, \sigma^2)}{g(\mathbf{w}_{s-1}; \mathbf{X}, \mathbf{t}, \sigma^2)} = \frac{p(\widetilde{\mathbf{w}}_s | \sigma^2)}{p(\mathbf{w}_{s-1} | \sigma^2)} \frac{p(\mathbf{t} | \widetilde{\mathbf{w}}_s, \mathbf{X})}{p(\mathbf{t} | \mathbf{w}_{s-1}, \mathbf{X})}.$$

This ratio will always be positive as the density functions are always positive. If it is one or greater, we accept the sample ($\mathbf{w}_s = \widetilde{\mathbf{w}}_s$). If r is less than 1, we accept the sample with probability equal to r. In other words, if we propose a set of parameters that corresponds to a higher value of the posterior density than $\mathbf{w}_{s-1}$, we always accept it ($r > 1$). If we propose a set that corresponds to a lower value of posterior density, we accept it sometimes, but not always. The algorithm is depicted in Figure 4.10. Notice that we have described the accept/reject step in more detail. If $r < 1$, we should accept with probability r. This is achieved by drawing a value (u) from a uniform distribution between 0 and 1. Because it is uniform, the probability that u will be less than or equal to r is equal to r. Hence, we accept the proposal if $u \leq r$ and reject otherwise. The whole process is best illustrated with an example.

Figure 4.11 shows the Metropolis–Hastings algorithm in action, sampling from an arbitrary density (indicated by contours) (MATLAB script: `mhexample.m`). The starting point, $\mathbf{w}_1$ is shown in Figure 4.11(a). Our proposal density is Gaussian with $\boldsymbol{\Sigma} = \mathbf{I}$. From the starting point, the first proposal made is $\widetilde{\mathbf{w}}_2$, shown in Figure 4.11(b). The proposal causes an increase in posterior density and is therefore accepted: $\mathbf{w}_2 = \widetilde{\mathbf{w}}_2$. This acceptance is indicated by the solid line in Figure 4.11(b). The next proposal $\widetilde{\mathbf{w}}_3$ causes a slight decrease in posterior density but is accepted nonetheless (remember that, if the proposal causes a decrease, there is still a probability of acceptance). This is shown by the new solid line in Figure 4.11(c). The next proposal $\widetilde{\mathbf{w}}_4$ causes a large decrease in the posterior density value. Such a proposal is highly unlikely to be accepted (the ratio is much less than 1) and in this instance it isn't. This is represented by the dashed line in Figure 4.11(c). Hence, $\mathbf{w}_4 \neq \widetilde{\mathbf{w}}_4$ and is instead set to $\mathbf{w}_4 = \mathbf{w}_3$. This process continues in Figures 4.11(d) and 4.11(e) by which time we have ten samples. Along the way, three proposals were rejected and in each of those instances the sample is set to be equal to the value of the previous (accepted) sample. Continuing this process, we can see the first 300 accepted samples in Figure 4.11(f). These samples look reasonably consistent with the density contours – samples seem to be more concentrated towards the centre of the density and very sparse around the edges.

The density we are sampling from in this example happens to be a Gaussian. So, we can go some way towards convincing ourselves that we are indeed sampling from the correct density by computing the mean and covariance of the samples and seeing if they correspond to the mean and covariance of the actual density. The actual mean and covariance are given by

$$\mu = \begin{bmatrix} 1 \\ 1 \end{bmatrix}, \quad \mathbf{S} = \begin{bmatrix} 3 & 0.4 \\ 0.4 & 3 \end{bmatrix}.$$

After $N_s = 10,000$ samples, we can compute the sample-based approximations to the mean and covariance $(\mu', \mathbf{S}')$ as follows:

$$\mu' = \frac{1}{N_s} \sum_{s=1}^{N_s} \mathbf{w}_s, \quad \mathbf{S}' = \frac{1}{N_s} \sum_{s=1}^{N_s} (\mathbf{w}_s - \mu')(\mathbf{w}_s - \mu')^\mathsf{T}.$$

These work out as

$$\mu' = \begin{bmatrix} 0.9770 \\ 1.0928 \end{bmatrix}, \quad \mathbf{S}' = \begin{bmatrix} 3.0777 & 0.4405 \\ 0.4405 & 2.8983 \end{bmatrix},$$

which are both very similar to the true values.

Before we move on to applying MH to our binary response model, we need to discuss two related concepts – **burn-in** and **convergence**. As we can start our sampler from anywhere (there is no restriction on $\mathbf{w}_1$), we don't necessarily know if we are starting the sampler in an area that we should be generating samples from (it might be an area of very low posterior density). Therefore, the first few samples may not be representative and should be discarded. This period between the starting point and convergence of the sampler is known as the burn-in period. Sadly, it is not possible to conclusively determine how long this period should be. In the example described above, it is no more than a couple of samples but in some applications it could easily be hundreds or thousands. To overcome this problem we need a method for determining convergence. This is not convergence to a particular *value*, but convergence to a particular *distribution*. In other words, are the samples we are seeing coming from the correct distribution?

A popular method is to start several samplers simultaneously from different starting points. When all of the samplers are generating samples with similar characteristics (mean, variance, etc.), it suggests that they have all converged to the same distribution – the one we are trying to sample from.

We will now return to our binary response model. Using the MH scheme described above, we generate 10,000 samples from $p(\mathbf{w}|\mathbf{X}, \mathbf{t}, \sigma^2)$ (MATLAB script: logmh.m). Our proposal density is a Gaussian with $\Sigma = \gamma^2\mathbf{I}$ where $\gamma^2 = 0.5$. In Figure 4.12(a) we show every tenth sample (plotting all 10,000 samples makes for a very crowded plot) along with the posterior contours. The samples and the contours look reasonably coherent. If we like, we can use the samples to create marginal posterior densities for the two individual parameters. Recall from Section 2.2.6 that to marginalise w_2 from the posterior we would need to integrate (or sum, if the random variable is discrete) over all values w_2 could take:

$$p(w_1|\mathbf{X}, \mathbf{t}, \sigma^2) = \int p(w_1, w_2|\mathbf{X}, \mathbf{t}, \sigma^2) \, dw_2,$$

where $p(w_1, w_2|\mathbf{X}, \mathbf{t}, \sigma^2)$ is another way of writing $p(\mathbf{w}|\mathbf{X}, \mathbf{t}, \sigma^2)$. To get a sample-based approximation, we take each of our samples, $\mathbf{w}_s$, and ignore w_2. In other words, if we throw away the value of w_2 from each sample, we are left with a set of samples from $p(w_1|\mathbf{X}, \mathbf{t}, \sigma^2)$. In Figures 4.12(b)–4.12(d), we show three popular ways of visualising these samples. In the first, (Figure 4.12(b)) we have split the range of possible values into 20 sections and counted the number of samples that fall in each section. The black bars show the numbers for w_1 and the grey bars for w_2. If we were to take the number of samples falling into a particular section and divide it by the total number of samples, the numbers obtained could be thought of as the posterior probabilities that the w_1 (or w_2) falls into each of these sections. In the second example (Figure 4.12(c)), we have just plotted all 10,000 samples for w_1 (a similar plot for w_2 looks almost identical). This plot gives us confidence that the sampler has converged very quickly. If it hadn't, we might see an overall increasing or decreasing trend. In Figure 4.12(d) we show two continuous density functions that have been fitted to the samples. This is, in itself, a machine learning task for which there are various possible solutions. If the samples looked like they had come from a Gaussian, we could fit Gaussian densities to the two sets of samples (see Exercise 2.8). In this example, we have used a more general technique known as kernel density estimation. This can be performed in MATLAB using the `ksdensity` function. We won't go into any more detail here – the important point is that there are many ways to visualise the samples and it is possible to turn them into (approximate) continuous density functions.

Finally we turn our attention back to the predictive probability, $P(T_\text{new} = 1|\mathbf{x}_\text{new}, \mathbf{X}, \mathbf{t}, \sigma^2)$. When using the Laplace approximation, we approximated this quantity by drawing samples $\mathbf{w}_1, \ldots, \mathbf{w}_{N_s}$ from the approximate posterior and then computing

$$P(T_\text{new} = 1|\mathbf{x}_\text{new}, \mathbf{X}, \mathbf{t}, \sigma^2) = \frac{1}{N_s} \sum_{s=1}^{N_s} \frac{1}{1 + \exp(-\mathbf{w}_s^\mathsf{T} \mathbf{x}_\text{new})}.$$

We now have a set of samples from the true posterior, $p(\mathbf{w}|\mathbf{X}, \mathbf{t}, \sigma^2)$ and we can use them in exactly the same way. Figure 4.12(e) shows the predictive probability contours computed using these true posterior samples. Remember that these contours give the probability of classifying an object at any particular location as a square. The shape of the contours looks rather like the shape in Figure 4.7(b), which is not very surprising, as we saw in Figure 4.6(b) that the Laplace approximation didn't look too different from the true posterior. The only noticeable difference is that the contours in Figure 4.12(e) are slightly less tightly curved around the areas in which the data lie. This suggests that the probability reduces rather more slowly as we move away from the squares. The MH sampler is sampling from the true posterior and so the contours in Figure 4.12(e) should be considered closer to the truth than those for the Laplace approximation in Figure 4.6(a). This comparison is really just giving us an indication of how good the Laplace approximation is *at making predictions*. Figure 4.12(f) shows the decision boundaries corresponding to 20 of the MH samples picked at random (c.f. Figure 4.7(a)) (see Exercises 4.6, 4.7 and 4.8).

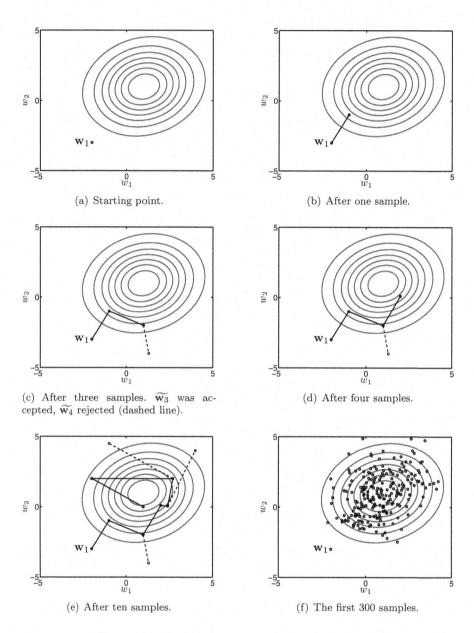

(a) Starting point.

(b) After one sample.

(c) After three samples. $\widetilde{\mathbf{w}}_3$ was accepted, $\widetilde{\mathbf{w}}_4$ rejected (dashed line).

(d) After four samples.

(e) After ten samples.

(f) The first 300 samples.

FIGURE 4.11 Example of the Metropolis–Hastings agorithm in operation.

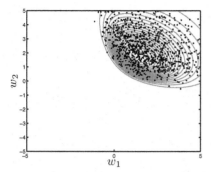

(a) One thousand of the MH samples along with the posterior contours.

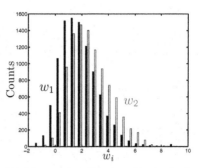

(b) Histograms of the samples for both w_1 (black) and w_2 (grey).

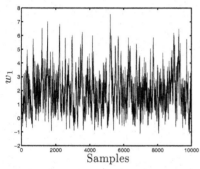

(c) All of the w_1 samples plotted against iteration, s.

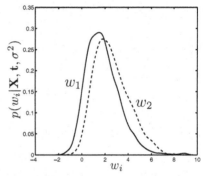

(d) Continuous densities fitted to the w_1 and w_2 samples.

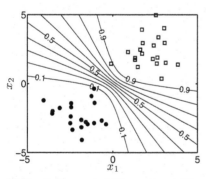

(e) Predictive probability contours. The contours show the probability of classifying an object at any location as a square. The probability of classifying an object as a circle at any point is 1 minus this value.

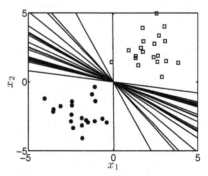

(f) Decision boundaries created from 20 randomly selected MH samples.

FIGURE 4.12 Results of applying the MH sampling algorithm to the binary response model.

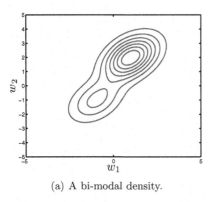

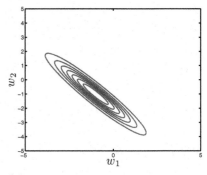

(a) A bi-modal density.

(b) A density with high parameter correlation.

FIGURE 4.13 Two densities that would be tricky to sample from with MH.

4.5.3 The art of sampling

The Metropolis–Hastings algorithm seems to work well for our binary response model. This will not always be the case – sampling methods (like MH) can be tricky to use. The difficulty lies in the (often unknown) shape of the density from which we are attempting to sample. Consider the density shown in Figure 4.13(a). This density has two modes, one at $\mathbf{w} = [-1 \; -1]^\mathsf{T}$ and one at $\mathbf{w} = [2, 2]^\mathsf{T}$. MH likes to move towards the modes, as these are moves that increase the posterior density and are therefore always accepted. Imagine $\mathbf{w}_s$ somewhere near the mode at $\mathbf{w} = [2, 2]^\mathsf{T}$. To move from here to the mode at $\mathbf{w} = [-1, -1]^\mathsf{T}$ would require many downhill steps in a row. Although this is possible, it is incredibly unlikely. This is where the relationship between the theory and practice of algorithms like MH breaks down. In theory, we will move from the top of one mode to the top of the other at some point in the future (just because it is unlikely doesn't mean that it won't happen eventually). In practice, we might get very old while we wait. We will happily explore one of the modes without ever realising that the other exists.

A second problem is illustrated by the density in Figure 4.13(b). Here, we have a density with only one mode but the two variables w_1 and w_2 are very dependent or highly correlated. If the value of w_1 is known, it is possible to narrow w_2 down to quite a small range. Densities such as this make it very difficult to choose proposal distributions: $p(\widetilde{\mathbf{w}}_s | \mathbf{w}_{s-1})$. Pick any position on the density in Figure 4.13(b) and imagine proposing a movement based on a Gaussian density with a diagonal covariance matrix (as we used in all of our examples) which would have circular contours when plotted. The density shown in Figure 4.13(b) is far from circular, and, because the shape of the proposal density is so different from the shape of the density we are attempting to sample from, many samples will be rejected: the vast majority of moves that we sample from our proposal will involve moving steeply down the probability gradient.

These are not the only problems. For example, how do we know when we have taken enough samples? How do we know how many samples we need to discard at the beginning? Fortunately, there are ways to overcome all of these problems: more sophisticated algorithms, ways of choosing proposal densities, quantities that we can evaluate that indicate convergence, etc. Further details are provided in the suggested reading.

4.6 CHAPTER SUMMARY

The motivation for this chapter was the desire to do things in the Bayesian way when we are not able to compute the distributions of interest analytically. We have shown examples of three general techniques. Firstly, finding the highest point of the posterior (the MAP estimate). This is a single value, and single values are not very Bayesian but it incorporates the prior and could therefore be considered a step up from the maximum likelihood solution. The second approach was to approximate the posterior with another density. We chose the Laplace approximation which approximates the posterior with a Gaussian. In many applications, this density could be used to compute the required expectations (predictions) analytically. In our binary response application, the expectation was not analytically tractable, but sampling from a Gaussian is easy and so we approximated (again) with a sample-based approximation. The third approach involved using the Metropolis–Hastings algorithm to generate samples from the true posterior which could be used to compute expectations. This comes at additional computational cost but (in theory at least) we get predictions that reflect the true posterior.

4.7 EXERCISES

4.1 For a data set consisting of N observations $\mathbf{x}_n$ (each of which is D-dimensional) and *real* valued targets t_n, a linear regression model is defined as

$$p(t_n|\mathbf{x}_n, \mathbf{w}) = \mathcal{N}(\mathbf{w}^\mathsf{T}\mathbf{x}_n, 1).$$

Making the standard IID assumption and assuming a Gaussian prior over the D-dimensional parameters $\mathbf{w}$, show that the Laplace approximation is equal to the true posterior.

4.2 In Chapter 3 we computed the posterior density over r, the probability of a coin giving heads, using a beta prior and a binomial likelihood. Recalling that the beta prior with parameters α and β is given by:

$$p(r|\alpha, \beta) = \frac{\Gamma(\alpha + \beta)}{\Gamma(\alpha)\Gamma(\beta)} r^{\alpha-1}(1 - r)^{\beta-1}$$

and the binomial likelihood, assuming y heads in N throws, is given by:

$$p(y|r, N) = \left(\begin{array}{c} y \\ N \end{array} \right) r^y(1 - r)^{N-y},$$

compute the Laplace approximation to the posterior. (Note: You should be able to obtain a closed-form solution for the MAP value, $\widehat{r}$, by setting the log posterior to zero, differentiating and equating to zero.)

4.3 Plot the true beta posterior and the Laplace approximation computed in Exercise 4.2 for various values of α, β, y and N.

4.4 Given the expression for the area of a circle, $A = \pi r^2$, and using only uniformly distributed random variates, devise a sampling approach for computing π.

4.5 Rearrange the logistic function

$$P(T_{\text{new}} = 1|\mathbf{x}_{\text{new}}, \widehat{\mathbf{w}}) = \frac{1}{1 + \exp(-\widehat{\mathbf{w}}^\mathsf{T}\mathbf{x}_{\text{new}})}$$

to show that $P(T_{\text{new}} = 1|\mathbf{x}_{\text{new}}, \widehat{\mathbf{w}}) = 0.5$ implies $\widehat{\mathbf{w}}^\mathsf{T}\mathbf{x}_{\text{new}} = 0$.

4.6 Assume that we observe N vectors of attributes, $\mathbf{x}_1, \ldots, \mathbf{x}_N$ and associated integer counts $t_1, \ldots, t_N$. A Poisson likelihood would be suitable:

$$p(t_n|\mathbf{x}_n, \mathbf{w}) = \frac{f(\mathbf{x}_n; \mathbf{w})^{t_n} \exp\{-f(\mathbf{x}_n; \mathbf{w})\}}{t_n!}.$$

Assuming a Gaussian prior on $\mathbf{w}$, derive the gradient and Hessian needed to use a Newton–Raphson routine to find the MAP solution for the parameters $\mathbf{w}$.

4.7 Derive the Laplace approximation for the model in Exercise 4.6.

4.8 Implement a Metropolis–Hastings sampling scheme for the model of Exercise 4.6 and compare the posterior with the Laplace approximation derived in Exercise 4.7.

4.8 FURTHER READING

[1] Christophe Andrieu, Nando de Freitas, Arnaud Doucet, and Michael Jordan. An introduction to MCMC for machine learning. *Machine Learning*, 50:5–43, 2003.

> A tutorial introduction to MCMC techniques from the specific point of view of Machine Learning.

[2] Siddhartha Chib. Understanding the Metropolis–Hasting algorithm. *The American Statistican*, 49(4):327–335, 1995.

> An excellent tutorial on the Metropolis–Hasting algorithm. A good starting point to look deeper into this family of algorithms.

[3] Arnaud Doucet, Nando de Freitas, and Neil Godron, editors. *Sequential Monte Carlo Methods in Practice*. Springer, 2010.

> We have not covered sequential Monte Carlo techniques in this book, but they are becoming increasingly popular for performing Bayesian inference in complex models, particularly models with a temporal component, like target tracking.

[4] Andrew Gelman, John B. Carlin, Hal S. Stern, and Donald B. Rubin. *Bayesian Data Analysis*. Chapman and Hall/CRC, second edition, 2004.

> This is an excellent resource for practical Bayesian inference. In particular, it provides a solid introduction to other sampling techniques as well as procedures for determining if Metropolis-Hastings and other sampling algorithms have converged.

[5] W. R. Gilks, S. Richardson, and D. Spiegelhalter, editors. *Markov Chain Monte-Carlo in Practice*. Chapman and Hall/CRC, 2005.

An edited volume providing several interesting practical sampling examples.

[6] Mark Girolami and Ben Calderhead. Riemann manifold Langevin and Hamiltonian Monte Carlo methods. *Journal of the Royal Statistical Society: Series B (Statistical Methodology)*, 73(2):123–214, 2011.

A recent paper by the authors describing a sophisticated Metropolis algorithm for sampling from distributions with complex forms.

[7] Jun Liu. *Monte Carlo Strategies in Scientific Computing*. Springer, 2008.

[8] Carl Rasmussen and Christopher Williams. *Gaussian Processes for Machine Learning*. The MIT Press, 2006.

In this chapter we briefly mentioned the non-parametric Gaussian process as an alternative to the parametric model. This book provides a comprehensive introduction to the use of Gaussian processes for both classification and regression.

[9] Simon Rogers, Richard Scheltema, Mark Girolami, and Rainer Breitling. Probabilistic assignment of formulas to mass peaks in metabolomics experiments. *Bioinformatics*, 25(4):512–518, 2009.

A paper by the authors that described an alternative Bayesian sampling method (Gibbs sampling) being applied to the problem of detecting metabolites in mass spectrometry experiments.

[10] Michael Tipping. Sparse Bayesian learning and the relevance vector machine. *Journal of Machine Learning Research*, 1:211–244, 2001.

An example of both regression and classification based on a linear model. The Laplace approximation is used in the classification example.

[11] Christopher Williams and David Barber. Bayesian classification with Gaussian Processes. *IEEE Transactions on Pattern Analysis and Machine Intelligence*, 20(12):1342–1351, 1998.

One of the first papers to use Gaussian processes for classification. A good introduction into some real approximate Bayesian inference.

CHAPTER 5

Classification

In the previous chapters, we have introduced many of the main concepts that underpin machine learning methods. We have seen how, for a particular model, we can choose parameters and make predictions based on observed data. This has been done in three ways – finding the parameters that minimise a loss function, finding those that maximise a likelihood function and by treating the parameters as random variables. We will meet some of these approaches again in this and subsequent chapters as we tackle the main algorithmic families that make up the field of machine learning: classification, clustering and projection.

In this chapter we will deal with classification. The field of Machine learning can boast of many classification algorithms and this set grows on a daily basis. We have chosen to introduce just four algorithms here. The four comprise a broad foundation to classification techniques in general and knowledge of these will enable the reader to solve a wide range of classification problems and explore the rest of the literature.

The four algorithms that we cover can be split into two types – those that produce probabilistic outputs and those that produce non-probabilistic outputs. Both types have their advantages and the choice will always be dataset dependent.

5.1 THE GENERAL PROBLEM

Typically, we will be presented with a set of N training objects, $\mathbf{x}_1, \ldots, \mathbf{x}_N$. Each is a vector with dimension D. For each object we are also provided with a label t_n that will describe which class object n belongs to. This label will typically take an integer value. For example, if there are two classes in our data, $t_n = \{0, 1\}$ or $t_n = \{-1, 1\}$. More generally, if there are C classes, $t_n = \{1, 2, \ldots, C\}$. Our task is to predict the class t_{new} for an unseen object $\mathbf{x}_{\mathsf{new}}$.

It is worthwhile drawing parallels between this setup and the one we saw in Chapters 1 to 3. In those chapters, we were provided with a set of objects $x_1, \ldots, x_N$ and associated real-valued labels. For many examples, the objects were Olympic years and the labels (responses) winning times for the men's 100 m sprint. Our aim was to predict the winning time for future Olympic games. The classification setup is very similar – it is just that in classification the response variable is an integer indicating a particular class rather than a real value. In fact, we have already seen an example of a classifier in Chapter 4. The binary response model is a well-known binary classification algorithm known as logistic regression.

Classification algorithms have been used successfully in many domains. Two particularly challenging examples are automatic disease diagnosis, where we are interested in predicting whether a patient is healthy or unhealthy based on medical observations, and text classification, where we are interested in classifying documents into topics or as relevant/irrelevant for a particular user. These two examples illustrate the diverse applications in which classification techniques can be found. Different domains each have their own associated problems. In the first example, how do we handle the uneven cost of making errors? In the second, how do we handle complex data objects like text? We will address both of these issues in later sections.

5.2 PROBABILISTIC CLASSIFIERS

Probabilistic and non-probabilistic classifiers differ in the type of output they produce. In the probabilistic case, the output is the probability of a new object belonging to a particular class. Expressing the training data in matrix and vector form $(\mathbf{X}, \mathbf{t})$, this probability for class c is

$$P(T_{\text{new}} = c|\mathbf{x}_{\text{new}}, \mathbf{X}, \mathbf{t}). \tag{5.1}$$

As a probability it must satisfy the following constraints:

$$0 \leq P(T_{\text{new}} = c|\mathbf{x}_{\text{new}}, \mathbf{X}, \mathbf{t}) \leq 1$$
$$\sum_{c=1}^{C} P(T_{\text{new}} = c|\mathbf{x}_{\text{new}}, \mathbf{X}, \mathbf{t}) = 1.$$

At first glance, obtaining a probability as an output may seem unnecessary. After all, we just said that our task was to predict the class T_{new}. If we are primarily interested in an assignment, then we might choose a non-probabilistic classifier. However, in many applications, the probability is useful, as it provides a level of *confidence* in the output. For example, consider a disease diagnosis application with two classes, healthy (0) and diseased (1). Providing the probability $P(T_{\text{new}} = 1|\mathbf{x}_{\text{new}}, \mathbf{X}, \mathbf{t})$ is much more informative than simply stating that $t_{\text{new}} = 1$. $P(T_{\text{new}} = 1|\mathbf{x}_{\text{new}}, \mathbf{X}, \mathbf{t}) = 0.6$ and $P(T_{\text{new}} = 1|\mathbf{x}_{\text{new}}, \mathbf{X}, \mathbf{t}) = 0.9$ both suggest that $\mathbf{x}_{\text{new}}$ should be classified as diseased, but in the former case, the model is much less certain. Perhaps more tests are required before a decision can be made.

5.2.1 The Bayes classifier

Our first probabilistic classifier is known as the Bayes classifier, taking its name from the equation on which it is based. Given a set of training points from C classes, our aim is to be able to compute the predictive probabilities (Equation 5.1) for each of C potential classes. These probabilities can then form the basis of a decision-making process (e.g. assign $\mathbf{x}_{\text{new}}$ to the class with the highest probability) or be used to compute an expectation.

From Bayes' rule (see Section 2.2.7 and Chapters 3 and 4), we can obtain an expression for the predictive probability:

$$P(T_{\text{new}} = c|\mathbf{x}_{\text{new}}, \mathbf{X}, \mathbf{t}) = \frac{p(\mathbf{x}_{\text{new}}|T_{\text{new}} = c, \mathbf{X}, \mathbf{t})P(T_{\text{new}} = c|\mathbf{X}, \mathbf{t})}{p(\mathbf{x}_{\text{new}}|\mathbf{X}, \mathbf{t})}.$$

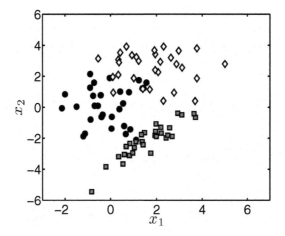

FIGURE 5.1 Three-class classification dataset.

The marginal likelihood, $p(\mathbf{x}_{new}|\mathbf{X}, \mathbf{t})$ can be expanded to a sum over the C possible classes, resulting in the following equation that defines the Bayes classifier:

$$P(T_{new} = c|\mathbf{x}_{new}, \mathbf{X}, \mathbf{t}) = \frac{p(\mathbf{x}_{new}|T_{new} = c, \mathbf{X}, \mathbf{t})P(T_{new} = c|\mathbf{X}, \mathbf{t})}{\sum_{c'=1}^{C} p(\mathbf{x}_{new}|T_{new} = c', \mathbf{X}, \mathbf{t})P(T_{new} = c'|\mathbf{X}, \mathbf{t})}. \qquad (5.2)$$

We are left with the task of defining $p(\mathbf{x}_{new}|T_{new} = c, \mathbf{X}, \mathbf{t})$ and $P(T_{new} = c|\mathbf{X}, \mathbf{t})$, the likelihood of $\mathbf{x}_{new}$ belonging to the cth class and the prior probability of the cth class. We will now discuss each of these in turn.

5.2.1.1 Likelihood – class-conditional distributions

The likelihood term in Equation 5.2, $p(\mathbf{x}_{new}|T_{new} = c, \mathbf{X}, \mathbf{t})$, is a distribution specific to the cth class (it is conditioned on $T_{new} = c$), evaluated at $\mathbf{x}_{new}$. To create a Bayes classifier, we need to define C of these class-conditional distributions. It is common to use the same type of distribution for each class, although there is no reason why this has to be the case. As with any choice of distribution, our decision should be based on the type of data being modelled and any additional knowledge we have about this data. Once we have chosen the distribution for the cth class, we are left with the job of choosing its parameters. For example, if we choose a Gaussian distribution, we need to choose the mean and (co)variance. Any parameters required to define the distribution for class c will be set using just the training data for class c. This stage in itself could be thought of as a machine learning problem and we will discuss it further in Section 5.2.1.3.

5.2.1.2 Prior class distribution

The second quantity in Equation 5.2 is $P(T_{new} = c|\mathbf{X}, \mathbf{t})$. This is the probability that the object belongs to class c conditioned on just the training data, $\mathbf{X}, \mathbf{t}$. It enables us to specify any prior beliefs in the class of $\mathbf{x}_{new}$ *before* we see it. This allows us to account for uneven class sizes. For example, perhaps there is a class c that is extremely rare. Before we see the data, we might like to bias against this class (choose $P(T_{new} = c|\mathbf{X}, \mathbf{t})$ to be very low) so that we will only classify $\mathbf{x}_{new}$ as belonging to it if it has a very high likelihood. Alternatively, class c may be very rare but we always want to detect it – it may be crucial not to misclassify these rare instances. In this case, we might set $P(T_{new} = c|\mathbf{X}, \mathbf{t})$ to be high. This will result in more potential $\mathbf{x}_{new}$ vectors being classified as class c. Of course, some of them will be incorrect (they truly belong to a different class) but we will not miss many that really belong to class c. These issues can also be resolved when we make a decision based on the set of predictive probabilities. We will discuss these issues at length in Section 5.4.

Regardless of our motives, the only technical restriction in the choice of $p(T_{new} = c|\mathbf{X}, \mathbf{t})$ is that they are positive and $\sum_c P(T_{new} = c|\mathbf{X}, \mathbf{t}) = 1$. Two popular choices are

1. Uniform prior: $P(T_{new} = c|\mathbf{X}, \mathbf{t}) = \frac{1}{C}$.
2. Class size prior: $P(T_{new} = c|\mathbf{X}, \mathbf{t}) = \frac{N_c}{N}$, where N is the number of objects in the training set and N_c is the number of objects in the training set belonging to class c.

Note that, although we have written the prior as being conditioned on $\mathbf{X}$ and $\mathbf{t}$, it is not necessarily dependent on them. Neither example above uses $\mathbf{X}$ in the prior definition and only the second example uses $\mathbf{t}$ (through N_c).

5.2.1.3 Example – Gaussian class-conditionals

The data shown in Figure 5.1 has been generated from three classes. Each training object consists of a two-dimensional attribute vector $\mathbf{x}_n = [x_{n1}, x_{n2}]^\mathsf{T}$ and an associated label $t_n = \{1, 2, 3\}$. Class 1 is plotted as black circles, class 2 as white diamonds and class 3 as grey squares. Given that the attributes are real valued, we will use Gaussian class-conditional distributions:

$$p(\mathbf{x}_n|t_n = c, \mathbf{X}, \mathbf{t}) = \mathcal{N}(\boldsymbol{\mu}_c, \boldsymbol{\Sigma}_c) \tag{5.3}$$

where $\boldsymbol{\mu}_c$ and $\boldsymbol{\Sigma}_c$ need to be chosen based on the training points associated with class c. We will denote these points as $\mathbf{X}^c$. This is itself a machine learning task – we have some data ($\mathbf{X}^c$) and wish to infer something about the parameters of a model. In this example we will find the parameters $\boldsymbol{\mu}_c$ and $\boldsymbol{\Sigma}_c$ that maximise the likelihood of the observations $\mathbf{X}^c$. As an alternative, we could use a Bayesian approach. For example, defining a prior density for these parameters, $p(\boldsymbol{\mu}_c, \boldsymbol{\Sigma}_c)$, we could compute a posterior from Bayes' rule:

$$p(\boldsymbol{\mu}_c, \boldsymbol{\Sigma}_c|\mathbf{X}^c) = \frac{p(\mathbf{X}^c|\boldsymbol{\mu}_c, \boldsymbol{\Sigma}_c)p(\boldsymbol{\mu}_c, \boldsymbol{\Sigma}_c)}{p(\mathbf{X}^c)}$$

and then compute the likelihood of $\mathbf{x}_{new}$ by taking the expectation

$$p(\mathbf{x}_{new}|T_{new} = c, \mathbf{X}, \mathbf{t}) = \mathbf{E}_{p(\boldsymbol{\mu}_c, \boldsymbol{\Sigma}_c|\mathbf{X}^c)} \{p(\mathbf{x}_{new}|\boldsymbol{\mu}_c, \boldsymbol{\Sigma}_c)\}.$$

Assuming that the choice of prior $p(\boldsymbol{\mu}_c, \boldsymbol{\Sigma}_c)$ is conjugate with the Gaussian likelihood, the posterior and expectation could both be obtained analytically. Performing this analysis in a Bayesian manner is likely to be most useful when there is little data, and hence our estimates of $\boldsymbol{\mu}_c$ and $\boldsymbol{\Sigma}_c$ are uncertain. See Exercises 5.1 and 5.2.

The maximum likelihood estimates for the mean and covariance of a Gaussian given a set of N data points can be obtained by differentiating the log-likelihood with respect to each parameter, setting to zero and solving (just as we did in Chapter 2 for the linear model). Omitting the details (see Exercise 5.3), the maximum likelihood estimates are

$$\boldsymbol{\mu}_c = \frac{1}{N_c} \sum_{n=1}^{N_c} \mathbf{x}_n \tag{5.4}$$

$$\boldsymbol{\Sigma}_c = \frac{1}{N_c} \sum_{n=1}^{N_c} (\mathbf{x}_n - \boldsymbol{\mu}_c)(\mathbf{x}_n - \boldsymbol{\mu}_c)^\mathsf{T}, \tag{5.5}$$

where the summations are only over the data instances from the cth class. The three class-conditional distributions are shown (along with the data) in Figure 5.2 (MATLAB script: plotcc.m).

We are left with the task of deciding on the prior, $P(T_{\text{new}} = c|\mathbf{X}, \mathbf{t})$. As mentioned earlier, a common choice is $P(T_{\text{new}} = c|\mathbf{X}, \mathbf{t}) = \frac{N_c}{N}$, the proportion of training points in class c. In our example, there are $N_c = 30$ in each class and therefore $P(T_{\text{new}} = c|\mathbf{X}, \mathbf{t}) = \frac{1}{3}$.

5.2.1.4 Making predictions

Armed with the class-conditional distributions and the prior, we are able to make predictions. As a worked example, we will compute the posterior class probabilities for $\mathbf{x}_{\text{new}} = [2, 0]^\mathsf{T}$. We summarise the various quantities that we need to compute and their values for $\mathbf{x}_{\text{new}}$ in Table 5.1. The final column gives us the numerator of Equation 5.2. To convert these values into probabilities, we have to divide each value by the sum of the three values: $0.0046 + 0.0020 + 0.0001 = 0.0067$. The resulting probabilities are

$$P(T_{\text{new}} = 1|\mathbf{x}_{\text{new}}, \mathbf{X}, \mathbf{t}) = 0.6890$$
$$P(T_{\text{new}} = 2|\mathbf{x}_{\text{new}}, \mathbf{X}, \mathbf{t}) = 0.3024$$
$$P(T_{\text{new}} = 3|\mathbf{x}_{\text{new}}, \mathbf{X}, \mathbf{t}) = 0.0087,$$

from which we can see that $\mathbf{x}_{\text{new}}$ is approximately twice as likely to belong to class 1 (black circles) than class 2 (white diamonds) and is very unlikely to belong to class 3 (grey squares).

By evaluating the classification probabilities over a grid of many $\mathbf{x}_{\text{new}}$ values, we can draw the contours of the classification probabilities. These can be seen in Figure 5.3 (MATLAB script: bayesclass.m). For each class the model assigns a high probability to the area of the space populated by training points of that class. However, there are some odd effects. Take 5.3(a) as an example: It has a high probability, > 0.9, in the area around the middle left of the plot where most class 1 (black circles) data is located. However, it also has a high probability in the bottom right of the plot where there is no class 1 data (or data from any class). Similarly, the

TABLE 5.1 Likelihood and priors for $\mathbf{x}_{\text{new}} = [2, 0]^{\top}$ for the Gaussian class-conditional Bayesian classification example.

c	$p(\mathbf{x}_{\text{new}}|T_{\text{new}} = c, \boldsymbol{\mu}_c, \boldsymbol{\Sigma}_c)$	$P(T_{\text{new}} = c|\mathbf{X}, \mathbf{t})$	$p(\mathbf{x}_{\text{new}}|T_{\text{new}} = c, \boldsymbol{\mu}_c, \boldsymbol{\Sigma}_c)P(T_{\text{new}} = c|\mathbf{X}, \mathbf{t})$
1	0.0138	$\frac{1}{3}$	0.0046
2	0.0061	$\frac{1}{3}$	0.0020
3	0.0002	$\frac{1}{3}$	0.0001

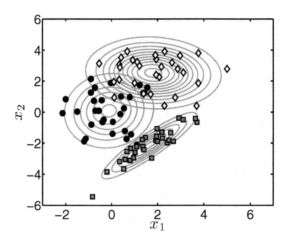

FIGURE 5.2 Three-class classification dataset with the density contours for the three class-conditional distributions fitted using Equations 5.4 and 5.5.

contours for class 2 (Figure 5.3(b)) give a high probability in the middle right of the plot where there is no data belonging to class 2. These effects can be explained by noticing the steepness of the class-conditional contours for class 3 (Figure 5.2) when compared with those for classes 1 and 2. Its density decays so much faster than those for classes 1 and 2 that to the right of class 3, the density functions for both classes 1 and 2 are higher. This is an unfortunate property – it does not seem sensible to label points to the bottom right of the plots as belonging with high probability to either class 1 or 2. It would be far better if, as in the binary response model we saw in Chapter 4, the probabilities would become less certain as we move away from the vicinity of the data.

5.2.1.5 The naive-Bayes assumption

In the previous example, we used two-dimensional Gaussians for the class-conditional distributions. These distributions were able to capture dependencies between the two attribute variables for each class. For example, we can see how the class-conditional distribution for class 3 was able to capture the strong dependency that exists between x_1 and x_2 for the training data in class 3. Fitting a two-Dimensional Gaussian

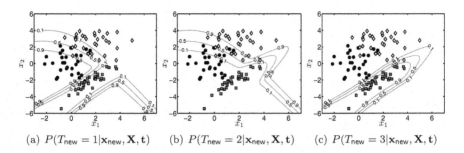

(a) $P(T_{new} = 1|\mathbf{x}_{new}, \mathbf{X}, \mathbf{t})$ (b) $P(T_{new} = 2|\mathbf{x}_{new}, \mathbf{X}, \mathbf{t})$ (c) $P(T_{new} = 3|\mathbf{x}_{new}, \mathbf{X}, \mathbf{t})$

FIGURE 5.3 Contour plots of the classification probabilities for the Bayesian classifier with Gaussian class-conditional distributions.

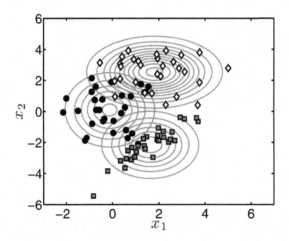

FIGURE 5.4 Density contours for Gaussian class-conditionals with the Naive Bayes assumption.

involves choosing five parameter values: two for $\boldsymbol{\mu}$ and three for $\boldsymbol{\Sigma}$ ($\boldsymbol{\Sigma}$ is symmetric so the two off-diagonal elements must be equal). This was perfectly feasible given that we had 30 training points in each class. Problems arise when the number of dimensions starts increasing. In general, fitting a D-dimensional Gaussian requires $D + D + \frac{D(D-1)}{2}$ parameters (D for the mean and $D + \frac{D(D-1)}{2}$ for the covariance matrix). For 10 dimensions, it is likely that 30 data points would not be sufficient to fit the resulting 65 parameters reliably.

A common way to partly overcome this problem (lack of data can only be completely solved by getting more data) is to make the *Naive Bayes* assumption: the D-dimensional class-conditional distributions can be factorised into a product of D univariate distributions. In other words, conditioned on a particular class, the dimensions (e.g. x_1 and x_2) are independent. A univariate Gaussian requires two parameters – μ and σ^2. Therefore, fitting D of these requires $2D$ parameters – 45 fewer in 10 dimensions than a single 10-dimensional Gaussian. The price we pay for this decrease in number of parameters is a decrease in model flexibility. In our Gaussian example, it means that we are restricting the shapes of the class-conditional distributions to be aligned with the axis – they cannot model any within-class dependencies. This is clear from Figure 5.4, where we see the density contours for the class-conditional distributions when we make the Naive Bayes assumption:

$$p(\mathbf{x}_n | t_n = k, \mathbf{X}, \mathbf{t}) = \prod_{d=1}^{2} p(x_{nd} | t_n = k, \mathbf{X}, \mathbf{t}).$$

Comparing this with Figure 5.2, it is clear that the model for class 3 no longer accurately reflects the characteristics of the data. Figure 5.5 shows the classification probability contours for the three classes (MATLAB script: `bayesclass.m`). It is interesting to note that, although we know that the class-conditional distribution for class 3 is not particularly appropriate, the classification contours are still reasonable (notwithstanding the lack of uncertainty as we move away from the data).

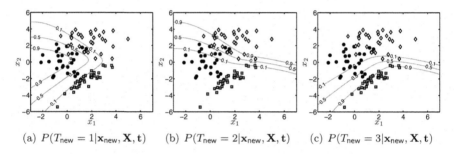

(a) $P(T_{\text{new}} = 1 | \mathbf{x}_{\text{new}}, \mathbf{X}, \mathbf{t})$ (b) $P(T_{\text{new}} = 2 | \mathbf{x}_{\text{new}}, \mathbf{X}, \mathbf{t})$ (c) $P(T_{\text{new}} = 3 | \mathbf{x}_{\text{new}}, \mathbf{X}, \mathbf{t})$

FIGURE 5.5 Contour plots of the classification probabilities for the Bayesian classifier with Gaussian class-conditional distributions and the Naive Bayes assumption.

5.2.1.6 Example – classifying text

Machine learning is widely used to perform automatic text classification. Learning from data makes a lot of sense within this domain – it is not straightforward to manually build a set of rules or models that could be used to classify text, but at the same time there is a lot of data with which a classifier could be trained.

The 20 newsgroups dataset is a popular benchmark dataset on which to evaluate new algorithms. It consists of approximately 20,000 documents, each of which is a post to one of 20 newsgroups. Considering each of these 20 newsgroups as a different class, we will build a classification system that can automatically assign a new document to one of these 20 classes. The groups cover a diverse set of topics including sport, computing and religion.

The algorithms that we have introduced work with numerical data and we therefore need a way of encoding a document as a vector of numerical values. The most common way of doing this is to use the *bag-of-words* model. If the total number of unique words in all documents (the vocabulary) is M, each document is represented as an M-dimensional vector. The vector for the nth document, $\mathbf{x}_n$, is made up of the counts of the number of times each word appears. x_{nm} is therefore the number of times word m appears in document n.

Given that the vocabulary is likely to be large, we will make the naive-Bayes assumption. Therefore our class-conditional distribution can be decomposed into a product over the words in the vocabulary:

$$p(\mathbf{x}_n|T_n = c, \ldots) = \prod_{m=1}^{M} p(x_{nm}|T_n = c, \ldots).$$

This assumption means that the number of parameters we require to define each class-conditional will be roughy equal (depending on the choice of distribution function) to the number of words. Adding any form of dependency between words would cause an explosion in the number of parameters that we would have to fit. For example, if we looked at pair-wise dependencies, we would need of the order of M^2 parameters. Given that a typical vocabulary might include some $50,000$ words, this is already a significant challenge.

The bag-of-words model also assumes that the ordering of the words is not important. For example, $\mathbf{x}_n$ would be identical for the following two sentences despite the fact that the second is nonsense:

1. The quick brown fox jumps over the lazy dog.
2. Dog quick lazy the jumps fox brown the over.

This assumption is not too restrictive: if our classifier is given a document that includes many instances of the word 'baseball' it is likely that this document is about sport regardless of the particular ordering of the words. Note that the bag-of-words model ignores ordering but does not necessarily imply independence. We could still define class-conditional distributions that allowed for dependencies between the elements of $\mathbf{x}_n$.

We will use multinomials (introduced in Section 2.3.3) for the class-conditional distributions. The multinomial distribution for the vector $\mathbf{x}_n$ is defined as

$$P(\mathbf{x}_n|\mathbf{q}) = \left(\frac{s_n!}{\prod_{m=1}^{M} x_{nm}!} \right) \prod_{m=1}^{M} q_m^{x_{nm}} \tag{5.6}$$

where $s_n = \sum_{m=1}^{M} x_{nm}$ and $\mathbf{q} = [q_1, \ldots, q_M]^\mathsf{T}$ are a set of parameters, each of which is a probability ($\sum_m q_m = 1$). Note that the multinomial distribution automatically makes the Naive Bayes assumption through the product over m.

There will be one multinomial (and hence one $\mathbf{q}$) for each class. Therefore, we need to determine the value of $\mathbf{q}_c$ (the vector of probabilities for the cth class) based on the set of training objects – $\mathbf{x}_n$ – corresponding to class c. We can do this with maximum likelihood (see Exercise 5.4), resulting in

$$q_{cm} = \frac{\sum_{n=1}^{N_c} x_{nm}}{\sum_{m'=1}^{M} \sum_{n=1}^{N_c} x_{nm'}}$$

where the summations over n just include objects from class C. Defining the prior distribution $P(T_\mathsf{new} = c|\mathbf{X}, \mathbf{t}) = \frac{1}{C}$, we could make predictions using Equation 5.2. However, before we do that, there is a problem that needs to be addressed.

5.2.1.7 Smoothing

It is quite feasible that a particular word (say m) will never appear in documents from one class (say c) – not many religious newsgroup posts are likely to mention 'baseball'. This will result in $q_{cm} = 0$. Look back at Equation 5.6 – if any one or more q_{cm} is zero with non-zero x_{nm}, the product $\prod_{m=1}^{M} q_{cm}^{x_{nm}}$ will be zero. In other words, if we are trying to compute the classification probability for a new document $\mathbf{x}_{\text{new}}$ that happens to include word m, the likelihood ($p(\mathbf{x}_{\text{new}}|T_{\text{new}} = c, \mathbf{q}_c)$) will equal zero and hence $P(T_{\text{new}} = c|\mathbf{x}_{\text{new}}, \mathbf{X}, \mathbf{t}) = 0$. A document including a word that doesn't appear in any of the training documents will have probability 0 of belonging to all classes. This is another example of over-fitting to the training data and we can overcome this by placing a prior density on $\mathbf{q}$ that encodes the belief that all probabilities are greater than 0. Once we have defined this prior, we can set $\mathbf{q}$ with the MAP estimate (see Chapter 4) rather than the maximum likelihood estimate. We could also take expectations with respect to the posterior density of $\mathbf{q}$ (see Exercises 5.5 and 5.6).

A suitable prior density for a vector of probabilities is the Dirichlet density, defined as

$$p(\mathbf{q}_c|\boldsymbol{\alpha}) = \frac{\Gamma\left(\sum_{m=1}^{M} \alpha_m\right)}{\prod_{m=1}^{M} \Gamma(\alpha_m)} \prod_{m=1}^{M} q_{cm}^{\alpha_m - 1}. \tag{5.7}$$

We will simplify this further by assuming that $\alpha_m = \alpha$ – i.e. the parameter used to define the Dirichlet is the same for each word. The MAP estimate can be obtained by maximising the prior multiplied by the multinomial likelihood (or the log of this product). Omitting the details here (see Exercise 5.7), the MAP estimate for q_{cm} is

$$q_{cm} = \frac{\alpha - 1 + \sum_{n=1}^{N_c} x_{nm}}{M(\alpha - 1) + \sum_{m'=1}^{M} \sum_{n=1}^{N_c} x_{nm'}}. \tag{5.8}$$

Once again, summations are only over the training objects from class c. For $\alpha > 1$, $q_{cm} > 0$ and the issue of zeros is no longer a problem. This technique is often referred to as *smoothing* – if we keep increasing α, each word probability q_{cm} will get closer and closer to $\frac{1}{M}$. This could also be considered as another example of regularisation (see Section 1.6).

The newsgroup data has been split into training and test sets holding $\approx 11,000$ and $\approx 7,000$ documents, respectively. Setting $\alpha = 2$, using Equation 5.8 to determine $\mathbf{q}_c$ and setting the prior classification probability to $1/20$ (a uniform prior over the 20 classes), we can compute the classification probabilities using Equation 5.2 where $p(\mathbf{x}_{\text{new}}|t_{\text{new}} = c, \mathbf{X}, \mathbf{t})$ is given by Equation 5.6, with $\mathbf{x}_n$ substituted for $\mathbf{x}_{\text{new}}$.

For each of the $\approx 7,000$ $\mathbf{x}_{\text{new}}$ vectors, we have a set of 20 probabilities. The simplest way to evaluate how well the classifier is working is to assign each $\mathbf{x}_{\text{new}}$ to the class for which it has the highest probability and compare these assignments to the known labels. If we do this, we find that the classifier is correct 78% of the time – not bad given that we have used the simplest possible model and have not attempted to optimise it in any way.

Figure 5.6 provides a graphical representation of the classification probabilities for the $\approx 7,000$ test points (MATLAB script: `newspred.m`). Each row corresponds to a single test point and the rows are ordered by true class. Each column corresponds to a predicted class. For example, the values in column 10 give the probabilities of

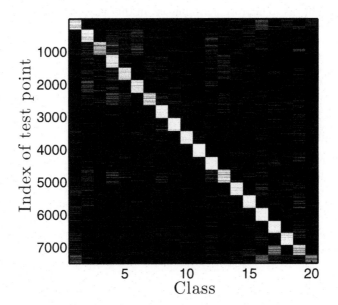

FIGURE 5.6 Graphical representation of the predictive probabilities for the Bayesian classifier on the 20 newsgroups data. Each row corresponds to one test point and the test points are ordered by true class. The whiter the colour, the higher the probability.

test points being classified as belonging to class 10. The block-like structure present tells us that the algorithm is doing reasonably well – the probabilities are high where they ought to be. A plot like this also allows us to see whether there is any pattern in the errors being made. For example, it seems that a large number of test points belonging to class 19 (the penultimate block) are wrongly classified as belonging to class 17. These two classes are from the newsgroups `talk.politics.guns` and `talk.politics.misc` and so it is not surprising that there might be some confusion here – many popular words will be shared by the two classes. Another example is the confusion between classes 20 and 16 for data points whose true class is 20. These two are from `talk.religion.misc` and `soc.religion.christian`, which are also clearly related. An analysis of the types of mistakes being made by classification algorithms will often enable us to improve performance. In this example, it may be sensible to consider whether classes 16 and 20 should be amalgamated into a larger class. If not, it might suggest that we should attempt to obtain more data (documents) from these two classes.

There are several ways to analyse the results being produced by a classification algorithm. We will look at these in more detail later in this chapter (Section 5.4). In the meantime, we will move onto our second probabilistic classifier.

5.2.2 Logistic regression

Although we called it a binary response model, Chapter 4 was entirely devoted to a binary classifier known as logistic regression. In Chapter 4 we didn't really discuss it from the viewpoint of classification but as a model for which analytical Bayesian inference was not possible. However, everything that one would need to use this method is there in Chapter 4 and we will not reproduce it here. There are, however, a couple of points that are worth discussing – the motivation for what we called the 'squashing function' and generalisations to this type of model.

5.2.2.1 Motivation

In Chapter 4 we motivated the logistic likelihood,

$$P(T_{\text{new}} = 1|\mathbf{x}_{\text{new}}, \mathbf{w}) = \frac{1}{1 + \exp(-\mathbf{w}^\mathsf{T}\mathbf{x}_{\text{new}})},$$

by arguing that we wanted to use our familiar linear model ($\mathbf{w}^\mathsf{T}\mathbf{x}$) but needed to transform it so that the output was a probability ($0 \leq P(T_{\text{new}} = 1|\mathbf{x}_{\text{new}}, \mathbf{w}) \leq 1$).

Whilst there is nothing wrong with this as a motivation, the use of the logistic likelihood is usually more formally derived as a result of modelling the *log-odds ratio*. This is the log of the ratio between $P(T_{\text{new}} = 1|\mathbf{x}_{\text{new}}, \mathbf{w})$ and $P(T_{\text{new}} = 0|\mathbf{x}_{\text{new}}, \mathbf{w})$:

$$\log\left(\frac{P(T_{\text{new}} = 1|\mathbf{x}_{\text{new}}, \mathbf{w})}{P(T_{\text{new}} = 0|\mathbf{x}_{\text{new}}, \mathbf{w})}\right).$$

There are no constraints on this value – it can take any real value. If $P(T_{\text{new}} = 1|\mathbf{x}_{\text{new}}, \mathbf{w}) \ll P(T_{\text{new}} = 0|\mathbf{x}_{\text{new}}, \mathbf{w})$, the log ratio will take on a large negative value, and, if $P(T_{\text{new}} = 1|\mathbf{x}_{\text{new}}, \mathbf{w}) \gg P(T_{\text{new}} = 0|\mathbf{x}_{\text{new}}, \mathbf{w})$ it will take a large positive one. Therefore, this quantity is a sensible candidate for modelling with our familiar linear model:

$$\log\left(\frac{P(T_{new} = 1|\mathbf{x}_{new}, \mathbf{w})}{P(T_{new} = 0|\mathbf{x}_{new}, \mathbf{w})}\right) = \mathbf{w}^\mathsf{T}\mathbf{x}_{new}. \tag{5.9}$$

With a bit of rearranging, and noting that

$$P(T_{new} = 0|\mathbf{x}_{new}, \mathbf{w}) = 1 - P(T_{new} = 1|\mathbf{x}_{new}, \mathbf{w}),$$

we can obtain an expression for $P(T_{new} = 1|\mathbf{x}_{new}, \mathbf{w})$:

$$\log\left(\frac{P(T_{new} = 1|\mathbf{x}_{new}, \mathbf{w})}{P(T_{new} = 0|\mathbf{x}_{new}, \mathbf{w})}\right) = \mathbf{w}^\mathsf{T}\mathbf{x}_{new}$$

$$\frac{P(T_{new} = 1|\mathbf{x}_{new}, \mathbf{w})}{P(T_{new} = 0|\mathbf{x}_{new}, \mathbf{w})} = \exp(\mathbf{w}^\mathsf{T}\mathbf{x}_{new})$$

$$\frac{P(T_{new} = 1|\mathbf{x}_{new}, \mathbf{w})}{1 - P(T_{new} = 1|\mathbf{x}_{new}, \mathbf{w})} = \exp(\mathbf{w}^\mathsf{T}\mathbf{x}_{new})$$

$$P(T_{new} = 1|\mathbf{x}_{new}, \mathbf{w})(1 + \exp(\mathbf{w}^\mathsf{T}\mathbf{x}_{new})) = \exp(\mathbf{w}^\mathsf{T}\mathbf{x}_{new})$$

$$P(T_{new} = 1|\mathbf{x}_{new}, \mathbf{w}) = \frac{\exp(\mathbf{w}^\mathsf{T}\mathbf{x}_{new})}{1 + \exp(\mathbf{w}^\mathsf{T}\mathbf{x}_{new})}$$

$$P(T_{new} = 1|\mathbf{x}_{new}, \mathbf{w}) = \frac{1}{1 + \exp(-\mathbf{w}^\mathsf{T}\mathbf{x}_{new})}.$$

By using the logistic likelihood for $P(T_{new} = 1|\mathbf{x}_{new}, \mathbf{w})$, we are actually modelling the log-odds ratio with a linear model. In the statistics community, approaches like this are known as *generalised linear models* – linear models that are passed through some transformation to model the quantity of interest.

5.2.2.2   Non-linear decision functions

The decision boundaries for individual $\mathbf{w}$ values in Chapter 4 were all straight lines. The probability contours obtained with the Laplace approximation and the Metropolis–Hastings algorithm were curved as the result of averaging over many straight lines. By expanding $\mathbf{x}_n$ to include terms like x_n^2, we can obtain non-linear decision boundaries in logistic regression in a manner similar to the way we obtained non-linear regression functions in Chapter 1. For example, the data in Figure 5.7(a) shows a binary classification dataset that may require a non-linear decision boundary. Using x_1 and x_2 to denote the individual attributes ($\mathbf{x} = [x_1, x_2]^\mathsf{T}$), we could use the following model for the log-odds ratio:

$$\log\left(\frac{P(T_{new} = 1|\mathbf{x}_{new}, \mathbf{w})}{P(T_{new} = 0|\mathbf{x}_{new}, \mathbf{w})}\right) = w_0 + w_1 x_1 + w_2 x_2 + w_3 x_1^2 + w_4 x_2^2. \tag{5.10}$$

To show that this is able to produce non-linear decision boundaries, we find the MAP estimate $\widehat{\mathbf{w}}$ of the parameters assuming a Gaussian prior $p(\mathbf{w}|\sigma^2) = \mathcal{N}(\mathbf{0}, \sigma^2\mathbf{I})$ (see Section 4.3). We could, of course, submit this model to the more Bayesian treatments introduced in Chapter 4 if desired.

Plugging $\widehat{\mathbf{w}}$ into the logistic likelihood allows us to compute the classification probabilities:

$$P(T_{new} = 1|\mathbf{x}_{new}, \widehat{\mathbf{w}}) = \frac{1}{1 + \exp(-\widehat{\mathbf{w}}^\mathsf{T}\mathbf{x}_{new})}.$$

Evaluating this over a grid of $\mathbf{x}_{new}$ values enables us to plot contours of the probability

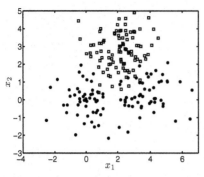

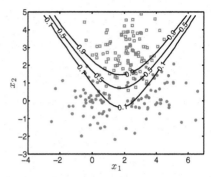

(a) Dataset that might be better modelled with a non-linear decision boundary.

(b) Classification probabilities for a model with up to second-order terms (see Equation 5.10). These are based on a point estimate of the parameters – $\widehat{\mathbf{w}}$ – obtained using a Newton–Raphson optimisation.

FIGURE 5.7 Binary data and classification probability contours for the logistic regression model described by Equation 5.10.

of belonging to class 1 over the space of attributes. The non-linear decision boundary can be seen in Figure 5.7(b) (the training points have been greyed out a little to make the contours easier to see) (MATLAB script: `nonlinlogreg.m`). This is an appealing property of logistic regression but it is important to remember that the problems of over-fitting and poor generalisation we saw when making the linear model more and more complex in Chapter 1 are just as troublesome in the classification domain. Remember that this is for a single value of $\mathbf{w}$: we obtained non-linear decision boundaries in the Laplace and Metropolis–Hastings cases in Chapter 4, but only by averaging over many different straight lines.

5.2.2.3 Non-parametric models – the Gaussian process

Throughout this book, we have restricted ourselves to models of the form $\mathbf{w}^\mathsf{T}\mathbf{x}$. This model has a set of parameters $\mathbf{w}$ in which it is linear. For any particular expansion of $\mathbf{x}$ (e.g. adding squared terms), this function belongs to a particular family of functions. For example, if we had squared terms, it is a member of the quadratic family. The choice of a family places restrictions on the flexibility of the function – if we choose $w_0 + w_1 x$, we can only model things with straight lines. If we choose $w_0 + w_1 x + w_2 x^2 + w_3 x^3$, we can only model things with cubic (third-order) polynomials. Models such as these are known as *parametric*, as they belong to a particular parametric family and the particular function within that family is determined by a set of parameters, $\mathbf{w}$.

It is worth briefly mentioning a very flexible alternative – non-parametric models. Rather than being defined as a function of some parameters (e.g. $f(\mathbf{x}; \mathbf{w})$), non-parametric models are defined in a more general manner. For example, a popular non-parametric model is the Gaussian process (GP). In parametric models, we place a prior distribution on the parameters $\mathbf{w}$ which in turn implies a prior distribution over the output values of the function. With a GP we place the prior distribution *directly* onto the output values of the function. Note that non-parametric does not mean that the GP does not have *any* parameters, but that it does not assume a parametric form for the function.

The GP is characterised by two functions – a mean function $\mu(\mathbf{x})$ that describes the average function value as a function of the attribute x (x can be a scalar or a vector) and a covariance function $c(\mathbf{x}_n, \mathbf{x}_m)$ that defines how similar the function output at $\mathbf{x}_n$ should be to that at $\mathbf{x}_m$. In practice, the mean function is often assumed to be 0.

For any finite set of N data points, the Gaussian process essentially becomes an N-dimensional Gaussian distribution with mean $\boldsymbol{\mu} = [\mu(\mathbf{x}_1), \ldots, \mu(\mathbf{x}_N)]^\mathsf{T}$ and covariance matrix

$$\mathbf{C} = \begin{bmatrix} c(\mathbf{x}_1, \mathbf{x}_1) & c(\mathbf{x}_1, \mathbf{x}_2) & \ldots & c(\mathbf{x}_1, \mathbf{x}_N) \\ c(\mathbf{x}_2, \mathbf{x}_1) & c(\mathbf{x}_2, \mathbf{x}_2) & \ldots & c(\mathbf{x}_2, \mathbf{x}_N) \\ \vdots & \vdots & \ddots & \vdots \\ c(\mathbf{x}_N, \mathbf{x}_1) & c(\mathbf{x}_N, \mathbf{x}_2) & \ldots & c(\mathbf{x}_N, \mathbf{x}_N) \end{bmatrix}$$

Sampling a vector from this Gaussian gives a value for the output of the function at each of the N data objects.

GPs have become increasingly popular within machine learning due to their flexibility – a GP is not restricted to a particular parametric family. They can be thought of as a replacement for a parametric model in any particular algorithm. For example, we could have used a GP to model the Olympics data, or as a replacement for $\mathbf{w}^\mathsf{T}\mathbf{x}_n$ in the logistic regression algorithm. We discuss GPs more thoroughly in Chapter 8.

5.3 NON-PROBABILISTIC CLASSIFIERS

We now turn our attention to non-probabilistic classifiers. Rather than providing a probability of class membership, $P(T_\text{new} = c | \mathbf{x}_\text{new}, \mathbf{x}, \mathbf{t})$, their output is an assignment of an object to a class, $t_\text{new} = c$. We will look at two different algorithms – K-nearest neighbours and the Support Vector Machine. Both are very popular within machine learning due to their excellent empirical performance. The Support Vector Machine will also provide us with an introduction to the area of kernel methods.

5.3.1 K-nearest neighbours

Our first approach, K-nearest neighbours (KNN), is very popular due to simplicity and excellent empirical performance. It can handle both binary and multiclass data and makes no assumptions about the parametric form of the decision boundary. KNN does not have a training phase and is best described through the simple process used to classify new objects, $\mathbf{x}_\text{new}$.

Consider our normal scenario – we have N training objects, each of which is represented by a set of attributes $\mathbf{x}_n$ and a label t_n. To classify $\mathbf{x}_\text{new}$ with KNN, we first find the K training points that are closest to $\mathbf{x}_\text{new}$. t_new is then set to be

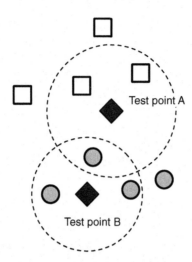

FIGURE 5.8 Cartoon depicting the operation of KNN ($K = 3$). Circles and squares denote the training points and diamonds the test points. Test point A will be assigned to the 'square' class and B to the circles.

the majority class amongst these neighbours. This is illustrated in Figure 5.8. The training data consists of data points belonging to one of two classes (grey circles and white squares). Two test points are indicated by black diamonds, and in both cases, the dotted circles enclose their $K = 3$ nearest neighbours. The neighbours of test point A include two from the square class and one from the circle class, and so it will be classified as belonging to the square class. All of the neighbours of test point B belong to the circle class, to which B is therefore assigned.

One drawback of the K-nearest neighbours approach is the issue of ties – two or more classes having an equal number of votes. For example, if $K = 8$ in Figure 5.8, we will always have four neighbours belonging to each class and no majority. One option is to assign the class randomly from the set of tied classes. This may not always be sensible, as it means that the same x_{new} may be assigned to different classes if it is tested more than once. For binary classification, a neater solution is to always use an odd number of neighbours. More generally, we can weight the votes according to distance such that the votes from closer points have greater influence making ties highly unlikely.

In Figure 5.8 we have used Euclidean distance to determine which points are neighbours of the test point. However, we are free to choose any distance measure we like. KNN is therefore very flexible – it can be used for any data type for which we can define a distance between two objects. Examples of other data types for which KNN has been used successfully include strings, graphs and images.

5.3.1.1 Choosing K

Once we have some data and have chosen a suitable distance measure, the only thing that remains is the choice of K. If K is too small, our classification can be

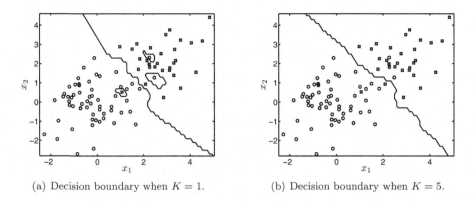

(a) Decision boundary when $K = 1$.   (b) Decision boundary when $K = 5$.

FIGURE 5.9 Binary classification dataset and decision boundaries for $K = 1$ and $K = 5$.

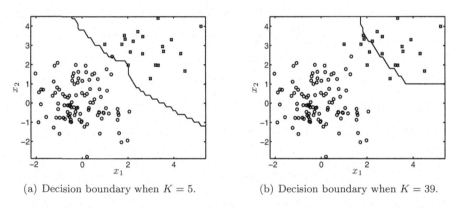

(a) Decision boundary when $K = 5$.   (b) Decision boundary when $K = 39$.

FIGURE 5.10 Second binary classification dataset and decision boundaries for $K = 5$ and $K = 39$.

heavily influenced by noise. This is demonstrated in Figure 5.9(a) (MATLAB script: knnexample.m) where we have plotted the decision boundary (consisting of points equidistant from a single neighbour in each class) for some binary data with $K = 1$. Whilst the majority of the boundary looks reasonable, there are three 'islands' that look like the result of over-fitting. Each island guards a large area of input space on what looks like the wrong side of the decision boundary. The three points in the centre of the islands are likely to be noise (i.e. mislabeled points). This problem is easily rectified by increasing K. Figure 5.9(b) shows the same data along with the $K = 5$ decision boundary. The inclusion of more neighbours has had the effect of regularising the boundary, removing the three islands.

We have seen that a very small value of K can be dangerous. What happens if K gets too big? As we increase K, we are using neighbours from further away from $\mathbf{x}_{new}$. Up to a point, this is useful. It has a regularising effect that reduces the chance of over-fitting. However, if we go too far, we will lose the true patterns in

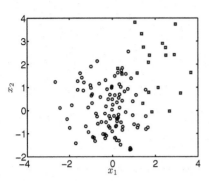

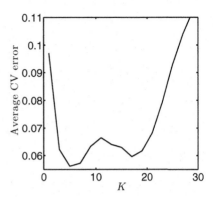

(a) Binary classification dataset. Note the class inbalance: the grey squares class has fewer members than the white circles.

(b) Average cross-validation error as K is increased.

FIGURE 5.11 Using cross-validation to find the best value of K. Ten-fold cross-validation was used and the reported error is averaged both over the folds and over 100 different partitions of the data into folds.

the data that we are attempting to model. Consider this extreme example: in some hypothetical training data there are $N_0 = 50$ and $N_1 = 10$ points from classes 0 and 1, respectively. Given that $N_1 = 10$, no test point can have more than 10 neighbours belonging to class 1. Therefore, if $K \geq 21$, $\mathbf{x}_{\mathsf{new}}$ can never be classified as belonging to class 1 – we have smoothed to such an extent that everywhere belongs to class 0! A less extreme example can be seen in Figures 5.10(a) and 5.10(b), where we show a dataset that has 50 points in class 0 (white circles) and only 20 points in class 1 (grey squares). The $K = 5$ decision boundary in Figure 5.10(a) looks reasonable whilst the $K = 39$ boundary in Figure 5.10(b) is being pushed up into the top right corner as the larger class exerts its influence.

Datasets with uneven numbers of objects in each class are known as *imbalanced* and are common in machine learning and something we must be aware of when we undertake any classification analysis. We will discuss this particular problem in more detail in Section 5.4.

The most popular method for choosing K is cross-validation (see Section 1.5.2). In previous sections when t was continuous, we used cross-validation to optimise the squared loss. We now need something suitable for our discrete (classification) t. We will discuss various other measures in Section 5.4 but for the moment we will use the simple measure that we used with the newsgroups data in Section 5.2.1.6 – the proportion of times the classifier makes a mistake. Figure 5.11(b) shows how the percentage error (0/1 loss) changes as K increases for the synthetic data given in Figure 5.11(a) (MATLAB script: `knncv.m`). Ten-fold cross-validation was used and, to remove the effect of any particular partitioning of the data into the ten folds, the entire process was repeated 100 times. The errors plotted are therefore an average of $10 \times 100 = 1000$ fold errors. As K increases, the classification error drops to a minimum corresponding to $K = 5$ and then starts increasing (with a little bump at $K = 17$).

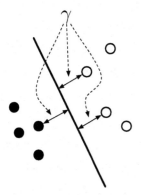

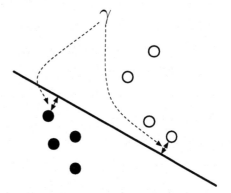

(a) The decision bound-
ary that maximises the
margin.

(b) A non-optimal decision boundary.

FIGURE 5.12 The classification margin γ, defined as the perpendicular distance from the decision boundary to the closest points on either side.

5.3.2 Support vector machines and other kernel methods

Our second non-probabilistic classifier is the Support Vector Machine (SVM). SVMs are binary classifiers (although multiclass extensions have been proposed) and have been used successfully across a wide range of machine learning applications. Their success is due to their excellent empirical performance and for many applications they are hard to beat. They have been found to be particularly useful in applications where the number of attributes is much larger than the number of training objects. This is because the number of parameters that must be set for the SVM is related to the number of training objects and not the number of attributes.

The standard SVM uses a linear decision boundary, given by $\mathbf{w}^\mathsf{T}\mathbf{x}_{new} + b$, to classify new data objects. Objects lying on one side of the line are put into class $t_{new} = 1$ and objects on the other side into $t_{new} = -1$ (note that the class labels are $\{1, -1\}$ rather than $\{0, 1\}$).

The SVM decision function for a test point $\mathbf{x}_{new}$ is therefore given as

$$t_{new} = \text{sign}(\mathbf{w}^\mathsf{T}\mathbf{x}_{new} + b). \tag{5.11}$$

The learning task involves choosing the values of $\mathbf{w}$ and b based on the training data. This is achieved by finding the parameters that maximise a quantity called the *margin*. This is much the same way that we minimised the loss in Chapter 1, maximised the likelihood in Chapter 2 and found the MAP solution in Chapter 3.

5.3.2.1 The margin

The margin is defined as the perpendicular distance from the decision boundary to the closest points on either side. This is illustrated in Figure 5.12, where the margin is denoted by γ.

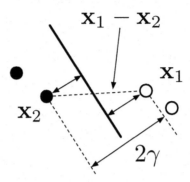

FIGURE 5.13 Illustrating the steps taken to compute the margin, γ. 2γ is equal to the component of the vector $\mathbf{x}_1 - \mathbf{x}_2$ in the direction perpendicular to the boundary.

The toy examples in Figures 5.12(a) and 5.12(b) demonstrate why the margin is a sensible quantity to maximise. Intuitively, the boundary corresponding to the larger margin (Figure 5.12(a)) looks more sensible. In particular, the decision boundary in Figure 5.12(b) will classify points towards the top left and bottom right as belonging to the white and black classes, respectively whereas common sense would suggest the opposite. Notice how in Figure 5.12(b) the margin is computed as the distance between the decision boundary and a *different* set of training points than in Figure 5.12(a). The margin is defined as the distance between the boundary and the *closest* points, the set of which will change as the boundary does.

5.3.2.2 Maximising the margin

It is easiest to compute the margin using one point from each class. Figure 5.13 shows how this is done. $\mathbf{x}_1$ and $\mathbf{x}_2$ are the closest points from the two classes. 2γ (i.e. double the boundary) is equal to the component of the vector joining $\mathbf{x}_1$ and $\mathbf{x}_2$ in the direction perpendicular to the boundary.

The vector joining $\mathbf{x}_1$ and $\mathbf{x}_2$ is given by $\mathbf{x}_1 - \mathbf{x}_2$ and the direction perpendicular to the decision boundary is given by $\mathbf{w}/||\mathbf{w}||$. The inner product between these two quantities gives us the quantity that we require:

$$2\gamma = \frac{1}{||\mathbf{w}||}\mathbf{w}^\mathsf{T}(\mathbf{x}_1 - \mathbf{x}_2).$$

Our decision function, $t_{\text{new}} = \text{sign}(\mathbf{w}^\mathsf{T}\mathbf{x}_{\text{new}}+b)$, is invariant to scaling its argument by a positive constant. This means that we can multiply $\mathbf{w}^\mathsf{T}\mathbf{x}_{\text{new}} + b$ by a positive constant λ and the output of the sign function will be unchanged. Therefore, we can decide to fix the scaling of $\mathbf{w}$ and b such that $\mathbf{w}^\mathsf{T}\mathbf{x} + b = \pm 1$ for the closest points on either side. This restriction allows us to simplify our expression for γ:

$$
\begin{aligned}
2\gamma &= \frac{1}{||\mathbf{w}||}\mathbf{w}^{\mathsf{T}}(\mathbf{x}_1 - \mathbf{x}_2) \\
&= \frac{1}{||\mathbf{w}||}(\mathbf{w}^{\mathsf{T}}\mathbf{x}_1 - \mathbf{w}^{\mathsf{T}}\mathbf{x}_2) \\
&= \frac{1}{||\mathbf{w}||}(\mathbf{w}^{\mathsf{T}}\mathbf{x}_1 + b - \mathbf{w}^{\mathsf{T}}\mathbf{x}_2 - b) \\
&= \frac{1}{||\mathbf{w}||}(1 + 1) \\
\gamma &= \frac{1}{||\mathbf{w}||}.
\end{aligned}
\tag{5.12}
$$

Comment 5.1 – Constrained optimisation with Lagrange multipliers: At various points in this book we will need to perform constrained optimisations – finding the values of a set of parameters that maximise (or minimise) an objective function but that also satisfy some constraints. This can be done using *Lagrange* multipliers. In particular, we make a new objective function which includes the original plus an additional term for each constraint. The form of these terms is chosen such that the optimum of the new function is equal to the optimum of the constrained problem.

For example, suppose we wish to minimise $f(w)$ subject to the constraint $g(w) \le a$:

$$
\underset{w}{\mathrm{argmin}} \quad f(w)
$$
$$
\text{subject to} \quad g(w) \le a.
$$

The new objective function is produced by adding a Lagrangian term of the form $\lambda(a - g(w))$ and optimised over both w *and* the Lagrange multiplier λ:

$$
\underset{w,\lambda}{\mathrm{argmin}} \quad f(w) - \lambda(g(w) - a)
$$
$$
\text{subject to} \quad \lambda > 0.
$$

We are not going to go into the details of how this works here. Whenever we perform constrained optimisation, we will state the necessary Lagrangian terms without any further details. For more details, see the suggested reading at the end of this chapter.

To maximise the margin, we must therefore maximise $\frac{1}{||\mathbf{w}||}$. There are, however, some constraints. Recall that we decided that, for the closest points in class 1: $\mathbf{w}^{\mathsf{T}}\mathbf{x}_n + b = 1$. Therefore, $\mathbf{w}$ has to be chosen to satisfy $\mathbf{w}^{\mathsf{T}}\mathbf{x}_n + b \ge 1$ for all points in class 1. Similarly, it must satisfy $\mathbf{w}^{\mathsf{T}}\mathbf{x}_n + b \le -1$ for those in class -1. Defining the labels as ± 1 allows us to express these two sets of constraints succinctly as

$$
t_n(\mathbf{w}^{\mathsf{T}}\mathbf{x}_n + b) \ge 1.
$$

Therefore, our learning task is to find the largest value of $\gamma = \frac{1}{||\mathbf{w}||}$ that satisfies these N constraints (where N is the number of points in the training set). It will actually be easier to *minimise* $\frac{1}{2}||\mathbf{w}||^2$ and so we shall do this instead. Formally, our optimisation problem has become

$$\operatorname*{argmin}_{\mathbf{w}} \quad \frac{1}{2}||\mathbf{w}||^2$$

$$\text{subject to} \quad t_n(\mathbf{w}^\mathsf{T}\mathbf{x}_n + b) \geq 1, \text{ for all } n.$$

This is the first time we have come across a constrained optimisation problem. To solve it, we need to incorporate the constraints into the objective function through a set of Lagrange multipliers. Lagrange multipliers add a new term in our objective function for each constraint such that the optimum of the new objective function corresponds to the optimum of the original, constrained problem. In our case, we need N Lagrangian terms. Each has an associated Lagrange multiplier, which is itself constrained to be positive. Without going into any more details of Lagrange multipliers, our new objective function is

$$\operatorname*{argmin}_{\mathbf{w},\alpha} \quad \frac{1}{2}\mathbf{w}^\mathsf{T}\mathbf{w} - \sum_{n=1}^{N} \alpha_n(t_n(\mathbf{w}^\mathsf{T}\mathbf{x}_n + b) - 1)$$

$$\text{subject to} \quad \alpha_n \geq 0, \text{ for all } n,$$

where we've used the fact that $||\mathbf{w}||^2 = \mathbf{w}^\mathsf{T}\mathbf{w}$. At an optimum of this new objective function, the partial derivatives of the objective function with respect to $\mathbf{w}$ and b must be zero. These derivatives are

$$\frac{\partial}{\partial \mathbf{w}} = \mathbf{w} - \sum_{n=1}^{N} \alpha_n t_n \mathbf{x}_n$$

$$\frac{\partial}{\partial b} = -\sum_{n=1}^{N} \alpha_n t_n.$$

Equating these two expression to zero gives us the following two identities that must be satisfied at the optimum:

$$\mathbf{w} = \sum_{n=1}^{N} \alpha_n t_n \mathbf{x}_n \tag{5.13}$$

$$\sum_{n=1}^{N} \alpha_n t_n = 0. \tag{5.14}$$

Substituting the first of these identities back into the objective function gives us a new objective function which must be *maximised* with respect to the α_n rather than w:

$$\frac{1}{2}\mathbf{w}^\mathsf{T}\mathbf{w} - \sum_{n=1}^{N} \alpha_n \left(t_n(\mathbf{w}^\mathsf{T}\mathbf{x}_n + b) - 1 \right)$$

$$= \frac{1}{2}\left(\sum_{m=1}^{N} \alpha_m t_m \mathbf{x}_m^\mathsf{T}\right)\left(\sum_{n=1}^{N} \alpha_n t_n \mathbf{x}_n\right) - \sum_{n=1}^{N} \alpha_n \left(t_n \left(\sum_{m=1}^{N} \alpha_m t_m \mathbf{x}_m^\mathsf{T}\mathbf{x}_n + b\right) - 1 \right)$$

$$= \frac{1}{2}\sum_{n,m=1}^{N} \alpha_m \alpha_n t_m t_n \mathbf{x}_m^\mathsf{T}\mathbf{x}_n - \sum_{n,m=1}^{N} \alpha_m \alpha_n t_m t_n \mathbf{x}_m^\mathsf{T}\mathbf{x}_n - \sum_{n=1}^{N} \alpha_n t_n b + \sum_{n=1}^{N} \alpha_n$$

$$= \sum_{n=1}^{N} \alpha_n - \frac{1}{2}\sum_{n,m=1}^{N} \alpha_m \alpha_n t_m t_n \mathbf{x}_m^\mathsf{T}\mathbf{x}_n,$$

where we used the fact that $\sum_{n=1}^{N} \alpha_n t_n = 0$ to remove the third term in the penultimate line. This expression is known as the dual optimisation problem and has to be maximised subject to the following constraints:

$$\alpha_n \geq 0, \quad \sum_{n=1}^{N} \alpha_n t_n = 0,$$

the second of which comes from Equation 5.14. Notice that $\mathbf{w}$ doesn't feature at all in this optimisation problem.

This optimisation problem is a constrained quadratic programming task, quadratic because of the $\alpha_m \alpha_n$ term. There is no analytical solution, but it is reasonably straightforward to solve numerically. For example, the MATLAB function `quadprog` solves problems such as these.

5.3.2.3 Making predictions

Given a set of optimal α_n, how do we go about making predictions? Our decision function, $t_{\text{new}} = \text{sign}(\mathbf{w}^\mathsf{T}\mathbf{x}_{\text{new}} + b)$, is based on $\mathbf{w}$ and b, not α_n. To convert it into a function of α_n, we substitute the expression for $\mathbf{w}$ given in Equation 5.13, resulting in

$$t_{\text{new}} = \text{sign}\left(\sum_{n=1}^{N} \alpha_n t_n \mathbf{x}_n^\mathsf{T}\mathbf{x}_{\text{new}} + b\right). \tag{5.15}$$

To find b, we will use the fact that, for the closest points, $t_n(\mathbf{w}^\mathsf{T}\mathbf{x}_n + b) = 1$. Substituting Equation 5.13 into this expression and rearranging allows us to calculate b (note that $1/t_n = t_n$):

$$b = t_n - \sum_{m=1}^{N} \alpha_m t_m \mathbf{x}_m^\mathsf{T}\mathbf{x}_n \tag{5.16}$$

where x_n is any one of the closest points. This gives us everything we need to be able to classify any $\mathbf{x}_{\text{new}}$.

5.3.2.4 Support vectors

The set of points closest to the maximum margin decision boundary are known collectively as the support vectors. The name comes from the fact that they define,

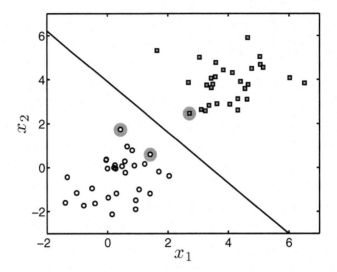

FIGURE 5.14 Decision boundary and support vectors for a linear SVM.

or support, the decision boundary. As the decision boundary is found by maximising the margin and as the margin only depends on the closest points, we could discard all of the other data and end up with just the same decision boundary. This is reflected by the fact that, at the optimum, all of the α_n that do not correspond to support vectors will be zero. If they were non-zero, they would have an influence on the decision function (see Equation 5.15). In many applications, this will lead to a sparse solution – the decision is a function of only a small subset of the training examples. For large problems, this can be a very useful feature. Consider classifying a test point using KNN when the training set consists of several thousand objects. To find the set of neighbours, distances must be computed between the new object and all of the training objects. For an SVM trained on the same data, the decision function might just involve a small subset of the training data.

Figure 5.14 shows a binary dataset and the resulting decision boundary ($\mathbf{w}^\mathsf{T}\mathbf{x} + b = 0$, where $\mathbf{w} = \sum_{n=1}^{N} \alpha_n t_n \mathbf{x}_n$) along with the three support vectors (large grey circles) (MATLAB script: svmhard.m). These are the only points for which $\alpha_n > 0$ and hence the only points that need to be used when classifying new data.

Although it could be considered efficient to base our decision on (in this case) only three of the training points, it will not always be a good thing. To illustrate why, consider Figure 5.15 (MATLAB script: svmhard.m). This is the same data that we saw in Figure 5.14 with one difference – the support vector from the class denoted by grey squares has been moved closer to the other class. Moving this single data point has had a large effect on the position of the decision boundary. This is another example of over-fitting – we are allowing the data to have too much influence. To see why this happens, we need to look at our original constraints:

$$t_n(\mathbf{w}^\mathsf{T}\mathbf{x}_n + b) \geq 1. \tag{5.17}$$

This means that all training points *have* to sit on the correct side of the decision boundary. This type of SVM is known as a *hard margin* SVM. It will sometimes

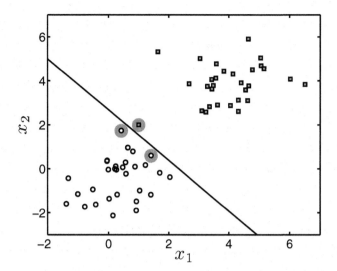

FIGURE 5.15 Decision boundary and support vectors for a linear SVM. The support vector from the grey square class appears to be exerting too much influence.

be sensible (and lead to better generalisation performance) to relax this constraint. Fortunately, this is straightforward using a *soft margin*.

5.3.2.5 Soft margins

To allow points to potentially lie on the wrong side of the boundary, we need to slacken the constraints in our original formulation. In particular, we need to adapt Equation 5.17 so that it admits the possibility of some points lying closer to (or on the wrong side of) the decision boundary. To achieve this, the constraint becomes

$$t_n(\mathbf{w}^\mathsf{T}\mathbf{x}_n + b) \geq 1 - \xi_n, \tag{5.18}$$

where $\xi_n \geq 0$. If $0 \leq \xi_n \leq 1$, the point lies on the correct side of the boundary but within the boundary of the margin. If $\xi_n > 1$, the point lies on the wrong side of the boundary. Our optimisation task becomes

$$\underset{\mathbf{w}}{\operatorname{argmin}} \quad \frac{1}{2}\mathbf{w}^\mathsf{T}\mathbf{w} + C\sum_{n=1}^{N}\xi_n$$

$$\text{subject to } \xi_n \geq 0 \quad \text{and} \quad t_n(\mathbf{w}^\mathsf{T}\mathbf{x}_n + b) \geq 1 - \xi_n \text{ for all } n.$$

The new parameter C controls to what extent we are willing to allow points to sit within the margin band or on the wrong side of the decision boundary. If we follow the same steps that we took for the hard margin class we find that this change in the model has only a very small effect on the maximisation problem. Omitting the details (see Exercise 5.8), we now need to find the maximum of the following

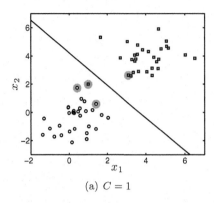

(a) $C = 1$

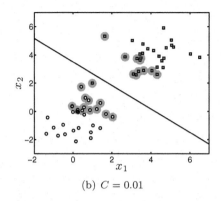

(b) $C = 0.01$

FIGURE 5.16 Decision boundary and support vectors for a linear SVM with a soft margin for two values of the margin parameter C. The influence of the stray support vector has been reduced.

quadratic programming problem:

$$\operatorname*{argmax}_{\alpha} \quad \sum_{n=1}^{N} \alpha_n - \frac{1}{2} \sum_{n,m=1}^{N} \alpha_n \alpha_m t_n t_m \mathbf{x}_n^\mathsf{T} \mathbf{x}_m$$

$$\text{subject to} \quad \sum_{n=1}^{N} \alpha_n t_n = 0 \text{ and } 0 \leq \alpha_n \leq C, \text{ for all } n.$$

The only difference is an upper bound (C) on α_n. The influence of each training point in our decision function is proportional to α_n. We are therefore imposing an upper bound on the influence that any one training point can have. For the example in Figure 5.15, the support vector from the grey class had $\alpha_n = 5.45$. Setting C to 1 would result in a change in the decision boundary (some other α_n will have to become non-zero from the grey square class), moving it back towards the other objects in the grey square class. This is exactly what happens, as we can see from Figure 5.16, where we plot the decision boundary and support vectors for $C = 1$ and $C = 0.01$ (MATLAB script: svnsoft.m). As C decreases, the maximum potential influence of each training point is eroded and so more and more of them become active in the decision function.

Using a soft margin gives us a free parameter (C) that needs to be fixed. As with K for KNN, we can set this using cross-validation. The procedure and error measure are identical to those for KNN and so we omit details here. A final practical point is the computation of b. We can no longer use any support vector to compute it, as they will not all satisfy $t_n(\mathbf{w}^\mathsf{T}\mathbf{x}_n + b) = 1$. Support vectors within the margin band (or on the wrong side) will have $t_n(\mathbf{w}^\mathsf{T}\mathbf{x}_n + b) < 1$. To overcome this problem, find the support vector with the highest value of $\mathbf{w}^\mathsf{T}\mathbf{x}_n$ (or $\sum_m \alpha_m t_m \mathbf{x}_m^\mathsf{T}\mathbf{x}_n$) and compute b from Equation 5.16.

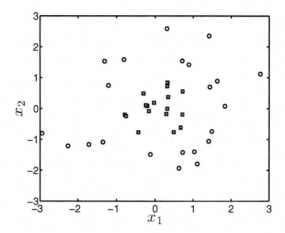

FIGURE 5.17 A binary dataset for which a linear decision boundary would not be appropriate.

5.3.2.6 Kernels

Our study of SVMs thus far has been restricted to linear decision boundaries. The soft margin allows training points to reside on the wrong side of the decision boundary but this will not help if the data, like that shown in Figure 5.17, is more complex. When we wanted a non-linear function from linear regression, we added some terms to $\mathbf{x}$ and extended $\mathbf{w}$. With SVMs, we take a very different approach. The model remains the same (a linear decision boundary) but for data that has been transformed into some new space. The transformation is done in such a way as to make the transformed data classifiable with a linear decision boundary.

To illustrate this idea, consider the data in Figure 5.17. The data cannot be separated by a straight line. However, if, instead of representing each data point by $\mathbf{x}_n = [x_{n1}, x_{n2}]^\mathsf{T}$, we represented them by their distance from the origin, $z_n = x_{n1}^2 + x_{n2}^2$, we could separate them with a straight line: the points in the circle class look consistently further from the origin than those in the square class. Using z_n instead of $\mathbf{x}_n$ in the SVM, we do not need to modify the algorithm at all. When we have a test point, $\mathbf{x}_{\mathsf{new}}$, we compute z_{new} and then classify it in the normal manner. In general, we will use $\phi(\mathbf{x}_n)$ to denote a transformation of the nth training object.

Perhaps the most important characteristic of the SVM framework is that we never actually have to perform the transformations. In our objective and decision function, the data $\mathbf{x}_n, \mathbf{x}_m, \mathbf{x}_{\mathsf{new}}$ appear exclusively within inner (or dot) products: $\mathbf{x}_n^\mathsf{T}\mathbf{x}_m, \mathbf{x}_n^\mathsf{T}\mathbf{x}_{\mathsf{new}}$, etc. We never see an $\mathbf{x}$ on its own. After applying the transformation, we need to calculate these inner products in the new space, $\phi(\mathbf{x}_n)^\mathsf{T}\phi(\mathbf{x}_m)$. We could explicitly transform each data point and compute the inner products in the transformed space. However, we do not actually need to think in terms of transformations at all. Instead, if we can show that some function $k(\mathbf{x}_n, \mathbf{x}_m) = \phi(\mathbf{x}_n)^\mathsf{T}\phi(\mathbf{x}_m)$ for *some* transformation $\phi(\cdot)$, we are free to use $k(\mathbf{x}_n, \mathbf{x}_m)$ in our expression in place of any inner product in the original space. Functions that correspond to inner products in some space are known as *kernel* functions.

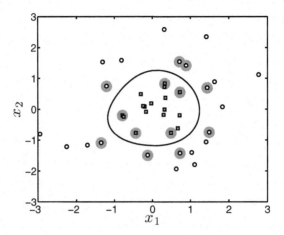

FIGURE 5.18 Decision boundary and support vectors for the dataset in Figure 5.17 using a Gaussian kernel with the kernel parameter $\gamma = 1$ and $C = 10$.

Our optimisation and decision function (soft margin version) rewritten to include kernel functions are

$$\underset{\alpha}{\text{argmax}} \qquad \sum_{n=1}^{N} \alpha_n - \frac{1}{2} \sum_{n,m=1}^{N} \alpha_n \alpha_m t_n t_m k(\mathbf{x}_n, \mathbf{x}_m)$$

$$\text{subject to} \qquad \sum_{n=1}^{N} \alpha_n t_n = 0 \text{ and } 0 \leq \alpha_n \leq C, \text{ for all } n.$$

$$t_{\text{new}} = \text{sign} \left(\sum_{n=1}^{N} \alpha_n t_n k(\mathbf{x}_n, \mathbf{x}_{\text{new}}) + b \right).$$

There are plenty of off-the-shelf kernel functions (each equivalent to an inner product after some transformation) that we can use. The following are probably the three most popular:

$$\text{linear} \quad k(\mathbf{x}_n, \mathbf{x}_m) = \mathbf{x}_n^{\mathsf{T}} \mathbf{x}_m.$$

$$\text{Gaussian} \quad k(\mathbf{x}_n, \mathbf{x}_m) = \exp \left\{ -\gamma (\mathbf{x}_n - \mathbf{x}_m)^{\mathsf{T}} (\mathbf{x}_n - \mathbf{x}_m) \right\}. \qquad (5.19)$$

$$\text{polynomial} \quad k(\mathbf{x}_n, \mathbf{x}_m) = (1 + \mathbf{x}_n^{\mathsf{T}} \mathbf{x}_m)^{\gamma}.$$

The linear kernel is equivalent to the SVM that we have been using thus far. The Gaussian and polynomial kernels are more flexible and both have additional parameters (γ) that must be set by the user – normally via cross-validation.

The results of using a Gaussian kernel for the data shown in Figure 5.17 can be seen in Figure 5.18 for $\gamma = 1$ and $C = 10$ (all $\alpha_n < C$, so this is effectively a hard margin) (MATLAB script: svmgauss.m). The decision boundary looks reasonable. For the original SVM, we could compute the decision boundary exactly, as it consisted of the values of $\mathbf{x}$ that satisfied

$$\mathbf{w}^\mathsf{T}\mathbf{x} + b = 0.$$

We can no longer compute $\mathbf{w}$ as it would be given by $\sum_n \alpha_n t_n \phi(\mathbf{x}_n)$ and we do not necessarily know $\phi(\mathbf{x}_n)$ (we only know $k(\mathbf{x}_n, \mathbf{x}_m) = \phi(\mathbf{x}_n)^\mathsf{T}\phi(\mathbf{x}_m)$). Therefore, to draw this decision boundary, we have had to evaluate $\sum_n \alpha_n t_n k(\mathbf{x}_n, \mathbf{x}_{\text{new}})$ over a grid of $\mathbf{x}_{\text{new}}$ values and then use the MATLAB contour function to draw the contour corresponding to $\sum_n \alpha_n t_n k(\mathbf{x}_n, \mathbf{x}_{\text{new}}) = 0$.

What happens if we change γ? Modifying γ changes the (implicit) transformation $\phi(\mathbf{x}_n)$, which will in turn change the kind of decision boundaries we might expect to see when we view them in the original space (remember that they will be linear in the transformed space). For the Gaussian kernel, increasing γ has the effect of increasing the complexity of the decision boundaries in the original space. This is clear when we compare Figures 5.19(a) and 5.19(b), where we have used $\gamma = 0.01$ and $\gamma = 50$, respectively (MATLAB script: svmgauss.m). In Figure 5.19(a), the decision boundary is too simple – it is not able to curve rapidly enough in the original space to surround just the data from the square class. Conversely, when $\gamma = 50$ (Figure 5.19(b)), the decision boundary has too much flexibility, resulting in a decision boundary that looks far too complex. In both cases, it is also worth noticing that the number of support vectors has increased dramatically (c.f. Figure 5.18) and the solution can no longer be considered sparse.

This model complexity problem is exactly the same as the one we encountered in Chapter 1. There we found that increasing the polynomial order beyond a certain point resulted in poor predictions for our Olympic 100 m model. Here, models that are too simple (Figure 5.19(a)) or too complex (Figure 5.19(b)) will also produce bad predictions. In the too-simple case, it looks like the model will predict a grey square too often and in the too-complex case, the opposite. Just as in Chapter 1, we must be careful to set γ such that the complexity is just right using, for example, cross-validation. To make matters worse, the parameters C and γ will affect the model in a coupled manner. We cannot optimise one and then optimise the other; we must do both at the same time. This is particularly problematic if our training dataset is large (N is high). The SVM solves an N-dimensional optimisation problem. For large N this might be very time consuming, and a cross-validation-based search over two parameters (C, γ) will result in performing this optimisation many times.

The SVM is not the only algorithm that can be kernelised. Many machine learning algorithms can be expressed in such a way that the data only appear inside inner products. This means that, in a large number of algorithms, we can solve complex problems (e.g. fit highly non-linear decision boundaries) without any additional algorithmic complexity. We will see another example when we look at clustering in the next chapter. We can also kernelise our other non-probabilistic classifier, KNN. KNN requires the computation of distances between $\mathbf{x}_{\text{new}}$ and each $\mathbf{x}_n$. This distance can be expressed as

$$(\mathbf{x}_{\text{new}} - \mathbf{x}_n)^\mathsf{T}(\mathbf{x}_{\text{new}} - \mathbf{x}_n).$$

If we multiply this out, we obtain just inner products:

$$\mathbf{x}_{\text{new}}^\mathsf{T}\mathbf{x}_{\text{new}} - 2\mathbf{x}_{\text{new}}^\mathsf{T}\mathbf{x}_n + \mathbf{x}_n^\mathsf{T}\mathbf{x}_n.$$

Replacing this with its kernelised equivalent,

$$k(\mathbf{x}_{\text{new}}, \mathbf{x}_{\text{new}}) - 2k(\mathbf{x}_{\text{new}}, \mathbf{x}_n) + k(\mathbf{x}_n, \mathbf{x}_n),$$

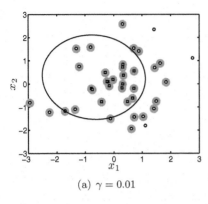

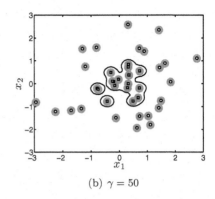

(a) $\gamma = 0.01$ (b) $\gamma = 50$

FIGURE 5.19 Decision boundary and support vectors for the dataset in Figure 5.17 using a Gaussian kernel with different values of the kernel parameter γ and $C = 10$.

gives us kernelised KNN.

5.3.3 Summary

In the previous sections we have described four popular classification algorithms and described how each can be used. These four algorithms provide a solid base from which one can experiment with data and explore the literature of other classification techniques.

Being able to apply a particular algorithm is only part of a classification analysis. It is also crucial to be able to reliably assess how well a particular classification is performing and that is the focus of the final section in this chapter.

5.4 ASSESSING CLASSIFICATION PERFORMANCE

In the following discussion we shall assume that we are interested in assessing performance based on the predictions for some set of N independent test examples, $\mathbf{x}_1, \ldots, \mathbf{x}_N$, with known labels, $t_1^*, \ldots, t_N^*$, to distinguish them from the labels predicted by the classifier – $t_1, \ldots, t_N$. These could be from a completely independent dataset or could be the data held out in a particular cross-validation fold.

5.4.1 Accuracy – 0/1 loss

When we have needed to express a measure of performance, we have used raw classification accuracy, also known as 0/1 loss. It is given this name, as, for a particular test point, the loss is either 0 or 1, depending on whether the prediction is correct $(t_n = t_n^*)$ or incorrect $(t_n \neq t_n^*)$. When averaged over the N objects in the test set, this quantity gives the proportion of objects for which the classifier is *wrong*. This could be interpreted as an estimate of the probability that some random test point is incorrectly classified. Clearly, the lower this value the better. Although widely used, this measure does have some drawbacks. In particular, it is not always easy to place this quantity in context – i.e. how good is 0.2? Consider two hypothetical binary classification problems: In the first we observe roughly the same number of objects from each class and in the second, 80% of the objects we see come from class 1 and 20% from class 2. In the former case, an average 0/1 loss of 0.2 might represent very good performance. In the latter, it does not: we could always classify objects as belonging to class 1 and get an average loss of 0.2. We should therefore be very careful using 0/1 loss in applications where the classes are *imbalanced*. We will now introduce an alternative that overcomes this problem.

5.4.2 Sensitivity and specificity

Imagine a binary classification task that involves detecting disease. $t = 0$ corresponds to a healthy patient ($\mathbf{x}$) and $t = 1$ diseased. If we are attempting to detect a rare disease, 0/1 loss is a bad idea – diagnosing everyone as healthy will give us a very low 0/1 loss. Analysing two quantities known as sensitivity and specificity is a better idea. To compute sensitivity and specificity we need to extract four summary values from our classification results. These are the numbers of

- True positives (TP) – the number of objects with $t_n^* = 1$ that are classified as $t_n = 1$ (diseased people diagnosed as diseased).

- True negatives (TN) – the number of objects with $t_n^* = 0$ that are classified as $t_n = 0$ (healthy people diagnosed as healthy).

- False positives (FP) – the number of objects with $t_n^* = 0$ that are classified as $t_n = 1$ (healthy people diagnosed as diseased).

- False negatives (FN) – the number of objects with $t_n^* = 1$ that are classified as $t_n = 0$ (diseased people diagnosed as healthy).

Given these values, we compute sensitivity as

$$S_e = \frac{TP}{TP + FN} \tag{5.20}$$

and specificity as

$$S_p = \frac{TN}{TN + FP}. \tag{5.21}$$

Both values lie between 0 and 1.

Broadly speaking, these two quantities tell us how good we are at detecting diseased and healthy people, respectively. The sensitivity is the proportion of the diseased people $(TP + FN)$ that we correctly classify as being diseased (TP). Specificity is the proportion of all of the healthy people $(TN + FP)$ that we correctly classify as being healthy (TN).

Considering our rare disease example, if we diagnosed everyone as healthy, we would have a specificity of 1 (very good – we diagnose all healthy people correctly), but a sensitivity of 0 (we diagnose all unhealthy people incorrectly) which is very bad. Ideally we would like $S_e = S_p = 1$ – perfect sensitivity and specificity. This is unrealistic in all but the most trivial applications and we need a way to define how optimal a pair of sensitivity/specificity values is. For example, is $S_p = 0.9, S_e = 0.8$

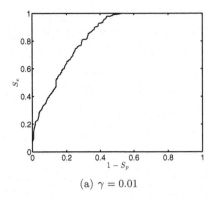

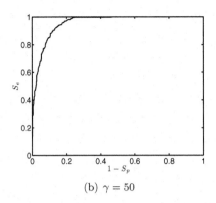

(a) $\gamma = 0.01$ (b) $\gamma = 50$

FIGURE 5.20 ROC curves for the SVMs shown in Figures 5.19(a) and (b).

better or worse than $S_p = 0.8, S_e = 0.9$? The answer will be application dependent. In our rare disease diagnosis, we do not want to misdiagnose any diseased people but are probably happy to tolerate diagnosing some healthy people as diseased (they are likely to be subject to more tests and later discovered to be healthy). As such, we might be happy to reduce S_p in order to increase S_e. In other applications, we may have completely opposite pressures.

It is often convenient to be able to combine sensitivity and specificity into a single value. This can be achieved through evaluating the area under the *receiver operating characteristic* (ROC) curve.

5.4.3 The area under the ROC curve

In many classification algorithms we are provided with a real-valued output that is then thresholded to give a classification. For example, in (binary) Bayesian classification and logistic regression, we are provided with $P(T_{new} = 1|\mathbf{x}_{new}, \mathbf{X}, \mathbf{t})$ – a value between 0 and 1. In the SVM, we are provided with a real value that was then thresholded at 0 (passed through a sign function). We could use any threshold we liked for any of these algorithms to obtain a hard classification. For example, we may decide that, if $P(T_n = 1|\mathbf{x}_n, \mathbf{X}, \mathbf{t}) > 0.7$, then $\mathbf{x}_n$ should belong to class 1. For the SVM we might decide to threshold at 0.2 rather than 0, making it slightly less likely that $\mathbf{x}_n$ will be classified as belonging to class 1.

The receiver operating characteristic (ROC) curve lets us examine how the performance varies as we change this threshold. The sensitivity and specificity are calculated for a range of threshold values, and sensitivity is plotted against the complementary specificity or false positive rate $(1 - S_p)$, giving a curve that will typically look like those shown in Figure 5.20 (MATLAB script: svmroc.m). These curves are for the too-simple and too-complex models shown in Figures 5.19(a) and (b) evaluated on an independent test set of 1000 objects. We know what we want to make S_e and S_p as high as possible. Therefore, the closer the curve gets to the top left of the plot ($S_e = 1, 1 - S_p = 0$), the better. If the curve hits the top left corner, it

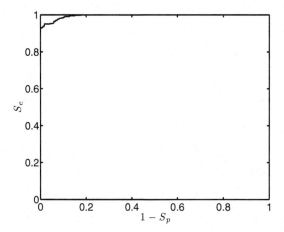

FIGURE 5.21 ROC curve for the SVM shown in Figure 5.18. The curve is hard to see because either $1 - S_p = 0$ or $S_e = 1$ for most threshold values.

tells us that there is a threshold we can choose that will classify the data perfectly. The curve will always start at $S_e = 0, 1 - S_p = 0$, corresponding to a threshold that never classifies anything as belonging to class 1, and finish at $S_e = 1, 1 - S_p = 1$, corresponding to a classifier that never classifies anything as belonging to class 0 (-1 in the SVM case). As the classifier gets worse, the curve will get closer to a straight line from $(0, 0)$ to $(1, 1)$. This is equivalent to randomly guessing the class.

Based on the plots in Figure 5.20, the SVM with $\gamma = 50$ gets closer to the top left corner and so is better than the one with $\gamma = 0.01$. We can quantify this performance by computing the area under the ROC curve (known as the AUC). A classifier that is able to perfectly classify the data will have an AUC of 1 (the curve will go straight up the left hand side and then straight across the top), a classifier that is guessing randomly will have an AUC of 0.5 (the curve will be approximately a straight line from $(0, 0)$ to $(1, 1)$, as mentioned in the previous paragraph). The two curves in Figure 5.20 have AUCs of 0.8348 and 0.9551, respectively. In Figure 5.21, we show the ROC curve for $\gamma = 1$ (the SVM plotted in Figure 5.18). The AUC in this case is 0.9936 – the best of the three, as we would expect.

The AUC is, in most applications, a better way of evaluating performance than the 0/1 loss. It takes class imbalance into account through its use of sensitivity and specificity. One drawback is that it does not generalise to the multiclass setting. One way of using it within a multiclass problem is to analyse the results of the classification as several binary problems. For example, if we have three classes, we might do three ROC analyses where each one looks at the binary problem created by considering class c against the rest. This would provide useful information about each classifier, but it is not clear how the three AUC values could be combined. We will now look at one final performance analysis tool that is easily generalised to (and very useful for) multiclass classification.

TABLE 5.2 A binary confusion matrix.

		True class	
		1	0
Predicted class	1	TP	FP
	0	FN	TN

5.4.4 Confusion matrices

The four quantities (TP, TN, FP, FN) introduced in Section 5.4.2 are often usefully visualised in a table. In the case of two classes, this table will have two rows and two columns. The rows correspond to predicted class (t) and the columns to true class (t^*). The structure of this table is illustrated in Table 5.2 and it is known as a *confusion matrix*. Confusion matrices for binary problems just summarise these four values. However, where confusion matrices really come into their own is in multi-class problems. A confusion matrix for the 20-class newsgroup data would have 20 rows and 20 columns and would let us explore in detail what the algorithm was getting right and what it was getting wrong. This table can be seen in Table 5.3. At first glance, it looks rather unwieldy, but it is reasonably straightforward to extract useful information. For example, the high values on the diagonals tell us that, on the whole, the classifier is doing pretty well. High off-diagonal elements tell us about mistakes that are being made regularly within the data. For example, 68 documents belonging to class 20 are incorrectly classified as belonging to class 16 – a phenomenon we discussed in Section 5.2.1.6. Similarly, a large number of documents belonging to class 19 are incorrectly classified as belonging to class 17. This analysis not only lets us uncover where the mistakes are being made (details not available if we simply compute the 0/1 loss) but they also provide suggestions for how to improve performance. In Section 5.2.1.6 we saw that classes 20 and 16 were very similar, as were classes 19 and 17. Perhaps it is too difficult to distinguish between them. Class 20 appears to be the class that is misclassified most often and so if we wanted to improve performance perhaps we should concentrate here – maybe we could collect more data or consider combining it with another class.

TABLE 5.3 Confusion matrix for the 20-class newsgroup data.

		True class																		
		1	2	3	4	5	6	7	8	9	10	11	12	13	14	15	16	17	18	19	20
Predicted class	1	242	3	3	0	1	0	0	1	0	4	2	0	2	10	4	7	1	12	7	47
	2	0	296	33	8	8	42	9	1	1	0	0	4	18	7	8	2	0	1	1	3
	3	0	6	209	15	9	8	4	0	0	0	0	1	0	1	0	1	0	0	0	0
	4	0	12	60	303	36	12	46	2	0	1	0	1	28	3	0	0	0	0	0	0
	5	0	8	10	22	277	2	21	0	0	1	0	2	7	0	0	1	1	0	0	0
	6	1	21	30	2	2	304	0	1	0	3	0	1	3	0	1	2	0	0	1	0
	7	0	1	0	5	5	1	235	5	1	2	0	1	1	4	0	0	1	0	0	0
	8	0	3	1	6	4	0	31	356	25	3	1	0	9	0	0	0	2	2	1	0
	9	0	2	2	0	1	2	5	4	353	1	0	0	2	1	1	0	1	1	0	1
	10	0	0	2	0	1	1	0	2	2	348	4	0	0	0	0	0	1	1	0	0
	11	1	0	1	1	0	0	1	0	0	16	382	0	1	0	1	1	1	1	0	0
	12	1	16	16	5	4	10	3	1	1	2	0	360	45	3	4	0	3	4	3	1
	13	1	4	1	24	16	0	9	5	1	2	0	3	260	3	4	1	0	0	0	0
	14	2	3	4	0	8	0	2	0	1	0	2	2	6	324	4	0	1	0	3	3
	15	3	7	4	1	2	3	3	2	0	0	1	0	4	3	336	0	2	0	7	5
	16	39	4	5	0	0	1	3	1	1	3	2	2	5	17	4	376	3	7	2	68
	17	4	0	0	0	3	1	1	5	4	1	0	9	0	3	1	3	325	3	95	19
	18	7	1	0	0	0	1	3	1	2	2	1	0	2	6	2	1	2	325	4	5
	19	7	2	9	0	6	2	5	8	5	8	4	8	0	10	21	1	16	19	185	7
	20	10	0	1	0	0	0	1	0	0	0	0	1	0	1	1	2	4	0	1	92

5.5 DISCRIMINATIVE AND GENERATIVE CLASSIFIERS

In our discussion, we subdivided classifiers into probabilistic and non-probabilistic approaches. Another common way of partitioning classifiers is to split them depending on whether they are generative or **discriminative**. Generative classifiers define a model for each class and then assign new objects to the model that suits them best. On the other hand, discriminative classifiers explicitly define a decision boundary between classes. The Bayesian classifier (Section 5.2.1) is an example of a generative classifier and the SVM (Section 5.3.2) and logistic regression (Section 5.2.2) examples of discriminative classifiers.

5.6 CHAPTER SUMMARY

In this chapter we have introduced four popular classification algorithms – two that provide probabilistic outputs and two that provide hard classifications. In the space available to us, it is impossible to do them all justice – whole books have been written on SVMs and other kernel methods alone. However, the material presented here should be enough for the reader to be able to implement and experiment with these algorithms. In addition, it should provide enough background knowledge about the general problem of classification and the various *types* of classification algorithm that the reader can explore other algorithms and place them into some kind of context.

In addition to describing algorithms, we have also looked at how we might evaluate whether a classifier is doing well and some of the problems we might come up against. Again, we have only scraped the surface. There are many other performance measures favoured by different application areas and plenty of other problems that we might come up against.

5.7 EXERCISES

5.1 Assuming $\Sigma_c = \mathbf{I}$ for all classes, compute the posterior density $p(\boldsymbol{\mu}_c|\mathbf{X}^c)$ for the parameter $\boldsymbol{\mu}_c$ of a Bayesian classifier where the set of training objects in class c is given by $\mathbf{x}_1, \ldots, \mathbf{x}_{N_c}$. Assume a Gaussian prior on $p(\boldsymbol{\mu}_c)$.

5.2 Using the posterior computed in the previous exercise, compute the expected likelihood:

$$p(\mathbf{x}_{\text{new}}|T_{\text{new}} = c, \mathbf{X}, \mathbf{t}) = \mathbf{E}_{p(\boldsymbol{\mu}_c, \Sigma_c|\mathbf{X}^c)} \left\{ p(\mathbf{x}_{\text{new}}|\boldsymbol{\mu}_c, \Sigma_c) \right\}.$$

5.3 Compute the maximum likelihood estimates of $\boldsymbol{\mu}_c$ and Σ_c for class c of a Bayesian classifier with Gaussian class-conditionals and a set of N_c objects belonging to class c, $\mathbf{x}_1, \ldots, \mathbf{x}_{N_c}$.

5.4 Compute the maximum likelihood estimates of q_{mc} for class c of a Bayesian classifier with multinomial class-conditionals and a set of N_c, M-dimensional objects belonging to class c, $\mathbf{x}_1, \ldots, \mathbf{x}_{N_c}$.

5.5 For a Bayesian classifier with multinomial class-conditionals with M-dimensional parameters $\mathbf{q}_c$, compute the posterior Dirichlet for class c when the prior over $\mathbf{q}_c$ is a Dirichlet with constant parameter α and the observations belonging to class c are the N_c observations $\mathbf{x}_1, \ldots, \mathbf{x}_{N_c}$.

5.6 Using the posterior computed in the previous exercise, compute the expected likelihood:

$$p(\mathbf{x}_{\text{new}}|T_{\text{new}} = c, \mathbf{X}, \mathbf{t}) = \mathbf{E}_{p(\mathbf{q}_c|\mathbf{X}^c)}\{p(\mathbf{x}_{\text{new}}|\mathbf{q}_c)\}.$$

5.7 Compute the MAP estimate of q_{cm} for the setup described in Exercise 5.4.

5.8 Derive the dual optimisation problem for a soft margin SVM.

5.8 FURTHER READING

[1] Ken Binmore and Joan Davies. *Calculus: Concepts and Methods*. Cambridge University Press, 2002.

> Includes good descriptions of the use of Lagrangian terms in optimisation.

[2] N. Cristianini and J. Shawe-Taylor. *An Introduction to Support Vector Machines and Other Kernel-Based Learning Methods*. Cambridge University Press, 2000.

> A comprehensive introduction to Support Vector Machines and other kernel techniques.

[3] Richard Duda, Peter Hart, and David Stork. *Pattern Classification*. Wiley-Interscience, second edition, 2000.

> A comprehensive textbook on the subject of classification.

[4] T. Furey et al. Support vector machine classification and validation of cancer tissue samples using microarray expression data. *Bioinformatics*, 16(10):906–914, 2000.

> One of the first papers to apply the Support Vector Machine to very high dimension microarray data. Also describes a simple feature selection technique.

[5] Brian Ripley. *Pattern Recognition and Neural Networks*. Cambridge University Press, 1996.

> A classic pattern recognition textbook from the late 1990s.

[6] J. Shawe-Taylor and N. Cristianini. *Kernel Methods for Pattern Analysis*. Cambridge University Press, 2004.

> An accessible introduction to kernel techniques with examples of their use in many applications. This is a broader and more practically minded text than the other by the same authors.

CHAPTER 6

Clustering

Thus far we have been concerned with supervised learning. In all tasks, we have been provided with a set of data objects $\mathbf{x}_1, \ldots, \mathbf{x}_N$ and their associated labels (or targets), $t_1, \ldots, t_N$. For example, objects consisting of Olympic years and targets corresponding to 100 m winning times; objects consisting of documents and targets consisting of document categories. It is the presence of the targets, t_n, that makes the tasks supervised.

Sometimes we will just be supplied with objects $\mathbf{x}_n$ without labels. The analysis of this kind of data requires unsupervised Machine Learning techniques. At first glance it is perhaps hard to understand what can be done with such data. There is certainly not much that can be done if we were told just the years of the modern Olympics.

In this and the following chapter, we will see two families of techniques that are used extensively in Machine Learning for exactly these unsupervised scenarios. In this chapter, we will look at the first: clustering. In particular, we will consider two clustering methods – K-means and mixture models.

6.1 THE GENERAL PROBLEM

The aim of cluster analysis is to create a grouping of objects such that objects within a group are similar and objects in different groups are not similar. There are many ways of defining what it means for two objects to be similar and many ways of performing the grouping once similarity is defined. Before we look at some in more detail, we shall first motivate cluster analysis with some examples.

Customer preference Imagine you run a large online store and would like to personalise users' shopping experience. Your motives are not entirely altruistic – you hope that by improving their shopping experience, users will buy more. One way to do this is to provide each user with a set of unique recommendations that they see when they access your site. You do not *directly* know each user's personal preferences and tastes but you do have lots of data – records of all purchases made by each user. This is classic Machine Learning territory – no fundamental model but lots of data.

Assuming that we can define a measure of similarity between customers based on their purchasing history, we could use cluster analysis to group customers into K

groups. Within each group, customers have similar shopping patterns. Differences between customers in the same group could form the basis of a recommender system. For example, customers A and B are in the same cluster because they share a number of purchases – perhaps they both have an interest in a particular sport. However, customer A has additionally bought several items that customer B has not. On the strength of their similarity, it might make sense for customer B to be recommended these items.

A recommender system could also be created by clustering the items based on the customers they were bought by. If items 1 and 2 were both bought by customers A, D, E and G, then they could be considered similar. Customers could then be recommended items that were similar (in this sense) to items they had already bought.

Gene function prediction A large proportion of research effort in molecular biology involves categorising genes into particular functional classes – i.e. the role does a particular gene plays; its purpose. One potential source of information is mRNA microarray data – numerical values describing how active each gene is in a particular biological sample. For a collection of genes, this activity can be measured over time. If genes are clustered based on this representation, we obtain a grouping of genes such that genes in a particular group exhibit similar behaviour over time. Consider one such group (cluster) consisting of ten genes. Half of the genes have a known function, whereas the function of the other half is unknown. Given no additional evidence, it might be reasonable to assume that the unknown half has the same or similar function as those for which function is known. This will not always give the correct function, but it is a good starting point for additional analysis.

In this example, the structure present in the data exposed by cluster analysis has allowed us to make some prediction about the objects. It is interesting to note that this problem could alternatively be considered as a supervised classification problem where the genes with known function form the training set (the class labels consist of the different functions) and the unknown is a test set to be labeled by the algorithm.

6.2 K-MEANS CLUSTERING

Consider the data shown in Figure 6.1. It consists of 100 objects, $\mathbf{x}_1, \ldots, \mathbf{x}_{100}$, each represented by two attributes, $\mathbf{x} = [x_1, x_2]^\mathsf{T}$. When we plotted classification data, objects belonging to different classes were plotted with different symbols. Now we have no class information – all of the dots look the same.

If you were to partition these objects into groups by hand such that groups contained similar objects, you might come to the conclusion that there were three groups. Most objects fall quite obviously into one of these three groups, although there are a few that are more ambiguous (e.g. the point at $\mathbf{x} \approx [2.5, -1]^\mathsf{T}$).

By clustering the data in this manner, we have implicitly defined what 'similar' means – similar objects are those that are close to one another in terms of squared distance (i and j are similar if $(\mathbf{x}_i - \mathbf{x}_j)^\mathsf{T}(\mathbf{x}_i - \mathbf{x}_j) = (x_{i1} - x_{j1})^2 + (x_{i2} - x_{j2})^2$ is low). Provided with no additional information about the data or the purpose of the cluster analysis, this is a reasonable measure of similarity. There are other ways of defining similarity that may be more appropriate, for example, the **Mahanalobis**

distance, $(\mathbf{x}_i - \mathbf{x}_j)^T \mathbf{A}(\mathbf{x}_i - \mathbf{x}_j)$. Both of these distances are suitable for real-valued data. For data of other types (for example, text), different distance measures would be required.

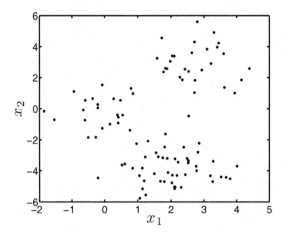

FIGURE 6.1 Synthetic dataset for clustering examples.

To develop an algorithm that can perform this grouping automatically, we need to define what a cluster is more formally. K-means defines a cluster as a representative point, just like one of the data objects. The point is defined as the mean of the objects that are assigned to the cluster (hence the name K-means). We will use $\boldsymbol{\mu}_k$ to define the mean point for the kth cluster and z_{nk} as a binary indicator variable that is 1 if object n is assigned to cluster k and 0 otherwise. Each object has to be assigned to one, and only one cluster, i.e. $\sum_k z_{nk} = 1$. This leads us to the following expression for $\boldsymbol{\mu}_k$:

$$\boldsymbol{\mu}_k = \frac{\sum_n z_{nk} \mathbf{x}_n}{\sum_n z_{nk}}. \tag{6.1}$$

Each object is assigned to the cluster to which it is closest, i.e., the cluster k that gives the minimum value of $(\mathbf{x}_n - \mu_k)^T(\mathbf{x}_n - \mu_k)$ (or some other suitable distance).

This is a circular argument: the clusters are defined as the centres of the points assigned to them, and the points are assigned to their closest clusters. If we know the clusters, $\boldsymbol{\mu}_1, \ldots, \boldsymbol{\mu}_K$, we can compute the assignments, but without the assignments we cannot compute the clusters. K-means clustering overcomes this problem with an iterative scheme. Starting with initial (random) values for the cluster means, $\boldsymbol{\mu}_1, \ldots, \boldsymbol{\mu}_K$:

1. For each data object, $\mathbf{x}_n$, find k that minimises $(\mathbf{x}_n - \boldsymbol{\mu}_k)^T(\mathbf{x}_n - \boldsymbol{\mu}_k)$ (i.e. find the closest cluster mean) and set $z_{nk} = 1$, and $z_{nj} = 0$ for all $j \neq k$.

2. If all of the assignments (z_{nk}) are unchanged from the previous iteration, stop.

3. Update each $\boldsymbol{\mu}_k$ with Equation 6.1.

4. Return to 1.

Figure 6.2 illustrates the operation of the algorithm for the data shown in Figure 6.1 (MATLAB script: `kmeansexample.m`). Figure 6.2(a) shows the initial guesses for the means (large symbols) with the data objects given the symbol corresponding to their closest mean. The means are now updated according to Equation 6.1 and Figure 6.2(b) shows the means moving to their new locations. Now that the means have changed, the objects must be reassigned, and the new assignments as well as the resulting change in the means can be seen in Figure 6.2(c). Figures 6.2(d) and 6.2(e) show the status after three and five iterations respectively. After eight iterations, the algorithm has converged, and the final assignments (the clustering) can be seen in Figure 6.2(f). The point at $\mathbf{x}_n = [2.5, -1]^\mathsf{T}$ appears to be incorrectly assigned – this is simply due to the scaling of the axis.

This iterative scheme is guaranteed to converge to a local minimum of the following quantity:

$$D = \sum_{n=1}^{N}\sum_{k=1}^{K} z_{nk}(\mathbf{x}_n - \boldsymbol{\mu}_k)^\mathsf{T}(\mathbf{x}_n - \boldsymbol{\mu}_k), \qquad (6.2)$$

which can be interpreted as the total distance between the objects and their respective cluster centres. However, it is not guaranteed to reach the lowest possible value (the global minimum). Whether it does or not will depend on the initial guesses of the cluster means. For K-means, this problem can never be totally overcome unless we evaluate every possible way of assigning all N points to K clusters, which is infeasible for even small values of N and K. A more common way to partly overcome this limitation is to run the algorithm from several random starting points and use the solution that gives the lowest value of the total distance.

6.2.1 Choosing the number of clusters

In order to use K-means, we need to choose a value of K – the number of clusters. Determining the number of clusters is a common problem in cluster analysis. Recall that K-means produces a clustering that corresponds to a local minima of Equation 6.2. Unfortunately, in much the same way that likelihood turned out to be a poor model selection criterion (recall that it monotonically increases as models become more complex, e.g. Figure 2.11(a)), D is no good either. Figure 6.3 shows $\log D$ as K is increased (MATLAB script: `kmeansK.m`). For each value of K we used 50 random initialisations of the algorithm and the boxplots show the median value, the 25th and 75th percentiles and any outliers. It is clear that $\log D$ (and hence D) decreases as K is increased. As K increases, large clusters will be broken down into smaller and smaller parts. The smaller each cluster, the closer each point will get (on average) to its cluster mean, reducing its contribution to D. Taken to the extreme case of $K = N$, it is possible to get $D = 0$ when each cluster contains just one object and $\boldsymbol{\mu}_k = \mathbf{x}_n$.

There is no straightforward solution to this model selection problem. To overcome it, it is often useful to look beyond the clustering to the overall aim of the analysis. For example, in the introduction to this chapter, we mentioned a recommendation system that clustered customers. The grouping is done in order to obtain a compact representation of the data and provide customer-product recommendations. Therefore, it makes sense to choose the number of clusters that produces the

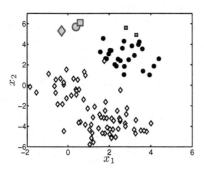

(a) Data and initial random means. Means are depicted by large symbols. Each data object is given the symbol of its closest mean.

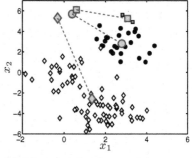

(b) Means updated according to assigned objects.

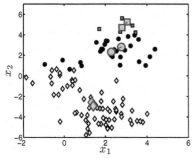

(c) Objects re-assigned to new means and means updated again.

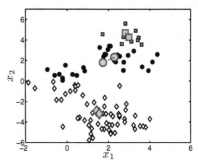

(d) Means updated after three iterations.

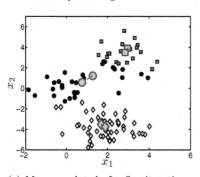

(e) Means updated afterfive iterations.

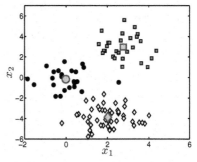

(f) Means updated after eight iterations. Algorithm has converged.

FIGURE 6.2 Illustration of the K-means algorithm. Data objects are represented as small symbols, means as large symbols. Objects are given the symbol of the mean to which they're assigned.

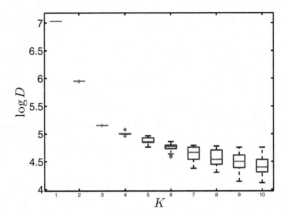

FIGURE 6.3 $\log D$ (where D is defined in Equation 6.2) as K increases for the data shown in Figure 6.1. Each boxplot is the result of 50 random initialisations of the K-means algorithm.

best recommendations, perhaps on some validation data. Similarly, clustering is a popular choice for **feature selection** in classification – clustering features based on their values across objects rather than clustering objects ($\mathbf{X}^\mathsf{T}$ rather than $\mathbf{X}$). In this instance, K should be chosen to give the best classification performance.

6.2.2 Where K-means fails

Figure 6.4 shows two datasets on which K-means has failed to extract what looks like the true cluster structure. In both cases, the objects in the true clusters do not necessarily conform to our current notion of similarity (distance). In the first example, Figure 6.4(a), the data exist in concentric circles. It is clear that standard K-means can never work in this setting, as, the means of both circles are in the same place. In the second example, Figure 6.4(b), the clusters are stretched in such a way (check the scaling of the axes) that objects at the top of the right hand cluster are closer to the mean of the left hand cluster (the means are shown in this plot as large symbols).

In the next section, we will cluster the data in Figure 6.4(a) by kernelising the K-means algorithm. For the data in Figure 6.4(b) we will turn, from Section 6.3 onwards to an alternative clustering method: mixture models.

6.2.3 Kernelised K-means

We can extend K-means using the kernel substitution trick that we introduced in Chapter 5. At an abstract level, the idea is the same: rather than making the algorithm more complex, we will transform the data into a space in which our simple algorithm works. We shall highlight this approach using the data shown in Figure 6.4(a).

We have seen that, rather than actually performing the transformation of the

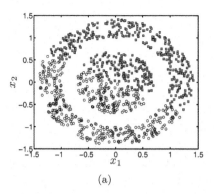
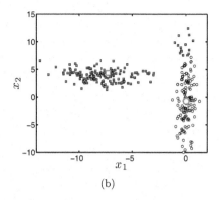

(a)   (b)

FIGURE 6.4 Two datasets in which K-means fails to capture the clear cluster structure.

data, kernel methods use kernel functions to directly compute inner (dot) products in the transformed space. As such, any algorithm where the data objects, $\mathbf{x}_1, \ldots, \mathbf{x}_N$, only appear as inner products ($\mathbf{x}_i^\mathsf{T}\mathbf{x}_j$ etc.) can be given the kernel treatment, making it more powerful without any significant additional cost. Key to the operation of K-means is the computation of the distance between the nth object and the kth mean:

$$d_{nk} = (\mathbf{x}_n - \boldsymbol{\mu}_k)^\mathsf{T}(\mathbf{x}_n - \boldsymbol{\mu}_k),$$

where the mean, $\boldsymbol{\mu}_k$, is calculated according to Equation 6.1. Substituting this into the expression for d_{nk} gives:

$$d_{nk} = \left(\mathbf{x}_n - \frac{1}{N_k}\sum_{m=1}^{N} z_{mk}\mathbf{x}_m\right)^\mathsf{T}\left(\mathbf{x}_n - \frac{1}{N_k}\sum_{r=1}^{N} z_{rk}\mathbf{x}_r\right),$$

where $N_k = \sum_{n=1}^{N} z_{nk}$, the number of objects assigned to cluster k.

Multiplying out this expression results in the data ($\mathbf{x}_n$) only appearing in product terms:

$$d_{nk} = \mathbf{x}_n^\mathsf{T}\mathbf{x}_n - \frac{2}{N_k}\sum_{m=1}^{N} z_{mk}\mathbf{x}_n^\mathsf{T}\mathbf{x}_m + \frac{1}{N_k^2}\sum_{m=1}^{N}\sum_{r=1}^{N} z_{mk}z_{rk}\mathbf{x}_m^\mathsf{T}\mathbf{x}_r.$$

All that remains is to replace the inner products with kernel functions to give a kernelised distance:

$$d_{nk} = K(\mathbf{x}_n, \mathbf{x}_n) - \frac{2}{N_k}\sum_{m=1}^{N} z_{mk}K(\mathbf{x}_n, \mathbf{x}_m) + \frac{1}{N_k^2}\sum_{m=1}^{N}\sum_{r=1}^{N} z_{mk}z_{rk}K(\mathbf{x}_m, \mathbf{x}_r). \quad (6.3)$$

This distance is purely a function of the data and the current assignments; the cluster means do not appear. In fact, it is not, in general, possible to actually compute the cluster means in the transformed space. The original expression for the mean of cluster k is

$$\boldsymbol{\mu}_k = \frac{\sum_{n=1}^{N} z_{nk}\mathbf{x}_n}{\sum_{n=1}^{N} z_{nk}},$$

and the kernelised version is

$$\boldsymbol{\mu}_k = \frac{\sum_{n=1}^{N} z_{nk}\phi(\mathbf{x}_n)}{\sum_{n=1}^{N} z_{nk}}.$$

Within this expression, data objects appear on their own and not as inner products. In Chapter 5 we discussed how, for most kernel functions, we cannot compute the transformation $(\mathbf{x}_n \to \phi(\mathbf{x}_n))$; we can only compute inner products in the transformed space $(\phi(\mathbf{x}_n)^\mathsf{T}\phi(\mathbf{x}_m))$. If we are unable to compute the transformation, we cannot compute $\boldsymbol{\mu}_k$.

Equation 6.3 suggests the following procedure for kernelised K-means:

1. Randomly initialise z_{nk} for each n (see below).
2. Compute $d_{n1}, \ldots, d_{nK}$ for each object using Equation 6.3.
3. Assign each object to the cluster with the lowest d_{nk}.
4. If assignments have changed, return to step 2, otherwise stop.

In standard K-means, we initialised the algorithm by randomly setting the means $\boldsymbol{\mu}_1, \ldots, \boldsymbol{\mu}_K$. In kernel K-means we do not have access to the means and we therefore initialise the algorithm via the object-cluster assignments, z_{nk}. We could do this completely randomly – for each n set one z_{nk} to 1 and all of the others $(z_{nl},\ l \neq k)$ to 0 but, given that we know K-means to be sensitive to initial conditions, it might be better to be more careful. Alternatively, we could run standard K-means and use the values of z_{nk} at convergence. This has the advantage that we can be sure that objects within the same cluster will be reasonably close to one another (something that we cannot guarantee if we set them randomly). A second alternative would be to assign $N - K + 1$ objects to cluster 1 and the remaining $K - 1$ objects to their own individual clusters. The performance of each iteration scheme will depend on the particular characteristics of the data being clustered.

Figure 6.5 shows the result of applying the kernel K-means algorithm to the data shown in Figure 6.4(a) (MATLAB script: **kernelkmeans.m**). In this case, we have initialised by assigning all but one object to the 'circle' cluster and the remaining object to the 'square' cluster. A Gaussian kernel was used with $\gamma = 1$ (see Equation 5.19). Figure 6.5(a) shows the assignments one iteration after initialisation. As the algorithm progresses through 5, 10 and 30 iterations (Figures 6.5(b), 6.5(c) and 6.5(d), respectively) the smaller cluster grows to take up the central circle. At convergence (Figure 6.5(d)), we can see that the algorithm has captured the interesting structure in the data.

Not only does kernel K-means allow us to find clusters that do not conform to our original idea of similarity, it also opens the door to performing analysis on other data types. We can cluster any type of data for which a kernel function exists, and it is hard to find a data type for which there does not. Obvious examples are kernels for text (each object is a document) and kernels for graphs or networks. The latter is used widely in computational biology.

6.2.4 Summary

In the previous sections we introduced the K-means algorithm and showed how it could be kernelised. One of the great advantages of K-means is its simplicity – it is

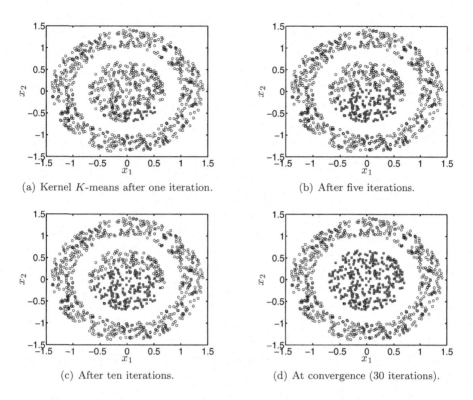

(a) Kernel K-means after one iteration.

(b) After five iterations.

(c) After ten iterations.

(d) At convergence (30 iterations).

FIGURE 6.5 Result of applying kernelised K-means to the data shown in Figure 6.4(a).

very easy to use and poses no great computational challenge. However, its simplicity is also a drawback: assuming that a cluster can be represented by a single point will often be too crude. In addition, there is no objective way to determine the number of clusters if our aim is just to cluster (remember that we mentioned how the number of clusters could be chosen as the one that gave best performance in some later task like classification). To overcome some of these drawbacks, we will now describe clustering with statistical mixture models. These models share some similarities with K-means but offer far richer representations of the data.

6.3 MIXTURE MODELS

In Figure 6.4(b) we showed a dataset for which the original K-means failed. The two clusters were stretched in such a way that some objects that should have belonged to one were in fact closer to the centre of the other. The problem our K-means algorithm had here was that its definition of a cluster was too crude. The characteristics of these stretched clusters cannot be represented by a single point and the squared distance. We need to be able to incorporate a notion of shape. Statistical mixtures represent each cluster as a probability density. This generalisation leads to a powerful approach, as we can model clusters with a wide variety of shapes in almost any type of data.

6.3.1 A generative process

In Section 2.1.1 we motivated a probabilistic treatment of the linear model described in Chapter 1 by creating a process by which the data could have been generated. In that case, we combined (by adding them together) a deterministic function of the form $\mathbf{w}^\top \mathbf{x}_n$ with a Gaussian random variable with zero mean and variance σ^2. Data generated in this way was qualitatively similar to our real data. Note that we never tried to claim that this *was* the process by which the data was generated, it was merely an abstraction that would allow us to build a better model. We will use much the same motivation to move from K-means to statistical mixture models.

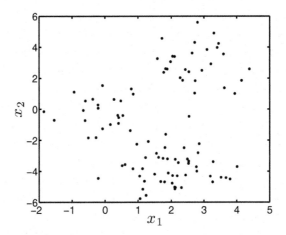

FIGURE 6.6 Synthetic dataset for clustering examples.

Our synthetic clustering dataset is reproduced in Figure 6.6. How could we generate data that *looks* like this? The data in Figure 6.6 does not look like samples from any density function that we have encountered. There appear to be three disjoint regions in which data are concentrated. None of the density functions that we have seen can produce data with this complex structure. However, each of the three regions looks simple enough to generate on its own. In fact, they all look a bit like samples from two-dimensional Gaussians.

Assuming that the data was generated by three separate Gaussians suggests a two-step procedure for sampling the nth data object, $\mathbf{x}_n$:

1. Select one of the three Gaussians.

2. Sample $\mathbf{x}_n$ from this Gaussian.

Both of these steps are straightforward. Step 1 involves choosing one value from a discrete set, like rolling a die. To do this, we just need to define the probability of each outcome, π_k, subject to the constraint $\sum_k \pi_k = 1$. Having chosen which Gaussian to sample from, the second step is straightforward.

To illustrate this process, we will sample some data from a setup with $K = 2$ Gaussians. As in K-means, we will use z_{nk} as an indicator variable. If we choose the kth component as the source of the nth object, we set $z_{nk} = 1$, and $z_{nj} = 0$ for all $j \neq k$. We will use $\boldsymbol{\mu}_k$ and $\boldsymbol{\Sigma}_k$ to denote the parameters of the kth Gaussian.

The density function for $\mathbf{x}_n$ given that it was produced by the kth component ($z_{nk} = 1$) is a Gaussian with mean and covariance $\boldsymbol{\mu}_k$ and $\boldsymbol{\Sigma}_k$, respectively:

$$p(\mathbf{x}_n | z_{nk} = 1, \boldsymbol{\mu}_k, \boldsymbol{\Sigma}_k) = \mathcal{N}(\boldsymbol{\mu}_k, \boldsymbol{\Sigma}_k).$$

For our example, we will use the following means and covariances for the two components:

$$\boldsymbol{\mu}_1 = [3, 3]^\mathsf{T}, \; \boldsymbol{\Sigma}_1 = \begin{bmatrix} 1 & 0 \\ 0 & 2 \end{bmatrix} \quad \boldsymbol{\mu}_2 = [1, -3]^\mathsf{T}, \; \boldsymbol{\Sigma}_2 = \begin{bmatrix} 2 & 0 \\ 0 & 1 \end{bmatrix}. \tag{6.4}$$

Finally, we need to define π_k. Assuming that component 1 is more likely than component 2, we will use $\pi_1 = 0.7$, $\pi_2 = 0.3$. Figure 6.7 shows the first 50 generated data objects and the density functions of the two Gaussians (MATLAB script: mixgen.m). For the first point, $k = 2$ is chosen and the object sampled from the second (lower) component – Figure 6.7(a). Figure 6.7(b) shows the first five objects (the most recent is always denoted as a larger circle). We notice that all but the first one have come from the first component. This is not surprising, as the first component is more likely than the second: $\pi_1 > \pi_2$. Figures 6.7(c) and 6.7(d) show the first 10 and 50 data objects, respectively. If we compare Figure 6.7(d) with Figure 6.6, we can see that, although the datasets are different, they share certain qualities. In particular, it looks like the data in Figure 6.6 *could* have been generated in a similar manner to the generative procedure shown in Figure 6.7.

The generative procedure that we have described is the generative procedure for a mixture model – the data are assumed to have been sampled from a *mixture* of several individual density functions. Mixture models find a wide variety of uses in data modelling, as fitting a set of simple distributions is often more straightforward than fitting one more complex one. Within the context of clustering, each individual component can be viewed as a cluster – all objects for which $z_{nk} = 1$ are in the kth cluster. Our learning task is to infer, from the observed data, the component parameters $(\boldsymbol{\mu}_k, \boldsymbol{\Sigma}_k)$ and the assignments of objects to components. As with K-means, this is a circular argument: the component parameters would be easy to compute if we knew the assignments, and the assignments would be easy to compute if we knew the component parameters. Without either, it is hard to know where to start. The answer comes in the form of the Expectation-Maximisation (EM) algorithm – an iterative maximum likelihood technique that is used for a wide range of models and has parallels with the K-means algorithm we introduced earlier in the chapter.

6.3.2 Mixture model likelihood

To derive the steps required in the EM algorithm, we need an expression for the likelihood. To keep this as general as possible, we will work with $p(\mathbf{x}_n | z_{nk} = 1, \Delta_k)$ where Δ_k denotes the parameters of the kth density (not necessarily Gaussian).

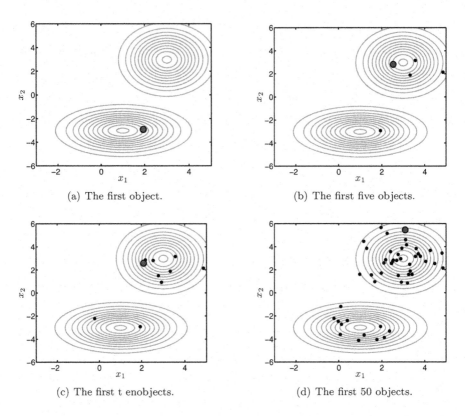

(a) The first object.

(b) The first five objects.

(c) The first t enobjects.

(d) The first 50 objects.

FIGURE 6.7 Generating data from two Gaussians.

In addition, Δ will denote the collection of the parameters of all of the mixture components $\Delta = \{\Delta_1, \ldots, \Delta_K\}$ and we will collect all of the π_k together into a vector $\boldsymbol{\pi} = \{\pi_1, \ldots, \pi_K\}$.

We require the likelihood of the data objects $\mathbf{x}_n$ under the whole model: $p(\mathbf{x}_n | \Delta, \boldsymbol{\pi})$. To obtain this expression, we start with the likelihood of a particular data object conditioned on $z_{nk} = 1$:

$$p(\mathbf{x}_n | z_{nk} = 1, \Delta) = p(\mathbf{x}_n | \Delta_k).$$

To obtain $p(\mathbf{x}_n | \Delta, \boldsymbol{\pi})$, we need to get rid of z_{nk}. To do this, we first multiply both sides by $p(z_{nk} = 1)$, which we have defined as π_k:

$$
\begin{aligned}
p(\mathbf{x}_n | z_{nk} = 1, \Delta) p(z_{nk} = 1) &= p(\mathbf{x}_n | \Delta_k) p(z_{nk} = 1) \\
p(\mathbf{x}_n, z_{nk} = 1 | \Delta, \boldsymbol{\pi}) &= p(\mathbf{x}_n | \Delta_k) \pi_k.
\end{aligned}
$$

Summing both sides over k (marginalising over the individual components) yields the likelihood:

$$\sum_{k=1}^{K} p(\mathbf{x}_n, z_{nk} = 1 | \Delta, \boldsymbol{\pi}) = \sum_{k=1}^{K} p(\mathbf{x}_n | \Delta_k) \pi_k$$

$$p(\mathbf{x}_n | \Delta, \boldsymbol{\pi}) = \sum_{k=1}^{K} \pi_k p(\mathbf{x}_n | \Delta_k).$$

Making the standard independence assumption, we can extend this to the likelihood of all N data objects:

$$p(\mathbf{X} | \Delta, \boldsymbol{\pi}) = \prod_{n=1}^{N} \sum_{k=1}^{K} \pi_k p(\mathbf{x}_n | \Delta_k). \tag{6.5}$$

6.3.3 The EM algorithm

We shall now demonstrate the use of the EM algorithm to maximise the likelihood given in Equation 6.5. It is normally easier to work with the logarithm of the likelihood and so, taking the natural logarithm of Equation 6.5 gives

$$L = \log p(\mathbf{X} | \Delta, \boldsymbol{\pi}) = \sum_{n=1}^{N} \log \sum_{k=1}^{K} \pi_k p(\mathbf{x}_n | \boldsymbol{\mu}_k, \boldsymbol{\Sigma}_k). \tag{6.6}$$

The summation inside the logarithm makes finding the optimal parameter values, $\boldsymbol{\mu}_k, \boldsymbol{\Sigma}_k, \boldsymbol{\pi}$, challenging. The EM algorithm overcomes this problem by deriving a *lower bound* on this likelihood (a function of $\mathbf{X}, \Delta$ and $\boldsymbol{\pi}$ that is *always* lower than or equal to L). Instead of maximising L directly, we instead maximise the lower bound.

To obtain a lower bound on L we can use the following relationship between logs of expectations and expectations of logs, which is a known as Jensen's inequality:

$$\log \mathbf{E}_{p(z)} \{f(z)\} \geq \mathbf{E}_{p(z)} \{\log f(z)\}, \tag{6.7}$$

i.e. the log of the expected value of $f(z)$ is always greater than or equal to the expected value of $\log f(z)$.

In order to use Jensen's inequality to lower bound our likelihood, we need to make the right hand side of Equation 6.6 look like the log of an expectation. To do this, we multiply and divide the expression inside the summation over k by a new variable q_{nk}:

$$L = \sum_{n=1}^{N} \log \sum_{k=1}^{K} \pi_k p(\mathbf{x}_n | \boldsymbol{\mu}_k, \boldsymbol{\Sigma}_k) \frac{q_{nk}}{q_{nk}}.$$

If we restrict q_{nk} to be positive and satisfy the summation constraint $\sum_{k=1}^{K} q_{nk} = 1$ (i.e. q_{nk} is some probability distribution over the K components for the nth object), we can rewrite this as an expectation with respect to q_{nk}:

$$L = \sum_{n=1}^{N} \log \sum_{k=1}^{K} q_{nk} \frac{\pi_k p(\mathbf{x}_n | \boldsymbol{\mu}_k, \boldsymbol{\Sigma}_k)}{q_{nk}}$$

$$= \sum_{n=1}^{N} \log \mathbf{E}_{q_{nk}} \left\{ \frac{\pi_k p(\mathbf{x}_n | \boldsymbol{\mu}_k, \boldsymbol{\Sigma}_k)}{q_{nk}} \right\}.$$

Applying Jensen's inequality, we can lower bound this expression:

$$L = \sum_{n=1}^{N} \log \mathbf{E}_{q_{nk}} \left\{ \frac{\pi_k p(\mathbf{x}_n | \boldsymbol{\mu}_k, \boldsymbol{\Sigma}_k)}{q_{nk}} \right\} \geq \sum_{n=1}^{N} \mathbf{E}_{q_{nk}} \left\{ \log \frac{\pi_k p(\mathbf{x}_n | \boldsymbol{\mu}_k, \boldsymbol{\Sigma}_k)}{q_{nk}} \right\}.$$

The right hand side of this expression is the bound (we will denote it $\mathcal{B}$) that we shall optimise. Expanding the expression gives us something more manageable:

$$
\begin{aligned}
\mathcal{B} &= \sum_{n=1}^{N} \mathbf{E}_{q_{nk}} \left\{ \log \frac{\pi_k p(\mathbf{x}_n | \boldsymbol{\mu}_k, \boldsymbol{\Sigma}_k)}{q_{nk}} \right\} \\
&= \sum_{n=1}^{N} \sum_{k=1}^{K} q_{nk} \log \left(\frac{\pi_k p(\mathbf{x}_n | \boldsymbol{\mu}_k, \boldsymbol{\Sigma}_k)}{q_{nk}} \right) \\
&= \sum_{n=1}^{N} \sum_{k=1}^{K} q_{nk} \log \pi_k + \sum_{n=1}^{N} \sum_{k=1}^{K} q_{nk} \log p(\mathbf{x}_n | \boldsymbol{\mu}_k, \boldsymbol{\Sigma}_k) - \sum_{n=1}^{N} \sum_{k=1}^{K} q_{nk} \log q_{nk}.
\end{aligned}
$$

$$(6.8)$$

Value of $q_{nk}, \boldsymbol{\pi}, \boldsymbol{\mu}_k, \boldsymbol{\Sigma}_k$ that correspond to a local maxima of this bound will also correspond to a local maxima of the log-likelihood, L.

As we mentioned earlier, the EM algorithm produces an iterative procedure. This will involve updates for each of the quantities in the model that we will repeat until convergence. To obtain each update, we will take the partial derivative of the bound $\mathcal{B}$ with respect to the relevant parameter, set it to zero and solve. We will now do this for each parameter in turn.

6.3.3.1 Updating π_k

Only the first term of $\mathcal{B}$ contains π_k (the partial derivative of all other terms with respect to π_k is zero). π_k is a probability and therefore $\sum_k \pi_k = 1$. Hence, the optimisation with respect to π_k is constrained. As we saw for the SVM in Section 5.3.2.2, we can use Lagrangian terms to incorporate constraints into our objective function (in this case, $\mathcal{B}$). The relevant part of $\mathcal{B}$ along with the suitable Lagrangian term (and associated Lagrange multiplier λ; see Comment 5.1) is

$$\mathcal{B} = \sum_{n=1}^{N} \sum_{k=1}^{K} q_{nk} \log \pi_k - \lambda \left(\sum_{k=1}^{K} \pi_k - 1 \right) + \dots$$

Taking partial derivatives with respect to π_k, setting to zero and rearranging results in

$$\frac{\partial \mathcal{B}}{\partial \pi_k} = \frac{\sum_{n=1}^{N} q_{nk}}{\pi_k} - \lambda = 0$$

$$\sum_{n=1}^{N} q_{nk} = \lambda \pi_k.$$

$$(6.9)$$

The final step requires computing λ. To do this, we sum both sides over k:

$$\sum_{k=1}^{K}\sum_{n=1}^{N} q_{nk} = \lambda \sum_{k=1}^{K} \pi_k$$

$$\sum_{n=1}^{N} 1 = \lambda$$

$$\lambda = N$$

where we have used the fact that $\sum_{k=1}^{K} q_{nk} = 1$ and $\sum_{k=1}^{K} \pi_k = 1$ by definition. Substituting $\lambda = N$ into Equation 6.9 gives us the expression for π_k:

$$\pi_k = \frac{1}{N}\sum_{n=1}^{N} q_{nk}.$$

We will discuss the intuition behind this and the other expression in Section 6.3.3.5.

6.3.3.2 Updating μ_k

Next, we will look at μ_k. Only the second term of $\mathcal{B}$ includes μ_k. If we explicitly write $p(\mathbf{x}_n|\mu_k, \Sigma_k)$ as a multivariate Gaussian (e.g. Equation 2.28) and expand, we obtain

$$\mathcal{B} \propto \sum_{n=1}^{N}\sum_{k=1}^{K} q_{nk} \log\left(\frac{1}{(2\pi)^{d/2}|\Sigma_k|^{1/2}} \exp\left(-\frac{1}{2}(\mathbf{x}_n - \mu_k)^{\mathsf{T}}\Sigma_k^{-1}(\mathbf{x}_n - \mu_k)\right)\right)$$

$$= -\frac{1}{2}\sum_{n=1}^{N}\sum_{k=1}^{K} q_{nk} \log\left((2\pi)^d|\Sigma_k|\right) - \frac{1}{2}\sum_{n=1}^{N}\sum_{k=1}^{K} q_{nk}(\mathbf{x}_n - \mu_k)^{\mathsf{T}}\Sigma_k^{-1}(\mathbf{x}_n - \mu_k)$$

The first term does not involve μ_k and can therefore be ignored. Making use of the identity (see Table 1.4)

$$f(\mathbf{w}) = \mathbf{w}^{\mathsf{T}}\mathbf{C}\mathbf{w}, \quad \frac{\partial f(\mathbf{w})}{\partial \mathbf{w}} = 2\mathbf{C}\mathbf{w},$$

and using the chain rule, we can take the partial derivative of $\mathcal{B}$ with respect to μ_k:

$$\frac{\partial \mathcal{B}}{\partial \mu_k} = -\frac{1}{2}\sum_{n=1}^{N} q_{nk} \times \frac{\partial\,(\mathbf{x}_n - \mu_k)^{\mathsf{T}}\Sigma_k^{-1}(\mathbf{x}_n - \mu_k)}{\partial\,(\mathbf{x}_n - \mu_k)} \times \frac{\partial\,(\mathbf{x}_n - \mu_k)}{\partial\,\mu_k}$$

$$= \sum_{n=1}^{N} q_{nk}\Sigma_k^{-1}(\mathbf{x}_n - \mu_k).$$

Equating to zero and rearranging gives us an expression for $\boldsymbol{\mu}_k$:

$$\sum_{n=1}^{N} q_{nk}\boldsymbol{\Sigma}_k^{-1}(\mathbf{x}_n - \boldsymbol{\mu}_k) = 0$$

$$\sum_{n=1}^{N} q_{nk}\boldsymbol{\Sigma}_k^{-1}\mathbf{x}_n = \sum_{n=1}^{N} q_{nk}\boldsymbol{\Sigma}_k^{-1}\boldsymbol{\mu}_k$$

$$\sum_{n=1}^{N} q_{nk}\mathbf{x}_n = \boldsymbol{\mu}_k\sum_{n=1}^{N} q_{nk}$$

$$\boldsymbol{\mu}_k = \frac{\sum_{n=1}^{N} q_{nk}\mathbf{x}_n}{\sum_{n=1}^{N} q_{nk}}. \tag{6.10}$$

6.3.3.3 Updating $\boldsymbol{\Sigma}_k$

Thirdly, we will look at $\boldsymbol{\Sigma}_k$. As with $\boldsymbol{\mu}_k$, we only need to look at the $p(\mathbf{x}_n|\boldsymbol{\mu}_k, \boldsymbol{\Sigma}_k)$ term of $\mathcal{B}$. We have already seen this term expanded to:

$$\mathcal{B} \propto -\frac{1}{2}\sum_{n=1}^{N}\sum_{k=1}^{K} q_{nk}\log\left((2\pi)^d|\boldsymbol{\Sigma}_k|\right) - \frac{1}{2}\sum_{n=1}^{N}\sum_{k=1}^{K} q_{nk}(\mathbf{x}_n - \boldsymbol{\mu}_k)^{\mathsf{T}}\boldsymbol{\Sigma}_k^{-1}(\mathbf{x}_n - \boldsymbol{\mu}_k)$$

Ignoring the constant (2π) part of the first term, we are left with

$$\mathcal{B} \propto -\frac{1}{2}\sum_{n=1}^{N}\sum_{k=1}^{K} q_{nk}\log\left(|\boldsymbol{\Sigma}_k|\right) - \frac{1}{2}\sum_{n=1}^{N}\sum_{k=1}^{K} q_{nk}(\mathbf{x}_n - \boldsymbol{\mu}_k)^{\mathsf{T}}\boldsymbol{\Sigma}_k^{-1}(\mathbf{x}_n - \boldsymbol{\mu}_k)$$

To take partial derivatives with respect to the matrix $\boldsymbol{\Sigma}_k$, we need two more useful identities. Firstly

$$\frac{\partial\log|\mathbf{C}|}{\partial\mathbf{C}} = (\mathbf{C}^{\mathsf{T}})^{-1},$$

and

$$\frac{\partial\mathbf{a}^{\mathsf{T}}\mathbf{C}^{-1}\mathbf{b}}{\partial\mathbf{C}} = -(\mathbf{C}^{\mathsf{T}})^{-1}\mathbf{a}\mathbf{b}^{\mathsf{T}}(\mathbf{C}^{\mathsf{T}})^{-1}.$$

Using these two identities, we take partial derivatives with respect to $\boldsymbol{\Sigma}_k$:

$$\frac{\partial\mathcal{B}}{\partial\boldsymbol{\Sigma}_k} = -\frac{1}{2}\sum_{n=1}^{N} q_{nk}\boldsymbol{\Sigma}_k^{-1} + \frac{1}{2}\sum_{n=1}^{N} q_{nk}\boldsymbol{\Sigma}_k^{-1}(\mathbf{x}_n - \boldsymbol{\mu}_k)(\mathbf{x}_n - \boldsymbol{\mu}_k)^{\mathsf{T}}\boldsymbol{\Sigma}_k^{-1}.$$

Note that, as it is a covariance matrix, $\boldsymbol{\Sigma}_k$ is symmetric and therefore $\boldsymbol{\Sigma}_k^{\mathsf{T}} = \boldsymbol{\Sigma}_k$. Equating this expression to zero and rearranging gives

$$-\frac{1}{2}\sum_{n=1}^{N} q_{nk}\boldsymbol{\Sigma}_k^{-1} + \frac{1}{2}\sum_{n=1}^{N} q_{nk}\boldsymbol{\Sigma}_k^{-1}(\mathbf{x}_n - \boldsymbol{\mu}_k)(\mathbf{x}_n - \boldsymbol{\mu}_k)^{\mathsf{T}}\boldsymbol{\Sigma}_k^{-1} = 0$$

$$\frac{1}{2}\sum_{n=1}^{N} q_{nk}\boldsymbol{\Sigma}_k^{-1} = \frac{1}{2}\sum_{n=1}^{N} q_{nk}\boldsymbol{\Sigma}_k^{-1}(\mathbf{x}_n - \boldsymbol{\mu}_k)(\mathbf{x}_n - \boldsymbol{\mu}_k)^{\mathsf{T}}\boldsymbol{\Sigma}_k^{-1}$$

Pre- and post-multiplying both sides by $\boldsymbol{\Sigma}_k$ allows us to cancel all of the $\boldsymbol{\Sigma}_k^{-1}$:

$$\boldsymbol{\Sigma}_k \sum_{n=1}^{N} q_{nk} \boldsymbol{\Sigma}_k^{-1} \boldsymbol{\Sigma}_k = \boldsymbol{\Sigma}_k \boldsymbol{\Sigma}_k^{-1} \sum_{n=1}^{N} q_{nk}(\mathbf{x}_n - \boldsymbol{\mu}_k)(\mathbf{x}_n - \boldsymbol{\mu}_k)^{\mathsf{T}} \boldsymbol{\Sigma}_k^{-1} \boldsymbol{\Sigma}_k$$

$$\boldsymbol{\Sigma}_k \sum_{n=1}^{N} q_{nk} = \sum_{n=1}^{N} q_{nk}(\mathbf{x}_n - \boldsymbol{\mu}_k)(\mathbf{x}_n - \boldsymbol{\mu}_k)^{\mathsf{T}}$$

$$\boldsymbol{\Sigma}_k = \frac{\sum_{n=1}^{N} q_{nk}(\mathbf{x}_n - \boldsymbol{\mu}_k)(\mathbf{x}_n - \boldsymbol{\mu}_k)^{\mathsf{T}}}{\sum_{n=1}^{N} q_{nk}}. \tag{6.11}$$

6.3.3.4 Updating q_{nk}

Finally, we need to derive an update for q_{nk}. This appears in all three terms in $\mathcal{B}$. In addition, it is subject to the constraint $\sum_{k=1}^{K} q_{nk} = 1$ and so, like the update for π_k, we will need a Lagrangian term (see Comment 5.1). The bound, complete with Lagrangian term, is

$$\mathcal{B} = \sum_{n=1}^{N} \sum_{k=1}^{K} q_{nk} \log \pi_k + \sum_{n=1}^{N} \sum_{k=1}^{K} q_{nk} \log p(\mathbf{x}_n | \boldsymbol{\mu}_k, \boldsymbol{\Sigma}_K)$$
$$- \sum_{n=1}^{N} \sum_{k=1}^{K} q_{nk} \log q_{nk} - \lambda \left(\sum_{k=1}^{K} q_{nk} - 1 \right).$$

Taking partial derivatives with respect to q_{nk} gives

$$\frac{\partial \mathcal{B}}{\partial q_{nk}} = \log \pi_k + \log p(\mathbf{x}_n | \boldsymbol{\mu}_k, \boldsymbol{\Sigma}_k) - (1 + \log q_{nk}) - \lambda$$

Comment 6.1 – The product rule of differentiation: The product rule is used when we need to differentiate a product of two functions of the same variable with respect to the variable. For example, if

$$f(a) = g(a)h(a),$$

the product rule states that

$$\frac{\partial f(a)}{\partial a} = g(a) \frac{\partial h(a)}{\partial a} + \frac{\partial g(a)}{\partial a} h(a).$$

For example, to differentiate $a \log a$ with respect to a, this gives

$$a \times \frac{1}{a} + 1 \times \log(a) = 1 + \log(a).$$

---

where we have used the product rule (see Comment 6.1) to differentiate the $q_{nk} \log q_{nk}$ term. Setting to zero, rearranging and exponentiating gives us an expression for q_{nk}:

$$1 + \log q_{nk} + \lambda = \log \pi_k + \log p(\mathbf{x}_n | \boldsymbol{\mu}_k, \boldsymbol{\Sigma}_k)$$
$$\exp(\log q_{nk} + (\lambda + 1)) = \exp(\log \pi_k + \log p(\mathbf{x}_n | \boldsymbol{\mu}_k, \boldsymbol{\Sigma}_k))$$
$$q_{nk} \exp(\lambda + 1) = \pi_k p(\mathbf{x}_n | \boldsymbol{\mu}_k, \boldsymbol{\Sigma}_k). \tag{6.12}$$

As with the update for π_k, to find the constant term (in this case, $\exp(\lambda + 1)$), we sum both sides over k:

$$\exp(\lambda + 1) \sum_{k=1}^{K} q_{nk} = \sum_{k=1}^{K} \pi_k p(\mathbf{x}_n | \boldsymbol{\mu}_k, \boldsymbol{\Sigma}_k)$$

$$\exp(\lambda + 1) = \sum_{k=1}^{K} \pi_k p(\mathbf{x}_n | \boldsymbol{\mu}_k, \boldsymbol{\Sigma}_k). \quad (6.13)$$

Substituting Equation 6.13 into Equation 6.12 gives us our expression for q_{nk}:

$$q_{nk} = \frac{\pi_k p(\mathbf{x}_n | \boldsymbol{\mu}_k, \boldsymbol{\Sigma}_k)}{\sum_{j=1}^{K} \pi_j p(\mathbf{x}_n | \boldsymbol{\mu}_j, \boldsymbol{\Sigma}_j)}. \quad (6.14)$$

6.3.3.5 Some intuition

The four update equations are

$$\pi_k = \frac{1}{N} \sum_{n=1}^{N} q_{nk}. \quad (6.15)$$

$$\boldsymbol{\mu}_k = \frac{\sum_{n=1}^{N} q_{nk} \mathbf{x}_n}{\sum_{n=1}^{N} q_{nk}}. \quad (6.16)$$

$$\boldsymbol{\Sigma}_k = \frac{\sum_{n=1}^{N} q_{nk} (\mathbf{x}_n - \boldsymbol{\mu}_k)(\mathbf{x}_n - \boldsymbol{\mu}_k)^{\mathsf{T}}}{\sum_{n=1}^{N} q_{nk}}. \quad (6.17)$$

$$q_{nk} = \frac{\pi_k p(\mathbf{x}_n | \boldsymbol{\mu}_k, \boldsymbol{\Sigma}_k)}{\sum_{j=1}^{K} \pi_j p(\mathbf{x}_n | \boldsymbol{\mu}_j, \boldsymbol{\Sigma}_j)}. \quad (6.18)$$

The first three expressions rely heavily on q_{nk}: π_k is the mean value of q_{nk} for a particular k, $\boldsymbol{\mu}_k$ is the average of the data objects weighted by q_{nk} and $\boldsymbol{\Sigma}_k$ is a weighted covariance. What does q_{nk} represent? Equation 6.18 can provide some intuition. At first glance, it looks a lot like Bayes' rule with a prior π_k, a likelihood $p(\mathbf{x}_n | \boldsymbol{\mu}_k, \boldsymbol{\Sigma}_k)$ and a normalising constant obtained by averaging over the k components. In fact, it could be interpreted as computing a posterior probability of object n belonging to class k (it looks very similar to the Bayesian classification version of Bayes' rule given in Equation 5.2). In particular,

$$p(z_{nk} = 1 | \mathbf{x}_n, \boldsymbol{\pi}, \Delta) = \frac{p(z_{nk} = 1 | \pi_k) p(\mathbf{x}_n | \boldsymbol{\mu}_k, \boldsymbol{\Sigma}_k)}{\sum_{j=1}^{K} p(z_{nj} = 1 | \pi_j) p(\mathbf{x}_n | \boldsymbol{\mu}_j, \boldsymbol{\Sigma}_j)} = q_{nk}. \quad (6.19)$$

For particular values of the model parameters $\boldsymbol{\pi}, \boldsymbol{\mu}_1, \ldots, \boldsymbol{\mu}_K, \boldsymbol{\Sigma}_1, \ldots, \boldsymbol{\Sigma}_K$, q_{nk} tells us the posterior probability of object n belonging to component k. In light of this, Equations 6.15, 6.16 and 6.17 make sense. Equation 6.15 is the average of all posterior probabilities of belonging to class k or, in other words, the expected proportion of the data belonging to class k. Imagine a scenario where the components are so distinct that the posterior probabilities are all either 1 or 0. In this case, π_k is just the proportion of the data assigned to component k. $\boldsymbol{\mu}_k$ and $\boldsymbol{\Sigma}_k$ are the mean and variance of the data objects where each object is weighted by the posterior probability of belonging to component k – objects that have a high probability of belonging to component k have a strong influence on the mean and variance of component k.

Keeping the previous discussion in mind, we can split the four updates into two sets. The first set consists of updating our current estimates of the model components $\pi_k, \boldsymbol{\mu}_k$ and $\boldsymbol{\Sigma}_k$ with q_{nk}, the assignment probabilities, fixed. In the second step, we update the assignments q_{nk} to reflect the new values of the model parameters. This procedure is very similar to the K-means algorithm introduced earlier. Updating q_{nk} is analogous to updating z_{nk} in K-means and updating $\boldsymbol{\mu}_k, \boldsymbol{\Sigma}_k, \boldsymbol{\pi}$ is analogous to updating $\boldsymbol{\mu}_k$ in K-means. The key difference is that we are computing posterior probabilities of cluster memberships rather than making hard assignments and the fact that we are inferring the component covariances (although this is a design choice – we could simply make the assumption that $\boldsymbol{\Sigma}_k = \mathbf{I}$). Replacing q_{nk} with z_{nk} in Equation 6.16 gives us exactly the mean update from K-means, Equation 6.1.

The four update equations make up an example of the EM algorithm. The first three updates, $\pi_k, \boldsymbol{\mu}_k, \boldsymbol{\Sigma}_k$, make up the so-called 'M' (maximisation) step where the bound is maximised conditioned on the values of q_{nk}. The update of q_{nk} is known as the 'E' (expectation) step, as it actually involves computing the expected value of the unknown assignments, z_{nk}, although we have not derived them in this way. The reader is encouraged to explore other uses of EM in the literature to see alternative derivations.

6.3.4   Example

The synthetic data we have used throughout this chapter is reproduced in Figure 6.8 and we will use it to illustrate the operation of the EM algorithm we derived in the previous section (MATLAB script: `gmix.m`). Much like K-means, we must specify the number of components we expect to see a priori and in this case, we will use $K = 3$. Unlike K-means, there is a useful measure that we can use to infer this from the data and we shall come to this in due course.

Before we can start performing the updates provided in Equations 6.15 to 6.18 we need to initialise some of the parameters. We do this by randomly choosing the means and covariances of the three mixture components. The three resulting Gaussian pdfs are plotted in Figure 6.9(a). In addition, before we can compute q_{nk} using Equation 6.18, we need to initialise π_k. We do this by assuming a uniform prior distribution over the three components: $\pi_k = 1/K$. We now have all we need to compute q_{nk} through Equation 6.18 (the 'E' step) and then subsequently update $\pi_k, \boldsymbol{\mu}_k, \boldsymbol{\Sigma}_k$ using Equations 6.15, 6.16 and 6.17, respectively (the 'M' step). The resulting Gaussians can be seen in Figure 6.9(b). We notice that, after only one iteration, the Gaussians are beginning to reflect the cluster structure in the data. After this first large step, progress becomes a little slower. In Figure 6.9(c) we see the Gaussians after five EM iterations – the top right component has become more distinct (completely separated from the other two) whilst the other two are gradually diverging. Two iterations later, these two components have moved apart, as can be seen in Figure 6.9(d), and from here it is only a few iterations until the algorithm converges – updating q_{nk} and the model parameters causes no change in their values. The converged solution can be seen in Figure 6.9(e), where the distinct cluster structure is clearly visible. Finally, in Figure 6.9(f) we can see the evolution of the bound $\mathcal{B}$ and the log-likelihood L. Both increase as required.

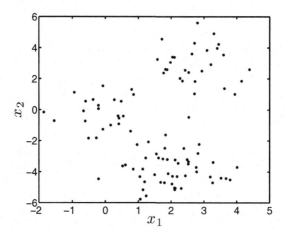

FIGURE 6.8 The synthetic clustering data encountered earlier in the chapter.

Often we are not interested in the Gaussians themselves but the assignments of objects to components – the *clustering*. These are provided by the values of q_{nk} – the posterior probability of objects belonging to components. If we want a single assignment of objects to components, we can assign each object to the component for which it has the highest posterior probability. It is worth pointing out that, a hard assignment like this might not always be sensible. Consider an object (object n) that has the following values of q_{nk} at convergence:

$$q_{n1} = 0.53, \quad q_{n2} = 0.45, \quad q_{n3} = 0.02.$$

If we must assign it to a particular component, number 1 is most appropriate, but in doing so, we are throwing away useful information about the relationship object n has with component 2.

At this point, you could be forgiven for wondering why we have bothered deriving this rather complex way of doing something that K-means seemed to do in a much more straightforward manner – the clusterings produced by K-means and the mixture model are almost identical *and* K-means can be kernelised. In the next two sections, we will see that mixture models have some key advantages over K-means due, predominantly, to their probabilistic nature.

Before we move on, we will revisit the data that motivated our move from K-means to the mixture model (Figure 6.10(a)). Using $K = 2$, and the update equations derived in this section, we can apply a mixture model to this data and the result is seen in Figure 6.10(b). It is clear that the mixture model has successfully extracted the interesting cluster structure.

6.3.5 EM finds local optima

As with K-means, the solution to which the EM algorithm will converge will depend upon the specific initialisation. It is only guaranteed to reach a local maximum of

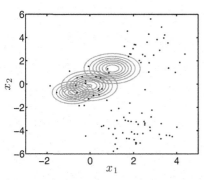

(a) The three randomly initialised Gaussian mixture components.

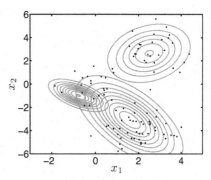

(b) The three components after one iteration of the EM algorithm.

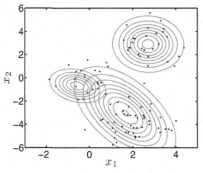

(c) The three components after five iterations of the EM algorithm.

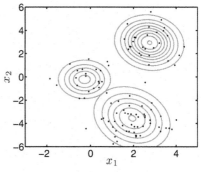

(d) The three components after seven iterations of the EM algorithm.

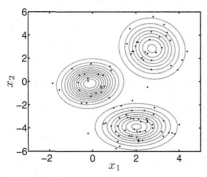

(e) The three components at convergence of the EM algorithm.

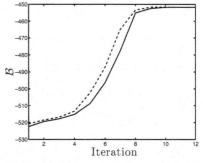

(f) The evolution of the bound $\mathcal{B}$ (solid line, Equation 6.8) and log-likelihood L (dashed line, Equation 6.5).

FIGURE 6.9 Example of the Gaussian mixture algorithm in action.

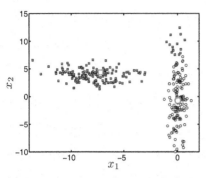

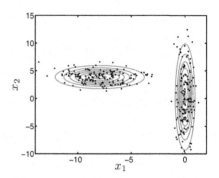

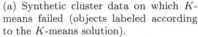

(a) Synthetic cluster data on which K-means failed (objects labeled according to the K-means solution).

(b) The converged mixture model with $K = 2$ Gaussian components.

FIGURE 6.10   The data on which K-means failed and the successful mixture model solution.

the likelihood and not necessarily the global maximum. In fact, there will always be more than one global maximum, as redefining the component labels must result in the same likelihood (renaming $\boldsymbol{\mu}_k, \boldsymbol{\Sigma}_k$ as, say, $\boldsymbol{\mu}_j, \boldsymbol{\Sigma}_j$). As for K-means, we cannot solve this problem analytically and have to resort to running the algorithm from many starting points. We can use the likelihood (Equation 6.5) to evaluate which of the converged solutions is better (as we did with D, Equation 6.2, in K-means).

6.3.6   Choosing the number of components

As with K-means, we have to specify the number of clusters by choosing the number of components. We saw earlier that this choice, within the context of K-means, was nontrivial – the only quantity at our disposal was the total distance between objects and their cluster centres, and this kept decreasing as the number of components increased. The same problem eliminates the use of the log-likelihood L (and the bound $\mathcal{B}$) for the mixture model. Figure 6.11(a) shows how the log-likelihood L increases with the number of mixture components K. To understand why this is the case, consider the clustering with $K = 10$ shown in Figure 6.11(b). Each of the three original components (Figure 6.9(e)) is now represented by several smaller components. Imagine these Gaussians plotted in 3D (as we did in Figure 2.8). Because their volume must equal 1 (they are densities), the smaller area they occupy in the input space (i.e. the smaller the ellipses in Figure 6.11(b)) the higher they must be. The likelihood for the dataset, which is the product of the heights at each of the data objects (or sum of the log of the heights for the log-likelihood, L), will be higher. As we add more and more components, the area they need to take up decreases and the likelihood increases still further.

Fortunately, we can overcome this problem by computing the likelihood on a validation set using, for example, cross-validation. The results of performing a 10-fold cross validation can be seen in Figure 6.12 (MATLAB script: `gmixcv.m`). The line and bars show the mean and standard deviation of the likelihood on the held-

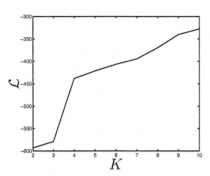

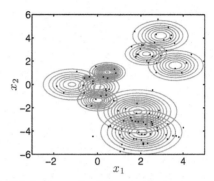

(a) The increase in model likelihood as the number of components increases.

(b) An example of the model at convergence for $K = 10$.

FIGURE 6.11 The log-likelihood L increases with the number of components, K.

out data. The results are not conclusive in the sense that they strongly suggest a particular number of components but they do give us an indication that the likely number lies somewhere between, say, 3 and 8. In our experience, this is about as much precision as one can expect with this quantity of data but it offers a considerable advantage over K-means, where it is hard to get any indication of how many clusters are present.

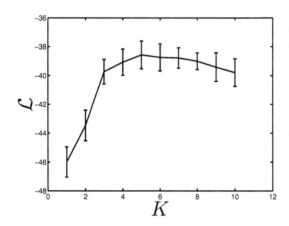

FIGURE 6.12 Result of ten-fold cross-validation for a Gaussian mixture model on the data shown in Figure 6.8.

Of course, if the clustering is just one step in a larger analysis, we can use some other figure of merit (classification accuracy, for example) to choose the number of clusters. In addition, recently developed non-parametric techniques enable the number of components to be sampled within a Markov chain Monte Carlo scheme (like the Metropolis–Hastings method described in Chapter 4). These techniques are introduced in Chapter 10 and the interested reader is also referred to the growing body of literature in this area given in the reading list at the end of the chapter.

6.3.7 Other forms of mixture component

The second advantage of mixture models over K-means is their immense flexibility. In particular, $p(\mathbf{x}_n|\ldots)$ can take the form of any probability density. In the previous example, we used (and derived updates for) a Gaussian. Many other forms of components are regularly used. We will demonstrate this with a binary dataset, but before we do that, it is worth spending a little more time with the Gaussian, as it often appears in slightly different forms.

In particular, it is often necessary to put restrictions on the mixture component covariance matrices, as there is not enough data to reliably estimate a full covariance matrix. For example, if we had ten-dimensional data rather than two-dimensional data, we would need a lot more data to be able to estimate the 55 parameters required in each covariance matrix. To overcome this, it is common to assume that the covariance matrix has only diagonal elements. You should recall from Chapter 2 that this is equivalent to assuming that the dimensions are independent. The only difference to the EM algorithm is in the update for $\boldsymbol{\Sigma}_k$, which can now be separated into an update for the variance of each dimension d, σ_{kd}^2 (see Exercise 6.1). An even more extreme case is when the covariance is assumed to be *isotropic* (diagonal, with the same value on each diagonal element), $\boldsymbol{\Sigma}_k = \sigma_k^2\mathbf{I}$. Once again, the only difference to the algorithm is in the update for $\boldsymbol{\Sigma}_k$ (see Exercise 6.2).

We will now briefly describe a mixture model for binary data. Each data object, $\mathbf{x}_n$, is a collection of D binary values. For example, in $D = 10$ dimensions, an example data object might be

$$\mathbf{x}_n = [0, 1, 0, 1, 1, 1, 0, 0, 0, 1].$$

An example ten-dimensional dataset is shown in Figure 6.13. Each row represents one data object. Assuming that the dimensions are independent within a particular component, $p(\mathbf{x}_n|\ldots)$ could be represented as a product of Bernoulli distributions (see Section 2.3.1):

$$p(\mathbf{x}_n|\mathbf{p}_k) = \prod_{d=1}^{D} p_{kd}^{x_{nd}}(1 - p_{kd})^{1-x_{nd}}, \qquad (6.20)$$

where $\mathbf{p}_k = [p_{k1}, \ldots, p_{kD}]^\mathsf{T}$ is a vector of dimension-specific probabilities for the kth component (i.e. $0 \leq p_{kd} \leq 1$). There will be two differences to our EM algorithm. Firstly, when updating q_{nk}, Equation 6.18 becomes

$$q_{nk} = \frac{\pi_k p(\mathbf{x}_n|\mathbf{p}_k)}{\sum_{j=1}^{K} \pi_j p(\mathbf{x}_n|\mathbf{p}_j)} \qquad (6.21)$$

where $p(\mathbf{x}_n|\mathbf{p}_k)$ is given by Equation 6.20. Secondly, an update for $\mathbf{p}_k$ will replace the updates for $\boldsymbol{\mu}_k$ and $\boldsymbol{\Sigma}_k$ (Equations 6.16 and 6.17).

To derive this update, we can extract the data-dependent term from the bound

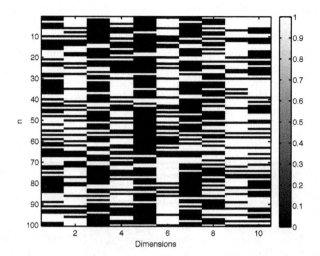

FIGURE 6.13 An example binary dataset with $N = 100$ objects and $D = 10$ dimensions. Each row represents one data object.

$\mathcal{B}$ (Equation 6.8). This term becomes

$$
\begin{aligned}
\mathcal{B} &= \sum_{n=1}^{N} \sum_{k=1}^{K} q_{nk} \log p(\mathbf{x}_n | \mathbf{p}_k) + \dots \\
&= \sum_{n=1}^{N} \sum_{k=1}^{K} q_{nk} \log \prod_{d=1}^{D} p_{kd}^{x_{nd}} (1 - p_{kd})^{1 - x_{nd}} + \dots \\
&= \sum_{n=1}^{N} \sum_{k=1}^{K} q_{nk} \sum_{d=1}^{D} (x_{nd} \log p_{kd} + (1 - x_{nd}) \log(1 - p_{kd})) + \dots
\end{aligned}
$$

Keeping only p_{kd} terms results in

$$
\mathcal{B} = \sum_{n=1}^{N} q_{nk} \left(x_{nd} \log p_{kd} + (1 - x_{nd}) \log(1 - p_{kd}) \right) + \dots
$$

Taking partial derivatives with respect to p_{kd} gives us

$$
\frac{\partial \mathcal{B}}{\partial p_{kd}} = \sum_{n=1}^{N} q_{nk} \left(\frac{x_{nd}}{p_{kd}} - \frac{1 - x_{nd}}{1 - p_{kd}} \right).
$$

Setting to zero and rearranging gives us an update for p_{kd} setting to zero and solving gives (see Exercise 6.3)

$$
p_{kd} = \frac{\sum_{n=1}^{N} q_{nk} x_{nd}}{\sum_{n=1}^{N} q_{nk}}, \tag{6.22}
$$

which is the weighted average of the dth data dimension, much like the update for $\boldsymbol{\mu}_k$

in the Gaussian mixture (Equation 6.16). Our new EM algorithm involves iterating between updating q_{nk} from Equation 6.21 (the 'E' step) and updating $\mathbf{p}_k$ and π_k using Equations 6.22 and 6.15, respectively. Just as with the Gaussian example, we need to initialise π_k and the component parameters which, once again, we do by setting $\pi_k = 1/K$ and randomly setting each p_{kd} to a value between 0 and 1. Using $K = 5$ and running the algorithm until convergence gives the clusters shown in Figure 6.14, where each block is one cluster (MATLAB script: binmix.m). We can see clear cluster structure – for example, in cluster 1 (top), all objects have a 1 in dimension 9 and a zero in dimensions 10, 7 and 2.

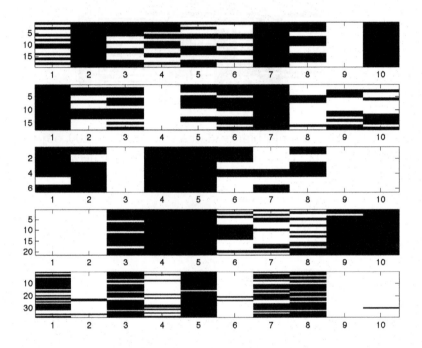

FIGURE 6.14 $K = 5$ clusters extracted from the data shown in Figure 6.13 using the mixture model with binary components.

In much the same way, we could derive an EM algorithm for many other component densities (see Exercise 6.6).

6.3.8 MAP estimates with EM

If we have a limited quantity of data, it might be useful to be able to regularise the parameter estimates obtained via EM. A straightforward way to do this is by multiplying the likelihood by suitable prior densities for the parameters and obtaining the MAP estimate (the value of the parameters that maximise the posterior, see Section 4.3). For example, in the binary example described above, we might use independent beta priors (see Section 2.5.2) for each of the parameters p_{kd}:

$$p(\mathbf{p}_1, \ldots, \mathbf{p}_K | \alpha, \beta) = \prod_{k=1}^{K} \prod_{d=1}^{D} \frac{\Gamma(\alpha + \beta)}{\Gamma(\alpha)\Gamma(\beta)} p_{kd}^{\alpha-1}(1 - p_{kd})^{\beta-1}.$$

This adds an extra p_{kd} term in the bound $\mathcal{B}$. The relevant terms are now

$$\begin{aligned}\mathcal{B} &= (\alpha - 1)\log p_{kd} + (\beta - 1)\log(1 - p_{kd}) \\ &+ \sum_{n=1}^{N} q_{nk}\left(x_{nd}\log p_{kd} + (1 - x_{nd})\log(1 - p_{kd})\right) + \ldots\end{aligned}$$

Taking partial derivatives, setting to zero and solving in the normal way gives (see Exercise 6.4

$$p_{kd} = \frac{\alpha - 1 + \sum_{n=1}^{N} q_{nk} x_{nd}}{\alpha + \beta - 2 + \sum_{n=1}^{N} q_{nk}}. \tag{6.23}$$

Note that $\alpha = \beta = 1$ recovers Equation 6.22. The regularising effect is clear. If $x_{nd} = 1$ for all n or $x_{nd} = 0$ for all n, Equation 6.22 would give $p_{kd} = 1$ and $p_{kd} = 0$. If a new data object did not have $x_{nd} = 1$ (or 0), it would have a likelihood of zero of belonging to this cluster regardless of its values in the other $D - 1$ dimensions. Equation 6.23 overcomes this problem by effectively bounding p_{kd} to minimum and maximum values of

$$\frac{\alpha - 1}{\alpha + \beta - 2}$$

and

$$\frac{\alpha - 1 + N}{\alpha + \beta - 2 + N},$$

respectively.

MAP solutions can be obtained via EM for many prior and likelihood combinations. See Exercise 6.5 for another example.

6.3.9 Bayesian mixture models

Obtaining point estimates that correspond to the maximum likelihood or MAP solutions via EM is not the only way to cluster with a mixture model. In particular, it is possible to use an MCMC scheme to sample cluster assignments and the associated component parameters. This has various advantages, not least the fact that it is possible to get around the problem of fixing the number of components (as mentioned at the end of Section 6.3.6). The result is not a single clustering but many samples from a *distribution* over clusterings. In a pure modelling sense, this is a good thing – we are explicitly acknowledging the fact that there is uncertainty present in the number of clusters (components) and the associated assignments. In the presence of such uncertainty, insisting on a single clustering comes with all the pitfalls of any other point estimate. However, it comes with problems of interpretability. For many applications, it is hard to imagine how we can use a distribution over clusterings, and often people resort to picking the sampled clustering that has maximum likelihood. MCMC approaches to mixture models *are* useful when the desired end result can be expressed as an expectation with respect to the distribution over clusterings. For example, if we want to compute the probability that two objects, $\mathbf{x}_n$ and $\mathbf{x}_m$, are in the same cluster, we can simply count the number of samples in which they are and divide this by the total number of samples. We could not calculate this quantity using a maximum likelihood or MAP solution via EM.

6.4 CHAPTER SUMMARY

In this chapter we have provided an introduction to clustering through two families of algorithms: K-means (including kernel K-means) and mixture models. The simplicity of K-means (and the flexibility of kernel K-means) makes it a popular approach. The diverse range of different component models available means that mixture models (and subtle variants) are appearing in more and more applications. These techniques also have drawbacks – in particular, the K-means algorithm and the EM algorithm for mixture models are both only guaranteed to reach local optima. In other words, they will reach an optimum of their respective objective function but it will not necessarily be the global optima (the overall best solution). In both cases, the particular solution that is reached depends on the initialisation – different random values of $\boldsymbol{\mu}_k$ and $\boldsymbol{\Sigma}_k$ will lead to different clusterings.

It is also important to remember that there are many other approaches available that we could never have covered in a single chapter, and the reader is strongly encouraged to investigate other popular methods, for example, hierarchical clustering (widely used in computational biology), spectral clustering and functional clustering.

6.5 EXERCISES

6.1 Derive the EM update for the variance of the dth dimension and the kth component, σ_{kd}^2, when the cluster components have a diagonal Gaussian likelihood

$$p(\mathbf{x}_n|z_{nk}=1,\mu_{k1},\ldots,\mu_{KD},\sigma_{k1}^2,\ldots,\sigma_{kD}^2) = \prod_{d=1}^{D}\mathcal{N}(\mu_{kd},\sigma_{kd}^2).$$

6.2 Repeat Exercise 6.1 with isotropic Gaussian components:

$$p(\mathbf{x}_n|z_{nk}=1,\boldsymbol{\mu}_k,\sigma_k^2) = \prod_{d=1}^{D}\mathcal{N}(\mu_{kd},\sigma_k^2).$$

6.3 Derive the EM update expression for the parameter p_{kd} given in Equation 6.22.

6.4 Derive the MAP EM update expression for the parameter p_{kd} given in Equation 6.22.

6.5 Derive the MAP update for a mixture model with Gaussian components that are independent over the D dimensions

$$p(\mathbf{x}_n|z_{nk}=1,\mu_{k1},\ldots,\mu_{KD},\sigma_{k1}^2,\ldots,\sigma_{kD}^2) = \prod_{d=1}^{D}\mathcal{N}(\mu_{kd},\sigma_{kd}^2),$$

assuming an independent Gaussian prior on each μ_{kd} with mean m and variance s^2.

6.6 Derive an EM algorithm for fitting a mixture of Poisson distributions. Assume you observe N integer counts, $x_1,\ldots,x_N$. The likelihood is

$$p(\mathbf{x}|\Delta) = \prod_{n=1}^{N}\sum_{k=1}^{K}\pi_k\frac{\lambda_k^{x_n}\exp\{-\lambda_k\}}{x_n!}.$$

6.6   FURTHER READING

[1] David Blei, Andrew Ng, and Michael Jordan. Latent Dirichlet Allocation. *Journal of Machine Learning Research*, 3:993–1022, 2003.

> This paper describes a complex mixture-type model for text data. The model is based on a more complex generative process than that described in this book. This particular model has proved to be very popular in the machine learning and information retrieval literature.

[2] Igor Cadez, David Heckerman, Christopher Meek, Padhraic Smyth, and Steven White. Model-based clustering and visualization of navigation patterns on a web site. *Data Mining and Knowledge Discovery*, pages 399–424, 2003.

> Mixture models can be defined with any type of component density. Here, a model is developed that uses Markov chains as the component densities, parameterised by a set of transition probabilities. The model is used to analyse internet browsing behaviour.

[3] Guojun Gan, Chaogun Ma, and Jianhong Wu. *Data Clustering: Theory, Algorithms, and Applications*. Society for Industrial Mathematics, 2007.

[4] A. K. Jain, M. N. Murty, and P. J. Flynn. Data clustering: A review. *ACM Computing Reviews*, 1999.

> A review of clustering techniques with discussions of applications in areas such as information retrieval, image segmentation and object recognition.

[5] Anil K. Jain. Data clustering: 50 years beyond k-means. *Pattern Recognition Letters*, 31:651–666, 2010.

> A recent tutorial paper providing an overview of the clustering problem and various clustering algorithms.

[6] Anil K. Jain and R. C. Dubes. *Algorithms For Clustering Data*. Prentice Hall, 1988.

> A clustering textbook that is now out of print but available free from the authors' website: http://www.cse.msu.edu/~jain/Clustering_Jain_Dubes.pdf

[7] G. McLachlan and D. Peel. *Finite Mixture Models*. Wiley, 2000.

> A comprehensive description of statistical mixture models.

[8] Carl Rasmussen. The infinite Gaussian mixture model. In *Advances in Neural Information Processing Systems 12*, pages 554–560, 2000.

> One of the first papers to describe the use of a Dirichlet process for overcoming the problem of fixing the number of components in a mixture model.

CHAPTER 7

Principal Components Analysis and Latent Variable Models

In the previous chapter we introduced two unsupervised methods that could be used to perform clustering – the partitioning of data objects into a finite number of disjoint groups such that objects in the same group share some similarity. We now turn our attention to a second class of unsupervised methods that could broadly be classed as **projection** techniques.

We will see how these methods can be used to take datasets in very high dimensions and project them down to a smaller number of dimensions for, for example, visualisation and feature selection. These techniques fall within the larger scope of latent variable models and we shall use the visualisation example to help provide an introduction to this area.

7.1 THE GENERAL PROBLEM

Our starting point is a dataset of N objects, $\mathbf{y}_n$. Each object is an M-dimensional vector. The number of parameters in many models increases with the number of dimensions, M. Therefore, if M is large, it can make parameter estimation challenging. Also, data in many dimensions is difficult to visualise. For these reasons, it is often useful to transform the M-dimensional representation $\mathbf{y}_n$ into a D-dimensional representation, $\mathbf{x}_n$. This process is known as projection. We are projecting M-dimensional data into D-dimensions in a manner that will hopefully preserve the properties of interest.

Figure 7.1 illustrates this problem in a more familiar setting. Both Figure 7.1(a) and Figure 7.1(b) show projections (shadows) of a three-dimensional object (a hand) onto a two-dimensional surface. In Figure 7.1(c) we see the idea of projection in a more mathematical setting. Here, some two-dimensional data ($\mathbf{y}_n$) has been projected onto one dimension. The projected dimension happens to be one of the original two dimensions, but this is not necessary. To draw an analogy with Figures 7.1(a) and 7.1(b), the original objects $\mathbf{y}_n$ correspond to the hand, and $\mathbf{x}_n$ to the shadow.

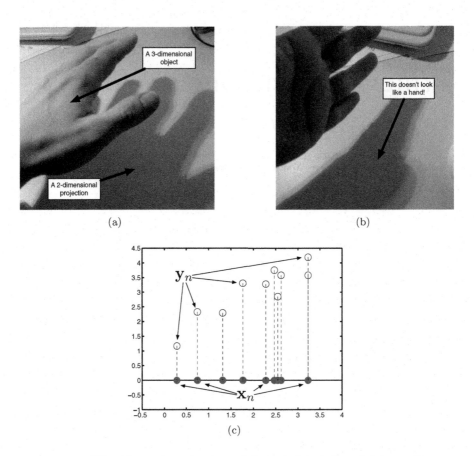

FIGURE 7.1 The idea of projection. (a) and (b) A hand (three dimensions) being projected onto a table (two dimensions) by a light. (c) two-dimensional data $\mathbf{y}_n$ being projected into one dimension $\mathbf{x}_n$. In this case, the projection is aligned with one of the original axes. This will not necessarily be the case.

7.1.1 Variance as a proxy for interest

When performing the projection, we would like to retain as much of the interesting structure in our data as possible. What do we mean by *interesting*? Figures 7.1(a) and 7.1(b) are both projections of the same 'data'. It is fairly clear in this case that the projection in Figure 7.1(a) maintains more of the characteristics of the original object (the hand) than Figure 7.1(b). In general, however, we will not be aware of the structure in the original representation and so cannot use this to optimise our projection.

In Figure 7.2(a) we can see a cloud of data points that have been generated from a single Gaussian distribution. The data has been projected onto two lines, A and

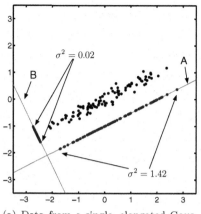

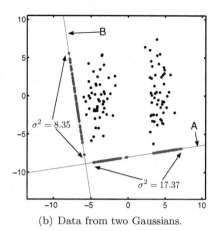

(a) Data from a single, elongated Gaussian.

(b) Data from two Gaussians.

FIGURE 7.2 Examples showing the variance of different projections of two synthetic two-dimensional datasets. In both cases, two different one-dimensional projections are shown (labeled A and B) as well as the variance of the data in each projection (σ^2).

B. Each line gives a different one-dimensional representation of the two-dimensional data. Note that, unlike in Figure 7.1(c), the lines do not correspond to either of the original dimensions. The representation in either one-dimensional space (the position on either line) is given by a linear combination of the original dimensions. In particular, $x_n = w_1 y_{n1} + w_2 y_{n2}$ (where $\mathbf{y}_n = [y_{n1}, y_{n2}]^\mathsf{T}$) or, in vector notation, $x_n = \mathbf{w}^\mathsf{T} \mathbf{y}_n$, where $\mathbf{w} = [w_1, w_2]^\mathsf{T}$.

We can compute the variance of the data in each one-dimensional space as

$$\sigma^2 = \frac{1}{N} \sum_{n=1}^{N} (x_n - \mu_x)^2,$$

and it is obvious that it will be higher for projection A than for projection B. Given no other information, if we must project into one-dimension, we should probably choose A. Put another way, if we are forced to throw one of A and B away, it feels safer to throw away the information present in B.

Figure 7.2(b) gives a more interesting example. We now have data that exhibits cluster structure. Projecting onto A preserves this cluster structure whilst projecting onto B does not. Cluster structure is an interesting property and so it looks like the projection onto A will be of more interest than that onto B. The variance of the data after projection A is more than double that for projection B. This is due to the cluster structure – all points are a large distance from the mean. If cluster structure is present in the data, using the projection with the highest variance is likely to preserve this structure.

For this reason, variance is seen as a good quantity to maximise when deciding on projection directions. It is the quantity that is maximised in the most popular projection technique, Principal Components Analysis.

7.2 PRINCIPAL COMPONENTS ANALYSIS

Principal Components Analysis (PCA) is perhaps the most widely used statistical technique for projecting data into a lower-dimensional space. It is very popular within machine learning for visualisation and feature selection. PCA defines a linear projection: each of the projected dimensions is a linear combination of the original dimensions. That is, if we are projecting from M to D dimensions, PCA will define D vectors, $\mathbf{w}_d$, each of which is M-dimensional. The dth element of the projection, x_{nd} (where $\mathbf{x}_n = [x_{n1}, \ldots, x_{nD}]^\mathsf{T}$), is computed as

$$x_{nd} = \mathbf{w}_d^\mathsf{T} \mathbf{y}_n.$$

The learning task is therefore to choose how many dimensions we want to project into (D) and then pick a projection vector, $\mathbf{w}_d$, for each.

PCA uses variance in the projected space as the criterion to choose $\mathbf{w}_d$. In particular, $\mathbf{w}_1$ will be the projection that makes the variance in the x_{n1} as high as possible. The second projected dimension is also chosen to maximise the variance but $\mathbf{w}_2$ must be orthogonal to $\mathbf{w}_1$ ($\mathbf{w}_1^\mathsf{T} \mathbf{w}_2 = 0$). The third component, $\mathbf{w}_3$, must maximise the variance and be orthogonal to both $\mathbf{w}_1$ and $\mathbf{w}_2$, etc. In general

$$\mathbf{w}_i^\mathsf{T} \mathbf{w}_j = 0, \ \forall j \neq i.$$

This set of constraints tells us that, if we set $D = M$, performing PCA amounts to rotating a rotation of the original data, without any loss of information.

In addition, PCA imposes the constraint that each $\mathbf{w}_i$ must have a length of 1, $\mathbf{w}_i^\mathsf{T} \mathbf{w}_i = 1$. This does not restrict the technique, as it is only the direction of each $\mathbf{w}$ that is important.

The problem that PCA solves in order to find the projections, $\mathbf{w}_1, \ldots, \mathbf{w}_D$, can be derived in a number of ways. We are going to do it by deriving an expression for the variance of x_{n1}, as this is perhaps the most intuitive. The reader is encouraged to explore other approaches within the statistics and machine learning literature.

Before we start the derivation, it is useful to make the assumption that each of the original dimensions has zero mean:

$$\bar{\mathbf{y}} = \frac{1}{N} \sum_{n=1}^{N} \mathbf{y}_n = 0.$$

This can be enforced by subtracting the mean, $\bar{\mathbf{y}}$, from each $\mathbf{y}_n$.

We shall start by finding a projection into $D = 1$ dimension. In other words, we are only interested in finding one $\mathbf{w}$ vector. In this case, the projection results in a scalar value, x_n, for each observation, given by

$$x_n = \mathbf{w}^\mathsf{T} \mathbf{y}_n.$$

The variance, σ_x^2, is given by:

$$\sigma_x^2 = \frac{1}{N} \sum_{n=1}^{N} (x_n - \bar{x})^2. \tag{7.1}$$

We can simplify this expression due to our assumption that $\bar{\mathbf{y}} = 0$:

$$
\begin{aligned}
\bar{x} &= \frac{1}{N} \sum_{n=1}^{N} \mathbf{w}^{\mathsf{T}} \mathbf{y}_n \\
&= \mathbf{w}^{\mathsf{T}} \left(\frac{1}{N} \sum_{n=1}^{N} \mathbf{y}_n \right) \\
&= \mathbf{w}^{\mathsf{T}} \bar{\mathbf{y}} = 0.
\end{aligned}
$$

Equation 7.1 becomes:

$$
\sigma_x^2 = \frac{1}{N} \sum_{n=1}^{N} x_n^2.
$$

Substituting the definition of x_n gives

$$
\begin{aligned}
\sigma_x^2 &= \frac{1}{N} \sum_{n=1}^{N} (\mathbf{w}^{\mathsf{T}} \mathbf{y}_n)^2 \\
&= \frac{1}{N} \sum_{n=1}^{N} \mathbf{w}^{\mathsf{T}} \mathbf{y}_n \mathbf{y}_n^{\mathsf{T}} \mathbf{w} \\
&= \mathbf{w}^{\mathsf{T}} \left(\frac{1}{N} \sum_{n=1}^{N} \mathbf{y}_n \mathbf{y}_n^{\mathsf{T}} \right) \mathbf{w} \\
\sigma_x^2 &= \mathbf{w}^{\mathsf{T}} \mathbf{C} \mathbf{w},
\end{aligned}
\tag{7.2}
$$

where $\mathbf{C}$ is the sample covariance matrix, defined as

$$
\mathbf{C} = \frac{1}{N} \sum_{n=1}^{N} (\mathbf{y}_n - \bar{\mathbf{y}})(\mathbf{y}_n - \bar{\mathbf{y}})^{\mathsf{T}},
$$

but where $\bar{\mathbf{y}} = 0$ in our case. Note that this expression tells us that we didn't lose anything by transforming our data to force $\bar{\mathbf{y}}$ to be 0. $\mathbf{C}$ would be the same whether we did this or not.

Our aim is to find the value of $\mathbf{w}$ that maximises σ^2 and therefore also maximises $\mathbf{w}^{\mathsf{T}} \mathbf{C} \mathbf{w}$. We could keep increasing $\mathbf{w}^{\mathsf{T}} \mathbf{C} \mathbf{w}$ by increasing the value of the elements in $\mathbf{w}$, and this is why $\mathbf{w}$ is constrained to have a length of 1, $\mathbf{w}^{\mathsf{T}} \mathbf{w} = 1$. As with the constraints in the SVM optimisation in Chapter 5 and the EM derivation in Chapter 6, we can incorporate this constraint into our optimisation through the use of a Lagrangian term (see Comment 5.1). In particular, we wish to find the $\mathbf{w}$ that maximises:

$$
L = \mathbf{w}^{\mathsf{T}} \mathbf{C} \mathbf{w} - \lambda(\mathbf{w}^{\mathsf{T}} \mathbf{w} - 1).
$$

Taking partial derivatives with respect to $\mathbf{w}$, equating to zero and rearranging gives

$$
\begin{aligned}
\frac{\partial L}{\partial \mathbf{w}} &= 2\mathbf{C}\mathbf{w} - \lambda \mathbf{w} = 0 \\
\mathbf{C}\mathbf{w} &= \lambda \mathbf{w}
\end{aligned}
\tag{7.3}
$$

(where we have incorporated the factor of 2 into the constant λ).

Comment 7.1 – Eigenvectors and eigenvalues: The eigenvector/eigenvalue equation for some square matrix **A** is given as

$$\lambda_i \mathbf{u}_i = \mathbf{A} \mathbf{u}_i. \tag{7.4}$$

The solutions to this equation are pairs of eigenvalues (λ_i) and eigenvectors ($\mathbf{u}_i$).

The figure on the right provides some intuition for this equation. Multiplying an M-dimensional vector **u** by an $M \times M$ matrix **B** results in another M-dimensional vector. Therefore, we can consider the matrix **B** as defining a rotation of the vector **u**. Different **B** matrices will produce different rotations. The solutions to Equation 7.3, for a particular matrix **A**, are the vectors **u** for which applying the rotation **A** only results in a change in the length of **u**. The magnitude of this change is given by the scalar λ.

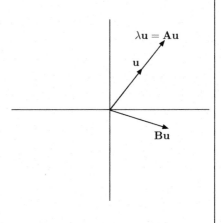

In general, if the matrix **A** has M rows and M columns, there are M eigenvector/eigenvalue pairs that solve Equation 7.4. The M eigenvectors will be orthogonal. We are not going to go into the detail about how to solve the eigenvalue/eigenvector equation. Routines for doing it are common, for example, the `eigs` function in MATLAB.

Equation 7.3 is of a very common form, known as the eigenvector/eigenvalue equation (see Comment 7.1). Comparing Equation 7.3 with Equation 7.4, we can see that the projection **w** that maximises the variance is one of the eigenvectors of the covariance matrix C. However, there will be M of these; how do we know which one corresponds to the highest variance? Our expression for σ_x^2 is

$$\sigma_x^2 = \mathbf{w}^\mathsf{T} \mathbf{C} \mathbf{w}.$$

Remember that $\mathbf{w}^\mathsf{T}\mathbf{w} = 1$, and we can therefore multiply the left hand side of this expression by $\mathbf{w}^\mathsf{T}\mathbf{w}$:

$$\sigma^2 \mathbf{w}^\mathsf{T}\mathbf{w} = \mathbf{w}^\mathsf{T}\mathbf{C}\mathbf{w}.$$

Removing a $\mathbf{w}^\mathsf{T}$ from each side leaves us with something that looks very similar to Equation 7.3:

$$\sigma^2 \mathbf{w} = \mathbf{C}\mathbf{w},$$

telling us that, given an eigenvalue/eigenvector pair $(\lambda, \mathbf{w})$, λ corresponds to the variance of the data in the projected space defined by **w**. If we find the M eigenvector/eigenvalue pairs of the covariance matrix **C**, the pair with the highest eigenvalue corresponds to the projection with maximal variance, $\mathbf{w}_1$. The second highest eigenvalue corresponds to $\mathbf{w}_2$, the third to $\mathbf{w}_3$, etc.

To summarise, performing PCA on a set of data objects, $\mathbf{y}_1, \ldots, \mathbf{y}_N$, requires performing the following steps (the expressions in parentheses are the corresponding matrix operations if we define $\mathbf{Y} = [\mathbf{y}_1, \ldots, \mathbf{y}_N]^\mathsf{T}$):

1. Transform the M-dimensional data to have zero mean by subtracting $\bar{\mathbf{y}}$ from each object where $\bar{\mathbf{y}} = \frac{1}{N} \sum_{n=1}^N \mathbf{y}_n$.

2. Compute the sample covariance matrix $\mathbf{C} = \frac{1}{N} \sum_{n=1}^N \mathbf{y}_n \mathbf{y}_n^\mathsf{T}$ (or $\mathbf{C} = \frac{1}{N} \mathbf{Y}^\mathsf{T} \mathbf{Y}$).

3. Find the M eigenvector/eigenvalue pairs of the covariance matrix. This can be done using, for example, the `eigs` function in MATLAB.

4. Find the eigenvectors corresponding to the D highest eigenvalues, $\mathbf{w}_1, \ldots, \mathbf{w}_D$.

5. Create the dth dimension for object n in the projection, $x_{nd} = \mathbf{w}_d^\mathsf{T} \mathbf{y}_n$, (or $\mathbf{X} = \mathbf{Y}\mathbf{W}$, where $\mathbf{W} = [\mathbf{w}_1, \ldots, \mathbf{w}_D]$, i.e. the $M \times D$ matrix created by placing the D eigenvectors alongside one another and $\mathbf{X}$ is the $N \times D$ matrix defined as $\mathbf{X} = [\mathbf{x}_1, \ldots, \mathbf{x}_N]^\mathsf{T}$).

To see a simple example of this, we can look back at Figure 7.2. In both plots, the directions we chose to project onto were the principal components. As we were working in two dimensions, there was a maximum of two components (a 2×2 covariance matrix has only two eigenvectors; it is impossible to have more than two orthogonal directions in two dimensions). When looking at these plots, remember that the procedure only defines the *direction* of the lines we have projected onto. We have moved the lines down a bit (for A) and left a bit (for B) to aid visualisation.

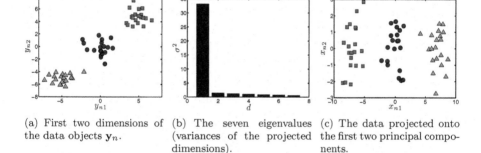

(a) First two dimensions of the data objects $\mathbf{y}_n$.

(b) The seven eigenvalues (variances of the projected dimensions).

(c) The data projected onto the first two principal components.

FIGURE 7.3 Synthetic PCA example where one projected dimension is all that is required. The data objects $\mathbf{y}_n$ are seven-dimensional. The first two dimensions have the cluster structure shown in (a). The remainder are made up of values sampled from $\mathcal{N}(0, 1)$.

Figure 7.3 shows a more complex example (MATLAB script: `pcaexample.m`). Here, we have generated a dataset where each object is drawn from one of three clusters (see Figure 7.3(a)). We then make the data more complex by adding an additional five dimensions whose values are drawn from $\mathcal{N}(0, 1)$:

$$y_{nd} \sim \mathcal{N}(0, 1), \ d = 3, \ldots, 7, \ n = 1, \ldots, N.$$

In other words, there is structure in the first two dimensions and noise in the remainder. This might correspond to a real example where we have measured various attributes of some objects, but do not know a priori which, if any, are interesting. After mean-centering the data, Figure 7.3(b) shows the values of the seven eigenvalues of the covariance matrix, $\mathbf{C} = \mathbf{Y}^\mathsf{T}\mathbf{Y}$, ordered by magnitude. Recall that these values correspond to the variance in each of the D potential projection dimensions. We can see that the highest eigenvalue is far higher than any of the others – it looks like we could capture most of the variance in our original 7 dimensional space with just one projected dimension. This might seem strange given that our original cluster structure was in two dimensions. However, looking back at Figure 7.3(a), the cluster structure is really only one dimensional, as the clusters all lie on the line $y_{n1} = y_{n2}$. One projected dimension will suffice. Plotting the data in the first two projected dimensions makes this clear (Figure 7.3(c)). The first projected dimension x_{n1} holds all the cluster structure.

This example shows us an important feature of PCA. The eigen-spectrum (magnitudes of the eigenvalues; Figure 7.3(b)) gives us some indication of how many *interesting* features there are in our data. In particular, Figure 7.3(b) tells us that we are unlikely to gain much by using two projected dimensions rather than one.

A second example can be seen in Figure 7.4 (MATLAB script: `pcaexample2.m`). Figure 7.4(a) shows a different cluster structure in the first two dimensions (the other five dimensions are constructed as in the previous example). We now have four clusters in an orientation that could not be explained using only one dimension. There is no single linear projection that would keep all of the clusters separate. We would therefore expect more than one large eigenvalue. Figure 7.4(b) shows that this is indeed the case – the first two eigenvalues are now both much higher than the remainder. The data projected onto these first two components can be seen in Figure 7.4(c), and it is clear that the cluster structure is preserved in the reduced space.

Before we proceed, it is worth reiterating a couple of important points from these examples. Firstly, remember that in both examples we added five 'random' dimensions. Hence, the problem is not as trivial as Figures 7.3(a) and 7.4(a) suggest. Secondly, although we have labeled the data objects differently when plotting them (circles, squares, etc.), this information is not used by PCA – it is unsupervised. Finally, the fact that we happened to put the cluster structure into the first two dimensions is irrelevant. If we shuffled up the columns of $\mathbf{Y}$ (i.e. reordered the dimensions), the result would be exactly the same.

7.2.1 Choosing D

In the previous section we used the eigen-spectrum (and our knowledge of the data) to inform how many dimensions we should project into. In general, our choice of D will be very application specific. For example, if we are performing PCA as a visualisation step that lets us *see* our high-dimensional data, then we are restricted to the number of dimensions we can visualise in a practical way: normally a maximum of three.

For other uses, the eigen-spectrum provides some useful information but its interpretation is highly subjective (we will not always get plots that send as clear a message as Figures 7.3(b) and 7.4(b)). If PCA is being used as part of a larger system, it is important to consider more objective measures. For example, a common

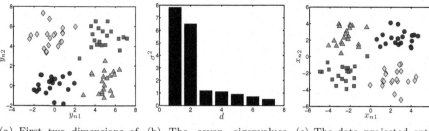

(a) First two dimensions of the data objects $\mathbf{y}_n$.

(b) The seven eigenvalues (variances of the projected dimensions).

(c) The data projected onto the first two principal components.

FIGURE 7.4 Synthetic PCA example where two projected dimensions are required.

use of PCA is as a feature extraction technique prior to classification. If the data used in Figure 7.4 was actually a four-class classification problem, consisting of a data matrix $\mathbf{Y}$ and some labels $\mathbf{t}$, it might be sensible to perform the classification with the projected data $\mathbf{X}$ rather than the original data $\mathbf{Y}$. In this case, D should really be chosen to be the value that gives the best classification performance via, perhaps, cross-validation.

7.2.2 Limitations of PCA

PCA has been successfully applied in many application areas but, like all models, it has clear limitations. In particular, it implicitly makes two assumptions about the data:

1. The data are real valued.

2. There are no missing values in the data.

Many problems will give rise to data that fulfils both of these criteria but just as many will not. For example, missing values are a common occurrence in scientific data where quantities being measured go outside the dynamic range of the measurement equipment. Datasets of purchasing records (whether someone bought something or not) are binary and not real valued. An obvious example that fails both criteria is a dataset of movie ratings. Imagine a matrix with a row for each viewer and a column for each movie. The value in the ith row and jth column is the rating that the ith viewer gives to the jth movie. Typically, this value will be an integer (0 to 5 stars; not real valued) and it is highly unlikely that a single viewer would be able to watch and rate each movie, so many values will be missing.

In the remainder of this chapter, we shall use these limitations of classical PCA as an opportunity to introduce the general concept of *latent variable models* and how we can perform inference or learning within these models. We should stress that there are many types of and uses for latent variable models beyond the PCA-like domain – we've already seen one – mixture models – in Chapter 6. However, addressing the limitations of classical PCA gives us a good route in. We will also use this opportunity to introduce variational inference – a method of approximating an intractable posterior density that has become very popular throughout the machine learning community in recent years due to its appealing combination of good empirical performance and low computational overhead.

7.3 LATENT VARIABLE MODELS

In many applications there will be characteristics of the objects of interest that are not provided in the data we are given. These *latent* variables (also known as hidden variables) can be placed into two categories:

1. Variables corresponding to a real feature of the object that have not been measured (e.g. maybe the technology to measure it is not available).

2. Abstract qualities that do not really exist but arise from our modelling assumptions and might be useful.

There are many examples of the former in the analysis of biological data. Consider a biological system consisting of three molecular species: A, B and C. A and C are easy to measure whilst B, for whatever reason, is not. In other words, A and C are observed whilst B is hidden. In this situation, we can explicitly model B as a hidden variable and use the data for A and C to learn something about B.

We are more interested in the second type of latent variable in this chapter. PCA is a good example – we observe some M-dimensional vectors, $\mathbf{y}_n$, and use these to construct a set of D-dimensional vectors $\mathbf{x}_n$. The input vectors are likely to be measurements of something that actually exists in the world. The $\mathbf{x}_n$, however, are latent variables that we have created based on assumptions within our model – they do not necessarily exist 'in the wild'. We created them in the hope that they might be more useful than the original variables for, for example, visualisation.

We shall return to PCA-like models in due course. Firstly, it will be useful to take a model that we have already seen and place it into the latent variable framework.

7.3.1 Mixture models as latent variable models

In Section 6.3, we introduced mixture models as a powerful clustering technique. By means of an introduction, we described a procedure for generating data that involved, for each data object we wished to generate, choosing one of K possible components and then sampling the object from this component. We introduced a set of indicator variables, z_{nk}, where $z_{nk} = 1$ if the nth object was generated by the kth component. These indicator variables are latent variables – they do not necessarily exist in reality – that enabled us to build the mixture models. When deriving the algorithm for inferring the parameters of the mixture model, we did not explicitly use z_{nk}, although in Equation 6.19 we showed that the q_{nk} parameters could be interpreted as the posterior probability that object n was generated by component k, $p(z_{nk} = 1 | \mathbf{x}_n, \boldsymbol{\pi}, \Delta)$. Our model definition implied the existence of a set of latent variables and we were able to learn something about the values they might have taken.

7.3.2 Summary

At the start of this chapter, we introduced PCA as a tool for *projecting M*-dimensional data into a *D*-dimensional space (where $D < M$). This can be useful for visualisation (when $D \leq 2$) or as a more generic unsupervised preprocessing tool before other analyses (classification, clustering, etc.). There are some drawbacks to PCA (ability to handle just real-valued data, inability to cope with missing data) which we will overcome in the remainder of this chapter. To set the scene for this, we have shown that PCA is one of a family of techniques known collectively as *latent variable models*, to which the mixture models introduced in Chapter 6 also belong. To be able to perform inference within a probabilistic PCA model, we will need to make some approximations. We have already seen ways of doing this in Chapter 4, and here we will introduce another technique, Variational Bayes.

7.4 VARIATIONAL BAYES

Variational Bayes (VB) is an approximate inference technique that has become popular within machine learning due to its good empirical performance and relatively low computational cost. Like the Laplace approximation introduced in Section 4.4, it allows us to approximate an intractable posterior with something tractable. The parameters of the approximate posterior are optimised to make the approximation as close to the true posterior as possible.

Although VB is used to construct an approximate posterior, it is not its primary motivation. The posterior approximation appears when we attempt to maximise the log marginal likelihood.

Consider a very general case where we have some data $\mathbf{Y}$ and a model that implies some parameters/latent variables $\boldsymbol{\theta}$. Note that we are lumping all model parameters and latent variables into the same symbol ($\boldsymbol{\theta}$). Within a Bayesian framework, the distinction between how we deal with latent variables and parameters becomes a little blurred: they are all things that we do not know so we treat them all as random variables. The marginal likelihood, $p(\mathbf{Y})$, is defined as

$$p(\mathbf{Y}) = \int p(\mathbf{Y}, \boldsymbol{\theta}) d\boldsymbol{\theta}. \tag{7.5}$$

In this expression, we have omitted conditioning on all things that are constant. This could include the model type, prior parameters, hyperparameters, etc. All of these things are model/problem specific, so we stick with this general expression but will be more precise when examining particular examples. An example of a more specific version of this equation is given in Section 3.4, where we first encountered marginal likelihoods.

Note that this expression is also commonly given with the joint density $p(\mathbf{Y}, \boldsymbol{\theta})$ broken up into its constituent parts:

$$p(\mathbf{Y}) = \int p(\mathbf{Y}|\boldsymbol{\theta}) p(\boldsymbol{\theta}) d\boldsymbol{\theta}.$$

The marginal likelihood computed in Equation 7.5 is therefore the result of averaging the likelihood ($p(\mathbf{Y}|\boldsymbol{\theta})$) over all values of the parameters (and latent variables), weighted by the prior, $p(\boldsymbol{\theta})$. This expression can be maximised with respect to all of the things on which the whole expression is conditioned (model structure, prior parameters). Unfortunately, maximising it is almost always very difficult due to the integral over the potentially high-dimensional parameter space. One way in which we can make progress is to lower bound the log marginal likelihood in a manner similar to that which we used in the EM derivation in Chapter 6. There, we used Jensen's inequality (see Equation 6.7), which we will repeat here:

$$\log \mathbf{E}_{p(z)} \{f(z)\} \geq \mathbf{E}_{p(z)} \{\log f(z)\}.$$

The log marginal likelihood is given by

$$\log p(\mathbf{Y}) = \log \int p(\mathbf{Y}, \boldsymbol{\theta}) d\boldsymbol{\theta}.$$

We start by introducing an arbitrary distribution over $\boldsymbol{\theta}$, $Q(\boldsymbol{\theta})$, into the right hand side:

$$\log p(\mathbf{Y}) = \log \int Q(\boldsymbol{\theta}) \frac{p(\mathbf{Y}, \boldsymbol{\theta})}{Q(\boldsymbol{\theta})} d\boldsymbol{\theta}.$$

Recall from Equation 6.7 that Jensen's inequality tells us that the log of an expectation is always greater than the expectation of a log. The right hand side of our expression can be interpreted as an expectation (of $p(\mathbf{Y}, \boldsymbol{\theta})/Q(\boldsymbol{\theta})$) with respect to $Q(\boldsymbol{\theta})$ so we use Jensen's inequality to construct a lower bound, $\mathcal{L}(Q)$:

$$
\begin{aligned}
\log p(\mathbf{Y}) &= \log \int Q(\boldsymbol{\theta}) \frac{p(\mathbf{Y}, \boldsymbol{\theta})}{Q(\boldsymbol{\theta})} d\boldsymbol{\theta} \\
&\geq \int Q(\boldsymbol{\theta}) \log \frac{p(\mathbf{Y}, \boldsymbol{\theta})}{Q(\boldsymbol{\theta})} d\boldsymbol{\theta} = \mathcal{L}(Q).
\end{aligned}
\tag{7.6}
$$

Computing the difference between the true log marginal likelihood and our new bound reveals how we can obtain an approximate posterior:

$$
\begin{aligned}
\log p(\mathbf{Y}) - \mathcal{L}(Q) &= \log p(\mathbf{Y}) - \int Q(\boldsymbol{\theta}) \log \frac{p(\mathbf{Y}, \boldsymbol{\theta})}{Q(\boldsymbol{\theta})} d\boldsymbol{\theta} \\
&= \log p(\mathbf{Y}) - \int Q(\boldsymbol{\theta}) \log \frac{p(\boldsymbol{\theta}|\mathbf{Y})p(\mathbf{Y})}{Q(\boldsymbol{\theta})} d\boldsymbol{\theta} \\
&= \log p(\mathbf{Y}) - \int Q(\boldsymbol{\theta}) \log \frac{p(\boldsymbol{\theta}|\mathbf{Y})}{Q(\boldsymbol{\theta})} d\boldsymbol{\theta} - \int Q(\boldsymbol{\theta}) \log p(\mathbf{Y}) d\boldsymbol{\theta} \\
&= \log p(\mathbf{Y}) - \int Q(\boldsymbol{\theta}) \log \frac{p(\boldsymbol{\theta}|\mathbf{Y})}{Q(\boldsymbol{\theta})} d\boldsymbol{\theta} - \log p(\mathbf{Y}) \int Q(\boldsymbol{\theta}) d\boldsymbol{\theta} \\
&= \log p(\mathbf{Y}) - \int Q(\boldsymbol{\theta}) \log \frac{p(\boldsymbol{\theta}|\mathbf{Y})}{Q(\boldsymbol{\theta})} d\boldsymbol{\theta} - \log p(\mathbf{Y}) \\
\log p(\mathbf{Y}) - \mathcal{L}(Q) &= -\int Q(\boldsymbol{\theta}) \log \frac{p(\boldsymbol{\theta}|\mathbf{Y})}{Q(\boldsymbol{\theta})} d\boldsymbol{\theta} = -\text{KL}[Q(\boldsymbol{\theta})||p(\boldsymbol{\theta}|\mathbf{Y})].
\end{aligned}
\tag{7.7}
$$

The final expression is known as the Kullback–Leibler (KL) divergence between the posterior, $p(\boldsymbol{\theta}|\mathbf{Y})$, and $Q(\boldsymbol{\theta})$; see Comment 7.2.

Comment 7.2 – Kullback–Leibler divergence: It is often important to be able to quantify the difference between two probability distributions. For example, if we are trying to find an approximate posterior that is similar to the true posterior, we need to define what we mean by similar! The Kullback–Leibler divergence is one such quantity that appears in the derivation of Variational Bayesian techniques. It is defined for discrete and continuous distributions as

$$KL[q(x)||p(x)] = \int q(x) \log \frac{p(x)}{q(x)} \, dx \quad \text{(continuous)}$$

$$KL[q(x)||p(x)] = \sum_x q(x) \log \frac{p(x)}{q(x)} \quad \text{(discrete)}$$

For continuous distributions it is almost always intractable to compute due to the integral over a potentially high-dimensional space.

An important property of the KL divergence is its asymmetry – $KL[q(x)||p(x)] \neq KL[p(x)||q(x)]$. KL divergence is always less than or equal to zero, with the maximum value of zero being reached when $p(x) = q(x)$.

The left hand side of Equation 7.7 must always be greater than or equal to zero (remember that $\mathcal{L}(Q)$ is a lower bound on $\log p(\mathbf{Y})$). The KL divergence is a measure of dissimilarity between two distributions that takes the value 0 if the two distributions are identical and is otherwise less than 0. Maximising $\mathcal{L}(Q)$ by varying Q reduces the negative of the KL divergence, and therefore has the effect of making $Q(\boldsymbol{\theta})$ more and more similar to the true posterior $p(\boldsymbol{\theta}|\mathbf{Y})$. If $Q(\boldsymbol{\theta})$ and $p(\boldsymbol{\theta}|\mathbf{Y})$ are identical, the bound is equal to the true log marginal likelihood (see Exercise 7.1).

7.4.1 Choosing $Q(\boldsymbol{\theta})$

We have seen that, if we maximise the bound with respect to $Q(\boldsymbol{\theta})$, we are making $Q(\boldsymbol{\theta})$ a better and better approximation to the posterior. We need to choose the form of $Q(\boldsymbol{\theta})$, and it makes sense to choose it in such a way that makes it relatively straightforward to maximise the bound given in Equation 7.6. There is a clear trade-off here – more complex forms for $Q(\boldsymbol{\theta})$ are likely to make the bound harder to optimise but will provide us with a better approximation. Simple forms for $Q(\boldsymbol{\theta})$ will potentially make optimisation easy, but the resulting approximation will probably be poor. A popular assumption is to assume independence across the different parameters/latent variables with $\boldsymbol{\theta}$:

$$Q(\boldsymbol{\theta}) = \prod_{l=1}^{L} Q_l(\boldsymbol{\theta}_l) \tag{7.8}$$

where each $l = 1 \ldots L$ is a different individual or set of parameters or latent variables. For example, a model may have M vectors of parameters $\mathbf{w}_m$ and N latent variable vectors $\mathbf{x}_n$ collectively known as $\mathbf{W}$ and $\mathbf{X}$, respectively. We might decide to assume independence across these sets of parameters:

$$Q(\mathbf{W}, \mathbf{X}) = Q_{\mathbf{W}}(\mathbf{W}) Q_{\mathbf{X}}(\mathbf{X}).$$

We could go one step further and assume that either or both of these distributions was independent over its M (or N) components:

$$Q_{\mathbf{W}}(\mathbf{W}) = \prod_{m=1}^{M} Q_{\mathbf{w}_m}(\mathbf{w}_m), \quad \text{and/or} \quad Q_{\mathbf{X}}(\mathbf{X}) = \prod_{n=1}^{N} Q_{\mathbf{x}_n}(\mathbf{x}_n).$$

Going even further, we could, for example, assume independence across the D-dimensions of $\mathbf{x}_n$:

$$Q_{\mathbf{X}}(\mathbf{X}) = \prod_{n=1}^{N} \prod_{d=1}^{D} Q_{x_{nd}}(x_{nd}).$$

Given that the parameters are likely to be dependent in the true posterior, the more independence assumptions we make, the worse our approximation is likely to become. This is an example of the trade-off we just mentioned: greater independence assumptions will make the bound easier to optimise but will result in a poorer approximate posterior.

7.4.2   Optimising the bound

If we construct $Q(\boldsymbol{\theta})$ in the manner described by Equation 7.8, the bound is optimised by distributions of the form

$$Q_l(\boldsymbol{\theta}_l) = \frac{\exp\left(\mathbf{E}_{k \neq l}\left\{\log p(\mathbf{Y}, \boldsymbol{\theta})\right\}\right)}{\int \exp\left(\mathbf{E}_{k \neq l}\left\{\log p(\mathbf{Y}, \boldsymbol{\theta})\right\}\right) d\boldsymbol{\theta}_l} \tag{7.9}$$

where the expectation is over all of the individual distributions making up the product in Equation 7.8 except the lth one.

The expression is not as ominous as it appears at first glance. The denominator is simply a normalising constant, which will often be defined by the form of the terms involving $\boldsymbol{\theta}_l$ in the numerator. For example, the presence of linear ($\boldsymbol{\theta}_l^\mathsf{T}\mathbf{b}$) and quadratic ($\boldsymbol{\theta}_l^\mathsf{T}\mathbf{A}\boldsymbol{\theta}_l$) terms suggests that $Q_l(\boldsymbol{\theta}_l)$ is Gaussian, for which we know the normalising constant.

Computing each $Q_l(\boldsymbol{\theta}_l)$ requires taking an expectation with respect to each other $Q_k(\boldsymbol{\theta}_k)$. Much like the EM algorithm in Chapter 6, this means that we will require an iterative procedure to optimise our approximate posterior.

7.5   A PROBABILISTIC MODEL FOR PCA

To illustrate Variational Bayes, we will start with a probabilistic PCA-like model. Assume that we observe $n = 1 \ldots N$ M-dimensional input vectors $\mathbf{y}_n$. We would like to find a D-dimensional representation $\mathbf{x}_n$ (where $D < M$). We will link $\mathbf{y}_n$ and $\mathbf{x}_n$ with the model

$$\mathbf{y}_n = \mathbf{W}\mathbf{x}_n + \mathbf{v}$$

where $\mathbf{W}$ is an $M \times D$ matrix and $\mathbf{v}$ is an $M \times 1$ noise vector. The graphical representation (see Section 3.6) of this model can be seen in Figure 7.5. We will

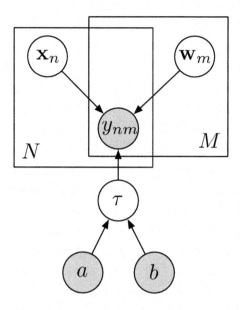

FIGURE 7.5 Graphical representation of the probabilistic PCA model.

make the following prior assumptions:

$$p(\mathbf{x}_n) = \mathcal{N}(\mathbf{0}, \mathbf{I}_D)$$

$$p(\mathbf{W}) = \prod_{m=1}^{M} p(\mathbf{w}_m)$$

$$p(\mathbf{w}_m) = \mathcal{N}(\mathbf{0}, \mathbf{I}_D)$$

$$p(y_{nm}) = \mathcal{N}(\mathbf{w}_m^{\mathsf{T}} \mathbf{x}_n, \tau^{-1})$$

$$p(\tau | a, b) = \Gamma(a, b) = \frac{b^a \tau^{a-1} e^{-b\tau}}{\Gamma(a)}$$

where $\mathbf{W} = [\mathbf{w}_1, \dots, \mathbf{w}_M]^{\mathsf{T}}$ and, for convenience, we have defined a **precision** rather than variance parameter for the noise, τ $(\tau^{-1} = \sigma^2)$.

We will now use Variational Bayes to infer an approximate posterior over $\mathbf{X} = [\mathbf{x}_1, \dots, \mathbf{x}_N]^{\mathsf{T}}$, $\mathbf{W}$ and τ. The first step is to decide how we shall decompose $Q(\mathbf{W}, \mathbf{X}, \tau)$. We will do the following:

$$Q(\mathbf{W}, \mathbf{X}, \tau) = Q_\tau(\tau) \left[\prod_{n=1}^{N} Q_{\mathbf{x}_n}(\mathbf{x}_n) \right] \left[\prod_{m=1}^{M} Q_{\mathbf{w}_m}(\mathbf{w}_m) \right],$$

i.e. assume independence across the three sets of parameters (for brevity, we will refer to the latent variables $\mathbf{x}_n$ as parameters from now on) and, additionally, independence across the various vector components of $\mathbf{X}$ and $\mathbf{W}$.

To obtain expressions for each $Q_l(\boldsymbol{\theta}_l)$, we need, from Equation 7.9, to take expectations of $\log p(\mathbf{Y}, \boldsymbol{\theta})$. In our example, this is (making the standard IID assumption)

$$p(\mathbf{Y}, \mathbf{X}, \mathbf{W}, \tau) \;=\; p(\tau|a, b)\left[\prod_{m=1}^{M} p(\mathbf{w}_m)\right]\left[\prod_{n=1}^{N} p(\mathbf{x}_n)p(\mathbf{y}_n|\mathbf{W}, \mathbf{x}_n, \tau)\right]$$

$$\log p(\mathbf{Y}, \mathbf{X}, \mathbf{W}, \tau) \;=\; \log p(\tau|a, b) + \sum_{m=1}^{M} \log p(\mathbf{w}_m) + \sum_{n=1}^{N} \log p(\mathbf{x}_n)$$

$$+ \sum_{n=1}^{N} \log p(\mathbf{y}_n|\mathbf{W}, \mathbf{x}_n, \tau).$$

Because of our assumption that the noise vector $\mathbf{v}$ has diagonal covariance, the final term on the right hand side can be further expanded to each individual element of $\mathbf{y}_n$:

$$\log p(\mathbf{Y}, \mathbf{X}, \mathbf{W}, \tau) \;=\; \log p(\tau|a, b)$$

$$+ \sum_{m=1}^{M} \log p(\mathbf{w}_m)$$

$$+ \sum_{n=1}^{N} \log p(\mathbf{x}_n)$$

$$+ \sum_{n=1}^{N}\sum_{m=1}^{M} \log p(y_{nm}|\mathbf{w}_m, \mathbf{x}_n, \tau), \qquad (7.10)$$

where

$$p(y_{nm}|\mathbf{w}_m, \mathbf{x}_n, \tau) = \mathcal{N}(\mathbf{w}_m^{\mathsf{T}}\mathbf{x}_n, \tau^{-1}).$$

We will now define each component of the approximate posterior in turn.

7.5.1 $Q_\tau(\tau)$

From Equation 7.9 we know that

$$Q_\tau(\tau) \propto \exp\left(\mathbf{E}_{Q_{\mathbf{X}}(\mathbf{X})Q_{\mathbf{W}}(\mathbf{W})}\left\{\log p(\mathbf{Y}, \mathbf{X}, \mathbf{W}, \tau)\right\}\right).$$

Any terms within the expectation that do not include τ can be ignored, as they will be swallowed up by the normalisation constant. The only terms that do depend on τ in Equation 7.10 are the first and the last. Writing these terms in full gives us

$$\log p(\mathbf{Y}, \mathbf{X}, \mathbf{W}, \tau) \quad \propto \quad a\log b + (a - 1)\log\tau - b\tau - \log\Gamma(a)$$

$$-\frac{NM}{2}\log 2\pi + \frac{NM}{2}\log\tau - \frac{\tau}{2}\sum_n\sum_m(y_{nm} - \mathbf{w}_m^{\mathsf{T}}\mathbf{x}_n)^2$$

Removing new terms that do not depend on τ leaves (and remembering that $\exp(A + B) = \exp(A)\exp(B)$)

$$Q_\tau(\tau) \quad \propto \quad \exp\left(\mathbf{E}_{Q_{\mathbf{X}}(\mathbf{X})Q_{\mathbf{W}}(\mathbf{W})}\left\{\log p(\mathbf{Y}, \mathbf{X}, \mathbf{W}, \tau)\right\}\right)$$

$$\propto \quad \exp\left((a - 1)\log\tau - b\tau + \frac{NM}{2}\log\tau\right)$$

$$\times \exp\left(-\frac{\tau}{2}\mathbf{E}_{Q_{\mathbf{X}}(\mathbf{X})Q_{\mathbf{W}}(\mathbf{W})}\left\{\sum_n\sum_m(y_{nm} - \mathbf{w}_m^{\mathsf{T}}\mathbf{x}_n)^2\right\}\right).$$

Bearing in mind that

$$\mathbf{E}_{p(a)}\{f(a) + g(a)\} = \mathbf{E}_{p(a)}\{f(a)\} + \mathbf{E}_{p(a)}\{g(a)\},$$

we can take the expectations of all of the terms in the summation separately. Also y_{nm}^2 is the observed data and therefore

$$\mathbf{E}_{Q_{\mathbf{x}_n}(\mathbf{x}_n)Q_{\mathbf{w}_m}(\mathbf{w}_m)}\{y_{nm}^2\} = y_{nm}^2.$$

We are left with

$$\exp\left(-\frac{\tau}{2}\sum_{n,m}\left(y_{nm}^2 + \mathbf{E}_{Q_{\mathbf{x}_n}(\mathbf{x}_n)Q_{\mathbf{w}_m}(\mathbf{w}_m)}\left\{-2\mathbf{w}_m^\mathsf{T}\mathbf{x}_n + \mathbf{x}_n^\mathsf{T}\mathbf{w}_m\mathbf{w}_m^\mathsf{T}\mathbf{x}_n\right\}\right)\right).$$

At first glance, this still looks difficult, but consider the expectation

$$\mathbf{E}_{p(a)p(b)}\{f(a)f(b)\}.$$

Writing it out in full gives us

$$\begin{aligned}
\mathbf{E}_{p(a)p(b)}\{f(a)f(b)\} &= \iint p(a)p(b)f(a)f(b)\,da\,db \\
&= \iint p(a)f(a)\,da\,p(b)f(b)\,db \\
&= \int \mathbf{E}_{p(a)}\{f(a)\}\,p(b)f(b)\,db \\
&= \mathbf{E}_{p(a)}\{f(a)\}\,\mathbf{E}_{p(b)}\{f(b)\}. \tag{7.11}
\end{aligned}$$

Using this result, we can evaluate the first argument inside our expectation:

$$\mathbf{E}_{Q_{\mathbf{x}_n}(\mathbf{x}_n)Q_{\mathbf{w}_m}(\mathbf{w}_m)}\left\{-2\mathbf{w}_m^\mathsf{T}\mathbf{x}_n\right\} = -2\mathbf{E}_{Q_{\mathbf{x}_n}(\mathbf{x}_n)}\{\mathbf{x}_n\}^\mathsf{T}\mathbf{E}_{Q_{\mathbf{w}_m}(\mathbf{w}_m)}\{\mathbf{w}_m\},$$

which is the expected (mean) value of $\mathbf{x}_n$ multiplied by the expected value of $\mathbf{w}_m$. Before we continue, it is worth introducing a more useful notation, as we are going to see a lot of expressions like this. From now on, we will denote expectations such as this as

$$\mathbf{E}_{Q_{\boldsymbol{\theta}_l}(\boldsymbol{\theta}_l)}\{f(\boldsymbol{\theta}_l)\} = \langle f(\boldsymbol{\theta}_l)\rangle.$$

The first term in the expectation becomes

$$\mathbf{E}_{Q_{\mathbf{x}_n}(\mathbf{x}_n)Q_{\mathbf{w}_m}(\mathbf{w}_m)}\left\{-2\mathbf{w}_m^\mathsf{T}\mathbf{x}_n\right\} = -2\langle\mathbf{x}_n\rangle^\mathsf{T}\langle\mathbf{w}_m\rangle.$$

The second term is a bit trickier. We cannot write it as $f(\mathbf{x}_n)g(\mathbf{w}_m)$ so we have to do the expectations one at a time:

$$\begin{aligned}
\mathbf{E}_{Q_{\mathbf{x}_n}(\mathbf{x}_n)Q_{\mathbf{w}_m}(\mathbf{w}_m)}\left\{\mathbf{x}_n^\mathsf{T}\mathbf{w}_m\mathbf{w}_m^\mathsf{T}\mathbf{x}_n\right\} &= \mathbf{E}_{Q_{\mathbf{x}_n}(\mathbf{x}_n)}\left\{\mathbf{x}_n^\mathsf{T}\left\langle\mathbf{w}_m\mathbf{w}_m^\mathsf{T}\right\rangle\mathbf{x}_n\right\} \\
&= \left\langle\mathbf{x}_n^\mathsf{T}\left\langle\mathbf{w}_m\mathbf{w}_m^\mathsf{T}\right\rangle\mathbf{x}_n\right\rangle.
\end{aligned}$$

Putting everything back together, we have

$$\begin{aligned}
Q_\tau(\tau) \quad\propto\quad &\exp\left((a-1)\log\tau - b\tau + \frac{NM}{2}\log\tau\right. \\
&\left. -\frac{\tau}{2}\sum_{n,m}\left(y_{nm}^2 - 2\langle\mathbf{w}_n\rangle^\mathsf{T}\langle\mathbf{x}_n\rangle + \left\langle\mathbf{x}_n^\mathsf{T}\left\langle\mathbf{w}_m\mathbf{w}_m^\mathsf{T}\right\rangle\mathbf{x}_n\right\rangle\right)\right).
\end{aligned}$$

This can be written as

$$Q_\tau(\tau) \propto \tau^{e-1} \exp\{-\tau f\}, \tag{7.12}$$

where

$$e = a + \frac{NM}{2}$$

$$f = b + \frac{1}{2} \sum_{n,m} \left(y_{nm}^2 - 2 \langle \mathbf{w}_n \rangle^\mathsf{T} \langle \mathbf{x}_n \rangle + \langle \mathbf{x}_n^\mathsf{T} \langle \mathbf{w}_m \mathbf{w}_m^\mathsf{T} \rangle \mathbf{x}_n \rangle \right).$$

The form of Equation 7.12 tells us that $Q_\tau(\tau)$ is a gamma distribution, with parameters e, f. If you are unsure of why this is the case, take the log of a gamma density with parameters e and f and remove terms that do not depend on τ – you will get the right hand side of Equation 7.12.

To summarise

$$Q_\tau(\tau) = \Gamma(e, f).$$

We will now derive $Q_{\mathbf{x}_n}(\mathbf{x}_n)$ and $Q_{\mathbf{w}_m}(\mathbf{w}_m)$ – once we know the forms of these we will be able to compute the expectations required to calculate e and f.

7.5.2 $Q_{\mathbf{x}_n}(\mathbf{x}_n)$

The steps required to obtain $Q_{\mathbf{x}_n}(\mathbf{x}_n)$ are much the same as those we needed to get $Q_\tau(\tau)$. To start with, we extract the terms we need from $\log p(\mathbf{Y}, \mathbf{X}, \mathbf{W}, \tau)$, ignoring everything that does not involve $\mathbf{x}_n$:

$$Q_{\mathbf{x}_n}(\mathbf{x}_n) \propto \exp\left(\mathbf{E}_{Q_\mathbf{W}(\mathbf{W})Q_\tau(\tau)} \left\{ \log p(\mathbf{x}_n) + \sum_{m=1}^{M} p(y_{nm}|\mathbf{w}_m, \mathbf{x}_n, \tau) \right\} \right).$$

Note that the expectation should also be with respect to all $Q_{\mathbf{x}_l}(\mathbf{x}_l)$ for all $l \neq n$. However, there are no $\mathbf{x}_l$ terms in our expression, and subsequently the expectations vanish. Expanding the two terms in the expectation and removing non $\mathbf{x}_n$ terms, we have

$$
\begin{aligned}
Q_{\mathbf{x}_n}(\mathbf{x}_n) &\propto \exp\left(\mathbf{E}_{Q_\mathbf{W}(\mathbf{W})Q_\tau(\tau)} \left\{ -\frac{1}{2}\mathbf{x}_n^\mathsf{T}\mathbf{x}_n \right.\right. \\
&\qquad \left.\left. -\frac{1}{2}\tau \sum_m \left(-2y_{nm}\mathbf{x}_n^\mathsf{T}\mathbf{w}_m + \mathbf{x}_n^\mathsf{T}\mathbf{w}_m\mathbf{w}_m^\mathsf{T}\mathbf{x}_n \right) \right\} \right) \\
&= \exp\left(-\frac{1}{2}\mathbf{x}_n^\mathsf{T}\mathbf{x}_n - \frac{1}{2}\langle\tau\rangle \sum_m \left(-2y_{nm}\mathbf{x}_n^\mathsf{T}\langle\mathbf{w}_m\rangle + \mathbf{x}_n^\mathsf{T}\langle\mathbf{w}_m\mathbf{w}_m^\mathsf{T}\rangle\mathbf{x}_n \right) \right) \\
&= \exp\left(-\frac{1}{2}\left(\mathbf{x}_n^\mathsf{T}\left[\mathbf{I}_D + \langle\tau\rangle \sum_m \langle\mathbf{w}_m\mathbf{w}_m^\mathsf{T}\rangle \right]\mathbf{x}_n \right.\right. \\
&\qquad \left.\left. -2\langle\tau\rangle\,\mathbf{x}_n^\mathsf{T}\sum_m y_{nm}\langle\mathbf{w}_m\rangle \right) \right).
\end{aligned}
$$

The presence of the linear and quadratic terms within the expectation tells us that this is a Gaussian:

$$Q_{\mathbf{x}_n}(\mathbf{x}_n) = \mathcal{N}(\boldsymbol{\mu}_{\mathbf{x}_n}, \boldsymbol{\Sigma}_{\mathbf{x}_n}).$$

Equating coefficients lets us read off expressions for $\boldsymbol{\mu}_{\mathbf{x}_n}$ and $\boldsymbol{\Sigma}_{\mathbf{x}_n}$:

$$\mathbf{x}_n^{\mathsf{T}} \boldsymbol{\Sigma}_{\mathbf{x}_n}^{-1} \mathbf{x}_n \equiv \mathbf{x}_n^{\mathsf{T}} \left[\mathbf{I}_D + \langle \tau \rangle \sum_m \left\langle \mathbf{w}_m \mathbf{w}_m^{\mathsf{T}} \right\rangle \right] \mathbf{x}_n$$

$$\boldsymbol{\Sigma}_{\mathbf{x}_n} = \left[\mathbf{I}_D + \langle \tau \rangle \sum_m \left\langle \mathbf{w}_m \mathbf{w}_m^{\mathsf{T}} \right\rangle \right]^{-1} \tag{7.13}$$

$$-2\mathbf{x}_n^{\mathsf{T}} \boldsymbol{\Sigma}_{\mathbf{x}_n}^{-1} \boldsymbol{\mu}_{\mathbf{x}_n} \equiv -2 \langle \tau \rangle \mathbf{x}_n^{\mathsf{T}} \sum_m y_{nm} \langle \mathbf{w}_m \rangle$$

$$\boldsymbol{\mu}_{\mathbf{x}_n} = \langle \tau \rangle \boldsymbol{\Sigma}_{\mathbf{x}_n} \sum_m y_{nm} \langle \mathbf{w}_m \rangle . \tag{7.14}$$

Note that the expression for the covariance matrix $\boldsymbol{\Sigma}_{\mathbf{x}_n}$ has no dependence on n. It can be computed once and used for all $\mathbf{x}_n$.

7.5.3 $Q_{\mathbf{w}_m}(\mathbf{w}_m)$

The method for computing $Q_{\mathbf{w}_m}(\mathbf{w}_m)$ is essentially identical to that for computing $Q_{\mathbf{x}_n}(\mathbf{x}_n)$. We start by removing everything that doesn't have a $\mathbf{w}_m$ term:

$$Q_{\mathbf{w}_m}(\mathbf{w}_m) \propto \exp\left(\mathbf{E}_{Q_{\mathbf{X}}(\mathbf{X})Q_\tau(\tau)} \left\{ \log p(\mathbf{w}_m) + \sum_{n=1}^{N} p(y_{nm}|\mathbf{w}_m, \mathbf{x}_n, \tau) \right\} \right).$$

Once again, the expectations with respect to $Q_{\mathbf{w}_l}(\mathbf{w}_l)$ for all $l \neq m$ vanish. Expanding, noticing that $\mathbf{w}_m^{\mathsf{T}} \mathbf{x}_n \equiv \mathbf{x}_n^{\mathsf{T}} \mathbf{w}_m$:

$$Q_{\mathbf{w}_m}(\mathbf{w}_m) \propto \exp\left(\mathbf{E}_{Q_{\mathbf{X}}(\mathbf{X})Q_\tau(\tau)} \left\{ -\frac{1}{2}\mathbf{w}_m^{\mathsf{T}}\mathbf{w}_m \right. \right.$$

$$\left. \left. -\frac{1}{2}\tau \sum_n \left(-2y_{nm}\mathbf{w}_m^{\mathsf{T}}\mathbf{x}_n + \mathbf{w}_m^{\mathsf{T}}\mathbf{x}_n\mathbf{x}_n^{\mathsf{T}}\mathbf{w}_m \right) \right\} \right)$$

$$= \exp\left(-\frac{1}{2}\mathbf{w}_m^{\mathsf{T}}\mathbf{w}_m - \frac{1}{2} \langle \tau \rangle \sum_n \left(-2y_{nm}\mathbf{w}_m^{\mathsf{T}} \langle \mathbf{x}_n \rangle + \mathbf{w}_m^{\mathsf{T}} \left\langle \mathbf{x}_n\mathbf{x}_n^{\mathsf{T}} \right\rangle \mathbf{w}_m \right) \right)$$

$$\propto \exp\left(-\frac{1}{2}\left(\mathbf{w}_m^{\mathsf{T}} \left[\mathbf{I}_D + \langle \tau \rangle \sum_n \left\langle \mathbf{x}_n\mathbf{x}_n^{\mathsf{T}} \right\rangle \right] \mathbf{w}_m \right. \right.$$

$$\left. \left. -2 \langle \tau \rangle \mathbf{w}_m^{\mathsf{T}} \sum_n y_{nm} \langle \mathbf{x}_n \rangle \right) \right).$$

This is clearly another Gaussian:

$$Q_{\mathbf{w}_m}(\mathbf{w}_m) = \mathcal{N}(\boldsymbol{\mu}_{\mathbf{w}_m}, \boldsymbol{\Sigma}_{\mathbf{w}_m})$$

$$\boldsymbol{\Sigma}_{\mathbf{w}_m} = \left[\mathbf{I}_D + \langle \tau \rangle \sum_n \left\langle \mathbf{x}_n\mathbf{x}_n^{\mathsf{T}} \right\rangle \right]^{-1}$$

$$\boldsymbol{\mu}_{\mathbf{w}_m} = \langle \tau \rangle \boldsymbol{\Sigma}_{\mathbf{w}_m} \sum_n y_{nm} \langle \mathbf{x}_n \rangle .$$

As with $\boldsymbol{\Sigma}_{\mathbf{x}_n}$, the covariance matrix $\boldsymbol{\Sigma}_{\mathbf{w}_m}$ has no dependence on m and so can be computed once for all $\mathbf{w}_m$.

7.5.4 The required expectations

Each of the components of our approximate posterior, $Q_{\mathbf{x}_n}(\mathbf{x}_n), Q_{\mathbf{w}_m}(\mathbf{w}_m), Q_\tau(\tau)$, depends on expectations (e.g. $\langle \mathbf{x}_n \rangle$ and $\langle \mathbf{w}_m \mathbf{w}_m^{\mathsf{T}} \rangle$) with respect to the other components. As all of the components are well known distributions, these expectations are all standard results. $Q_{\mathbf{x}_n}(\mathbf{x}_n)$ and $Q_{\mathbf{w}_m}(\mathbf{w}_m)$ are both Gaussian and therefore

$$\langle \mathbf{x}_n \rangle = \boldsymbol{\mu}_{\mathbf{x}_n} \qquad \langle \mathbf{x}_n \mathbf{x}_n^{\mathsf{T}} \rangle = \boldsymbol{\Sigma}_{\mathbf{x}_n} + \boldsymbol{\mu}_{\mathbf{x}_n} \boldsymbol{\mu}_{\mathbf{x}_n}^{\mathsf{T}}$$

$$\langle \mathbf{w}_m \rangle = \boldsymbol{\mu}_{\mathbf{w}_m} \qquad \langle \mathbf{w}_m \mathbf{w}_m^{\mathsf{T}} \rangle = \boldsymbol{\Sigma}_{\boldsymbol{\mu}_m} + \boldsymbol{\mu}_{\mathbf{w}_m} \boldsymbol{\mu}_{\mathbf{w}_m}^{\mathsf{T}}.$$

$Q_\tau(\tau)$ is a gamma distribution so

$$\langle \tau \rangle = \frac{e}{f}.$$

The final expectation we need is $\langle \mathbf{x}_n^{\mathsf{T}} \langle \mathbf{w}_m \mathbf{w}_m^{\mathsf{T}} \rangle \mathbf{x}_n \rangle$. This is of the form $\langle \mathbf{z}^{\mathsf{T}} \mathbf{A} \mathbf{z} \rangle$, which, if $p(\mathbf{z}) = \mathcal{N}(\boldsymbol{\mu}, \boldsymbol{\Sigma})$, is equal to

$$\langle \mathbf{z}^{\mathsf{T}} \mathbf{A} \mathbf{z} \rangle = \mathrm{Tr}(\mathbf{A}\boldsymbol{\Sigma}) + \boldsymbol{\mu}^{\mathsf{T}} \mathbf{A} \boldsymbol{\mu}.$$

Therefore:

$$\langle \mathbf{x}_n^{\mathsf{T}} \langle \mathbf{w}_m \mathbf{w}_m^{\mathsf{T}} \rangle \mathbf{x}_n \rangle = \mathrm{Tr}\left(\langle \mathbf{w}_m \mathbf{w}_m^{\mathsf{T}} \rangle \boldsymbol{\Sigma}_{\mathbf{x}_n} \right) + \boldsymbol{\mu}_{\mathbf{x}_n}^{\mathsf{T}} \langle \mathbf{w}_m \mathbf{w}_m^{\mathsf{T}} \rangle \boldsymbol{\mu}_{\mathbf{x}_n}.$$

7.5.5 The algorithm

We now have everything we need to obtain an approximate posterior $Q(\mathbf{W}, \mathbf{X}, \tau)$ using VB. We must first initialise the various parameters. We will start by initialising $\langle \tau \rangle = a/b$ (its expected prior value) and then sample each $\langle \mathbf{w}_m \rangle$ from $\mathcal{N}(\mathbf{0}, \mathbf{I}_D)$ and compute $\langle \mathbf{w}\mathbf{w}^{\mathsf{T}} \rangle = \mathbf{I}_D + \langle \mathbf{w}_m \rangle \langle \mathbf{w}_m \rangle^{\mathsf{T}}$. We can now compute $\boldsymbol{\mu}_{\mathbf{x}_n}$ and $\boldsymbol{\Sigma}_{\mathbf{x}_n}$ and hence $\langle \mathbf{x}_n \rangle$ and $\langle \mathbf{x}_n \mathbf{x}_n^{\mathsf{T}} \rangle$. We proceed as follows:

1. For all n, compute $\boldsymbol{\Sigma}_{\mathbf{x}_n}$ and $\boldsymbol{\mu}_{\mathbf{x}_n}$ and update $\langle \mathbf{x}_n \rangle$ and $\langle \mathbf{x}_n \mathbf{x}_n^{\mathsf{T}} \rangle$.

2. Using the new values of $\langle \mathbf{x}_n \rangle$ and $\langle \mathbf{x}_n \mathbf{x}_n^{\mathsf{T}} \rangle$, compute $\boldsymbol{\mu}_{\mathbf{w}_m}$ and $\boldsymbol{\Sigma}_{\boldsymbol{\mu}_w}$ and update $\langle \mathbf{w}_m \rangle$ and $\langle \mathbf{w}_m \mathbf{w}_m^{\mathsf{T}} \rangle$ for all m.

3. Compute $\langle \mathbf{x}_n^{\mathsf{T}} \langle \mathbf{w}_m \mathbf{w}_m^{\mathsf{T}} \rangle \mathbf{x}_n \rangle$ for all n and m.

4. Compute e and f and update $\langle \tau \rangle$.

5. If not converged, return to 1.

To check convergence, we can either monitor how much the various parameters are changing, or compute the bound, $\mathcal{L}(\boldsymbol{\theta})$ (Equation 7.6), which will increase until convergence and then remain unchanged. The bound is given by

$$\begin{aligned} \mathcal{L}(\mathbf{X}, \mathbf{W}, \tau) &= \int Q(\mathbf{X}, \mathbf{W}, \tau) \log \frac{p(\mathbf{Y}, \mathbf{X}, \mathbf{W}, \tau)}{Q(\mathbf{X}, \mathbf{W}, \tau)} \, dQ(\mathbf{X}, \mathbf{W}, \tau) \\ &= \int Q(\cdot) \log p(\cdot) \, dQ(\cdot) - \int Q(\cdot) \log Q(\cdot) \, dQ(\cdot). \end{aligned}$$

Making use of the independence assumptions and noting that both expressions are expectations with respect to $Q(\cdot)$, we can further decompose these two terms as

$$
\int Q(\cdot) \log p(\cdot)\, dQ(\cdot) \;=\; \mathbf{E}_{Q_\tau(\tau)} \{\log p(\tau|a,b)\}
$$
$$
+ \sum_{n=1}^{N} \mathbf{E}_{Q_{\mathbf{x}_n}(\mathbf{x}_n)} \{\log p(\mathbf{x}_n)\}
$$
$$
+ \sum_{m=1}^{M} \mathbf{E}_{Q_{\mathbf{w}_m}(\mathbf{w}_m)} \{\log p(\mathbf{w}_m)\}
$$
$$
+ \sum_{n=1}^{N} \sum_{m=1}^{M} \mathbf{E}_{Q_{\mathbf{x}_n}(\mathbf{x}_n)} \{\log p(y_{nm}|\mathbf{x}_n, \mathbf{w}_m, \tau)\},
$$

and

$$
\int Q(\cdot) \log Q(\cdot)\, dQ(\cdot) \;=\; \mathbf{E}_{Q_\tau(\tau)} \{\log Q_\tau(\tau)\}
$$
$$
+ \sum_{n=1}^{N} \mathbf{E}_{Q_{\mathbf{x}_n}(\mathbf{x}_n)} \{\log Q_{\mathbf{x}_n}(\mathbf{x}_n)\}
$$
$$
+ \sum_{m=1}^{M} \mathbf{E}_{Q_{\mathbf{w}_m}(\mathbf{w}_m)} \{\log Q_{\mathbf{w}_m}(\mathbf{w}_m)\}.
$$

It is left to the reader (see Exercise 7.2) to show that these individual terms give the following bound (each line corresponds to one of the expectations, in the same order as above):

$$
\mathcal{L}(\mathbf{X}, \mathbf{W}, \tau) \;=\; a \log b + (a-1)\langle \log \tau \rangle - b\langle \tau \rangle - \log \Gamma(a)
$$
$$
- \frac{ND}{2} \log 2\pi - \frac{1}{2} \sum_n \left(\mathrm{Tr}(\mathbf{\Sigma}_{\mathbf{x}_n}) + \boldsymbol{\mu}_{\mathbf{x}_n}^{\mathsf{T}} \boldsymbol{\mu}_{\mathbf{x}_n} \right)
$$
$$
- \frac{MD}{2} \log 2\pi - \frac{1}{2} \sum_m \left(\mathrm{Tr}(\mathbf{\Sigma}_{\mathbf{w}_m}) + \boldsymbol{\mu}_{\mathbf{w}_m}^{\mathsf{T}} \boldsymbol{\mu}_{\mathbf{w}_m} \right)
$$
$$
- \frac{NM}{2} \log 2\pi + \frac{NM}{2} \langle \log \tau \rangle - \frac{1}{2} \langle \tau \rangle \sum_{n,m} \left\langle (y_{nm} - \mathbf{w}_m^{\mathsf{T}} \mathbf{x}_n)^2 \right\rangle
$$
$$
- \left(e \log f + (e-1)\langle \log \tau \rangle - f\langle \tau \rangle - \log \Gamma(e) \right)
$$
$$
- \left(-\frac{ND}{2} \log 2\pi - \frac{ND}{2} - \frac{1}{2} \sum_n \log |\mathbf{\Sigma}_{\mathbf{x}_n}| \right)
$$
$$
- \left(-\frac{MD}{2} \log 2\pi - \frac{MD}{2} - \frac{1}{2} \sum_m \log |\mathbf{\Sigma}_{\mathbf{w}_m}| \right)
$$

where

$$
\left\langle (y_{nm} - \mathbf{w}_m^{\mathsf{T}} \mathbf{x}_n)^2 \right\rangle = y_{nm}^2 - 2 y_{nm} \langle \mathbf{x}_n \rangle^{\mathsf{T}} \langle \mathbf{w}_m \rangle + \left\langle \mathbf{x}_n^{\mathsf{T}} \left\langle \mathbf{w}_m \mathbf{w}_m^{\mathsf{T}} \right\rangle \mathbf{x}_n \right\rangle,
$$

all of which we have already computed. The only term in the bound that we have not seen before is $\langle \log \tau \rangle$. We are forced to approximate this term and can do so by sampling. If we take S samples, $\tau^1, \ldots, \tau^S$, the approximation is given by

$$\langle \log \tau \rangle \approx \frac{1}{S} \sum_{s=1}^{S} \log \tau^s.$$

7.5.6 An example

Figure 7.6(a) shows a dataset generated in the same manner as that used in the example depicted in Figure 7.4 (MATLAB script: `ppcaexample.m`). The first two dimensions are shown, in which there is clear cluster structure. To this, an additional five dimensions are added ($y_{nm} \sim \mathcal{N}(0, 1)$). The evolution of the bound, $\mathcal{L}(\mathbf{X}, \mathbf{W}, \tau)$ as the algorithm progresses (with $D = 2$) can be seen in Figure 7.6(b). The bound increases monotonically until convergence, which is after only a small number of iterations. In Figure 7.6(c) we can see the posterior means of the latent variables. These are analogous to the standard PCA projections (see, e.g. Figure 7.4(c)). It is clear that the cluster structure is captured in the latent space.

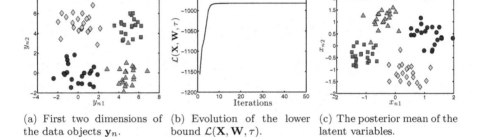

(a) First two dimensions of the data objects $\mathbf{y}_n$.

(b) Evolution of the lower bound $\mathcal{L}(\mathbf{X}, \mathbf{W}, \tau)$.

(c) The posterior mean of the latent variables.

FIGURE 7.6 Synthetic probabilistic PCA example.

7.6 MISSING VALUES

One of our motivations for moving to a probabilistic representation was its ability to handle missing values. In the model we defined in the previous section, the easiest way to achieve this is to only define the model for the data that we observe. To this end, we introduce a new set of binary variables z_{nm} which are equal to 1 if we observe feature m for object n and 0 otherwise. Collecting all of the z_{nm} together into a matrix $\mathbf{Z}$, we have

$$p(\mathbf{Y}, \mathbf{X}, \mathbf{W}, \tau | \mathbf{Z}) = p(\tau | a, b) \left[\prod_{m=1}^{M} p(\mathbf{w}_m) \right] \left[\prod_{n=1}^{N} p(\mathbf{x}_n) \prod_{m=1}^{M} p(y_{nm} | \mathbf{w}_m, \mathbf{x}_n, \tau)^{z_{nm}} \right]$$

$$\log p(\mathbf{Y}, \mathbf{X}, \mathbf{W}, \tau | \mathbf{Z}) = \log p(\tau | a, b) + \sum_{m=1}^{M} \log p(\mathbf{w}_m) + \sum_{n=1}^{N} \log p(\mathbf{x}_n) \qquad (7.15)$$

$$+ \sum_{n=1}^{N} \sum_{m=1}^{M} z_{nm} \log p(y_{nm} | \mathbf{w}_m, \mathbf{x}_n, \tau).$$

The binary variables act as switches, only switching on the terms for which we observe data. Note how everything is conditioned on $\mathbf{Z}$. It is left as an exercise (see Exercise 7.3) for the reader to follow the steps detailed in the previous section to derive the necessary variational distributions. These are

$$Q_{\mathbf{x}_n}(\mathbf{x}_n) = \mathcal{N}(\boldsymbol{\mu}_{\mathbf{x}_n}, \boldsymbol{\Sigma}_{\mathbf{x}_n})$$

$$\boldsymbol{\Sigma}_{\mathbf{x}_n} = \left[\mathbf{I}_D + \langle \tau \rangle \sum_m z_{nm} \left\langle \mathbf{w}_m \mathbf{w}_m^\mathsf{T} \right\rangle \right]^{-1}$$

$$\boldsymbol{\mu}_{\mathbf{x}_n} = \langle \tau \rangle \boldsymbol{\Sigma}_{\mathbf{x}_n} \sum_m z_{nm} y_{nm} \langle \mathbf{w}_m \rangle$$

$$Q_{\mathbf{w}_m}(\mathbf{w}_m) = \mathcal{N}(\boldsymbol{\mu}_{\mathbf{w}_m}, \boldsymbol{\Sigma}_{\mathbf{w}_m})$$

$$\boldsymbol{\Sigma}_{\mathbf{w}_m} = \left[\mathbf{I}_D + \langle \tau \rangle \sum_n z_{nm} \left\langle \mathbf{x}_n \mathbf{x}_n^\mathsf{T} \right\rangle \right]^{-1}$$

$$\boldsymbol{\mu}_{\mathbf{w}_m} = \langle \tau \rangle \boldsymbol{\Sigma}_{\mathbf{w}_m} \sum_n z_{nm} y_{nm} \langle \mathbf{x}_n \rangle$$

$$Q_\tau(\tau) = \Gamma(e, f)$$

$$e = a + \frac{1}{2} \sum_{n,m} z_{nm}$$

$$f = b + \frac{1}{2} \sum_{n,m} z_{nm} \left(y_{nm}^2 - 2 \langle \mathbf{w}_m \rangle^\mathsf{T} \langle \mathbf{x}_n \rangle + \left\langle \mathbf{x}_n^\mathsf{T} \left\langle \mathbf{w}_m \mathbf{w}_m^\mathsf{T} \right\rangle \mathbf{x}_n \right\rangle \right).$$

In the previous section, we noted that the equations for $\boldsymbol{\Sigma}_{\mathbf{x}_n}$ and $\boldsymbol{\Sigma}_{\mathbf{w}_m}$ had no dependence on n and m, respectively, and therefore did not have to be computed for each n and m. Due to the presence of z_{nm} in both expressions, this is no longer the case and a different $\boldsymbol{\Sigma}_{\mathbf{x}_n}$ must be computed for each $\mathbf{x}_n$ (and a $\boldsymbol{\Sigma}_{\mathbf{w}_m}$ for each $\mathbf{w}_m$). Both $\mathbf{x}_n$ and $\mathbf{w}_m$ are D-dimensional and so, for large N, M or D, this is a considerable additional computational overhead. In Section 7.4.1 we mentioned the possibility of making additional independence assumptions when defining the components of the approximate posterior. In particular

$$Q_{\mathbf{x}_n}(\mathbf{x}_n) = \prod_{d=1}^{D} Q_{x_{nd}}(x_{nd})$$

would result in us having to work with scalar variances rather than the $D \times D$ covariance matrices, $\boldsymbol{\Sigma}_{\mathbf{x}_n}$. This would represent a considerable computational saving

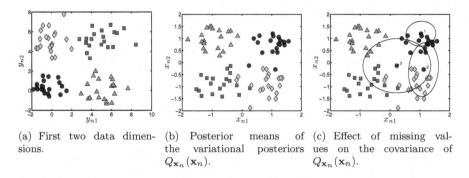

(a) First two data dimensions.

(b) Posterior means of the variational posteriors $Q_{\mathbf{x}_n}(\mathbf{x}_n)$.

(c) Effect of missing values on the covariance of $Q_{\mathbf{x}_n}(\mathbf{x}_n)$.

FIGURE 7.7 Variational Bayesian PPCA model with missing values. The data is the same as that shown in Figure 7.6 with each value made y_{nm} removed with a probability of 0.05.

but would come at the cost of a poorer approximation to the posterior.

Figure 7.7 gives an example of the PPCA model with missing values (MATLAB script: `ppcamvexample.m`). Figure 7.7(b) shows the posterior means of the variational posteriors $Q_{\mathbf{x}_n}(\mathbf{x}_n)$. The data is the same as in the previous examples (cluster structure in the first two dimensions, shown in Figure 7.7(a), noise in the remaining five), with each observation y_{nm} removed with probability 0.05. As we might expect, the effect of removing data is that the cluster structure becomes less distinct. The individual covariance matrices make this effect easy to visualise. In Figure 7.7(c), we have visualised the covariance matrices as ellipses for three objects belonging to the 'circle' class. The ellipses show us the level of uncertainty that the model ascribes to the values of the latent variables. Object 1 has no values missing in the two dimensions that encode the cluster structure and sits comfortably with the other objects of the same class. Object 2 is missing its value for y_{n2} and hence the information that determines whether it is in the circle or diamond class (see Figure 7.7(a)). This is reflected in both its mean and covariance in Figure 7.7(c) – the model places it half way between the two groups, but the allows the possibility that it could be in either. Finally, object 3 is missing values for both y_{n1} and y_{n2} – all of the non-noise features. The model places it close to the origin (remember that the prior $p(\mathbf{x}_n) = \mathcal{N}(\mathbf{0}, \mathbf{I}_D)$) but with very high uncertainty – it could belong to any group.

It is clear that the covariance information shown in Figure 7.7(c) is a useful output of the model. It is important to know if there is a high level of uncertainty about the position, $\mathbf{x}_n$, of an object in the latent space. In other words, if we just saw Figure 7.7(c), we could potentially deduce that we should not draw any serious conclusions about the position of object 3 – the covariance is high because many values are missing. In Section 7.7.2 we shall see an interesting example where covariance information is useful.

7.6.1 Missing values as latent variables

In the previous section we saw how the VB framework allowed us to solve the problem of missing values – we only included the observed values in our model. The increased uncertainty that should be present when many values are missing is naturally handled through the individual covariance matrices, $\boldsymbol{\Sigma}_{\mathbf{x}_n}$. Individual covariance matrices come with an additional computational load which may, in some cases, be prohibitive. Alternatively, it is possible to consider the missing values as additional latent variables. Introducing the superscripts h and o to denote hidden and observed, respectively, this corresponds to the following joint log-likelihood:

$$
\begin{aligned}
\log p(\mathbf{Y}, \mathbf{X}, \mathbf{W}, \tau | \mathbf{Z}) \;=\; & \log p(\tau | a, b) + \sum_{m=1}^{M} \log p(\mathbf{w}_m) + \sum_{n=1}^{N} \log p(\mathbf{x}_n) \\
& + \sum_{n=1}^{N} \sum_{m=1}^{M} z_{nm} \log p(y_{nm}^{o} | \mathbf{w}_m, \mathbf{x}_n, \tau) \\
& + \sum_{n=1}^{N} \sum_{m=1}^{M} (1 - z_{nm}) \log p(y_{nm}^{h} | \mathbf{w}_m, \mathbf{x}_n, \tau).
\end{aligned}
$$

In addition, we require another set of variational posteriors, $Q_{y_{nm}^{h}}(y_{nm}^{h})$. We will omit the derivation of the VB algorithm here but will just state the important results. Firstly, the additional variational posteriors:

$$
Q_{y_{nm}^{h}}(y_{nm}^{h}) = \mathcal{N}\left(\langle \mathbf{w}_m \rangle^{\mathsf{T}} \langle \mathbf{x}_n \rangle, \langle \tau \rangle^{-1} \right).
$$

Therefore, $\langle y_{nm}^{h} \rangle = \langle \mathbf{w}_m \rangle^{\mathsf{T}} \langle \mathbf{x}_n \rangle$. $Q_{\mathbf{x}_n}(\mathbf{x}_n)$ is given by a Gaussian with parameters:

$$
\begin{aligned}
\boldsymbol{\Sigma}_{\mathbf{x}_n} \;=\; & \left[\mathbf{I}_D + \langle \tau \rangle \sum_m z_{nm} \left\langle \mathbf{w}_m \mathbf{w}_m^{\mathsf{T}} \right\rangle + \langle \tau \rangle \sum_m (1 - z_{nm}) \left\langle \mathbf{w}_m \mathbf{w}_m^{\mathsf{T}} \right\rangle \right]^{-1} \\
\;=\; & \left[\mathbf{I}_D + \langle \tau \rangle \sum_m \left\langle \mathbf{w}_m \mathbf{w}_m^{\mathsf{T}} \right\rangle \right]^{-1} \qquad\qquad\qquad (7.16) \\
\boldsymbol{\mu}_{\mathbf{x}_n} \;=\; & \langle \tau \rangle \, \boldsymbol{\Sigma}_{\mathbf{x}_n} \sum_m \left(z_{nm} y_{nm}^{o} + (1 - z_{nm}) \left\langle y_{nm}^{h} \right\rangle \right) \langle \mathbf{w}_m \rangle \\
\;=\; & \langle \tau \rangle \, \boldsymbol{\Sigma}_{\mathbf{x}_n} \sum_m y_{nm}^{*} \langle \mathbf{w}_m \rangle
\end{aligned}
$$

where $\mathbf{y}_n^{*}$ is a vector with elements y_{nm}^{o} and $\langle y_{nm}^{h} \rangle$ depending on whether the particular parameter is observed or not. $Q_{\mathbf{w}_m}(\mathbf{w}_m)$ and $Q_{\tau}(\tau)$ follow similarly.

It is clear from Equation 7.16 that the covariance of $Q_{\mathbf{x}_n}(\mathbf{x}_n)$ no longer depends on n and so we no longer require specific covariance matrices for each object. In fact, one can view the resulting VB algorithm as identical to our original VB PCA algorithm where we insert the value that the model expects for y_{nm} (i.e. $\langle \mathbf{w}_m \rangle^{\mathsf{T}} \langle \mathbf{x}_n \rangle$) into each missing value. This gives us a large computational saving but we lose the object-specific covariance matrices, $\boldsymbol{\Sigma}_{\mathbf{x}_n}$. All objects have the same covariance in the latent space, regardless of how many values are observed/missing because the expected values of the unobserved data, $\langle y_{nm}^{h} \rangle$, are given the same influence as the actual observations. If there are very few missing values, this is unlikely to be a problem. If there are many, it should be avoided.

7.6.2 Predicting missing values

One of the benefits of considering the missing values as latent variables is that it automatically imputes the missing values. However, we can still achieve this with the original missing value model. In particular, the expected value of y_{nm}^h with respect to the variational posteriors is

$$\mathbf{E}_{Q(\cdot)}\left\{y_{nm}^h\right\} = \mathbf{E}_{Q(\cdot)}\left\{\mathbf{w}_m^\mathsf{T}\mathbf{x}_n + \epsilon\right\}$$
$$= \left\langle \mathbf{w}_m \right\rangle^\mathsf{T} \left\langle \mathbf{x}_n \right\rangle$$

where $\epsilon \, \mathcal{N}(0, \tau^{-1})$. The variance of the predicted value is given by

$$\text{var}\{y_{nm}^h\} = \mathbf{E}_{Q(\cdot)}\left\{(y_{nm}^h)^2\right\} - \mathbf{E}_{Q(\cdot)}\left\{y_{nm}^h\right\}^2$$
$$= \left\langle \mathbf{x}_n^\mathsf{T} \left\langle \mathbf{w}_m \mathbf{w}_m^\mathsf{T} \right\rangle \mathbf{x}_n \right\rangle + \left\langle \tau \right\rangle^{-1} - \left\langle \mathbf{x}_n \right\rangle^\mathsf{T} \left\langle \mathbf{w}_m \right\rangle \left\langle \mathbf{w}_m \right\rangle^\mathsf{T} \left\langle \mathbf{x}_n \right\rangle.$$

As an example, consider object 2 in Figure 7.7(c) – using these expressions, the missing value y_{n2}^h has a mean of 0.5839 and variance of 5.4070.

7.7 NON-REAL-VALUED DATA

Wanting to handle non-real-valued data was the second motivation we discussed in Section 7.2.2 for moving to a probabilistic representation. In our derivation for VB PPCA, we used a Gaussian likelihood. Using the same steps, we can use VB inference for PCA-like models with alternative likelihoods. An interesting dataset that consists of both non-real data and missing values is the voting history of British members of parliament (MPs) available from the Public Whip (http://www.publicwhip.org. uk). British MPs are appointed for a parliament at a general election. A parliament typically lasts four or five years, in which time there will be > 1000 divisions (votes) in which they may take part. Each division consists of a binary choice (the MP is either for or against whatever is being proposed). MPs do not have to vote – they can abstain or they might simply not be present in parliament on a particular day. Hence, the data is both non-real valued (binary) and contains many missing values.

As we have already seen in Chapter 4, likelihoods for binary data normally come with analytical problems. Rather than going over the material in that chapter again, we will now show an alternative approach based on introducing an auxiliary (or hidden) variable. It is not our intention to suggest this is the only way of solving this problem for PPCA-like models but it is a good example of a more general technique for handling binary likelihoods. An alternative probabilistic binary PCA algorithm is given in the suggested reading at the end of this chapter.

7.7.1 Probit PPCA

We potentially observe M votes for N MPs. For each vote, assuming the value is not missing (i.e. $z_{nm} = 1$), we observe $y_{nm} = \pm 1$. As before, we will assume that there exist some D-dimensional unobserved latent variables $\mathbf{x}_n$ which are then projected by a set of vectors $\mathbf{w}_m$. In our previous examples, we used a Gaussian likelihood for $p(y_{nm}|\mathbf{w}_m, \mathbf{x}_n)$. To model the binary MP data, we will use the *probit* likelihood instead. The probit function (also known as the normal cdf function) is defined as

$$\phi(z) = \int_{-\infty}^{z} \exp\left\{-\frac{1}{2}x^2\right\} dx$$

and transforms a real-valued argument, z, into the range 0 to 1 (like the sigmoid function we used for logistic regression in Chapter 4). In particular, we will define

$$P(y_{nm} = 1|\mathbf{w}_m, \mathbf{x}_n) = \phi(\mathbf{w}_m^\mathsf{T}\mathbf{x}_n) \qquad (7.17)$$

and

$$P(y_{nm} = -1|\mathbf{w}_m, \mathbf{x}_n) = 1 - P(y_{nm} = 1|\mathbf{w}_m, \mathbf{x}_n).$$

Unfortunately, if we tried to derive variational posteriors $Q_{\mathbf{x}_n}(\mathbf{x}_n)$, etc., we would discover that they were not of any recognisable form. At this point, we make use of a slightly odd trick. We start by introducing a new set of (real-valued) variables, q_{mn}:

$$p(q_{nm}|\mathbf{w}_m, \mathbf{x}_n) = \mathcal{N}(\mathbf{w}_m^\mathsf{T}\mathbf{x}_n, 1),$$

which we link to the observed data y_{nm} through the likelihood

$$P(y_{nm} = 1|q_{nm}) = \delta(q_{nm} > 0)$$

and

$$P(y_{nm} = -1|q_{nm}) = \delta(q_{nm} < 0).$$

To justify this choice, consider the joint distribution over q_{nm} and y_{nm}:

$$p(y_{nm} = 1, q_{nm}|\mathbf{w}_m, \mathbf{x}_n) = P(y_{nm} = 1|q_{nm})p(q_{nm}|\mathbf{w}_m, \mathbf{x}_n).$$

Choosing $P(y_{nm} = 1|q_{nm}) = \delta(q_{nm} > 0)$ means that, if we marginalise over q_{nm}, we get back to our original probit likelihood (Equation 7.17):

$$
\begin{aligned}
P(y_{nm} = 1|\mathbf{w}_m, \mathbf{x}_n) &= \int p(y_{nm} = 1, q_{nm}|\mathbf{w}_m, \mathbf{x}_n)\, dq_{nm} \\
&= \int P(y_{nm} = 1|q_{nm})p(q_{nm}|\mathbf{w}_m, \mathbf{x}_n)\, dq_{nm} \\
&= \int_{-\infty}^{\infty} \delta(q_{nm} > 0)\mathcal{N}(\mathbf{w}_m^\mathsf{T}\mathbf{x}_n, 1)\, dq_{nm} \\
&= \int_{0}^{\infty} \mathcal{N}(\mathbf{w}_m^\mathsf{T}\mathbf{x}_n, 1)\, dq_{nm} \\
&= \int_{-\mathbf{w}_m^\mathsf{T}\mathbf{x}_n}^{\infty} \mathcal{N}(0, 1)\, dq_{nm} \\
&= \int_{-\infty}^{\mathbf{w}_m^\mathsf{T}\mathbf{x}_n} \mathcal{N}(0, 1)\, dq_{nm} = \phi(\mathbf{w}_m^\mathsf{T}\mathbf{x}_n).
\end{aligned}
$$

This suggests that we can think of the probit likelihood as the result of a model with an additional parameter, q_{nm}, that has been integrated out. It turns out that, if the parameter is left in (we treat q_{nm} as a latent variable and infer its value), the VB algorithm becomes quite simple, even though there are an additional $N \times M$ parameters. The graphical representation of this model can be seen in Figure 7.8.

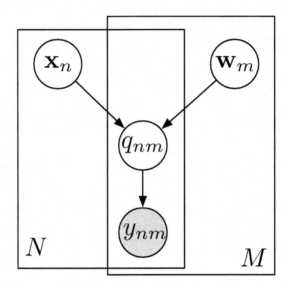

FIGURE 7.8 Graphical representation of probit PCA model.

Collating all of the q_{nm} into an $N \times M$ matrix $\mathbf{Q}$ gives us the following starting point for VB:

$$
\begin{aligned}
\log p(\mathbf{Y}, \mathbf{X}, \mathbf{W}, \mathbf{Q}) &= \log \left[\prod_{m=1}^{M} p(\mathbf{w}_m) \right] \left[\prod_{n=1}^{N} p(\mathbf{x}_n) \right] \\
&\quad \times \left[\prod_{n=1}^{N} \prod_{m=1}^{M} p(y_{nm}|q_{nm})^{z_{nm}} p(q_{nm}|\mathbf{w}_m, \mathbf{x}_n)^{z_{nm}} \right] \\
&= \sum_{m=1}^{M} \log p(\mathbf{w}_m) + \sum_{n=1}^{N} \log p(\mathbf{x}_n) \\
&\quad + \sum_{n=1}^{N} \sum_{m=1}^{M} z_{nm} \left[\log p(y_{nm}|q_{nm}) + \log p(q_{nm}|\mathbf{w}_m, \mathbf{x}_n) \right].
\end{aligned}
$$

For our variational approximation, we need $Q_{\mathbf{x}_n}(\mathbf{x}_n)$ and $Q_{\mathbf{w}_m}(\mathbf{w}_m)$ as before and, additionally, $Q_{q_{nm}}(q_{nm})$. Gathering together the terms involving $\mathbf{x}_n$ and $\mathbf{w}_m$, we notice that they are identical to the terms in our real-valued model but with y_{nm} replaced by q_{nm}, which has a variance of 1 rather than τ^{-1}. Therefore, we already know what the respective variational distributions will be:

$$Q_{\mathbf{x}_n}(\mathbf{x}_n) = \mathcal{N}(\boldsymbol{\mu}_{\mathbf{x}_n}, \boldsymbol{\Sigma}_{\mathbf{x}_n})$$

$$\boldsymbol{\Sigma}_{\mathbf{x}_n} = \left[\mathbf{I}_D + \sum_m z_{nm} \left\langle \mathbf{w}_m \mathbf{w}_m^\mathsf{T} \right\rangle \right]^{-1}$$

$$\boldsymbol{\mu}_{\mathbf{x}_n} = \boldsymbol{\Sigma}_{\mathbf{x}_n} \sum_m z_{nm} \langle q_{nm} \rangle \langle \mathbf{w}_m \rangle$$

$$Q_{\mathbf{w}_m}(\mathbf{w}_m) = \mathcal{N}(\boldsymbol{\mu}_{\mathbf{w}_m}, \boldsymbol{\Sigma}_{\mathbf{w}_m})$$

$$\boldsymbol{\Sigma}_{\mathbf{w}_m} = \left[\mathbf{I}_D + \sum_n z_{nm} \left\langle \mathbf{x}_n \mathbf{x}_n^\mathsf{T} \right\rangle \right]^{-1}$$

$$\boldsymbol{\mu}_{\mathbf{w}_m} = \boldsymbol{\Sigma}_{\mathbf{w}_m} \sum_n z_{nm} \langle q_{nm} \rangle \langle \mathbf{x}_n \rangle.$$

For $Q_{q_{nm}}(q_{nm})$ we need to do a bit of work. Recalling Equation 7.9, we know that $Q_{q_{nm}}(q_{nm})$ will be given by

$$Q_{q_{nm}}(q_{nm}) \propto \exp\left(\mathbf{E}_{Q_{\mathbf{x}_n}(\mathbf{x}_n)Q_{\mathbf{w}_m}(\mathbf{w}_m)} \{\log p(y_{nm}|q_{nm}) + \log p(q_{nm}|\mathbf{w}_m, \mathbf{x}_n)\}\right)$$

Isolating terms only involving q_{nm}, we have

$$Q_{q_{nm}}(q_{nm}) \propto p(y_{nm}|q_{nm}) \exp\left\{-\frac{1}{2}(q_{nm}^2 - 2q_{nm} \langle \mathbf{w}_m \rangle^\mathsf{T} \langle \mathbf{x}_n \rangle)\right\},$$

which is $p(y_{nm}|q_{nm})$ multiplied by a Gaussian:

$$Q_{q_{nm}}(q_{nm}) \propto p(y_{nm}|q_{nm})\mathcal{N}(\langle \mathbf{w}_m \rangle^\mathsf{T} \langle \mathbf{x}_n \rangle, 1).$$

For the time being, we shall assume that $y_{nm} = 1$. Therefore, we have

$$\begin{aligned} Q_{q_{nm}}(q_{nm}) &\propto \delta(q_{nm} > 0)\mathcal{N}(\langle \mathbf{w}_m \rangle^\mathsf{T} \langle \mathbf{x}_n \rangle, 1) \\ &= \mathcal{N}^+(\langle \mathbf{w}_m \rangle^\mathsf{T} \langle \mathbf{x}_n \rangle, 1), \end{aligned}$$

where $\mathcal{N}^+(\cdot)$ is used to denote a Gaussian *truncated* (see Comment 7.3) such that q_{nm} must be positive. If $y_{nm} = -1$, we end up with $\mathcal{N}^-(\langle \mathbf{w}_m \rangle^\mathsf{T} \langle \mathbf{x}_n \rangle, 1)$ – a Gaussian with the same mean truncated such that q_{nm} must be negative.

To compute $Q_{\mathbf{x}_n}(\mathbf{x}_n)$ and $Q_{\mathbf{w}_m}(\mathbf{w}_m)$, we need $\langle q_{nm} \rangle$. This is the expected value of a Gaussian truncated to be positive or negative (depending on the value of y_{nm}). General expressions to compute this are given in Comment 7.3. Defining $\mu_{nm} = \langle \mathbf{w}_m \rangle^\mathsf{T} \langle \mathbf{x}_n \rangle$ and $\sigma = 1$, these are

$$y_{nm} = 1: \qquad \langle q_{nm} \rangle = \mu_{nm} + \frac{\mathcal{N}_{\mu_{nm}}(0, 1)}{1 - \phi(-\mu_{nm})}$$

$$y_{nm} = -1: \qquad \langle q_{nm} \rangle = \mu_{nm} - \frac{\mathcal{N}_{\mu_{nm}}(0, 1)}{\phi(-\mu_{nm})}.$$

This completes the expressions required for the VB algorithm. In the next section, we shall show an example of the algorithm in operation.

Comment 7.3 – Truncated Gaussian densities: A truncated Gaussian density is a Gaussian density with an additional restriction placed on the random variable. We will only be interested in Gaussian densities truncated above or below the origin.

The figure on the right shows a standard Gaussian density (with mean 0.5 and variance 1) as well as the positively and negatively truncated densities. The truncated densities have the same shape as the standard density but are both higher. This is because they must still integrate to 1 over their reduced range.

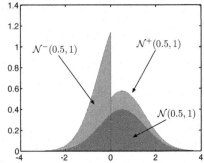

Sampling from a truncated Gaussian is fairly straightforward – one can just sample from the untruncated density and throw away samples that do not fulfil the necessary constraint. The expected values of positively and negatively truncated Gaussians are given by

$$p(x) = \mathcal{N}^+(\mu, \sigma^2), \qquad \langle x \rangle = \mu + \frac{\mathcal{N}_{\mu/\sigma}(0,1)}{1 - \phi(-\mu/\sigma)}$$

$$p(x) = \mathcal{N}^-(\mu, \sigma^2), \qquad \langle x \rangle = \mu - \frac{\mathcal{N}_{\mu/\sigma}(0,1)}{\phi(-\mu/\sigma)}$$

where $\mathcal{N}_a(0,1)$ is the standard Gaussian pdf evaluated at a, and $\phi(a)$ is the standard normal cdf function evaluated at a.

7.7.2 Visualising parliamentary data

The motivation for developing this model was the vote data for members of parliament. We shall look at data for the UK parliament that sat between 2005 and 2010. To show the benefit of sensibly handling the missing values *and* using a suitable likelihood, we will compare the model with the simplest approach we could use for visualising this data – standard, non-probabilistic principal components where we will use a value of zero for the missing values (i.e. a value half way between the possible votes, ± 1) and not make any concessions to the fact that the data are not real-valued.

To get a feel for the complexity of the problem, the dataset consists of voting records for some 657 MPs and 1288 divisions (votes). The average number of votes attended per MP is 853 (66%). The most active MP voted 1237 times (96%) and the least active 20 times (1.6%).

The result of running standard PCA on the data can be seen in Figure 7.9(a). Clear cluster structure is present in the latent space. In Figure 7.9(b) we label the MPs on the plot by their party affiliation and it becomes clear that the cluster structure corresponds to the three main political parties (Labour, Conservative and Liberal Democrats). The cluster structure present is not surprising, as MPs often

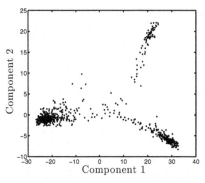

(a) MPs plotted onto the first two principal components.

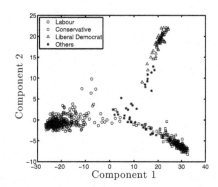

(b) MPs labeled according to party affiliations (only three main parties shown)

FIGURE 7.9 Standard PCA visualisation of the 2005 MP voting data. Each point corresponds to an MP.

vote according to party affiliations. However, it is reassuring that it appears clearly in the first two principal components.

Some MPs seem to also be being pulled towards the origin. This could be interpreted as a measure of rebelliousness – these MPs do not vote as often along party lines. However, unfortunately, what it is showing is that these MPs simply do not vote very often. To illustrate this, we can plot the number of votes made against distance from the origin in this PCA plot, as shown in Figure 7.10. It is clear that the large number of missing values is having an unhelpful effect on the analysis – position in the latent space is a function of both political preference *and* attendance.

The results of using the VB binary PCA algorithm can be seen in Figure 7.11(a) (MATLAB script: `mpvis.m`). This plot shows $\langle \mathbf{x}_n \rangle$ and cluster structure is again clearly present. In Figure 7.11(b) we can see the MPs labeled according to party affiliations. Once again, the cluster structure corresponds to the different political parties. Because we are modelling the missing values correctly, we no longer get the pull towards the origin. To demonstrate this, Figure 7.12 shows the number of votes cast versus distance from the origin – the very clear relationships present in Figure 7.10 are no longer so pronounced. The variations we can see in Figure 7.11(a) show political tendencies and not attendance tendencies.

This point is well illustrated by considering some of the smaller parties within the parliament. Figure 7.13 highlights the position of four small parties – the Democratic Unionist Party (DUP), Plaid Cymru (PC), Scottish National Party (SNP) and the Social Democratic and Labour Party (SDLP). In the traditional PCA analysis, it looks like the DUP members' votes sit within the cluster of Conservative MPs (see Figure 7.9(b)) and, to a lesser extent, PC and SNP members sit with the Liberal Democrats. However, comparing with the output of the binary PCA algorithm, we can see that the DUP form their own coherent cluster, away from the Conservatives whilst the SNP and PC members form a very tight cluster of their own. It looks like

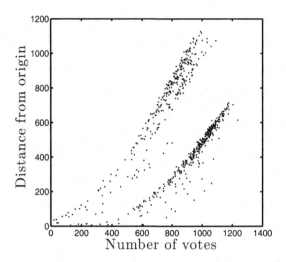

FIGURE 7.10 Number of votes cast versus distance from the origin (of the PCA plot).

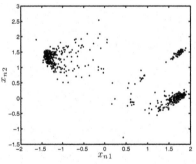

(a) The posterior mean latent variables.

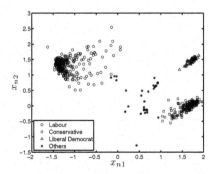

(b) MPs labeled according to party affiliations (only three main parties shown).

FIGURE 7.11 Probabilistic binary principal components visualisation of the 2005 MP voting data. Each point corresponds to an MP.

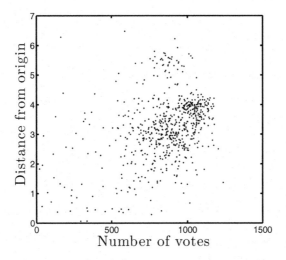

FIGURE 7.12 Number of votes cast versus distance from the origin for the probabilistic binary PCA.

the position of these groups in the original PCA was heavily influenced by the poor modelling of the missing data.

Finally, because of the way we have chosen to model the missing values, we have an individual covariance matrix $\Sigma_{\mathbf{x}_n}$ for each MP. In Figure 7.14 we visualise, with ellipses, the covariance matrices of the 20 MPs for which the model is least certain. These MPs tend to be those who cast the least votes. It is clear that there is no real pattern to where they are located – the model does not pull MPs who do not vote often towards the origin.

Much more interesting analysis could be done with this data but is beyond the scope of this book. The important point is that a model based on sensible assumptions that can correctly handle missing values (the binary probabilistic PCA) is likely to be able to give us more insight into interesting variability amongst the MPs than using basic PCA.

7.7.2.1 Aside – relationship to classification

Before we finish, it is worth trying to get an intuitive feel for how this model works. On the face of it, it appears rather complex, but perhaps the easiest way to look at it is as a classification model. The training data consists of labels for M classification tasks (one for each vote) but no input features. The model infers a set of latent observations (the $\mathbf{x}_n$) and M classification functions (defined by the $\mathbf{w}_m$) such that we can satisfy as many of the classification labels as possible. Figure 7.15 shows four example votes (input features) and the corresponding decision boundary in the latent space. MPs are plotted at their posterior mean position and labeled according to how they voted (circle/square for ±1, light grey dot for missing value). The model has positioned the MPs in the latent space and constructed decision boundaries in such a way as to enable as many of the classification labels to be satisfied as possible.

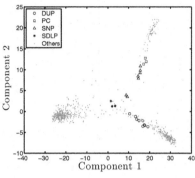
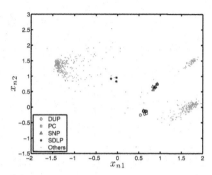

(a) Visualisation of smaller parties in traditional PCA.

(b) Visualisation of smaller parties in VB binary PCA.

FIGURE 7.13   Visualisation of the small parties using the two PCA methods.

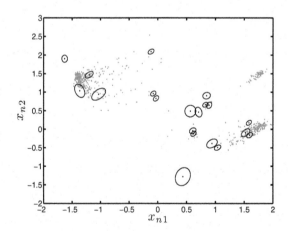

FIGURE 7.14   Covariance matrix visualisation for the 20 MPs corresponding to the highest uncertainty.

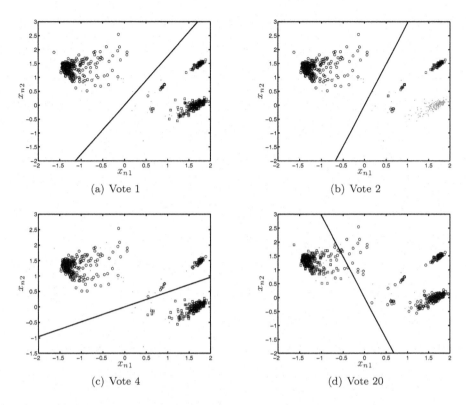

(a) Vote 1

(b) Vote 2

(c) Vote 4

(d) Vote 20

FIGURE 7.15 Example of four of the votes – each MP is displayed as a circle or square depending on how they voted (light grey if they didn't vote).

It is not always possible to satisfy all of the labels – see, for example, the circles to the right of the boundary in vote 1.

7.8 CHAPTER SUMMARY

In this chapter, we have used Principal Components Analysis (PCA) and some probabilistic variants to introduce the concepts of latent variable models and the inference technique Variational Bayes. There are many other latent variable models being used for diverse applications – the field of information retrieval is particularly full of them – and our hope is that the techniques introduced here will enable the reader to understand some of these more application-specific models.

Variational Bayes (VB) is an increasingly popular inference technique within the field of machine learning. With any posterior approximation technique, we are making a trade-off between accuracy of approximation and computational difficulty. The empirical evidence suggests that VB finds a good balance between tractability and accuracy. It is important to remember that other methods can be used for performing inference in latent variable models – we saw the EM algorithm in Chapter 6 being used for a mixture model. Also, the use of the auxiliary variable trick with the probit likelihood is certainly not the only way we can overcome tricky binary likelihoods – we saw alternatives in Chapter 4.

7.9 EXERCISES

7.1 Show that the bound given in Equation 7.6 is maximised (i.e. equal to the true log marginal likelihood) when $Q(\boldsymbol{\theta})$ is identical to the true posterior $p(\boldsymbol{\theta}|\mathbf{X})$.

7.2 Compute each term in the lower bound, $\mathcal{L}(\boldsymbol{\theta})$, for the probabilistic PCA model given in Section 7.5.

7.3 Compute the components of the variational posterior for the probabilistic PCA model with missing values described by Equation 7.15.

7.10 FURTHER READING

[1] Christopher M. Bishop. Variational principal components. In *Proceedings of the Ninth International Conference on Artificial Neural Networks, ICANN'99*, pages 509–514, 1999.

> An example of a probabilistic principal components model where the inference is performed using Variational Bayes. A prior is used to encourae sparsity in the latent dimensions which goes some way towards avoiding having to choose the size of the latent space.

[2] I. T. Jolliffe. *Principal Component Analysis*. Springer, second edition, 2002.

> A comprehensive textbook on Principal Components Analysis.

[3] M. Jordan, Z. Ghahramani, T. S. Jaakkola, and L. K. Saul. An introduction to variational methods for graphical models. *Machine Learning*, 37:183–233, 1999.

[4] Arto Klami and Samuel Kaski. Probabilistic approaches to detecting dependencies between data sets. *Neurocomputing*, 72:39–46, 2008.

> An interesting latent variable model that extends the ideas of probabilistic PCA into the scenario where two datasets are being analysed together. Also provides an example of the EM algorithm and Variational Bayes.

[5] S. Roweis and Z. Ghahramani. A unifying review of linear Gaussian models. *Neural Computation*, 11(2):305–345, 1999.

> An excellent, accessible review of linear Gaussian models giving many examples.

[6] Michael Tipping. Probabilistic visualisation of high-dimensional binary data. In *Proceedings of the 1998 Conference on Advances in Neural Information Processing Systems II*, pages 592–598, Cambridge, MA, USA, 1999. MIT Press.

> A probabilistic binary PCA algorithm using the logistic likelihood we saw in Chapter 4 and an EM-like inference algorithm.

[7] Michael Tipping and Christopher Bishop. Probabilistic principal component analysis. *Journal of the Royal Statistical Society. Series B (Statistical Methodology)*, 61(3):611–622, 1999.

> An interesting application of maximum likelihood. Here it is applied to one of the first probabilistic approaches to the the classical statistical problem of Principal Component Analysis.

II

Advanced Topics

CHAPTER 8

Gaussian Processes

In the last decade, **Gaussian process** models have become very popular in many ML applications due to their incredible flexibility. To do Gaussian processes justice, a whole book is required (see the references at the end of this chapter for a very good one!) but their popularity suggests that they are worthy of being introduced in a book such as this one. In this chapter we restrict ourselves to the basics of Gaussian process regression and classification, providing pointers to more advanced topics. Our aim is that, once you are familiar with the material in this chapter, you are ready to tackle the vast academic literature being produced in this area!

8.1 PROLOGUE – NON-PARAMETRIC MODELS

In Part 1 we introduced several key Machine Learning concepts through the use of linear regression. Recall that, in the linear regression model, the targets (t_n) were modelled as a linear function of a set of parameters $(\mathbf{w})$:

$$t_n = \mathbf{w}^\mathsf{T}\mathbf{x}_n.$$

Initially, we trained the model by finding the parameters that minimised the loss before explicitly incorporating noise into the model and finding the parameters that maximised the likelihood. In Chapter 3 we adopted a Bayesian approach by placing a prior distribution over the parameters, computing the posterior distribution (once the data had been observed) and then made predictions by averaging over this posterior distribution.

Assuming that the prior over $\mathbf{w}$ is Gaussian with zero mean and identity covariance, the Bayesian linear regression model was defined as

$$\begin{aligned} p(\mathbf{w}) &= \mathcal{N}(\mathbf{0}, \mathbf{I}_D) \\ p(\mathbf{t}|\mathbf{w}, \mathbf{X}, \sigma^2) &= \mathcal{N}(\mathbf{X}\mathbf{w}, \sigma^2\mathbf{I}_N), \end{aligned}$$

where, for first-order polynomials (i.e. straight lines)

$$\mathbf{w} = \begin{bmatrix} w_0 \\ w_1 \end{bmatrix}, \quad \mathbf{X} = \begin{bmatrix} 1 & x_1 \\ 1 & x_2 \\ \vdots & \vdots \\ 1 & x_N \end{bmatrix}, \quad \mathbf{t} = \begin{bmatrix} t_1 \\ t_2 \\ \vdots \\ t_N \end{bmatrix},$$

and $\mathbf{I}_D$ and $\mathbf{I}_N$ are $D \times D$ ($D = 2$) and $N \times N$ identity matrices. For given values of $x_1, \ldots, x_N$ and σ^2, we can use this model to generate values of $\mathbf{t}$ – i.e. what kind of data does the model expect – by first sampling a $\mathbf{w}$ from $p(\mathbf{w})$ and then a value of $\mathbf{t}$ from $p(\mathbf{t}|\mathbf{w}, \mathbf{X}, \sigma^2)$. Some examples are shown in Figure 8.1. In these plots we have used the Olympic number for x, to allow comparison with, e.g., Figure 3.20 ($x = 0$ corresponds to 1896, $x = 27$ corresponds to 2008), and $\sigma^2 = 1$.

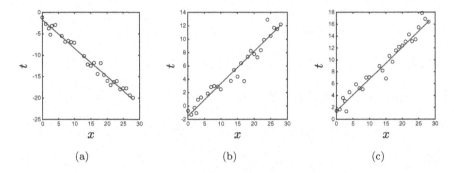

(a)   (b)   (c)

FIGURE 8.1   Three example sets of $\mathbf{t}$ generated from the Bayesian linear regression model.

As the prior $p(\mathbf{w})$ and likelihood $p(\mathbf{t}|\mathbf{w}, \mathbf{X}, \sigma^2)$ are both Gaussian, we can integrate out $\mathbf{w}$ from our model to get a distribution for $\mathbf{t}$ conditioned only on $\mathbf{X}$ and σ^2. The joint density of $\mathbf{w}$ and $\mathbf{t}$ is

$$p(\mathbf{t}, \mathbf{w}|\mathbf{X}, \sigma^2) = p(\mathbf{t}|\mathbf{w}, \mathbf{X}, \sigma^2)p(\mathbf{w}).$$

Integrating this with respect to $\mathbf{w}$ gives us

$$\int p(\mathbf{t}|\mathbf{w}, \mathbf{X}, \sigma^2)p(\mathbf{w}) \, d\mathbf{w} = p(\mathbf{t}|\mathbf{X}, \sigma^2) = \mathcal{N}(\mathbf{0}, \sigma^2 \mathbf{I}_N + \mathbf{X}\mathbf{X}^\mathsf{T}). \qquad (8.1)$$

Note that we have computed this exact quantity before – it is the marginal likelihood we computed in Chapter 3 (see Equation 3.23), with prior mean $\boldsymbol{\mu}_0 = \mathbf{0}$ and prior covariance $\boldsymbol{\Sigma}_0 = \mathbf{I}_D$. Some values of $\mathbf{t}$ sampled from this distribution can be seen in Figure 8.2.

Sampling $\mathbf{t}$ conditioned on $\mathbf{w}$ or sampling $\mathbf{t}$ directly from the marginal are obviously statistically equivalent. However, removing $\mathbf{w}$ from our model (making it non-parametric) opens the door to many interesting avenues, some of which we will explore later in this chapter. Before we do, let's look a bit more closely at the marginal distribution over $\mathbf{t}$.

In the original model, we placed a prior distribution on the model parameters $\mathbf{w}$. This, coupled with the original assumption that the model should be a first order polynomial, and the assumption of Gaussian noise results in a distribution over the values of the function ($\mathbf{t}$), as visualised by the samples shown in Figure 8.1. When we marginalise $\mathbf{w}$, we can think of the resulting distribution over $\mathbf{t}$ as a prior distribution

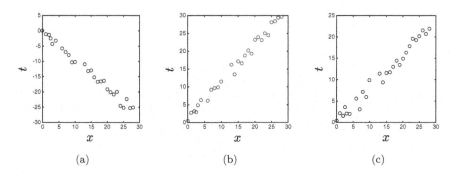

FIGURE 8.2   Three example sets of **t** generated from the Bayesian linear regression model where the parameters **w** have been marginalised.

placed *directly on the values of the function*. This is not an easy concept to grasp: in the original formulation, the relationship between the data (x) and the function value (t) is clear, whilst in the marginalised formulation, it is far less obvious as **X** is hidden inside the covariance matrix. To get a feel for what is happening, let's assume that there are only two Olympic years in our dataset, 1896 and 1900. $p(\mathbf{t}|\mathbf{X}, \sigma^2)$ is now two-dimensional and is visualised in Figure 8.3.

The density is sloping, which tells us that the two random variables (t_{1896} and t_{1900}) are dependent – if the value of t_{1896} is high, then the value of t_{1900} is also likely to be high (and vice versa). This makes complete sense. The two values of the function correspond to very similar inputs (they are consecutive Olympic years) and we would therefore expect the function values to be the same too (we don't expect the 100 m winning time to change very quickly). In the original model formulation, this dependence came through **w**. As $t_n = \mathbf{w}^\mathsf{T}\mathbf{x}_n$, similar values of **x** would give similar values of t. The difference now is that, in the marginalised model, this dependence is defined directly between the t_n via the covariance matrix.

To further illustrate this, we can look at the prior density for two very different Olympic years. The density for t_{1896} and t_{2008} is shown in Figure 8.4 (the smaller density in the figure is Figure 8.3 replicated for comparison). There is now no discernible dependence between the two variables (there will be dependence, but it's very weak, and impossible to see in this plot), suggesting that t_{1896} doesn't tell us much about t_{2008}. Again this makes sense, as we might expect the winning time to change quite considerably in 112 years.

Also of note is the fact that the density is much broader for t_{2008} than it was for t_{1900}. This is a consequence of our original model assumptions. The best way to demonstrate this is by sampling lots of values of **t**, as can be seen in Figure 8.5. The much wider spread of values for later Olympic years is obvious. Our original prior on **w** favours lines that pass close to the origin and therefore typically get further from the origin as x increases.

At this point, you might reasonably ask why we bother marginalising the **w**. Indeed, in this particular example, it hasn't really helped us at all – we have the same model (as far as **t** is concerned). However, this is one specific example of a very powerful idea. We have shown that, rather than assume some parametric form

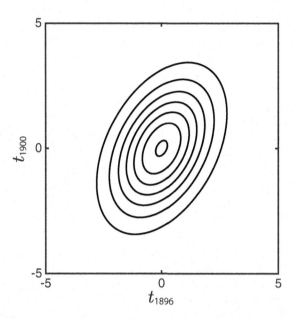

FIGURE 8.3 $p(\mathbf{t}|\mathbf{X}, \sigma^2)$ for just two Olympic years (1896 and 1900).

for the function (i.e. first-order polynomial) and placing a prior distribution on its parameters, we can place a prior distribution directly on the N-dimensional vector of function values $\mathbf{t}$. In our example, we obtained this prior by first assuming a parametric form and then marginalising the parameters $\mathbf{w}$, but we don't need to do things this way. We are free to choose any distribution for $\mathbf{t}$ that we like; it doesn't have to be derived from a parametric model. A popular choice is to assume a Gaussian distribution, resulting in models that make up the subject of this chapter – Gaussian process models.

8.2 GAUSSIAN PROCESS REGRESSION

As alluded to in the previous section, Gaussian process (GP) regression models assume that the vector of targets (e.g. $\mathbf{t}$) comes from a Gaussian distribution. Rather than choosing a parametric form for the regression function, we instead choose the mean vector and covariance matrix for this Gaussian. In the following, we'll start with the noise-free regression case, before adding noise, and then move on to using GPs for classification.

8.2.1 The Gaussian process prior

As in Chapter 1, we are interested in fitting a function $f(x)$ based on a set of training examples so that we can make predictions at previously unseen values of x. For reasons that will become obvious later, we will define the output of the function for

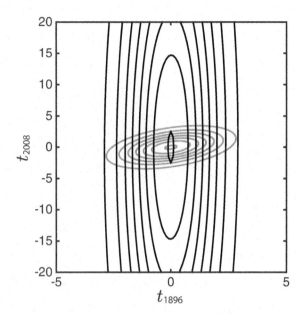

FIGURE 8.4 $p(\mathbf{t}|\mathbf{X}, \sigma^2)$ for two distant Olympic years (1896 and 2008). The smaller density in the center is the one for 1896 and 1900 repeated from Figure 8.3.

the nth data point, x_n, as f_n rather than t_n and collect them together into a vector $\mathbf{f}$. The central assumption made by the GP is that the collection of function outputs f_n at all possible input values x_n are jointly Gaussian distributed. This feels a bit strange – in many examples there will be infinitely many different possible inputs, implying an infinite-dimensional vector $\mathbf{f}$ and therefore an infinite-dimensional Gaussian! However, a key property of the multivariate Gaussian density is that, if a vector $\mathbf{f}$ follows a multivariate Gaussian, then any subset of the elements of $\mathbf{f}$ also follow a multivariate Gaussian with their mean and covariance simply extracted from the overall mean vector and covariance matrix (see Comment 8.1). We therefore don't need to worry about all the x_n that we will never see and just stick to those that appear in our training and test sets.

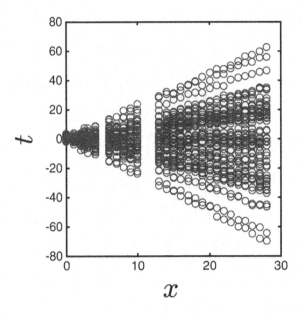

FIGURE 8.5 Fifty samples of **t** from the marginalised model.

Comment 8.1 – Gaussian Marginals: Consider a random vector $\mathbf{z} = [z_1, z_2, z_3, z_4]^T$ following a multivariate Gaussian distribution with mean and covariance given by

$$\boldsymbol{\mu} = \begin{bmatrix} \mu_1 \\ \mu_2 \\ \mu_3 \\ \mu_4 \end{bmatrix}, \quad \mathbf{C} = \begin{bmatrix} c_{11} & c_{12} & c_{13} & c_{14} \\ c_{21} & c_{22} & c_{23} & c_{24} \\ c_{31} & c_{32} & c_{33} & c_{34} \\ c_{41} & c_{42} & c_{43} & c_{44} \end{bmatrix}.$$

The marginal distribution of any subset of these four variables obtained by integrating over the remaining ones can be easily extracted by simply extracting out the relevant elements of $\boldsymbol{\mu}$ and $\mathbf{C}$. For example, $p(z_2, z_3)$ is a Gaussian, with mean and covariance given by

$$\boldsymbol{\mu} = \begin{bmatrix} \mu_2 \\ \mu_3 \end{bmatrix}, \quad \mathbf{C} = \begin{bmatrix} c_{22} & c_{23} \\ c_{32} & c_{33} \end{bmatrix},$$

$p(z_1, z_3)$ is a Gaussian with mean and covariance given by

$$\boldsymbol{\mu} = \begin{bmatrix} \mu_1 \\ \mu_3 \end{bmatrix}, \quad \mathbf{C} = \begin{bmatrix} c_{11} & c_{13} \\ c_{31} & c_{33} \end{bmatrix},$$

and $p(z_4)$ is a Gaussian with mean μ_4 and variance c_{44}, etc.

The GP is typically specified through mean and **covariance functions**, $\mu(x_n)$ and $c(x_n, x_m)$ (in our examples we'll assume that the inputs are one dimensional, but everything is the same for vectors $\mathbf{x}_n$). These are used to compute the elements of the mean vector and covariance matrix that define the Gaussian distribution. A popular choice for the mean function is $\mu(x_n) = 0$ (i.e. the Gaussian mean is a vector of zeros). Many different covariance functions have been used, one of the most popular of which is the RBF function (that we saw being used as an SVM kernel in Chapter 5):

$$c(x_n, x_m) = \alpha \exp(-\gamma(x_n - x_m)^2). \tag{8.2}$$

The covariance matrix is built by evaluating this function for all pairs of x values in our training set and setting the value at the nth row and mth column of the matrix as $c(x_n, x_m)$. Defining a fine grid of x values between -5 and 5, and choosing a value for γ, we can sample vectors $\mathbf{f}$ from the GP prior, $\mathcal{N}(\mathbf{0}, \mathbf{C})$, and then plot the elements of the N-dimensional vector $\mathbf{f} = [f_1, \ldots, f_N]^\mathsf{T}$ against $x_1, \ldots, x_N$. Some examples for different values of γ (with $\alpha = 1$) can be seen in Figure 8.6 (MATLAB script: `gpprior.m`) (see Exercise 8.1). Each series of dots is one sample from the N-dimensional Gaussian (there are five on each plot). When plotted this way, these samples look like standard parametric functions of x. Crucially, however, we have produced these 'functions' without having to make any explicit parametric assumptions. All we have done is chosen a covariance function.

As we vary γ, the complexity of the resulting functions changes – high γ produces more complex looking functions. Drawing samples from the prior and varying covariance parameters in this way gives us an indication of the enormous flexibility of GP models (and hence their popularity). The RBF covariance function alone allows us to fit functions and make predictions for a huge range of problems.

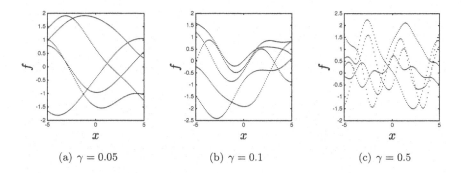

(a) $\gamma = 0.05$ (b) $\gamma = 0.1$ (c) $\gamma = 0.5$

FIGURE 8.6 Samples from the GP prior with zero mean and an RBF covariance function with parameter γ. As γ is increased, the functions become more complex.

As with the marginalised linear regression model we looked at at the start of this chapter, we can gain some insight into our GP prior with an RBF covariance function by visualising the prior for pairs of data points. The RBF covariance function only depends on the difference between x_n and x_m (see Equation 8.2) so we can visualise it as a function of this difference. Figure 8.7 shows the covariance function for four values of $|x_n - x_m|$ with $\gamma = 0.1$ (and $\alpha = 1$). For the smallest difference (0.5), the covariance function shows high dependence between f_n and f_m – similar inputs (x_n and x_m) should produce similar function values. In other words, knowing the value of the function at x_n tells us a lot about the value of the function at x_m. As the difference increases, the dependence drops until f_n and f_m are effectively independent at $|x_n - x_m| = 10$. This maps clearly to the functions in Figure 8.6(b). If the value of x changes by 0.5, the function doesn't change very much, but if it changes by 10.0 (the width of the plot) the function can change an awful lot and therefore the value of the function at x_n tells us very little about the value of it at x_m.

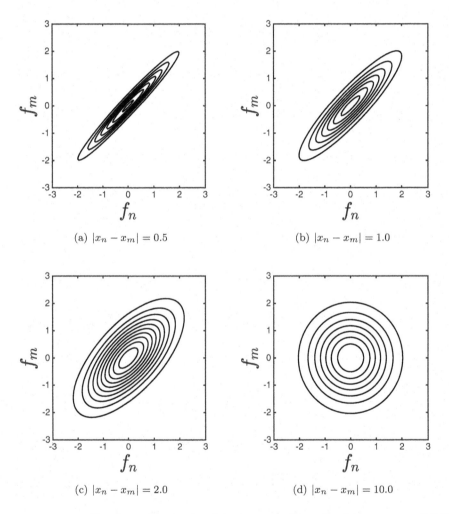

(a) $|x_n - x_m| = 0.5$

(b) $|x_n - x_m| = 1.0$

(c) $|x_n - x_m| = 2.0$

(d) $|x_n - x_m| = 10.0$

FIGURE 8.7 GP prior for pairs of function values f_n, f_m using an RBF covariance with $\gamma = 0.1$.

8.2.2   Noise-free regression

We have seen how the GP prior allows us to place a prior distribution directly onto the space of functions. How then do we use this to perform regression tasks? Fortunately, the process is straightforward due to another useful property of the multivariate Gaussian distribution – a subset of the variables conditioned on the others is also distributed as a multivariate Gaussian (see Comment 8.2).

Comment 8.2 – Gaussian Conditionals: Consider a random vector $\mathbf{z}$ consisting of variables that can be split into two sets, $\mathbf{z}_1$ and $\mathbf{z}_2$:

$$\mathbf{z} = \begin{bmatrix} \mathbf{z}_1 \\ \mathbf{z}_2 \end{bmatrix}.$$

Assume that $\mathbf{z}$ follows a Gaussian distribution:

$$p(\mathbf{z}) = \mathcal{N}(\boldsymbol{\mu}, \boldsymbol{\Sigma})$$

$$\boldsymbol{\mu} = \begin{bmatrix} \boldsymbol{\mu}_1 \\ \boldsymbol{\mu}_2 \end{bmatrix}, \qquad \boldsymbol{\Sigma} = \begin{bmatrix} \boldsymbol{\Sigma}_{11} & \boldsymbol{\Sigma}_{12} \\ \boldsymbol{\Sigma}_{21} & \boldsymbol{\Sigma}_{22} \end{bmatrix}.$$

(Note that $\boldsymbol{\Sigma}_{21} = \boldsymbol{\Sigma}_{12}^{\mathsf{T}}$ as covariance matrices must be symmetric.) If we observe the value of one of the sets of variables (say $\mathbf{z}_1$), the conditional density of the other set is also Gaussian:

$$p(\mathbf{z}_2|\mathbf{z}_1) = \mathcal{N}(\mathbf{a}, \mathbf{B})$$

$$\mathbf{a} = \boldsymbol{\mu}_2 + \boldsymbol{\Sigma}_{12}^{\mathsf{T}}\boldsymbol{\Sigma}_{11}^{-1}(\mathbf{z}_1 - \boldsymbol{\mu}_1), \qquad \mathbf{B} = \boldsymbol{\Sigma}_{22} - \boldsymbol{\Sigma}_{12}^{\mathsf{T}}\boldsymbol{\Sigma}_{11}^{-1}\boldsymbol{\Sigma}_{12}.$$

Figure 8.8 shows some training data that we would like to use to build a regression model. The circles denote the training (x_n, f_n) pairs and the dashed lines show the values of x at which we would like to make predictions. Using $*$ to distinguish the points at which we'd like to make predictions from the points at which we have training data, we have

$$\mathbf{x} = \begin{bmatrix} x_1 \\ x_2 \\ \dots \\ x_N \end{bmatrix}, \quad \mathbf{f} = \begin{bmatrix} f_1 \\ f_2 \\ \dots \\ f_N \end{bmatrix}, \quad \mathbf{x}^* = \begin{bmatrix} x_1^* \\ x_2^* \\ \dots \\ x_L^* \end{bmatrix}, \quad \mathbf{f}^* = \begin{bmatrix} f_1^* \\ f_2^* \\ \dots \\ f_L^* \end{bmatrix},$$

where L denotes the number of points in our prediction set, $f_n = f(x_n)$ and $f_n^* = f(x_n^*)$. The GP assumes that the function values at all points of interest (training and predictive) follow a Gaussian density. Therefore, if we combine $\mathbf{f}$ and $\mathbf{f}^*$ into a single vector,

$$\hat{\mathbf{f}} = \begin{bmatrix} \mathbf{f} \\ \mathbf{f}^* \end{bmatrix},$$

this vector must follow a Gaussian density. We now use our covariance function to define three covariance matrices. A covariance matrix for the training points:

$$\mathbf{C} = \begin{bmatrix} c(x_1, x_1) & c(x_1, x_2) & \dots & c(x_1, x_N) \\ c(x_2, x_1) & c(x_2, x_2) & \dots & c(x_2, x_N) \\ \vdots & \vdots & \ddots & \vdots \\ c(x_N, x_1) & c(x_N, x_2) & \dots & c(x_N, x_N) \end{bmatrix},$$

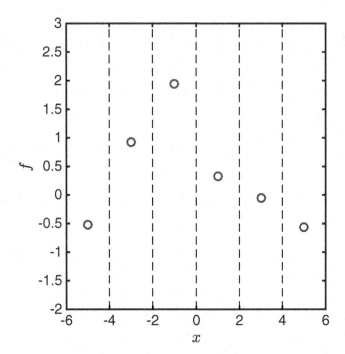

FIGURE 8.8 Some training data for the noise-free GP regression example.

a covariance matrix for the testing points:

$$
\mathbf{C}^* = \begin{bmatrix}
c(x_1^*, x_1^*) & c(x_1^*, x_2^*) & \cdots & c(x_1^*, x_L^*) \\
c(x_2^*, x_1^*) & c(x_2^*, x_2^*) & \cdots & c(x_2^*, x_L^*) \\
\vdots & \vdots & \ddots & \vdots \\
c(x_L^*, x_1^*) & c(x_L^*, x_2^*) & \cdots & c(x_L^*, x_L^*)
\end{bmatrix},
$$

and an $N \times L$ cross-covariance matrix:

$$
\mathbf{R} = \begin{bmatrix}
c(x_1, x_1^*) & c(x_1, x_2^*) & \cdots & c(x_1, x_L^*) \\
c(x_2, x_1^*) & c(x_2, x_2^*) & \cdots & c(x_2, x_L^*) \\
\vdots & \vdots & \ddots & \vdots \\
c(x_N, x_1^*) & c(x_N, x_2^*) & \cdots & c(x_N, x_L^*)
\end{bmatrix}.
$$

Assuming zero mean, the GP prior over $\hat{\mathbf{f}}$ is given by

$$
p(\hat{\mathbf{f}}) = \mathcal{N}\left(\mathbf{0}, \begin{bmatrix} \mathbf{C} & \mathbf{R} \\ \mathbf{R}^\mathsf{T} & \mathbf{C}^* \end{bmatrix}\right).
$$

This one distribution is the complete definition of our model. It tells us how all of the elements in $\hat{\mathbf{f}}$ (the function values at the training and prediction points) co-vary.

Making predictions amounts to manipulating this distribution to give the distribution over the function values at the prediction points conditioned on the observed values at the training points, $p(\mathbf{f}^*|\mathbf{f})$. As the joint distribution is Gaussian, this is a straightforward operation (see Comment 8.2) and the conditional distribution is given as

$$p(\mathbf{f}^*|\mathbf{f}) = \mathcal{N}(\boldsymbol{\mu}^*, \boldsymbol{\Sigma}^*)$$
$$\boldsymbol{\mu}^* = \mathbf{R}^\mathsf{T}\mathbf{C}^{-1}\mathbf{f}, \quad \boldsymbol{\Sigma}^* = \mathbf{C}^* - \mathbf{R}^\mathsf{T}\mathbf{C}^{-1}\mathbf{R}. \tag{8.3}$$

This gives us a joint Gaussian distribution over the predictions at all of the prediction points (the dashed lines in Figure 8.8). We can easily extract individual marginal distributions for the test points by taking the relevant components from the mean vector and covariance matrix (see Comment 8.1). These distributions are shown in Figure 8.9, with circles denoting the mean values and lines showing plus and minus one standard deviation (MATLAB script: gppred.m).

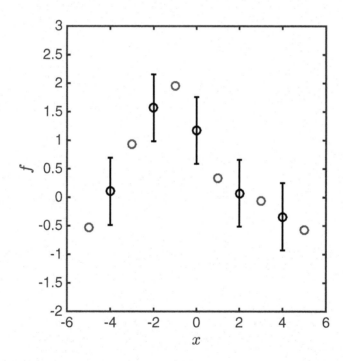

FIGURE 8.9 Marginal predictions at the test points shown as dashed lines in Figure 8.8.

The predictions look very reasonable. Creating a finer grid of predictive points, we can better visualise the overall regression results. Figure 8.10 shows predictions over a fine grid (subsequent test points separated by 0.1) that have been joined together to show a smooth function. The solid line gives the predictive mean, and the dashed lines show plus and minus one standard deviation.

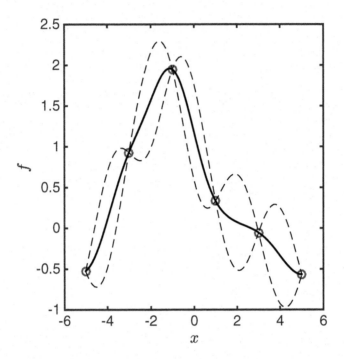

FIGURE 8.10 Predictions over a finer grid of points let us visualise the GP function. The solid line shows the predictive mean and the dashed line plus and minus one standard deviation.

The predictions shown in both Figures 8.9 and 8.10 are all based only on the marginal distributions of each test point (the error bars and three standard deviation envelope are both computed from the marginal variances, given by the diagonal elements of Σ^*). The GP prediction gives us much more than this – the full covariance structure of the function at the predictive points. The best way to visualise this is by sampling values of $\mathbf{f}^*$ from the predictive Gaussian (Equation 8.3). Figure 8.11 shows ten samples from this predictive distribution. All of the functions perfectly match the training points (a consequence of our implicit assumption of no noise that will be removed later) but show a wide range of behaviours between the training points. We can think of the posterior as the set of all functions defined by the prior that pass exactly through all of the training points.

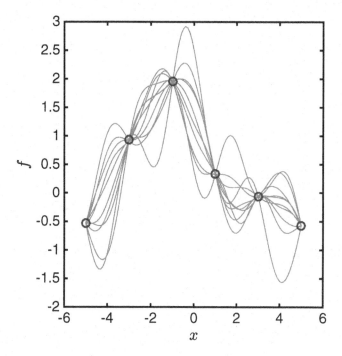

FIGURE 8.11 Ten sample functions from the predictive distribution given in Equation 8.3.

8.2.3 Noisy regression

The GP regression in the previous section assumed (implicitly) that the observed values were the true values of the function. Often the examples we observe will be corrupted by noise. In Chapter 2 we saw how we could include additive Gaussian noise in our linear regression model. We will now do exactly the same within the GP framework.

Assume that, instead of observing the true function values, we observe t_n where

$$t_n = f_n + \epsilon_n,$$

and $p(\epsilon_n) = \mathcal{N}(0, \sigma^2)$. That is, the observed value is the true function value with additive Gaussian noise, where the values of the noise (ϵ_n) are independent across the observations. Combining all values of t into a vector as previously, we have the following distribution for t conditioned on f:

$$p(t|f, \sigma^2) = \mathcal{N}(f, \sigma^2 I_N).$$

Because this is Gaussian, and the GP prior on f is Gaussian, we can integrate out f and place the prior directly on t:

$$p(t|\sigma^2) = \int p(t|f, \sigma^2)p(f) \; df = \mathcal{N}(0, C + \sigma^2 I_N).$$

As before, we want to make predictions at a set of inputs $\mathbf{x}^*$. Normally, we will be interested in predicting $\mathbf{f}^*$, the function value, rather than $\mathbf{t}^*$, the corrupted function value, although this will be application dependent. We will assume that it's $\mathbf{f}^*$ that we are after. To make the prediction, we need to construct the joint density as before. This is Gaussian, and is very similar to that for the noise-free case except that $\mathbf{C}$ is replaced with the new prior covariance $\mathbf{C} + \sigma^2 \mathbf{I}_N$:

$$p(\hat{\mathbf{f}}|\sigma^2) = \mathcal{N}\left(\mathbf{0}, \begin{bmatrix} \mathbf{C} + \sigma^2 \mathbf{I}_N & \mathbf{R} \\ \mathbf{R}^\mathsf{T} & \mathbf{C}^* \end{bmatrix}\right),$$

where

$$\hat{\mathbf{f}} = \begin{bmatrix} \mathbf{t} \\ \mathbf{f}^* \end{bmatrix}.$$

Note that if we wanted instead to predict $\mathbf{t}^*$, the bottom right component of the covariance matrix would be $\mathbf{C}^* + \sigma^2 \mathbf{I}_L$ rather than $\mathbf{C}^*$.

We obtain the predictive conditional distribution, $p(\mathbf{f}^*|\mathbf{t}, \sigma^2)$ in exactly the same manner as for the noise-free case (see Comment 8.2). The distribution is

$$p(\mathbf{f}^*|\mathbf{t}, \sigma^2) = \mathcal{N}(\boldsymbol{\mu}^*, \boldsymbol{\Sigma}^*)$$
$$\boldsymbol{\mu}^* = \mathbf{R}^\mathsf{T}(\mathbf{C} + \sigma^2 \mathbf{I}_N)^{-1}\mathbf{t}, \quad \boldsymbol{\Sigma}^* = \mathbf{C}^* - \mathbf{R}^\mathsf{T}(\mathbf{C} + \sigma^2 \mathbf{I}_N)^{-1}\mathbf{R}. \tag{8.4}$$

An example of this in action can be seen in Figure 8.12, where we have used the same data as in the noise-free example but with Gaussian noise added ($\sigma^2 = 0.1$) (MATLAB script: gpprednoise.m). Now that noise has been included we see that the predictive variance has increased (compare, e.g. Figure 8.12(b) with 8.9). The sampled functions are also no longer restricted to pass through the training data. It is also interesting to note that the GP tends to pull the predictions closer to zero than the training points. This is a direct consequence of the assumption of a zero mean GP. The effect of this assumption is particularly clear if we move significantly away from the region in which we observe data. Figure 8.13 shows the predictions as we move away from the region in x on which we've been concentrating. As we do, the mean predictions become closer and closer to the GP prior mean (zero) and the spread converges to the prior marginal standard deviation, which is equal to $\sqrt{c(x_n, x_n)}$ (which is equal to $\sqrt{\alpha}$ in the case of the RBF covariance function).

8.2.4 Summary

In these sections we have introduced GP regression with and without noise. We have seen that GP regression amounts to little more than some matrix manipulation due to the nice analytical properties of multivariate Gaussian distributions (see Comment 8.1 and Comment 8.2). These properties hold when the noise is Gaussian but things become a bit trickier for other likelihood functions. Later in this chapter, we will see how to use GPs for non-Gaussian likelihoods when we use them for classification, and the same general process we will use there holds for other, non-Gaussian likelihoods.

Before we move on to classification, we will go through an alternative way of deriving the distributions required to do regression in the presence of Gaussian noise. It is not really necessary to follow these steps, but it can often be useful to see a route through the algebra.

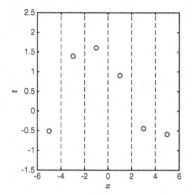

(a) Training data. Values of x where we would like to make predictions are shown by dashed lines.

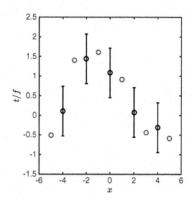

(b) Predictions. Mean prediction shown by circles, lines show plus and minus one standard deviation.

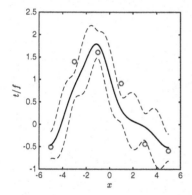

(c) Predcitions over a finer grid to show overall function. Solid line shows predictive mean, dashed line plus and minus one standard deviation.

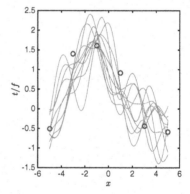

(d) Ten samples from the predictive distribution.

FIGURE 8.12 An example of GP regression with noise, using the same data as in the noise-free example, corrupted with Gaussian noise with $\sigma^2 = 0.1$.

8.2.5 Noisy regression – an alternative route

In the previous section, we included Gaussian noise through adding the noise variance to the diagonal elements of the covariance matrix $\mathbf{C}$. We could then choose whether or not to add this variance to the predictive variance, depending on whether or not we wish to make predictions of f^* or t^*. We can reach the same predictive distribution through an alternative route, and it is worthwhile doing so, as it will

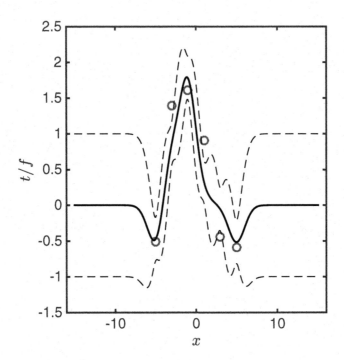

FIGURE 8.13 As we move away from the area where we observe data, the predictions converge to the GP prior.

help when we come to non-Gaussian likelihood functions, such as those needed for classification problems.

We would like to compute $p(\mathbf{f}^*|\mathbf{t}, \sigma^2)$ and can do so via

$$p(\mathbf{f}^*|\mathbf{t}, \sigma^2) = \int p(\mathbf{f}^*|\mathbf{f})p(\mathbf{f}|\mathbf{t}, \sigma^2) \, d\mathbf{f}.$$

The first term in the integral is the standard noise-free GP regression:

$$p(\mathbf{f}^*|\mathbf{f}) = \mathcal{N}(\mathbf{R}^\mathsf{T}\mathbf{C}^{-1}\mathbf{f}, \mathbf{C}^* - \mathbf{R}^\mathsf{T}\mathbf{C}^{-1}\mathbf{R}).$$

The second term can be computed via Bayes' rule:

$$\begin{aligned}
p(\mathbf{f}|\mathbf{t}, \sigma^2) &\propto \mathcal{N}(\mathbf{t}|\mathbf{f}, \sigma^2\mathbf{I})\mathcal{N}(\mathbf{f}|\mathbf{0}, \mathbf{C}) \\
&\propto \exp\left\{-\frac{1}{2}(\mathbf{t} - \mathbf{f})^\mathsf{T} \left(\sigma^2\mathbf{I}\right)^{-1}(\mathbf{t} - \mathbf{f})\right\} \exp\left\{-\frac{1}{2}\mathbf{f}^\mathsf{T}\mathbf{C}^{-1}\mathbf{f}\right\} \\
&= \mathcal{N}(\boldsymbol{\mu}_\mathbf{f}, \boldsymbol{\Sigma}_\mathbf{f}),
\end{aligned}$$

where

$$\boldsymbol{\Sigma}_\mathbf{f} = \left[\mathbf{C}^{-1} + \frac{1}{\sigma^2}\mathbf{I}\right]^{-1}, \quad \boldsymbol{\mu}_\mathbf{f} = \frac{1}{\sigma^2}\boldsymbol{\Sigma}_\mathbf{f}\mathbf{t}.$$

To compute the integral, we need to make use of the following result:

$$\int \mathcal{N}(\mathbf{a}|\mathbf{Bc},\mathbf{D})\mathcal{N}(\mathbf{c}|\mathbf{e},\mathbf{F})\,dc = \mathcal{N}(\mathbf{Be},\mathbf{D}+\mathbf{BFB}^{\mathsf{T}}).$$

In our case, this tell us that

$$p(\mathbf{f}^*|\mathbf{t},\sigma^2) = \mathcal{N}\left(\mathbf{R}^{\mathsf{T}}\mathbf{C}^{-1}\boldsymbol{\mu}_{\mathbf{f}}, \mathbf{C}^* - \mathbf{R}^{\mathsf{T}}\mathbf{C}^{-1}\mathbf{R}+\mathbf{R}^{\mathsf{T}}\mathbf{C}^{-1}\boldsymbol{\Sigma}_{\mathbf{f}}\mathbf{C}^{-1}\mathbf{R}\right).$$

To demonstrate that this is the same as the predictive distribution computed previously, we need to show that the means are equal:

$$\mathbf{R}^{\mathsf{T}}\mathbf{C}^{-1}\boldsymbol{\mu}_{\mathbf{f}} = \mathbf{R}^{\mathsf{T}}\left(\mathbf{C}+\sigma^2\mathbf{I}\right)^{-1}\mathbf{t}$$

and so are the covariances:

$$\mathbf{C}^* - \mathbf{R}^{\mathsf{T}}\left(\mathbf{C}+\sigma^2\mathbf{I}\right)^{-1}\mathbf{R} = \mathbf{C}^* - \mathbf{R}^{\mathsf{T}}\mathbf{C}^{-1}\mathbf{R}+\mathbf{R}^{\mathsf{T}}\mathbf{C}^{-1}\boldsymbol{\Sigma}_{\mathbf{f}}\mathbf{C}^{-1}\mathbf{R}.$$

Taking the first one,

$$
\begin{aligned}
\mathbf{R}^{\mathsf{T}}\mathbf{C}^{-1}\boldsymbol{\mu}_{\mathbf{f}} &= \mathbf{R}^{\mathsf{T}}\left(\mathbf{C}+\sigma^2\mathbf{I}\right)^{-1}\mathbf{t}\\
\frac{1}{\sigma^2}\mathbf{R}^{\mathsf{T}}\mathbf{C}^{-1}\boldsymbol{\Sigma}_{\mathbf{f}}\mathbf{t} &= \mathbf{R}^{\mathsf{T}}\left(\mathbf{C}+\sigma^2\mathbf{I}\right)^{-1}\mathbf{t}\\
\frac{1}{\sigma^2}\mathbf{R}^{\mathsf{T}}\mathbf{C}^{-1}\left(\mathbf{C}^{-1}+\frac{1}{\sigma^2}\mathbf{I}\right)^{-1}\mathbf{t} &= \mathbf{R}^{\mathsf{T}}\left(\mathbf{C}+\sigma^2\mathbf{I}\right)^{-1}\mathbf{t}.
\end{aligned}
$$

Noting that

$$\mathbf{A}^{-1}\mathbf{B}^{-1} = (\mathbf{AB})^{-1},$$

and

$$\mathbf{C}\mathbf{C}^{-1} = \mathbf{I},$$

we have

$$
\begin{aligned}
\frac{1}{\sigma^2}\mathbf{R}^{\mathsf{T}}\left(\mathbf{I}+\frac{1}{\sigma^2}\mathbf{C}\right)^{-1}\mathbf{t} &= \mathbf{R}^{\mathsf{T}}\left(\mathbf{C}+\sigma^2\mathbf{I}\right)^{-1}\mathbf{t}\\
\mathbf{R}^{\mathsf{T}}\left(\sigma^2\mathbf{I}+\mathbf{C}\right)^{-1}\mathbf{t} &= \mathbf{R}^{\mathsf{T}}\left(\mathbf{C}+\sigma^2\mathbf{I}\right)^{-1}\mathbf{t},
\end{aligned}
$$

as required. For the second term,

$$
\begin{aligned}
\mathbf{C}^* - \mathbf{R}^{\mathsf{T}}\left(\mathbf{C}+\sigma^2\mathbf{I}\right)^{-1}\mathbf{R} &= \mathbf{C}^* - \mathbf{R}^{\mathsf{T}}\mathbf{C}^{-1}\mathbf{R}+\mathbf{R}^{\mathsf{T}}\mathbf{C}^{-1}\boldsymbol{\Sigma}_{\mathbf{f}}\mathbf{C}^{-1}\mathbf{R}\\
\mathbf{R}^{\mathsf{T}}\left(\mathbf{C}+\sigma^2\mathbf{I}\right)^{-1}\mathbf{R} &= \mathbf{R}^{\mathsf{T}}\mathbf{C}^{-1}\mathbf{R}-\mathbf{R}^{\mathsf{T}}\mathbf{C}^{-1}\boldsymbol{\Sigma}_{\mathbf{f}}\mathbf{C}^{-1}\mathbf{R}\\
\left(\mathbf{C}+\sigma^2\mathbf{I}\right)^{-1} &= \mathbf{C}^{-1}-\mathbf{C}^{-1}\boldsymbol{\Sigma}_{\mathbf{f}}\mathbf{C}^{-1}\\
&= \mathbf{C}^{-1}-\mathbf{C}^{-1}\left(\mathbf{C}^{-1}+\frac{1}{\sigma^2}\mathbf{I}\right)^{-1}\mathbf{C}^{-1}\\
&= \mathbf{C}^{-1}-\left(\mathbf{I}+\frac{1}{\sigma^2}\mathbf{C}\right)^{-1}\mathbf{C}^{-1}\\
&= \mathbf{C}^{-1}-\sigma^2\left(\sigma^2\mathbf{I}+\mathbf{C}\right)^{-1}\mathbf{C}^{-1}\\
\mathbf{I} &= (\mathbf{C}+\sigma^2\mathbf{I})\mathbf{C}^{-1}-\sigma^2\mathbf{C}^{-1}\\
&= \mathbf{I}+\sigma^2\mathbf{C}^{-1}-\sigma^2\mathbf{C}^{-1}\\
&= \mathbf{I},
\end{aligned}
$$

as required. In other words, the predictive distribution we obtain through this process is identical to the previous one (it has to be – all we have done is apply some rules of probability). This may seem like a lot of effort compared to the solution we obtained by adding a diagonal term to the covariance matrix. However, when we look at non-Gaussian likelihoods (for, e.g. classification), we will not be able to fold the likelihood into the covariance function, and we will be forced to do things this way.

8.2.6 Alternative covariance functions

The RBF covariance function used in the previous sections is probably the most popular – it can perform very well in a wide range of applications. However, there are many others, some of which we describe below. For a more thorough treatment, see the references at the end of this chapter. For generality, we will provide the covariance functions for multidimensional input vectors $\mathbf{x}_n$, although all plots will be for one-dimensional inputs.

8.2.6.1 Linear

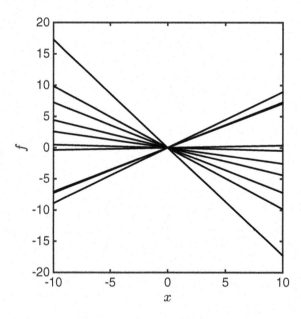

FIGURE 8.14 Ten functions drawn from a GP prior with a linear covariance function.

The linear covariance function is defined as

$$c(\mathbf{x}_n, \mathbf{x}_m) = \alpha \mathbf{x}_n^\mathsf{T} \mathbf{x}_m \tag{8.5}$$

and produces functions that are straight lines. Some example functions drawn from a GP prior with a linear covariance function for one-dimensional data (and $\alpha = 1$) can be seen in Figure 8.14 (note that in this and the following examples we have used a large number of input points to enable us to plot smooth functions). The prior covariance matrix (using our standard method of stacking all of the input vectors into one matrix $\mathbf{X}$) can be computed as

$$\mathbf{C} = \mathbf{X}\mathbf{X}^\mathsf{T}.$$

If we include a noise term, this becomes

$$\mathbf{C} = \mathbf{X}\mathbf{X}^\mathsf{T} + \sigma^2 \mathbf{I}_N,$$

which is exactly the same as the covariance matrix of the Gaussian distribution we obtained when marginalising the weights $\mathbf{w}$ from the linear model at the start of this chapter.

All of the functions in Figure 8.14 pass through the origin. If we add a constant to the covariance function

$$c(\mathbf{x}_n, \mathbf{x}_m) = \alpha(1 + \mathbf{x}_n^\mathsf{T} \mathbf{x}_m),$$

(which is equivalent to adding a column of 1s to $\mathbf{X}$), we get functions that do not pass through the origin, as can be seen in Figure 8.15. To get a feel for why this is the case, consider the original linear covariance function ($c(\mathbf{x}_n, \mathbf{x}_m) = \alpha \mathbf{x}_n^\mathsf{T} \mathbf{x}_m$). If the GP has a zero mean function, then, for $x_n = 0$, both the prior mean and covariance will be zero, so the function value *has* to be zero. The addition of the constant term means that the covariance at $x_n = 0$ will be α, allowing the function to move away from the origin if necessary.

8.2.6.2 Polynomial

Another popular covariance function is the polynomial

$$c(\mathbf{x}_n, \mathbf{x}_m) = \alpha(1 + \mathbf{x}_n^\mathsf{T} \mathbf{x}_m)^u, \tag{8.6}$$

where u controls the order of the polynomial. Example functions with $u = 2$ and $\alpha = 1$ are shown in Figure 8.16.

We have seen that, when we add a noise term to the linear covariance function, it is identical to the covariance of the marginal likelihood of a linear regression model. Consider adding a quadratic term to the linear regression model (with one-dimensional input) by adding a column to $\mathbf{X}$ consisting of x_n^2. The marginal covariance is still computed as $\mathbf{X}\mathbf{X}^\mathsf{T} + \sigma^2 \mathbf{I}_N$, but $\mathbf{X}$ has one additional column. Ignoring the noise term, the n, mth element of this matrix is

$$1 + x_n x_m + x_n^2 x_m^2.$$

How does this compare with the polynomial covariance function with $u = 2$? To find out, we can set $u = 2$ and multiply out the polynomial covariance function for one-dimensional inputs. Assuming $\alpha = 1$, this is

$$(1 + x_n x_m)^2 = 1 + 2 x_n x_m + x_n^2 x_m^2,$$

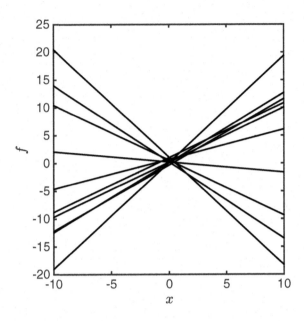

FIGURE 8.15 Ten functions drawn from a GP prior with a linear covariance function including an offset term.

which is very similar to the term from the marginal likelihood of the linear model, only differing in the constant in the $x_n x_m$ term. In fact, if we premultiplied the column in $\mathbf{X}$ corresponding to the x_n terms by $\sqrt{2}$, the two models would be identical. The only effect of this change would be to modify the optimal value of w_1 (it would become $w_1/\sqrt{2}$). Hence the two models are essentially equivalent (the same applies to higher values of u).

8.2.6.3 Neural network

An important characteristic of covariance functions is whether or not they are **stationary**. Stationary covariance functions do not depend on absolute values of $\mathbf{x}_n$ and $\mathbf{x}_m$, but only on differences between them. The RBF is an example of a stationary covariance function and this can be seen in the fact that functions drawn from a GP prior with an RBF covariance function seem to have the same degree of curvature across all of the values of $\mathbf{x}_n$ (the functions don't get more or less wiggly as we move along the x-axis). More formally, consider one-dimensional inputs x_n and x_m. A stationary covariance function would have the property that $c(x_n, x_m) = c(x_n + a, x_m + a)$ – shifting the points up or down has no effect. This also means that $c(x_n, x_n) = c(x_n + a, x_n + a)$ and therefore that the marginal variance of the function is constant (for the RBF this is α). The linear and polynomial functions are non-stationary. Consider Figure 8.14 – it is very clear that the variance in the

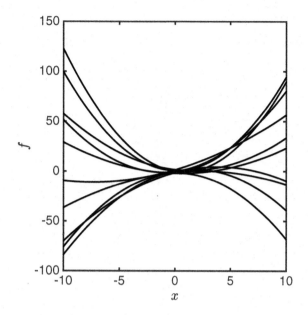

FIGURE 8.16 Ten functions drawn from a GP prior with a polynomial (second-order) covariance function.

function varies with x. At $x = 0$ the variance is zero, whereas the variance at $x = 10$ is very high (the same applies in Figure 8.16).

Another popular non-stationary covariance function is the neural network covariance function, so called because it is obtained by marginalising the parameters from a neural network model (similar in spirit to our marginalisation of the parameters in a linear model). The neural network covariance function is given as

$$c(\mathbf{x}_n, \mathbf{x}_m) = \frac{2}{\pi} \sin^{-1} \left(\frac{2\tilde{\mathbf{x}}_n \boldsymbol{\Sigma} \tilde{\mathbf{x}}_m}{\sqrt{(1 + 2\tilde{\mathbf{x}}_n \boldsymbol{\Sigma} \tilde{\mathbf{x}}_n)(1 + 2\tilde{\mathbf{x}}_m \boldsymbol{\Sigma} \tilde{\mathbf{x}}_m)}} \right), \qquad (8.7)$$

where

$$\tilde{\mathbf{x}}_n = \begin{bmatrix} 1 \\ \mathbf{x}_n \end{bmatrix}.$$

Example functions where

$$\boldsymbol{\Sigma} = \begin{bmatrix} 2 & 0 \\ 0 & 10 \end{bmatrix}$$

are shown in Figure 8.17. These functions look quite odd – they have high variability when x is close to zero, but saturate and become fairly constant as x moves away from 0. Such covariance functions are useful in a wide range of practical situations. One common example is for modelling chemical processes that often exhibit rapid changes before converging to a steady state. For more details on the derivation of

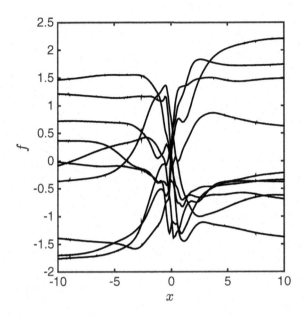

FIGURE 8.17 Ten functions drawn from a GP prior with a neural network covariance function.

the neural network covariance function, and the role of Σ, see the references at the end of the chapter.

8.2.7 ARD

Consider the following covariance function:

$$c(\mathbf{x}_n, \mathbf{x}_m) = \alpha \exp\left\{ -\sum_d \gamma_d (x_{nd} - x_{md})^2 \right\}. \tag{8.8}$$

This looks like the RBF, but now has one γ parameter per dimension. Low values of γ_d (γ_d must be greater than or equal to zero) reduce the contribution of dimension d to the covariance and hence the model. High values give dimensions high influence. Because it is possible to infer γ_d (and other covariance parameters; see Section 8.4), covariance functions like this are known as Automatic Relevance Detection (ARD) covariance functions. Such covariance functions are very useful in applications where it is likely that not all dimensions will be relevant, but which ones are relevant is not known a priori. There is a linear ARD covariance function too:

$$c(\mathbf{x}_n, \mathbf{x}_m) = \sum_d \gamma_d x_{nd} x_{md}.$$

For more details on ARD covariance functions, see the references at the end of the chapter.

8.2.8 Composite covariance functions

It is possible to combine individual covariance functions to form composite functions. In particular, if we have $j = 1 \ldots J$ covariance functions $c_1(\mathbf{x}_n, \mathbf{x}_m), \ldots, c_J(\mathbf{x}_n, \mathbf{x}_m)$, one common way to combine them is to take a weighted sum:

$$c_{(}\mathbf{x}_n, \mathbf{x}_m) = \sum_{j=1}^{J} \alpha_j c_j(\mathbf{x}_n, \mathbf{x}_m), \tag{8.9}$$

where $\alpha_j \geq 0$ are the mixing weights.

Composite covariance functions allow us to fit functions that may not naturally correspond to one particular covariance function. We leave it as an exercise to experiment with combining the various covariance described above (see Exercise 8.2).

8.2.9 Summary

In the previous sections we have introduced GP regression (both noisy and noise free) as well as describing some of the most popular covariance functions that are used with GPs. These covariance functions are not only for regression problems – they can be used in any problem with a GP prior – and there are many more of them available.

We will leave regression now and move onto GP classification. Unfortunately, for non-Gaussian likelihoods, we lose tchapter) or sampling approaches (see Chapter 9). As with regression, our aim is to provide a taste of the vast body of literature about GP approaches and not cover the field in great detail.

8.3 GAUSSIAN PROCESS CLASSIFICATION

In the previous section we saw how to use a GP to perform regression in the presence of Gaussian noise. The combination of a GP prior and Gaussian noise (a Gaussian likelihood) enabled us to analytically compute the posterior over the function values at the training and test points. In many cases, a Gaussian likelihood term will not be appropriate and, while the general process remains unchanged we will have to resort to approximate inference (e.g. Variational Bayes that we met in Chapter 7) or MCMC sampling schemes (e.g. the Metropolis–Hastings algorithm that we met in Chapter 4 or Gibbs sampling that we will meet in Chapter 9). A common example where a Gaussian likelihood is inappropriate is classification, and that is the subject of this section.

8.3.1 A classification likelihood

The GP places a prior density over functions whose domain is real valued (i.e. f_n is a real number). In classification, we would like to predict whether or not a test object belongs to a particular class. In particular, for binary classification (with the classes labelled as 0 and 1), we would like to be able to compute

$$P(t^* = 1 | \mathbf{x}^*, \mathbf{X}, \mathbf{t}),$$

i.e. the probability that the test point is in class 1 (the probability that it is in class 0 is one minus this value). As a probability, this value has to be between 0 and 1 and can therefore not be directly modelled by the type of functions given by GP priors. We met this exact same problem in Chapter 4 when performing logistic regression with a linear model: the output of the linear model $(\mathbf{w}^\mathsf{T}\mathbf{x})$ had to be squashed through a logistic function to provide a value between 0 and 1 that could be interpreted as a probability. We can do exactly the same here and squash the GP function value through a logistic function:

$$P(t_n = 1|f_n) = \frac{1}{1 + \exp(-f_n)}.$$

In the regression example, f_n, the GP output, had an intuitive meaning – it represented the *true* value of the function before it had been corrupted by noise. The idea of a true real-valued function in classification doesn't necessarily make much sense, so it is much harder to understand what this value means. One way to get a feel for it is through the process that this model (a GP prior with a logistic likelihood) assumes was responsible for generating the data, as illustrated in Figure 8.18 (MATLAB script: `gpclass.m`).

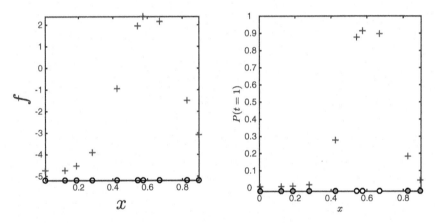

(a) One-dimensional training points (circles) with latent function values (crosses) drawn from a GP prior.

(b) Squashed function values (crosses) and sampled class labels (denoted by the shading of the circles).

FIGURE 8.18 Generating classification data from a GP prior. First we generate the latent function values at the training points (a). These are then passed through a squashing function (crosses in (b)) to give probabilities from which we can sample class labels (circles in (b)).

Figure 8.18(a) shows some one-dimensional data points (circles on the x-axis) and values for f_n (crosses) drawn from a GP prior with mean zero and RBF covariance ($\alpha = 10, \gamma = 10$). These function values are then passed through the logistic function, resulting in the probabilities (crosses) shown in Figure 8.18(b). The class labels are then randomly generated according to these probabilities. The sampled class labels are shown as the colours of the circles in Figure 8.18(b).

Five of the points have been assigned to class 0 (grey) and three to class 1 (white). When using a GP to perform classification, we are making the implicit assumption that the class labels (t) were generated this way from the input data (x) – i.e. we are assuming that there *was* some latent function f that was passed through a logistic function to produce probabilities from which the labels were sampled. In a real application where we are presented with x and t, our task is therefore to infer the values of the latent function. If we know the latent function, we can use standard GP regression to obtain the function values at test points and pass these values through the logistic function to obtain the desired classification probabilities at the test points.

8.3.2 A classification roadmap

Ultimately, we are interested in computing predictive probabilities (note that, in the following, we omit hyperparameters (e.g. γ and α) for clarity):

$$P(t^* = 1|\mathbf{x}^*, \mathbf{X}, \mathbf{t}).$$

Note that $\mathbf{f}$ doesn't appear in this expression – that's because it's not something we can observe, so we integrate it out:

$$P(t^* = 1|\mathbf{x}^*, \mathbf{X}, \mathbf{t}) = \int p(t^* = 1|f^*)p(f^*|\mathbf{x}^*, \mathbf{X}, \mathbf{t}) \, df^*.$$

The first term in the integrand is the logistic function. The second term is a noise-free GP regression, where we have integrated out the latent function values $\mathbf{f}$. It can therefore further be expanded as

$$P(t^* = 1|\mathbf{x}^*, \mathbf{X}, \mathbf{t}) = \iint p(t^* = 1|f^*)p(f^*|\mathbf{f}, \mathbf{x}^*)p(\mathbf{f}|\mathbf{X}, \mathbf{t}) \, d\mathbf{f} \, df^*. \tag{8.10}$$

The final term is the posterior density over the latent function evaluated at the training points. This can be computed via Bayes' law as

$$p(\mathbf{f}|\mathbf{X}, \mathbf{t}) = \frac{p(\mathbf{t}|\mathbf{f}, \mathbf{X})p(\mathbf{f}|\mathbf{X})}{p(\mathbf{t}|\mathbf{X})}. \tag{8.11}$$

So, in order to compute $P(t^* = 1|\mathbf{x}^*, \mathbf{X}, \mathbf{t})$, we have three distinct steps:

1. Compute the posterior density over the latent functions at the training points, $p(\mathbf{f}|\mathbf{X}, \mathbf{t})$.

2. Compute the predictive density for f^* using a GP regression based on the posterior density for $\mathbf{f}$, $p(f^*|\mathbf{x}^*, \mathbf{X}, \mathbf{t}) = \int p(f^*|\mathbf{f})p(\mathbf{f}|\mathbf{X}, \mathbf{t}) \, d\mathbf{f}$.

3. Compute the predictive probabilities by taking the expectation of the logistic function with respect to this predictive density.

Unfotunately, this process is not analytically tractable. For example, the posterior density over $\mathbf{f}$ is not available in closed form for the logistic likelihood, and the expectation in the final step can also not be computed exactly. We therefore must resort to sampling, or approximations, or both.

8.3.3 The point estimate approximation

We will start with the simplest approximation possible – replacing each density with a single point estimate. In particular, for step 2:

$$p(f^*|\mathbf{x}^*, \mathbf{X}, \mathbf{t}) = \int p(f^*|\mathbf{f})p(\mathbf{f}|\mathbf{X}, \mathbf{t}) \, d\mathbf{f} \approx p(f^*|\hat{\mathbf{f}}, \mathbf{x}^*),$$

where $\hat{\mathbf{f}}$ is the *maximum a posteriori* (MAP) value of $\mathbf{f}$ (the value that maximises $p(\mathbf{f}|\mathbf{X}, \mathbf{t})$, see Chapter 4). Similarly for step 3:

$$P(t^* = 1|\mathbf{x}^*, \mathbf{X}, \mathbf{t}) = \int p(t^* = 1|f^*)p(f^*|\mathbf{x}^*, \mathbf{X}, \mathbf{t}) \, df^* \approx P(t^* = 1|\hat{f}^*),$$

where $\hat{f}^*$ is the value of f^* that maximises $p(f^*|\hat{\mathbf{f}}, \mathbf{x}^*)$.

As mentioned above, computing $p(\mathbf{f}|\mathbf{X}, \mathbf{t})$ is not analytically tractable due to the combination of the GP prior and the logistic likelihood. $\hat{\mathbf{f}}$ (the value that maximises $p(\mathbf{f}|\mathbf{X}, \mathbf{t})$) is also not immediately available. As in Chapter 4, we will find it using the Newton–Raphson numerical optimisation procedure. The process here is very similar to that used to find $\hat{\mathbf{w}}$ for the logistic regression model (see Section 4.3 and Comment 4.1).

The expression for $p(\mathbf{f}|\mathbf{X}, \mathbf{t})$ is given in Equation 8.11. As we are interested in finding the value of $\mathbf{f}$ that maximises this expression, we can ignore the denominator on the right hand side, as it is independent of $\mathbf{f}$. We can also (as with logistic regression) maximise $\log p(\mathbf{f}|\mathbf{X}, \mathbf{t})$ rather than $p(\mathbf{f}|\mathbf{X}, \mathbf{t})$. This leaves us with the following problem:

$$\hat{\mathbf{f}} = \underset{\mathbf{f}}{\text{argmax}} \ \log p(\mathbf{t}|\mathbf{f}) + \log p(\mathbf{f}|\mathbf{X}). \tag{8.12}$$

Using the shorthand $P_n = P(t_n = 1|f_n) = 1/(1 + \exp(-f_n))$, assuming a GP prior with zero mean and covariance matrix $\mathbf{C}$, and removing terms that do not include $\mathbf{f}$, this expression becomes

$$
\begin{aligned}
\hat{\mathbf{f}} &= \underset{\mathbf{f}}{\text{argmax}} \left[\sum_n \log \left(P_n^{t_n} (1 - P_n)^{1-t_n} \right) \right] - \frac{1}{2}\mathbf{f}^\mathsf{T}\mathbf{C}^{-1}\mathbf{f} \\
&= \underset{\mathbf{f}}{\text{argmax}} \left[\sum_n t_n \log P_n + (1 - t_n) \log(1 - P_n) \right] - \frac{1}{2}\mathbf{f}^\mathsf{T}\mathbf{C}^{-1}\mathbf{f} \quad (8.13) \\
&= \underset{\mathbf{f}}{\text{argmax}} \ g(\mathbf{f}).
\end{aligned}
$$

The Newton–Raphson approach maximises $\mathbf{f}$ by repeatedly applying the following update rule until convergence:

$$\mathbf{f}' = \mathbf{f} - \left(\frac{\partial^2 g(\mathbf{f})}{\partial \mathbf{f} \partial \mathbf{f}^\mathsf{T}} \right)^{-1} \frac{\partial g(\mathbf{f})}{\partial \mathbf{f}}, \tag{8.14}$$

i.e. we subtract the inverse of the matrix of second partial derivatives multiplied by the vector of first partial derivatives (both evaluated at the current estimate, $\mathbf{f}$). To compute these, we will need to compute the partial derivative of P_n with respect to f_n. Using the chain rule, this is

$$
\begin{aligned}
P_n &= \frac{1}{1 + \exp(-f_n)} \\
\frac{\partial P_n}{\partial f_n} &= -\frac{1}{(1 + \exp(-f_n))^2} \frac{\partial(1 + \exp(-f_n))}{\partial f_n} \\
&= \frac{\exp(-f_n)}{(1 + \exp(-f_n))^2} \\
&= \frac{1}{1 + \exp(-f_n)} \frac{\exp(-f_n)}{1 + \exp(-f_n)} \\
&= P_n(1 - P_n).
\end{aligned}
$$

From this expression, and further use of the chain rule, we can see that

$$
\frac{\partial \log P_n}{\partial f_n} = (1 - P_n), \quad \text{and} \quad \frac{\partial \log(1 - P_n)}{\partial f_n} = -P_n.
$$

Using these definitions, we can differentiate $g(\mathbf{f})$ with respect to $\mathbf{f}$ to give

$$
\frac{\partial g(\mathbf{f})}{\partial \mathbf{f}} = \mathbf{q} - \mathbf{C}^{-1}\mathbf{f}, \tag{8.15}
$$

where $\mathbf{q} = [q_1, \ldots, q_N]^{\mathsf{T}}$ and

$$
q_n = t_n(1 - P_n) - (1 - t_n)P_n = t_n - P_n.
$$

The matrix of second derivatives follows as

$$
\frac{\partial^2 g(\mathbf{f})}{\partial \mathbf{f} \partial \mathbf{f}^{\mathsf{T}}} = -\mathbf{P} - \mathbf{C}^{-1} \tag{8.16}
$$

where $\mathbf{P}$ is an $N \times N$ matrix where the nth diagonal element is $P_n(1 - P_n)$ and all off-diagonal elements are zero. The Newton–Raphson maximisation procedure is therefore

1. Start with an initial guess for $\mathbf{f}$.

2. Compute P_n for $n = 1 \ldots N$.

3. Compute the vector of first derivatives and the matrix of second derivatives, evaluated at the current value of $\mathbf{f}$, as described in Equations 8.15 and 8.16.

4. Compute $\mathbf{f}'$, as described in Equation 8.14.

5. Set $\mathbf{f} = \mathbf{f}'$ and either stop if converged or return to step 2.

Figure 8.19 shows a one-dimensional example of finding $\hat{\mathbf{f}}$ (MATLAB script: gpclass.m). In Figure 8.19(a) the circles represent the one-dimensional training data. The shading of the circle represents the class label (the first five points are in class 0 and the second five in class 1; note that the position of the points on the vertical axis is arbitrary). The crosses show the MAP approximation to $\mathbf{f}$, $\hat{\mathbf{f}}$. As we would expect, the MAP values are higher for points in class 1 than for those in class 0 (corresponding to high $P(t_n = 1)$ for points in class 1 and low $P(t_n = 1)$ for points in class 0). Figure 8.19(b) shows the evolution of $\mathbf{f}$ through the Newton–Raphson iterations. In this case, $\mathbf{f}$ was initialised to a vector of zeros, and it is clear that, after

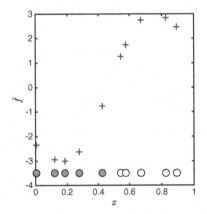

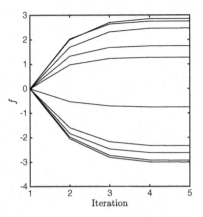

(a) Example binary data (circles; their position on the vertical axis has no meaning and their shading denotes their class label) and MAP estimate of **f** (crosses).

(b) Evolution of **f** through the Newton–Raphson procedure. **f** was initialised as a vector of zeros.

FIGURE 8.19 Example binary classification data and the MAP approximation of **f**.

five iterations, we have converged to a maximum. In this (and subsequent) examples, a zero-mean GP prior was used with an RBF covariance matrix with $\alpha = \gamma = 10$.

Now that we have $\hat{\mathbf{f}}$, we need to compute f^* for any test points of interest (collectively $\mathbf{f}^*$). This is nothing more than the noise-free GP regression that we saw earlier in the chapter with training targets $\hat{\mathbf{f}}$. Using the same notation as earlier in the chapter (see Section 8.2.2), $p(\mathbf{f}^*|\hat{\mathbf{f}})$ is given by Equation 8.3 as

$$p(\mathbf{f}^*|\hat{\mathbf{f}}) = \mathcal{N}(\boldsymbol{\mu}^*, \boldsymbol{\Sigma}^*) \tag{8.17}$$
$$\boldsymbol{\mu}^* = \mathbf{R}^\mathsf{T}\mathbf{C}^{-1}\hat{\mathbf{f}}, \qquad \boldsymbol{\Sigma}^* = \mathbf{C}^* - \mathbf{R}^\mathsf{T}\mathbf{C}^{-1}\mathbf{R}.$$

In our current approximation, we are interested in only a point MAP estimate for $\mathbf{f}^*$. Given that this is a Gaussian density, the MAP estimate is given by its mean:

$$\hat{\mathbf{f}^*} = \mathbf{R}^\mathsf{T}\mathbf{C}^{-1}\hat{\mathbf{f}}.$$

For illustration, we will use a large, finely spaced set of test values of x^* so that we can plot $\hat{\mathbf{f}^*}$ as a smooth curve. This is shown in Figure 8.20(a). As we would expect from a noise-free regression, the curve passes perfectly through the 'training' points ($\hat{\mathbf{f}}$) and is therefore high in areas of the input space corresponding to class 1 and low in areas corresponding to class 0.

The final stage in making predictions is converting $\hat{\mathbf{f}^*}$ into probabilities by passing the individual values through the logistic function. The result is shown in Figure 8.20(b), where we have also converted the training values ($\hat{\mathbf{f}}$) into probabilities (MATLAB script: `gpclass.m`). As expected, the probabilities are close to zero where

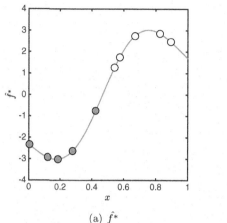

(a) $\hat{f}^*$

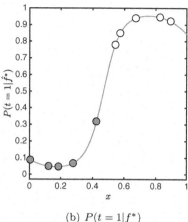

(b) $P(t = 1|\hat{f}^*)$

FIGURE 8.20 $\hat{f}^*$ and $P(t = 1|\hat{f}^*)$ for the illustrative binary example. The test points are 100 evenly spaced values between 0 and 1, allowing us to draw the predictions as a smooth function. Note that we have now plotted the training points at their respective values of $\hat{f}$ and $P(t = 1|f)$.

we have training data from class 0 and close to 1 where we have training data from class 1.

Before we move away from point estimates, it is helpful to look at an example with two-dimensional input data. The process is identical, but we just plot things slightly differently. The example can be seen in Figure 8.21. Note that in Figure 8.21(a) we have plotted the training data at $f = 0$ in the 3D plot (MATLAB script: gpclass2d.m).

8.3.4 Propagating uncertainty through the sigmoid

Given $\hat{\mathbf{f}}$, we use a noise-free GP regression to get the latent function at the test points, $\mathbf{f}^*$. We will now look at the effect of using the full distribution for $\mathbf{f}^*$ in our predictions, rather than the point estimate $\hat{\mathbf{f}}^*$. In essence, for a single test point, we would like to compute

$$P(t^* = 1|\mathbf{x}^*, \mathbf{X}, \hat{\mathbf{f}}) = \int P(t^* = 1|f^*)p(f^*|\mathbf{x}^*, \mathbf{X}, \hat{\mathbf{f}}) \, df^*, \qquad (8.18)$$

rather than the approximation used in the previous section,

$$P(t^* = 1|\mathbf{x}^*, \mathbf{X}, \hat{\mathbf{f}}) \approx P(t^* = 1|\hat{f}^*),$$

where $\hat{f}^*$ is the mean of $p(f^*|\mathbf{x}^*, \mathbf{X}, \hat{\mathbf{f}})$.

The first term in the integrand in Equation 8.18 is the logistic function, whilst

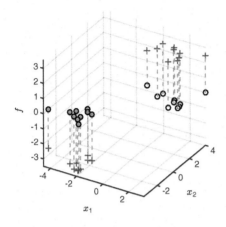

(a) Data and $\hat{\mathbf{f}}$ for a two-dimensional GP classification example. Data points are denoted by circles at $f = 0$ with their colour representing their class. The crosses show $\hat{\mathbf{f}}$ obtained via Newton–Raphson optimisation.

(b) Evolution of $\mathbf{f}$ through the Newton–Raphson procedure.

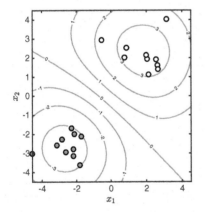

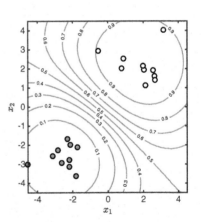

(c) Contours of f^*. The test points are places on a fine grid, enabling us to consider the predictions as a surface.

(d) Contours of $P(t = 1|f^*)$.

FIGURE 8.21 A GP binary classification example with two-dimensional input data.

the second is a Gaussian. Unfortunately, an analytical solution to this integral is not available, but it is easy to approximate through sampling. In particular, if $f^{*,1}, \ldots, f^{*,S}$ are S samples from $p(f^* | \mathbf{x}^*, \mathbf{X}, \hat{\mathbf{f}})$, we can approximate the integral as

$$P(t^* = 1 | \mathbf{x}^*, \mathbf{X}, \hat{\mathbf{f}}) \approx \frac{1}{S} \sum_{s=1}^{S} P(t^* = 1 | f^{*,s}) = \frac{1}{S} \sum_{s=1}^{S} \frac{1}{1 + \exp(-f^{*,s})}.$$

Conditioned on $\hat{\mathbf{f}}$, $\mathbf{f}^*$ for a set of test points is obtained via a noise-free GP regression. $p(\mathbf{f}^* | \mathbf{X}^*, \mathbf{X}, \hat{\mathbf{f}})$ is therefore given by (see Section 8.2.2)

$$p(\mathbf{f}^* | \hat{\mathbf{f}}) = \mathcal{N}(\boldsymbol{\mu}^*, \boldsymbol{\Sigma}^*)$$
$$\boldsymbol{\mu}^* = \mathbf{R}^\mathsf{T} \mathbf{C}^{-1} \hat{\mathbf{f}}, \qquad \boldsymbol{\Sigma}^* = \mathbf{C}^* - \mathbf{R}^\mathsf{T} \mathbf{C}^{-1} \mathbf{R}.$$

From this multivariate density, we can extract $p(f^* | \mathbf{x}^*, \mathbf{X}, \hat{\mathbf{f}})$ for each test point by extracting the relevant component of the mean vector and diagonal component of the covariance matrix (see Comment 8.1).

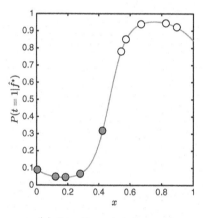

(a) One-dimensional example.

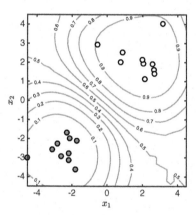

(b) Two-dimensional example.

FIGURE 8.22 The result of using a sampling approximation to solve the integral in Equation 8.18.

Returning to our one- and two-dimensional examples, approximating the integral with 10,000 samples results in the probability function and surface given in Figure 8.22. Comparing these to their point estimate counterpoint (Figures 8.20(b) and 8.21(d), respectively) we notice that they are almost identical, suggesting that, in this instance, the point approximation is not doing much harm.

8.3.5 The Laplace approximation

In the previous section we used a point approximation for $\mathbf{f}$ to overcome the fact that the posterior density was not analytically tractable. An alternative is to use an approximating distribution. In particular, we will use the Laplace approximation that we have already seen in Chapter 4 to approximate the posterior density over parameters for a logistic regression model. Recall that the Laplace approximation approximates a density with a Gaussian density. The mean of the Gaussian is placed at the mode of the density we are approximating, while the covariance matrix is set to the negative inverse Hessian matrix evaluated at the mode. We already have both of these objects, having needed them for the Newton–Raphson optimisation in the previous section.

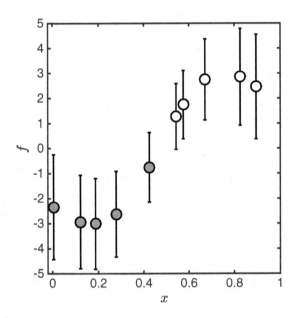

FIGURE 8.23 Visualisation of the Laplace approximation to the posterior. For each training point, we have plotted the posterior mean plus and minus the marginal posterior standard deviation.

Figure 8.23 visualises the Laplace approximation to the posterior $p(\mathbf{f}|\mathbf{X}, \mathbf{t})$. Recall that this distribution is N-dimensional (where N is the number of training points). For each training point, we have plotted the mean (with the circle, shaded according to class) and the marginal standard deviation (the square root of the diagonal element of the covariance matrix for this point). The bars are quite large – there is quite a lot of uncertainty in this distribution – however, there is still a clear separation between the points in each class.

In our original GP classification equation (Equation 8.10), $\mathbf{f}$ is marginalised from the model. As the Laplace is a Gaussian approximation, and this is then used in a noise-free GP regression, we can do this marginalisation analytically. To do this, we consider our approximate posterior over $\mathbf{f}$ as a GP prior for the regression, and continue as we did in Section 8.2.5. Using $\boldsymbol{\mu}_{\mathbf{f}}$ and $\boldsymbol{\Sigma}_{\mathbf{f}}$ to denote the mean and covariance of our Laplace approximation, this yields the following Gaussian density over the latent function at the test points:

$$p(\mathbf{f}^*|\mathbf{X}, \mathbf{t}, \mathbf{X}^*) \ = \ \mathcal{N}(\boldsymbol{\mu}^*, \boldsymbol{\Sigma}^*)$$
$$\boldsymbol{\mu}^* \ = \ \mathbf{R}^\mathsf{T} \mathbf{C}^{-1} \boldsymbol{\mu}_\mathbf{f}$$
$$\boldsymbol{\Sigma}^* \ = \ \mathbf{C}^* - \mathbf{R}^\mathsf{T} \mathbf{C}^{-1} \mathbf{R} + \mathbf{R}^\mathsf{T} \mathbf{C}^{-1} \boldsymbol{\Sigma}_\mathbf{f} \mathbf{C}^{-1} \mathbf{R}$$
$$\ = \ \mathbf{C}^* - \mathbf{R}^\mathsf{T} \mathbf{C}^{-1} \left[\mathbf{I} + \boldsymbol{\Sigma}_\mathbf{f} \mathbf{C}^{-1} \right] \mathbf{R}.$$

Samples from this distribution (grey lines) as well as the mean plus and minus one standard deviation can be seen in Figure 8.24. Also shown is the mean plus and minus one standard deviation of $\mathbf{f}$ (from Figure 8.23). We can see that the high variability in $\mathbf{f}$ produces similarly variable predictive functions.

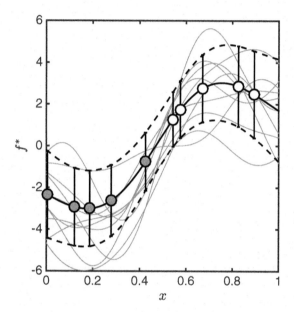

FIGURE 8.24 Mean (solid dark line), plus and minus one standard deviation (dashed line), and samples (grey lines) from the distribution over $\mathbf{f}^*$ obtained by marginalising $\mathbf{f}$.

If we pass each sampled function through the logistic function, we can also visualise the different predictive probabilities for each. This is shown for the both the one-dimensional and two-dimensional examples in Figure 8.25. For the one-dimensional example, we plot the predictive probability as a function of x for 10 samples of $\mathbf{f}^*$ whilst for the two-dimensional example, we plot the contour corresponding to a probability of 0.5 for three samples. In both cases, the probabilities are highly variable, but also seem to capture the essence of the problem. For example, the three contours in the two-dimensional example are very different, but all do a fairly good job of separating one class from the other.

Finally, in Figure 8.26, we plot the probability function obtained by averaging

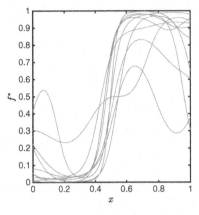

(a) One-dimensional example.

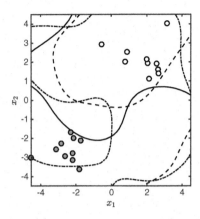

(b) Two-dimensional example.

FIGURE 8.25 Samples from $\mathbf{f}^*$ passed through the logistic function. In the two-dimensional example, we plot the contour corresponding to $P(t^* = 1|f^*) = 0.5$ in each case.

the result of passing 1000 samples through the logistic function (MATLAB script: gpclasslaplace.m). In the one-dimensional example we have also shown the original predictions (using the MAP approximation $\hat{\mathbf{f}}$), and it is clear that the additional uncertainty captured by the Laplace approximation has the effect of slightly pulling the predictive probabilities towards 0.5. This effect is even clearer in the two-dimensional example. Comparing Figure 8.26(b) with the MAP approximation in Figure 8.21(d), we can see that the MAP approximation gives much more confident predictions, particularly as we move away from the training data. We saw the exact same effect when comparing the Laplace approximation (and MCMC) with the MAP approximation for logistic regression (see Chapter 4).

8.3.6 Summary

In this section we have presented a quick tour of GP classification with both point parameter estimates and the Laplace approximation to the posterior. As you can see, it's a slightly more complex process that GP regression with Gaussian noise, but the end result is a powerful classifier that has been successfully used in many applications.

In our examples, we have stuck with the RBF covariance function. One of the strengths of the GP approach is that plugging in different covariance functions makes no difference to the computation – as with the SVM (see Chapter 5) we get many classifiers for the price of one!

Other inference techniques are possible. Amongst the references at the end of this chapter you will find an example of Variational Bayes being used and in Chapter 9 we will use GP classification as an example for an MCMC algorithm called Gibbs sampling.

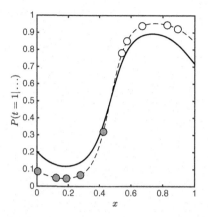

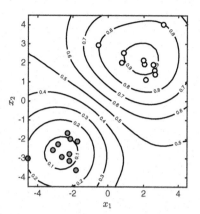

(a) One-dimensional example. Solid line shows the predictive probabilities from the full Laplace approximation. Dashed line shows the probabilities for predictions when we used the MAP point estimate for **f**.

(b) Two-dimensional example.

FIGURE 8.26 Predictive probabilities for the full Laplace approximation where **f** is marginalised.

We will now briefly look at how the hyperparameters within the covariance function can be estimated before wrapping the chapter up with some pointers to some other interesting extensions to the standard GPs that we have presented here.

8.4 HYPERPARAMETER OPTIMISATION

All of the covariance functions we have seen require parameters to be set (α, γ, u, etc.). These parameters are known as hyperparameters, to distinguish them from standard model parameters (e.g. the **w** in logistic regression). In previous chapters we have used empirical methods (e.g. cross-validation) to set unknown model parameters, and the same could be done here. However, when working with GPs, there is another method that can be used: setting the parameters by maximising the *marginal likelihood*.

Consider the noisy GP regression model:

$$y_n = f_n + \epsilon, \ \mathbf{f} \sim \mathcal{N}(\mathbf{0}, \mathbf{C}), \ \epsilon \sim \mathcal{N}(0, \sigma^2).$$

Integrating over **f** allows us to compute the log marginal likelihood of all N observations, **y** conditioned only on the data **X**, the noise variance σ^2, and any hyperparameters in the covariance function:

$$
\begin{aligned}
\log p(\mathbf{y}|\mathbf{X}, \sigma^2) &= \log \int \mathcal{N}(\mathbf{y}|\mathbf{f}, \sigma^2 \mathbf{I}_N) \mathcal{N}(\mathbf{f}|\mathbf{0}, \mathbf{C}) \, d\mathbf{f} \\
&= -\frac{N}{2} \log 2\pi - \frac{1}{2} \log |\mathbf{C} + \sigma^2 \mathbf{I}_N| - \frac{1}{2} \mathbf{y}^\top (\mathbf{C} + \sigma^2 \mathbf{I}_N)^{-1} \mathbf{y}.
\end{aligned}
$$

Figure 8.27 shows an example of using the marginal likelihood to optimise hyperparameters (MATLAB script: gphyper.m). Figure 8.27(a) shows some data drawn from a noisy GP regression with an RBF covariance with $\gamma = 5$ and $\sigma^2 = 0.05$ ($\alpha = 1$ is assumed fixed throughout). Figure 8.27(b) shows how the log marginal likelihood varies as γ and σ^2 are varied on a log scale. On the plot we have highlighted four points – the true values (True), the values that maximise the log marginal likelihood (Max) and two others, A and B. In Figure 8.27(c) we show the mean predictive functions corresponding to these four sets of parameters. The parameters that maximise the marginal likelihood are fairly close to the true values, resulting in fairly similar predictive functions that pass close to the true values of the functions at the training points (white circles). Note that the predictive function at the true parameter values will typically not be identical to the true function as the dataset is corrupted with random noise.

The contours in Figure 8.27(b) highlight a relationship between γ and σ^2. If we decrease γ, we reduce the complexity (curvature) of the model, forcing the GP to increase the noise variance to attempt to explain the data. This is demonstrated by point B, which can be seen in Figure 8.27(c) to correspond to a fairly flat function. The function doesn't capture much of the true variability in the data and hence σ^2 is increased (note that the axis in Figure 8.27(b) has a log scale, so that σ^2 at B is approximately double the true value). At the other end, point A corresponds to a more complex function (see Figure 8.27(c)). As the function is more complex, it can get closer to the training data and therefore tolerate smaller values of σ^2.

At both points A and B, the marginal likelihood is lower than it is at the true values, showing that the marginal likelihood penalises both under- and over-fitting. However, in travelling from B to the true values to A, the marginal likelihood changes fairly slowly (they all represent models that are OK). Towards the other corners of the plot the likelihood changes more rapidly. As we move towards the top right, the models become more complex and the noise variance becomes larger. Such complexity is unnecessary to explain this data and Bayesian methods naturally penalise excessive complexity. Moving towards the bottom left is where the likelihood drops most rapidly. This area corresponds to simple models with low noise – models that are clearly inappropriate for this data.

The marginal likelihood is a useful quantity to maximise when choosing GP hyperparameters. Unlike cross-validation, it is able to use all of the data at once (not requiring it to be split into training and test sets). It is also able to penalise under- and over-fitting as it does not monotonically increase with model complexity (as standard likelihood did for our linear model in Chapter 2). In practice, one doesn't perform a search over parameter values as done here. Instead, it is common to use numerical optimisation to find the values that maximise the log marginal likelihood. For many covariance functions, it is possible to compute the derivatives of the log marginal likelihood with respect to the covariance parameters, and gradient-based optimisers can be used. It is also not restricted to regression models – marginal likelihood optimisation can be used on any GP model. For more details on optimising marginal likelihoods, see the references at the end of this chapter.

8.5   EXTENSIONS

Finally, we will briefly point to some extensions to the standard GP models we have seen in this chapter. More details can be found in the references at the end of the chapter.

8.5.1   Non-zero mean

All of our GP models have involved assuming a GP prior with zero mean function. It is straightforward to extend this to a non-zero mean and we leave the derivation for the predictive distributions to the reader.

8.5.2   Multiclass classification

Various multiclass GP classifiers have been proposed. These typically fit one latent regression function per class and use the *softmax* function (a multiclass generalisation of the logistic function) to squash the latent functions into probabilities. The latent function for a particular class ought to be high in areas of the input space where there is a high density of examples in this class, and low elsewhere. As with the binary case, inference of the posterior over the latent functions is analytically intractable, requiring approximations (e.g. Laplace) or sampling. One interesting feature of multiclass GP classifiers is that one can use different covariance functions (or different hyperparameters) for the different functions.

8.5.3   Other likelihood functions and models

GPs are not restricted to classification and regression likelihoods. For example, integer count data can be modelled using a continuous GP latent function and a Poisson likelihood (see Exercise 8.4), robust regression (regression less susceptible to outliers) can be performed using likelihood functions with heavier tails than the Gaussian (e.g. the Student-T distribution) and ordinal regression can be achieved by using a combination of probit (see Chapter 7) functions. Again, inference in these models is not analytically tractable, requiring approximation or sampling schemes.

8.5.4   Other inference schemes

In this chapter we used the Laplace approximation when the posterior over $\mathbf{f}$ wasn't available analytically (in binary classification). Other approximate schemes can also be used. Common alternatives include Variational Bayes (as seen in Chapter 7) and **Expectation propagation** (EP). Sampling is also an option. For example, in the binary classification example, Metropolis–Hastings could be used to sample values of $\mathbf{f}$ from $p(\mathbf{f}|\mathbf{X}, \mathbf{t})$. For each sample, a GP regression could be done to give a predictive density for $\mathbf{f}^*$ from which predictive probabilities can be computed. These probabilities would then be averaged over all samples generated from $p(\mathbf{f}|\mathbf{X}, \mathbf{t})$ (see Exercise 8.5).

8.6 CHAPTER SUMMARY

In this chapter we have given a quick tour of GP models for regression and classification. GPs have become very popular within Machine Learning in the last few years. The ability to fit complex functions without having to specify a parametric form has obvious advantages, as does their probabilistic nature.

When a Gaussian likelihood is used for regression, GP inference is straightforward, requiring little more than some standard matrix manipulation. When we require a non-Gaussian likelihood (for, e.g. classification) things get a bit more complex, but not dauntingly so. GP classifiers offer a useful probabilistic alternative to non-probabilistic methods such as support vector machines (SVMs; see Chapter 5).

The references below will serve as a useful starting point to begin exploring the vast research literature that makes use of GPs for regression and classification, as well as ordinal regression and projection.

8.7 EXERCISES

8.1 Write some code to sample from a GP prior. In particular, define some one-dimensional input points (x), compute the covariance matrix by computing the covariance function at all pairs of points in x and then sample from the multivariate Gaussian with zero mean and covariance equal to the covariance matrix. Vary the covariance function and its associated parameters. Note that occasionally you may find that you cannot sample, as your covariance matrix is singular. When this happens, add a small constant to the diagonal elements of the matrix.

8.2 Using your code from the previous question, experiment with what happens if you combine a linear covariance function with an RBF covariance function using the weighted combination given in Equation 8.9. What kind of functions do you expect? Experiment with the weights, α_j, and the covariance parameters.

8.3 Use a numerical optimisation routine to find the values of σ^2 and γ that maximise the marginal likelihood for GP regression using an RBF covariance matrix (with $\alpha = 1$). Use data generated from a GP. How close are the optimised parameters to their true values?

8.4 For some one-dimensional input data (x), generate a real-valued latent function using a GP prior with an RBF covariance function. For each value, sample a random integer from a Poisson distribution with rate $\lambda = \exp(f)$, i.e. the probability of getting the value z is equal to

$$P(z) = \frac{\lambda^z \exp(-\lambda)}{z!}$$

From this data, we would like to reverse-engineer the latent function. Compute the gradient and Hessian required to find the MAP solution to $\mathbf{f}$ and compare the inferred value to the true value from which the data were generated.

8.5 Use Metropolis–Hastings to perform inference in the binary GP classifier. The MH sampler should repeatedly resample values of $\mathbf{f}$. For each sample, do a noise-free regression to compute f^* and then feed this through the logistic function to get a probability sample.

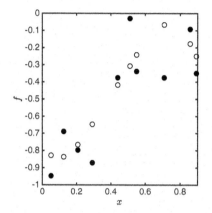

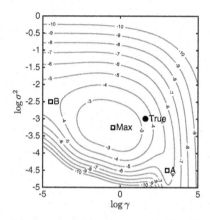

(a) True function values (white circles) and noisy training examples (black circles).

(b) Contours of the log marginal likelihood as the hyperparameters are varied.

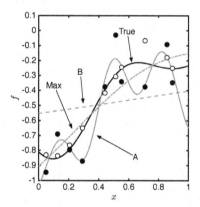

(c) Predictive functions with various sets of hyperparameters.

FIGURE 8.27 Example of choosing hyperparameters by optimising the marginal likelihood. Note that the predictive function with the true parameters (black line in (c)) is not necessarily the same as the *true* function.

8.8 FURTHER READING

[1] Wei Chu and Zoubin Ghahramani. Gaussian processes for ordinal regression. *Journal of Machine Learning Research*, 6:1019–1041, 2005.

An example of a Gaussian process being used for ordinal regression (classification with ordered classes).

[2] Lehel Csató and Manfred Opper. Sparse representation for Gaussian Process models. In T. K. Leen, T. G. Dietterich, and V. Tresp, editors, *Advances in Neural Information Processing Systems 13*, pages 444–450. MIT Press, 2001.

GPs at their heart, require the inversion of an $N \times N$ covariance matrix. This can become computationally challenging as N increases. In this paper, a sparse approach is proposed whereby unnecessary training points are not used, thus decreasing the computational burden.

[3] Mark Girolami and Simon Rogers. Variational Bayesian multinomial probit regression with Gaussian process priors. *Neural Computation*, 18(8):1790–1817, 2006.

A multi-class GP classification method that uses Variational Bayes inference and a multiclass probit likelihood.

[4] Neil Lawrence. Gaussian process latent variable models for visualisation of high dimensional data. In *Proceedings of the 2004 conference on Advances in neural information processing systems*. The MIT Press, 2004.

Using GPs as a prior over mappings from a latent space to the observed space, much like PCA.

[5] Carl Rasmussen and Christopher Williams. *Gaussian Processes for Machine Learning*. The MIT Press, 2006.

This book provides a comprehensive introduction to the use of Gaussian processes, including a detailed discussion of the different covariance functions available and inference schemes. The associated MATLAB code is very useful, providing a wide range of functionality.

CHAPTER 9

Markov Chain Monte Carlo Sampling

In Chapter 4 we saw that, for logistic regression, it was not possible to analytically obtain the posterior density over the model parameters. We described how to overcome this problem with three alternatives: the MAP solution (a point estimate of the parameters that maximises the posterior), the Laplace approximation (where the posterior is approximated with a Gaussian density) and sampling from the posterior using the Metropolis–Hastings algorithm.

Unfortunately, this situation is not exceptional. The relatively small number of conjugate prior and likelihood pairs means that, in many applications, we will not be able to get an analytical expression for the posterior.

When compared with point estimates and approximations, sampling methods (such as Metropolis–Hastings) have the benefit of providing samples from the true posterior at the expense of more computational work. As computational power has become less of an issue, sampling methods have increased in popularity across many machine learning applications.

For this reason, we feel that our brief introduction to Metropolis–Hastings in Chapter 4 is insufficient, and sampling methods require a chapter all to themselves. We will start by introducing a common alternative to Metropolis–Hastings: Gibbs sampling. Gibbs sampling is very popular, possibly due to the lack of user-tunable parameters, but is restricted to problems where the conditional distribution of each parameter (conditioned on values for all others) is available. After Gibbs, we will spend a little time looking at the theory behind Markov chain Monte Carlo (MCMC) techniques.

Unfortunately, although these methods are often quite easy to implement, getting them to work properly is quite another matter, and we devote a section to some MCMC practicalities. Finally, we will conclude the chapter with a quick tour of a few of the more advanced sampling algorithms that are currently found within machine learning.

9.1 GIBBS SAMPLING

Our motivation for sampling has been cases where we cannot obtain an analytical expression for the posterior density over parameters for a Bayesian model. The samples that we draw can be used to compute the expectations involved in our ultimate goal – making predictions. For the logistic regression model described in Chapter 4, we could compute something proportional to the posterior – the prior multiplied by the likelihood – but could not normalise it. Metropolis–Hastings was appropriate because we only ever required the ratio of the posterior value for two different parameter values, and in the ratio the normalising constant canceled.

In some cases, we cannot compute the posterior but we can compute the conditional densities of each parameter conditioned on the others. For example, consider a model with M parameters $\boldsymbol{\theta} = [\theta_1, \ldots, \theta_M]^\mathsf{T}$. If we observe some data $\mathbf{X}$, the posterior is given by

$$p(\boldsymbol{\theta}|\mathbf{X}) = \frac{p(\mathbf{X}|\boldsymbol{\theta})p(\boldsymbol{\theta})}{p(\mathbf{X})},$$

which we assume that we cannot compute. However, we *can* compute the conditional densities for each parameter conditioned on values for all of the other parameters:

$$p(\theta_1|\theta_2, \ldots, \theta_N, \mathbf{X})$$
$$p(\theta_2|\theta_1, \theta_3, \ldots, \theta_N, \mathbf{X})$$
$$\vdots$$
$$p(\theta_N|\theta_1, \ldots, \theta_{N-1}, \mathbf{X}).$$

This might appear to be an unlikely situation – computing all of these things looks harder than computing the posterior itself! But in many cases the conditional distributions are straightforward to compute and sample from even when the posterior is inaccessible. In these situations Gibbs sampling can be used.

Armed with the conditional distributions, **Gibbs sampling** is very straightforward. For notational convenience, we will assume we are sampling from $p(\boldsymbol{\theta})$ and drop the dependence on $\mathbf{X}$. We start with a guess of the values of the parameters, $\boldsymbol{\theta}^0 = [\theta_1^0, \ldots, \theta_M^0]^\mathsf{T}$. When using Gibbs sampling to sample from a posterior over parameters, a sample from the prior would be sensible. We then resample each parameter conditioned on the most recent values of all other parameters. Assuming we go through the parameters in numerical order (we don't have to but it makes it easier to draw), this process is depicted in Figure 9.1. We start by sampling a new value for θ_1 (θ_1^1). The most recent values of all of the other parameters are $\theta_2^0, \ldots, \theta_M^0$ and so we condition on these. Now we move to θ_2. The most recent value of θ_1 is now θ_1^1 and the most recent values of the other parameters are $\theta_3^0, \ldots, \theta_M^0$ so we condition on $\theta_1^1, \theta_3^0, \ldots, \theta_M^0$. We continue until we have resampled all M parameters, at which point the most recent values will be $\boldsymbol{\theta}^1 = [\theta_1^1, \ldots, \theta_M^1]$. $\boldsymbol{\theta}^1$ represents our first sample from $p(\boldsymbol{\theta})$. The process is now repeated as many times as we wish to draw samples. We call each loop through all of the individual parameters a cycle and each cycle produces one sample from $p(\boldsymbol{\theta})$.

We will illustrate Gibbs sampling by demonstrating how it can be used to sample from a two-dimensional Gaussian (MATLAB script: `gibbsgauss.m`). Clearly, we can sample from multivariate Gaussians directly (we did it a lot when dealing with Gaussian processes in Chapter 8) but it helps to illustrate the concept of Gibbs

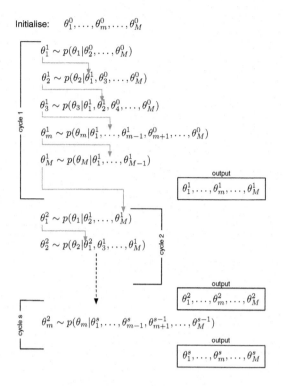

Initialise: $\theta_1^0, \ldots, \theta_m^0, \ldots, \theta_M^0$

$\theta_1^1 \sim p(\theta_1 | \theta_2^0, \ldots, \theta_M^0)$

$\theta_2^1 \sim p(\theta_2 | \theta_1^1, \theta_3^0, \ldots, \theta_M^0)$

$\theta_3^1 \sim p(\theta_3 | \theta_1^1, \theta_2^1, \theta_4^0, \ldots, \theta_M^0)$

$\theta_m^1 \sim p(\theta_m | \theta_1^1, \ldots, \theta_{m-1}^1, \theta_{m+1}^0, \ldots, \theta_M^0)$

$\theta_M^1 \sim p(\theta_M | \theta_1^1, \ldots, \theta_{M-1}^1)$

cycle 1

output

$\theta_1^1, \ldots, \theta_m^1, \ldots, \theta_M^1$

$\theta_1^2 \sim p(\theta_1 | \theta_2^1, \ldots, \theta_M^1)$

$\theta_2^2 \sim p(\theta_2 | \theta_1^2, \theta_3^1, \ldots, \theta_M^1)$

cycle 2

output

$\theta_1^2, \ldots, \theta_m^2, \ldots, \theta_M^2$

cycle s

$\theta_m^2 \sim p(\theta_m | \theta_1^s, \ldots, \theta_{m-1}^s, \theta_{m+1}^{s-1}, \ldots, \theta_M^{s-1})$

output

$\theta_1^s, \ldots, \theta_m^s, \ldots, \theta_M^s$

FIGURE 9.1 A schematic of the Gibbs sampling process. Parameters are repeatedly resampled conditioned on the current values of all other parameters.

sampling before we progress to something more realistic where direct sampling is not an option.

Consider the Gaussian shown shown in Figure 9.2. It has mean and covariance given by

$$\boldsymbol{\mu} = \begin{bmatrix} 1 \\ 2 \end{bmatrix} \quad \boldsymbol{\Sigma} = \begin{bmatrix} 1 & 0.8 \\ 0.8 & 2 \end{bmatrix}. \tag{9.1}$$

Because this is a Gaussian density, we can analytically obtain the conditional densities for x_1 (conditioned on x_2) and x_2 conditioned on x_1 (see Comment 8.2):

$$p(x_1 | x_2, \boldsymbol{\mu}, \boldsymbol{\Sigma}) = \mathcal{N}(\mu_1, \sigma_1^2) \tag{9.2}$$

$$\mu_1 = 1 + \frac{0.8}{2}(x_2 - 2) \qquad \sigma_1^2 = 1 - \frac{0.8^2}{2}$$

$$p(x_2 | x_1, \boldsymbol{\mu}, \boldsymbol{\Sigma}) = \mathcal{N}(\mu_2, \sigma_2^2) \tag{9.3}$$

$$\mu_2 = 1 + \frac{0.8}{1}(x_1 - 1) \qquad \sigma_1^2 = 2 - \frac{0.8^2}{1}$$

We start with the guesses of our two parameters, θ_1^0 and θ_2^0. We then resample

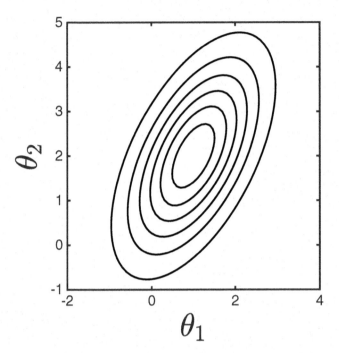

FIGURE 9.2 A 2D Gaussian density.

each parameter in turn, conditioning on the current value of the other parameters. So we first sample a new value for θ_1 (θ_1^1) by conditioning on $\theta_2 = \theta_2^0$. Then we sample θ_2 (θ_2^1) by conditioning on $\theta_1 = x_1^1$. θ_1 is then resampled to give θ_1^2 by conditioning on $\theta_2 = \theta_2^1$, etc. Once we are confident that the effects of the random initialisation have been removed (more on this later), the samples, θ_1^s, θ_2^s are samples from $p(\theta_1, \theta_2|\boldsymbol{\mu}, \boldsymbol{\Sigma})$. Note that the order in which the parameters are updated doesn't matter, as long as every sample is conditioned on the most recent values of all other parameters. In practice, we often randomise the order of parameters in each cycle.

Figure 9.3 shows Gibbs sampling in action for our 2D Gaussian example where the required conditional densities are given in Equations 9.2 and 9.3 (MATLAB script: gibbs_gaussian.m). We start with an initial guess, $\boldsymbol{\theta}^0 = [-1.5, 4]^\mathsf{T}$ (shown by the open circle). In the first step, we sample a new value of θ_1 from Equation 9.2, shown by the small solid circle. Based on this new value for θ_1, we sample a new value of θ_2 using Equation 9.3. This is one cycle of the sampler and we have transitioned from our initial value $\boldsymbol{\theta}^0$ to a new value $\boldsymbol{\theta}^1$. In Figure 9.3(d) we see the effect of 2 cycles (4 updates; 2 for each parameter) and in Figures 9.3(e) and 9.3(f) the state after 5 and 100 cycles, respectively. Visually, the samples look like they are coming from the full 2-dimensional Gaussian (shown by the contours). To check more objectively, we can calculate the mean and covariance of the samples, and compare

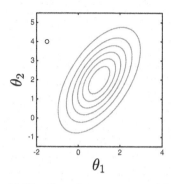

(a) The Gaussian contours and initial value, $\mathbf{x}^0$.

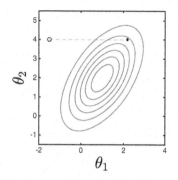

(b) θ_1 is updated by sampling from $p(\theta_1|\theta_2^0,\ldots)$ to give θ_1^1.

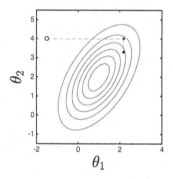

(c) θ_2 is updated by sampling from $p(\theta_2|\theta_1^1,\ldots)$ to give θ_2^1.

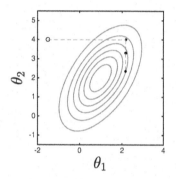

(d) The first two full cycles of the sampler.

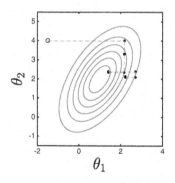

(e) The first five full cycles.

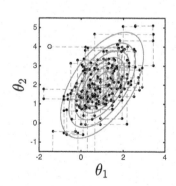

(f) The first 100 full cycles.

FIGURE 9.3 Gibbs sampling from a 2D Gaussian.

them with the true values. After 100 samples, the sample mean and covariance are

$$\mu^{100} = \begin{bmatrix} 0.93 \\ 2.11 \end{bmatrix} \quad \Sigma^{100} = \begin{bmatrix} 0.92 & 0.74 \\ 0.74 & 2.30 \end{bmatrix}.$$

These are similar to the true values given in Equation 9.1. Are they close enough? It's hard to say, but, if the scheme is working, we ought to get closer to the true values the more samples we take. Below are the values after 1000 samples, which are now much closer to the true values.

$$\mu^{1000} = \begin{bmatrix} 0.95 \\ 1.92 \end{bmatrix} \quad \Sigma^{1000} = \begin{bmatrix} 1.00 & 0.80 \\ 0.80 & 2.05 \end{bmatrix}.$$

As well as samples from the joint distribution, if we only look at the samples generated for θ_1 (or θ_2), we have samples from the marginal density $p(\theta_1)$ (or $p(\theta_2)$). This is a useful property that we will use in the following, more realistic example (see Exercise 9.1).

9.2 EXAMPLE: GIBBS SAMPLING FOR GP CLASSIFICATION

The two-dimensional Gaussian is a nice density to introduce Gibbs sampling, but we could, if we wanted to, sample from the Gaussian directly. We will now look at a more realistic example where we cannot directly sample from the distribution of interest but do have access to all of the conditionals.

The example we will use is binary Gaussian process (GP) classification using a probit likelihood function. GP classification was introduced in Chapter 8, where we used point and Laplace approximations to overcome the non-conjugacy of the GP prior and the logistic likelihood. Here we will swap the logistic likelihood for the probit likelihood and demonstrate how, using the auxiliary variable trick introduced in Chapter 7, we can perform inference using Gibbs sampling.

Assume that we observe N training examples, each consisting of a one-dimensional observation x_n and a binary target value $t_n \in \{0, 1\}$ (extension to multivariate input data is straightforward). We assume that the observed targets were generated by pushing a real value (f_n) through a squashing function to give a probability and then sampling a value of 1 or 0 according to this probability. Rather than the logistic squashing function used in Chapter 8, we will use the probit function (see Section 7.7)

$$P(t_n = 1|f_n) = \phi(f_n) = \int_{-\infty}^{f_n} \mathcal{N}(y|0,1) \, dy,$$

which is the probability that a random variable from a standard Gaussian density is below f_n.

Recall from Chapter 8 that performing GP classification has three steps:

1. computing the posterior density over the latent function (f_n),

2. using this posterior to perform a GP regression to predict the function values at test points,

3. pushing the predicted latent function values through the squashing function to produce predictive posteriors.

Placing all of the observations $x_1, \ldots, x_N$ into $\mathbf{X}$, all of the labels t_n into $\mathbf{t}$ and the N latent function values f_n into $\mathbf{f}$, we can begin to think about a sampling scheme. Using the superscript $*$ to denote predictive quantities, here is one possible cycle (that would be repeated S times to generate S samples):

- Sample $\mathbf{f}^s$ from $p(\mathbf{f}|\mathbf{t}, \mathbf{X})$ (sample from the posterior density over the latent function).

- Sample $\mathbf{f}^{*,s}$ from a GP regression based on $\mathbf{f}^s$.

- Sample $\mathbf{t}^{*,s}$ from the probabilities provided by squashing $\mathbf{f}^{*,s}$ through the probit function.

The final predictive probabilities could then be computed by averaging over the S values of $\mathbf{t}^{*,s}$, i.e., for each test point, the probability that it is in class 1 is the proportion of samples its t^* value was equal to 1 and not 0.

The problem with this scheme lies in the first step which requires samples from the posterior over the latent function values. We cannot sample from this density directly because of the non-conjugacy of the GP prior and the probit likelihood. However, using the same scheme that is introduced in Section 7.7, we can introduce a set of auxiliary variables, $\mathbf{y}$, that sit between the latent function and the labels such that we can sample directly from the conditional densities $p(\mathbf{y}|\mathbf{f}, \mathbf{t})$ and $p(\mathbf{f}|\mathbf{y}, \mathbf{X})$ and obtain the samples of $\mathbf{f}$ as required.

To do this, we first rearrange the probit likelihood:

$$
\begin{aligned}
P(t_n = 1|f_n) &= \int_{-\infty}^{f_n} \mathcal{N}(y|0, 1) \, dy \\
&= \int_{-\infty}^{0} \mathcal{N}(y| - f_n, 1) \, dy \\
&= \int_{0}^{\infty} \mathcal{N}(y|f_n, 1) \, dy \\
&= \int_{-\infty}^{\infty} \delta(y > 0)\mathcal{N}(y|f_n, 1) \, dy, \quad (9.4)
\end{aligned}
$$

where $\delta(y > 0)$ is 1 if $y > 0$ and 0 otherwise. Now, consider the following model:

$$
\begin{aligned}
P(t_n = 1|y_n) &= \delta(y_n > 0) \\
p(y_n|f_n) &= \mathcal{N}(y_n|f_n, 1) \\
p(t_n = 1, y_n|f_n) &= \delta(y_n > 0)\mathcal{N}(y_n|f_n, 1). \quad (9.5)
\end{aligned}
$$

The probit likelihood is therefore equivalent to this extended model with the y_n variables integrated out (Equation 9.4 is just Equation 9.5 integrated over all possible values of y).

As with the probabilistic PCA model in Section 7.7, if we keep the auxiliary variables (y_n) in the model, inference becomes more straightforward. In the PCA example, it enabled us to perform Variational Bayes inference, and in this case it will allow us to use Gibbs sampling. The final definition we need is $P(t_n = 0|y_n)$. Because $P(t_n = 0|y_n) + P(t_n = 1|y_n) = 1$, this has to be equal to $\delta(y_n < 0)$.

Our Gibbs sampling procedure becomes

- Sample $\mathbf{y}^s$ from $p(\mathbf{y}|\mathbf{f}^{s-1}, \mathbf{t})$

- Sample $\mathbf{f}^s$ from $p(\mathbf{f}|\mathbf{y}^s, \mathbf{X})$
- Sample $\mathbf{f}^{*,s}$ from a GP regression based on $\mathbf{f}^s$
- Sample $\mathbf{t}^{*,s}$ from the probabilities provided by squashing $\mathbf{f}^{*,s}$ through a probit function,

and compute the final predictive probabilities by averaging over the $\mathbf{t}^{*,s}$. Note that we could make the predictions by sampling auxiliary variables for the test points, $\mathbf{y}^*$, and then assigning the elements of $\mathbf{t}^*$ depending on whether the particular components of y^* are positive or negative. That is, for each test point, we sample from $\mathcal{N}(y^*|f^{*,s}, 1)$ and then assign $t^{*,s} = 1$ if $y^* > 0$ and $t^{*,s} = 0$ otherwise. The two procedures are identical for exactly the reason we can perform the auxiliary variable trick in the first place – as far as t is concerned, the two processes (marginalising y or not) are statistically identical.

The inclusion of the auxiliary variables $\mathbf{y}$ has allowed us to use Gibbs sampling to sample from the joint density $p(\mathbf{f}, \mathbf{y}|\mathbf{X}, \mathbf{t})$ by repeatedly sampling $\mathbf{f}$ conditioned on $\mathbf{y}$ and $\mathbf{y}$ conditioned on $\mathbf{f}$. Recall that, in the last section, we claimed that, if we only look at the samples generated for one of the parameters, these are samples from the marginal density of that parameter. In this example, the marginal density for $\mathbf{f}$ is

$$\int p(\mathbf{f}, \mathbf{y}|\mathbf{t}, \mathbf{X}) \, d\mathbf{y} = p(\mathbf{f}|\mathbf{X}, \mathbf{t}),$$

which is exactly the posterior density we wished to sample from. In other words, the inclusion of the additional variables now enables us to generate samples from the original posterior density over $\mathbf{f}$.

9.2.1 Conditional densities for GP classification via Gibbs sampling

The joint posterior density over $\mathbf{f}$ and $\mathbf{y}$ is given by

$$p(\mathbf{f}, \mathbf{y}|\mathbf{t}, \mathbf{X}) = \frac{p(\mathbf{t}|\mathbf{y})p(\mathbf{y}|\mathbf{f})p(\mathbf{f}|\mathbf{X})}{p(\mathbf{t}|\mathbf{X})}.$$

We will use Gibbs sampling to sample from this density and therefore need conditional densities for each parameter (or set of parameters) conditioned on the others. Note that we will consider $\mathbf{f}$ as one parameter (we could obtain Gibbs conditionals for all of the individual components conditioned on all others but this isn't necessary) but will consider each element of $\mathbf{y}$ separately (out of necessity). The two densities that we need are therefore $p(\mathbf{f}|\mathbf{y}, \mathbf{X})$ and $p(\mathbf{y}|\mathbf{f}, \mathbf{X})$ which, because we assume that the elements of $\mathbf{y}$ are independent conditioned on $\mathbf{f}$ can be factored into N one-dimensional densities, $p(y_n|t_n, f_n)$.

Consider the identity

$$p(a|b) = \frac{p(a, b)}{p(b)},$$

which comes from the fact that $p(a, b) = p(a|b)p(b)$. Now, the denominator on the right hand side does not involve a, so we can say that $p(a|b) \propto p(a, b)$ – the conditional density is proportional to the joint density. Returning to the joint density of interest

$$p(\mathbf{f}|\mathbf{y}, \mathbf{t}, \mathbf{X}) \propto p(\mathbf{f}, \mathbf{y}|\mathbf{t}, \mathbf{X}) = \frac{p(\mathbf{t}|\mathbf{y})p(\mathbf{y}|\mathbf{f})p(\mathbf{f}|\mathbf{X})}{p(\mathbf{t}|\mathbf{X})}$$
$$\propto p(\mathbf{t}|\mathbf{y})p(\mathbf{y}|\mathbf{f})p(\mathbf{f}|\mathbf{X})$$
$$\propto p(\mathbf{y}|\mathbf{f})p(\mathbf{f}|\mathbf{X}),$$

where at each stage we have removed terms that do not depend on $\mathbf{f}$. This final expression looks familiar – the distribution of interest is proportional to a prior ($p(\mathbf{f}|\mathbf{X})$) multiplied by a likelihood ($p(\mathbf{y}|\mathbf{f})$) – Bayes' rule! In the case of $\mathbf{f}$, the prior is Gaussian (it is a GP prior) and the likelihood is also Gaussian

$$p(y_n|f_n) = \mathcal{N}(f_n, 1), \quad \text{and therefore} \quad p(\mathbf{y}|\mathbf{f}) = \mathcal{N}(\mathbf{f}, \mathbf{I}),$$

so the conditional distribution we are trying to compute must be Gaussian too. To compute the mean and covariance of this Gaussian, we equate the coefficients of $\mathbf{f}$, exactly as we did for $\mathbf{w}$ when computing the posterior distribution over parameters for the model of the Olympic data in Section 3.8:

$$\mathcal{N}(\mathbf{f}|\boldsymbol{\mu}_\mathbf{f}, \boldsymbol{\Sigma}_\mathbf{f}) \propto \mathcal{N}(\mathbf{y}|\mathbf{f}, \mathbf{I})\mathcal{N}(\mathbf{f}|\mathbf{0}, \mathbf{C})$$
$$\exp\left\{-\frac{1}{2}(\mathbf{f} - \boldsymbol{\mu}_\mathbf{f})^\mathsf{T}\boldsymbol{\Sigma}_\mathbf{f}^{-1}(\mathbf{f} - \boldsymbol{\mu}_\mathbf{f})\right\} \propto \exp\left\{-\frac{1}{2}(\mathbf{y} - \mathbf{f})^\mathsf{T}\mathbf{I}(\mathbf{y} - \mathbf{f}) - \frac{1}{2}\mathbf{f}^\mathsf{T}\mathbf{C}^{-1}\mathbf{f}\right\}$$
$$\mathbf{f}^\mathsf{T}\boldsymbol{\Sigma}_\mathbf{f}^{-1}\mathbf{f} = \mathbf{f}^\mathsf{T}\left[\mathbf{C}^{-1} + \mathbf{I}\right]\mathbf{f}$$
$$\boldsymbol{\Sigma}_\mathbf{f} = \left[\mathbf{C}^{-1} + \mathbf{I}\right]^{-1}$$
$$\mathbf{f}^\mathsf{T}\boldsymbol{\Sigma}_\mathbf{f}^{-1}\boldsymbol{\mu}_\mathbf{f} = \mathbf{f}^\mathsf{T}\mathbf{y}$$
$$\boldsymbol{\mu}_\mathbf{f} = \boldsymbol{\Sigma}_\mathbf{f}\mathbf{y}.$$

Similarly, $p(y_n|f_n, t_n)$ is proportional to the full posterior and we can start by ignoring all terms that do not depend on y_n and f_n. This leaves

$$p(y_n|f_n, t_n) \propto p(t_n|y_n)p(y_n|f_n).$$

If we take an example where $t_n = 1$, this becomes

$$p(y_n|f_n, t_n = 1) \propto P(t_n = 1|y_n)p(y_n|f_n) = \delta(y_n > 0)\mathcal{N}(y_n|f_n, 1),$$

which is a Gaussian with mean f_n truncated to be positive. Sampling from this density is straightforward: simply sample from the untruncated Gaussian and throw away all of the samples until a positive one arrives. For examples where $t_n = 0$, the density is

$$p(y_n|f_n, t_n = 0) \propto \delta(y_n < 0)\mathcal{N}(y_n|f_n, 1),$$

a Gaussian truncated to be negative.

We now have everything we need to generate samples from $p(\mathbf{f}, \mathbf{y}|\mathbf{X}, \mathbf{t})$ and therefore $p(\mathbf{f}|\mathbf{X}, \mathbf{t})$ (by just looking at the $\mathbf{f}$ samples). The procedure is as follows:

1. Initialise $\mathbf{y}$ with some sensible values (i.e. it would make sense for all y_n for which $t_n = 1$ to be positive)

2. Repeat for each desired sample:

   (a) Update $\mathbf{f}$ by sampling from $p(\mathbf{f}|\mathbf{y}, \mathbf{X})$.

    (b) Update each y_n by sampling from $p(y_n|f_n, t_n)$.

    (c) If making predictions, for a sample of $\mathbf{f}$, perform a GP regression to find $\mathbf{f}^*$.

    (d) Sample $\mathbf{y}^*$ from $p(\mathbf{y}^*|\mathbf{f}^*) = \mathcal{N}(\mathbf{f}^*, \mathbf{I})$.

    (e) Set $\mathbf{t}^{*,s}$ to one or zero depending on whether the corresponding elements of $\mathbf{y}^*$ are positive or negative.

3. Compute the predictive probabilities by averaging over $\mathbf{t}^{*,s}$.

We will now demonstrate this with an example (MATLAB script: `gibbs_gp_class.m`). Figure 9.4(a) shows some example 1-dimensional classification data. The class of the training examples is depicted by their height on the y axis and the shading of the plot symbol. Using the scheme described above, we can obtain posterior samples of the latent function at these training points. The mean plus and minus one standard deviation of $S = 10,000$ such samples can be seen in Figure 9.4(b), where we have used an RBF covariance function (see Equation 8.2) with $\alpha = 1, \gamma = 10$. For each new sample of $\mathbf{f}$, we can perform a (noise-free) GP regression to produce a sample of the latent function at a set of test points, $\mathbf{f}^*$ (in this case, we have constructed a fine grid of 100 test points in the range $0 < x < 1$). Figure 9.4(c) shows the posterior mean of the predictive function (solid black line), the mean plus and minus one standard deviation (dashed black lines) as well as a randomly chosen subset of 10 of the 10,000 samples (the plot also shows the posterior mean and standard deviation of $\mathbf{f}$, as in Figure 9.4(b)). Finally, for each sample of $\mathbf{f}^*$, we can sample a $\mathbf{y}^*$ and then assign 1 or 0 to the components of $\mathbf{t}^*$ depending on whether the respective components of $\mathbf{y}^*$ are positive or negative. After S samples, we can average these values of t to give a predictive probability. This probability is shown in Figure 9.4(d). We can see that the predictive probabilities seem reasonable – for areas of the input space (x) where we see a high density of training points with $t_n = 0$, the probability is low. Where we see training points with $t_n = 1$, the probability is higher.

Here, the initial model was not amenable to Gibbs sampling but it became so through the introduction of the auxiliary variables. The addition of extra variables has made posterior inference more straightforward – all of the conditionals are easy to sample from. We could have sampled from the posterior via Metropolis–Hastings and we leave it as an exercise to compare the two (see Exercise 9.2). In Chapter 10 we will see another model where Gibbs sampling is a natural choice for posterior inference.

Finally, you may have noticed that, in the Gibbs sampler for GP classification, we updated the whole vector $\mathbf{f}$ by sampling from $p(\mathbf{f}|\mathbf{y}, \mathbf{X})$ rather than updating each variable in turn. We could have done the latter – $p(\mathbf{f}|\mathbf{y}, \mathbf{X})$ is a Gaussian and so all of the conditional densities are available – but there seems little point if we can do it all in one go, and in this case it is also much more efficient (see Section 9.4.2 and Exercise 9.1). In general, when building a Gibbs sampler, we can either update each parameter individually or in blocks (assuming conditionals are available in both cases). In many cases, the choice of blocks is obvious ($\mathbf{f}$ is a natural collection of parameters) and larger blocks tend to lead to greater efficiency.

9.2.2 Summary

In this section we have introduced Gibbs sampling and demonstrated its use through sampling from a Gaussian as well as a Gaussian process classification model. Whilst

Metropolis–Hastings can, in theory, be used to sample from any posterior for which we can compute the product of prior and likelihood, Gibbs sampling is restricted to those models for which the conditional distribution of each parameter conditioned on all others is available.

Up to now, we have presented Metropolis–Hastings and Gibbs sampling as recipes for generating samples, without any thought about why they work. This is the subject of the next section. For those of you who are just keen to get started and want some hints on how to use these techniques in the wild, you can skip straight to Section 9.4.

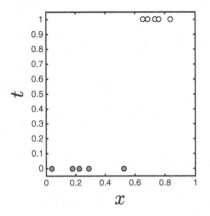

(a) Some example one-dimensional classification data. The y-axis (and plot symbol) denotes the class.

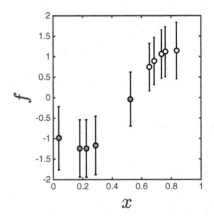

(b) Marginal posterior means and standard deviations over f_n from the Gibbs sampler.

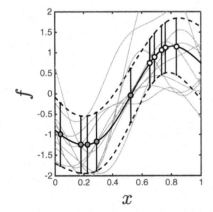

(c) Predictive latent function values at a fine grid of test points. The solid black line gives the posterior mean prediction, the dashed lines ± one standard deviation and the grey lines show 10 example samples.

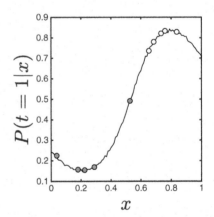

(d) Predictive probabilities for a fine grid of test points.

FIGURE 9.4 Gibbs sampling for GP classification.

9.3   WHY DOES MCMC WORK?

To understand why Metropolis–Hastings and Gibbs sampling work, we have to take a step back and learn a little about the theory of **Markov chains**. Figure 9.5 shows a system consisting of five boxes and a single token. The *state* of the system is defined as which box the token is in. At every second, the token is moved randomly according to the following rule: with probability equal to 0.5 it moves one square to the left, and with probability equal to 0.5 it moves one square to the right. The end states wrap around so that, if the token is in the far right state and it moves right, it ends up in the far left state. This system satisfies the *Markovian* property – the state of the system (location of the token) at time t depends only on its state at $t-1$. In other words, to decide where to move the token to at time $t+1$, we need only know where it is at time t, not where it was at any previous times.

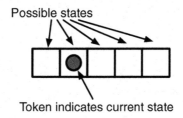

FIGURE 9.5   A simple state-space model consisting of five states (boxes) and one token to indicate the current state.

This state-space model is an example of a Markov chain. The probabilities of moving from one state to another are known as **transition probabilities**. Our simple example has a discrete state space (i.e. there is a set of distinct states) but Markov chains can also be defined over continuous state spaces. Consider the plots in Figure 9.3. Here we have a system moving through a continuous state space where the next position is dependent only on the current position (via the conditional distributions used in Gibbs sampling) – like Metropolis–Hastings, a set of samples generated via Gibbs sampling is an example of a Markov chain (hence the name Markov chain Monte Carlo).

Imagine you left the system in Figure 9.5 running for a long time and then came back: what is the probability that it will be in a particular state? This set of probabilities over states is known as the *stationary distribution* of the chain. For our example it will actually be a uniform distribution over the five states. Now consider Gibbs sampling or Metropolis–Hastings. If we start off a Gibbs or Metropolis–Hastings Markov chain to sample from some density $p(\theta)$, leave it alone for a while and then come back, the probability of the chain being in state θ is $P(\theta)$ – that's the distribution it is sampling over. Gibbs sampling and Metropolis–Hastings work by creating Markov chains with stationary distributions equal to the distribution of interest.

To firm up the relationship between the sampling methods we have seen and Markov chains, let's see how we can use our five-state model to sample from a distribution (MATLAB script: `sampleworld.m`). If we simply let the chain run and log the states it visits, we are effectively generating samples from a uniform distribution over the five states (that's the stationary distribution of the chain). Can we get it to sample from an arbitrary distribution over the five states? The answer is yes – this is exactly what Metropolis–Hastings allows us to do. We will use it to sample from the following distribution over the five states:

$$1:0.1, \ 2:0.1, \ 3:0.4, \ 4:0.2, \ 5:0.1 \qquad (9.6)$$

Metropolis–Hastings works by first proposing a new state and then deciding whether or not to accept it. For the proposal distribution, we will use the state transition probabilities described above, i.e. the probability of going from state 1 to state 2 is 0.5, as is the probability of going from state 1 to state 5. All other states have probability 0 from state 1. From state 2 we can either go to state 1 (probability 0.5) or state 3 (probability 0.5), etc. We will denote the transition probability of going from state θ_j to state θ_i with $q(\theta_i|\theta_j)$. Recall that the Metropolis–Hastings acceptance probability of a move from θ_j to θ_i is given by the ratio:

$$r = \frac{p(\theta_i)}{p(\theta_j)} \frac{q(\theta_j|\theta_i)}{q(\theta_i|\theta_j)}.$$

As the proposal is symmetric (the transition probability from state i to state j is equal to the transition probability from state j to state i), the second part of the ratio will cancel and so the acceptance probability reduced to the ratio of state probabilities. For example, the acceptance probability of going from state 3 to state 4 is $0.2/0.4 = 0.5$. If the sample is rejected, we stay in the same place. The probabilities obtained by averaging over 2000 posterior samples can be seen in Figure 9.6 (along with the true probabilities) and its clear that the method is indeed sampling from the correct distribution (MATLAB script: **state_chain.m**). This result isn't dependent on our choice of transition probabilities (i.e. our proposal).

So, how do the transition rules used by Gibbs sampling (sampling from conditional distributions) and Metropolis–Hastings (accepting based on the computed acceptance probability) create Markov chains with the distribution of interest as the stationary distribution? To describe this in detail is beyond the scope of this book. However, it can be shown (we won't) that, for a particular set of transition rules to converge to a particular stationary distribution, the rules and the desired stationary distribution must satisfy **detailed balance**. Detailed balance says that being in some state θ_i and moving into some other state θ_j has to be equally likely to being in state θ_j and moving into θ_i. If we use $p(\theta_j|\theta_i)$ to denote the probability of moving from state θ_i into state θ_j, detailed balance says

$$p(\theta_i)p(\theta_j|\theta_i) = p(\theta_j)p(\theta_i|\theta_j). \qquad (9.7)$$

Note that it is important to make the distinction between the proposal distribution $(q(\theta_i|\theta_j))$ and the movement distribution $(p(\theta_i|\theta_j))$, particularly in the context of Metropolis–Hastings. Proposing a move from θ_j to θ_i does not necessarily mean it will happen. $p(\theta_i|\theta_j)$ is the probability that we propose to move from θ_j to θ_i *and that it is accepted.*

One way of interpreting detailed balance is that if you start your chain, go away and then come back and observe two consecutive states, you're just as likely

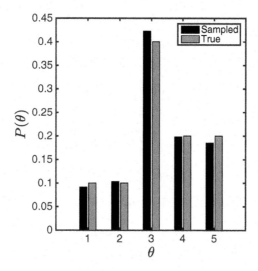

FIGURE 9.6 Samples obtained from the distribution described in Equation 9.6 using Metropolis–Hastings with the state-space model drawn in Figure 9.5. The black bars are the sample approximations and the grey bars the true values.

to observe θ_i, θ_j as you are θ_j, θ_i. Inspecting the samples we obtained when using Metropolis–Hastings with our five-state model, we can see that this is indeed the case. For example, the number of times we saw state 2 followed by state 3 was 100. The number of times we saw state 3 followed by state 2 was 105 – very similar values, despite the fact that we are in state 3 approximately four times as often as we are in state 2. Detailed balance also tells us that if it is possible to be in state θ_j (i.e. $p(\theta_j) > 0$) and possible to move to θ_i ($p(\theta_i|\theta_j) > 0$) then the opposite must also be possible.

For a particular distribution of interest $(p(\theta))$, any set of transition probabilities $(p(\theta_i|\theta_j))$ that satisfies detailed balance will give us a sampler that converges to $p(\theta)$. It is informative to see how the transition schemes defined by Metropolis–Hastings and Gibbs sampling both satisfy detailed balance. In both cases we use $p(\boldsymbol{\theta})$ to denote the distribution of interest (where $\boldsymbol{\theta}$ could be a vector or a scalar), and use $\boldsymbol{\theta}_i$ and $\boldsymbol{\theta}_j$ to be two different states of $\boldsymbol{\theta}$. We will now demonstrate how the transition probabilities implied by the two methods satisfy Equation 9.7.

Starting with Metropolis–Hastings, we can always label the two states such that $p(\boldsymbol{\theta}_j) \geq p(\boldsymbol{\theta}_i)$ and to start with we will assume that the proposal density $(q(\boldsymbol{\theta}_j|\boldsymbol{\theta}_i))$ is symmetric. The acceptance ratio is computed as:

$$r = \frac{p(\boldsymbol{\theta}_j)}{p(\boldsymbol{\theta}_i)} \frac{q(\boldsymbol{\theta}_i|\boldsymbol{\theta}_j)}{q(\boldsymbol{\theta}_j|\boldsymbol{\theta}_i)},$$

where the second term is 1 (due to the symmetry of the proposal) and the first term is greater than or equal to 1 (due to our labelling of the points). Therefore the sample is accepted. The left hand side of Equation 9.7 becomes:

$$p(\boldsymbol{\theta}_i)q(\boldsymbol{\theta}_j|\boldsymbol{\theta}_i)$$

For the right hand side, the acceptance ratio is:

$$r = \frac{p(\boldsymbol{\theta}_i)}{p(\boldsymbol{\theta}_j)}\frac{q(\boldsymbol{\theta}_j|\boldsymbol{\theta}_i)}{q(\boldsymbol{\theta}_i|\boldsymbol{\theta}_j)}.$$

Again, the second term is 1. However r is now less than 1, so the sample is accepted with probability r. The right hand side of Equation 9.7 is therefore:

$$p(\boldsymbol{\theta}_j)q(\boldsymbol{\theta}_i|\boldsymbol{\theta}_j)\frac{p(\boldsymbol{\theta}_i)}{p(\boldsymbol{\theta}_j)}.$$

For detailed balance, these two sides must be equal. The full detailed balance equation is therefore

$$p(\boldsymbol{\theta}_i)q(\boldsymbol{\theta}_j|\boldsymbol{\theta}_i) = p(\boldsymbol{\theta}_j)q(\boldsymbol{\theta}_i|\boldsymbol{\theta}_j)\frac{p(\boldsymbol{\theta}_i)}{p(\boldsymbol{\theta}_j)},$$

which, given the symmetry of the proposal is clearly the case.

What about the more general case then when the proposal is not symmetric. In this case, we will label the states such that $p(\boldsymbol{\theta}_j)q(\boldsymbol{\theta}_i|\boldsymbol{\theta}_j) \geq p(\boldsymbol{\theta}_i)q(\boldsymbol{\theta}_j|\boldsymbol{\theta}_i)$, which ensures a ratio greater than 1 (and therefore guarantees acceptance) for a move from $\boldsymbol{\theta}_i$ to $\boldsymbol{\theta}_j$. The left hand side of Equation 9.7 is therefore:

$$p(\boldsymbol{\theta}_i)q(\boldsymbol{\theta}_j|\boldsymbol{\theta}_i),$$

as before. For the right hand side, the second term in the acceptance ratio no longer cancels, leaving:

$$p(\boldsymbol{\theta}_j)q(\boldsymbol{\theta}_i|\boldsymbol{\theta}_j)\frac{p(\boldsymbol{\theta}_i)}{p(\boldsymbol{\theta}_j)}\frac{q(\boldsymbol{\theta}_j|\boldsymbol{\theta}_i)}{q(\boldsymbol{\theta}_i|\boldsymbol{\theta}_j)}.$$

Cancelling terms leaves:

$$p(\boldsymbol{\theta}_i)q(\boldsymbol{\theta}_j|\boldsymbol{\theta}_i),$$

which is identical to the left hand side, as required. We can conclude that Metropolis–Hastings satisfies detailed balance.

We should take a moment here to clarify the exact naming of this algorithm. Technically, when the proposal is symmetric, we are dealing with the Metropolis algorithm. It becomes the Metropolis–Hastings algorithm when the proposal is asymmetric – the Metropolis acceptance ratio is corrected so that detailed balance is still satisfied when the proposal is asymmetric.

Now let's see how Gibbs sampling satisfies detailed balance. Consider a set of parameters $\boldsymbol{\theta} = [\theta_1, \theta_2, \ldots, \theta_N]^{\mathsf{T}}$. Consider a second set of parameters $\boldsymbol{\theta}' = [\theta'_1, \theta_2, \ldots, \theta_N]^{\mathsf{T}}$ that differs only in its value of θ_1. Detailed balance is then

$$p(\boldsymbol{\theta})p(\boldsymbol{\theta}'|\boldsymbol{\theta}) = p(\boldsymbol{\theta}')p(\boldsymbol{\theta}|\boldsymbol{\theta}').$$

Consider a slight variation on the Gibbs sampling method we described above – rather than looping through the individual variables, we select them at random. The left hand side is therefore

$$p(\boldsymbol{\theta})\frac{1}{N}p(\theta'_1|\theta_2, \ldots, \theta_N)$$

where the $\frac{1}{N}$ term comes from the random choice of parameter 1. Doing the same to the right hand side leaves us with the following expression:

$$p(\boldsymbol{\theta})\frac{1}{N}p(\theta_1'|\theta_2,\ldots,\theta_N) = p(\boldsymbol{\theta}')\frac{1}{N}p(\theta_1|\theta_2,\ldots,\theta_N).$$

To show that this is true (and hence that detailed balance holds for Gibbs sampling), we need to expand the conditional distributions. In particular, from the relationship between conditional and joint distributions:

$$p(\theta_1'|\theta_2,\ldots,\theta_N)p(\theta_2,\ldots,\theta_N) = p(\boldsymbol{\theta}')$$

and therefore

$$p(\theta_1'|\theta_2,\ldots,\theta_N) = \frac{p(\boldsymbol{\theta}')}{p(\theta_2,\ldots,\theta_N)}.$$

Doing the same for $p(\theta_1|\theta_2,\ldots,\theta_N)$ and substituting into our detailed balance equation, we have

$$p(\boldsymbol{\theta})\frac{1}{N}\frac{p(\boldsymbol{\theta}')}{p(\theta_2,\ldots,\theta_N)} = p(\boldsymbol{\theta}')\frac{1}{N}\frac{p(\boldsymbol{\theta})}{p(\theta_2,\ldots,\theta_N)}.$$

Detailed balance is therefore satisfied for Gibbs sampling.

We have seen how Metropolis–Hastings and Gibbs sampling satisfy detailed balance and therefore that chains using the transition probabilities defined by Gibbs sampling and Metropolis–Hastings have the desired distribution as their stationary distribution. What we haven't done is convince you why detailed balance is the right thing to satisfy! That would be beyond the scope of this book, and readers who want to learn more are encouraged to explore the references provided at the end of this chapter.

9.4   SOME SAMPLING PROBLEMS AND SOLUTIONS

In theory, sampling (via either Gibbs sampling or Metropolis–Hastings) appears straightforward. In practice things are not quite so easy. In this section we will look at two of the key practical issues facing sampling methods when used in the wild: assessing convergence and reducing autocorrelation.

9.4.1   Burn-in and convergence

In our description of Gibbs sampling and Metropolis–Hastings, we paid very little attention to the initialisation of the algorithm – i.e., where to start. In theory, it does not matter where we start, but in practice a poor choice of starting position can result in the chain taking a long time to converge to the desired distribution. Some initialisation methods are likely to be more sensible than others. For example, when sampling from a posterior distribution, initialising with a sample from the prior might be more sensible than plucking a value out of thin air. Even with what looks like a sensible choice, our starting point may not be in an area of significant posterior density. Initial samples will therefore be quite unrepresentative of the posterior. We therefore need a method of determining whether or not our chain has converged and is sampling from the intended distribution. As we aren't able to evaluate the true distribution (if we could, we probably wouldn't have decided to sample), this is not straightforward. But, if we change the question slightly, we we can devise a proxy

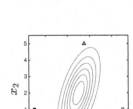

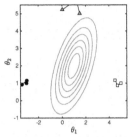

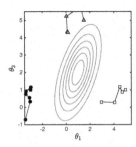

(a) Initial values.   (b) After 5 samples.   (c) After 20 samples.

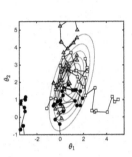

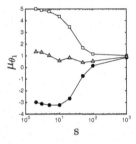

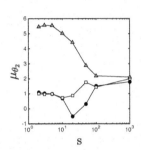

(d) After 50 samples.   (e) Estimate of mean of θ_1.   (f) Estimate of mean of θ_2.

FIGURE 9.7 Three chains sampling from a two-dimensional Gaussian density. The final plots show the estimates of the Gaussian mean obtained from increasing numbers of samples.

for convergence. In particular, rather than trying to determine if a single chain has converged to the *true* distribution, we try and assess if multiple chains (with different initialisations) have all converged to the *same* distribution. This is illustrated in Figure 9.7 (MATLAB script: `convergence.m`), where we show three Metropolis–Hastings chains (with a symmetric Gaussian proposal density with $\sigma^2 = 0.4$ for both dimensions) sampling from a two-dimensional Gaussian density. To visually assess whether the chains have converged to the same distributions, the final two plots in Figure 9.7 show the estimates of the mean of the Gaussian using increasing numbers of samples (note the logarithmic scale on the x-axis).

In practice, we can use a slightly formal idea of convergence, also taking into account the variance between and within the chains. The procedure that we will describe is introduced in *Bayesian Data Analysis* (see reference at the end of the chapter) and the reader is referred to that book for a more detailed discussion.

Assume that, for each parameter of interest, we have $s = 1 \ldots S$ samples from each of $c = 1 \ldots C$ chains, where the sth sample in the cth chain is denoted θ_{sc}. In our example, we have $S = 1000$ samples from $C = 3$ chains. We start by computing the mean (μ_c) and variance (σ_c^2) of the samples within each chain:

$$\mu_c = \frac{1}{S}\sum_{s=1}^{S}\theta_{sc}, \quad \sigma_c^2 = \frac{1}{S-1}\sum_{s=1}^{S}(\theta_{sc} - \mu_c)^2.$$

We then average the mean values to obtain a global mean, $\mu = \frac{1}{C}\sum_{c=1}^{C}\mu_c$, and use these three quantities to compute within and between chain variances, W and B:

$$W = \frac{1}{C}\sum_{c=1}^{C}\sigma_c^2, \quad B = \frac{S}{C-1}\sum_{c=1}^{C}(\mu_c - \mu)^2.$$

Finally, we compute the measure of interest, $\hat{R}$, as

$$\hat{R} = \sqrt{\frac{V}{W}}, \tag{9.8}$$

where V is an estimate of the marginal posterior variance of θ, computed as a weighted sum of B and W:

$$V = \frac{S-1}{S}W + \frac{1}{S}B.$$

$\hat{R}$, converges to 1 as the number of samples approaches infinity. We therefore sample until this quantity becomes sufficiently close to 1 for all parameters. How close *sufficiently close* is depends on the application, but waiting for values below 1.01 is quite common in practice. A value of $\hat{R}$ that seems to stop decreasing at a higher value is possibly indicative of a problem with your sampler. Figure 9.8 shows the evolution of $\hat{R}$ for our example. The solid line corresponds to x_1 and the dashed to x_2. After 2000 samples, the value of $\hat{R}$ for both parameters is well below 1.01.

This gives us an objective procedure for determining whether or not our sampler has converged. Start multiple chains from diverse starting positions (the more chains the better). Monitor $\hat{R}$ for each parameter, and, when it has fallen to a value below some predetermined threshold (say 1.01) for all parameters, consider the chains to have converged. At this point we can start our sampling proper. The convergence of the chains just tells us that they are all sampling from the same distribution (which we assume must be the true one) and so we can confidently start collecting samples to use. Typically, all of the initial samples are discarded, and this initial sampling is known as the burn-in phase (see Exercise 9.3).

9.4.2 Autocorrelation

Once we have decided that our chains have converged, there is still another potential hurdle to overcome – **autocorrelation**. We will often be using the samples to approximate an expectation. For example,

$$\int f(\theta)p(\theta)\,d\theta \approx \frac{1}{S}\sum_{s=1}^{S}f(\theta^s).$$

For this approximation to work, the S samples $\theta^1, \ldots, \theta^S$ need to be independent samples from $p(\theta)$. Unfortunately, the nature of most sampling algorithms means

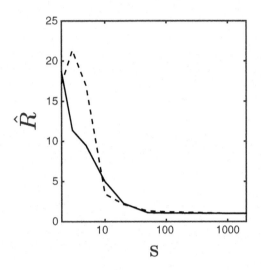

FIGURE 9.8 Evolution of $\hat{R}$ computed from the chains shown in Figure 9.7. The solid line corresponds to x_1 and the dashed to x_2.

that consecutive samples that are produced are very dependent on one another. This is particularly obvious for Metropolis–Hastings, where new samples are proposed by moving a small distance away from the current sample. If the proposed value is accepted, the new sample will be similar to (dependent on) the old one. If the proposed value is rejected, the new sample will be identical to (very dependent upon!) the old one.

There are two ways in which we can overcome this problem. Firstly, design our sampler to produce samples that are as independent as possible and, secondly, remove any remaining dependence by throwing lots of samples away (known as **thinning**). For example, we could keep only every tenth sample, throwing the rest away.

The choice of sampling algorithm will influence the extent to which we can use these two approaches, and, in practice, both will be required. For example, when using Metropolis–Hastings, the choice of proposal distribution will have a significant role in determining the dependence between successive samples, but it's unlikely that you will find a proposal distribution that completely removes the need for thinning. When using Gibbs sampling, it is sometimes possible to update parameters in blocks, or integrate one set of parameters out when sampling another. Both will reduce the dependence between consecutive samples, but only up to a point.

The dependence between samples can be measured by computing the autocorrelation of the samples. Autocorrelation measures the correlation between samples in the same chain separated by some lag. For example, the lag 1 autocorrelation is the correlation of consecutive samples, θ^s and θ^{s+1}. The lag 2 autocorrelation is the correlation between samples two steps apart (e.g. samples θ^1 and θ^3, and θ^2 and θ^4, etc.).

Autocorrelation is computed separately for each chain, so for notational simplicity we can drop the chain subscript and consider $s = 1 \ldots S$ samples, θ_s for each chain. The autocorrelation (at a lag of k; a_k) is then computed as

$$a_k = \frac{1}{(S-k)\sigma^2} \sum_{s=1}^{S-k} (\theta_s - \mu)(\theta_{s+k} - \mu),$$

where θ_{s+k} is the sample k steps after the sth one, μ is the mean of the S samples, and σ^2 the variance. The summation is over all pairs of samples separated by k steps (the first pair will be θ_1 and θ_{1+k} and the last pair θ_{S-k} and θ_S). In the extreme case of $k = 0$, this expression simplifies to $\sigma^2/\sigma^2 = 1$, which is the maximum value of autocorrelation possible (see Exercise 9.4).

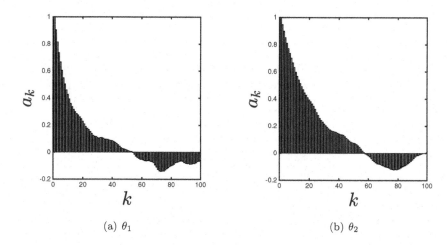

(a) θ_1 (b) θ_2

FIGURE 9.9 Autocorrelation for samples of x_1 and x_2 for one of the three chains shown in Figure 9.7.

Often autocorrelation is plotted as a function of k to provide a useful visual diagnosis of the degree of autocorrelation in the samples. The plots for θ_1 and θ_2 from our Metropolis–Hastings example above are given in Figure 9.9.

These plots show very high autocorrelation – our samples are very dependent on one another, even at quite large lags. An autocorrelation plot for independent samples would have a value of 1 for lag 0 and then values of zero (or very close to zero) elsewhere. If faced with plots like these, one ought to thin the samples considerably to try and leave a set of independent samples. The plots suggest that the autocorrelation reaches zero at a lag of approximately 40. So, we should thin by keeping the first one, discarding the next 40, keeping the 42nd one, discarding the next 40 etc. This comes at a considerable computational cost (we are discarding almost all samples we draw), but thinning at this or higher levels is not uncommon in practice. Fortunately, in this case, we can improve things through other means. These samples were drawn with an isotropic Gaussian proposal density that had a variance of 0.4 for both dimensions. Increasing this value will lead to bigger movements and

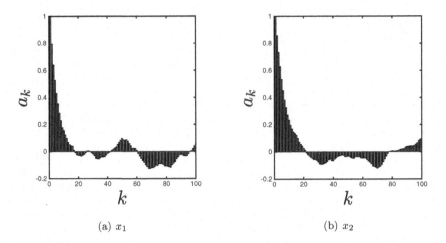

FIGURE 9.10 Autocorrelation for samples of x_1 and x_2 for one of the three chains shown in Figure 9.7 with a proposal density with variance increased to 3.

therefore autocorrelation that decays rapidly. The resulting autocorrelation is shown in Figure 9.10 and we can indeed see that the autocorrelation decays more rapidly but still pretty slowly. Thinning these samples would still be required.

In general, when sampling (particularly with Metropolis–Hastings and similar methods), it is useful to compute the **acceptance ratio**, which is defined as the proportion of proposed samples that are accepted. In this example, when the proposal variance was 0.4, the value was around 0.6. When the variance was increased to 3, the value was closer to 0.3. It drops because, as the steps get bigger, there is an increased chance that a bad new value will be proposed. An acceptance rate of 0.3 means that most of the time (about 70%) the proposed sample is rejected and the current sample is used again. This will obviously affect the autocorrelation – if too many samples are rejected, the copying of samples for many steps will give very high autocorrelation. There is therefore a trade-off between high autocorrelation due to small steps (that are regularly accepted) and high correlation due to steps that are too big and often rejected. In practice, varying proposal densities and monitoring autocorrelation is a crucial step in designing an efficient sampler. Optimal acceptance ratios have been theoretically derived for various distributions. See the references at the end of the chapter for more information.

For comparison, we can plot the autocorrelation for a Gibbs sampler for the same density. This is shown in Figure 9.11. The autocorrelation drops much more rapidly, and one could just thin every other sample to obtain samples that were practically independent. Why is this the case? Let's just consider θ_1. In Metropolis–Hastings, a new value of θ_1 is proposed based on the old value. There is therefore a direct dependence between the consecutive values. In Gibbs sampling, the old value of θ_1 is used when sampling a new value of θ_2, which is then used when sampling the new value of θ_1. In this case, the dependence is indirect (mediated by θ_2), and the

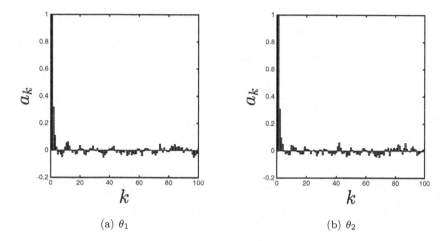

(a) θ_1 (b) θ_2

FIGURE 9.11 Autocorrelation for samples of θ_1 and θ_2 for a Gibbs sampler.

dependence therefore depends on the strength of the relationship between θ_1 and θ_2. It seems unsurprising that this weakens the effective dependence between successive values of θ_1 as measured by the autocorrelation.

This will generally be the case – if we have the choice between Metropolis–Hastings and Gibbs for the same set of parameters, we would typically go for Gibbs. However, the situation gets muddier when you consider updating groups of variables at a time. For example, Metropolis–Hastings lets us update as many parameters as we like at once, whereas with Gibbs we are limited to what we can compute the conditional distributions for (we might be able to group things, we might not). When conditional distributions for blocks are unavailable, there will be examples where it is more efficient to do Metropolis–Hastings on the blocks than Gibbs sampling on the individual parameters. We saw an example of a Gibbs block update earlier in this chapter. When we built the GP classification model, we computed a conditional density for the vector $\mathbf{f}$, rather than the individual elements f_n. We leave it as an exercise (Exercise 9.1) to derive the individual updates and assess the (in)efficiency of sampling them all individually.

It is worth remembering that, in many problems, the choice between Gibbs and Metropolis–Hastings (or others) is not one we have. We can use Metropolis–Hastings on any model, as long as we can compute the prior and likelihood. Gibbs sampling can only be used on a small subset of models for which the conditional distributions are available.

9.4.3 Summary

In this section we have described two important measures for diagnosing how well our sampler is operating. $\hat{R}$ can be used to determine if multiple chains are sampling from the same distribution, whilst the autocorrelation can tell us how (in)dependent our samples are. Careful use of these measures can help ensure that samplers are working correctly (they will often not be!) and that the samples being produced can legitimately be used to compute expectations, etc.

Other tools are available for assessing convergence and reducing sample dependence. For example, although it is subjective, visual inspection is a useful tool. Re-parameterisation of the model can also be very helpful to, for example, remove parameters that cannot be identified from the data available. It is also possible to marginalise parameters (particularly in Gibbs sampling), and we will see an example of this in Chapter 10.

In the final part of this chapter we will provide a brief introduction to various advanced sampling techniques that are currently popular in machine learning.

9.5   ADVANCED SAMPLING TECHNIQUES

9.5.1   Adaptive proposals and Hamiltonian Monte Carlo

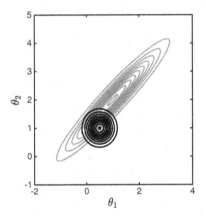
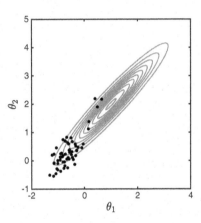

(a) An isotropic proposal (dark contours) being used to sample from a distribution with high covariance.

(b) The first 100 samples using the proposal shown in (a).

FIGURE 9.12   An example of Metropolis–Hastings when the proposal distribution is not well matched to the distribution being sampled from.

The efficiency of Metropolis–Hastings is partly dependent on the relationship between the distribution being sampled from and the proposal distribution. If the proposal distribution is likely to often propose very poor movements, many samples will be rejected. Figure 9.12(a) shows an example where the proposal is poorly matched to the distribution being sampled from (MATLAB script: `badmh.m`). The distribution being sampled from (light contours) exhibits high covariance, whereas the proposal distribution (darker contours) is isotropic. Given the current value of θ (the centre of the proposal distribution), we can see that the proposal distribution is highly likely to propose a poor new value of θ. Regardless of the position of the current sample, many samples will be rejected. One way to overcome this would be to reduce the variance of the proposal distribution, resulting in proposals being (on average) closer to the current value. This makes it less likely that proposals will be rejected (shorter moves are less likely to result in large drops in the posterior value) but it will make the autocorrelation between samples higher (resulting in the need for a greater degree of thinning) and mean that the sampler takes much longer to explore the full distribution.

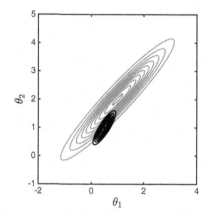
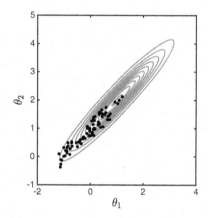

(a) A Gaussian proposal with covariance equal to 0.2 multiplied by the empirical covariance from the samples shown in Figure 9.12(b).

(b) The first 100 samples using the adapted proposal.

FIGURE 9.13 Adapting the proposal based on previous samples.

A second solution is to make the proposal more representative of the true distribution. For example, the distribution in Figure 9.12(a) would benefit from a proposal distribution that favoured moves roughly along the line $\theta_1 = \theta_2$. Without knowledge of the distribution being sampled from, we can add useful covariance structure to the proposal by basing it on samples already drawn. In our example, we can use the covariance matrix of the 100 samples shown in Figure 9.12(b) (multiplied by a small constant) to replace the covariance of the original proposal distribution. This new proposal distribution should produce a more efficient sampler than the original one.

Figure 9.12(b) shows this in action. The proposal density shown has as its covariance the covariance of the samples shown in Figure 9.12(b) multiplied by a small constant (0.2). The first 100 samples using this new proposal are shown in Figure 9.13(b). We can see that the new sampler is able to explore the space more efficiently.

Of course, the more samples on which we base the proposal the better. There is nothing stopping us from continually adapting the proposal as we learn more about the covariance structure of the distribution being sampled from. In this example, the constant we multiplied the empirical covariance by (0.2) was chosen fairly arbitrarily. See the references at the end of this chapter for pointers to where choices of this value are discussed.

An alternative to adapting the proposal covariance in this way is through the use of **Hamiltonian Monte Carlo** (HMC, also known as hybrid Monte Carlo). We will not give a full description of HMC here – see the references at the end of the chapter for suggestions for further reading.

HMC uses information about the gradient of the distribution to inform our proposal. In particular, for each variable being sampled, HMC introduces an additional momentum parameter and samples from the joint distribution of the original and momentum parameters. Calling the momentum parameters $\mathbf{v}$, we sample from

$$p(\boldsymbol{\theta}, \mathbf{v}) = p(\boldsymbol{\theta})p(\mathbf{v}),$$

where $p(\mathbf{v})$ is user defined and will affect the efficiency of the sampler. The proposal step starts by drawing a new value of $\mathbf{v}$ from $p(\mathbf{v})$. This is followed by a user-defined number of steps, in each of which the momentum is updated according to the derivative of the log of the distribution with respect to $\boldsymbol{\theta}$, and $\boldsymbol{\theta}$ is moved based on the momentum. After the steps are complete, the acceptance probability is computed as in standard Metropolis–Hastings but with the ratio of the proposals replaced with the ratio of $p(\mathbf{v})$ after and before the iterative steps. Although we are technically accepting both $\mathbf{x}$ and $\mathbf{v}$, we aren't interested in the values of $\mathbf{v}$, so don't need to store them from one sample to the next.

Figure 9.14 illustrates this proposal procedure. We start by sampling a momentum. The current value of $\boldsymbol{\theta}$ gets moved in this momentum direction. The momentum

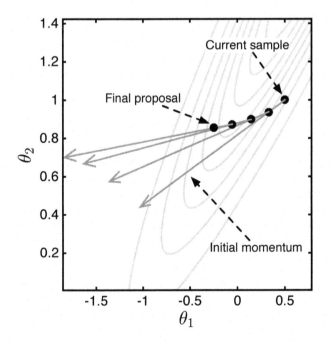

FIGURE 9.14 A single proposal step in the HMC algorithm.

is then updated based on the gradient of $\log p(\boldsymbol{\theta})$, which makes it point slightly more uphill, and $\boldsymbol{\theta}$ is updated again. After several steps, the procedure is stopped and the value of $\boldsymbol{\theta}$ is used as the proposed value. This proposal is still random (it's based on the initial value of $\mathbf{v}$), but it is biased to move up the gradient of $p(\boldsymbol{\theta})$. A proof of how this procedure obeys detailed balance is beyond our scope but, needless to say, it does, and it can make sampling much more efficient. Figure 9.15 shows the first 100 samples obtained from our distribution using HMC (MATLAB script: badmh.m). Comparing with the standard Metropolis–Hastings approach (Figure 9.12(b)), we can see that it explores the distribution much more efficiently.

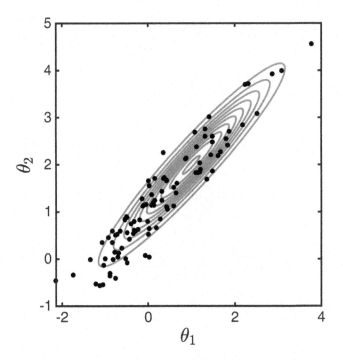

FIGURE 9.15 One hundred samples obtained using HMC.

Because it uses information about the gradient of the distribution, HMC will often be more efficient than standard Metropolis–Hastings. However, we can only use HMC when we do have access to the derivative information, which, for some complex models, may not be the case.

9.5.2 Approximate Bayesian computation

When using Metropolis–Hastings (and related techniques, e.g. HMC) to perform Bayesian inference, we have to be able to compute the likelihood of the observed data for the current and proposed set of parameters. In all of our applications, we have been able to do this easily. However, there exist applications where computing the likelihood is either impossible or very computationally expensive. **Approximate Bayesian computation** (ABC) has been developed for these situations and is a technique that allows us to sample from the posterior density without having to compute the likelihood at all.

Recall the fairground coin game that we used as our first example of Bayesian inference in Chapter 3. We observed a certain number of heads (n) from a certain number of tosses of a coin (N). We showed how we were able to analytically compute the posterior density over the probability that any individual toss was a head (r) when the likelihod was a Bernoulli distribution and the prior a beta density.

Say we observe $n = 3$ heads in $N = 10$ tosses and we assume that we know nothing about the coin so choose a uniform prior ($\alpha = \beta = 1$). At the fairground you don't have access to the means of computing the posterior exactly, but you do have a way of generating possible coins from this uniform prior which, coincidentally, is exactly the scenario in which you could use ABC!

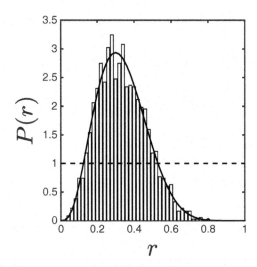

FIGURE 9.16 Example of ABC for the coin game example introduced in Chapter 3.

To use ABC, we generate lots of samples from the prior. For each sample, we generate a dataset according to the generative process defined by the likelihood. Note that, in this and many other scenarios, this doesn't require calculating the likelihood – we simply toss the coin $N = 10$ times, and count n, the number of heads. If the number of heads is equal to the number of heads we observed in reality (three), we accept the prior sample. If not, we throw it away. The magic of ABC is that the accepted samples are samples from the posterior density! We can intuitively see why this is the case. The posterior should give non-zero weight to all values of r that could produce three heads from ten tosses. This is all values except $r = 0$ and

$r = 1$, but samples of r corresponding to areas of high posterior density (in this case, around 0.3) will be more likely to produce three heads from ten tosses and therefore be accepted far more often than those at much higher and lower values.

Figure 9.16 shows the empirical posterior density obtained by sampling (white bars) along with the true posterior (solid black line) and the prior (dashed black line) (MATLAB script: abc.m). The empirical distribution was obtained by generating 20,000 samples from the prior, of which 1819 (9%) were accepted. This is pretty inefficient – 90% of the samples we obtain are rejected, and this figure gets worse the more complex we make the problem. For example, if we increase N to 20 and observe $n = 6$ heads, we only accept 5% of the samples and if $N = 50$ and $n = 15$, we only accept 2% of samples. For many real applications the situation is worse, and efficiency is very low.

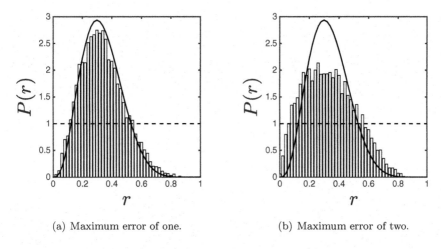

(a) Maximum error of one.   (b) Maximum error of two.

FIGURE 9.17 ABC sampling for the coin game when we accept samples that generate a number of heads maximally one and two different from the true value (three).

Our set of samples is an exact sample from the posterior – there is no approximation here. So why the 'approximation' in the name? Well, for many likelihoods, even with the true parameters we would never generate a dataset that was identical to the true one. Consider doing Bayesian inference over the posterior density of the mean of a Gaussian for which we have observed one data point. Even if we knew the true mean, we would never sample *exactly* the value we had previously observed.

To overcome this, ABC allows prior samples to be accepted if the dataset they produce is sufficiently similar to the true data. This makes things more efficient (we accept more parameters) but we no longer know that we are sampling from the true posterior density and there is not really any way of knowing how close to the true posterior the distribution we are sampling from is.

In our coin example, we can relax our acceptance criteria by accepting a sample if it generates a number of heads that differs by the true value by a maximum of one or a maximum of two. Plots of the true and empirical posteriors for both cases can be seen in Figure 9.17. As expected, the efficiency increases (27% and 40% of samples are accepted, respectively) but the empirical posterior becomes quite different from the true one, spreading across more values of r.

When comparing the true and generated datasets, one can compare the data directly or compare summary statistics of the data. This is what we have done above – we haven't compared the exact sequence of heads and tails obtained in the ten tosses, but just the number of heads. In this example, the data (the sequence of heads and tails) and summary statistic (number of heads) will both give the exact posterior (if we don't relax the acceptance criteria). We can get a feeling for why this is the case by looking at what happens when you normally compute the posterior analytically. The posterior is given by

$$p(r|n, N, \alpha, \beta) = \frac{\Gamma(\alpha + \beta)}{\Gamma(\alpha)\Gamma(\beta)} r^{\alpha+n-1}(1 - r)^{\beta+N-n+1}.$$

which only uses the number of heads (and not their order). So, somehow, all of the information that we require is captured by the number of heads. If we only accepted identical sequences, all prior samples of r would be less likely to be accepted, but this drop in probability would not depend on the particular value of r. So, we would end up with the same distribution, just fewer samples.

Similarly, if we are interested in inferring the mean of a Gaussian density (with known variance, σ^2) based on observing N values from the Gaussian $(x_1, \ldots, x_N)$ and a Gaussian prior with mean μ_0 and variance σ_0^2, the posterior is Gaussian with mean and variance given by

$$\sigma_N^2 = \left(\frac{1}{\sigma_0^2} + \frac{N}{\sigma^2}\right)^{-1}, \quad \mu_N = \sigma_N^2 \left(\frac{\mu_0}{\sigma_0^2} + \frac{1}{\sigma^2}\sum_n x_n\right),$$

in which the data only appear as a summation. That is all we need to know to compute the posterior. So, if we were willing to wait a long time, we could accept samples that generated datasets with the same sum as the real data and get samples from the true posterior. Statistics such as these that encapsulate all of the information in the data that we need to do inference are examples of *sufficient statistics*.

Finally, we will demonstrate how ABC allows us to get approximate samples from the posterior density of the mean of a Gaussian (with known variance). We will use a scheme where a prior sample is accepted if the absolute difference of the mean of the generated data is less than some tunable parameter ϵ. Figure 9.18 shows empirical and true posteriors for increasing values of ϵ. In all cases, the empirical sample was generated by taking 50,000 samples from the prior (mean zero, unit variance; dashed line on the plots). As ϵ increases, we can clearly see the trade-off between efficiency and accuracy. For $\epsilon = 0.01$, we have the samples most representative of the posterior (they must be, as the acceptance is at its most stringent), but very few of them (only 0.13% of samples) were accepted. At the other extreme ($\epsilon = 0.5$), we have many more accepted samples (although still only 8.5%) but the empirical distribution is quite different from the true posterior. In this example, the middle value ($\epsilon = 0.1$) seems to represent a reasonable trade-off between number of samples (1.5%) and proximity to the true posterior.

Although ABC is approximate, it is increasingly popular in areas where likelihood computation is expensive (or impossible). Improving ABC techniques is an open area of research (see Exercise 9.5).

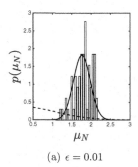

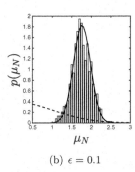

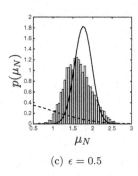

(a) $\epsilon = 0.01$ (b) $\epsilon = 0.1$ (c) $\epsilon = 0.5$

FIGURE 9.18 Using ABC to sample from the posterior density of the mean of a Gaussian with known variance. The three plots correspond to three values of ϵ, the maximum absolute difference between the means of the data and generated datasets for a sample to be accepted. The solid line is the true posterior and the dashed line the prior.

9.5.3 Population MCMC and temperature schedules

In Section 9.5.1 we saw that using Metropolis–Hastings in situations where parameters have high covariance can be challenging unless we can incorporate this information into our proposal (which we did via adapting the proposal covariance and using Hamiltonian Monte Carlo). Another feature of a distribution that can cause problems for samplers is multi-modality. Figure 9.19(a) shows such a distribution and 1000 samples from a Metropolis–Hastings sampler with an isotropic proposal density ($\sigma^2 = 0.05$). We can see that the sampler has explored one of the modes but no samples have been drawn from the other mode. In theory, the sampler will eventually reach all of the modes, but in practice, movement from one mode to another requires a large number of downhill moves which are collectively very unlikely. If we start multiple chains, as in Figure 9.19(b), each chain seems to get stuck in whichever mode it enters first. Fortunately, it is quite easy to detect this kind of problem – the $\hat{R}$ statistic introduced earlier will not converge as the samples from the individual chains will look so different. Unfortunately, it is not so easy to fix!

Population MCMC is a family of approaches that can help to overcome this problem. In essence, these approaches run multiple chains in parallel, and, as well as standard proposals that allow movement within a chain, more complex proposals that allow positions to be swapped between chains are also allowed. These swaps provide an efficient way for chains to jump out of local modes and provide more efficient sampling.

The individual chains do not all have to be sampling from the same distribution, as long as one of them is sampling from the distribution of interest. A particularly interesting approach for posterior sampling is when we use what is known as a temperature schedule. Here, we run chains in each of N distributions where the nth chain is sampling from:

$$p_n(\boldsymbol{\theta}|\mathbf{X}) \propto p(\mathbf{X}|\boldsymbol{\theta})^{t_n} p(\boldsymbol{\theta}),$$

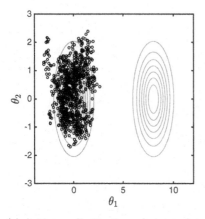 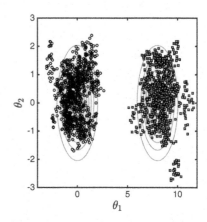

(a) A Metropolis–Hastings chain stuck in a single mode of a bi-modal density.

(b) Two chains, each stuck in different modes.

FIGURE 9.19 An example of Metropolis–Hastings getting stuck in individual modes of a bi-modal density.

where t_n ranges from 0 to 1. When t_n is equal to 0, $p_n(\boldsymbol{\theta}|\mathbf{X})$ is equal to the prior, and when t_n is equal to 1, the posterior. As t_n increases from 0, the distribution becomes less like the prior and more like the posterior. At each step in the sampler, we can update individual chains according to standard Metropolis–Hastings proposals or swap the states of adjacent chains (i.e. between the nth and the $n+1$th chain). We keep track of the state of all chains, but it is only the samples from the $t_n = 1$ chain that are of interest (samples from the posterior).

The rationale behind such an approach is that samplers in chains with low values of t_n should be able to move more easily around the space than those with higher values of t_n. Allowing swaps between adjacent chains means that this exploration can percolate up to the chains with higher t_n, giving them the opportunity to make larger moves and not get stuck in local optima.

For more detail on population MCMC and associated methods, see the suggested reading at the end of the chapter.

9.5.4 Sequential Monte Carlo

The final method we will look at is **sequential Monte Carlo** (SMC), often also called *particle filtering*. SMC techniques have been used widely to perform real-time inference for distributions that change over time (for example, tracking the movement of an object).

In its simplest setting, SMC represents the distribution over parameters at time t via a set of samples. These samples are then modified when we see the new observation. The simplest form of modification is to weight each of the current samples by the likelihood of the new observation and then create a new population by choosing current samples with probability proportional to their likelihood and applying some random modification to them. Crucially, samples are chosen from the current population with replacement, meaning that the same current sample could be chosen more than once. The modification to the parameters is often something simple, like moving them according to a simple Gaussian density (much like a Metropolis–Hastings proposal).

This simple process has been used in many applications due to its efficiency and speed, which are both particularly important in real-time tracking applications. More recently, it has also been shown to be useful for sampling for things that do not change over time. In these cases, time can be replaced with a temperature schedule (as described above). Starting with a large sample of the prior, we gradually increase the power to which the likelihood is raised, updating our sample at each step. Finally, we have a sample that can be interpreted as a sample from the posterior.

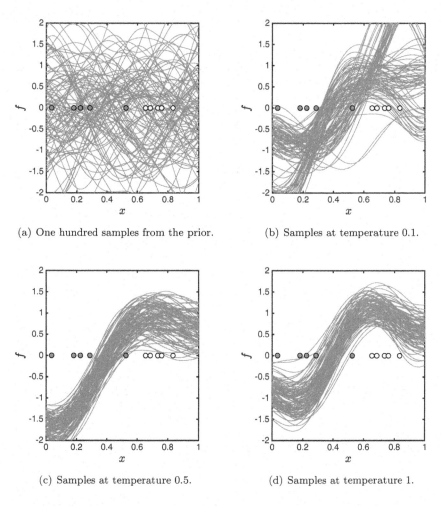

(a) One hundred samples from the prior.

(b) Samples at temperature 0.1.

(c) Samples at temperature 0.5.

(d) Samples at temperature 1.

FIGURE 9.20 GP classification with SMC.

Figure 9.20 shows this in action to sample from the posterior over latent functions for a one-dimensional GP classifier (MATLAB script: gp_smc.m) using the probit likelihood we used earlier in this chapter. We start with $N = 10$ observed data points in two classes (those in class 0 are denoted by grey circles, those in class 1 by white circles) and 100 sampled latent functions from the prior (Figure 9.20(a)), denoted by $\mathbf{f}^1, \ldots, \mathbf{f}^S$. Note that, in the plot, rather than plotting the samples directly (they are only defined at the values of x in the training set), we have plotted the functions given by doing a GP regression from the prior samples onto a fine grid over x. Assuming a temperature schedule that increases by 0.1 at each stage, we give each of these samples a weight of

$$
w_s = \left[\prod_{n=1}^{N} P(t_n = 1|f_n^s)^{t_n} (1 - P(t_n = 1|f_n^s))^{1-t_n} \right]^{0.1} \mathcal{N}(\mathbf{f}^s|\mathbf{C})
$$

We then normalise this weight and use the normalised weight to resample a new population of 100 samples. For each new sample, we move it slightly away from the original (say $\mathbf{f}^s$) by sampling from a Gaussian with mean $\mathbf{f}^s$ and a covariance matrix equal to $0.05\mathbf{C}$. This new population of samples can be seen in Figure 9.20(b), where we can see that already the samples look reasonable – having lower values on the left (class 0) than on the right (class 1). This process is repeated with the likelihood raised to increasing temperature values for each temperature up to 1 $(0.2, 0.3, \ldots, 1)$, at which point the samples have been weighted and resampled based on their posterior values. The population of samples at temperatures of 0.5 and 1.0 can be seen in Figures 9.20(c) and 9.20(d), respectively. The samples from the highest temperature look like what we might expect from the posterior – they are heavily concentrated around functions that are low where we see examples in class 0 and high where we see examples in class 1. In this example, we can compare them with the samples from the true posterior as shown in Figure 9.4(c) and they look pretty similar.

Using SMC in this way, we cannot really quantify how close to the true posterior our samples are. For example, when we regenerate samples, we pick one of the previous ones and perturb it a little. Choice of this perturbation will affect our final samples. However, the simplicity of the process has led to it being used in various applications.

9.6   CHAPTER SUMMARY

In this chapter we have built upon the brief introduction to Metropolis–Hastings that we provided in Chapter 4. As well as providing more detail on Metropolis–Hastings, we have introduced Gibbs sampling and briefly introduced various other sampling approaches. All of these methods are widely used for generating posterior samples that can be used to make predictions across many machine learning applications, and a knowledge of MCMC techniques is increasingly important for those working in machine learning.

Although theoretically quite straightforward, MCMC techniques are often tricky to use, particularly when sampling from complex distributions that exhibit high correlation between variables, or multiple modes. Being able to assess whether chains have converged and assessing the autocorrelation of the samples being produced are vital to producing useful samples. Although we have covered these areas, we strongly recommend practising building and evaluating sampling methods – it is the only way to really get a feel for these powerful approaches.

There is much ongoing research in this area, and many techniques that we have not described. However, we hope that from this introduction you are in a position to explore this area further and are able to make use of MCMC techniques. The suggested reading below provides a lot more detail in the areas we have covered, and more.

9.7 EXERCISES

9.1 For some one-dimensional input data, construct a GP RBF covariance matrix. Use Gibbs sampling to sample functions from this GP prior (samples from a GP prior are just samples from a multivariate Gaussian). Compare the samples with values obtained by sampling directly from the Gaussian. In particular, compute the autocorrelation of the function at one of the inputs across the two methods.

9.2 Use Metropolis–Hastings instead of Gibbs sampling to sample from the GP classification model. Note that you will no longer need to perform the auxiliary variable trick. Compare the predictions with those obtained from the Gibbs sampling approach.

9.3 Using the provided code for performing Gibbs sampling for binary GP classification, compute the $\hat{R}$ value for one of the training latent function values. How many samples need to be drawn before $\hat{R}$ is lower than 1.01?

9.4 For the same GP model as in Exercise 9.3, compute the autocorrelation of one of the training latent function values. How much thinning would be required to obtain independent samples?

9.5 Generate a regression dataset by sampling a function from a GP prior and then adding some noise. Use ABC to sample from the posterior. Each sample should be generated by first sampling from the GP prior and then adding noise. Use the Euclidean distance between the generated data and the original data to determine acceptance (experiment with different levels of tolerance). How efficient is your sampler? How do the samples compare with those from the true posterior (see Section 8.2.3)?

9.8 FURTHER READING

[1] Arnaud Doucet, Nando de Freitas, and Neil Gordon. *Sequential Monte Carlo Methods in Practice*. Springer, first edition, 2001.

   An excellent introduction to many sequential Monte Carlo algorithms.

[2] Andrew Gelman, John B. Carlin, Hal S. Stern, and Donald B. Rubin. *Bayesian Data Analysis*. Chapman and Hall/CRC, third edition, 2014.

   This is an excellent resource for practical Bayesian inference. In particular, it provides a solid introduction to several sampling techniques as well as procedures for determining if Metropolis–Hastings and other sampling algorithms have converged. It also includes discussion of suitable acceptance rates when sampling from different distributions.

[3] Walter Wilks, Sylvia Richardson, and David Spegelhalter. *Markov Chain Monte Carlo in Practice*. Springer, first edition, 1996.

   An excellent and practical introduction to many facets of MCMC approaches.

CHAPTER 10

Advanced Mixture Modelling

In Chapter 6 we introduced mixture models as a statistical method for clustering. Mixture models allow us to model complex distributions as combinations of simpler ones. This is particularly useful for clustering, as data that we might wish to cluster is likely to have multiple modes and it is natural to imagine each mode (cluster) being modelled by a separate distribution. To introduce inference in mixture models, we used the EM algorithm, which produces point estimates of the parameters of each component, and the component membership probabilities of each data point.

Mixture models are used across machine learning and so we have decided to devote a whole chapter to describe things that we didn't have space for in the clustering chapter. We will start by showing how we can use Gibbs sampling as a nice alternative to the EM algorithm. As well as giving samples from the posterior distribution over clusterings (rather than point estimates), the Gibbs sampler allows us to create an infinite mixture model, freeing us from having to specify the precise number of components in the data.

The infinite mixture model is closely related to a stochastic process that has gained a lot of traction in machine learning in recent years – the Dirichlet process. We will provide a high-level introduction to Dirichlet processes and their extension to Hierarchical Dirichlet processes.

Finally, topic models have become popular within machine learning, particularly for text modelling. These models relax the assumption that each data point was generated by one of the components, and allow data points to be modelled by multiple components. We will briefly discuss the most popular topic model – Latent Dirichlet Allocation.

10.1   A GIBBS SAMPLER FOR MIXTURE MODELS

In Chapter 9 we introduced Gibbs sampling, a Markov Chain Monte Carlo algorithm for sampling from joint distributions for which conditional distributions over all parameters (conditioned on the others) are available. With suitable prior distribution choices, mixture models fall into this category and Gibbs sampling is a popular alternative to the EM algorithm we described in Section 6.3.3. To illustrate this, we will construct a Gibbs sampler for a two-dimensional Gaussian Mixture.

Figure 10.1 shows a dataset that appears to consist of three clusters. Data in each cluster looks like it could have been derived from a two-dimensional Gaussian density, and we will assume in this example that each Gaussian has an identity

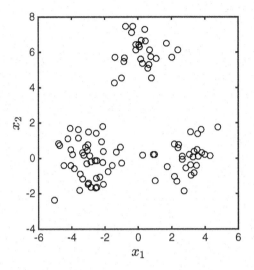

FIGURE 10.1 A dataset consisting of three Gaussian clusters.

covariance matrix (extending the model to include unknown covariance matrices is possible, but we have omitted it here, as the extra algebra might be a bit off-putting). We would therefore like to perform inference over the means of the Gaussians as well as infer which Gaussian each particular data point came from. We will do this with Gibbs sampling.

The mixture model likelihood for the nth observation $(\mathbf{x}_n)$ is given by

$$p(\mathbf{x}_n|\boldsymbol{\pi}, \boldsymbol{\mu}_1, \ldots, \boldsymbol{\mu}_K) = \sum_{k=1}^{K} \pi_k p(\mathbf{x}_n|\boldsymbol{\mu}_k),$$

where K is the number of components, $\boldsymbol{\pi} = [\pi_1, \ldots, \pi_K]^{\mathsf{T}}$ is the vector of prior component probabilities and, in this case, $p(\mathbf{x}_n|\boldsymbol{\mu}_k) = \mathcal{N}(\boldsymbol{\mu}_k, \mathbf{I})$.

When defining a mixture model, we are making the implicit assumption that each data point originated from one (and only one) of the K components (we will look at how this can be relaxed in Section 10.5). Part of our aim is to perform inference over which component each data point came from. To this end, we define a set of $N \times K$ binary parameters z_{nk}, where $z_{nk} = 1$ if observation n belongs to the kth component and 0 otherwise. Formally, if $z_{nk} = 1$, then $z_{nj} = 0$ for all $j \neq k$. We will collect all of these binary variables into an $N \times K$ matrix $\mathbf{Z}$ and we will use $\mathbf{z}_n$ to denote the $K \times 1$ binary membership vector for the nth data point.

If we know that $z_{nk} = 1$, our likelihood becomes

$$p(\mathbf{x}_n, \mathbf{z}_n|\boldsymbol{\pi}, \boldsymbol{\mu}_1, \ldots, \boldsymbol{\mu}_K) = \pi_k p(\mathbf{x}_n|\boldsymbol{\mu}_k),$$

i.e. the likelihood of $\mathbf{x}_n$ for the component that produced it, multiplied by the prior probability of that component producing a data point (π_k). In general, it's notationally easier to write this as

$$p(\mathbf{x}_n, \mathbf{z}_n | \boldsymbol{\pi}, \boldsymbol{\mu}_1, \ldots, \boldsymbol{\mu}_K) = \prod_{k=1}^{K} [\pi_k p(\mathbf{x}_n | \boldsymbol{\mu}_k)]^{z_{nk}},$$

which is identical – raising the likelihood of each component to the power z_{nk} has the effect of *switching on* the component to which this data point is assigned.

In reality we don't know $\mathbf{Z}$ – this is one of the things we are trying to learn. We therefore have three sets of unknown parameters: the means, $\boldsymbol{\mu}_1, \ldots, \boldsymbol{\mu}_K$, the component priors, $\boldsymbol{\pi}$, and the component memberships $\mathbf{Z}$. Gibbs sampling will give us samples from the joint posterior distribution of these three sets of variables. The final definitions we need are the various prior densities. We will assume a Gaussian prior over each of the mean vectors with mean $\boldsymbol{\mu}_0$ and covariance $\boldsymbol{\Sigma}_0$:

$$p(\boldsymbol{\mu}_k | \boldsymbol{\mu}_0, \boldsymbol{\Sigma}_0) = \mathcal{N}(\boldsymbol{\mu}_0, \boldsymbol{\Sigma}_0).$$

We will also assume that, under the prior, the different mean vectors are independent, allowing us to compute the joint prior density by taking a product over the K individual priors:

$$p(\boldsymbol{\mu}_1, \ldots, \boldsymbol{\mu}_K | \boldsymbol{\mu}_0, \boldsymbol{\Sigma}_0) = \prod_{k=1}^{K} \mathcal{N}(\boldsymbol{\mu}_k | \boldsymbol{\mu}_0, \boldsymbol{\Sigma}_0).$$

What is the prior for z_{nk}? If we think of our model generatively, we sample from the kth component with probability π_k. Therefore, isn't the prior probability that $z_{nk} = 1$ simply π_k? Not quite – we need to be a little more specific. If we set $z_{nk} = 1$, we also have to set $z_{nj} = 0$ for all other components. It is therefore the whole vector $\mathbf{z}_n$ that we are setting, of which only one element can be 1. $\mathbf{z}_n$ is therefore one draw from a multinomial distribution with parameters $\boldsymbol{\pi}$ (see Section 2.3.3). The multinomial distribution is defined as

$$P(\mathbf{z}_n | \boldsymbol{\pi}) = \frac{(\sum_k z_{nk})!}{\prod_{k=1}^{K} z_{nk}!} \prod_{k=1}^{K} \pi_k^{z_{nk}}.$$

Because we are only making one draw from the multinomial, both terms in the fraction evaluate to 1 ($\sum_k z_{nk} = 1$, and $z_{nk}! = 1$ for all k). The distribution therefore reduces to

$$P(\mathbf{z}_n | \boldsymbol{\pi}) = \prod_{k=1}^{K} \pi_k^{z_{nk}},$$

where only one term in the product is switched on (the one corresponding to the chosen component).

Comment 10.1 – The Dirichlet Distribution: A Dirichlet distribution in M dimensions is defined over all vectors of length M where each value is between 0 and 1 and the sum of the values equals 1. In particular, for vectors $\mathbf{y} = [y_1, \ldots, y_M]^\mathsf{T}$, the Dirichlet is defined over all vectors that satisfy: $0 \leq y_m \leq 1$, $\sum_m y_m = 1$. The pdf is given by

$$p(\mathbf{y}|\boldsymbol{\alpha}) = Dir(\alpha_1, \ldots, \alpha_M) = \frac{\Gamma\left(\sum_m \alpha_m\right)}{\prod_m \Gamma(\alpha_m)} \prod_{m=1}^{M} y_m^{\alpha_m - 1},$$

where $\Gamma(\cdot)$ is the gamma function that we have seen before (see, e.g. Section 2.5.2). As the vector has to sum to 1, the distribution is therefore really defined over an $M - 1$ dimensional subspace of the M dimensions. This is because the Mth dimension is completely determined by the other $M - 1$ ($y_M = 1 - \sum_{m=1}^{M-1} y_m$).

For $M = 2$, we therefore have a one-dimensional subspace (a line) on which the Dirichlet defines a probability density over y_1 and $y_2 = 1 - y_1$. Three examples, with different parameter values, are shown on the right. On the x axis is the value for y_1. The value for y_2 is not shown (it has to be $1 - y_1$).

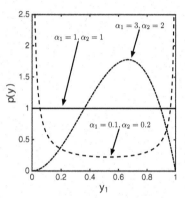

For $M = 3$, the valid points lie on the two-dimensional triangular surface with corners at $[1, 0, 0]$, $[0, 1, 0]$ and $[0, 0, 1]$. By varying the parameters, the distribution can be varied between something where the highest density is in the corners (producing sparse probability vectors with a small number of non-zero values) and something where it is in the centre. Examples with $\boldsymbol{\alpha} = [0.8, 0.8, 0.8]$ (left plot; high density in the corners) and $\boldsymbol{\alpha} = [3, 3, 3]$ (right plot; high density in the centre) can be seen below.

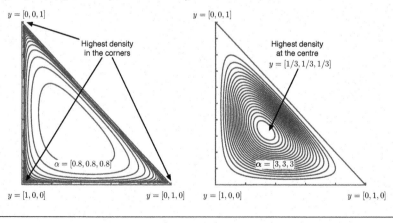

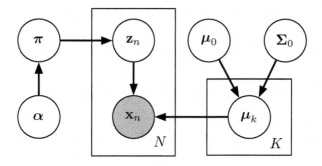

FIGURE 10.2 A plates diagram of the mixture model.

Finally, we need a prior for $\boldsymbol{\pi}$. As this is a vector of probabilities, all of its values have to be between 0 and 1 and the sum of the values must be equal to 1. A suitable prior distribution defined over vectors with these properties is the **Dirichlet** distribution (see Comment 10.1 and Equation 5.7). The pdf of the Dirichlet is

$$p(\boldsymbol{\pi}|\boldsymbol{\alpha}) = \frac{\Gamma\left(\sum_{k=1}^{K} \alpha_k\right)}{\prod_{k=1}^{K} \Gamma(\alpha_k)} \prod_{k=1}^{K} \pi_k^{\alpha_k - 1}.$$

This completes our model definition and a plates diagram of the model can be seen in Figure 10.2.

The joint posterior density over the three sets of unknown parameters is:

$$p(\mathbf{Z}, \boldsymbol{\pi}, \boldsymbol{\mu}_1, \ldots, \boldsymbol{\mu}_K | \mathbf{X}, \alpha, \boldsymbol{\mu}_0, \boldsymbol{\Sigma}_0) \propto \left[\prod_{n=1}^{N} \prod_{k=1}^{K} [\pi_k p(\mathbf{x}_n | \boldsymbol{\mu}_k)]^{z_{nk}} \right]$$

$$\times \left[\prod_{k=1}^{K} p(\boldsymbol{\mu}_k | \boldsymbol{\mu}_0, \boldsymbol{\Sigma}_0) \right] p(\boldsymbol{\pi}|\alpha). \quad (10.1)$$

We saw in Chapter 9 that the conditional distributions for each parameter are proportional to this joint posterior. For each parameter we can therefore ignore any terms that don't involve it on the right hand side and use the terms that remain to work out the form of the conditional distribution. Starting with $\boldsymbol{\pi}$, if we only keep terms involving $\boldsymbol{\pi}$ on the right hand side, we are left with

$$p(\boldsymbol{\pi}| \ldots) \propto p(\boldsymbol{\pi}|\alpha) \prod_{n=1}^{N} \prod_{k=1}^{K} \pi_k^{z_{nk}}.$$

Expanding the Dirichlet prior (and ignoring the constant, as it doesn't involve $\boldsymbol{\pi}$),

$$p(\boldsymbol{\pi}| \ldots) \propto \left[\prod_{k=1}^{K} \pi_k^{\alpha_k - 1} \right] \left[\prod_{n=1}^{N} \prod_{k=1}^{K} \pi_k^{z_{nk}} \right].$$

Because z_{nk} is binary, the second term can be rewritten as

$$\prod_{n=1}^{N} \prod_{k=1}^{K} \pi_k^{z_{nk}} = \prod_{k=1}^{K} \pi_k^{\sum_n z_{nk}},$$

and the whole thing can be expressed with one product over K:

$$p(\boldsymbol{\pi}|\ldots) \propto \prod_{k=1}^{K} \pi_k^{\alpha_k - 1 + \sum_n z_{nk}}.$$

So, the unnormalised conditional density for $\boldsymbol{\pi}$ has the form of a product over the components of $\boldsymbol{\pi}$, each raised to the power of $\alpha_k^* - 1$ where

$$\alpha_k^* = \alpha_k + \sum_{n=1}^{N} z_{nk}.$$

This is exactly the form of a Dirichlet distribution (see Comment 10.1) and so the conditional density of $\boldsymbol{\pi}$ has to be a Dirichlet. The fact that this distribution is a Dirichlet also tells us that the Dirichlet prior and the multinomial likelihood form a conjugate pair – a feature that has led to so-called Dirichlet-multinomial models being widely used, particularly in text modelling applications. Our Dirichlet is given as

$$p(\boldsymbol{\pi}|\ldots) = Dir(\alpha_1 + \sum_n z_{n1}, \ldots, \alpha_K + \sum_n z_{nK}). \tag{10.2}$$

Next we will derive the conditional distribution for $\boldsymbol{\mu}_k$. Taking the terms involving $\boldsymbol{\mu}_k$ from the right hand side of Equation 10.1, we are left with

$$p(\boldsymbol{\mu}_k|\ldots) \propto p(\boldsymbol{\mu}_k|\boldsymbol{\mu}_0, \boldsymbol{\Sigma}_0) \prod_{n=1}^{N} p(\mathbf{x}_n|\boldsymbol{\mu}_k)^{z_{nk}}. \tag{10.3}$$

The two terms on the right hand side could be interpreted as a Gaussian prior and a Gaussian likelihood and therefore we know that the conditional distribution will also be Gaussian. We leave it as an exercise (see Exercise 10.1) to show that the conditional distribution is

$$p(\boldsymbol{\mu}_k|\ldots) = \mathcal{N}(\mathbf{a}, \mathbf{B}), \tag{10.4}$$

where

$$\mathbf{B} = \left[\boldsymbol{\Sigma}_0^{-1} + \left(\sum_n z_{nk} \right) \mathbf{I} \right]^{-1}, \quad \mathbf{a} = \mathbf{B} \left[\boldsymbol{\Sigma}_0^{-1} \boldsymbol{\mu}_0 + \sum_n z_{nk} \mathbf{x}_n \right].$$

Finally, we need the conditional distribution for $\mathbf{z}_n$. Isolating terms involving $\mathbf{z}_n$ in the right hand side of Equation 10.1 we are left with

$$P(\mathbf{z}_n|\ldots) \propto \prod_{k=1}^{K} [\pi_k p(\mathbf{x}_n|\boldsymbol{\mu}_k)]^{z_{nk}}.$$

Consider the vector $\mathbf{z}_n$ that has its 1 in the kth position (all other entries must be 0). We will write the probability of this vector as $P(z_{nk} = 1|\ldots)$, with the implicit assumption that $z_{nj} = 0$ for all $j \neq k$. The unnormalised probability is

$$P(z_{nk} = 1|\ldots) \propto \pi_k p(\mathbf{x}_n|\boldsymbol{\mu}_k).$$

To normalise, all we need to do is divide by the summation over all possible values of $\mathbf{z}_n$, which is simply $\sum_j \pi_j p(\mathbf{x}_n|\boldsymbol{\mu}_j)$. In particular

$$P(z_{nk} = 1|\ldots) = \frac{\pi_k p(\mathbf{x}_n|\boldsymbol{\mu}_k)}{\sum_{j=1}^{K} \pi_j p(\mathbf{x}_n|\boldsymbol{\mu}_j)}. \tag{10.5}$$

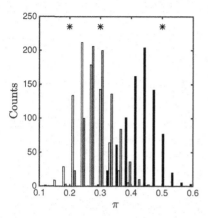

(a) Marginal posteriors for π_k. Stars show the true values.

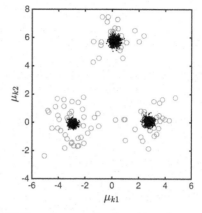

(b) Posterior samples of $\boldsymbol{\mu}_k$ (dots show samples and light circles the data).

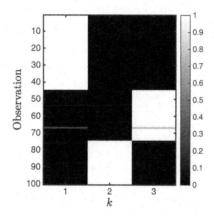

(c) Posterior probability of cluster membership.

FIGURE 10.3 Results of applying the Gibbs sampler to the mixture model. One thousand samples were drawn, with the first 200 discarded as a burn-in phase.

We now have all of the conditional distributions required to build our Gibbs sampler. The procedure is as follows:

1. Initialise $\boldsymbol{\mu}_1, \ldots, \boldsymbol{\mu}_K$ and $\boldsymbol{\pi}$ with samples from their respective prior densities.
2. Resample each $\mathbf{x}_n$ conditioned on $\boldsymbol{\mu}_1, \ldots, \boldsymbol{\mu}_K$ and $\boldsymbol{\pi}$, via Equation 10.5.
3. Resample each $\boldsymbol{\mu}_k$ conditioned on $\mathbf{Z}$, via Equation 10.4.
4. Resample $\boldsymbol{\pi}$ conditioned on $\mathbf{Z}$, via Equation 10.2.

5. Return to step 2 until enough samples have been generated.

We can see the result of this procedure in Figure 10.3 (MATLAB script: `gmix2d.m`). Here we have taken 1000 posterior samples and discarded the first 100 as a burn-in (see Section 9.4.1). K was set to 3 and $\boldsymbol{\alpha} = [1/3, 1/3, 1/3]$. $\boldsymbol{\mu}_0$ was set to a vector of zeros, and $\boldsymbol{\Sigma}_0$ to the identity matrix.

In Figure 10.3(a) we can see histograms of the posterior samples for the components of $\boldsymbol{\pi}$. The stars show the true values, and it is clear that the true values correspond to reasonably high posterior values. Note that, because we are only sampling $N = 100$ data points, we would expect to observe some deviation from the true value. Figure 10.3(b) shows posterior samples of the three cluster means. The samples are shown as black dots with the data shown (for reference) as lighter circles. We can see that the posterior samples for the means correspond very strongly to the positions of the true means. Finally, in Figure 10.3(c) we show the posterior probability of cluster membership, obtained by averaging over the number of times each data point was assigned to each cluster. In this case we can see that points are always assigned to the correct clusters (in the figure the data points (rows) are grouped in their clusters).

Gibbs sampling is popular for mixture models where the various prior and likelihood terms are chosen such that we can compute and sample from all of the conditional distributions. In this example, we assumed the covariance of the Gaussian components was known but this is not necessary. There is a conjugate prior for the mean and covariance of a Gaussian (the Normal-Inverse-Wishart) which would allow us to obtain posterior distributions over both the mean and covariance. Other conjugate prior-likelihood pairs, such as the beta-binomial and the Dirichlet-multinomial, also result in computationally attractive sampling schemes. To work through an example, see Exercise 10.3.

The sampler we have described appears to work very well (albeit on a very simple example). However, it actually only explores a small part of the posterior. We have defined three cluster components (call them 1, 2 and 3). The assignment of these components to the data clusters in Figure 10.1 is arbitrary. We could assign number 1 to the bottom left cluster, number 2 to the bottom right and number 3 to the top one, or any other combination. The value of the posterior for each assignment would be identical (the model doesn't change when we change the name of a cluster) and so we can deduce that the posterior has multiple identical nodes, one for each way of assigning the cluster names to the actual clusters. If you are not sure about this point, imagining implementing the sampler. You would perhaps have arrays storing the current values of $\boldsymbol{\mu}$, $\boldsymbol{\pi}$ and $\mathbf{Z}$. Let's assume that, in each case, the column of the array indicates the cluster (e.g. the kth column of $\mathbf{Z}$ gives the memberships to cluster k and the kth column of $\boldsymbol{\mu}$ gives the value of $\boldsymbol{\mu}_k$). If you permuted the columns of all arrays in the same way, the model wouldn't have changed at all.

Now, a good sampler ought to explore the whole of the posterior, but, in our example, it has only explored one mode (one mapping of columns to cluster). Because we know that all of the modes are identical, this is not a practical problem. In fact, it would make it harder to interpret the output of the sampler if it did explore them all. However, it is important to bear in mind, particularly if we are monitoring convergence using multiple chains, as two chains are unlikely to converge to the same mode (see Exercise 10.2).

So far, we have applied Gibbs sampling (from Chapter 9) to a mixture model (from Chapter 6). Although this is useful, we haven't done anything particularly new. We will now move on to show that within the Gibbs sampler, we can avoid having to specify the number of components (K). In fact, we will infer the posterior distribution over the number of components from the data. We will do this by first extending the mixture model to having an infinite number of components and then see how this can also be viewed from the perspective of **Dirichlet processes**. Before we do this, we must first see how Gibbs sampling allows us to get rid of some variables from the model (collapsed Gibbs sampling).

10.2   COLLAPSED GIBBS SAMPLING

In the previous section we described a Gibbs sampler for a mixture model. Part of the model was the prior distribution over mixture components, π. The kth component of π, π_k tells us the prior probability a data point should be assigned to component k (i.e. the probability before we see the actual value of the data point). As such, the posterior values of this variable reflect the proportion of points in each cluster.

We have some additional control over this parameter through a Dirichlet prior. By varying the Dirichlet parameters (α), we are able to provide an a priori preference for vectors π that are quite uniform (all values are roughly the same) or are quite non-uniform (some very high and some very low values). Being able to specify a prior over π feels quite useful, but are we actually interested in the posterior? Probably not – we are normally only interested in how the data points cluster. Because of the conjugacy of the Dirichlet prior and multinomial likelihood, it turns out that we can actually remove π from our sampler. Doing so will open up a useful way of extending our model to overcome the limitation of having to specify K.

Consider resampling the cluster membership of the nth data point $(\mathbf{z}_n)$. In the previous section, we derived the conditional distribution to be

$$P(z_{nk} = 1 | \ldots) \propto \pi_k p(\mathbf{x}_n | \boldsymbol{\mu}_k). \tag{10.6}$$

At this stage in the sampler, what do we know about π? We know its prior (a Dirichlet with parameters α) and we know the likelihood of the observed data (all of the other $\mathbf{z}_m$) given π (a multinomial). As the Dirichlet prior is conjugate to the multinomial, we can compute the posterior over π. Note that this is conditional on all of the other assignments so the posterior for π will potentially be different when resampling each data point.

To derive this posterior, we need to expand our notation a bit. We will use $\mathbf{Z}^{-n}$ to be the set of all assignments *except* the nth one, and c_k^{-n} to be the number of objects assigned to component k, not including the assignment of $\mathbf{x}_n$, i.e. $c_k^{-n} = \sum_{m \neq n} z_{mk}$. The likelihood of the other observations given π is given by

$$P(\mathbf{Z}^{-n} | \pi) \propto \prod_{m \neq n}^{K} \prod_{k=1}^{K} \pi_k^{z_{mk}} = \prod_{k=1}^{K} \pi_k^{c_k^{-n}},$$

where we have ignored the normalisation constant, as it does not depend on π. The prior is Dirichlet with parameter α, which is (again ignoring the constant) given by

$$p(\pi | \alpha) \propto \prod_{k=1}^{K} \pi_k^{\alpha_k - 1}.$$

Because the prior and likelihood are conjugate, we know that the posterior will also be a Dirichlet. The parameters of this posterior Dirichlet (call them $\boldsymbol{\beta}$) can be obtained by equating the posterior to the product of the likelihood and prior:

$$\prod_{k=1}^{K} \pi_k^{\beta_k - 1} = \left[\prod_{k=1}^{K} \pi_k^{\alpha_k - 1} \right] \left[\prod_{k=1}^{K} \pi_k^{c_k^{-n}} \right]$$

$$= \prod_{k=1}^{K} \pi_k^{\alpha_k + c_k^{-n} - 1}$$

$$\beta_k = \alpha_k + c_k^{-n}.$$

The posterior Dirichlet parameter for component k is simply the prior parameter plus the number of data points in the component. So, at this point in the sampler, there is no reason why we could not sample a value for $\boldsymbol{\pi}$ conditioned on $\mathbf{Z}^{-n}$ and $\boldsymbol{\alpha}$ and then use this to sample $\mathbf{z}_n$. But, we can actually go one step further and remove $\boldsymbol{\pi}$ from the expression completely.

If we were to sample a value for $\boldsymbol{\pi}$ and then $\mathbf{z}_n$, we would effectively be drawing a sample from the joint density over $\mathbf{z}_n$ and $\boldsymbol{\pi}$ conditioned on everything else: $p(\mathbf{z}_n, \boldsymbol{\pi} | \mathbf{Z}^{-n}, \boldsymbol{\mu}_1, \ldots, \boldsymbol{\mu}_K, \boldsymbol{\alpha}, \mathbf{x}_n)$. Decomposing this into the two separate steps gives

$$p(\mathbf{z}_n, \boldsymbol{\pi} | \mathbf{Z}^{-n}, \boldsymbol{\mu}_1, \ldots, \boldsymbol{\mu}_K, \boldsymbol{\alpha}, \mathbf{x}_n) = p(\mathbf{z}_n | \boldsymbol{\pi}, \mathbf{x}_n, \boldsymbol{\mu}_1, \ldots, \boldsymbol{\mu}_K) p(\boldsymbol{\pi} | \mathbf{Z}^{-n}, \boldsymbol{\alpha}),$$

where $p(\boldsymbol{\pi} | \mathbf{Z}^{-n}, \boldsymbol{\alpha})$ is the posterior Dirichlet that we just computed. Expanding the first term in the right hand side (and ignoring the normalisation over k), we have

$$p(\mathbf{z}_n, \boldsymbol{\pi} | \mathbf{Z}^{-n}, \boldsymbol{\mu}_1, \ldots, \boldsymbol{\mu}_K, \boldsymbol{\alpha}, \mathbf{x}_n) \propto \left[\prod_{k=1}^{K} \pi_k p(\mathbf{x}_n | \boldsymbol{\mu}_k) \right]^{z_{nk}} p(\boldsymbol{\pi} | \mathbf{Z}^{-n}, \boldsymbol{\alpha}).$$

If we look at a particular value of $\mathbf{z}_n$, say the one where the kth element is 1 (and all others are zero), this probability becomes

$$p(z_{nk} = 1, \boldsymbol{\pi} | \mathbf{Z}^{-n}, \boldsymbol{\mu}_1, \ldots, \boldsymbol{\mu}_K, \boldsymbol{\alpha}, \mathbf{x}_n) \propto \pi_k p(\mathbf{x}_n | \boldsymbol{\mu}_k) p(\boldsymbol{\pi} | \mathbf{Z}^{-n}, \boldsymbol{\alpha}),$$

which, because π_k is (by definition) $P(z_{nk} = 1 | \boldsymbol{\pi})$ (for the $\mathbf{z}_n$ that has a 1 in the kth element), we can further rewrite as

$$p(z_{nk} = 1, \boldsymbol{\pi} | \mathbf{Z}^{-n}, \boldsymbol{\mu}_1, \ldots, \boldsymbol{\mu}_K, \boldsymbol{\alpha}, \mathbf{x}_n) \propto p(\mathbf{x}_n | \boldsymbol{\mu}_k) p(z_{nk} = 1 | \boldsymbol{\pi}) p(\boldsymbol{\pi} | \mathbf{Z}^{-n}, \boldsymbol{\alpha}).$$

If we integrate both sides with respect to $\boldsymbol{\pi}$, we can remove it completely from the expression (using $\boldsymbol{\mu}$ to denote $\boldsymbol{\mu}_1, \ldots, \boldsymbol{\mu}_K$):

$$\int p(z_{nk} = 1, \boldsymbol{\pi} | \mathbf{Z}^{-n}, \boldsymbol{\mu}, \boldsymbol{\alpha}, \mathbf{x}_n) \, d\boldsymbol{\pi} \propto \int p(\mathbf{x}_n | \boldsymbol{\mu}_k) P(z_{nk} = 1 | \boldsymbol{\pi}) p(\boldsymbol{\pi} | \mathbf{Z}^{-n}, \boldsymbol{\alpha}) \, d\boldsymbol{\pi}$$

$$P(z_{nk} = 1 | \mathbf{Z}^{-n}, \boldsymbol{\mu}, \boldsymbol{\alpha}, \mathbf{x}_n) \propto p(\mathbf{x}_n | \boldsymbol{\mu}_k) \int P(z_{nk} = 1 | \boldsymbol{\pi}) p(\boldsymbol{\pi} | \mathbf{Z}^{-n}, \boldsymbol{\alpha}) \, d\boldsymbol{\pi}$$

$$\propto p(\mathbf{x}_n | \boldsymbol{\mu}_k) P(z_{nk} = 1 | \mathbf{Z}^{-n}, \boldsymbol{\alpha}).$$

So, if we can evaluate the integral on the right hand side, then we can update $\mathbf{z}_n$ without worrying about $\boldsymbol{\pi}$ at all. In fact, we need never worry about $\boldsymbol{\pi}$ in our sampler. Note that the right hand side of the final expression is proportional to the probability we want. But, as with the original expression, it is easy to normalise: we simply divide by the sum across all of the components:

$$P(z_{nk} = 1|\mathbf{Z}^{-n}, \boldsymbol{\mu}_1, \ldots, \boldsymbol{\mu}_K, \alpha, \mathbf{x}_n) = \frac{p(\mathbf{x}_n|\boldsymbol{\mu}_k)P(z_{nk} = 1|\mathbf{Z}^{-n}, \alpha)}{\sum_{j=1}^{K} p(\mathbf{x}_n|\boldsymbol{\mu}_j)P(z_{nj} = 1|\mathbf{Z}^{-n}, \alpha)}.$$

So, we need to be able to evaluate the following integral:

$$P(z_{nk} = 1|\mathbf{Z}^{-n}, \alpha) = \int P(z_{nk} = 1|\boldsymbol{\pi})p(\boldsymbol{\pi}|\mathbf{Z}^{-n}, \alpha) \, d\boldsymbol{\pi}. \qquad (10.7)$$

The first term is just π_k whilst the second term is the posterior Dirichlet that we derived earlier (with parameters $\beta_k = \alpha_k + c_k^{-n}$). Writing these out in full gives us

$$P(z_{nk} = 1|\mathbf{Z}^{-n}, \alpha) = \frac{\Gamma\left(\sum_{j=1}^{K} \beta_j\right)}{\prod_{j=1}^{K} \Gamma(\beta_j)} \int \pi_k \prod_{j=1}^{J} \pi_j^{\beta_j - 1} \, d\boldsymbol{\pi},$$

where we have taken the Dirichlet constant out of the integral, as it does not depend on $\boldsymbol{\pi}$. If we define δ_{jk} as 1 if $j = k$ and 0 otherwise, we can rewrite the integrand to give

$$P(z_{nk} = 1|\mathbf{Z}^{-n}, \alpha) = \frac{\Gamma\left(\sum_{j=1}^{K} \beta_j\right)}{\prod_{j=1}^{K} \Gamma(\beta_j)} \int \prod_{j=1}^{J} \pi_j^{\beta_j + \delta_{jk} - 1} \, d\boldsymbol{\pi}.$$

The integrand now looks like an unnormalised Dirichlet with parameters $\beta_j + \delta_{jk}$. Its integral *must* therefore be the inverse of the Dirichlet constant. Therefore, our expression becomes

$$P(z_{nk} = 1|\mathbf{Z}^{-n}, \alpha) = \frac{\Gamma\left(\sum_{j=1}^{K} \beta_j\right)}{\prod_{j=1}^{K} \Gamma(\beta_j)} \frac{\prod_{j=1}^{K} \Gamma(\beta_j + \delta_{jk})}{\Gamma\left(\sum_{j=1}^{K} \beta_j + \delta_{jk}\right)}.$$

This expression can be simplified considerably. Firstly, note that $\sum_{j=1}^{K} \delta_{jk} = 1$ and therefore

$$\Gamma\left(\sum_{j=1}^{K} \beta_j + \delta_{jk}\right) = \Gamma\left(1 + \sum_{j=1}^{K} \beta_j\right).$$

Secondly, because $\delta_{jk} = 0$ for all $j \neq k$, all of the product terms in the numerator and denominator cancel except for the terms where $j = k$. This leaves

$$P(z_{nk} = 1|\mathbf{Z}^{-n}, \alpha) = \frac{\Gamma\left(\sum_{j=1}^{K} \beta_j\right)}{\Gamma\left(1 + \sum_{j=1}^{K} \beta_j\right)} \frac{\Gamma(\beta_k + 1)}{\Gamma(\beta_k)}.$$

To simplify further, we need to make use of a property of the gamma function. In particular

$$\Gamma(z + 1) = z\Gamma(z)$$

In our expression we can make use of this twice and cancel almost everything:

$$P(z_{nk} = 1|\mathbf{Z}^{-n}, \alpha) = \frac{\Gamma\left(\sum_{j=1}^{K} \beta_j\right)}{\left(\sum_{j=1}^{K} \beta_j\right)\Gamma\left(\sum_{j=1}^{K} \beta_j\right)} \frac{\beta_k \Gamma(\beta_k)}{\Gamma(\beta_k)} = \frac{\beta_k}{\sum_{j=1}^{K} \beta_j}.$$

If we substitute $\beta_k = c_k^{-n} + \alpha_k$, we get

$$P(z_{nk} = 1 | \mathbf{Z}^{-n}, \boldsymbol{\alpha}) = \frac{c_k^{-n} + \alpha_k}{\sum_{j=1}^{K} c_j^{-n} + \alpha_j},$$

which is a remarkably simple expression. It tells us that the prior probability of assigning data point n to component k is proportional to the number of other points in component k plus the prior Dirichlet parameter. In other words, data points are more likely to be assigned to bigger clusters (high c_k^{-n}) than smaller clusters (low c_k^{-n}). The strength of this clustering force is controlled by α_k. If α_k is high, it will dominate and the probability won't change much as the cluster changes size. If α_k is small, then the number of other data points in the cluster will dominate.

It is important to realise that this clustering force, controlled by α, is not a feature of marginalising $\boldsymbol{\pi}$ (the marginalisation doesn't really *change* the model); it is a feature of our use of the Dirichlet prior for $\boldsymbol{\pi}$. The two plots in Comment 10.1 show how changing $\boldsymbol{\alpha}$ changes the Dirichlet from having its mode somewhere near the center (high α values) to having modes at each of the corners (low α values). This corresponds exactly with what we see in our new marginalised prior expression. Consider a Dirichlet where all parameters are the same: $\alpha_k = \alpha \; \forall k$. High α values dominate the marginalised prior expression, resulting in roughly constant cluster membership probabilities. This would result in (on average) a uniform number of points in each component, which is also reflected in the mode of the prior having roughly equal probabilities for each component (see plot in Comment 10.1). Low values of α would leave the c_k^{-n} to dominate, resulting in all of the points being drawn to a small number of large components, which is reflected in the prior mode of $\boldsymbol{\pi}$ being in a corner or an edge.

The result of our marginalisation is a new expression for the resampling of $\mathbf{z}_n$:

$$P(z_{nk} = 1 | \mathbf{Z}^{-n}, \boldsymbol{\mu}_1, \ldots, \boldsymbol{\mu}_K, \boldsymbol{\alpha}, \mathbf{x}_n) \propto \frac{c_k^{-n} + \alpha_k}{\sum_{j=1}^{K} c_j^{-n} + \alpha_j} p(\mathbf{x}_n | \boldsymbol{\mu}_k),$$

which we can substitute into our sampling procedure, allowing us to never bother sampling a value for $\boldsymbol{\pi}$. Note that, if we were interested in $\boldsymbol{\pi}$, we could still sample a value as before, but we will no longer use it anywhere else in the sampler. This is known as a **Collapsed Gibbs** sampler, as we have *collapsed* $\boldsymbol{\pi}$ from the sampler. The two parts in this expression can be considered as a prior:

$$\frac{c_k^{-n} + \alpha_k}{\sum_{j=1}^{K} c_j^{-n} + \alpha_j}$$

and a likelihood ($p(\mathbf{x}_n | \boldsymbol{\mu}_k)$). The prior is conditioned on all of the other assignments so it doesn't look like a prior we have seen before. However, it tells us the probabilities of the different components *without* considering the data, and so in that sense can very naturally be thought of as a prior and we will refer to it as that in the following.

Before we move on to see how this helps us overcome the problem of determining the number of components, we can use this procedure to remove another set of variables from our model: $\boldsymbol{\mu}_1, \ldots, \boldsymbol{\mu}_K$. Using exactly the same reasoning, we could, when resampling $\mathbf{z}_n$ compute the posterior over $\boldsymbol{\mu}_k$ based on the current assignments without the nth point ($\mathbf{Z}^{-n}$). We could then, if we wished, sample a $\boldsymbol{\mu}_k$ and then compute $p(\mathbf{x}_n|\boldsymbol{\mu}_k)$. But, the prior over $\boldsymbol{\mu}_k$ and the likelihood $p(\mathbf{x}_n|\boldsymbol{\mu}_k)$ are both Gaussian and therefore we can integrate out $\boldsymbol{\mu}_k$. We leave it as an exercise (see Exercise 10.4) to show that the posterior over $\boldsymbol{\mu}_k$ is given by

$$p(\boldsymbol{\mu}_k|\mathbf{Z}^{-n}, \mathbf{X}^{-n}, \boldsymbol{\mu}_0, \boldsymbol{\Sigma}_0) = \mathcal{N}(\mathbf{d}, \mathbf{E}),$$

where $\mathbf{X}^n$ is all of the data apart from $\mathbf{x}_n$ and

$$\mathbf{E} = \left(\boldsymbol{\Sigma}_0^{-1} + \mathbf{I}\sum_{m \neq n} z_{mk}\right)^{-1}, \quad \mathbf{d} = \mathbf{E}\left(\boldsymbol{\Sigma}_0^{-1}\boldsymbol{\mu}_0 + \sum_{m \neq n} z_{mk}\mathbf{x}_m\right),$$

and therefore

$$p(\mathbf{x}_n|\mathbf{Z}^{-n}, \mathbf{X}^{-n}, \boldsymbol{\mu}_0, \boldsymbol{\Sigma}_0) = \mathcal{N}(\mathbf{d}, \mathbf{E} + \mathbf{I}). \qquad (10.8)$$

This removes the need to sample $\boldsymbol{\mu}_k$ and leaves us with the following expression for resampling $\mathbf{z}_n$:

$$P(z_{nk} = 1|\mathbf{x}_n, \mathbf{Z}^{-n}, \boldsymbol{\mu}_0, \boldsymbol{\Sigma}_0, \boldsymbol{\alpha}) \propto \frac{c_k^{-n} + \alpha_k}{\sum_{j=1}^{K} c_j^{-n} + \alpha_j} \mathcal{N}(\mathbf{x}_n|\mathbf{d}, \mathbf{E} + \mathbf{I}).$$

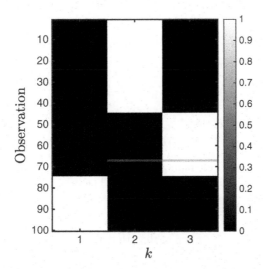

FIGURE 10.4 The posterior component memberships for the collapsed Gibbs sampler.

Our Gibbs sampler now only consists of resampling each $\mathbf{z}_n$ according to this expression! To demonstrate that this works, in Figure 10.4 we have plotted the posterior probabilities of component membership (MATLAB script: gmix2d_marg.m). We can see that these are very similar to those shown in Figure 10.3(c) (with a change in cluster labels – see the discussion of multiple symmetric modes at the end of the last section).

So far, we have not really justified *why* we might prefer a collapsed Gibbs sampler over sampling everything. Our primary motivation is that marginalising $\boldsymbol{\pi}$ will enable us to overcome the problem of having to specify the number of components. However, it has other benefits. In particular, removing parameters can often improve MCMC convergence (e.g. cluster memberships can change more quickly if not conditioned on particular values of $\boldsymbol{\mu}_k$ etc). We won't go into this in detail now but there are some pointers to further reading at the end of the chapter (see Exercise 10.5).

10.3 AN INFINITE MIXTURE MODEL

In the previous section we showed how $\boldsymbol{\pi}$ could be marginalised from the update for $\mathbf{z}_n$ to give a new expression for the prior probability of joining component k:

$$P(z_{nk} = 1|\boldsymbol{\alpha}, \mathbf{Z}^{-n}) = \frac{c_k^{-n} + \alpha_k}{\sum_{j=1}^{K} c_j^{-n} + \alpha_j}.$$

Often we will set all of the Dirichlet prior parameters, $\boldsymbol{\alpha}$, to the same value (we have no a priori reason to prefer any particular component over any other) and, for reasons that will become apparent in a little while, we will set this parameter to α/K – i.e. a constant tunable parameter α divided by the number of components K. Our Dirichlet prior is therefore

$$p(\boldsymbol{\pi}|\alpha) = Dir(\alpha/K, \ldots, \alpha/K)$$

and our sampling prior for $z_{nk} = 1$ becomes

$$P(z_{nk} = 1|\alpha, \mathbf{Z}^{-n}) = \frac{c_k^{-n} + \alpha/K}{\alpha + N - 1},$$

where we have used the fact that $\sum_{j=1}^{K} \alpha/K = \alpha$ and $\sum_{j=1}^{K} c_j^{-n} = N-1$, because all N data points must be in a component except the nth one that we are reassigning.

What happens to this expression if we make K very large? In particular, what if we have an infinite number of components: $K = \infty$? Well, if $K = \infty$, then $\alpha/K = 0$ (assuming that $\alpha > 0$, which it always will be). The prior expression becomes

$$P(z_{nk} = 1|\alpha, \mathbf{Z}^{-n}) = \frac{c_k^{-n}}{\alpha + N - 1}.$$

So, when resampling the allocation of the nth data point, the prior probability that it goes into the kth component is proportional to the number of objects currently in that component. The count, c_k^{-n}, can only be greater than zero for at most $N - 1$ of the infinite number of components. What is the probability of assigning to one of the currently empty ones? We cannot compute the probability of any individual cluster (there are an infinite number of empty ones so they can't each have a non-zero probability without the total probability exceeding 1). However, we can compute the probability that it doesn't go into a component that currently has members (i.e. it goes into *any* of the empty ones) by computing one minus the total probability of going into the non-empty components. Using k_* to denote the empty clusters

$$P(z_{nk_*} = 1|\alpha, \mathbf{Z}^{-n}) = 1 - \sum_{k=1}^{K} \frac{c_k^{-n}}{\alpha + N - 1} = 1 - \frac{N - 1}{\alpha + N - 1} = \frac{\alpha}{\alpha + N - 1}.$$

This expression tells us that, under our prior, a data point is assigned to a component that has members with probability proportional to the number of members and to any one of the empty components with probability proportional to α. Hence, if α is high, we will see lots of small components (many data points will go to currently empty components), and, if α is low, we will see a small number of very large components. We can see this in action by just doing Gibbs sampling with this prior (i.e. ignoring the original likelihood term $p(\mathbf{x}_n|\boldsymbol{\mu}_k)$ or the collapsed likelihood term $p(\mathbf{x}_n|\mathbf{Z}^{-n}, \boldsymbol{\mu}_0, \boldsymbol{\Sigma}_0)$, neither of which we actually know how to compute yet for empty components). We can start by assigning all data points to one component and then resample the assignment of each data point with probability

$$P(z_{nk} = 1|\mathbf{Z}^{-n}, \alpha) = \begin{cases} \frac{c_k^{-n}}{\alpha+N-1} & \text{for } c_k^{-n} > 0 \\ \frac{\alpha}{\alpha+N-1} & \text{for empty components} \end{cases}$$

We need a bit of extra bookkeeping. If we assign a data point to the empty components, we need to create a new component to put it in. If we are resampling a data point that is currently the only member of a component, when we remove it from the component to resample it, we must delete the now empty component. Although officially the number of components, K, is equal to infinity, in practice we use K to denote the number of *non-empty* components. Sampling from this prior therefore involves the following steps:

1. Randomly assign the N data points into K components (e.g. put them all in one component; $K = 1$).

2. For each data point $n = 1 \ldots N$:

    (a) Remove point n from its current component.

    (b) If its current component is now empty, delete it (and set $K = K - 1$).

    (c) Compute the probabilities of all non-empty components and the combined probability of empty components.

    (d) Sample a new component k.

    (e) If the component is non-empty, set $z_{nk} = 1$.

    (f) If it is empty, create a new component (set $K = K + 1$) and assign the nth point to it.

3. Return to 2 until enough samples have been drawn.

Both the assignment of data points and the number of non-empty components can change throughout this process. We have therefore moved from a prior that defines how things group together within a fixed number of components to a prior distribution over all possible ways we can partition the N data points into any number of components (in reality, we are limited to between 1 and N components – we cannot partition N objects into $> N$ components!).

This distribution is controlled by a single parameter: α. Figure 10.5 (MATLAB script: infprior.m) shows the number of non-empty components when we sample from this conditional prior for three different values of α (0.1,1,10). In each case, the sampler was initialised with all data points in a single component and then run for 5000 samples (i.e. the assignment of each data point was resampled 5000 times). As the parameter is increased (from left to right in Figure 10.5) we see more and more non-empty components. In this example, $N = 100$, so, when $\alpha = 10$, the probability

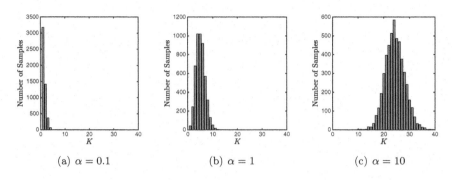

(a) $\alpha = 0.1$ (b) $\alpha = 1$ (c) $\alpha = 10$

FIGURE 10.5 Number of non-empty components at each sample for three different values of α. Five thousand samples were drawn in each case.

of a data point starting a new component is equal to $10/(10 + 100 - 1) = 0.09$ (new components are created approximately 10% of the time). When $\alpha = 0.1$, this probability drops to 0.001 (new components 0.1% of the time). It is clear why we see more components when α is increased!

Sampling partitions from the prior is one thing, but what we are really interested in is fitting our mixture model, and for that we need to include the data. Before we look at how that is done, we will describe a common analogy for this sampling scheme – the Chinese restaurant process.

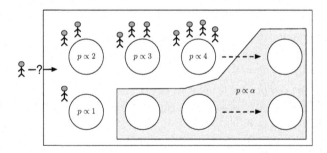

FIGURE 10.6 A cartoon depiction of the Chinese restaurant process. A new diner sits at a non-empty table with probability proportional to the number of diners and sits at a new table with probability proportonal to α.

10.3.1 The Chinese restaurant process

Imagine an enormous restaurant that has room for an infinite number of tables (!). Diners are sitting at some of the tables. Some diners are eating alone, some in groups. As you enter the restaurant, you need to decide where to sit. The **Chinese** restaurant process (CRP) is a stochastic process that defines the probabilities of you sitting at a particular table. We will use k to index the tables, and assume that the first K tables are occupied. c_k is the number of diners at table k, and the total number of diners in the restaurant is $\sum_{k=1}^{K} c_k = N$. The CRP defines the probabilities as

$$P(k) \propto \begin{cases} c_k & \text{a currently occupied table} \\ \alpha & \text{a currently empty table} \end{cases} \quad (10.9)$$

Normalising the probabilities is straightforward – we just divide each one by the total probability (you have to sit somewhere: $\alpha + \sum_{k=1}^{K} c_k = \alpha + N$). A cartoon depiction of the CRP can be seen in Figure 10.6 (see Exercise 10.6).

We can see a clear correspondence between the CRP and the sampling scheme we derived in the previous section (by marginalising $\boldsymbol{\pi}$ from our model). In fact, our prior is a CRP where we assume that the data point that we are resampling is always the last diner to arrive in the restaurant, and everyone else is already sitting (i.e. we condition on $\mathbf{Z}^{-n}$). In our previous expressions we have $N - 1$ diners sitting (because we have removed one) rather than N in this description of the CRP.

How can we explain α within the dining metaphor? Well, high α values correspond to populations of people who are slightly anti-social – they like starting new tables and are likely to end up dining alone. On the other hand, low α values make it likely that diners will be attracted to tables that already have many people at them – they are very social diners. We can see how this relates very clearly to the numbers of non-empty components shown in Figure 10.5.

We have included a description of the CRP for completeness – many machine learning papers that make use of infinite mixture models describe it, and it can often be a useful metaphor for describing extensions to the model, for example, the Hierarchical Dirichlet process (see Section 10.4.1).

10.3.2   Inference in the infinite mixture model

In Section 10.3 we saw how we could extend our model to have an infinite number of components and in doing so remove the need to fix the number of components. The result was a prior distribution for each z_{nk} conditioned on all of the other assignments. However, our expression is just a prior – it assigns probabilities to partitions of the N data points, but doesn't use the actual data to do so. In order to do inference in the new model, we must incorporate the data.

For non-empty components, this is no difference from the likelihood for the finite model. We can either use $p(\mathbf{x}_n | \boldsymbol{\mu}_k)$ or collapse the $\boldsymbol{\mu}_k$ and use $p(\mathbf{x}_n | \mathbf{Z}^{-n}, \mathbf{X}^{-n}, \boldsymbol{\mu}_0, \boldsymbol{\Sigma}_0)$. For empty components, things are not so straightforward – what is $\boldsymbol{\mu}_k$ for a component that doesn't have any data points assigned to it? If we were to update the value of $\boldsymbol{\mu}_k$ for all of the empty tables at each stage of the sampler, we would sample the values from the prior ($\mathcal{N}(\boldsymbol{\mu}_0, \boldsymbol{\Sigma}_0)$), as none of them have any data assigned to them. So we could (if the fact that there were an infinite number of them wasn't a problem) cycle through each one at each iteration and sample a new value from the prior. Given a value for $\boldsymbol{\mu}_k$ for each empty table, we could compute the likelihood.

However, we don't assign data points to *particular* empty tables – due to their infinite number, each one has probability zero. Instead we assign points to the set of empty tables. Therefore, we need to marginalise over all possible assignments to empty components. This sounds difficult, as there are an infinite number of these components, but, in fact, its quite straightforward. Recall that we can use samples to approximate expectations. For example, for S samples from $p(z)$, $z_1, \ldots, z_S$, we can approximate arbitrary expectations via

$$\int f(z)p(z) \ dz \approx \frac{1}{S} \sum_{s=1}^{S} f(z_s).$$

The more samples we draw, the better the approximation becomes, and, in the limit that we have an infinite number of samples, the expectation becomes exact. In our impossible sampling scheme, we have an infinite number of samples (one for each empty component) so averaging over them must be the same as computing the expectation

$$p(\mathbf{x}_n | \boldsymbol{\mu}_0, \boldsymbol{\Sigma}_0) = \int p(\mathbf{x}_n | \boldsymbol{\mu}) p(\boldsymbol{\mu} | \boldsymbol{\mu}_0, \boldsymbol{\Sigma}_0) \ d\boldsymbol{\mu},$$

which, in our example, is possible because $p(\mathbf{x}_n | \boldsymbol{\mu})$ is a Gaussian with mean $\boldsymbol{\mu}$ and identity covariance. The result is given by

$$p(\mathbf{x}_n | \boldsymbol{\mu}_0, \boldsymbol{\Sigma}_0) = \mathcal{N}(\boldsymbol{\mu}_0, \boldsymbol{\Sigma}_0 + \mathbf{I}). \tag{10.10}$$

In general, we may not be able to compute this expectation, but all is not lost – we can approximate it with any number of samples from the prior that we like. The more samples we draw the better, but even approximating the expectation by drawing one sample has been shown to work fairly well.

Our infinite collapsed Gibbs sampling scheme now involves resampling each $\mathbf{z}_n$ according to the probabilities:

$$P(z_{nk} = 1 | \ldots) \propto \begin{cases} c_k^{-n} p(\mathbf{x}_n | \mathbf{Z}^{-n}, \mathbf{X}^{-n}, \boldsymbol{\mu}_0, \boldsymbol{\Sigma}_0) & \text{non-empty component} \\ \alpha p(\mathbf{x}_n | \boldsymbol{\mu}_0, \boldsymbol{\Sigma}_0) & \text{empty component} \end{cases}$$
$$\tag{10.11}$$

where we have relegated the denominator of the prior to the overall normalisation constant, and $p(\mathbf{x}_n | \mathbf{Z}^{-n}, \mathbf{X}^{-n}, \boldsymbol{\mu}_0, \boldsymbol{\Sigma}_0)$ and $p(\mathbf{x}_n | \boldsymbol{\mu}_0, \boldsymbol{\Sigma}_0)$ are given by Equations 10.8 and 10.10, respectively.

We will illustrate this infinite sampling scheme with the same data we used for the finite mixture model at the start of this chapter (MATLAB script: `gibbsinf.m`). The data are shown in Figure 10.1, and, as before, we set $\boldsymbol{\mu}_0$ to a vector of zeros and $\boldsymbol{\Sigma}_0$ to the identity matrix. α was set to 1. As for the finite model, 1000 samples were taken, of which the first 200 were discarded as a burn-in phase. For the finite model, we plotted the posterior samples for $\boldsymbol{\mu}_k$ and $\boldsymbol{\pi}$ as well as the posterior component membership. For the infinite model we cannot plot any of these things – we no longer sample $\boldsymbol{\mu}_k$ and $\boldsymbol{\pi}$, and, as components are created and destroyed, there isn't a static set of components to compute posterior probabilities for. Interpreting the output of the infinite model is more challenging than for the finite model, and how we do it will often depend on what we are using the mixture model for. Two things that are often visualised are the marginal posterior over the number of non-empty components and the pairwise probabilities that two data points are in the same component. These

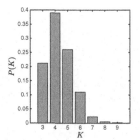

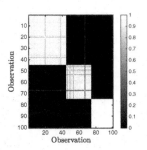

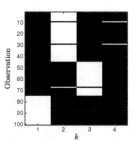

(a) Marginal posterior over the number of non-empty components.

(b) Marginal posterior over pairwise component membership.

(c) One randomly chosen posterior sample of component membership.

FIGURE 10.7 Output of the infinite mixture model for the data shown in Figure 10.1.

are shown in Figure 10.7. The marginal distribution over the number of non-empty components K is shown in Figure 10.7(a). To obtain this distribution we keep track of the number of non-empty components after each iteration of the sampler. The posterior seems to overestimate the number of components (there should be three). If we look at a randomly chosen set of assignments from the sampler (Figure 10.7(c)) we can see why. Whenever we resample the membership of a data point, there is a finite probability that it will form a new component. This component might attract one or two more members (see $k = 4$ in Figure 10.7(c)) but will most likely collapse again within a couple of iterations. So, there are always data points jumping out and forming new components that don't survive and hence we overestimate the number of components. One way of interpreting Figure 10.7(a) is that it needs *at least* $K = 3$ components (we never see $K = 2$), which seems reasonable.

Figure 10.7(b) visualises the pairwise membership probabilities. The posterior probability is indicated by the colour at a particular row and column. For example, the strong white colour in the upper left block indicates that the first 40 or so points almost always end up in the same component. We obtain these probabilities by counting how often each pair of data points was assigned to the same component (regardless of which component it was). The data points (observations) are ordered according to their true component, and we can clearly see the block structure that we would expect if the clustering was correct. It's not perfect though – there are some data points that don't always get assigned to the correct component. And, as we have already seen, each data point will occasionally jump off on its own.

This data is a bit easy to model, as the three groups of data are highly separated. In Figure 10.8(a) we show a tougher dataset where the groups (particularly the lower two) are significantly closer together. Figure 10.8(b) shows quite clearly the additional posterior uncertainty in this problem – although the majority of the first two components make up tidy blocks, there are a lot of data points that switch between the two. The final component is still quite separated (it is the top one in Figure 10.8(a)) and the posterior probabilities still form a nice clean block.

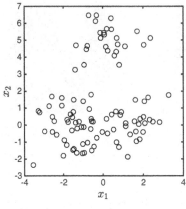
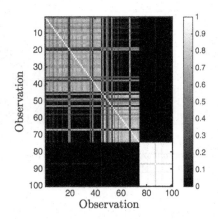

(a) A tricker dataset.

(b) Pairwise posterior membership probabilities.

FIGURE 10.8 The performance of the infinite mixture on a slightly tougher dataset.

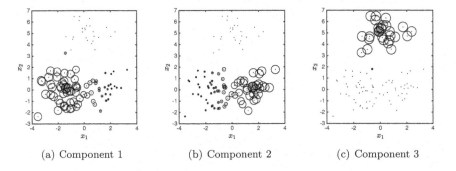

(a) Component 1

(b) Component 2

(c) Component 3

FIGURE 10.9 Visualising the pairwise probabilities between the point closest to the center of each component (shaded) and the other points. Circle area corresponds to probability, with the areas of the shaded points being 1 (points are always in the same component as themselves).

Finally, in Figure 10.9 we visualise the pairwise posterior probabilities in a different way. Here, for each of the three components, we show the pairwise probability between each data point and the data point closest to the true centre of that component (i.e. the centre used to generate the data). The circle size (area) corresponds to the probability. The shaded point is the one being compared to and therefore has a probability of 1 (it is always in the same component as itself). Focusing on components 1 and 2 (component 3 is far enough away that points rarely switch), we can see exactly what we might expect. The probability of being in the same membership as the central point in component 1 drops as we move towards component 2 – points in the middle flip between the components more often. None of the circles is as large as the shaded one, as all points will occasionally jump out into their own components.

The steps we have taken are not restricted to Gaussian densities. To try an example with a different prior and likelihood, see Exercise 10.7.

10.3.3 Summary

In this section we have introduced the idea of an *infinite mixture model* – a model that has an infinite number of components, only some of which will ever be occupied. This has removed the need to specify a priori how many components there are – the model fills up as many as it needs. This is a useful and computationally straightforward model that has found many uses within machine learning. The prior degree of clustering expected is controlled by α. High values of α lead to a preference towards many small clusters, low values to a smaller number of large clusters.

One drawback of this approach is interpretation of the output – it is hard to summarise the thousands of samples from the posterior because the number of components in each sample can be different. However, this problem can be overcome if what is ultimately of interest are marginal distributions (e.g. the number of components, pairwise probabilities, etc.), or expectations that can be computed from the samples (e.g. anything that involves a real-valued function that takes a clustering as its input).

We obtained this model via increasing K to infinity. In the following section we will see that this is in fact equivalent to a more general stochastic process – the Dirichlet process.

10.4 DIRICHLET PROCESSES

In this section we will provide a brief description of the Dirichlet process. Dirichlet processes are stochastic processes from which we can sample sequences of values that have interesting properties. To go into DPs in detail would require a deeper understanding of probability theory than we have provided, so we'll keep our description quite informal. At the end of the chapter are pointers to further reading for those wanting to explore more.

Let's assume we are interested in sampling continuous values θ. To define a DP, we will have to choose a *base* distribution for θ (more on this later). To stick with the most common DP notation, we will use H to represent this distribution. More specifically, because θ is a continuous random variable, it will have pdf $h(\theta)$. Recall that the probability that θ lies in some subset of possible values (e.g. the probability that θ is between 1 and 2) is obtained by integrating the pdf over that subset. In general, we will use A to denote subsets of possible θ values and use $H(A)$ to denote the probability that θ lies in the subset defined by A. For example, perhaps A is the subset of values between some values a and b:

$$H(A) = P(\theta \in A) = P(a < \theta < b) = \int_a^b h(\theta) \, d\theta.$$

As well as thinking of $H(A)$ as the integral of the pdf over A, we can also think of it more generally as a function that takes a subset of θ values and assigns a probability. You might find this a more useful approach when thinking about DPs. This touches on **measure theory** – a subset of mathematics that formalises probability. We won't go into any details here, but a couple of good introductory books are mentioned at the end of the chapter.

So far, this description has been very abstract. Don't worry – things will get more concrete later on! Now, consider a set of M subsets, such that all possible values of θ are in one and only one subset (a **partition**). If the mth subset is denoted A_m, the following must be true:

$$\sum_{m=1}^{M} H(A_m) = 1$$

because the subsets cover all possible values of θ and don't overlap.

Although it defines probabilites, H itself is deterministic – it always gives the same probability for some subset A. Would it be possible to produce some kind of function that acts on subsets of θ values and produces probabilities just as H does, but is itself stochastic and produces random probabilities? The answer is yes, and a DP is exactly this! In particular, consider a new function $G(A)$. G is a Dirichlet process if the vector of values $[G(A_1), \ldots, G(A_M)]$ is distributed according to the Dirichlet distribution (see Comment 10.1) with parameters $\alpha H(A_1), \ldots, \alpha H(A_M)$ where α is a positive constant.

Formally, G is a DP if:

$$[G(A_1), \ldots, G(A_M)] \sim Dir(\alpha H(A_1), \ldots, \alpha H(A_M)). \qquad (10.12)$$

This is quite an abstract definition. For some partition $A_1, \ldots, A_M$, we could sample vectors $[G(A_1), \ldots, G(A_M)]$ from the Dirichlet described above, but what then? Insight into the DP is obtained if we generate samples from it but it's not obvious how to do that from this expression. Fortunately, we can make some progress by marginalising G.

Consider two random variables x, y and the two conditional distributions $p(x|y)$ and $p(y|z)$. Assuming z is known, one way to sample values of x is to sample a value of y from $p(y|z)$ and then sample x from $p(x|y)$. Another way would be to marginalise y and just sample a value of x directly conditioned on z:

$$p(x|z) = \int p(x|y)p(y|z) \, dy.$$

As far as the samples of x are concerned, the two processes are statistically identical. We can do the same for our DP to marginalise the GP. In particular

$$
\begin{aligned}
P(\theta \in A_m|H) &= \int P(\theta \in A_m|G)P(G|H) \, dG \\
&= \int G(A_m)P(G(A_m|H) \, dG(A_m) = \mathbf{E}\left\{G(A_m)\right\},
\end{aligned}
$$

which is the expected value of $G(A_m)$. As $G(A_m)$ is the mth component of a Dirichlet, its expected value is the corresponding Dirichlet parameter divided by the sum of the Dirichlet parameters:

$$\mathbf{E}\left\{G(A_m)\right\} = \frac{\alpha H(A_m)}{\sum_{j=1}^{M} \alpha H(A_j)} = \frac{\alpha H(A_m)}{\alpha \sum_{j=1}^{M} H(A_j)} = H(A_m).$$

So, the probability of θ being in A_m is $H(A_m)$, which is just the base probability. We can therefore easily draw a single sample of θ from the DP: we just draw a sample from H. In other words, the pdf $g(\theta)$ is identical to the pdf $h(\theta)$.

This doesn't seem very interesting, but it gets more interesting when we consider multiple samples from a DP. A DP actually gives us a sequence of samples, each of which is sampled conditioned on the previous ones (it is a stochastic process): $g(\theta_1)$, $g(\theta_2|\theta_1)$, $g(\theta_3|\theta_1, \theta_2)$, etc. We will see some interesting properties of these samples below, but to give you a sneak preview, consider a Gaussian base distribution. The probability that any two values drawn directly from the base are identical is zero – we would never draw exactly the same value twice. In contrast, the probability that two (or more) identical values are drawn from a DP with this same Gaussian as its base is non-zero!

To see why, imagine the situation where we have observed N observations, $\theta_1, \ldots, \theta_N$. For some partition $A_1, \ldots, A_M$, our DP says that

$$[G(A_1), \ldots, G(A_M)] \sim Dir(\alpha H(A_1), \ldots, H(A_M)).$$

We can think of this as a prior over the probabilities of θ lying in each of the m regions. Having observed some data, we ought to update these probabilities – regions in which we have observed lots of θ values ought to get more likely, whilst regions in which we have observed very few ought to become less likely. If we use c_m to denote the number of samples that lie in A_m, we can therefore use a multinomial likelihood to update the Dirichlet. We have already seen that in a Dirichlet-multinomial model, the posterior Dirichlet has parameters equal to the prior parameters plus the associated counts. The posterior is therefore

$$[G(A_1), \ldots, G(A_M)]|\theta_1, \ldots, \theta_N \sim Dir(\alpha H(A_1) + c_1, \ldots, H(A_M) + c_M).$$

So, having observed some data, the vector $[G(A_1), \ldots, G(A_M)]$ is distributed according to a Dirichlet. If we can write the parameters of the Dirichlet as the product of a base (say H') and a parameter (α'), then this posterior must also be a DP. We can find H' and α' with a little algebra:

$$\alpha' H'(A_m) = \alpha H(A_m) + c_m$$
$$\sum_m \alpha' H'(A_m) = \sum_m \alpha H(A_m) + c_m$$
$$\alpha' = \alpha + N$$
$$\text{and therefore} \quad H'(A_m) = \frac{\alpha H(A_m) + c_m}{\alpha + N}.$$

It will be useful to write this slightly more generally and replace c_m with $\sum_{n=1}^{N} \delta_{\theta_n}(A_m)$ where $\delta_{\theta_n}(A_m)$ is 1 if $\theta_n \in A_m$ and 0 otherwise. Having observed some data, we therefore have a new DP with parameter $\alpha' = \alpha + N$ and base

$$H'(A) = \frac{\alpha H(A) + \sum_{n=1}^{N} \delta_{\theta_n}(A)}{\alpha + N}.$$

We already know how to take one sample from a DP – just generate a sample from the base. What would a sample from this new base look like? It helps to rewrite it:

$$H'(A) = \frac{\alpha}{\alpha + N} H(A) + \frac{1}{\alpha + N} \sum_{n=1}^{N} \delta_{\theta_n}(A).$$

This is a mixture where the first component is the original base and the second component is some function of the data that has been observed. The mixture weights are given by $\alpha/(\alpha+N)$ for the original base and $N/(\alpha+N)$ for all of the previous observations combined. We know how to sample from a mixture – we first choose a component based on the weights and then sample a value from the chosen component. If we choose the first component, we draw a sample from the original base. The second component is a bit more complex. In fact, as it is a summation, we can think of it as another mixture. Each component has equal weight and corresponds to one of the previous observations. Each of these components has the form

$$Q(A) = \delta_{\theta_n}(A),$$

i.e. the probability of the sample being in A is 1 if θ_n is in A and zero otherwise. How can we sample from Q? Well, all samples from Q must belong to any range A that includes θ_n. The only value of θ that can satisfy this is θ_n itself. So, a sample from this component has to be identical to θ_n.

So, to sample from the posterior DP we first decide whether or not to use the original base distribution with probability $\alpha/(\alpha+N)$. If we do, we generate a sample from the base. If we do not, we pick one of the previous samples (uniformly) and replicate it. Hence the non-zero probability of obtaining identical samples.

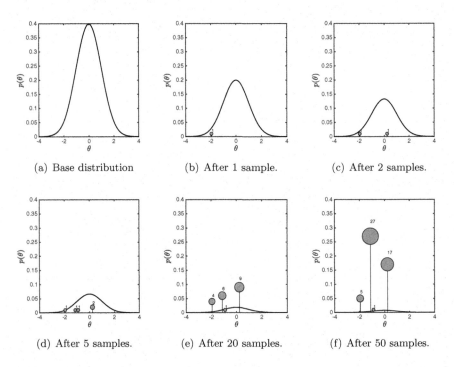

(a) Base distribution (b) After 1 sample. (c) After 2 samples.

(d) After 5 samples. (e) After 20 samples. (f) After 50 samples.

FIGURE 10.10 Samples from a DP with a Gaussian base distribution $(\mu = 0, \sigma^2 = 1)$ and $\alpha = 1$.

Let's consider a more concrete example. Assume that H is a Gaussian with zero mean and unit standard deviation. The first sample, θ_1, is simply a sample from this Gaussian. Assuming $\alpha = 1$ (more about this parameter later) when sampling the second sample, we have $N = 1$ previous samples, and therefore sample from H again with probability $1/(1+1) = 0.5$ and otherwise copy θ_1. This process then repeats for subsequent samples. The fact that, when sampling sets of values from a DP, there is a non-zero probability of many of them being identical is a key property of the DP. It is exactly this property that makes them very useful in mixture models. Before we see the connection, let's draw some samples from a real DP.

Figure 10.10 shows this sampling process for a DP with a Gaussian base distribution ($\mu = 0, \sigma^2 = 1$) and $\alpha = 1$ (MATLAB script: `dpsamp.m`). The first plot shows the base distribution from which the first sample will be drawn. This sample is shown in the second plot, along with the base distribution that we've reweighted by $\alpha/(\alpha + N)$ to show that for subsequent samples it is less likely that we will draw from it. The second sample will either be drawn from the base (with probability $1/(1 + 1) = 0.5$) or be equal to the first sample (also with probability 0.5). In this example, the base won and the new sample (with the base reweighted further) can be seen in the third plot. The state after five samples can be seen in the fourth plot. Four unique values have been drawn, one of which has been drawn twice (shown by a slightly larger circle, plotted slightly higher). After five samples, the probability of the sixth sample coming from the base is $1/(1+5) = 1/6$. This is lower than the value of 0.5 (after the first sample) and will keep decreasing as we generate more samples. In other words, the more samples we draw, the less likely it is that we will draw an original one, and the more likely that we will copy an old one (our re-weighting of the base in the figures is to demonstrate this). In the final two panels, we see the state of the DP after 20 and 50 samples. In the latter, we can clearly see that a small number of values are dominating. In fact, no new values have been sampled from the base – we have the same four values that we had after five samples (see Exercise 10.8).

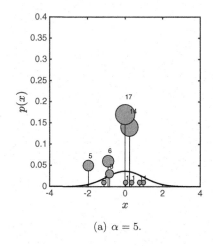

(a) $\alpha = 5$.

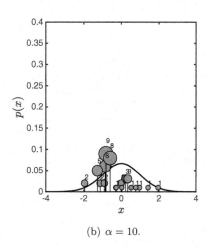

(b) $\alpha = 10$.

FIGURE 10.11 Fifty samples from a DP with $\alpha = 5$ and $\alpha = 10$.

Let's now look at what happens if we increase α. We know that, after N samples, the probability of generating a new value is equal to $\alpha/(\alpha + N)$, suggesting that increasing α will result in more new values and therefore more unique values after, say, 50 samples. Figure 10.11 shows the first 50 samples for $\alpha = 5$ and $\alpha = 10$ and we can see clearly the increase in unique values as α gets larger. Note also that the base is larger in these two plots than it was after 50 samples when $\alpha = 1$ (see Figure 10.10). This is because, when $\alpha = 10$, the probability of a new value after 50 samples is still quite large ($10/(10 + 50) = 1/6$, for $\alpha = 1$ the corresponding figure is $1/51$). In the DP world, α is known as the **concentration parameter**.

Hopefully you are beginning to see the parallels between this process and the infinite mixture model described previously. To help, we can rewrite our posterior base distribution a little. The posterior base is given by

$$H'(A) = \frac{\alpha}{\alpha + N} H(A) + \frac{1}{\alpha + N} \sum_{n=1}^{N} \delta_{\theta_n}(A).$$

Within the N previous samples there will be K unique values ($K \leq N$). Rather than pick from the previous samples uniformly, we can instead pick from the previous unique values with probability proportional to the number of times they have been sampled. Using n_k to denote the number of times unique value θ_k has been sampled, we have

$$H'(A) = \frac{\alpha}{\alpha + N} H(A) + \frac{1}{\alpha + N} \sum_{k=1}^{K} n_k \delta_{\theta_k}(A).$$

To sample from this, we first choose whether or not we should sample a new value, with probability proportional to α, and, if not, replicate a previous value with probability proportional to the number of times it has been sampled. If we replace the word value with component, this is exactly the prior we obtained for an infinite mixture model in Section 10.3! The value we are sampling in the DP is equivalent to the component mean (μ_k) in the infinite mixture model.

There is one distinction: In the infinite mixture, at any point in the sampler, we considered only K mean values. In the DP, every data point has its own mean value – we always sample a θ, but amongst the N values, there are only K unique ones. This distinction has no practical implications, but it is an important feature of the DP.

When used in mixture models, the DP is a prior on the component parameters for each observation. It gives a non-zero probability that multiple observations will have identical parameters and therefore belong to the same component. To complete the mixture model, we just need to add the likelihood term that links the component parameters with the observed data (e.g. a Gaussian). We can therefore generate data by first (for each data point) sampling component parameters from the DP and then sampling data conditioned on these components. Two example datasets drawn from such a model with a Gaussian base, $\alpha = 1$ and an isotropic Gaussian likelihood (with $\sigma^2 = 1$) can be seen in Figure 10.12 (MATLAB script: `dpsampdata.m`). The mean values from the DP prior are shown as filled circles; the data are the open circles and the contours show the base distribution. Unsurprisingly, these datasets have clear cluster structure. If we were to derive Gibbs updates for this model to perform inference, they would be identical to those derived for the infinite mixture in Section 10.3, so we won't repeat them here.

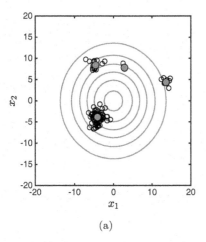
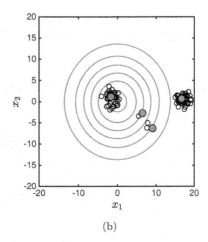

(a)   (b)

FIGURE 10.12 Two datasets drawn from a model with a DP prior with a Gaussian base (contours shown) and an isotropic Gaussian likelihood ($\sigma^2 = 1$).

10.4.1 Hierarchical Dirichlet processes

The standard clustering problem assumes that we have one dataset and would like to group the data into a set of components. In some applications we might have more than one dataset to cluster. We could cluster them separately, but it might be interesting to know if some of the clusters exist across multiple datasets. Hierarchical Dirichlet processes (HDPs) were created for exactly this problem. A separate DP prior is used for the data points in each file where the base distribution is itself a DP that is shared across all of the files. Formally, we can describe this as follows:

$$G_0 \sim DP(\gamma, H)$$
$$G_1 \sim DP(\alpha_1, G_0)$$
$$\vdots$$
$$G_J \sim DP(\alpha_J, G_0)$$

where there are $j = 1 \ldots J$ files.

At first glance this looks a bit daunting but we can gain some insight by imagining drawing samples. We will denote the nth sample in the jth file as θ_{jn}. For the first sample in the first file, we need a sample from G_1. No other samples have been drawn so this is just a sample from the base, G_0. No samples have been drawn from G_0 either, so we have to generate a new sample from its base, H. We will use β_k to denote the kth unique sample from G_0 and n_k to denote the number of times it has been sampled. So, for the first sample, we sample β_1 from the base and set n_1 to 1. Within file 1, we need to keep track of the number of different values we sample from G_0. We will denote the ith new value with δ_{ji}, so in this case, $\delta_{11} = \beta_1$ and $\theta_{11} = \delta_{11}$. To keep track of the number of objects assigned to δ_{ji}, we will use m_{ji}.

Therefore, $m_{11} = 1$. Now consider the second sample in file 1, θ_{12}. It will either be equal to δ_{11} (and therefore equal to θ_{11}) or we must sample a new value δ_{12} from G_0. If it is the former, G_0 is unchanged (G_0 only changes when we sample from it) and we set $\theta_{12} = \delta_{11}$ and $m_{11} = 2$. If the latter, we generate a sample from G_0, set δ_{12} to equal this value and set $m_{12} = 1$. This new sample could either be identical to β_1 or will be a new sample from H. Note that, if it is identical to β_1, then δ_{21} is also identical to δ_{11}! However, as these are separate draws from G_0, we must treat them as separate objects. This will be more obvious when we relate this process back to the Chinese restaurant (below).

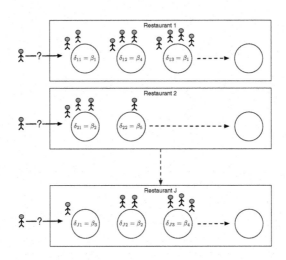

FIGURE 10.13 The Chinese restaurant franchise.

After two samples from file 1, we now consider the first sample from file 2. So far, we have no samples from G_2 so we must generate a new sample (δ_{21}) from G_0. This time there have already been samples from G_0, so δ_{21} could be, say, identical to β_1. Let's assume it is, so $\delta_{21} = \beta_1$ and $\theta_{21} = \delta_{21}$. Now imagine that we are also generating data, x_{jn}, which comes from a Gaussian with mean θ_{jn} and unit variance. x_{21} will have mean $\theta_{21} = \delta_{21} = \beta_1 = \delta_{11} = \theta_{11}$. In other words, x_{21} will share a Gaussian mean with x_{11}. With a small leap of faith, hopefully you can see that, when it comes to inference, this means that mixture components are effectively shared across the different files.

As we have just demonstrated, this is quite a tricky process to describe in words. Fortunately, the Chinese restaurant metaphor (see Figure 10.6) has been extended to this case resulting in the Chinese restaurant franchise. Each file is one branch of a chain of restaurants that all share the same menu. At each table, diners all eat the same item from this menu. This is depicted in Figure 10.13. Each of the diners has an associated θ_{jn} value which is equal to the δ_{ji} value of the table at which they are sitting. Each δ_{ji} value is identical to one of the dishes, β_k. In this example there are five unique dishes, $\beta_1, \ldots, \beta_5$.

As with the standard Chinese restaurant process, a diner sits at a table with probability proportional to the number of diners at the table, or at a new table with probability $\alpha_j/(\alpha_j + N_j)$ (where N_j is the number of diners in restaurant j). If they sit at a current table, their value of θ is set to the table's δ value. If a new table, we draw a δ from G_0. A sample from G_0 will be a dish (β) that already exists or a new dish. New dishes are generated with probability proportional to γ, whilst old dishes are resampled with probability proportional to the number of tables across the franchise that are using that dish. We can see now why it is important to keep track of all draws from G_0 within a restaurant (through the δs), even if the draw is identical to a β in use on another table in the same restaurant – it is still a new draw from G_0.

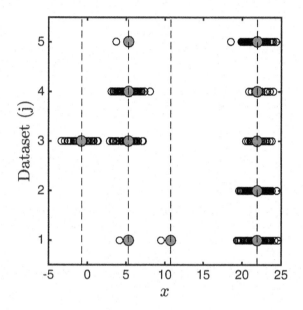

FIGURE 10.14 One hundred samples for each of five datasets. H is a Gaussian with mean 0 and $\sigma^2 = 100$. All concentration parameters are set to 1 ($\gamma = \alpha_1 = \ldots = \alpha_J = 1$).

An example of five one-dimensional datasets drawn from an HDP can be seen in Figure 10.14 (MATLAB script: hdp.m). In this example, the overall base was set to a Gaussian with $\mu = 0$ and $\sigma^2 = 100$. All concentration parameters ($\gamma, \alpha_1, \ldots, \alpha_J$) were set to 1. The data are one dimensional, and each dataset is shown at a different height on the y-axis. The filled circles show the cluster means, and the dashed lines the unique values of β. We can clearly see the sharing of clusters between datasets. The highest (rightmost) value of β is shared by all five datasets and all other values appear in one or more datasets. Changing the concentration parameters controls how much sharing goes on across the datasets. For example, if we set γ to a high value, then most samples from G_0 will be from the base, and we will get very few shared β values. Increasing individual α values changes how likely it is that a new draw from G_0 will be required in each dataset. Different datasets need not necessarily be given the same α_j values. We leave it as a practical exercise to experiment with the setting of these values (see Exercise 10.9).

We will not go into detail on the inference for HDPs here. Gibbs sampling is fairly straightforward (with some slightly more complex bookkeeping than the standard DP) and we leave it as an exercise (see Exercise 10.10). Readers are referred to the references at the end of the chapter for more information.

10.4.2 Summary

In the last two sections we have provided a quick, informal introduction to Dirichlet processes and Hierarchical Dirichlet processes. To go any deeper would require the reader to have some familiarity with measure theory, and that is a whole book in itself (see the references at the end of this chapter). Within the context of mixture models, the DP can be used as a prior distribution over the component parameters associated with each data point. Crucially, the DP has a non-zero probability that some of these parameters will be identical and hence data points can be thought of as coming from the same component. Hierarchical Dirichlet processes allow us to perform DP mixture modelling on separate datasets whilst sharing information between them.

Finally, we will look at what happens when we relax one of the key assumptions underpinning mixture models – that each data point is generated by one component.

10.5 BEYOND STANDARD MIXTURES – TOPIC MODELS

In the previous sections we have shown how we can use mixture models without specifying a priori how many components are required. This extension can, in theory, be used for any type of mixture component, although inference might be tricky if the prior and likelihood don't form a conjugate pair. When the pair is conjugate, deriving the updates required for Gibbs sampling is fairly formulaic, so we will not provide details of the updates for other conjugate pairs here. Instead, we will briefly introduce a model that relaxes the key mixture model assumption – that each data point is generated by one particular mixture component.

Consider clustering the text in web pages. We could use a standard mixture model that assumes each web page is generated by one mixture component. In this case, each mixture component would be defined by a multinomial distribution over words, a suitable prior for which is the Dirichlet. Each component could be considered to be a topic, and each page generated by that component is about that topic.

In reality, however, this definition is too restrictive. Many pages would be about more than one topic. For example, if we allowed humans to tag pages with topics, then a page about climate change might be tagged with two topics: *environment* and *politics*. A page about football transfers might be tagged with *football* and *economics*. Trying to model these documents with a mixture will result in many very specific mixture components that will not capture topics as humans might understand them.

Latent Dirichlet Allocation (LDA) is a probabilistic model that overcomes this limitation. It has proven very popular in many machine learning applications (including text modelling and biological data – see the references at the end of the chapter). Like a standard mixture model, LDA consists of K components (it can be made infinite, but we will stick to the finite version here). In the text example, each component is a multinomial distribution over words. The difference is that, rather than each document being generated by one topic, it is assumed to have been generated by multiple topics. The generative process is as follows:

1. For each document:

   (a) Sample a multinomial over the K topics, $\boldsymbol{\theta}_n$, from a Dirichlet $p(\boldsymbol{\theta}_n|\boldsymbol{\alpha})$.

   (b) For each word in the document:

      i. Sample a topic from the K topics where the kth topic has probability θ_{nk}.

      ii. Sample the word from the chosen topic.

This process reduces to the standard mixture if the distribution over topics ($\boldsymbol{\theta}_n$) for each document has probability 1 for one topic and probability 0 for all others. In other words, the standard mixture model is a special case of this more general model.

Given a set of documents (or other data types), inference in LDA is only a little more complex than for a standard mixture. The extra complexity lies in rather than keeping track of one set of indicator variables for each document, we now need to keep one set for each word in each document. Formally, the model is defined as

$$
\begin{aligned}
p(\boldsymbol{\theta}_n|\boldsymbol{\alpha}) &= Dir(\boldsymbol{\alpha}) \\
p(z_{ni} = k|\boldsymbol{\theta}_n) &= \theta_{nk} \\
P(x_{ni} = w|z_{ni} = k) &= \beta_{kw} \\
p(\boldsymbol{\beta}_k|\boldsymbol{\gamma}) &= Dir(\boldsymbol{\gamma})
\end{aligned}
$$

where i indexes the words in any particular document, $z_{ni} = k$ if the ith word in document n was generated by topic k and $x_{ni} = w$ if the ith word in document n is word w. $\boldsymbol{\beta}_k$ are the word probabilities that define the kth topic and $\boldsymbol{\alpha}$ and $\boldsymbol{\gamma}$ are the hyperparameters defining the Dirichlet priors over the document to topic multinomials and the topic to word multinomials.

Because we are only dealing with Dirichlets and multinomials, we can use collapsed Gibbs sampling to marginalise all of the multinomial parameters, resulting in a Gibbs sampling scheme that requires just updating z_{ni}. In particular, we leave it as an exercise (see Exercise 10.11) to show that the conditional probability that $z_{ni} = k$ is given by

$$
P(z_{ni} = k|x_{ni} = w, \ldots) \propto (c_{nk}^{-i} + \alpha_k) \times \frac{v_{kw} + \gamma_w}{\sum_{w'} v_{kw'} + \gamma_{w'}}. \tag{10.13}
$$

The first term comes from marginalising $\boldsymbol{\theta}_n$ and the second from marginalising $\boldsymbol{\beta}_k$. c_{nk}^{-i} is the number of other words in document n that are currently assigned to topic k, and v_{kw} is the number of other times word w has been assigned to topic k (across the whole dataset).

We will illustrate this with a simple example (MATLAB script: lda.m). We will use a vocabulary of $W = 5$ words and generate data from $K = 3$ topics. The word probabilities for each topic are each sampled from a Dirichlet with uniform parameter $\gamma = 0.1$. These three topics can be seen in Figure 10.15. For each of $N = 100$ documents, $\boldsymbol{\theta}_n$ is sampled from a Dirichlet with uniform parameter $\alpha = 10$ and for each document 50 words are sampled using the process described above.

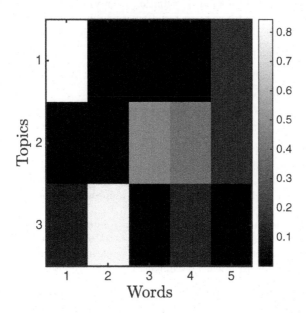

FIGURE 10.15 The true word parameters for the LDA example. Each row is a topic and each column a word.

We then use collapsed Gibbs sampling to sample from the posterior distribution over z_{ni}. Although we don't explicitly sample them, we are jointly inferring the distributions over topics for each document ($\boldsymbol{\theta}_n$) and the distribution over words for each topic ($\boldsymbol{\beta}_k$). At any point in the sampler, we can compute the posterior Dirichlet over each $\boldsymbol{\theta}_n$ and $\boldsymbol{\beta}_k$. In the former case, the distribution is Dirichlet with parameters $\alpha_k + c_{nk}$ and in the latter Dirichlet with parameters $v_{kw} + \gamma_w$ (if you're unsure about this, try Exercise 10.11). Comparing the expected value of $\boldsymbol{\beta}_k$ with the true value allows us to assess how well we are able to learn the true topics. The expected value of the posterior Dirichlet over the topic to word probabilities ($\boldsymbol{\beta}_k$) can be seen in Figure 10.16. Comparison with the true values in Figure 10.15 shows that the probabilities match very well, suggesting that the sampling scheme is indeed able to recreate the true topic probabilities.

LDA has been used successfully in many applications, from discovering scientific topics to modelling cellular processes (see the references at the end of the chapter). Inference in LDA is not restricted to collapsed Gibbs sampling. In fact, in the original paper (see references at the end of the chapter), a Variational Bayes (see Chapter 7) scheme is presented.

10.6   CHAPTER SUMMARY

In this chapter we have described some extensions to the standard mixture model. In particular, how we can remove the need to specify the number of components

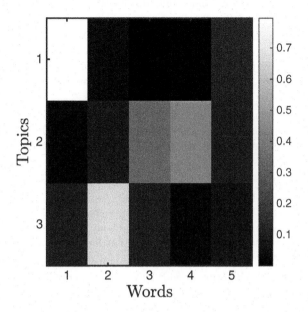

FIGURE 10.16 The inferred word parameters for the LDA example.

and how we can relax the original assumption that each observation comes from one component. Such extensions to standard mixture models have been very popular in machine learning in recent years, with many models being proposed and applied in a wide range of applications.

It was not our aim in this chapter to give a comprehensive survey of machine learning approaches in this area. Rather, we intended to provide an intuitive understanding of these approaches to give the reader the necessary background to explore and understand some of the interesting work in this area. The references presented below are a good starting point!

10.7 EXERCISES

10.1 For the mixture model where each component is a one-dimensional Gaussian with variance 1, show that the conditional distribution for the mean of the kth mixture component is that given by Equation 10.4.

10.2 Implement the Gibbs sampler for the mixture model. Compute $\hat{R}$ and the autocorrelation of the component means μ_k. How many samples are required for convergence? How much should the samples be thinned?

10.3 In Section 6.3.7 we used EM to fit a mixture model for binary data. Assuming a beta prior on the binomial parameters, derive the Gibbs sampler for this model.

10.4 Marginalise the Gaussian mean from the Gibbs sampler to give a conditional distribution for z_{nk} conditioned only on the other assignments and the prior parameters $(\mu_0, \Sigma_0, \alpha)$.

10.5 Implement the collapsed Gibbs sampler for the Gaussian mixture model. At each iteration in the sampler, sample the means μ_k even though they are not needed (sample them from the posterior you computed to marginalise them). Compare the autocorrelation and $\hat{R}$ for the μ_k with that obtained in Exercise 10.2.

10.6 Implement a sampler that samples from the Chinese restaurant process. Repeatedly resample assignment of customers to tables and plot a histogram over the number of tables. Investigate how the histogram changes as you change α.

10.7 Derive the Gibbs sampler for the infinite version of the binary mixture described in Exercise 10.3.

10.8 Write some code that will sample from a Dirichlet process. The code should store all previous samples and then copy previous samples or draw new samples from the base. Experiment with different base distributions and concentration parameters.

10.9 Using the MATLAB script provided (MATLAB script: `hdp.m`), experiment with setting the values of the concentration parameters for the top level DP (α) and the lower DPs ($\gamma_1, \ldots, \gamma_J$).

10.10 Derive a Gibbs sampling scheme for inference in the Hierarchical Dirichlet process. Assume that the base distribution is Gaussian ($H = \mathcal{N}(\mu_0, \sigma_0^2)$) and the observations are one-dimensional real values.

10.11 Derive the collapsed Gibbs sampler for LDA given in Equation 10.13.

10.8 FURTHER READING

[1] David Blei, Andrew Ng, and Michael Jordan. Latent Dirichlet Allocation. *Journal of Machine Learning Research*, 3:993–1022, 2003.

This is the original paper describing LDA, including a Variational Bayes algorithm for inference.

[2] Thomas Griffiths and Mark Steyvers. Finding scientific topics. *PNAS*, 101:5228–5235, 2004.

An interesting paper where LDA with collapsed Gibbs sampling is used to discover topics from the scientific literature.

[3] David Pollard. *A User's Guide to Measure Theoretic Probability*. Cambridge University Press, first edition, 2002.

Another good introduction to measure theory.

[4] Carl Rasmussen. The infinite Gaussian mixture model. In *Advances in Neural Information Processing Systems 12*, pages 554–560, 2000.

A very nice introduction to the infinite mixture model. This is a good starting point for further reading on Dirichlet processes

[5] Simon Rogers, Mark Girolami, Colin Campbell, and Rainer Breitling. The latent process decomposition of cDNA microarray data sets. *IEEE/ACM Trans. Comput. Biol. Bioinformatics*, 2(2):143–156, April 2005.

An article by the authors describing an LDA-inspired model for cDNA microarray data.

[6] Jeffrey Rosenthal. *A First Look at Rigorous Probability Theory*. World Scientific Publishing Co, second edition, 2007.

An accessible introduction to measure theory. Worth reading if you want to delve deeper into Dirichlet processes.

[7] Yee Whey Teh, Michael Jordan, Matther Beal, and David Blei. Hierarchical Dirichlet Processes. *Journal of the American Statistical Association*, 101:1566–1581, 2006.

The paper introducing hierarchical Dirichlet processes.

Glossary

Acceptance ratio In Metropolis–Hastings, the proportion of proposed samples that are accepted.

Analytical solution An analytical solution to a particular mathematical problem (e.g. optimising a quantity or evaluating an integral) is one in which the solution can be obtained exactly. Many of the problems that we will deal with will not have analytical solutions, necessitating the use of iterative algorithms or sampling techniques.

Approximate Bayesian computation A sampling method that is used when it is impossible (or inefficient) to evaluate the likelihood. Samples are drawn from the prior from which datasets are created. If the dataset is within some tolerance of the original data, the sample is accepted.

Autocorrelation The autocorrelation of a sequence of samples is the correlation between samples a certain number of steps apart. Within MCMC schemes, we would like to draw independent samples and so the autocorrelation should be close to zero for all steps. In practice we often need to throw many samples away (thinning) to achieve this.

Biased An estimator (e.g. $\widehat{\sigma^2}$ in Chapter 2) is said to be biased if, on average it does not equal the true value.

Binomial distribution A popular probability distribution that describes the number of successes in a set of binary trials.

Burn-in When generating samples using the Metropolis–Hastings algorithm, it is common to throw away the first N, as the algorithm may not have converged and hence these are not representative. Determining N is not straightforward.

Chinese restaurant process A way of visualising Dirichlet processes. Customers enter a restaurant with an infinite number of tables and decide which table to sit at. They sit at a currently occupied table with probability proportional to the number of customers, or, with probability proportional to a parameter α, sit at one of the empty ones.

Collapsed Gibbs sampling A sampling procedure obtained by marginalising unnecessary parameters from a Gibbs sampling scheme.

Concentration parameter The positive parameter in a Dirichlet process that controls how likely it is that new samples will come from the base or be replicates of previous samples.

Conditional independence Two (or more) random variables A and B are said to be conditionally independent if their joint distribution, conditioned on C, can be factorised as $P(A, B \mid C) = P(A \mid C)P(B \mid C)$. Conditional independence does not imply unconditional independence.

Conditional probabilities Conditional probabilities are used to describe the probability of events that depend on the outcome of other events. For example, if the value of the random variable A depends upon the value of the random variable B, we can write the probability of A given the value of C, as: $P(A \mid C)$.

Conjugate A prior and likelihood are said to be conjugate if they result in a posterior of the same form as the prior.

Continuous random variables Random variables defined on a sample space that cannot be systematically enumerated. For example, random variables defined over all real numbers.

Convergence (sampler) A sampler is said to have converged when the samples it is generating are all coming from the same distribution. Before the sampler has converged, the samples should not be used.

Covariance function A function, used in Gaussian processes, to define the covariance of the function value between two input points.

Covariance Covariance is the generalisation of variance to the distributions over several variables. The covariance matrix describes how the different variables co-vary – how they are related.

Cross-validation A technique used for validation and model selection. The data is randomly partitioned into K groups. The model is then trained K times, each time with one of the groups left out, on which it is evaluated.

Decision boundary A line separating two classes in a classification problem.

Deterministic Something that is not random. For example, our model in Chapter 1, $t = \mathbf{w}^\mathsf{T}\mathbf{x}$, is deterministic. The same value of $\mathbf{x}$ will always give the same value of t.

Dirichlet distribution A probability distribution defined over vectors with positive values that sum to 1.

Dirichlet process A stochastic process widely used as a prior in mixture models.

Discrete random variables Random variables defined over a sample space that can be systematically enumerated.

Discriminative classifier A classifier that explicitly defines (and optimises) decision boundaries between the classes.

Expectation propagation A recently proposed inference scheme. A popular alternative to EM and Variational Bayes.

Expectation For a (discrete) random variable, X, the expected value of some function of X, $f(X)$, is defined as

$$\mathbf{E}_{p(X)} \{f(X)\} = \sum_x P(x)f(x).$$

This can be thought of as an average weighted by how likely the different values of X are. For continuous random variables, the summation is exchanged for an integral.

Feature selection In some classification problems it is useful to reduce the number of attributes. This process is known as feature selection. Common techniques for feature selection are scoring functions (pick the attributes/features) with the highest scores, clustering (cluster the attributes and use the cluster means as the new attributes) and projection techniques such as Principal Components Analysis.

Fisher information The Fisher information is a measure of how much information a random variable provides about a particular model parameter.

Function A way of defining a relationship between two or more variables. For example,

$$t = f(x)$$

tells us that t depends on x – if we know x we can compute t.

Gaussian processes A popular class of models that allow us to place a prior directly onto functions rather than on parameters of a particular family of functions. They have been used in many Machine Learning applications, spanning regression, classification, ordinal regression, and projection.

Generalisation Generalisation is the ability to take something that has been learnt from one set of objects and apply it to previously unseen objects. For example, our Olympics model in Chapter 1 is generalising well if it makes good predictions for future Olympic sprints. In other words, an algorithm that exhibits good generalisation performance is one that is able to make good predictions on previously unseen data.

Generative model A generative model defines a process that could have generated the observed data. Thinking in terms of potential generative processes is often a useful abstraction when building models.

Gibbs sampling An MCMC scheme in which samples from a joint distribution are obtained by iteratively sampling from all conditional distributions.

Global optimum For a function that can have many maxima (or minima), the global optimum is described as the highest (or lowest).

Graphical model A graphical representation of a probability distribution in which nodes correspond to random variables and directed edges to dependency relationships.

Hamiltonian Monte Carlo An extension to Metropolis–Hastings that uses the gradient of the density to improve sampling efficiency.

Hessian matrix The matrix of second derivatives of a function with respect to each pair of variables. Developed and named after Ludwig Otto Hesse, a 19th century German mathematician.

Hyper-parameter A parameter controlling the prior over another parameter in a hierarchical Bayesian model.

Information theory The quantitative study of information. In particular, the information content of a random variable is linked to its probability distribution. A distribution that is very uncertain has a high information content.

Joint probability The joint probability of two random variables A and B is the probability that they each take a specific value. For example, the probability that A takes value a *and* B takes value b. This is written as, $P(A = a, B = b)$.

Latent Dirichlet Allocation A topic model that relaxes the standard mixture model assumption that each data point comes from only one mixture component. LDA has been particularly successful within the text modelling domain.

Likelihood The value of the density function (or distribution if the data are discrete) of the data, conditioned on any model parameters, evaluated at the data. This is a single numerical value, which is optimised with respect to the model parameters to produce the maximum likelihood solution.

Linear A function $t = f(x)$ is said to be linear if it satisfies the conditions

$$f(x_1 + x_2) = f(x_1) + f(x_2)$$
$$f(ax) = af(x)$$

A common example is $f(x) = wx$.

Mahanalobis distance The Mahanalobis distance between two objects $\mathbf{x}_n$ and $\mathbf{x}_m$ is defined as

$$(\mathbf{x}_i - \mathbf{x}_j)^T \mathbf{A} (\mathbf{x}_i - \mathbf{x}_j).$$

Substituing $\mathbf{A} = \mathbf{I}$, we recover the standard squared Euclidean distance. The matrix $\mathbf{A}$ creates a warping of the space such that distances are not the same in all directions. The set of points that have a particular squared Euclidean distance away from, say, $\mathbf{x}_n$ form a circle. The set of points a certain Mahanalobis distance away from $\mathbf{x}_n$ form an ellipse, the shape of which is defined by $\mathbf{A}$.

Marginal likelihood The denominator of Bayes' rule. A useful quantity for model comparison and choice.

Marginalisation The act of removing a random variable from a joint distribution by summing (or integrating if it is continuous) the joint distribution over all possible values that the random variable can take. For example

$$P(A = a) = \sum_b P(A = a, B = b).$$

Markov chain A system in which the next state depends only on the current state. Both Gibbs sampling and Metropolis–Hastings are Markov chains.

Maximum a posteriori A popular way of choosing point estimates for parameter values that extends maximum likelihood by adding a regularising prior term.

Maximum likelihood A popular parameter estimation scheme, where parameters are chosen that maximise the likelihood of the observed data.

Measure theory A branch of mathematics that offers a formal treatment of probability.

Metropolis–Hastings A popular algorithm for generating samples from a density that does not require evaluation of the normalising constant.

Model complexity A term used to describe how complex a model is. For example, $t = w_0 + w_1 x$ is less complex than $t = w_0 + w_1 x + w_2 x^2$ and as such, is not able to find as complex patterns in data.

Model selection The task of selecting which model to use for a particular task. The model choices could all come from the same family although they don't have to. For example, if we wish to use a polynomial function $t = \sum_{k=0}^{K} w_k x^k$, choosing a suitable value for K is a model selection problem.

Model A mathematical description of a process. For example, in Chapter 1 we proposed the model $t = w_0 + w_1 x$ to represent the winning time in a $100\,\mathrm{m}$ sprint in Olympic year x.

Mode The mode of a distribution over some random variable is the most likely value.

Monotonic function A monotonic function is one that increases or decreases indefinitely. A common example is $\log(x)$ that always increases as x increases. This has the useful property that the value of x that minimises $f(x)$ will also minimise $\log(f(x))$.

Monte Carlo approximation An approximation to an expectation performed by drawing samples from the appropriate distribution. An expectation of the form

$$\mathbf{E}_{p(x)}\{f(x)\} = \int f(x)p(x)\ dx,$$

is approximated by

$$\mathbf{E}_{p(x)}\{f(x)\} \approx \frac{1}{S} \sum_{s=1}^{S} f(x^s),$$

where $x^1, \ldots, x^S$ are S samples from $p(x)$.

Multinomial distribution A popular distribution over vectors of integers. For example, if I role a die N times and record the number of times I obtain each face value in a six-dimensional vector, this vector could be modelled as a random variable with a multinomial distribution.

Natural logarithm The logarithm to the base e, referred to here as log but often referred to as ln.

Noise Variability in data that is assumed to be not of interest for the problem at hand. For example, random fluctuations brought about by measurement error.

Over-fitting A model is said to be over-fitting if it is too complex and is using its surplus complexity to fit to noise. Over-fitted models usually generalise badly.

Parameters Variables used to define a model. For example, the model

$$t = w_0 + w_1 x$$

has two parameters – w_0 and w_1.

Partial derivatives Taking partial derivatives of a function of several variables involves differentiation with respect to each variable whilst treating other variables as constant. For example, if the function $t = f(x, y)$ is defined as

$$t = 2x^2 + 3y^3 + xy,$$

the partial derivatives with respect to x and y are

$$\frac{\partial f(x, y)}{\partial x} = 4x + y$$
$$\frac{\partial f(x, y)}{\partial y} = 9y^2 + x$$

Partition A partition of a space is a set of subsets of the space such that every possible value in the space is in one and only one subset. For example, the real values can be partitioned into those values less than 0 and those greater than or equal to 0.

Plate In graphical models, a shorthand used to show that there are several instances of a particular type of random variables.

Polynomial A polynomial function $t = f(x)$ has the form $t = \sum_{k=0}^{K} w_k x^k$. Common examples are the first-order (or linear) polynomial $t = w_0 + w_1 x = \sum_{k=0}^{1} w_k x^k$ (called first-order because the highest power to which x is raised is 1) and quadratic (second-order) polynomial $t = w_0 + w_1 x + w_2 x^2 = \sum_{k=0}^{2} w_k x^k$. Note that $x^0 = 1$.

Population MCMC A family of approaches that use multiple chains (often run in parallel) to perform efficient sampling.

Posterior distribution The posterior distribution is the distribution over our parameter values after we have observed some data.

Precision In hierarchical Bayesian models it is often convenient to work with the precision rather than the variance. The precision is defined as

$$\tau = \frac{1}{\sigma^2}.$$

Hence a Gaussian with mean μ and variance σ^2 can also be represented using precision τ as

$$\mathcal{N}(\mu, \tau^{-1}).$$

Prior distributions Distributions describing our knowledge of parameter values before any data has been observed.

Probability density function A probability density function (pdf) describes how the probability mass of a continuous random variable is distributed across its sample space. Probability density functions must always be positive, and the integral of the probability density function over the sample space must be equal to 1.

Probability distribution A function or set of values that describes the characteristics of a random variable.

Probability The probability of an event taking place is a number between 0 and 1 that describes how likely the event is to take place.

Projection algorithms A family of machine learning algorithms that project data from M dimensions into D dimensions ($D \ll M$). Projection techniques are useful for visualisation (with $D = 2$) and can also be used for data preprocessing for, for example, classification.

Quadratic A quadratic function $t = f(x)$ is a polynomial function where the highest power to which x is raised is 2. For example, $t = x^2$ and $t = w_0 + w_1 x + w_2 x^2$ are both quadratic functions.

Random events Events for which we cannot (or do not want or need to) define a deterministic model. For example, rolling a die or tossing a coin. Although we do not know the outcome of such events, it is likely that we will know the relative likelihoods of different outcomes.

Random variables A variable that stores the result of a random event. For example, if we toss a coin and assign the variable X the value 1 if the coin lands with the heads face up and 0 if it lands with the tails face up is a random variable.

Random walk A sequence of samples where each depends on the previous one.

Regularisation Regularisation is the act of placing restrictions on parameter values to limit the maximum complexity of a model.

Sample space The space of possible values that can be taken by a random variable. In other words, the set of the possible outcomes of a particular random event.

sequential Monte Carlo A sampling approach popular for models that evolve over time. The sample is represented as a set of *particles* from which a new set is resampled at each time instance.

Stationary covariance functions Covariance functions that depend only on the difference between two data points, and not their absolute values. An example is the RBF covariance function.

statistics Statistics describes the collection of techniques and principles concerning the collection and interpretation of data.

Supervised learning Machine learning tasks where one is provided with a set of data objects and some associated labels.

Symmetric matrix A square matrix $\mathbf{X}$ is symmetric if $x_{ij} = x_{ji}$ for all j, i. If this is the case, then it follows that $\mathbf{X}^\mathsf{T} = \mathbf{X}$.

Thinning The practice of throwing away samples generated by MCMC so that the remaining samples are independent.

Transition probabilities The set of probabilities used to describe how likely a Markov chain is to move from one state to another.

Unbiased An estimator (for example, $\hat{\mathbf{w}}$) is said to be unbiased if, on average, its value is equal to the true value.

Unsupervised learning Learning algorithms that do not require targets or labels. Examples include clustering and projection.

Validation data Data that is used to help choose model type and parameters that is not directly used to train the model.

Variance Variance is the expected squared difference between the random variable and its mean.

Index